W9-CBQ-975

Frommer's®

Tokyo

Here's what the critics say about Frommer's:

"Amazingly easy to use. Very portable, very complete."
—*Booklist*

♦

"The only mainstream guide to list specific prices. The Walter Cronkite of guidebooks—with all that implies."
—*Travel & Leisure*

♦

"Complete, concise, and filled with useful information."
—*New York Daily News*

♦

"Hotel information is close to encyclopedic."
—*Des Moines Sunday Register*

♦

"Detailed, accurate and easy-to-read information for all price ranges."
—*Glamour Magazine*

Other Great Guides for Your Trip:

Frommer's Japan

Frommer's®

6th Edition

Tokyo

by Beth Reiber

IDG Books Worldwide, Inc.
An International Data Group Company
Foster City, CA • Chicago, IL • Indianapolis, IN • New York, NY

ABOUT THE AUTHOR

Beth Reiber worked for several years in Tokyo as editor of the *Far East Traveler*. Now a freelance travel writer residing in Lawrence, Kansas, with her husband and two young sons, she is the author of several Frommer's guides including *Frommer's Japan* and *Frommer's Hong Kong*. She is a contributor to *Frommer's Europe from $60 a Day*, *Frommer's USA*, and *Frommer's Southeast Asia*.

IDG BOOKS WORLDWIDE, INC.

An International Data Group Company
919 E. Hillsdale Blvd.
Suite 400
Foster City, CA 94404

Find us online at **www.frommers.com**

ISBN 0-02-863451-9
ISSN 1045-9340

Editor: Jeff Soloway
Production Editor: M. Faunette Johnston
Photo Editor: Richard Fox
Design by Michele Laseau
Page Creation: Pete Lippincott, David Faust, and Elizabeth Brooks
Staff Cartographers: John Decamillis, Roberta Stockwell, and Elizabeth Puhl

SPECIAL SALES

For general information on IDG Books Worldwide's books in the U.S., please call our Consumer Customer Service department at 1-800-762-2974. For reseller information, including discounts, bulk sales, customized editions, and premium sales, please call our Reseller Customer Service department at 1-800-434-3422.

Manufactured in the United States of America

5 4 3 2 1

Contents

6 What to See & Do in Tokyo 140

7 Tokyo Strolls 168

8 Shopping 188

9 Tokyo After Dark 207

10 Side Trips from Tokyo 227

Appendix A: Tokyo in Depth 259

Appendix B: The Japanese Language   285

Index   293

List of Maps

ACKNOWLEDGMENTS

I would like to thank several fine and very special people who graciously offered their help in the preparation of this book: Marian Goldberg, Yoshimi Mizuno, and Nozomi Oishi of the Japan National Tourist Organization for their many years of support and hard work; Larry Estes and Debbie Howard for their moral support and friendship; and last but not least, my parents, the best baby-sitters in the world.

—Beth Reiber

AN INVITATION TO THE READER

In researching this book, we discovered many wonderful places—hotels, restaurants, shops, and more. We're sure you'll find others. Please tell us about them, so we can share the information with your fellow travelers in upcoming editions. If you were disappointed with a recommendation, we'd love to know that, too. Please write to:

Beth Reiber
Frommer's Tokyo, 6th Edition
IDG Travel
1633 Broadway
New York, NY 10019

AN ADDITIONAL NOTE

Please be advised that travel information is subject to change at any time—and this is especially true of prices. We therefore suggest that you write or call ahead for confirmation when making your travel plans. The authors, editors, and publisher cannot be held responsible for the experiences of readers while traveling. Your safety is important to us, however, so we encourage you to stay alert and be aware of your surroundings. Keep a close eye on cameras, purses, and wallets, all favorite targets of thieves and pickpockets.

WHAT THE SYMBOLS MEAN

✪ Frommer's Favorites

Our favorite places and experiences—outstanding for quality, value, or both.

The following abbreviations are used for credit cards:

AE	American Express	EC	Eurocard
CB	Carte Blanche	JCB	Japan Credit Bank
DC	Diners Club	MC	MasterCard
DISC	Discover	V	Visa
ER	enRoute		

FIND FROMMER'S ONLINE

www.frommers.com offers up-to-the-minute listings on almost 200 cities around the globe—including the latest bargains and candid, personal articles updated daily by Arthur Frommer himself. No other Web site offers such comprehensive and timely coverage of the world of travel.

A FEW WORDS ABOUT PRICES

All of the prices quoted in this book are given in both Japanese yen and U.S. dollars. The rate of exchange used to calculate the given dollar values was the actual conversion rate at the time of this writing: $1 = approximately ¥120, or ¥100 = 83¢.

However, please note that the conversion rate varies daily and can fluctuate dramatically—and there's no way we can tell you what the future holds for the Japanese yen or the U.S. dollar. So use the price conversions given in this book only as an approximate guide. Before you travel, be sure to check the current conversion rate with your bank, in the Sunday travel section of your local newspaper, or for up-to-the-minute conversion, point your Internet Web browser to www.cnn.com/travel/currency.

A NOTE ON JAPANESE SYMBOLS

Many hotels, restaurants, attractions, and other establishments in Japan do not have signs giving their names in Roman (English-language) letters. Section 2 of appendix B lists the Japanese symbols for all such places described in this guide. Each set of characters representing an establishment name has a number in the section that corresponds to the number that appears inside the oval before the establishment's name in the text. Thus, to find the Japanese symbol for, say, the restaurant **Hayashi** in Tokyo (p. 111), refer to no. 29 in section 2 of appendix B.

The Best of Tokyo

Describing Tokyo to someone who has never been here is a formidable task. After all, how do you describe a city that—as one of my friends visiting Tokyo for the first time put it—seems like it's part of another planet?

To be sure, Tokyo is very different from Western capitals, but what really sets it apart is its people. Approximately 12 million reside within Tokyo's 800 square miles, and almost one-fourth of Japan's total population lives within commuting distance of the city. This translates into a crush of humanity that packs the subways, crowds the sidewalks, and fills the department stores beyond belief. In some parts of the city, the streets are as crowded at 3am as they are at 3pm. Tokyo makes even New York seem like a sleepy town.

And yet, despite its limited space for harmonious living, Tokyo is one of the safest cities in the world, with remarkably little crime or physical aggression. No matter how lost I may become, I know that people will go out of their way to help me. Hardworking, honest, and helpful to strangers, the Japanese themselves are their country's greatest asset.

With Tokyo so densely packed, it comes as no shock to learn that land here is more valuable than gold and that buildings are built practically on top of each other, shaped like pieces in a jigsaw puzzle to fit the existing plots of real estate. More than perhaps any other city in the world, Japan's capital is a concrete jungle, with a few parks but not many trees to break the monotony, and it stretches on and on as far as the eye can see. Fires, earthquakes, wars, the zeal for modernization, and the price of land have all taken their toll on the city, eradicating almost all evidence of previous centuries. It's as though Tokyo were born only this morning, with all the messy aftermath of a city conceived without plan and interested only in the future.

Thus, first-time visitors to Tokyo are almost invariably disappointed. They come expecting an exotic Asian city, but instead find a megalopolis westernized to the point of drabness. Used to the grand edifices and monuments of Western cities, they look in vain for Tokyo's own monuments to its past—ancient temples, exquisite gardens, imperial palaces, or whatever else they've imagined. Instead they find what may be, quite arguably, one of the ugliest cities in the world.

So, while Tokyo is one of my favorite cities, it's an appreciation that came only with time. When I first moved here, I was tormented by the unsettling feeling that I was somehow missing out on the "real" Tokyo. Even though I was living and working here, Tokyo seemed beyond my grasp, elusive, vague, and undefined. I felt that the meaning of the city was out there somewhere, if only I knew where to look.

With time, I finally learned that I needn't look farther than my own front window. Tokyo has no center, but rather is made up of a series of small towns and neighborhoods clustered together, each with its own history, flavor, and atmosphere. There are narrow residential streets, ma-and-pa shops, fruit stands, and stores. There's the neighborhood tofu factory, the lunch-box stand, grocery shop, and the tiny police station, where the police know the residents by name and patrol the area by bicycle. There are carefully pruned bonsai trees gracing sidewalks, women in kimono bowing and shuffling down streets, and wooden homes on impossibly narrow streets. Walk in the old downtown neighborhoods of Asakusa or Ueno and you're worlds apart from the trendy quarters of Harajuku or the high-rises of Shinjuku. Neighborhoods like these make Tokyo lovable and livable.

What's more, once visitors get to know Tokyo better, they learn that you can't judge Tokyo by what it looks like on the outside, for this is a city of interiors. Even those concrete monsters may house interiors that are fascinating in design and innovation. In the basement of that drab building could well be a restaurant with wooden beams, mud walls, and thatched ceiling, imported intact from a farmhouse in the Japan Alps; on its roof could be a small shinto shrine, while the top floor could house a high-tech bar or a sophisticated French restaurant.

In addition, beneath Tokyo's concrete shell is a thriving cultural life left very much intact. In fact, if you're interested in Japan's performing arts as well as such diverse activities as the tea ceremony or sumo, Tokyo is your best bet for offering the most at any one time. Tokyo is also rich in museums and claims the largest repository of Japanese art in the world. I can't imagine being bored here, even for just a minute.

1 Frommer's Favorite Tokyo Experiences

- **Strolling Through Asakusa.** No place better conveys the atmosphere of old Tokyo than Asakusa. Sensoji Temple is the city's oldest and most popular temple, and Nakamise Dori, the pedestrian lane leading to the temple, is lined with shops selling souvenirs and traditional Japanese goods. As in days of yore, arrive by boat via the Sumida River.

- **Catching the Action at Tsukiji Fish Market.** Get up early your first morning in Japan (you'll be wide awake with jet lag, anyway) and head straight for the country's largest fish market, where you can watch the tuna auctions, browse through stalls of seafood, and sample the freshest sushi you'll ever have.

- **Viewing Treasures at the Tokyo National Museum.** It's a feast for the eyes at the largest museum of Japanese art in the world, where you can see everything from samurai armor and lacquerware to kimono and woodblock prints.

- **Sitting Pretty in Shinjuku.** On the 45th floor of the Tokyo Metropolitan Government Office (TMG), designed by well-known architect Kenzo Tange, an observatory offers a bird's-eye view of Shinjuku's cluster of skyscrapers, the never-ending metropolis, and on fine winter days, Mt. Fuji. Best of all, it's free.

- **Time Traveling in the Edo-Tokyo Museum.** Housed in a high-tech modern building, this ambitious museum chronicles the fascinating and somewhat

Japan

tumultuous history of Tokyo (known as Edo during the Feudal Period), with models, replicas, artifacts, and dioramas.

- **Hanging Out in Harajuku.** Nothing beats Sunday in Harajuku, where you can begin the day leisurely with brunch, stroll the promenade of Omotesando Dori, shop the area's many boutiques, take in a museum or two and perhaps a flea market, and then relax over drinks at a sidewalk cafe watching the hordes of teenyboppers parading past.
- **Paying Respects at Meiji Jingu Shrine.** Tokyo's most venerable and refined Shinto shrine honors Emperor Meiji and his empress with simple yet dignified architecture surrounded by dense forest, making it a great refuge in the heart of the city. In June, be sure to see the Irish Garden.
- **Escaping Big-City Life in the Temple Town of Yanaka.** With its many temples, offbeat attractions, sloping hills, and peaceful narrow streets, the neighborhood of Yanaka makes for a wonderful half-day escape from the crowds of Tokyo.
- **Walking the Imperial Moat.** It's an easy, 3-mile walk around the Imperial Palace moat, beautiful especially in spring when the many cherry blossoms are aflame. Don't miss the attached (and free) East Garden.
- **Taking Part in a Festival.** Tokyo offers a myriad of annual festivals, ranging from processions of portable shrines to ladder-top acrobatics. Be ready to battle good-natured crowds, as festivals can be unbelievably packed.
- **Strolling a Japanese Landscaped Garden.** There's no better escape from Tokyo's urban jungle than a stroll through one of its landscaped gardens, especially in spring, when irises, wisteria, peonies, azaleas, and other flowers are in bloom. Top picks are Hama Rikyu Garden, Koishikawa Korakuen, and Shinjuku Gyoen.
- **Viewing Cherry Blossoms at Ueno Park.** Ueno Park is famous throughout Japan for its 1,000 cherry trees, attracting multitudes of company employees and organizations. It's not, however, the communing with nature you might think, as everyone drinks, eats, dances, and sings karaoke, seemingly oblivious to the shimmering blossoms above. Observing Tokyoites at play here is a cultural experience you won't soon forget.
- **Watching the Fat Guys Wrestle.** Nothing beats watching huge, almost-nude sumo wrestlers, most weighing well over 300 pounds, throw each other around. Matches are held in Tokyo in January, May, and September; catch one on TV if you can't make it in person. Great fun and not to be missed.
- **Attending a Baseball Game.** After sumo, baseball is Japan's most popular spectator sport, and watching a game in a stadium full of avid fans can be quite entertaining and enlightening. Top Tokyo teams include the Giants and the Swallows.
- **Getting a Massage.** After a hard day of work or sightseeing, nothing beats a relaxing massage followed by a hot bath. Shiatsu, or pressure-point massage, is available at virtually all first-class and most medium-range Tokyo hotels, as well as at a number of clinics in the city, many of which offer acupuncture as well.
- **Appreciating the Beauty of Ikebana.** After seeing how flowers, branches, and vases can be combined into works of art, you'll never be able to simply throw flowers into a vase again. You can learn the basics of ikebana, Japanese flower arranging, at several schools in Tokyo. Exhibitions of ikebana are held regularly at Yasukuni Shrine and department stores.
- **Experiencing the Serenity of the Tea Ceremony.** Developed in the 16th century as a means to achieve inner harmony with nature, the tea ceremony is a highly ritualized process that takes years to learn. You can experience a shortened version, with instruction in English, at several Tokyo hotels.

- **Browsing the Electronic Shops of Akihabara Electric Town.** Even if you don't buy anything, it's great fun—and very educational—to see the latest in electronic gadgets in Japan's largest electronics district, where you'll see many products unknown in Western markets.
- **Hunting for Bargains at Flea Markets.** Who knows what treasure you might find at one of Tokyo's monthly outdoor flea markets, where vendors sell everything from used kimono to antiques and curios. Go early, and be sure to bargain.
- **Getting the Royal Treatment at Department Stores.** Tokyo's department stores are huge, spotless, and filled with merchandise you never knew existed; many also have first-rate art galleries. Shibuya and Ginza boast the greatest concentration of department stores. Tobu, in Ikebukuro, is the city's largest—a virtual city in itself. Service in a Japanese department store is an unparalleled experience: Be there when it opens, and you'll see employees lined up at the front door, bowing to incoming customers.
- **Shopping for Japanese Designer Clothes.** Japanese designer clothing is often outrageous, occasionally practical, but always fun. Department stores, designer boutiques in Aoyama, and secondhand shops in Ebisu are the places to try on the digs—assuming you've got both the money and the figure.
- **Feasting on a Kaiseki Meal.** Although expensive, a kaiseki feast, consisting of dish after dish of artfully displayed delectables, may well be the most beautiful and memorable meal you'll ever have. Splurge at least once on the most expensive kaiseki meal you can afford, and you'll feel like royalty.
- **Dining Alfresco on a Rooftop.** During the summer months, the rooftops of office buildings, department stores, and hotels sprout so-called beer gardens, albeit with artificial grass. For a more down-to-earth experience, spend an evening under the paper lanterns of the lovely Hanezawa Beer Garden.
- **Rubbing Elbows in a Yakitori-ya.** A yakitori-ya is the drinking man's pub, usually a tiny affair with a single counter and skewered grilled chicken on offer in addition to beer. It's a good place to meet the natives, and inexpensive as well. You'll find them in every nightlife district in Tokyo.
- **Taking a Spin Through Kabuki-cho.** Shinjuku's Kabuki-cho has the craziest nightlife in all of Tokyo, with countless strip joints, porn shops, restaurants, bars, and the greatest concentration of neon (and drunks) you're likely to see anywhere. A fascinating place for an evening's stroll.
- **Attending a Kabuki Play at the Kabukiza Theater.** Kabuki has served as the most popular form of entertainment for the masses since the Edo Period. Watch the audience as they yell their approval; watch the stage for its gorgeous costumes, stunning settings, and easy-to-understand dramas of love, duty, and revenge.
- **Clubbing in Roppongi.** You can dance the night away in the madness that's Roppongi; most revelers party 'til dawn.

2 Best Bets for Accommodation

- **Best Historic Hotel:** Established in 1937, the **Hilltop Hotel,** 1–1 Surugadai, in Kanda (☎ **03/3293-2311**), boasts an art-deco facade and was once a favorite haunt of writers. It's changed little over the decades. Endearing touches include fringed lampshades, doilies, cherry-wood furniture, velvet curtains, old-fashioned heaters, and washlet toilets. A unique, old-fashioned hotel at reasonable prices.

- **Best for Business Travelers: The Imperial Hotel,** 1–1–1 Uchisaiwai-cho, in Hibiya (☎ **800/223-6800** in the U.S. and Canada, or 03/3504-1111), wins my vote as the best for business travelers with its central location close to the Ginza and financial districts, excellent service, twelve restaurants and bars, 24-hour room service, an extensively equipped business center, comfortable rooms complete with three phones, a safe large enough for a briefcase, free fax machine on request, and private e-mail address for each guest.
- **Best for a Romantic Getaway:** Nothing beats a weekend getaway to the historic **Fujiya Hotel,** in Hakone (☎ **0460/2-2211**). Established in 1878, it is one of Japan's finest, most majestic hotels, boasting great views, Japanese- and Western-style architecture, a wonderful 1930s dining hall, and a large landscaped garden perfect for moonlit walks.
- **Best Trendy Hotel: Hotel Sofitel,** 2–1–48 Ikenohata, in Ueno (☎ **800/ 221-4542** in the U.S. and Canada, or 03/5685-7111), is not only Tokyo's most uniquely shaped hotel—five trapezoids stacked on top of each other—but also Tokyo's best-kept secret. A sophisticated boutique hotel with only four rooms on each floor, it offers great views of Shinobazu Pond.
- **Best for Internet Buffs: The Royal Park Hotel,** 2–1–1 Nihombashi-Kakigara-cho (☎ **800/457-4000** in the U.S., or 03/3667-1111) offers a sophisticated TV center that provides Internet access and e-mail capability in all its rooms.
- **Best Lobby for Pretending You're Rich:** With its high rates, tons of marble, neoclassical columns, statuary, huge floral bouquets, palm trees, and attentive doormen, the **Westin Tokyo,** 1–4–1 Mita, in Ebisu (☎ **800/228-3000** in the U.S. and Canada, or 03/5423-7000), is a favorite among wealthy Japanese.
- **Best for Families: The National Children's Castle Hotel,** 5–53–1 Jingumae, in Aoyama (☎ **03/3797-5677**), is located in the same complex as Tokyo's best and most sophisticated indoor/outdoor playground and even offers some Japanese-style rooms where families can experience tatami living.
- **Best Moderately Priced Hotel:** Occupying the top floors of a Shinjuku skyscraper just a couple minutes' walk from Shinjuku Station, the **Hotel Century Southern Tower,** 2–2–1 Yoyogi (☎ **03/5354-0111**) offers great views, a convenient location, and comfortable rooms at reasonable prices.
- **Best Budget Accommodations:** Although the building itself is rather nondescript, **Ryokan Sawanoya,** 2–3–11 Yanaka, in Ueno (☎ **03/3822-2251**), is nestled in a delightful neighborhood of traditional shops and old wooden houses; the English-speaking owner goes out of his way to introduce the vicinity and make guests feel at home with such extras as complimentary tea and instant coffee and free laundry detergent. An added bonus is the free weekly lion dances performed by his son.
- **Best Japanese-Style Inn:** With a great location in historic Asakusa, just a stone's throw from famous Sensoji Temple, **Ryokan Shigetsu,** 1–31–11 Asakusa (☎ **03/ 3843-2345**), is a modern, moderately priced Japanese-style inn that combines the best of the old and the new with simple yet elegant interiors that utilize natural woods and artwork throughout. If you want to experience a Japanese inn but don't want to sleep on a futon, stay in one of Shigetsu's Western-style rooms, but don't pass up the public bath with views of the five-story pagoda.
- **Best Service: The Four Seasons Hotel Chinzan-So,** 2–10–8 Sekiguchi, in northwest Tokyo (☎ **800/332-3442** in the U.S., or 03/3943-2222), aims to please with its 24-hour concierge, an able staff, and such guest services as 24-hour room service, 24-hour laundry service, complimentary shoeshine, choice of free newspaper, complimentary in-room use of fax machine, free access to the health

club and pool, and—my favorite—complimentary limo service to anywhere in Tokyo.

- **Best Health Club:** Again the **Four Seasons Hotel Chinzan-So** wins. Its health spa boasts a gorgeous indoor swimming pool with a retractable glass ceiling, sunning terrace, indoor and outdoor Jacuzzis, sauna, steam room, fitness gym, and even hot-spring baths with thermal water shipped in from Izu Peninsula—all absolutely free for hotel guests, a rarity in Japan.
- **Best Hotel Pool: The Park Hyatt Tokyo,** 3–7–1–2 Nishi-Shinjuku, in Shinjuku (☎ **800/233-1234** in the U.S. and Canada, or 03/5322-1234), wins kudos for free entry for hotel guests to its dramatic, sunlit, 20-meter indoor pool, on the 47th floor with great views over Tokyo.
- **Best Views:** If it's winter, when Mt. Fuji is most likely to be visible, the **Park Hyatt Tokyo** in Shinjuku (see above) affords great views of Japan's tallest mountain. Otherwise, I love the views from the **Hotel Inter-Continental Tokyo Bay,** 1–16–2 Kaigan (☎ **800/327-0200** in the U.S. and Canada, or 03/5404-2222), located right on the waterfront with great views of Tokyo Bay and the chameleon Rainbow Bridge, even from the bathrooms.
- **Best Hotel for Spotting VIPs:** Located across from the American Embassy, the dignified **Hotel Okura,** 2–10–4 Toranomon, in Minato ward (☎ **800/ 223-6800** in the U.S., or 03/3582-0111), provides discreet refuge for visiting U.S. dignitaries and a wide range of celebrities, including the Rolling Stones, Vladimir Horowitz, Yo-Yo Ma, Henry Kissinger, and David Bowie.
- **Best Hotel Restaurant: The New York Grill** in the Park Hyatt Tokyo (see above) is Tokyo's current hot spot, boasting great food, excellent service, knockout views, live jazz, and tables booked weeks in advance.
- **Best Hotel Garden: The Hotel New Otani,** 4–1 Kioi-cho, in Akasaka (☎ **800/ 421-8795** in the U.S. and Canada, or 03/3265-1111), has a beautiful 400-year-old Japanese garden, once belonging to a feudal lord. It sprawls over 10 acres of ponds, waterfalls, bridges, bamboo groves, and manicured bushes.

3 Best Bets for Dining

- **Best Spot for a Romantic Dinner:** French cuisine, attentive but unobtrusive service, live music, and a bird's-eye view of the Imperial Palace and the fountain commemorating the crown prince's marriage make the **Crown Restaurant,** 1–1–1 Marunouchi, near Tokyo Station (☎ **03/3211-5211**), a perfect rendezvous for a romantic evening.
- **Best Spot for a Business Lunch:** The convenient Akasaka location and varied, international menu of **Trader Vic's,** 4–1 Kioi-cho (☎ **03/3265-4707**), make playing host or hostess here a cinch.
- **Best Spot for a Celebration: The New York Grill,** 3–7–1–2 Nishi-Shinjuku (☎ **03/5322-1234**), has all the makings for a joyous occasion: great food, excellent service, breathtaking views, and superb live jazz.
- **Best Decor:** In a city where presentation counts as much as the food itself, it's difficult to choose the best decor. For traditional surroundings, nothing beats the Japanese-style rooms of **Takamura** in Roppongi (☎ **03/3585-6600**), **Komagata Dojo** in Asakusa (☎ **03/3842-4001**), or **Kandagawa** in Kanda (☎ **03/ 3251-5031**). For offbeat decor, one of my favorites is **Tableaux** in Daikanyama (☎ **03/5489-2201**), with its whimsical, Russian-tearoom atmosphere. For high-tech Tokyo, head for **Manin** in Harajuku (☎ **03/3478-3778**) or **Ozawa** in Meguro (☎ **03/3442-1171**), both designed by Philippe Starck.

- **Best View: The New York Grill** (see above), located on the 52nd floor and surrounded by glass, offers breathtaking views of an endless city and, on clear days, Mt. Fuji, making this the closest you can get to dining on a cloud.
- **Best Wine List: The New York Grill** wins here, too, with 1,700 bottles in its cellar, featuring mostly California wines. **La Tour d'Argent,** New Otani Hotel, 4–1 Kioi-cho (☎ **03/3239-3111**), has an excellent choice of French wines.
- **Best for Kids:** Loud music, rock 'n' roll memorabilia, and familiar fare like burgers, chicken, and sandwiches make the **Hard Rock Cafe,** 5–4–20 Roppongi (☎ **03/3408-7018**), a sure winner with children and baby boomers alike.
- **Best American Cuisine:** New American cuisine is well represented by the Tokyo branch of **Spago,** 5–7–8 Roppongi (☎ **03/3423-4025**), a California institution. Its imaginative cuisine, cheerful dining room, and good California wines make dining here a pleasure.
- **Best French Cuisine: La Tour d'Argent,** New Otani Hotel, 4–1 Kioi-cho, in Akasaka (☎ **03/3239-3111**), is the Tokyo branch of this very famous Parisian restaurant, serving excellent classic French cuisine, including duckling flown in from Brittany. A beautiful, dramatic setting and superb service round out the experience.
- **Best Italian Cuisine: Carmine,** 1–19 Saiku-cho, in Ichigaya (☎ **03/3260-5066**), is out of the way yet always crowded because all of Tokyo seems to know that this unassuming restaurant offers the best Italian food at embarrassingly affordable prices.
- **Best Kaiseki:** Perched on a wooded hill in a 50-year-old traditional house, **Takamura,** 3–4–27 Roppongi (☎ **03/3585-6600**), offers eight private tatami rooms and exquisitely prepared kaiseki meals. Expensive but worth it.
- **Best Noodles:** Tokyo's most famous noodle restaurant, **Kanda Yabusoba,** 2–10 Awajicho, in Kanda (☎ **03/3251-0287**), features a traditional tatami house hidden behind a bamboo grove, hot and cold noodles, and a singing cashier.
- **Best Sushi:** If money is no object, head for **Sushiko,** 6–3–8 Ginza (☎ **03/3571-1968**), a fourth-generation restaurant with room for only eleven privileged diners. Otherwise, try **Sushi Dai,** located in Tsukiji Fish Market (☎ **03/3542-1111**), where the fish couldn't be any fresher.
- **Best Crossover Cuisine: Nobu,** 6–10–17 Minami Aoyama (☎ **03/5467-0022**), is Tokyo's hottest new restaurant, serving its own beautiful creations of East-meets-West cuisine with a unique blend of Pacific Rim ingredients.
- **Best Burgers:** Decorated like an American 1950s diner, **Johnny Rockets,** 3–11–10 Roppongi (☎ **03/3423-1955**), hits the spot with the best burgers in town, a real lifesaver when nothing else will do.
- **Best Pizza:** Italian-owned **Trattoria-Pizzeria Sabatini,** 2–13–5 Kita-Aoyama (☎ **03/3402-2027**), offers the closest thing to real pizza in Tokyo, with many ingredients flown in from Italy.
- **Best Late-Night Dining: La Boheme,** with several convenient locations around Tokyo, has made a name for itself by offering inexpensive Italian food daily until 5am. Otherwise, **Potomac,** in the Akasaka Prince Hotel (☎ **03/3234-1111**) is open 24 hours for steaks, sandwiches, and pasta.
- **Best Outdoor Dining:** Summer isn't summer until you've dined under the stars and paper lanterns of the **Hanezawa Beer Garden,** 3–12–15 Hiroo, near Ebisu (☎ **03/3400-6500**), with its lovely setting and cook-your-own barbecues.
- **Best People-Watching: Aux Bacchanales,** 1–6–1 Jingumae, in Harajuku (☎ **03/5474-0076**), with sidewalk seating, is a very civilized place from which

to watch the hordes of teenyboppers throng past as you dine on good bistro fare and cheap wine, thankful your own adolescent days are over.

- **Best for Japanese Desserts: Tatsutano,** 7–8–7 Ginza (☎ 03/3571-1850), has been popular with Japanese housewives for more than a century, especially for its anmitsu, a dessert made from beans, molasses, sweet-bean paste, and gelatin.
- **Best Weekend Brunch:** The weekend brunch at **The New York Grill** (see above) is so popular there's practically a waiting list.
- **Best Theatrics:** There's never a dull moment at **Inakaya,** 7–8–4 Roppongi (☎ 03/3405-9866), with yelling waiters shouting out orders, U-shaped counter seating, mountains of food, and kneeling cooks laboring over charcoal grills. Great fun.
- **Best Buffets: The Rainbow Room,** on the 17th floor of the Imperial Hotel, 1–1–1 Uchisaiwai-cho (☎ 03/3504-1111), with views of the Ginza and Hibiya, was a pioneer of all-you-can-eat buffets in Japan. After 40 years, it still offers great lunch and dinner buffets with mostly European dishes.
- **Best Place to Chill Out:** When the crowds get you down, escape to **Selan,** 2–1–19 Kita-Aoyama (☎ 03/3478-2200), with its glorious setting on a gingko-lined street, complete with sidewalk seating and an airy dining room with lots of windows. A good place to relax and do absolutely nothing.

2

Planning a Trip to Tokyo

This chapter is designed to guide you through the what, when, where, and how of travel to Tokyo—from what documents you should take with you to how to get around easily and economically, despite the language barrier.

1 Visitor Information

VISITOR INFORMATION

The **Japan National Tourist Organization (JNTO)** publishes a wealth of free, colorful brochures and maps covering Tokyo and other cities. These include a tourist map of Tokyo; Fuji-Hakone-Kamakura-Nikko, a brochure of popular destinations in the vicinity of Tokyo; "The Tourist's Language Handbook," a phrase booklet to help foreign visitors communicate with the Japanese; and "Your Traveling Companion, with Tips for Budget Travel," with money-saving advice on traveling, lodging, and dining in the Tokyo area.

THE JNTO OVERSEAS If you'd like information on Japan before leaving home, contact one of these JNTO offices:

In the **United States:** 401 N. Michigan Ave., Suite 770, Chicago, IL 60611 (☎ 312/222-0874; e-mail: jntochi@mcs.net); 515 S. Figueroa, Suite 1470, Los Angeles, CA 90071 (☎ 213/623-1952; e-mail: jntolax@mindspring.com); One Rockefeller Plaza, Suite 1250, New York, NY 10020 (☎ 212/757-5640; e-mail: jntonyc@interport.net); and 360 Post St., Suite 601, San Francisco, CA 94108 (☎ 415/989-7140; e-mail: sfjnto@msn.com).

In **Canada:** 165 University Ave., Toronto, ON M5H 3B8, Canada (☎ 416/366-7140; e-mail: jnto@interlog.com).

In the **United Kingdom:** Heathcoat House, 20 Savile Row, London W1X 1AE, England (☎ 0171/734-9638).

In **Australia:** Level 33, The Chifley Tower, 2 Chifley Sq., Sydney, NSW 2000, Australia (☎ 02/9232-4522).

THE JNTO ON-LINE You can also reach JNTO via the Internet at **www.jnto.go.jp**, where you can read up on what's new, view maps, and browse through information ranging from reasonable accommodations and hints on budget travel to regional events, museums, and attractions.

2 Entry Requirements & Customs

ENTRY REQUIREMENTS

Americans traveling to Japan as tourists with the intention of staying 90 days or less need only a valid passport to gain entry into the country. *Note:* Only American *tourists* don't need a visa—that is, those in the country for sightseeing, sports activities, family visits, inspection tours, business meetings, or short study courses. In other words, as a tourist, you cannot work in Japan or engage in any remunerative activity, including the teaching of English (though many young people ignore the law). No extensions of stay are granted, which means American tourists must absolutely leave the country after 90 days. If you're going to Japan to work or study and plan on staying longer, you'll need a visa; contact the Japanese embassy or consulate nearest you.

Australians and **New Zealanders** do not need a visa for stays of up to 90 days, while **Canadians** do not need a visa for stays of up to 3 months. Citizens of the **United Kingdom** and **Ireland** can stay for up to 6 months without a visa.

CUSTOMS

ENTERING JAPAN   If you're 20 or older, you can take duty-free into Japan up to 400 non-Japanese cigarettes or 500 grams of tobacco or 100 cigars; three bottles (760cc each) of alcohol; and 2 ounces of perfume. You can also bring in gifts and souvenirs whose total market value is less than ¥200,000 ($1,667).

GOING HOME   Returning **U.S. citizens** who have been away for 48 hours or more are allowed to bring back, once every 30 days, $400 worth of merchandise duty-free, including (for those 21 and older) 1 liter of wine or spirits. Beyond that, the next $1,000 worth of goods is assessed at a flat rate of 10% duty. Be sure to have your receipts handy. On gifts, the duty-free limit is $100. You're allowed to send up to $50 per package back by mail duty-free. You cannot bring fresh foodstuffs into the United States; tinned foods, however, are allowed.

Citizens of the **U.K.** returning from Japan have a customs allowance of: 200 cigarettes; 50 cigars; 250g of smoking tobacco; 2 liters of still table wine; 1 liter of spirits or strong liqueurs (over 22% volume); 2 liters of fortified wine, sparkling wine or other liqueurs; 60cc (ml) perfume; 250cc (ml) of toilet water; and £145 worth of all other goods, including gifts and souvenirs. People under 17 cannot have the tobacco or alcohol allowance.

Passport Tips

Safeguard your passport in an inconspicuous, inaccessible place like a money belt. If you lose it, visit the nearest consulate of your native country as soon as possible for a replacement. *Note:* Foreigners are required to carry with them at all times either their passports or, for those who have been granted longer stays, their alien registration cards. The police generally do not stop foreigners, but if you're caught without the proper identification, you'll be taken to the local police headquarters. It happened to me once, and believe me, I can think of better ways to spend an hour and a half than explaining in detail who I am, what I'm doing in Japan, where I live, and what I plan on doing for the rest of my life. Afterwards, I had to write a statement explaining how it was that I rushed out that day without my passport, apologizing and promising never to do such a thoughtless thing again. The policemen at the station were very nice and polite—they were simply doing their duty.

Canada gives its citizens a $500 exemption, and permits them to bring back duty-free 200 cigarettes, 2.2 pounds of tobacco, 40 imperial ounces of liquor, and 50 cigars. In addition, you're allowed to mail gifts to Canada from abroad at the rate of Can$60 a day, provided they're unsolicited and don't contain alcohol or tobacco (write on the package "unsolicited gift, under $60 value"). All valuables should be declared on the Y-38 form before departure from Canada, including serial numbers of valuables you already own, such as expensive foreign cameras. *Note:* The $500 exemption can only be used once a year and only after an absence of 7 days.

The duty-free allowance in **Australia** is A$400 or, for those under 18, A$200. Returning citizens can bring in 250 cigarettes or 250 grams of loose tobacco, and 1,125ml of alcohol. If you're returning with valuable goods you already own, such as foreign-made cameras, you should file form B263.

The duty-free allowance for **New Zealand** is NZ$700. Citizens over 17 can bring in 200 cigarettes, or 50 cigars, or 250 grams of tobacco (or a mixture of all three if their combined weight doesn't exceed 250 grams); plus 4.5 liters of wine and beer, or 1.125 liters of liquor. New Zealand currency does not carry import or export restrictions. Fill out a certificate of export, listing the valuables you are taking out of the country; that way, you can bring them back without paying duty.

3 Money

CURRENCY   The currency in Japan is called the **yen,** symbolized by ¥. Coins come in denominations of ¥1, ¥5, ¥10, ¥50, ¥100, and ¥500. Bills come in denominations of ¥1,000, ¥2,000, ¥5,000, and ¥10,000. You'll find all coins used (though you may find it hard getting rid of ¥1 coins); you'll want to keep plenty of change handy for riding local transportation, including buses and subways. Although change machines are virtually everywhere, even on buses where you can change larger coins and ¥1,000 bills, you'll find it faster to have the exact amount on hand.

Although the **conversion rate** varies daily and can fluctuate dramatically, the prices in this book are based on the rate of U.S. $1 to ¥120, or ¥100 to U.S. 83¢.

Personal checks are not used in Japan. Most Japanese pay with either **credit cards** or **cash**—and because the country has such a low crime rate, you can feel safe walking around with lots of money (though of course you should always exercise caution whenever you're traveling). When I worked as editor of a travel magazine in Tokyo, I was paid in cash; I often left the office for a night on the town with a whole month's salary in my purse. The only time you really need to be alert to possible pickpockets in Japan is when you're riding a crowded subway during rush hour.

CURRENCY EXCHANGE   Although some people like to arrive in a foreign country with that country's currency already on hand, I do not find it necessary for Japan. **Narita Airport** has several exchange counters that are open for all incoming international flights and that offer a better exchange rate than what you'd get abroad. In addition, all banks displaying an "Authorized Foreign Exchange" sign can exchange currency, with exchange rates usually displayed at the appropriate foreign-exchange counter. **Banks** are generally open Monday through Friday from 9am to 3pm. If you need to exchange money outside of banking hours, inquire at one of the larger first-class **hotels**—some of them will cash traveler's checks or exchange money, even if you're not their guest (you'll need to show your passport). Likewise, large **department stores** in major cities also offer exchange services and are often open until 7:30 or 8pm. Note, however, that hotels and department stores may charge a handling fee, offer a slightly less favorable exchange rate, and require a passport for all transactions.

The Japanese Yen

For American Readers   At this writing $1 = approximately ¥120, or ¥100 = 83¢; [*handwritten: 109*] [*handwritten: 92¢*] this was the rate of exchange used to calculate the dollar values given in this guide (rounded off to the nearest nickel for prices less than $10 and to the nearest dollar for prices more than $10). To roughly figure the price of something in dollars, calculate $8 for every ¥1,000; or multiply the yen amount by .008. For example, if something costs ¥2,000, that's approximately $16, close to the actual $16.65.

For British Readers   At this writing £1 = approximately ¥190, or ¥100 = 53£; this was the rate of exchange used to calculate the pound values in the table below. The Euro is approximately worth ¥129.

¥	U.S.$	U.K.£	¥	U.S.$	U.K.£
10	.08	.05	1,500	12.50	7.90
25	.21	.13	2,000	16.65	10.50
50	.42	.26	2,500	20.85	13.15
75	.62	.39	3,000	25.00	15.80
100	.83	.53	4,000	33.35	21.05
200	1.65	1.05	5,000	41.65	26.30
300	2.50	1.60	6,000	50.00	31.60
400	3.35	2.10	7,000	58.35	36.85
500	4.15	2.65	8,000	66.65	42.10
600	5.00	3.15	9,000	75.00	47.35
700	5.85	3.70	10,000	83.35	52.65
800	6.65	4.20	15,000	125.00	78.95
900	7.50	4.75	20,000	166.65	105.25
1,000	8.35	5.25	25,000	208.35	31.60

A note on exchange rates: The most difficult task of writing a guide is to set the rate of exchange, especially for Japan; if I could advise you accurately on the future exchange rate, I'd be too rich to be a guidebook writer. Since these rates will surely fluctuate, check the rate again when you travel to Japan and use this table only as an approximate guide.

GETTING CASH USING YOUR CREDIT OR ATM CARD   You can also use bank-issued credit cards and ATM cards to get cash, though access outside Japanese cities is very limited. For cash advances from a bank, only Sumitomo Bank handles **Visa. MasterCard** cashing service is available at Union Credit (UC) banks and some Sumitomo banks, Citibanks, Mitsubishi-Tokyo banks, and affiliated banks. Note, however, that MasterCard or Visa cards issued by Bank of America are accepted only at Bank of America, 1–12–32 Akasaka, Tokyo. There is no public American Express office in Japan.

   ATMs (automated teller machines) are a convenient way to get cash at an excellent exchange rate, but note that most accept only Japan-issued cards. Nonetheless, **ATMs** that accept foreign bank cards are located at many convenient locations in Tokyo (see "Fast Facts: Tokyo," in chapter 3).

What Things Cost in Tokyo	U.S. $
Narita Express Train from airport to city center	24.50
Subway ride from Akasaka to Roppongi	1.35
Local telephone call (per minute)	.08
Double room at the Imperial Hotel (deluxe)	292.00
Double room at the Hotel Sofitel (moderate)	183.00
Double room at the Ryokan Sawanoya (inexpensive)	75.00
Lunch for one at Munakata (moderate)	21.00
Lunch for one at Mominoki House (inexpensive)	8.35
Dinner for one, without drinks, at Inakaya (deluxe)	100.00
Dinner for one, without drinks, at Komagata Dojo (moderate)	40.00
Dinner for one, without drinks, at Ganchan (inexpensive)	21.00
Glass of beer	4.15–5.85
Coca-Cola	3.40–4.15
Cup of coffee	1.65–4.15
Roll of ASA 100 Fujicolor film (36 exposures)	4.00
Admission to the Tokyo National Museum	3.50
Movie ticket	15.00
Theater ticket to Kabuki	5.00–20.00

TRAVELER'S CHECKS Traveler's checks in U.S. and other denominations can be exchanged for yen at most banks with exchange services and at major hotels, but note that you'll need your passport every time you cash a check. Traveler's checks have a slight advantage in that they generally fetch a better exchange rate than cash. Note, however, that in some very remote areas, even banks won't cash them.

CREDIT CARDS Credit cards are convenient for obtaining cash in Tokyo and for paying for accommodations, meals at expensive restaurants, and for major purchases, with the exchange rate better than what you can get for either cash or traveler's checks at a bank. They are a safe way to carry money and provide a convenient record of all your expenses.

The most readily accepted cards are American Express, MasterCard (also called Eurocard), Visa, and the Japanese credit card JCB (Japan Credit Bank); many tourist-oriented facilities also accept Diners Club. Shops and restaurants accepting credit and charge cards will usually post which cards they accept at the door or on or near the cash register. However, some establishments may be reluctant to accept cards for small purchases and inexpensive meals; inquire beforehand. In addition, note that the vast majority of Tokyo's smaller and least-expensive businesses, including many restaurants, noodle shops, fast-food joints, ma-and-pa establishments, and some of the cheapest accommodations, do not accept credit cards.

4 When to Go

Although Tokyo's busiest foreign-tourist season is in summer, the city lends itself to visiting year-round. In fact, when the rest of Japan is besieged with vacationing

Japanese during Golden Week (Apr 29 to May 5) and summer vacation (mid-July through Aug), Tokyo is usually blissfully empty, as Tokyoites pour out of the city to the countryside. Keep in mind, however, that in mid-February, hotel rooms may be in short supply as high-school students from around the nation converge in Tokyo to compete in entrance exams to the city's prestigious universities. In addition, popular tourist destinations outside Tokyo, such as Nikko, Kamakura, and Hakone, will be jam-packed on major holidays. And from the end of December through the first 3 or 4 days of January, it seems as though the entire nation shuts down, including most restaurants and museums.

CLIMATE   The Japanese are very proud of the fact that Japan has four distinct seasons; they place much more emphasis on the seasons than people do in the West. Kimono, dishes and bowls used for kaiseki, and even Noh plays change with the seasons, and most festivals are tied to seasonal rites.

Summer, which begins in June, is heralded by the rainy season, which lasts from about mid-June to mid-July in Tokyo. July has, on the average, 10 rainy days, but even though it doesn't rain every day, umbrellas are imperative. When the rain stops, it gets unbearably hot and humid through August—you might want to head for Hakone for a bit of fresh air. Otherwise, you'll be most comfortable in light cottons, but be sure to pack a light jacket for unexpected cool evenings and air-conditioned rooms. The period from the end of August through September is typhoon season, though most storms stay out at sea and vent their fury on land only as thunderstorms.

Autumn, which lasts from September through November, is one of the best times to visit Japan. The days are pleasant and slightly cool, the skies are a brilliant blue, and the maples turn scarlet. Bring a warm jacket.

Winter lasts from about December to March in Tokyo, with days that are generally clear and cold with extremely low humidity. Tokyo doesn't get much snow, but it can snow, so be prepared. I remember one winter when it snowed a slushy mush through March. In any case, the temperature is usually above freezing.

Spring is ushered in with a magnificent fanfare of plum and cherry blossoms in March and April, an exquisite time of year when all of Japan is set ablaze in whites and pinks. The blossoms themselves last only a few days, symbolizing to the Japanese the fragile nature of beauty and of life itself. Tokyo can still have cool, rainy weather until May, so be sure to bring a light jacket or sweater.

Tokyo's Average Daytime Temperatures & Rainfall

	Jan	Feb	Mar	Apr	May	June	July	Aug	Sept	Oct	Nov	Dec
Temp. (°F)	37	39	45	54	65	71	77	80	73	62	51	41
Temp. (°C)	3	4	7	13	18	22	25	27	23	17	11	5
Days of Rain	4.3	6.1	8.9	10	9.6	12.1	10	8.2	10.9	8.9	6.4	3.8

HOLIDAYS   National holidays are January 1 (New Year's Day), January 15 (Coming-of-Age Day), February 11 (National Foundation Day), March 20 or 21 (Vernal Equinox Day), April 29 (Greenery Day), May 3 (Constitution Memorial Day), May 5 (Children's Day), July 20 (Marine Day), September 15 (Respect-for-the-Aged Day), September 23 or 24 (Autumn Equinox Day), October 10 (Health and Sports Day), November 3 (Culture Day), November 23 (Labor Thanksgiving Day), and December 23 (Emperor's Birthday). When a national holiday falls on a Sunday, the following Monday becomes a holiday.

The most important holidays for the Japanese are at **New Year's, Golden Week** (Apr 29 to May 5), and the **Obon Festival** time (in mid-July or mid-Aug).

Avoid traveling on these dates at all costs, since all long-distance trains and most accommodations are booked solid (and are also often more expensive), including most of those listed in chapter 10, "Side Trips from Tokyo." The weekends before and after these holidays are also likely to be very crowded. Luckily, Tokyo is an exception—since the major exodus is back to hometowns or the countryside, holidays such as Golden Week can be almost blissful in the metropolis. Another busy travel time is during summer school holidays, from July 19 through August, when Japanese take their vacations en masse.

Although government offices (including JNTO's Tourist Information Centers) and some businesses are closed on public holidays, restaurants and most stores remain open. The exception is during the New Year's celebration, the end of December through January 3, when almost all restaurants, public and private offices, and stores close up shop; during that time you'll have to dine in hotels.

All **museums** close for New Year's, for 1 to 4 days, but most major museums remain open for the other holidays. If a public holiday falls on a Monday (when most museums are closed), many museums will remain open but will close instead the following day, on Tuesday. Note that privately owned museums, however, such as art museums or special-interest museums, generally close on public holidays. To avoid disappointment, be sure to phone ahead if you plan on visiting a museum on or the day following a holiday.

FESTIVALS   Because Japan has two major religions, Shintoism and Buddhism, it celebrates festivals throughout the year. Every major shrine and temple observes at least one annual festival with events that might include traditional dances, archery, or colorful processions.

Listed below in the "Tokyo Calendar of Events" are major festivals and events held in Tokyo and cities close by. However, in Tokyo alone, there are so many small, neighborhood festivals that you could probably visit one almost every week of the year. For more information consult *Tokyo Journal,* which reports on current happenings in the capital city, or stop by the **Tourist Information Center** for a monthly leaflet called "Calendar Events."

Tokyo Calendar of Events

January

- **New Year's Day,** nationwide. The most important national holiday in Japan, it's a time of family reunions and gatherings with friends to drink sake and eat special New Year's dishes. Because the Japanese spend this holiday with their families, and because almost all businesses, restaurants, shops, and museums close down, it's not a particularly rewarding time of the year for foreigners to visit. January 1.
- **Dezomeshiki (New Year's Parade of Firemen),** on Chuo Dori in the Harumi district. This annual event features agile firemen in traditional costumes who prove their worth with acrobatic stunts atop tall bamboo ladders. January 6.
- **Coming-of-Age Day,** nationwide. This national holiday honors young people who have reached the age of 20, when they are allowed to vote, drink alcohol, and assume other responsibilities. Young women wear kimono. At Meiji Shrine, there's a traditional archery ceremony. January 15.

February

- **Setsubun (Bean-Throwing Festival),** at leading temples throughout Japan. This festival celebrates the last day of winter according to the lunar calendar. People throng to temples to participate in the traditional ceremony of throwing beans to drive away imaginary devils. In Tokyo, popular sites include Kanda Myojin Shrine, Hie Shrine, and Sensoji Temple. February 3 or 4.

- **Hari-kuyoo, Awashimado,** near Sensoji Temple in Asakusa. This unique event is considered an advantageous time for women, who bring broken pins and needles to Awashimado and stick them into squares of tofu, a custom since the Edo Period. February 8.
- **National Foundation Day (Kigensetsu),** a national holiday. February 11.

March

- **Hinamatsuri (Doll Festival),** observed throughout Japan. This festival is held in honor of young girls to wish them a future of happiness. In homes where there are girls, dolls dressed in ancient costumes representing the emperor, empress, and dignitaries are set up on a tier of shelves, along with miniature household articles. Many hotels also showcase doll displays in their lobbies. March 3.
- **Daruma Ichi Doll Festival,** Jindaiji Temple (take the Keio Line to Tsutsujigaoka Station). A *daruma* is a pear-shaped legless doll modeled after Bodhidharma, who founded the Zen sect in the 6th century and is said to have lost the use of his limbs from sitting 9 years in the lotus position on the way to enlightenment. Stalls here sell daruma with blank spots for eyes—according to custom, you're supposed to paint in one eye while making a wish; when your wish is fulfilled, you paint in the other eye. March 3 and 4.
- **Vernal Equinox Day,** a national holiday. Throughout the week, Buddhist temples hold ceremonies to pray for the souls of the departed. March 20 or 21.

April

- ✪ **Sakura Matsuri (Cherry-blossom Season).** The bursting forth of cherry blossoms represents the birth of spring for Tokyoites, who gather en masse under the trees to drink sake, eat, and be merry. Popular cherry-viewing spots in Tokyo include Ueno Park, Yasukuni Shrine, Shinjuku Gyoen, Aoyama Bochi Cemetery, Sumida Koen Park in Asakusa, and the moat encircling the Imperial Palace, especially Chidorigafuchi Park. Early to mid-April.
- **Buddha's Birthday,** nationwide. Ceremonies are held at all Buddhist temples, where a small image of Buddha is displayed and doused with a sweet tea called *amacha* in an act of devotion. April 8.
- ✪ **Jibeta Matsuri,** Kanayama Shrine, Kawasaki (just outside Tokyo). This festival extols the joys of sex and fertility, featuring a parade of giant phalluses. Needless to say, it's not your average festival, and you can get some unusual photographs here. Generally the second or third Sunday in April.
- **Kamakura Matsuri,** Tsurugaoka Hachimangu Shrine in Kamakura. Held in honor of heroes from the past, including Yoritomo Minamoto, who made Kamakura his shogunate capital back in 1192; highlights include horseback archery (truly spectacular to watch), a parade of portable shrines, and sacred dances. Second to third Sunday in April.
- **Yayoi Matsuri,** Futarasan Shrine in Nikko. This festival features a parade of gaily decorated floats. April 16 and 17.
- **Greenery Day,** a national holiday. The birthday of the former emperor Hirohito, who died in January 1989 and was known for his love of nature. April 29.
- **Golden Week,** a major holiday period throughout Japan. It's a crowded time to travel, making reservations a must. Because so many factories and businesses close during the week, this is said to be the best time of year for a clear view of the city and beyond from atop Tokyo Tower. April 29 to May 5.

May

- **Constitution Memorial Day,** a national holiday. May 3.
- **Children's Day,** a national holiday. This festival is for all children but especially honors young boys. Throughout Japan colorful streamers of carp are flown from poles to symbolize perseverance and strength, considered desirable attributes for young boys. May 5.
- ✪ **Kanda Myojin Festival,** Kanda Myojin Shrine. This festival, which commemorates Tokugawa Ieyasu's famous victory at Sekigahara in 1600, began during the Feudal Era as the only time townsmen could enter the shogun's castle and parade before him. Today it features a parade of dozens of portable shrines carried through the district, plus geisha dances and a tea ceremony. Held every other year in odd-numbered years on the Saturday and Sunday closest to May 15.
- **Grand Festival of Toshogu Shrine,** in Nikko. Commemorating the day in 1617 when Tokugawa Ieyasu's remains were brought to his mausoleum in Nikko, this festival re-creates that drama, with more than 1,000 armor-clad men escorting three palanquins through the streets. May 17 and 18.
- ✪ **Sanja Matsuri,** Asakusa Shrine. One of Tokyo's best-known and most colorful festivals, featuring a parade of 100 portable shrines carried through the streets of Asakusa on the shoulders of men and women dressed in traditional garb. Friday, Saturday, and Sunday closest to May 18.

June

- **Sanno Festival,** Hie Shrine. This festival, held every other year, first began in the Edo Period and features the usual portable shrines transported through the busy streets of the Akasaka district. June 10 to 16 in 2000 and 2002.

July

- **Ueki Ichi (Potted Plant Fair),** on the streets around Fuji Sengen Shrine near Asakusa on the Ginza subway line. On display are different kinds of potted plants and bonsai (miniature trees), as well as a miniature Mount Fuji symbolizing the opening of the official climbing season. July 1.
- **Tanabata (Star Festival),** celebrated throughout Japan. According to myth, the two stars Vega and Altair, representing a weaver and a shepherd, are allowed to meet only once a year on this day. If the skies are cloudy, however, the celestial pair cannot meet and must wait another year. July 7.
- **Hozuki Ichi (Ground Cherry Pod Fair),** on the grounds of Asakusa's Sensoji Temple. Hundreds of street stalls sell ground cherry pods and colorful wind bells. July 9 and 10.
- **Obon Festival,** nationwide. A festival in memory of dead ancestors, who, according to Buddhist belief, revisit the world during this period. Obon Odori folk dances are held in neighborhoods everywhere. Many Japanese return to their hometowns for the event, especially if a member of the family has died recently. As one Japanese, whose grandmother had died a few months before, told me, "I have to go back to my hometown—it's my grandmother's first Obon." Mid-July or mid-August.
- **Marine Day,** a national holiday. Commemorates the vital role of the sea in Japan's livelihood and honors those involved in the marine industry. July 20.
- ✪ **Hanabi Taikai (Fireworks Display).** Tokyo's largest summer celebration features a spectacular fireworks display over the Sumida River in Asakusa. Get there early and spread a blanket on the bank of the river or in Sumida Koen Park (near Kototoibashi and Komagatabashi bridges). Last Saturday of July, or early August.

August
- **Waraku Odori,** in Nikko. This is one of the most popular events for folk dances, with thousands of people dancing to the accompaniment of music. August 5 and 6.

September
- **Respect-for-the-Aged Day,** a national holiday. September 15.
- **Yabusame (Horseback Archery),** Tsurugaoka Hachimangu Shrine in Kamakura. The archery performances by riders on horseback recall the days of the samurai. September 16.
- **Akibasho (Autumn Sumo Match),** at the Kokugikan. The last sumo match of the year. Mid-September.
- **Autumnal Equinox Day,** a national holiday. September 23 or 24.

October
- **Health and Sports Day,** a national holiday. October 10.
- **Oeshiki Festival,** Hommonji Temple. This is the largest of Tokyo's commemorative services held for Nichiren (1222–82), a Buddhist leader exiled for his beliefs. Followers march toward the temple carrying large lanterns decorated with paper flowers. October 11 to 13.
- **Autumn Festival of Toshogu Shrine,** Toshogu Shrine in Nikko. A parade of warriors in early-17th-century dress are accompanied by spear-carriers, gun-carriers, flag-bearers, Shinto priests, pages, court musicians, and dancers as they escort a sacred portable shrine. October 17.

November
- **Culture Day,** a national holiday. November 3.
- **Daimyo Gyoretsu,** in Hakone. On this day the old Tokaido Highway that used to link Kyoto and Tokyo comes alive again with a faithful reproduction of a feudal lord's procession in the olden days. November 3.
- **Shichi-go-san (Children's Shrine-Visiting Day),** held throughout Japan. Shichi-go-san literally means "seven-five-three"; it refers to children of these ages who are dressed in kimono best and taken to shrines by their elders to express thanks and pray for their future. In Tokyo the most popular sites are Meiji, Yasukuni, Kanda Myojin, Asakusa, and Hie shrines. November 15.
- **Tori-no-Ichi (Rake Fair),** Otori Shrine in Asakusa. This fair features stalls selling rakes lavishly decorated with paper and cloth, which are thought to bring good luck and fortune. The date, based on the lunar calendar, changes each year. Mid-November.
- **Labor Thanksgiving Day,** a national holiday. November 23.

December
- **Gishi-sai,** Sengakuji Station. This memorial service honors 47 masterless samurai (*ronin*), who avenged their master's death by killing his rival and parading his head; for their act, all were ordered to commit suicide. Forty-seven men dressed as the ronin travel to Sengakuji Temple (site of their master's burial) with the enemy's head to place on their master's grave. December 14.
- **Hagoita-Ichi (Battledore Fair),** Sensoji Temple. Popular since Japan's feudal days, this fair features decorated paddles of all types and sizes. Most have designs of Kabuki actors—images made by pasting together silk and brocade—and make great souvenirs and gifts. December 17 to 19.
- **Emperor's Birthday,** celebrated nationwide. The birthday of Akihito, Japan's 125th emperor, is a national holiday. December 23.

✪ **New Year's Eve,** celebrated nationwide. At midnight many temples ring huge bells 108 times to signal the end of the old year and the beginning of the new (each peal represents a sin). Many families visit temples and shrines to pray for good luck and prosperity and to usher in the coming year. In Tokyo, Meiji Shrine is the place to be for this popular family celebration; many coffee shops and restaurants in nearby Harajuku stay open all night to serve the revelers. Other popular sites are Kanda Myojin Shrine, Sensoji Temple, and Sanno Hie Shrine.

5 Health & Insurance

You don't need any **inoculations** to enter Japan.

Prescriptions can be filled at Japanese pharmacies only if they're issued by a Japanese doctor. To avoid the hassle, be sure to bring more of your medications than you think you'll need, clearly labeled in the original vials, and packed in your

---

The Masterless Samurai

Every Japanese schoolchild knows the story of the 47 *ronin* (masterless samurai), a story also immortalized in a popular Kabuki play. In 1701, a feudal lord (*daimyo*) named Kira was ordered by the Tokugawa shogun to instruct another daimyo, Asano, in the etiquette of court ritual in preparation for a visit from an imperial entourage from Kyoto. The two quarreled, and the quick-tempered Asano, angered at the insults hurled by the older daimyo, drew his sword. Since the drawing of a sword in Edo Castle was strictly forbidden, Asano was ordered to commit ritual suicide, his family was disinherited and turned out of its home, his estate and castle were confiscated by the shogun, and his retainers, or samurai, became masterless. Kira, on the other hand, was found innocent and went unpunished.

In those days, masterless samurai were men without a future. Their loyalty in question, they were unlikely to find daimyo willing to retain them, so many turned to a life of crime, hiring themselves out as mercenaries or becoming highway robbers. The 47 ronin, however, decided to avenge their master's death by killing Kira. Knowing that Kira was on the lookout for revenge, they bided their time, until one snowy December night in 1702, they attacked Kira's mansion, cut off his head, and paraded it through the streets of Edo on the way to their master's grave. Although the public was sympathetic toward the ronin for the steadfast loyalty they had shown their dead master, the shogun ordered all of them to commit ritual suicide through disembowelment.

In Tokyo today, all that remains of Kira's mansion, located near the Kokugikan sumo stadium at 3–13–9 Ryogoku, is a white-and-black wall crowned by a weeping willow and a small inner courtyard. The 47 ronin, on the other hand, are memorialized with tombs at **Sengakuji Temple,** 2–11–1 Takanawa (subway: Sengakuji, a 2-min. walk) and a small museum (open daily 9am to 4pm) containing clothing, armor, and personal items belonging to the ronin. Admission to the temple and tombs is free; admission to the museum is ¥200 ($1.65) for adults and ¥100 (85¢) for children. Every December 14, in a reenactment of the parade, 47 men dressed as ronin deliver a replica of Kira's head to Sengakuji Temple.

carry-on luggage. Over-the-counter items are easy to obtain, though name brands are likely to be different from back home, some ingredients allowed elsewhere may be forbidden in Japan, and prices are likely to be higher.

If you get sick, you may want to speak to the **concierge** at your hotel—some hotels have in-house doctors or clinics. You can also contact the **International Association for Medical Assistance to Travelers (IAMAT)** (☎ **716/754-4883** or 416/652-0137; www.sentex.net/~iamat). This organization lists many local English-speaking doctors. In Tokyo, the **U.S. embassy** can provide a list of area doctors who speak English. If you can't find a doctor who can help you right away, try the **emergency room** at the local hospital. Many emergency rooms have walk-in-clinics for emergency cases that are not life-threatening, though there are usually limited visiting hours.

INSURANCE

There are three kinds of travel insurance: trip cancellation, medical, and lost luggage coverage. **Trip cancellation insurance** is a good idea if you have paid a large portion of your vacation expenses up front. The other two types of insurance, however, don't make sense for most travelers. Rule number one: Check your existing policies before you buy any additional coverage. In the case of **medical insurance,** your existing health plan will provide all the coverage you need; just be sure to carry your identification card in your wallet. And your homeowner's insurance, for example, should cover **stolen luggage.** Also, the airlines are responsible for $1,250 on domestic flights if they lose your luggage; if you plan to carry anything more valuable than that, keep it in your carry-on bag.

6 Tips for Travelers with Special Needs

TRAVELERS WITH DISABILITIES

Tokyo can be a nightmare for travelers with disabilities. City sidewalks can be so jam-packed that getting around on crutches or in a wheelchair is exceedingly difficult. Most subways are accessible only by stairs, and although the trains have seating for handicapped passengers—located in the first and last compartments of the train and indicated by a white circle with a blue seat—subways can be so crowded that there's barely room to move. Moreover, the seats for the handicapped are almost always occupied by commuters—so unless you look visibly handicapped, no one is likely to offer you a seat. Even Japanese homes are not very accessible, since the main floor is always raised about a foot above the entrance-hall floor.

When it comes to **facilities for the blind,** however, Japan has a very advanced system. At subway stations and on many major sidewalks in Tokyo, there are raised dots and lines on the ground to guide blind people at intersections and to subway platforms. In some cities, street lights chime a certain theme when the signal turns green east-west, and another for north-south. Even Japanese yen notes are identified by a slightly raised circle—the ¥1,000 note has one circle in a corner, while the ¥10,000 note has two. And finally, many elevators have floors indicated in Braille, and some hotels identify rooms in Braille.

In any case, a disability shouldn't stop anyone from traveling. There are more resources out there than ever before. You can join **The Society for the Advancement of Travel for the Handicapped (SATH),** 347 Fifth Ave., Suite 610, New York, NY 10016 (☎ **212/447-7284;** fax 212-725-8253; www.sath.org), for $45 annually, $30 for seniors and students, to gain access to its vast network of connections in the travel industry. The society provides information sheets on travel destinations and referrals to tour operators that specialize in traveling with disabilities. Its quarterly magazine, *Open World for Disability and Mature Travel*, is full of good information and resources. A year's subscription is $13.00 ($21 outside the U.S.).

GAY & LESBIAN TRAVELERS

While there are many gay and lesbian establishments in Tokyo, the gay community in Japan is not a vocal one, and in any case information in English is hard to come by. The **International Gay & Lesbian Travel Association (IGLTA)** (☎ 800/448-8550 or 954/776-2626; fax 954/776-3303; www.iglta.org), which has around 1,200 members, links travelers up with the appropriate gay-friendly service organization or tour specialist. It offers quarterly newsletters, marketing mailings, and a membership directory that's updated quarterly. Membership often includes gay or lesbian businesses but is open to individuals for $150 yearly, plus a $100 administration fee for new members. Members are kept informed of gay and gay-friendly hoteliers, tour operators, and airline and cruise-line representatives. Contact the IGLTA for a list of its member agencies.

General gay and lesbian travel agencies in the U.S. include **Family Abroad** (☎ 800/999-5500 or 212/459-1800; gay and lesbian), and **Above and Beyond Tours** (☎ 800/397-2681; mainly gay men).

SENIORS

A few museums in Tokyo offer **free admission** to senior citizens over 65 (be sure to have your passport handy), including the **Tokyo National Museum** and the **Edo-Tokyo Museum,** while several others in Tokyo and elsewhere offer discounts. In general, however, seniors do not receive a discount for admission to museums and other attractions. In addition, visitors to Japan should be aware that there are many stairs to navigate in metropolitan areas, particularly in subway and train stations and even pedestrian overpasses.

Before leaving home, consider becoming a member of the **American Association of Retired Persons (AARP),** 601 E St. NW, Washington, DC 20049 (☎ 800/ 424-3410 or 202/434-2277), which brings such benefits as a subscription to *Modern Maturity* magazine and a monthly newsletter and also discounts on airfares. The **National Council of Senior Citizens,** 8403 Colesville Rd., Suite 1200, Silver Spring, MD 20910 (☎ 301/578-8800), a nonprofit organization, offers a newsletter six times a year (partly devoted to travel tips); annual dues are $13 per person or couple.

If you want something more than the average vacation or guided tour, try **Elderhostel,** 75 Federal St., Boston, MA 02110-1941 (☎ 877/426-8056; www.elderhostel.org), or the University of New Hampshire's **Interhostel** (☎ 800/733-9753), both variations on the same theme: educational travel for senior citizens. Elderhostel arranges study programs for those aged 55 and over (and a spouse or companion of any age) in the U.S. and in 77 countries around the world, including Japan. Most courses last about 3 weeks and many include airfare, accommodations in student dormitories or modest inns, meals, and tuition. Write or call for a free catalog, which lists upcoming courses and destinations. Interhostel takes travelers 50 and over (with companions over 40), and offers 2- and 3-week trips, mostly international. The courses in both these programs are ungraded, involve no homework, and often focus on the liberal arts. They're not luxury vacations, but they're fun and fulfilling.

FAMILIES

The Japanese are very fond of children, which makes traveling in Japan with kids a delight. All social reserve seems to be waived for children. While the average Japanese will not approach foreign adults, if you bring a child with you the Japanese will not only talk to you but even invite you home. Taking along some small and easy-to-carry gifts for your kids to give out to other children you meet is a great icebreaker.

While children may not like such foreign customs as eating raw fish, they will find many other Japanese customs to their taste. What child could resist taking baths *en famille* and actually getting to splash? If you go to a ryokan, chances are your kids will love wearing *yukata* (cotton kimono) and clattering around in *geta* (wooden sandals). Your children will be pampered and played with and receive presents and lots of attention.

As for the food, the transition from kid-favorite spaghetti to udon noodles is easy, and udon and soba shops are inexpensive and ubiquitous. In addition, most family-style restaurants, especially those in department stores, offer a special children's meal that often includes a small toy or souvenir. For those real emergencies, Western fast-food places such as McDonald's and Kentucky Fried Chicken are everywhere in Tokyo.

Tourist spots in Japan almost always have a table or counter with a stamp and ink pad so that visitors can commemorate their trip; you might wish to give your children a small notebook so that they can collect imprints of every attraction they visit.

Children 6 to 11 years old generally are charged half-price for everything from temple admission to train tickets, while children under 6 are often admitted free. If your child under 6 sleeps with you, you generally won't even have to pay for him or her in most hotels and ryokans. However, it's always advisable to ask in advance.

Safety also makes Japan a good destination for families. Still, plan your itinerary with care. To avoid crowds, visit tourist sights on weekdays. Never travel on city transportation during rush hour or on trains during popular public holidays. And remember that with all the stairways and crowded sidewalks, strollers are less practical than baby backpacks. Many of Tokyo's major hotels provide baby-sitting services, although they are almost prohibitively expensive. Expect to fork over about $80 for 2 hours of baby-sitting.

STUDENTS

Students sometimes receive discounts at museums, though occasionally discounts are available only to students enrolled in Japanese schools. Furthermore, discounted prices are often not displayed in English. Your best bet is to bring along an International Student Identity Card (ISIC; see below) along with your university student ID, and to show them at museum ticket windows.

The best resource for students is the **Council on International Educational Exchange,** or CIEE (www.ciee.org). They can set you up with an ID card, and their travel branch, **Council Travel Service** (☎ **800/226-8624;** www.counciltravel.com), is the biggest student travel agency operation in the world, offering discounts on plane tickets and the like.

From CIEE you can obtain the student traveler's best friend, the $18 **International Student Identity Card (ISIC).** It's the only officially acceptable form of student identification, good for discounts to museums and attractions. It also provides you with basic health and life insurance and a 24-hour help line. If you're no longer a student but are still under 26, you can get a **GO 25 card** from the same people, which will get you the insurance and some of the discounts (but not student admission prices in museums).

In Canada, **Travel CUTS,** 200 Ronson St., Suite 320, Toronto, ONT M9W 5Z9 (☎ **800/667-2887** or 416/614-2887; www.travelcuts.com), offers similar services. **Campus Travel,** 52 Grosvenor Gardens, London SW1W 0AG (☎ **0171/ 730-3402;** www.campustravel.co.uk), opposite Victoria Station, is Britain's leading specialist in student and youth travel.

SINGLE TRAVELERS

Traveling alone poses no difficulty, even for women. The main obstacle is expense, since the price of accommodations is cheaper for couples and groups. Single travelers, therefore, should do what traveling businessmen do: Stay at so-called **business hotels.** With their large number of single rooms, they cater almost exclusively to solo businessmen.

An alternative is to register with **Travel Companion** (☎ **516/454-0880**), one of the nation's oldest roommate finders for single travelers, where you can find a trustworthy travel mate who will split the cost of the room with you and be around as little, or as often, as you like during the day.

7 Flying to Japan

Most visitors to Tokyo arrive by air, at the **New Tokyo International Airport,** located outside Tokyo in **Narita** (and usually referred to as the Narita Airport).

THE AIRLINES

Since the flying time to Tokyo is about 12 hours from Los Angeles and 13½ hours from Chicago or New York, you'll want to consider on-board services and even mileage programs (you'll earn lots of miles on this round-trip!) as well as ticket price when choosing your carrier. Airlines flying to Tokyo from North America, England, Australia, and New Zealand include the following.

Air Canada (☎ **800/268-7240** in Canada, 800/426-7000 in the United States; www.cdnair.ca) offers flights from Vancouver to Tokyo daily and from Toronto to Tokyo five times a week.

Air New Zealand (☎ **0800/737-000** in New Zealand; 800/262-1234 in the United States; www.airnz.co.nz) flies from Auckland to Tokyo.

All Nippon Airways (☎ **800/235-9262;** www.fly-ana.com) is Japan's largest domestic carrier. It offers daily round-trip service from New York, Washington, D.C., Chicago, and Los Angeles to Tokyo, as well as frequent service from San Francisco and Honolulu to Tokyo. It also flies from London and Sydney to Tokyo. ANA has a code share alliance with United Airlines (meaning that both airlines can sell each other's tickets; you can also get United frequent-flier miles with ANA). ANA passengers can also receive discounts at ANA hotels in Japan with free baggage transfers.

American Airlines (☎ **800/433-7300;** www.aa.com) offers flights daily from Seattle, Dallas, San Jose, and Chicago to Tokyo and code shares with Japan Airlines.

British Airways (☎ **03/4522-2111** in Britain; www.british-airways.com) flies from London to Tokyo.

Continental Airlines (☎ **800/523-3273;** www.flycontiental.com), offers daily flights from Newark, Houston, and Honolulu to Tokyo.

Delta Airlines (☎ **800/241-4141;** www.delta-air.com) offers daily flights from Los Angeles and Portland, Oregon, to Tokyo.

Japan Airlines (☎ 800/525-3663; www.japanair.com), Japan's flagship carrier, offers more international flights to Japan than any other carrier and is noted for its excellent service. Another plus to flying Japan Airlines is that JAL international passengers can make advance seat reservations at JAL overseas offices for Shinkansen bullet trains, a great convenience if you're traveling during peak times, and can purchase Japan Rail Passes (see "Getting Around," in chapter 3). JAL flies to Tokyo from New York, Chicago, San Francisco, Los Angeles, Dallas, Las Vegas, and Vancouver as well as England, New Zealand, and Australia.

Northwest Airlines (☎ 800/447-4747; www.nwa.com) offers more flights than any other American carrier serving Japan, with daily flights to Tokyo. North American gateways are Los Angeles, San Francisco, Seattle, Las Vegas, Detroit, New York, Minneapolis–St. Paul, and Honolulu; Japan-bound flights also depart from Singapore, Manila, Bangkok, Taipei, Kaohsiung, Seoul, Beijing, Shanghai, Guam, Saipan, Hong Kong, and Kuala Lumpur. The fact that Northwest (which shares mileage programs with KLM and Continental) flies to so many Asian destinations makes it easy to coordinate onward travel plans, say, to Hong Kong or Bangkok. And the airline's stellar service has even attracted the hard-to-please Japanese, who regularly fly Northwest.

Qantas (☎ 131313 in Australia; ☎ 800/227-4500; www.qantas.com) flies from Sydney, Melbourne, and Brisbane to Tokyo.

United Airlines (☎ 800/538-2929; www.ual.com) has daily flights from San Francisco, Los Angeles, Chicago, and New York to Tokyo. It shares codes with ANA.

AIRFARES

BUSINESS & FIRST CLASS   Because the flight to Japan is such a long one, you may wish to splurge for upgraded service and a roomier seat in business or first class. Other benefits include special counters for check-in, private lounges at the airport, and better meals. Northwest's regular round-trip business-class fares to Tokyo are $5,288 from New York and $4,007 from Seattle, San Francisco, or Los Angeles; Northwest's first-class fares to Tokyo are $9,670 from New York and $7,688 from Seattle, San Francisco, or Los Angeles.

ECONOMY & APEX   Full-fare economy class tickets offer little in terms of pampering on board but have few purchase restrictions and are certainly less expensive than first and business class. On Northwest, a full-fare round-trip economy seat costs $2,644 from New York and $2,038 from the West Coast. APEX (Advance Purchase Excursion) fares are less expensive, but are usually loaded with restrictions and vary according to the season. There are three fare seasons: peak season (summer) is the most expensive, basic season (winter) is the least expensive, and shoulder season is between the other two in time and in price. In all three seasons, APEX fares are a little higher on weekends. Reservations, ticketing, and payment for the nonrefundable APEX fare usually must be completed no later than 21 days prior to departure. There's also a limited time to complete your round trip, usually not less than one week and not more than six months. A few airlines offer inexpensive last-minute tickets with all the APEX restrictions except the advance-purchase time limit, in order to achieve full-passenger capacity. Northwest's APEX fare can be as low as $1,329 for a winter weekday flight from Los Angeles.

FLYING FOR LESS: TIPS FOR GETTING THE BEST AIRFARES

Passengers within the same airplane cabin are rarely paying the same fare for their seats. You'll save money by purchasing your ticket in advance, for example, and flying on a weekend. Here are a few other easy ways to save.

1. **Check your newspaper for advertised discounts or call the airlines directly and ask whether any promotional rates or special fares are available.** Periodically airlines lower prices on their most popular routes. If your schedule is flexible, ask if you can secure a cheaper fare by staying an extra day or by flying midweek. (Many airlines won't volunteer this information.) If you already hold a ticket when a sale breaks, it may even pay to exchange your ticket, which usually incurs a $50–$75 charge. Note, however, that the lowest-priced fares are often nonrefundable, require advance purchase of 21 days, and carry penalties for changing dates of travel.

2. **Look for discount fares.** Some companies provide deeply discounted tickets—sometimes saving more than 50% on economy fares and around 30% on APEX fares—with no restrictions, depending on availability. You can buy your ticket through them well in advance or, if you're lucky, at the last moment. Among such firms that deal with travel to Japan are **Nippon Travel,** 5028 Wisconsin Ave. NW, Suite 403, Washington, DC 20016 (☎ **202/362-0039**), and **Japan Associates Travel,** 2000 17th St. NW, Washington, DC 20009 (☎ **202/ 939-8853**).

   Consolidators, also known as bucket shops, are another good place to find low fares. Consolidators buy seats in bulk from the airlines and then sell them back to the public at prices below even the airlines' discounted rates. Their small, boxed ads usually run in the Sunday travel section at the bottom of the page. Before you pay, however, ask for a confirmation number from the consolidator and then call the airline itself to confirm your seat. Be prepared to book your ticket with a different consolidator—there are many to choose from—if the airline can't confirm your reservation. Also be aware that bucket shop tickets are usually nonrefundable or rigged with stiff cancellation penalties, often as high as 50% to 75% of the ticket price.

   Council Travel (☎ **800/226-8624;** www.counciltravel.com) caters especially to young travelers, but their bargain-basement prices are available to people of all ages. Other reliable consolidators include **1-800-FLY-CHEAP** (**www.1800flycheap. com**) and **TFI Tours International** (☎ **800-745-8000** or 212/736-1140), which serves as a clearinghouse for unused seats.

3. **Search the Internet for cheap fares**—though it's still best to compare your findings with the research of a dedicated travel agent, if you're lucky enough to have one, especially when you're booking more than just a flight. A few of the better-respected virtual travel agents are **Travelocity** (www.travelocity.com) and **Microsoft Expedia** (www.expedia.com). Each has its own little quirks—Travelocity and Expedia, for example, require you to register with them—but they all provide variations of the same service. Just enter the dates you want to fly and the cities you want to visit, and the computer roots out the lowest fares.

4. **Check out the great last-minute deals that are also available through free e-mail services, provided directly by the airlines.** Each week, the airline sends you a list of discounted flights, usually leaving the upcoming Friday or Saturday, and returning the following Monday or Tuesday. You can sign up for all the major airlines at once by logging on to Smarter Living (www.smarterliving.com), or go to each individual airline's web site (see the list of airlines serving Japan, above).

5. **Book a seat on a charter flight.** Discounted fares have pared the number available, but they can still be found. Most charter operators advertise and sell their seats through travel agents, thus making these local professionals your best source of information for available flights. Before deciding to take a charter flight,

however, check the restrictions on the ticket: You may be asked to purchase a tour package, to pay in advance, to be amenable if the day of departure is changed, to pay a service charge, to fly on an airline you're not familiar with (this usually is not the case), and to pay harsh penalties if you cancel—but be understanding if the charter doesn't fill up and is canceled up to 10 days before departure. Summer charters fill up more quickly than others and are almost sure to fly, but if you decide on a charter flight, seriously consider cancellation and baggage insurance.

TIPS FOR FLYING IN COMFORT

A major consideration for visitors flying to Japan, especially on long flights from North America, is **jet lag.** For some reason, flying west has slightly less effect than flying east, which means the hardest flight to overcome is the journey from Japan back to North America.

To minimize the adverse effects of jet lag—primarily fatigue and slow adjustment to your new time zone—refrain from consuming carbonated drinks or alcohol during the flight. In addition, eat light meals high in vegetable and cereal content the day before, during, and the day after your flight, and drink plenty of water to prevent dehydration. Further, exercise your body during the flight by walking around the cabin every so often and by flexing your arms, hands, legs, and feet. It also helps to set your watch (and your mental clock) to the time zone of your destination as soon as you board the plane.

Once you reach your destination, schedule your day according to your new time zone. Put in a normal day, even if you're tired. Go for a walk in the sunlight, and once in your hotel, turn on the lights as brightly as you can until it's time to go to bed in the evening. If you follow these instructions, your body should be back to normal within 2 days.

Consider also the following:

- You'll find the most legroom in a **bulkhead seat,** in the front row of each airplane cabin. Consider, however, that you will have to store your luggage in the overhead bin, and you won't have the best seat in the house for the in-flight movie.
- When you check in, ask for one of the **emergency-exit-row seats,** which also have extra legroom. They are assigned at the airport, usually on a first-come, first-served basis. In the unlikely event of an emergency, however, you'll be expected to open the emergency-exit door and help direct traffic.
- **Seat position** can be important. To be one of the first to disembark after the gangway is in place, ask for a seat toward the front of the plane. If, however, you are traveling with a large carry-on, ask for a seat toward the **back of the plane,** so that you can be assured of boarding first and finding space in the overhead bin.
- Pack some **toiletries** for long flights. Airplane cabins are notoriously dry places. Take a travel-size bottle of moisturizer or lotion to refresh your face and hands at the end of the flight, as well as a toothbrush. If you wear contact lenses, take them out before you get on board and wear glasses instead.
- If you're flying with a cold or chronic sinus problems, use a **decongestant** ten minutes before ascent and descent, to minimize pressure buildup in the inner ear.
- If you're flying with **kids,** don't forget a deck of cards, toys, extra bottles, pacifiers, diapers, and chewing gum to help them relieve ear pressure buildup during ascent and descent. Most airlines provide amenities and services for children. Northwest, for example, provides bassinets (reserve in advance), warms baby bottles, and stocks baby food on all international flights.

ARRIVING AT NARITA AIRPORT

Tokyo has two airports. International flights land at the **New Tokyo International Airport** in Narita (usually referred to as the Narita Airport), about 40 miles outside Tokyo. (If you're arriving in Tokyo from elsewhere in Japan, your flight will probably land at **Haneda Airport,** used primarily for domestic flights; see below.)

The Narita Airport consists of two terminals, Terminals 1 and 2, connected by free shuttle service. Arrival lobbies in both terminals have banks for money exchange and are connected to all ground transportation to Tokyo.

A **Tourist Information Center (TIC),** managed by the Japan National Tourist Organization, is located in the arrival lobbies of both Terminal 1 (☎ 0476/ 30-3383) and Terminal 2 (☎ 0476/34-6251). The TIC offers free maps and pamphlets and can direct you to your hotel or inn. Both are open daily 9am to 8pm; if you don't yet have a hotel room and want one at a modest price, you can make reservations here free of charge Monday through Friday from 9am to 7:30pm.

Other **facilities** at both terminals include post offices; Kokusai Denshin Denwa (KDD) offices, where you can make an international telephone call or send a telegram; and medical clinics (open Monday to Saturday 9am to 10pm). There are also shower rooms, day rooms for napping, and children's playrooms open and free of charge, and, in Terminal 2, a business center open daily 7am to 9pm.

GETTING FROM NARITA AIRPORT TO TOKYO

Everyone grumbles about Narita Airport because it's so far away from Tokyo. In fact, Narita is a different town altogether, with miles of rice paddies, bamboo groves, pine forests, and urban sprawl in between.

BY TAXI Obviously, jumping into a taxi is the easiest way to get to Tokyo, but it's also prohibitively expensive—and may not even be the quickest method during rush hours. Expect to spend ¥22,000 to ¥24,000 ($183 to $200) for this 1- to 2-hour taxi ride from Narita.

BY AIRPORT BUS The most popular way to get from Narita to Tokyo is via the **Airport Limousine Bus** (☎ 03/3665-7220), which picks up passengers and their luggage directly from just outside the arrival lobbies of both terminals. This is the best mode of transportation if you have heavy baggage or are staying at one of the many hotels served by the bus. Buses operate most frequently to the Tokyo City Air Terminal (TCAT) in downtown Tokyo; the trip takes about 70 minutes. Buses also go to Tokyo Station and Shinjuku Station, with departures up to four or five times an hour during peak times. They also serve more than 40 major hotels on a slightly less frequent schedule, generally once or twice an hour, and it can take almost 2 hours to reach a hotel in Shinjuku. Check with the staff at the Airport Limousine Bus counter in the arrival lobbies to inquire which bus stops nearest your hotel and the time of departure. Fares for the limousine bus average ¥2,900 to ¥3,000 ($24 to $25), based on distance traveled; children 6 to 12 are charged half price, and children 6 and younger ride free.

If you take a limousine bus into Tokyo, plenty of **taxis** are available at the end of the line. TCAT, Shinjuku Station, and Tokyo Station are also served by **public transportation.** TCAT is connected to the subway Hanzomon Line's end stop, Suitengu-mae, via moving walkways and escalators; Shinjuku and Tokyo stations are hubs for subway lines and commuter trains.

Though not as well known, **Airport Shuttle** (☎ 0476/35-6767) also operates buses to approximately 20 hotels in Tokyo but departures are not as frequent. Fares for this service also average ¥2,900 to ¥3,000 ($24 to $25), and you'll find the company's counters in the arrivals lobbies of both terminals.

BY TRAIN   The quickest way to reach Tokyo is by train, with several options available. Trains depart directly from the airport's two underground stations, called Narita Airport Station (which is in Terminal 1) and Airport Terminal 2.

The **JR Narita Express (NEX)** is the fastest way to reach Tokyo Station, Shinagawa, Shinjuku, Ikebukuro, and Yokohama, with departures approximately once an hour, or twice an hour during peak hours. The trip to Tokyo Station takes 53 minutes and costs ¥2,940 ($24). The trip to Shinagawa, Shinjuku or Ikebukuro costs ¥3,110 ($26). Note, however, that seats are occasionally sold out in advance, especially during peak travel times. If you want to reserve a seat for your return trip to Narita Airport—and I strongly urge that you do—you can do so here at the NEX counter, or at a JR Reservation Ticket Office or a View Plaza at major JR stations in Tokyo or at a travel agency.

If the NEX is sold out, you can take the slower **JR Airport Liner,** which will get you to Tokyo Station in 80 minutes and costs ¥1,280 ($11).

An alternative is the privately owned **Keisei Skyliner** train, which departs directly from both Narita Airport Station (Terminal 1) and Airport Terminal 2 and travels to Ueno Station in Tokyo in about 1 hour, with a stop at Nippori Station on the way. You'll find Keisei Skyliner counters in the arrival lobbies of both terminals. The fare from Narita Airport to Ueno Station in Tokyo is ¥1,920 ($17) one-way. Trains depart approximately every 30 or 40 minutes between 7:50am and 9:58pm. If you're on a strict budget, you can take one of Keisei's slower **limited express** trains to Ueno Station, with fares starting at ¥1,000 ($8.70) for the 75-minute trip. Upon reaching Ueno Station, you can take either the subway or the JR Yamanote Line to other parts of Tokyo. There are also plenty of taxis available.

RETURNING TO NARITA AIRPORT

If you're returning to Narita Airport via the Airport Limousine Bus (see above), the most convenient departure is from the Tokyo City Air Terminal (TCAT), located at Suitengu-mae Station on the Hanzomon Line, since there are more departures per hour from here than any other location. Some airlines, including Japan Airlines and Northwest Airlines, have full-service counters where you can check in your luggage and receive your boarding pass.

GETTING FROM HANEDA AIRPORT TO CENTRAL TOKYO

If you're arriving at **Haneda Airport,** located closer to the center of Tokyo and used mainly for domestic flights, you can take the **Airport Limousine Bus** to Shinjuku Station, Tokyo Station, the Tokyo City Air Terminal (TCAT) in downtown Tokyo, and hotels in Shinjuku, Ikebukuro, and Akasaka, with fares running from ¥900 to ¥1,200 ($7.50 to $10). Locals, however, are more likely to take the monorail from Haneda Airport to Hamamatsucho Station; the fare is ¥470 ($3.90) and the trip takes only 15 minutes. At Hamamatsucho, the Yamanote Line connects with major stations, including Tokyo Station and Shinjuku Station.

8 Organized Tours

ESCORTED TOURS

If you're the kind of traveler who doesn't like leaving such arrangements as accommodations, transportation, and itinerary to chance, you may wish to join an escorted tour of Japan. Among the many companies offering group tours to Tokyo

Arriving in Tokyo by Train

If you're getting to Tokyo by the Shinkansen bullet train, you'll probably arrive at **Tokyo Station** (note that some of the Tohoku and Joetsu Shinkansen lines terminate at Ueno Station). Tokyo Station is easily connected to the rest of the city via JR commuter trains and the subway. If you need assistance or information on Tokyo, stop by the **Information Bureau of Tokyo** (run by the Tokyo Metropolitan Government), located in Tokyo Station in the JR View Plaza, near the Yaesu Central Exit (open Monday through Saturday 9am to 6pm; closed Sunday and holidays).

---

are **Pacific Bestour,** 228 Rivervale Rd., Rivervale, NJ 07675 (☎ **800/688-3288** or 201/664-8778); and **TBI Tours,** 53 Summer St., Keene, NH 03431 (☎ **800/ 223-0266** or 603/357-5033). **Japan Airlines** (☎ **800/525-3663**), Japan's flagship carrier, also operates JALTOURS, which offers complete travel packages to Japan; call the airline or a travel agent for details.

PACKAGE TOURS

Package tours are not the same thing as escorted tours. They are simply a way to buy airfare and accommodations at the same time. For destinations like Tokyo, they are a smart way to go, because they save you a lot of money. That's because packages are sold in bulk to tour operators—who resell them to the public at a cost that drastically undercuts standard rates.

Packages, however, vary widely. Some offer a better class of hotels than others, while others offer the same hotels for lower prices or a range of hotel choices at different prices. Some offer flights on scheduled airlines, while others book charters. In some packages, your choice of accommodations and travel days may be limited. Some packages let you choose between escorted vacations and independent vacations; others will allow you to add on just a few excursions or escorted day trips (also at lower prices than you could locate on your own) without booking an entirely escorted tour.

FINDING A PACKAGE DEAL   The best place to start your search is the travel section of your local Sunday newspaper. Also check the ads in the back of national travel magazines like *Travel & Leisure, National Geographic Traveler,* and *Condé Nast Traveler.* Among the many tour companies offering independent packages to Tokyo, check **FultonEX** (☎ 888/345-1888); **Japan & Orient** (☎ 800/ 377-1080); **Nippon Travel Agency** (☎ 800/452-1682); **Pacific Bestour** (☎ 800/688-3288); **Pacifico Creative Service** (☎ 800/221-1081); and **TBI Tours** (☎ 800/223-0266).

Another good resource is the airlines themselves, which often package their flights together with accommodations. **All Nippon Airways** (☎ **800/235-9262**), Japan's largest domestic carrier, offers discounts at ANA hotels and can save you money on domestic flights planned in conjunction with your international flight. **Northwest World Vacations** (☎ **800/800-1504**) offers flight-and-hotel packages to Tokyo that allow you to choose from a range of hotels and provides options for additional nights and sightseeing tours. In addition, Northwest's **Cyber Saver Bargain Alerts,** posted on its Web site every Wednesday, offer special hotel rates, package deals, and discounted airline fares.

Getting to Know Tokyo

Tokyo's sheer size and the language barrier provide the greatest challenges facing newcomers. This chapter will help you to orient yourself in the city and answer some essential questions, from how to get around using public transportation to what numbers to call during an emergency.

1 Orientation

VISITOR INFORMATION

The **Japan National Tourist Organization (JNTO)** maintains three tourist offices, known as **Tourist Information Centers (TIC),** in the vicinity of Tokyo to handle inquiries from foreigners and the general public about Tokyo and the rest of Japan. All three are superbly equipped to answer questions about Tokyo and other destinations in Japan and to provide free maps and sightseeing materials. You can even make reservations here for inexpensive accommodations throughout Japan at no extra charge.

If you're arriving by plane at **Narita Airport,** you'll find a TIC in the arrival lobbies of both Terminal 1 (☎ **0476/30-3383**) and Terminal 2 (☎ **0476/34-6251**), both open daily from 9am to 8pm. Otherwise, there's another TIC in the heart of Tokyo at 3–5–1 Marunouchi (☎ **03/3201-3331**). It's buried (and rather hard to find) in a complex called the **Tokyo International Forum,** in the basement 1 concourse of the Glass Hall Building, a dramatic structure that resembles the hull of a ship. You can reach it by taking the subway to Yurakucho Station, from which it's a 1-minute walk, or by taking the Yamanote Line to JR Yurakucho Station (you can see the Tokyo International Forum building from the train platform). The staff here are courteous and efficient; I cannot recommend them highly enough. The office also has more information than any other tourist office in the rest of Japan, including pamphlets and brochures on major cities and attractions. Be sure to stop off here if you plan to visit other destinations, since information in English may not be available at the destinations themselves. Hours are Monday through Friday from 9am to 5pm and Saturday from 9am to noon; closed Sunday and national holidays. Note that the hotel reservation service is available only weekdays and is closed from 11:30am to 1pm.

Tokyo at a Glance

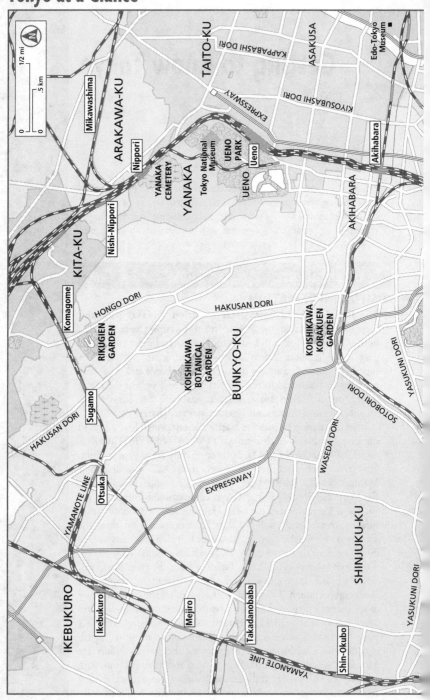

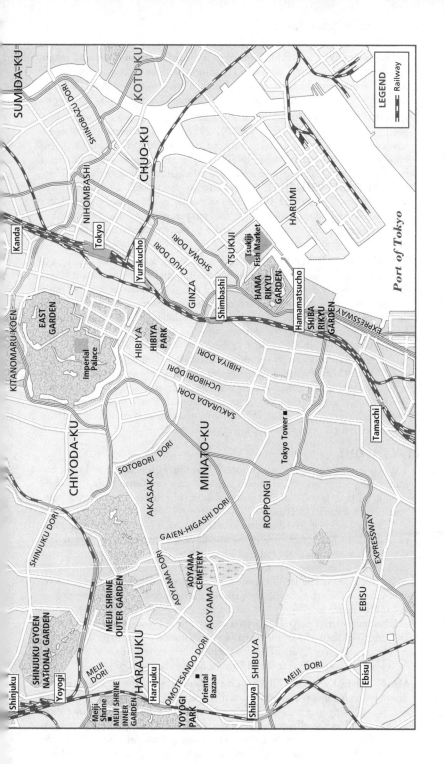

33

Another source of information on Tokyo is the **Information Bureau of Tokyo,** operated by the Tokyo Metropolitan Government, with locations at Tokyo Station near the Yaesu Central Entrance and in Shinjuku Station on the ground floor near the Central East Exit. Both are open Monday through Saturday from 9am to 6pm.

INFORMATION BY PHONE   If you want a quick rundown of what's happening in Tokyo, you can call ☎ **03/3201-2911** for a taped recording in English of what's going on in the city and its environs in the way of special exhibitions, performances, festivals, and events. JNTO also operates **Japan Travel-Phone,** a nationwide hot line offering travel advice and information in English. Inside Tokyo, call the TIC at ☎ **03/3201-3331;** outside Tokyo, you can call toll-free daily from 9am to 5pm at ☎ **0088-22-4800.** You can call Japan Travel-Phone not only for information but also for assistance—if, for example, you're having problems communicating with your innkeeper and need a translator, or even if you're lost and haven't a clue where the heck you are.

TOURIST PUBLICATIONS   The best publication for finding out what's going on in Tokyo is the *Tokyo Journal,* published monthly and available for ¥600 ($5) at foreign-language bookstores, restaurants, and bars. In addition to arts and entertainment listings, including Kabuki, concerts, and gallery exhibitions, it gives details on department-store sales, photography exhibitions, schools for learning Japanese, apartments for rent, and much more.

English-language newspapers such as the *Japan Times* and the *Daily Yomiuri* also carry information on theater, film, and special events. In addition, there are also free giveaways, the best of which is *Tokyo Classified,* filled mainly with classifieds for the ex-pat community but also containing nightlife information, events listings, movie reviews, and dining information. Other publications include *Tokyo Day & Night,* with nightlife information, and *Tokyo Weekender,* aimed at ex-pats living in Tokyo but also carrying a section on what's going on in the city.

CITY LAYOUT

Tokyo is located on the mideastern part of **Honshu,** Japan's largest and most historically important island, and sprawls westward onto the **Kanto Plain** (the largest plain in all Japan). It is bounded on the southeast by **Tokyo Bay,** which in turn, opens into the Pacific Ocean.

If you look at a map, you'll see that Tokyo retains some of its Edo-Period features, most notably a large green oasis in the middle of the city, site of the former Edo Castle and today home of the Imperial Palace and its grounds. Surrounding it is the castle moat; a bit farther out are remnants of another circular moat built by the Tokugawa shogun. The **JR Yamanote Line** forms another loop around the inner city; most of Tokyo's major hotels, nightlife districts, and attractions are near or inside this oblong loop.

For administrative purposes, Tokyo is broken down into 23 wards, known as *ku.* Its business districts of Marunouchi and Hibiya, for example, are in Chiyoda-ku, while Ginza is part of Chuo-ku (Central Ward). These two ku are the historic hearts of Tokyo, for it was here that the city had its humble beginnings.

MAIN STREETS & ARTERIES   One difficulty in finding your way around Tokyo is that hardly any streets are named. Think about what that means—12 million people living in a huge metropolis of nameless streets. Granted, major thoroughfares and some well-known streets in areas like Ginza and Shinjuku received names after World War II at the insistence of American occupation forces, and a few more have been labeled in the past decade. But for the most part, Tokyo's address system is based on a complicated number scheme that must make the postal worker's job here a nightmare. To make matters worse, most streets in Tokyo zigzag—an arrangement apparently left over from olden days, to confuse potential attacking enemies.

Among Tokyo's most important named streets are **Meiji Dori,** which follows the loop of the Yamanote Line and runs from Ebisu in the south through Shibuya, Harajuku, Shinjuku, and Ikebukuro in the north; **Yasukuni Dori** and **Shinjuku Dori,** which cut across the heart of the city from Shinjuku to Chiyoda-ku; and **Sotobori Dori, Chuo Dori, Harumi Dori,** and **Showa Dori,** which pass through Ginza. (*Dori* means avenue or street, as does *michi.*)

An intersection in Tokyo is called a crossing; it seems every district has a famous crossing. Ginza 4–chome Crossing is the intersection of Chuo Dori and Harumi Dori. Roppongi Crossing is the intersection of Roppongi Dori and Gaien-Higashi Dori.

FINDING AN ADDRESS Because streets did not have names when Japan's postal system was established, the country has a unique address system. A typical Tokyo address might read 7–8–4 Roppongi, Minato-ku, which is the address of the Inakaya restaurant. Minato-ku is the name of the ward. Wards are further divided into districts, in this case Roppongi. Roppongi itself is broken down into *chome,* here 7–chome. Number 8 refers to a smaller area within the chome—often an entire block, sometimes larger. Thus, houses on one side of the street will usually have a different middle number from houses on the other side. The last number, in this case 4, refers to the actual building. Although it seems reasonable to assume that next to a number 4 building will be a number 5, that's not always the case; buildings were assigned numbers as they were constructed, not according to location.

Addresses are usually, but not always, posted on buildings, beside doors, on telephone poles, and by streetlights, but often they are written only in *kanji* (Chinese characters.) In recent years Roman letters have been added to addresses posted below stoplights at major intersections.

FINDING YOUR WAY AROUND If you're traveling by subway or JR train, the first thing you should do upon reaching your destination is to look for signs posted on every platform that tell which exit to take for particular buildings, attractions, and chome. At Roppongi Station, for example, you'll find yellow signboards that tell you which exit to take for Roppongi 7–chome, which will at least get you pointed in the right direction once you emerge from the station. Stations also have maps of the area either inside the station or at the exit; these are your best plan of attack when trying to find a particular address.

As you walk around Tokyo, you will also notice maps posted beside sidewalks giving a breakdown of the postal numbering system for the area. The first time I tried to use one, I stopped first one Japanese, then another, and asked them to point out on the map where a particular address was. They both studied the map and pointed out the direction. Both turned out to be wrong. Not very encouraging, but if you learn how to read these maps, they're invaluable.

Another invaluable source of information is the numerous police boxes, called *koban,* located in every neighborhood throughout the city. Police officers have area maps and are very helpful. You should also never hesitate to ask a Japanese the way, but be sure to ask more than one. You'll be amazed at the conflicting directions you'll receive. Apparently, most Japanese would rather hazard a guess than impolitely shrug their shoulders and leave you standing there. The best thing to do is ask directions of several Japanese and then follow the majority opinion. You can also duck into a shop and ask someone where a nearby address is, although in my experience employees often do not even know the address of their own store.

MAPS   Before setting out on your own, arm yourself with a few maps. Maps are so much a part of life in Tokyo that they're often included as part of shop or restaurant advertisements, on business cards, and even in private-party invitations. Even though I've spent several years in Tokyo, I rarely venture forth without a map. One I find particularly useful is issued free by the Tourist Information Center; it's called **Tourist Map of Tokyo** and includes smaller, detailed maps of several districts (such as Shinjuku) as well as subway and greater-Tokyo train maps. With this map you should be able to locate at least the general vicinity of every place mentioned in this book. Hotels also sometimes distribute their own maps. In short, never pass up a free map.

For a detailed map, head to Tower Records and Books, Kinokuniya, Maruzen, or one of the other bookstores with an English-language section, where you'll find more than a dozen variations of city maps at various prices. My own personal favorite is Nippon Kokuseisha's **Map of Central Tokyo,** a compact map listing chome and chome subsections for major areas. Also useful is Shobunsa's **Tokyo Metropolitan Atlas,** which covers all 23 of Tokyo's wards with specific postal maps, as well as greater Tokyo and its vicinity, along with expressway and Tokyo area road maps. If you plan on spending a lot of time in Tokyo, consider Kodansha's heftier **Tokyo City Atlas,** which has both Japanese and English place names, along with rail and subway maps, district maps, and an index to important buildings, museums, and other places of interest.

Neighborhoods in Brief

Taken as a whole, Tokyo seems formidable, so the best strategy is to divide and conquer. It's best to think of Tokyo as nothing more than a variety of neighborhoods scrunched together, much like the pieces of a jigsaw puzzle. Holding the pieces together, so to speak, is the **Yamanote Line,** a commuter train loop around central Tokyo, passing through such important stations as Yurakucho, Tokyo, Ueno, Shinjuku, Harajuku, and Shibuya.

Hibiya   This is not only the business heart of Tokyo, but its spiritual heart as well. Hibiya is where the Tokugawa shogun built his magnificent castle, and was thus the center of old Edo. Today, it's no less important as the home of the **Imperial Palace,** built on the ruins of Edo Castle and today the residence of Japan's 125th emperor. Bordering the palace is the wonderful **East Garden.** Near Hibiya, located in the Chiyoda-ku ward, is the **Tourist Information Center** (see "Visitor Information," above).

Nihombashi   Back when Edo became Tokugawa's shogunate capital, Nihombashi was where merchants settled and set up shop, making it the commercial center of the city and therefore of all of Japan. Nihombashi, which stretches east of Tokyo Station, still serves as Tokyo's financial center; it's the home of the **Tokyo Stock Exchange** and headquarters for major banks and companies. The area takes its name from an actual **bridge,** Nihombashi, which means "Bridge of Japan," and served as the measuring point for all main highways leading out of the city to the provinces during the Edo Period.

Ginza   Ginza is the swankiest and most expensive shopping area in all Japan. When the country opened to foreign trade in the 1860s following 2 centuries of self-imposed seclusion, it was here that Western imports and adopted Western architecture were first displayed. Today, Ginza is where you'll find a multitude of department stores, boutiques, exclusive restaurants, hotels, art galleries, hostess clubs, and drinking establishments. Although Tokyo's younger generation favors less staid districts like Harajuku, Shibuya, and Shinjuku, the Ginza is still a good place to window-shop and dine, especially on Sundays, when several major thoroughfares are closed to vehicular traffic, giving it a festive atmosphere. On the edge of Ginza is **Kabukiza,** the nation's main venue for Kabuki productions.

Tsukiji   Located only two subway stops from Ginza, Tsukiji was born from reclaimed land during the Tokugawa shogunate; its name, in fact, means "reclaimed land." During the Meiji Period, it housed a large foreign settlement. Today it's famous for the **Tsukiji Fish Market,** one of the largest wholesale fish markets in the world. Nearby is the **Hama Rikyu Garden,** considered by some to be the best garden in Tokyo. From Hama Rikyu Garden, sightseeing boats depart for Asakusa in the north.

Asakusa   Located in the northeastern part of central Tokyo, Asakusa served as the pleasure quarters for old Edo. Today it's known throughout Japan as the site of the famous **Sensoji Temple,** one of Tokyo's top attractions. It also has a wealth of tiny shops selling traditional Japanese crafts, most clustered along a pedestrian street called **Nakamise Dori** which leads straight to Sensoji Temple; its atmosphere alone makes this one of the most enjoyable places to shop for Japanese souvenirs. When Tokyoites talk about *shitamachi* (old downtown), they are referring to the traditional homes and tiny narrow streets of the Asakusa and Ueno areas.

Ueno   Located not far from Asakusa, on the northern edge of the JR Yamanote Line loop, Ueno retains some of the city's old shitamachi atmosphere, especially at its spirited **Ameya Yokocho** food and flea market that spreads underneath the Yamanote train tracks. Ueno is most famous, however, for **Ueno Park,** a huge green space comprised of a zoo, concert hall, temple, shrine, and several acclaimed museums, including the **Tokyo National Museum,** which houses the largest collection of Japanese art and antiquities in the world. North of Ueno is **Yanaka,** a delightful residential area of traditional old homes, neighborhood shops, and temples; several of Tokyo's most affordable Japanese-style inns are located here.

Shinjuku   Originating as a post town in 1698 to serve the needs of feudal lords and their retainers traveling between Edo and the provinces, Shinjuku was hardly touched by the 1923 Great Kanto Earthquake, making it an attractive alternative for businesses wishing to relocate following the widespread destruction. In 1971, Japan's first skyscraper was erected with the opening of the Keio Plaza Hotel in western Shinjuku, setting a dramatic precedent for things to come. Today more than a dozen skyscrapers, including several hotels, dot the Shinjuku skyline, and with the opening of the new **Tokyo Metropolitan Government Office (TMG)** in 1991 (with a great observation floor), Shinjuku's transformation into the capital's upstart business district was complete. Eastern Shinjuku is known for its shopping, particularly the huge **Takashimaya Times Square** complex, and for its nightlife, especially in **Kabuki-cho,** one of Japan's most famous—as well as naughtiest—amusement centers, and in **Shinjuku 2–chome,** Tokyo's premier gay nightlife district. Separating eastern and western Shinjuku is **Shinjuku Station,** the nation's busiest commuter station, located on the western end of the Yamanote Line loop. An oasis in the middle of Shinjuku madness is **Shinjuku Gyoen Park,** a beautiful garden for strolling.

Harajuku   The mecca of Tokyo's younger generation, Harajuku swarms throughout the week with teenagers in search of fashion and fun. At its center is **Omotesando Dori,** a fashionable tree-lined avenue flanked by trendy shops, sidewalk cafes, and restaurants; it's a premier promenade for people-watching. Nearby is **Takeshita Dori,** a narrow pedestrian lane packed with young people looking for the latest in inexpensive clothing. Harajuku is also home to one of Japan's major attractions, **Meiji Jingu Shrine,** built in 1920 to deify Emperor and Empress Meiji; and the small but delightful Ota Memorial Museum of Art, with its woodblock prints. Another drawing card is the **Oriental Bazaar,** Tokyo's best shop for products and souvenirs of Japan; two Sundays a month, nearby **Togo Shrine** holds an antique flea market.

Aoyama   While Harajuku is for teenyboppers, nearby chic Aoyama serves as playground for Tokyo's trend setting yuppies, boasting sophisticated restaurants, expensive boutiques, and more designer-fashion outlets than anywhere else in the city. Located on the eastern end of **Omotesando Dori** (and an easy walk from Harajuku) and centered on **Aoyama Dori,** Aoyama is a must for its great array of tempting restaurants, as well as the fantastic **Japan Traditional Craft Center,** with its beautifully crafted traditional items.

Ikebukuro   Located north of Shinjuku on the Yamanote Line loop, Ikebukuro is the working man's Tokyo, less refined and a bit rougher around the edges. Ikebukuro is where you'll find **Seibu** and **Tobu,** two of the country's largest department stores, as well as the **Sunshine City Building,** one of Japan's tallest skyscrapers and home of a huge indoor shopping center.

Akihabara   Japan's foremost center for electronic and electrical appliances contains more than 600 shops offering a look at the latest in gadgets and gizmos. A stop on the Yamanote Line, this is a fascinating place for a stroll, even if you aren't interested in buying anything.

Shibuya   Located on the southwestern edge of the Yamanote Line loop, Shibuya serves as an important commuter nucleus and caters primarily to students and young office workers. More subdued than Shinjuku, more down to earth than Harajuku, and less cosmopolitan than Roppongi, it's a shopper's paradise for fashion and interior design, with as many as a dozen specialty department stores selling everything from designer clothing to housewares.

Ebisu   One station south of Shibuya on the JR Yamanote Line, Ebisu was a minor player in Tokyo's shopping and nightlife league until the 1995 debut of **Yebisu Garden Place,** a smart-looking planned community of apartments, concert halls, two museums (one highlighting Sapporo Beer, the other Japanese photography), restaurants, a department store, and a first-class hotel, all connected to Ebisu Station via moving walkway. The vicinity east of Ebisu Station, once a sleepy residential and low-key shopping district, has recently blossomed into a small but thriving nightlife mecca, popular with ex-pats who find Roppongi too crass or commercial. West of Ebisu Station is a handful of secondhand shops specializing in designer fashions.

Roppongi   Tokyo's best-known nightlife district for young Japanese and foreigners, Roppongi has more bars and nightclubs than any other district, as well as a multitude of restaurants serving international cuisine. The action continues until dawn. Nearby **Nishi Azabu,** once a residential neighborhood (many foreigners live here), offers a quieter and saner dining alternative to frenetic Roppongi.

Akasaka   With its several large hotels and a small nightlife district, Akasaka caters mostly to businessmen, making it of little interest to tourists.

Shinagawa   Once an important post station on the old Tokaido Highway, Shina-gawa remains an important crossroads due to **Shinagawa Station,** a major hub of the JR railway network located on the southern end of the Yamanote Line loop. Soon it will also be a stop on the Shinkansen bullet train; a subway station is also near completion. It's home to Sony headquarters and several major hotels, some of which offer fantastic views of Tokyo Bay, but otherwise there's little here to attract sightseers.

Ryogoku   Located outside the Yamanote Line loop east of the Sumida River, Ryo-goku has served as Tokyo's sumo town since the 17th century. Today it's home not only to Tokyo's large **sumo stadium and museum,** but also to about a dozen sumo stables, where wrestlers live and train. You can often see the giants as they stroll the district in their characteristic *yukata* robes. In 1993, Ryogoku became a tourist destination with the opening of the **Edo-Tokyo Museum,** which outlines the history of this fascinating city.

Odaiba   This is Tokyo's newest district, quite literally—it was constructed from reclaimed land in Tokyo Bay. Connected to the mainland by the **Rainbow Bridge** (famous for its chameleon colors after nightfall) and the Yurikamome Line mono-rail from Shimbashi Station, Odaiba is home to three hotels, Japan's largest convention space, several shopping complexes, futuristic buildings (including the Kenzo Tange–designed Fuji TV building), the Museum of Maritime Science, a man-made sandy beach complete with a boardwalk, and an amusement center sponsored by Toyota. For young Japanese, it's one of Tokyo's hottest dating spots; it's also a good escape from city life, with a seaside park and beach that capitalize on the city's bay location.

2 Getting Around

Your most frustrating moments in Tokyo will probably occur when you find you're totally lost. Maybe it will be in a subway or train station, when all you see are signs in Japanese, or on a street somewhere as you search for a museum, restaurant, or bar. At any rate, accept here and now that you will get lost if you are at all adventurous and strike out on your own. It's inevitable. But take comfort in the fact that Japanese get lost, too—even taxi drivers!

The second rule of getting around Tokyo: It will always take longer than you think. For short-term visitors, calculating travel times in Tokyo is tricky business. Taking a taxi is expensive and involves the probability of getting stuck interminably in traffic, with the meter ticking away. Taking the subway is usually more efficient, even though it's more complicated and harder on your feet: Choosing which route to take isn't always clear, and transfers between lines are sometimes quite a hike in themselves. If I'm going from one end of Tokyo to the other by subway, I usually allow anywhere from 30 to 60 minutes, depending on the number of transfers and the walking distance to my final destination. The journey from Roppongi or Shibuya to Ueno, for example, takes approximately a half hour because it's a straight shot on the subway, but the trip from Toranomon to Ueno can take three-quarters of an hour because it requires transfers. Traveling times to destinations within each line are posted on platform pillars.

Your best bet for getting around Tokyo is to take the subway or Japan Railways (JR) commuter train to the station nearest your destination. From there you can either walk, using a map and asking directions along the way, or take a taxi.

For all hotels, ryokan, restaurants, sights, shops, and nightlife venues listed in this book, I've included both the nearest station and, in parentheses, the number of minutes' walk required from the station to the destination.

BY TAXI

Taxis are shamefully expensive in Tokyo. Fares start at ¥660 ($5.50) for the first 2 kilometers (1¼ miles) and increase ¥80 (65¢) for each additional 274 meters (904 ft.) or 40 seconds of waiting time. There are also smaller, more compact taxis that start out slightly less, at ¥640 ($5.35) for the first 2 kilometers, but then increase ¥80 for each additional 290 meters (957 ft.). In 1997, when controls regulating taxi fares became less restrictive, some taxis began offering fares cheaper than the standard rates for short distances. Fares are posted on the back of the front passenger seat. If you're like me, however, you probably won't shop around—you'll just gratefully jump into the first taxi that stops. Note that from 11pm to 5am, an extra 30% is added to your fare.

With the exception of some major thoroughfares in the downtown area, you can hail a taxi from any street or go to a taxi stand or a major hotel. A red light will show above the dashboard if a taxi is free to pick up a passenger; a green light indicates the taxi is occupied. Be sure to stand clear of the back door—it swings open automatically. Likewise, it shuts automatically once you're in. Taxi drivers are quite perturbed if you try to maneuver the door yourself.

Unless you're going to a well-known landmark or hotel, it's best to have your destination written out in Japanese, since most taxi drivers don't speak English. But even that may not help. Tokyo is so complicated that even taxi drivers may not know a certain area, although they do have detailed maps. If a driver doesn't understand where you're going, he may refuse to take you. Otherwise, don't be surprised if he jumps out of the cab to inquire directions at a nearby shop—with the meter ticking.

There are many taxis cruising Tokyo and it seems that you can always find one easily—except when you need it most. That is, when it's raining and sometimes just after 1am on weekends, after all subways and trains have stopped. However, one surprising effect of the recession has been to increase the number of available taxis late at night; now that companies no longer pay for employees' expensive after-the-last-train taxi fares, nighttime revelers no longer have to stay out until 3am just to find a taxi.

One of these major taxi companies can be called for a pickup: **Nihon Kotsu** (☎ 03/3586-2151), **Kokusai** (☎ 03/3491-6001), **Daiwa** (☎ 03/3563-5151), or **Hinomaru** (☎ 03/3814-1111). Note, however, that only Japanese is spoken, and you'll be required to pay extra (usually not more than ¥500/$4.35). I've never telephoned for a taxi—just like in the movies, a taxi usually cruises by just when you raise your hand.

BY PUBLIC TRANSPORTATION

If you think you'll be using a combination of public transportation systems in one day—subway, JR train, and Toei bus (except double-decker buses)—consider purchasing a **Tokyo Free Kippu,** which, despite its name, costs ¥1,580 ($13) but does allow unlimited travel. It's available at all JR stations, JR View Plazas, and most subway stations.

There's a four-color **Tokyo Metro map,** with subway and train lines, on the inside front cover of this book.

BY SUBWAY

To get around Tokyo on your own, it's imperative that you learn how to ride its subways. Fortunately, the subway system is efficient, modern, clean, and easy to use, and all station names are written in English. Altogether, there are 14 subway lines crisscrossing underneath the city, and each line is color-coded. The Ginza Line, for example, is orange, which means all its trains and signs are orange. If you're transferring to the Ginza Line from another line, just follow the orange signs and circles to the Ginza Line platform. Before boarding, however, make sure the train is going in the right direction; otherwise you'll end up in the opposite end of the city.

TICKETS   **Vending machines** at all subway stations sell tickets, which begin at ¥160 ($1.35) for the shortest distance and increase according to how far you're traveling, with ¥300 ($2.50) charged for the longest distance. Children under 6 ride free; children 6 to 11 pay half-fare. Vending machines give change, and some even accept notes. To purchase your ticket, insert coins into the vending machine until the fare buttons light up, then push the amount for the ticket you want. Your ticket and change will drop onto a little platform at the bottom of the machine.

Fares are posted on a large subway map above the vending machines, but they're generally in Japanese only; major stations also post a smaller map listing fares in English, but you may have to search for it. An alternative is to look at your Tourist Information Center subway map—it lists stations in both Japanese and English. Once you know what the Japanese characters look like, you may be able to locate your station and the corresponding fare. If you still don't know the fare, just buy a basic-fare ticket for ¥160 ($1.35). When you exit at your destination, look for the **fare adjustment machine;** insert your ticket to find out how much more you owe, or look for a fare adjustment window where a subway employee will tell you how much you owe.

In any case, be sure to hang on to your ticket, since you must give it up at the end of your journey. In recent years, an automated ticketing system has been installed at most subway entrances and exits—simply insert your ticket and the doors to the wicket swing open.

If you think you'll be using Tokyo's subway system a lot or simply wish to avoid having to purchase an individual ticket for each ride, invest instead in an **SF Metro Card,** a prepaid card also sold at vending machines for ¥1,000 ($8.35), ¥3,000 ($25), and ¥5,000 ($42) worth of rides. Insert the card into the automatic ticket gates upon entering and exiting the subway wickets; the charge for your ride will be electronically deducted from the card. You can also use your Metro Card in the vending machine to purchase regular single tickets. Since rides on the subway can really add up, you'll find the ¥1,000 Metro Card useful even if you're staying in Tokyo only 3 or 4 days (six rides alone will probably end up costing more than ¥1,000). Although other types of tickets and passes are available, I find them too complicated for short-time visitors.

HOURS   Most subways run from about 5am to midnight, although the times of the first and last trains depend on the line, the station, and whether it's a weekday or weekend. Schedules are posted in the stations, and through most of the day trains arrive every 3 to 5 minutes.

Avoid taking the subway during the weekday morning **rush hour,** from 8 to 9am—the stories you've heard about commuters packed into trains like sardines are all true. There are even "platform pushers," men who push people into compartments so that the doors can close. If you want to witness Tokyo at its craziest, go to Shinjuku Station at 8:30am—but go by taxi unless you want to experience the crowding firsthand.

Another thing you'll want to keep in mind are **station exits,** which are always numbered. Once you reach your destination, look for the yellow signs designating which exit to take for major buildings, museums, and addresses. If you're confused

Transfers on the Subway and Train

You can transfer between subway lines without buying another ticket, and you can transfer between JR train lines on one ticket. However, your ticket or prepaid card does not allow a transfer between subway lines, JR train lines, and private train lines connecting Tokyo with outlying destinations such as Nikko. You usually don't have to worry about this, though, because if you exit through a wicket and have to give up your ticket, you'll know you have to buy another one.

There are instances, however, when you pass through a ticket wicket to transfer between subway lines (for example, when you transfer from the Yurakucho Line to the Hibiya Line at Hibiya Station). In this case, simply show your ticket when you pass through the wicket or insert it into the automatic gate, whereupon it will be returned. The general rule is that if your final destination and fare are posted above the ticket vending machines, you can travel all the way to your destination with only one ticket. But don't worry about this too much—the ticket collector will set you straight if you've miscalculated. Note, however, that if you pay too much for your ticket, the portion of the fare that's left unused is not refundable—so, again, the easiest thing to do if in doubt is to buy the cheapest fare.

about which exit to take from the station, ask someone at the window near the ticket gate. Taking the right exit can make a world of difference, especially in Shinjuku, where there are more than 60 station exits.

For more information on tickets, passes, and lines for the subway, stop by **information desks** located at Ginza, Shinjuku, Nihombashi, and Otemachi stations or call ☎ **03/3502-1461.**

BY JR TRAIN

As an alternative to subways, electric commuter trains operated by Japan Railways (JR) run above ground. These trains are also color-coded, with fares beginning at ¥130 ($1.10). Buy your ticket from vending machines the same as you would for the subway.

The **Yamanote Line** (green-colored coaches) is the best-known and most convenient JR line. It makes an oblong loop around the city, stopping at 29 stations along the way. In fact, you may want to take the Yamanote Line and stay on it for a roundup view of Tokyo; the entire trip takes about an hour, passing stations like Shinjuku, Tokyo, Harajuku, Akihabara, and Ueno on the way.

Another convenient JR line is the orange-colored **Chuo Line;** it cuts across Tokyo between Shinjuku and Tokyo stations. The yellow-colored **Sobu Line** runs between Shinjuku and Akihabara and beyond to Chiba. Since the Yamanote, Chuo, and Sobu lines are rarely identified by their specific names at major stations, look for signs that say, "JR Lines."

If you think you'll be traveling by JR lines quite a bit, consider purchasing an **IO Card,** a prepaid card similar to the SF Metro Card; it allows you to pass through automatic fare gates without having to purchase a separate JR ticket each time. These cards come in values of ¥3,000 ($25) and ¥5,000 ($42).

For more information on JR lines and tickets, stop by one of JR's **Information Centers** at Tokyo Station (Yaesu side) and Shinjuku Station (both the eastern and western sides). You can also call the JR's English-language telephone service at ☎ **03/3423-0111,** available Monday through Friday from 10am to 6pm.

BY BUS

Buses are difficult to use in Tokyo because destinations are often written only in Japanese and most bus drivers don't speak English. However, they are sometimes convenient for short distances. If you're feeling adventurous, board the bus at the front and drop the exact fare into a box by the driver. If you don't have the exact fare (usually ¥200/$1.65), a slot located next to the driver will accept coins only; your change will come out below, minus the fare. Another slot will accept ¥1,000 bills; the change comes out in the same place as if you insert a coin. When you wish to get off, press one of the buttons on the railing near the door or the seats. You can pick up a bus map at the Tourist Information Center.

BY BOAT

Although tourist destinations are all accessible by land transportation, there are some sights in Tokyo Bay or on the Sumida River that are served by sightseeing boat, an enjoyable way to travel and see the Tokyo skyline. Boats depart from **Hinode Pier** near Hamamatsucho Station and travel to **Asakusa** via the Sumida River, as well as to Tokyo Sea Life Park and the Museum of Maritime Science on **Odaiba**. The trip from Hinode Pier to Asakusa takes approximately 40 minutes and costs ¥660 ($5.50). You can also reach Asakusa by boat from Hama Rikyu Garden. Pick up a brochure at the TIC or call the **Tokyo Cruise Ship Co.** at ☎ **03/3457-7830.**

Fast Facts: Tokyo

If you can't find the information you need here, call the **Tourist Information Center** (☎ 03/3201-3331) Monday through Friday from 9am to 5pm and Saturday from 9am to noon. If you're staying in a first-class hotel, you should also try asking at the **guest-relations desk;** the staff there can tell you how to reach your destination, answer general questions, and even make restaurant reservations for you.

Airport   See "Flying to Japan" in chapter 2.

Baby-Sitters   Many major hotels provide baby-sitting services, but expect to pay about $80 for 2 hours. **Tokyo Domestic Service** (☎ 03/3584-4769) can provide bilingual sitters. There's a 3-hour minimum charge of ¥5,500 ($49.50), then ¥1,500 ($13.50) per hour after that. Parents are also required to pay transportation (¥1,000/$9 during the day, ¥1,500/$13.50 between 9 and 11pm, and ¥3,000/$27 after 11pm) and to provide meals.

Business Hours   **Government offices** and **private companies** are generally open Monday through Friday from 9am to 5pm. **Banks** are open Monday through Friday from 9am to 3pm, while **post offices** are open Monday through Friday from 9am to 5pm.

   Department stores are open from about 10am to 7:30 or 8pm, with irregular closing days one to four times a month (but always the same day of the week). Since closed days differ for each department store, you can always find several that are open, even on Sunday. **Smaller stores** are generally open from about 10am to 8pm and closed 1 day a week. **Convenience stores** are generally open 24 hours.

   Keep in mind that most **attractions** stop selling admission tickets at least 30 minutes before the actual closing time. Similarly, **restaurants** take their last orders at least 30 minutes before the posted closing time (even earlier for kaiseki restaurants).

ATMs   You can also use ATM machines in Japan to access your bank account at home and get Japanese currency at a good exchange rate. However, most ATMs in Japan accept only Japan-issued bank cards; access for foreign cards is extremely limited. You'll find ATMs for foreign cards at **Narita Airport,** as well as in the northeast corner of the basement of **Tokyo Station,** near Daimaru department store; on the 6th floor of **Matsuya department store,** located on Chuo Dori in the Ginza; adjacent to **Seibu department store** near Yurakucho Station; and on the 11th floor of **Takashimaya department store** in Shinjuku.

Currency   See "Money," in chapter 2 for an explanation of the yen and its dollar and British-pound equivalents.

Currency Exchange   You can exchange money in major banks throughout Tokyo, often indicated by a sign in English near the front door. Banks give a slightly better exchange rate for **traveler's checks** than for cash; you'll need your passport to exchange traveler's checks. If you need to exchange money outside banking hours, inquire at one of the larger first-class **hotels**—some of them will cash traveler's checks or exchange money even if you're not a guest, though note that you'll need a passport to change money in a hotel. At **Narita Airport** (which also has ATMs—see above), you can exchange money from 9am until the arrival of the last flight.

You can get also get cash advances using **Visa credit cards** at any Sumitomo bank and from **MasterCard** at Union Credit (UC) banks and some Sumitomo banks, Citibanks, Mitsubishi-Tokyo banks, and affiliated banks, with branches all over town; you'll have to show your passport for cash advances.

Dentists & Doctors   Many first-class hotels offer medical facilities or an in-house doctor. Otherwise, your embassy can refer you to English-speaking doctors, specialists, and dentists. In addition, the **AMDA International Medical Information Center** (☎ 03/5285-8088), available Monday through Friday 9am to 5pm, can provide information on English-speaking staff. The following are clinics with some English-speaking staff that are popular with foreigners living in Tokyo: **The International Clinic,** 1–5–9 Azabudai, Minato-ku, within walking distance of Roppongi Station (☎ **03/3582-2646;** open Monday through Friday 9am to noon and 2:30 to 5pm, Saturday 9am to noon; only walk-ins accepted); the **Ishikawa Clinic,** Azabu Sakurada Heights, Room 201, 3–2–7 Nishi-Azabu, Minato-ku, near Roppongi Station (☎ **03/3401-6340;** open Monday 8:30am to 12:30pm and 3 to 5pm, Tuesday to Friday 8:30am to 12:30pm and 3 to 7pm; both walk-ins and appointments accepted); **Tokyo Medical & Surgical Clinic,** 32 Mori Building, 3–4–30 Shiba-koen, Minato-ku, near Kamiyacho, Onarimon, or Shiba-koen stations and across from Tokyo Tower (☎ **03/3436-3028;** open Monday to Friday 9am to 1pm and 2 to 5pm, Saturday 9am to 1pm; appointments only). At the Tokyo Medical & Surgical Clinic, above, you'll also find the **Tokyo Clinic Dental Office** (☎ **03/3431-4225**). You can also make appointments to visit doctors at the hospitals listed below.

Drugstores   There is no 24-hour drugstore in Tokyo, but ubiquitous 24-hour convenience stores carry things like aspirin. If you're looking for specific pharmaceuticals, a good bet is the **American Pharmacy,** Hibiya Park Building, 1–8–1 Yurakucho, Chiyoda-ku (☎ **03/3271-4034;** open Monday through

Saturday 9:30am to 7:30pm, Sunday and holidays 10am to 6:30pm), which has many of the same over-the-counter drugs you can find at home (many of them imported from the U.S.) and can fill American prescriptions—but note that you must first visit a doctor in Japan before foreign prescriptions can be filled, so it's best to bring an ample supply of any prescription medication with you.

Earthquakes   Kobe's tragic 1995 earthquake brought attention to the fact that Japan is earthquake-prone, but in reality most earthquakes are too small to detect. However, in case of an earthquake you can feel, there are a few precautions you should take. If you're indoors, take cover under a doorway or against a wall and do not go outdoors. If you're outdoors, stay away from trees, power lines, and the sides of buildings; if you're surrounded by tall buildings, seek cover in a doorway. Never use elevators during a quake. You should be sure to note emergency exits wherever you stay. All hotels supply flashlights, usually found attached to your bedside table.

Electricity   The electricity throughout Japan is 100 volts AC, but there are two different cycles in use: In Tokyo and in regions northeast of the capital, it's 50 cycles, while in Nagoya, Kyoto, Osaka, and all points to the southwest, it's 60 cycles. Leading hotels in Tokyo often have two outlets, one for 110 volts and one for 220 volts; most hotels also have hair dryers in the rooms. You can use many American appliances, such as radios and hair dryers, because the American standard is 110 volts and 60 cycles, but they may run a little more slowly; note, too, that the flat, two-legged electrical plugs used in Japan are the same size and fit as in North America, but three-pronged appliances are not accepted. For sensitive equipment, either have it adjusted or use batteries if it's also battery-operated.

Embassies & Consulates   The visa or passport sections of most embassies are open only at certain times during the day, so it's best to call in advance. The **U.S. Embassy,** 1–10–5 Akasaka, Minato-ku, near the Toranomon subway station (☎ **03/3224-5000**), accepts telephone inquiries Monday to Friday 8:30am to 1pm and 2 to 5:30pm; its consular section is open Monday to Friday 8:30am to 12:30pm and 2 to 4pm. The **Canadian Embassy,** 7–3–38 Akasaka, Minato-ku, near Aoyama-Itchome Station (☎ **03/3408-2101**), has a consular section open Monday through Friday from 9am to 12:30pm and 1:30 to 5:30pm. The **British Embassy,** 1 Ichibancho, Chiyoda-ku, near Hanzomon Station (☎ **03/3265-5511**), has a consular section open Monday through Friday from 9am to noon and 2 to 4pm. The **Australian Embassy,** 2–1–14 Mita, Minato-ku (☎ **03/5232-4111**), is open from 9am to 12:30pm and 1:30 to 5pm; make an appointment for the consular section at ☎ 03/5232-4091. To reach it, take a taxi from Shiba-koen, Roppongi, Kamiyacho, Mita, or Hamamatsucho station. The **Embassy of Ireland,** 2–10–7 Kojimachi, Chiyoda-ku, near Hanzomon Station's exit 4 (☎ **03/3263-0695**), is open Monday through Friday from 10am to 12:30pm and 2 to 4pm; telephone inquiries are accepted Monday to Friday 9:30am to 5:30pm. The **New Zealand Embassy,** 20–40 Kamiyama-cho, Shibuya-ku, a 15-minute walk from Shibuya Station (☎ **03/3467-2271**), has a consular section open Monday through Friday from 9am to 12:30pm and 1:30 to 5:30pm.

Emergencies   The national emergency numbers are ☎ **110** for **police** and ☎ **119** for **ambulance** and **fire.** You do not need to insert any money into public telephones to call these numbers, but you must push a red button before dialing. Be sure to speak slowly and precisely.

Faxes   Your hotel probably can handle faxes. If not, you can send a fax from a **Kokusai Denshin Denwa** office (the name is equivalent to International Telephone & Telegraph); ask the hotel clerk where the office nearest your hotel is.

Holidays   See "When to Go," in chapter 2.

Home Visit System   You can spend a few evening hours visiting an English-speaking Japanese family in their home simply by applying the day before at the **Tourist Information Center** (☎ 03/3201-3331). See "Meeting the Japanese" under "Social Skills 101," in appendix A for details.

Hospitals   In addition to going to the following hospitals for an emergency, you can also make appointments at their clinics to see a doctor: the **International Catholic Hospital** (Seibo Byoin), 2–5–1 Naka-Ochiai, Shinjuku-ku, near Mei-jiro Station on the Yamanote Line (☎ 03/3951-1111; clinic hours Monday through Saturday 8 to 11am; closed third Saturday of each month; appointments required); **St. Luke's International Hospital** (Seiroka Byoin), 9–1 Akashi-cho, Chuo-ku, near Tsukiji Station on the Hibiya Line (☎ 03/3541-5151; Monday through Friday 8:30 to 11am); and the **Japan Red Cross Medical Center** (Nihon Sekijujisha Iryo Center), 4–1–22 Hiroo, Shibuya-ku (☎ 03/3400-1311; Monday through Friday 8:30 to 11am; walk-ins only), whose closest subway stations are Roppongi, Hiroo, and Shibuya—from there, you should take a taxi.

Information   Your best bet for travel information is the Tourist Information Center (or "TIC"; ☎ 03/3201-3331). See "Visitor Information," earlier in this chapter.

Internet Access   Most upper-range hotels in Tokyo are used to catering to international business travelers and therefore offer dataports for fax and computer hookups, as well as adapters to let you access the Internet (a few even offer in-room access via the TV). Many offer business centers as well, most equipped with computers for guest use (a fee may be charged). Otherwise, a company called NTT operates public telephones equipped with a modular jack for portable computer hookups, making it possible to scan Web sites and receive e-mail. Look for gray ISDN telephones—often found in lobbies of major hotels, airports, and train stations—which have English explanations of how to use them and accept prepaid telephone cards. Otherwise, **Cyberia,** 1–14–17 Nishi-Azabu (☎ 03/3423-0318), a 10-minute walk from Roppongi Station or a 7-minute walk from Nogizaka Station (exit 5), is a high-tech Internet cafe open daily from 11am to 11pm and offering a limited drink menu and rows of sophisticated computers (costing ¥500/$4.15 per 30 min.) where you can surf or send e-mail. **Kinko's,** located in the Hilton Hotel in West Shinjuku (☎ 03/ 3344-5245), a 2-minute walk from Nishi Shinjuku Station, is open 24 hours and charges ¥400 ($3.35) per 15 minutes of computer time, including Internet access.

Liquor Laws   The legal drinking age is 20. You'll find vending machines dispensing beer and whiskey in almost every neighborhood in Japan, but they close down at 11pm. *Note:* If you intend to drive in Japan, you are not allowed even one drink.

Lost Property   If you've forgotten something on a subway, in a taxi, or on a park bench, don't assume it's gone forever—if you're willing to trace it, you'll probably get it back. If you can remember where you last saw it, the first thing to do is telephone the establishment or return to where you left it; there's a good chance it will still be sitting there. If you've lost something on the street, go to the nearest police box (*koban*); items found in the neighborhood will stay there for about 3 days. After that, you should contact the **Central Lost and Found Office** of the Metropolitan Police Board, 1–9–11 Koraku, Bunkyo-ku (☎ **03/3814-4151**).

If you've lost something in a taxi, contact the **Taxi Kindaika Center,** 7–3–3 Minamisuma, Koto-ku (☎ **03/3648-0300**). For items lost on JR trains, have someone who speaks Japanese call or go to the **Lost and Found Section** at Tokyo JR Station (☎ **03/3231-1880**) or at Ueno JR Station (☎ **03/3841-8069**); or you can call the **JR East Infoline** at (☎ **03/3423-0111**). If you've lost something on a subway or bus, call the lost and found section of the **Tokyo Metropolitan Government,** 2–3–29 Hamamatsucho, Minato-ku (☎ **03/3431-1515**).

Luggage Storage/Lockers   Coin-operated lockers are located at all major JR stations, such as Tokyo, Shinjuku, and Ueno, as well as at most subway stations. Lockers cost ¥200 to ¥700 ($1.65 to $5.85), depending on the size.

Mail   If your hotel cannot mail letters for you, ask the concierge where the nearest post office is. Post offices are easily recognizable by the red logo of a capital T with a horizontal line over it. Mailboxes are bright orange-red. It costs ¥110 (90¢) to airmail letters weighing up to 25 grams and ¥70 (60¢) for postcards to North America and Europe. Domestic mail costs ¥80 (65¢) for letters weighing up to 25 grams and ¥50 (40¢) for postcards.

Although all post offices are open Monday through Friday from 9am to 5pm, the **Central Post Office,** just southwest of Tokyo Station at 2–7–2 Marunouchi, Chiyoda-ku (☎ **03/3284-9527**), has longer business hours than most: Monday through Friday 9am to 7pm, Saturday 9am to 5pm, Sunday and public holidays 9am to 12:30pm. An after-hours counter remains open throughout the night for mail and packages, making this the only 24-hour service facility in town. If you don't know where you'll be staying in Tokyo, you can also have your mail sent here c/o **Poste Restante,** Central Post Office, Tokyo, Japan.

As for mailing packages, your hotel may have a shipping service. Otherwise, it's only at larger post offices that you can mail packages abroad. Conveniently, they sell cardboard boxes in four sizes, with the necessary tape and string. Packages mailed abroad cannot weigh more than 20 kilograms (about 44 lb.). A package weighing 10 kilograms (about 22 lb.) will cost ¥6,750 ($56) to North America via surface mail and takes about a month. Express packages, which take 3 days to North America and can weigh up to 30 kilograms (66 lb.), cost ¥14,000 ($117). For English-language postal information call ☎ **03/5472-5851** Monday through Friday between 9:30am and 4:30pm.

Maps   Unless you're living in Japan or plan on doing extensive sightseeing, the free map offered by the **Tourist Information Center** is adequate for most sightseeing purposes. Otherwise, see "City Layout" earlier in this chapter for information on more detailed maps.

Measures   Before the metric system came into use in Japan, the country had its own standards for measuring length and weight. One of these old standards is still common—rooms are still measured by the number of **tatami** straw mats that will fit in them. A 6-tatami room, for example, is the size of 6 tatami mats, with a tatami roughly 3 feet wide and 6 feet long.

Newspapers & Magazines   Five English-language newspapers are published daily in Japan: the *Japan Times*, the *Mainichi Daily News*, the *Daily Yomiuri*, the

Asahi Evening News, and the *International Herald Tribune.* Hotels and major bookstores carry the international edition of such newsmagazines as *Time* and *Newsweek.* For details on what's going on in Tokyo, pick up a copy of *Tokyo Journal* or *Tokyo Classified.*

If you're interested in seeing the latest edition of your favorite magazine back home, your best bet is to drop in on the **World Magazine Gallery,** 3–13–10 Ginza, behind the Kabuki-za near Higashi-Ginza Station (☎ **03/3545-7227;** open Monday through Friday 11am to 7pm), which displays more than 1,200 magazines from 40 countries around the world. Magazines are for reading here only and are not for sale, but there is a coffee shop where you can peruse at leisure.

Police   The national emergency telephone number is ☎ **110.**

Radio   The **American Forces Network,** or AFN (at 810 kHz), is the English-language military radio station, with broadcasts of music, talk shows, and sports events from the United States, as well as Tokyo sumo matches. Tokyo's **J-Wave** (81.3 mHz) also broadcasts programs in English, with a wide range of music. **InterFM** (76.1 mHz) in Tokyo specializes in foreign-language broadcasts, including adult contemporary music and information, mostly in English but also in French, Chinese, Korean, Spanish, and other languages.

Rest Rooms   If you're in need of a rest room in Tokyo, your best bets are at train and subway stations (though these tend to be dirty), big hotels, department stores, and fast-food chains like McDonald's. Use of rest rooms is free in Japan, but since public facilities do not supply toilet paper, it's a good idea to carry a packet of tissues.

To find out whether a stall is empty, knock on the door. If it's occupied, someone will knock back. Similarly, if you're inside a stall and someone knocks, answer with a knock or else the person will just keep on knocking persistently and try to get in. And don't be surprised if you go into some rest rooms and find men's urinals and individual private stalls in the same room. Women are supposed to simply walk right past the urinals without noticing them.

Many toilets in Japan, especially those at train stations, are Japanese style: They're holes in the ground over which you squat facing the end that has a raised hood. Men stand and aim for the hole. Although Japanese lavatories may seem uncomfortable at first, they're actually much more sanitary because no part of your body touches anything.

Across Japan, the rage nowadays are **washlets,** combination toilet/bidets with heated toilet seats and buttons and knobs directing sprays of water of various intensities to various body parts. But alas, instructions are only in Japanese. The voice of experience: Don't stand up until you've figured out how to turn the darn spray off.

Safety   Tokyo is one of the safest cities in the world. Yet there are precautions you should always take when traveling: Stay alert and be aware of your immediate surroundings. Be especially careful with cameras, purses, and wallets, particularly in crowded subways. It never hurts to exercise caution at all times, even in the most heavily touristed areas. Some Japanese also caution women against walking through parks alone at night.

Salons   Virtually all major Tokyo hotels have beauty salons and barbershops, primarily to serve Japanese wedding parties. Otherwise, check *Tokyo Journal;* many salons advertise expertise in cutting foreigners' hair.

Shoe Repairs   All department stores have a shoe-repair counter, usually a **Mister Minit;** some stations, such as Yurakucho and Tokyo, have street-side shoe repairs.

Taxes   There's a 5% consumption tax imposed on goods and services in Japan, including hotel rates and restaurant meals. If your entire **hotel** charge per person, per night (including food, drinks, and a service charge) is ¥15,000 ($135) or less, a 5% government consumption tax will be added to your bill; if your hotel charge exceeds ¥15,000 per person per night, both a 5% consumption tax and a 3% local tax will be added to your bill. Some budget accommodations include the tax in their tariff, while others don't; be sure to ask whether rates include tax.

In **restaurants,** a 5% consumption tax is levied on meals costing ¥7,500 ($75) or less per person, while meals costing more than ¥7,500 are subject to an 8% tax (both consumption and local taxes).

In addition to these taxes, a 10% to 15% service charge will be added to your bill in lieu of **tipping** at most of the fancier restaurants and at moderately priced and upper-end hotels. Thus, the 18% to 23% in tax and service charge that will be added to your bill in the more expensive locales can really add up. Most ryokan, or Japanese-style inns, include a service charge but not a consumption tax in their rates. If you're not sure, ask. Inexpensive hotels and restaurants do not impose a service charge.

As for **shopping,** a 5% consumption tax is also levied on most goods (some of the smaller vendors are not required to levy tax). Travelers from abroad, however, are eligible for an exemption on goods taken out of the country, although only the larger department stores and specialty shops seem equipped to deal with the procedures. In any case, most department stores grant a **refund** on the consumption tax only when the total amount of purchases exceeds ¥10,000 ($83). You can obtain a refund immediately by having a sales clerk fill out a list of your purchases and then presenting the list to the tax-exemption counter of the department store; you will need to show your passport. Note that no refunds for consumption tax are given for food, drinks, tobacco, cosmetics, film, and batteries.

Telephones   For dialing Japan, the country code is **81.** If you're calling a Tokyo telephone number from outside Tokyo but within Japan, the **area code** for Tokyo is **03.** If you're calling Tokyo from abroad, drop the zero and dial only **3.** If you have questions, call the international operator in the country from which you are placing your call.

If you're staying in a medium- or upper-range **hotel,** you can make local, domestic, and international calls from your room. Some of the best hotels even offer in-room fax machines, most have business centers, and almost all will let you send a fax. For telephone calls, however, it's prudent to ask first whether you can make the call directly, whether you must go through the operator, and whether a surcharge will be added to your bill.

You can find **public telephones** virtually everywhere—in telephone booths on the sidewalk, on stands outside shops, on train platforms, in restaurants and coffee shops, even on bullet trains (but these require a magnetic telephone card; see below). A local call costs ¥10 (8¢) for the first minute, after which a warning chime will ring to tell you to insert more coins or you'll be disconnected. I usually insert two or three coins at the start so that I won't have to worry about being disconnected; ¥10 coins that aren't used are always returned at the end of the call. Some older, red models available for public use outside ma-and-pa shops accept only ¥10 coins, but most public phones accept both ¥10 and ¥100 coins, the latter convenient for long-distance calls. All gray, ISDN telephones are equipped for international calls. **Toll-free numbers** in Japan begin with **0120** or **0088.**

If you think you'll be making a lot of calls from public telephones and don't want to deal with coins, purchase a magnetic, **prepaid telephone card,** available in values of ¥500 ($4.15) and ¥1,000 ($8.35) and sold at vending machines (many of which are located right beside telephones), station kiosks, and even at tourist attractions, where cards are imprinted with photos of temples, castles, and other sights (but are also often more expensive than regular telephone cards, since they double as collectors' items). Green and gray telephones accept telephone cards. In fact, many nowadays accept only telephone cards; simply insert the card into the slot. In the gray ISDN telephones, there's a second slot for a second telephone card, convenient if the first one is almost used up or if you think you'll be talking a long time. Domestic long-distance calls are 20% to 40% cheaper at night, on weekends, and national holidays for calls of distances more than 60 kilometers (37 miles).

Of course, you can also avoid public telephones altogether by joining what seems like the rest of the population and using a **mobile phone,** a *keitai denwa.* Rental phones are available in Tokyo through the **NTT Mover Rental Center,** 2–2–1 Marunouchi in Chiyoda-ku (☎ **03/3282-0100;** open Monday through Friday 9am to 6pm). You will need to bring your passport and a credit card. Fees range from ¥1,500 ($12.50) per day for the first seven days to ¥20,580 ($171.50) for the month, plus a ¥20,000 ($167) deposit and service fees for domestic and international calls.

There are several ways to make **international calls.** You can, for example, make a collect call or place a call through a KDD operator anywhere in Japan by dialing ☎ **0051.** From a public telephone, look for a specially marked International and Domestic Card/Coin Telephone. Although many of the specially marked green telephones, the most common public telephone, accept both coins and magnetic telephone cards for international calls, most in larger cities such as Tokyo do not (due to illegal usage of telephone cards). Thus, if you wish to use a magnetic telephone card, which is certainly easier than having a lot of coins on hand, look for a gray ISDN public phone, found in the lobbies of major hotels, train stations, and airports. These telephones have slots for two telephone cards, convenient for long conversations. They even have dataports for hooking up to the Internet. Some hotels also have a KDD Credit Phone, KDD IC Global Phone, or a Japan Telecom Phone, which are special phones equipped to accept credit cards.

In addition, several telephone companies sell prepaid international telephone cards that can be used with any telephone. The **KDD Super World Card** is available in values of ¥1,000 ($8.35), ¥3,000 ($25), and ¥5,000 ($42) and can be purchased at major convenience stores and from vending machines located next to some ISDN telephones. A ¥3,000 card allows approximately 53 minutes worth of telephone calls to the United States. Similarly, IDC puts out its **0061 Love Home Card,** available at convenience stores and from vending machines. Essentially, they work like telephone cards issued by U.S. telephone companies, with an access number that must first be dialed, followed by a secret telephone number and then the number you wish to dial.

International rates vary according to when you call, which telephone company you use, and what type of service you use. Direct-dial service is cheaper than operator-assisted calls and is offered by both international public telephones and by hotels that advertise the service (though remember to ask about the surcharge). You can also save money by calling between 11pm and 8am Japan time, when rates are up to 40% cheaper than calling during a weekday. From 7 to 11pm, rates are 20% cheaper than daytime rates on weekdays. Weekend day-rates are also 20% cheaper than weekday rates. KDD's weekday prime-time rates are ¥450 ($3.75) for 3 minutes; after 11pm it drops to ¥350 ($2.90) for 3 minutes.

To make a direct-dial international call, you must first dial one of the following international access codes—**001** (KDD), **0041** (Japan Telecom), or **0061** (IDC)—followed by the country code. The country code for the **United States** and **Canada** is **1,** for the **United Kingdom** it's **44,** for **Australia** it's **61,** and for **New Zealand** it's **64.** To call the United States, for example, simply dial an access code such as 001, then country code 1, the area code, and the telephone number. If you're dialing from your hotel room, you must first dial for an outside line, usually 0.

If you wish to be connected with an operator in your home country, you can do so from green international telephones by dialing ☎ **0039,** followed by the country code (for the United States, dial 0039-111). These calls can be used for collect calls or credit-card calls. Some hotels and other public places are equipped with special phones that will link you to your home operator with the push of a button, and there are instructions in English.

Television   If you enjoy watching television, you've come to the wrong country. Almost nothing is broadcast in English; even foreign films are dubbed in Japanese. However, if you have what's called a **bilingual television,** you can switch from Japanese to the *original* language to hear programs and movies in English (in other words, if it's a Japanese program, it will not be available also in English). Most of the higher-class hotels offer bilingual TVs, though note that there are very few English movies and sitcoms broadcast each week (and most of these are fairly old). In my opinion, a major plus of bilingual TVs is that they allow you to listen to the nightly national news broadcast by NHK at 7 and 9pm. In addition, even if you don't understand Japanese, I suggest that you watch TV at least once; maybe you'll catch a samurai series. Commercials are also worth watching. Otherwise, major hotels also have cable TV with English-language programs, including CNN broadcasts and BBC World, as well as in-house pay movies. Note, however, that CNN is sometimes broadcast only in Japanese.

A word on those **pay video programs** offered by hotels and many resort ryokan: Upper-range hotels usually have a few choices in English, and these are charged automatically to your bill. Most business hotels usually offer only one kind of pay movie; since the descriptions are usually in Japanese only, I'll clear up the mystery—they're generally "adult entertainment" programs. If you're traveling with children, you'll want to be extremely careful about selecting your TV programs: Many adult video pay channels appear with a simple push of the channel-selector button, and they can be difficult to get rid of.

In budget accommodations, you may come across televisions with coin boxes attached to their sides. Sometimes this means that the TVs can be activated only by inserting coins into the box; I call these **coin-operated TVs.** But if the TV functions without having to insert coins, the coin box is for those special adult entertainment videos. Now you know.

Time Zone   Japan is 9 hours ahead of Greenwich mean time, 14 hours ahead of New York, 15 hours ahead of Chicago, and 17 hours ahead of Los Angeles. Since Japan does not go on daylight saving time, subtract 1 hour from the above times if you're calling the United States in the summer.

Because Japan is on the other side of the international date line, you lose a day when traveling from the United States to Asia (if you depart the U.S. on Tuesday, you'll arrive on Wednesday). Returning to North America, however, you gain a day, which means that you arrive on the same day you left. (In fact, it often happens that you arrive in the States at an earlier time than when you departed from Japan.)

Tipping   One of the delights of being in Japan is that there's no tipping—not even to waitresses, taxi drivers, or bellboys. If you try to tip them, they'll probably be confused or embarrassed. Instead, you'll have a 10% to 15% service charge added to your bill at higher-priced hotels and restaurants.

Water   The water is safe to drink anywhere in Japan, although some people claim it's too highly chlorinated. Bottled water is also readily available.

Weather   The *Japan Times* carries nearly a full page of weather information daily, including forecasts for Tokyo and other major Japanese cities and a weekly outlook.

Accommodations 4

Tokyo has no old, grand hotels in the tradition of the Peninsula in Hong Kong or the Raffles in Singapore; it has hardly any old hotels, period. But what the city's hotels may lack in quaintness or old grandeur is more than made up for by excellent service—for which the Japanese are legendary—as well as cleanliness and efficiency. Be prepared, however, for small rooms. Space is at a premium in Tokyo, so with the exception of some of the upper-range hotels, rooms seem to come in only three sizes: minuscule, small, and adequate.

Unfortunately, Tokyo also doesn't have many first-class *ryokan*, or Japanese-style inns; those that do exist rarely accept foreigners. I suggest, therefore, that you wait for your travels outside Tokyo (see chapter 10, "Side Trips from Tokyo," for recommended excursions) to experience a first-rate ryokan. Alternatively, most of Tokyo's upper-bracket hotels offer at least a few Japanese-style rooms, with tatami mats, a Japanese bathtub (deeper and narrower than the Western version), and futon. Although these rooms tend to be expensive, they're usually large enough for four people. There are also moderate and inexpensive Japanese-style inns willing to take in foreigners, and if you're traveling on a tight budget, a simple Japanese-style inn is often the cheapest way to go.

PRICE CATEGORIES The hotel recommendations below are arranged first according to price, then by geographical location, starting with the areas of the Ginza and Hibiya in the heart of the city and fanning out. Since Tokyo's attractions, restaurants, and nightlife are widely scattered, and the public transportation system is fast and efficient (I've provided nearest subway or train stations for each listing), there's no one location within Tokyo that is more convenient than others—and because this is one of the most expensive hotel cities in the world, the overriding factor in selecting accommodations will likely be one of cost. I've divided Tokyo's hotels into price categories based upon two people per night, excluding tax and service charge: **Very Expensive** hotels charge ¥35,000 ($292) and above, **Expensive** hotels charge ¥25,000 to ¥35,000 ($208 to $292), **Moderate** hotels offer rooms for ¥14,000 to ¥25,000 ($117 to $208), and **Inexpensive** accommodations offer rooms for ¥13,000 ($108) and less. Unless otherwise indicated, rooms are with private bath.

Impressions

Japan, a country combining a feverish proficiency in many of the habits of advanced civilization with uncompromising relics of feudal crystallization.
—George Curzon, *Tales of Travel* (1923)

TAXES & SERVICE CHARGES In addition to quoted prices, upper-class hotels and most medium-range hotels will add a **service charge** of 10% to 15% (cheaper establishments do not charge service, because no service is provided). Further, rates of more than ¥15,000 ($125) per person per night will require an additional 8% **tax;** rates of less than ¥15,000 per person will require an additional 5% tax. *Unless otherwise stated, the prices given in this chapter do not include tax or service.*

BUSY TIMES Although Tokyo doesn't suffer from a lack of hotel rooms during peak holidays (when most Japanese head for the hills and beaches), rooms may be in short supply because of **conventions** and other events. If possible, avoid coming to Tokyo in **mid-February** unless you book well in advance—that's when university entrance exams bring multitudes of aspiring high-school students and their parents to the capital for a shot at entering one of the most prestigious universities in the country. And in **summer,** when there are many foreign tourists in Japan, the cheaper accommodations are often the first to fill up.

It's always best, therefore, to **make your hotel reservations in advance,** especially if you're arriving in Tokyo after a long transoceanic flight and don't want the hassle of searching for a hotel room.

WELCOME INN RESERVATION CENTER If you're looking for help in booking moderately priced and budget accommodations, top on my list is to book a room through the Welcome Inn Reservation Center, operated in cooperation with the Japan National Tourist Organization. Some 100 modestly priced accommodations in Tokyo, mostly business hotels but also some tourist hotels and Japanese-style inns, are members of Welcome Inn; another 500 members are spread throughout Japan. Room rates are ¥8,000 ($67) or less per person per night. No fee is charged for the reservation service, nor is a deposit required, but note that there's a limit of three locations for each party. If you wish, you can make reservations for a Welcome Inn property before your departure for Japan, but you must first have a confirmed booking on a flight to Japan. Then you should contact your nearest **Japan National Tourist Organization (JNTO)** office (see "Visitor Information," in chapter 2) and request the Directory of Welcome Inns, which not only lists all the properties but also contains a reservation request form that you should then mail or fax to the **Tokyo Tourist Information Center** at least three weeks prior to your departure; you'll then receive a confirmation slip and detailed information and access maps to your selected accommodations. If you have access to the Internet, you can also access the e-mail reservation request form through JNTO's home page at **www.jnto.go.jp.**

If you're already in Japan, you can apply by mailing, faxing, or e-mailing your reservation request form, or by appearing in person at one of the two TIC offices in Tokyo—at Narita Airport (in the arrival lobbies of Terminals 1 and 2) or near Yurakucho Station in the heart of the city (see "Visitor Information" in chapter 3). Reservations are accepted at the Narita TIC daily from 9am to 7:30pm and at the Tokyo TIC Monday through Friday from 9:15 to 11:30am and 1 to 4:45pm. All reservation centers are closed on public holidays.

1 Japanese & Western-Style Accommodations

JAPANESE-STYLE ACCOMMODATIONS

RYOKAN   Although it can be very expensive, it's worth it to splurge at least once during your trip to spend the night in a traditional Japanese inn, called *ryokan* in Japanese. Unfortunately, you won't find many first-class ryokan in Tokyo itself. Unable to compete with the more profitable high-rise hotels, many have closed down. If you want to stay in a deluxe Japanese inn, therefore, it's best to do so at a resort or hot-spring spa, such as Hakone (see chapter 10). Alternatively, most of Tokyo's upper-class hotels offer Japanese-style rooms as well. If you don't have time for a sidetrip from Tokyo, however, you can still find some decent ryokan in the city, though they won't provide the full experience.

And the full ryokan experience is unforgettable. Nothing conveys the simplicity and beauty—indeed, the very atmosphere—of old Japan like these inns, with their gleaming polished wood, tatami floors, rice-paper sliding doors, and meticulously pruned gardens. Exquisitely prepared meals and personalized service by kimono-clad hostesses are the trademarks of such inns, and staying in one is like taking a trip back in time.

Traditionally, ryokan are small—only one or two stories high and containing about 10 to 30 rooms—and are made of wood with a tile roof. Most guests arrive at their ryokan between 4 and 5pm. The entrance is often through a gate and small garden; upon entering, you're met by a bowing woman in a kimono. Remove your shoes, slide on the proffered plastic slippers, and follow your hostess down long wooden corridors until you reach the sliding door of your room. After taking off your slippers, step into your tatami room, which is almost void of furniture: a low table in the middle of the room, floor cushions, an antique scroll hanging in an alcove, a simple flower arrangement, and best of all, a view past rice-paper sliding screens of a Japanese landscaped garden with bonsai, stone lanterns, and a meandering pond filled with carp. Notice there's no bed in the room.

Almost immediately your hostess brings you welcoming hot tea and a sweet, served at your low table so that you can sit there for a while and appreciate the view, the peace, and the solitude. Next comes your hot bath, either in your own room (if you have one), or in the communal bath. (Be sure to follow the procedure outlined in "Social Skills 101," in appendix A—soaping and rinsing yourself before getting into the tub.) After bathing and soaking away all tension, aches, and pains, change into your *yukata*, a cotton kimono provided by the ryokan.

When you return to your room, you'll find the maid ready to serve your kaiseki dinner, which consists of locally grown vegetables, fish, and various regional specialties, all spread out on many tiny plates; the menu is determined by the chef. Admire how each dish is in itself a delicate piece of artwork; it all looks too wonderful to eat, but finally hunger takes over. If you want, you can order sake or beer to accompany your meal.

After you've finished eating, the maid will return to clear away the dishes and to lay out your bed. The bed is really a futon, a kind of mattress with quilts, and is laid out on the tatami floor. The next morning the maid will wake you up, put away the futon, and serve a breakfast of fish, pickled vegetables, soup, dried seaweed, rice, and a raw egg to be mixed with the rice. Feeling rested, well fed, and pampered, you're then ready to pack your bags and pay your bill. Your hostess sees you off at the front gate, smiling and bowing as you set off for the rest of your travels.

Love Hotels

In addition to Japanese-style inns, Japan has another unique form of accommodation—so-called love hotels. Usually found close to entertainment districts such as Shinjuku and Shibuya, such hotels do not, as their name might suggest, provide sexual services themselves; rather, they offer rooms for rent by the hour to lovers. Even married couples use love hotels, particularly if they share small quarters with in-laws.

Altogether, there are an estimated 35,000 such love hotels in Japan, usually gaudy affairs shaped like ocean liners or castles and offering such extras as rotating beds, mirrored walls, video cameras, and fantasy-provoking decor. Love hotels are often clustered together. You'll know you've wandered into a love-hotel district when you notice discreet entryways and—a dead giveaway—hourly rates posted near the front door. Many also have fair reasonable overnight rates as well. I have friends who, finding themselves out too late and too far from home, have checked into a love hotel, solo.

Such is life at a good ryokan. Sadly, however, as I said, the number of upper-class ryokan diminishes each year. In addition, although ideally a ryokan is an old wooden structure that once served traveling daimyo or was perhaps the home of a wealthy merchant, many are actually modern concrete affairs with as many as 100 or more rooms. Meals are served in dining rooms. What they lack in intimacy and personal service, however, is made up for in slightly cheaper prices and such amenities as modern bathing facilities, and perhaps a bar and outdoor recreational facilities. Most guestrooms are fitted with a color TV, a telephone, a safe for locking up valuables, and a cotton yukata, as well as such amenities as soap, shampoo, razor, toothbrush, and toothpaste.

Rates are based on a per-person charge rather than on a straight room charge, and include breakfast, dinner, and often service; tax is extra. Thus, while rates may seem high, they're actually competitively priced compared to what you'd pay for a hotel room and comparable meals in a restaurant. Although rates can vary from ¥9,000 to an astonishing ¥150,000 ($75 to $1,250) per person, the average cost is generally ¥12,000 to ¥20,000 ($100 to $167). Even within a single ryokan the rates can vary greatly, depending on the room you choose, the dinner courses you select, and the number of people in your room. If you're paying the highest rate, you can be certain you're getting the best room, the best view of the garden, or perhaps even your own private garden, as well as a much more elaborate meal than lower-paying guests. All the rates for ryokan in this book are based on double occupancy; if there are more than two of you in one room, you can generally count on a slightly lower per-person rate.

Although I heartily recommend you try spending at least 1 night in a ryokan, there are a number of **disadvantages** to this style of accommodation. The most obvious problem is that you may find it uncomfortable sitting on the floor. And because the futon is put away during the day, there's no place to lie down for an afternoon nap or rest, except on the hard tatami-covered floor. In addition, some of the older ryokan, though quaint, are bitterly cold in the winter and may have only Japanese-style toilets. As for breakfast, you might find it difficult to swallow raw egg, rice, and seaweed in the morning (I've even been served grilled grasshopper—quite crunchy). Sometimes you can get a Western-style breakfast if you order it the night before, but more often than not the fried or scrambled eggs will arrive cold, leading you to suspect they were cooked right after you ordered them.

A ryokan is also quite rigid in its **schedule.** You're expected to arrive sometime after 4pm, take your bath, and then eat at around 6 or 7pm. Breakfast is served early, usually by 8am, and checkout is by 10am. That means you can't sleep in, and because the maid is continually coming in and out, you have a lot less privacy than you would in a hotel.

The main drawback of the ryokan, however, is that the majority of them will not take you. They simply do not want to deal with the problems inherent in accepting a foreign guest, including the language barrier and differing customs. I saw a number of beautiful old ryokan that I would have liked to include in this book, but I was turned away at their doors. The ryokan in this guide, therefore, are willing to take in foreigners, but because management and policies can change, you should always make reservations beforehand.

The Japan National Tourist Organization offers a free publication called "The Tourist's Handbook," which describes the rules of etiquette for staying in a ryokan, along with handy translations for common situations that may arise.

JAPANESE INN GROUP   If you want the experience of staying in a Japanese-style room but cannot afford the extravagance of a ryokan, you should consider staying in one of the participating members of the Japanese Inn Group. The Japanese Inn Group is a special organization of more than 80 Japanese-style inns throughout the country that offer inexpensive lodging and cater largely to foreigners. Although you may balk at the idea of staying at a place filled mainly with foreigners, remember that many inexpensive Japanese-style inns are not accustomed to guests from abroad and may be quite reluctant to take you in. I have covered many of the Japanese Inn Group members in this book over the years and have found the owners for the most part to be an exceptional group of friendly people eager to offer foreigners the chance to experience life on tatami and futon. In many cases, these are good places in which to exchange information with other world travelers, and they are popular with both young people and families.

Although many of the group members call themselves ryokan, they are not ryokan in the true sense of the word, because they do not offer the trademark personalized service nor the beautiful setting common to ryokan. However, they do offer simple tatami rooms that generally come with a TV and air conditioner (sometimes both are coin-operated); most also have towels and a cotton yukata kimono for your use. Some offer Western-style rooms as well, some offer rooms with private bathrooms (although rooms without are more common). Facilities generally include a coin-operated washer and dryer and a public bath. The average cost of a 1-night stay is about ¥4,500 to ¥7,500 ($37.50 to $62.50) per person, without meals. Breakfast is usually available by paying extra; dinner is also sometimes available.

This organization publishes a free pamphlet called "Japanese Inn Group," which lists the members and is available at the Tourist Information Center in Tokyo. Make reservations directly with the ryokan in which you wish to stay, though some member inns belong to the Welcome Inn group as well, which means you can also make reservations through the TIC offices listed above.

MINSHUKU   Technically, a minshuku is inexpensive Japanese-style lodging in a private home—the Japanese version of a bed-and-breakfast—usually located in resort areas or smaller towns. Because minshuku are family-run affairs, there's no personal service, which means that you're expected to lay out your own futon at night, stow it away in the morning, and tidy up your room. Most also do not supply a towel or yukata, nor do they have rooms with private bathrooms. Meals are served in a communal dining room.

Officially, what differentiates a ryokan from a minshuku is that the ryokan is more expensive and provides more services, but the difference is sometimes very slight. I've stayed in cheap ryokan providing almost no service and in minshuku too large and modern to be considered private homes. The average per-person cost for 1 night in a minshuku is generally ¥7,000 to ¥8,000 ($58 to $67), including two meals.

WESTERN-STYLE ACCOMMODATIONS

Western-style lodgings range from large first-class hotels to inexpensive ones catering primarily to Japanese businessmen.

When booking a hotel room, always ask what kinds of rooms are available. Many hotels, especially those in the upper and medium range, offer a variety of rooms at various prices, with room size the overwhelming factor in pricing. Other aspects that often have a bearing on rates include bed size, floor height (higher floors are more expensive), and in-room amenities. Views are generally not a factor (though some hotels near Tokyo Bay charge more for harbor views; Mt. Fuji in the far distance is generally visible only in the winter or rare, clear days). In Japan, a **twin room** usually refers to a room with two twin beds, while a **double room** refers to a room with one double bed, most hotels charge more for a twin room, but sometimes the opposite is the case. When making your reservation, therefore, inquire about the differences in rates and what they entail.

Once you decide on the type of room you want, ask for the best in that category. For example, if you want a standard room and deluxe rooms start on the 14th floor, ask for a standard on the 13th floor. In addition, be specific about the kind of room you want, whether it's a no-smoking room, a room with a view of Mt. Fuji, a room with a dataport for your computer modem, or a room away from traffic noise. If possible, give the hotel your approximate time of arrival, especially if you'll be arriving after 6pm, when untaken rooms are sometimes given away.

Price Categories

VERY EXPENSIVE & EXPENSIVE   Tokyo's top hotels can rival upper-range hotels anywhere in the world. Although many of the city's best hotels may not show much character from the outside, inside they're oases of subdued simplicity where hospitality reigns supreme. In addition to fine Japanese- and Western-style restaurants, they may also offer a travel agency, secretarial services, a guest relations officer to help with any problems or requests you may have (from making a restaurant reservation to finding an address), shopping arcades, cocktail lounges with live music, and a health club and swimming pool. Unfortunately, health clubs and swimming pools almost always cost extra—anywhere from ¥2,000 to an outrageous ¥5,000 ($17 to $42) per single use. In addition, outdoor pools are generally open only in July and August.

Rooms in upper-range hotels come with such standard features as a minibar, cable TV with CNN and pay movies, clock, radio, cotton kimono, hot-water pot and tea, hair dryer, and private bathrooms. Most also have Internet access, and many have "washlet" toilets, which are combination toilets and spray bidets. Because they're accustomed to foreigners, most upper-range hotels employ an English-speaking staff and offer no-smoking floors. Services provided include room

Tips for Saving on Your Hotel Room

Contrary to hotels, say, in the U.S., Japanese hotels have always remained pretty loyal to their published rack rates, always available at the front desk. The recession, however, has opened some possibilities for bargains.

- **Always ask politely whether a less expensive room is available.** The hotel usually has various types of rooms—at various prices. Ask whether there are corporate discounts or any promotional packages. If there are two of you, ask whether a double or a twin room is cheaper.
- **Dial direct.** When booking a room in a chain hotel, call the hotel's local line, as well as the toll-free number, and see where you get the best deal. Sometimes there are special packages, such as weekend or honeymoon packages, that central reservations desks will not be aware of.
- **Remember the law of supply and demand.** Resort hotels (see chapter 10) are most crowded and therefore usually more expensive on weekends and during peak travel periods such as Golden Week. Discounts, therefore, are often available for midweek and off-season stays. In Tokyo, some hotels catering to business travelers may offer weekend packages.
- **Avoid excess charges.** Find out before you dial whether your hotel imposes a surcharge on local or long-distance calls. A pay phone, however inconvenient, may save you money. Also, instead of using the minibar in your room, save money by buying drinks and snacks from convenience stores or vending machines.
- Some chain business hotels offer **hotel memberships,** with discounts on meals and free stays after a certain number of nights. Inquire at the front desk.
- **Consider a suite.** If you are traveling with your family or another couple, you can pack more people into a suite (which usually comes with a sofa bed), and perhaps reduce your per-person rate.

service, same-day laundry and dry-cleaning service, and complimentary English-language newspapers such as the *Japan Times.* Many hotels also offer executive floors with additional guest amenities, free continental breakfast and cocktails, free use of the health club, and extended checkout time; at just a few thousand yen more than regular rates, these can sometimes be quite economical.

MODERATE   Moderately priced accommodations vary from tourist hotels to business hotels, with business hotels making up the majority in this category. Catering primarily to traveling Japanese businessmen, a business hotel is a no-frills establishment with tiny, sparsely furnished rooms, most of them singles, with barely enough space to unpack your bags. If you're a large person, you may have trouble sleeping in a place like this. Primarily just a place to crash for the night, these rooms usually have everything you need—minuscule private bathroom, TV, telephone, radio, clock, hair dryer, and often a minibar. There's no room service, and sometimes not even a lobby or coffee shop, although usually there are vending machines that dispense beer and soda. Business hotels rarely have no-smoking rooms. On the plus side, they're usually situated in convenient locations. If you're interested simply in a clean and functional place to sleep rather than in roomy comfort, a nondescript business hotel may be the way to go.

Capsule Hotels

There's another inexpensive lodging option in Japan, but it's not for the claustrophobic. So-called capsule hotels, which became popular in the early 1980s, are used primarily by Japanese businessmen who have spent an evening out drinking with fellow workers and missed their last train home—a capsule hotel is cheaper than a taxi ride home. The units are small (no larger than a coffin) and contain a bed, private color TV, alarm clock, and radio; they're usually stacked two deep in rows down a corridor, and the only thing separating you from your probably inebriated neighbor is a curtain. A cotton kimono and locker are provided, and bath and toilets are communal. Most capsule hotels do not accept women.

INEXPENSIVE   It's difficult to find inexpensive lodgings in Tokyo; the price of land is simply prohibitive. You can, however, find rooms—tiny though they may be—for less than $90 a night for two people, which is pretty good considering that you're in one of the most expensive cities in the world. Inexpensive accommodations include a bed or futon and (usually) a phone, television, heating, and air-conditioning. Unless otherwise indicated, rooms also have private bathrooms. Facilities are generally spotless, and prices sometimes include tax. Inexpensive Japanese-style rooms make up the majority in this category; they're described in more detail above.

Many foreigners find Japan so expensive that they end up becoming **youth hostel** regulars, even though they may never consider staying in one in other countries. There's no age limit at hostels in Japan (though children younger than 4 may not be accepted), and although most require a youth-hostel membership card, they often let foreigners stay without one for about ¥600 ($5) extra per night. However, there are usually quite a few restrictions, such as a 9 or 10pm curfew, a lights-out policy shortly thereafter, an early breakfast time, and closed times through the day, generally from about 10am to 3pm. In addition, rooms are generally with many bunk beds or futon, affording little privacy. On the other hand, these are certainly the cheapest accommodations in Tokyo.

2 Very Expensive

GINZA & HIBIYA

Hotel Seiyo Ginza. 1–11–2 Ginza, Chuo-ku, Tokyo 104-0061. ☎ **03/3535-1111.** Fax 03/3535-1110. www.seiyo-ginza.com. E-mail: hsgsales@tkf.att.ne.jp. 79 units. A/C MINIBAR TV TEL. ¥48,000–¥72,000 ($400–$600) single or double; from ¥85,000 ($708) suite. AE, CB, DC, JCB, MC, V. Station: Ginza-Itchome or Kyobashi (2 min.).

Conveniently located between the Ginza and Nihombashi, this luxury hotel caters to famous personalities, royalty, and top executives. With only 79 guestrooms and suites, service is top-quality. The hotel isn't open to the public—that is, you must either be a hotel guest or have a reservation at one of its exclusive restaurants to go in the main entrance. The reception area resembles a living room more than a lobby, with check-in conducted at individual-sized desks fitted with comfortable chairs, and the atmosphere is one of hushed tranquility.

The large rooms—no two of which are alike—are comfortable homes-away-from-home, complete with humidity-control dials; safe; refrigerator stocked with complimentary beer, soda, and other drinks; fax machines; and VCR and on-

A Note on Prices

The prices quoted in this book were figured at ¥120 = U.S. $1 Because of fluctuations, however, in the exchange rate of the yen, the U.S. dollar equivalents given will probably vary during the lifetime of this edition. Be sure to check current exchange rates when planning your trip. In addition, the rates given below may increase, so be sure to ask for the current rate when making your reservation.

command videos. Telephones have two lines, and computerized do not disturb and maid service buttons prompt immediate response. Most of the large bathrooms boast mini-TVs and separate tub and shower areas.

Dining/Diversions: There's a tea lounge and a private guest and members bar. Diners can choose between French nouvelle, kaiseki, and Northern Italian cuisine.

Amenities: 24-hour room service; same-day laundry service; a personal secretary to organize business needs, travel arrangements, shopping, and sightseeing, two theaters; a small fitness room (free) and use of a nearby fitness center (fee: ¥3,000/$25).

○ **Imperial Hotel.** 1–1–1 Uchisaiwaicho, Chiyoda-ku, Tokyo 100-8558. ☎ **800/323-7500** in the U.S., or 03/3504-1111. Fax 03/3581-9146. www.imperialhotel.co.jp. 1,059 units. A/C MINIBAR TV TEL. ¥30,000–¥56,000 ($250–$467) single; ¥35,000–¥61,000 ($292–$508) double or twin; from ¥110,000 ($917) suite. AE, DC, JCB, MC, V. Station: Hibiya (1 min.).

Located across from Hibiya Park, within walking distance of Ginza and business districts, this modern structure is one of Tokyo's best-known hotels where foreigners (mostly business executives) make up about 40% of the guests. The Imperial's trademark is impeccable service: Guests are treated like royalty, and the atmosphere throughout is subdued and dignified. Although the Imperial's history goes back to 1922, when it opened as a much smaller hotel designed by Frank Lloyd Wright, the present hotel dates from 1970, with a 31-story tower added in 1983. (Part of the original structure survives at Meiji-Mura, an architectural museum outside Nagoya.)

Rooms in the main building are quite large for Tokyo. Tower rooms, while slightly smaller, are higher up, have floor-to-ceiling bay windows, and offer fantastic views of either the Imperial Palace or, my preference, Ginza and Tokyo Bay. All come equipped with the amenities you expect from a first-class hotel, including three telephones (including a hand-free phone), bedside controls for the curtains, a room safe large enough to stash a briefcase, cable TV with pay movies, a well-stocked minibar, freeze-dried coffee as well as tea, bathroom scales, fax machines, and a private e-mail address for transmission, reception, and Internet access.

Dining/Diversions: There are 13 restaurants, including Kamon serving teppan-yaki, and four bars. The signature restaurant, Les Saisons, serves exquisitely prepared French cuisine, while the Rainbow Room is popular for its lunch and dinner buffets. The Old Imperial Bar pays tribute to Frank Lloyd Wright.

Amenities: 24-hour room service, baby-sitting service (and an infant day-care center), in-house doctor and dentist, limousine and car-rental services, same-day laundry service, free newspaper. Impressive shopping arcade, barbershop and beauty parlor, extensively equipped bilingual business center, post office, tea-ceremony room, sauna, and a swimming pool, located on the 20th floor, with breathtaking views of Tokyo Bay (fee: ¥1,000/$8.35).

Ginza & Hibiya Accommodations, Dining & Nightlife

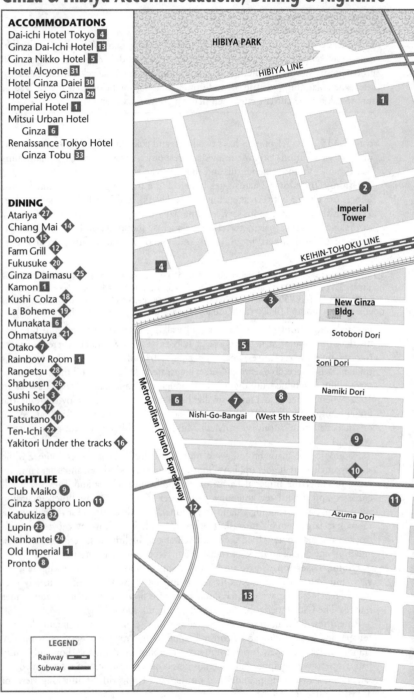

ACCOMMODATIONS
Dai-ichi Hotel Tokyo **4**
Ginza Dai-Ichi Hotel **13**
Ginza Nikko Hotel **5**
Hotel Alcyone **31**
Hotel Ginza Daiei **30**
Hotel Seiyo Ginza **29**
Imperial Hotel **1**
Mitsui Urban Hotel
    Ginza **6**
Renaissance Tokyo Hotel
    Ginza Tobu **33**

DINING
Atariya **27**
Chiang Mai **14**
Donto **15**
Farm Grill **12**
Fukusuke **20**
Ginza Daimasu **25**
Kamon **1**
Kushi Colza **18**
La Boheme **19**
Munakata **6**
Ohmatsuya **21**
Otako **7**
Rainbow Room **1**
Rangetsu **28**
Shabusen **26**
Sushi Sei **3**
Sushiko **17**
Tatsutano **10**
Ten-Ichi **22**
Yakitori Under the tracks **16**

NIGHTLIFE
Club Maiko **9**
Ginza Sapporo Lion **11**
Kabukiza **32**
Lupin **23**
Nanbantei **24**
Old Imperial **1**
Pronto **8**

LEGEND
Railway
Subway

HIBIYA PARK

HIBIYA LINE

Imperial
Tower

KEIHIN-TOHOKU LINE

New Ginza
Bldg.

Sotobori Dori

Soni Dori

Namiki Dori

Metropolitan (Shuto) Expressway

Nishi-Go-Bangai   (West 5th Street)

Azuma Dori

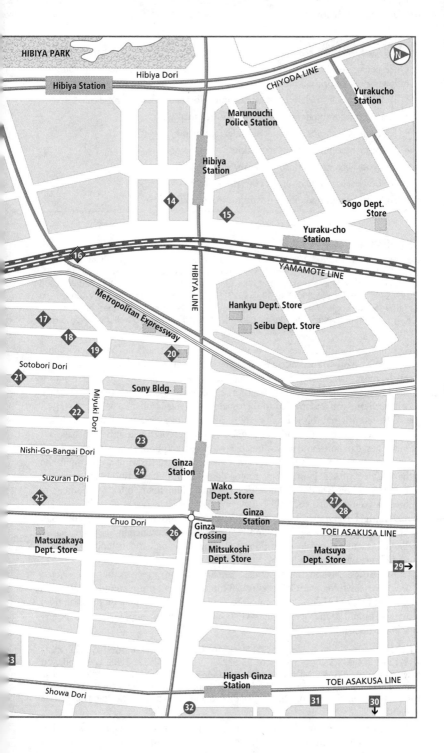

A Guide to Tokyo Maps

Once you've chosen a hotel or inn that appeals to you, you can locate it using the following neighborhood maps:

- To locate accommodations in **Ginza** and **Hibiya,** see map on page 62.
- To locate accommodations in **Shinjuku,** see map on page 66.
- To locate accommodations in **Akasaka,** see map on page 73.
- To locate accommodations in **Asakusa,** see map on page 81.
- To locate accommodations in **Ueno,** see map on page 83.
- To locate accommodations in **Harajuku,** see map on page 117.
- To locate accommodations in **Roppongi,** see map on page 127.

SHINJUKU

Century Hyatt Tokyo. 2–7–2 Nishi-Shinjuku, Shinjuku-ku, Tokyo 160-0023. ☎ **800/ 233-1234** in the U.S. and Canada, 03/3349-0111, or 03/3348-1234. Fax 03/3344-5575. www.centuryhyatt.co.jp/en/menu.html. 786 units. A/C MINIBAR TV TEL. ¥32,000–¥37,000 ($267–$308) single; ¥35,000–¥40,000 ($292–$333) double or twin. Regency Club, from ¥37,000 ($308) single; ¥40,000 ($333) double or twin. Discounts for longer stays. AE, DC, JCB, MC, V. Station: Nishi-Shinjuku (3 min.) or Shinjuku (a 10-min. walk, or a free 3-min. shuttle ride).

Located on Shinjuku's west side next to Shinjuku Central Park (popular with joggers), this 28-story hotel features an impressive seven-story atrium lobby with three of the most massive chandeliers you're likely to see anywhere. The excellent staff is used to the many foreigners (mostly American) who pass through the hotel's doors, which means you'll be treated to the usual high Hyatt standards.

The recently refurbished rooms are sizable and attractive, with English-language cable TV, pay movies, and voice mail. A quarter of the rooms also have fax machines, dataports, and a two-line, hand-free speakerphone. Room rates are based on size; ask for one on a high floor overlooking the park (in winter, you might also have a view of Mt. Fuji). Single rooms don't let in much sunshine; the twins are better, with big windows. The three Regency Club floors offer complimentary breakfast and evening cocktails.

Dining/Diversions: There are 10 restaurants and bars, including the well-known Hugo's, offering steaks and teppanyaki cuisine; Chenonceaux, an elegant French restaurant on the 27th floor with panoramic views; and Italian, Japanese, and Chinese restaurants.

Amenities: 24-hour room service, same-day laundry service, in-house doctor, free newspaper, free shuttle bus every 20 minutes to and from Shinjuku Station (in front of Odakyu Halc department store). Indoor swimming pool on the 28th floor with gym and sauna (fee: ¥2,000/$17), business center, shopping arcade, beauty salon, barbershop.

✪ **Park Hyatt Tokyo.** 3–7–1–2 Nishi-Shinjuku, Shinjuku-ku, Tokyo 163-1055. ☎ **800/ 233-1234** in the U.S. and Canada, or 03/5322-1234. Fax 03/5322-1288. www.parkhyatt tokyo.com. 178 units. A/C MINIBAR TV TEL. ¥47,000–¥58,000 ($392–$483) single or double; from ¥82,000 ($683) suite. AE, DC, JCB, MC, V. Station: Shinjuku (a 13-min. walk, or a 5-min. free shuttle ride); Hatsudai on the Keio Line (7 min.); Tochomae on the Toei No. 12 Line (8 min.).

Located in West Shinjuku on the 39th to 52nd floors of Kenzo Tange's granite-and-glass Shinjuku Park Tower, the Park Hyatt is among the most gorgeous and sophisticated hotels in Japan, a perfect reflection of high-tech, avant-garde Tokyo in the 21st century. If you can afford it, stay here. Check-in, on the 41st floor, is comfortably accomplished at one of three sit-down desks. Elevators reserved only for the guestroom floors offer privacy; if you do see other guests, they're likely to be personalities, fashion designers, or CEOs. In contrast to Shinjuku's other hotels, there's no off-the-street foot traffic here.

All rooms average more than 50 square meters (the largest in Tokyo) and offer original artwork, expansive views (including Mt. Fuji on clear days), two phone lines, dataport, fax machines, voice mail, deep tub (plus separate shower), washlet toilet, TV in the bathroom, walk-in closet, well-stocked minibar, CD and laser disc players (with free rentals), VCR and wide-screen TV (with cable), remote-control curtains, individually controlled air-conditioning, and more, including a Japanese/ English dictionary.

Dining/Diversions: The New York Grill, one of the most sophisticated restaurants in all of Tokyo, is on the 52nd floor; the adjacent New York Bar is a spectacular setting for live jazz. Kozue is tiered to provide views while you dine on impeccable original Japanese cuisine. High tea is served in the Peak Lounge; there's also a relaxed European-style cafe.

Amenities: 24-hour room service, same-day laundry service, free shuttle bus to Shinjuku Station one to three times an hour. On the 47th floor, a dramatic 20-meter indoor swimming pool, fully equipped gym, and professionally staffed aerobics studio (all free to hotel guests); on the 45th floor, Jacuzzi, sauna, steam bath, game room (fee: ¥4,000/$33); CD, laser disc, and book libraries; bakery; beauty salon; 24-hour parking; business center.

EBISU

Westin Tokyo. 1–4–1 Mita, Meguro-ku, Tokyo 153-8580. ☎ **800/WESTIN-1** in the U.S. and Canada, or 03/5423-7000. Fax 03/5423-7600. www.westin.co.jp. E-mail: wetok@westin. com. 444 units. A/C MINIBAR TV TEL. ¥31,000–¥38,000 ($258–$317) single; ¥36,000– ¥43,000 ($300–$358) double or twin; from ¥90,000 ($750) suite. Guest Office or Executive Club, ¥43,000 ($358) single; ¥48,000 ($400) double or twin. AE, DC, JCB, MC, V. Station: Ebisu (7 min.).

A black marble floor, neoclassical columns and statuary, huge floral bouquets, and palm trees set this smart-looking hotel apart from other Tokyo hotels—it would fit right in in Hong Kong. Opened in 1995 and set in the attractive Yebisu Garden Place (Tokyo's first planned community), it's still a hike from Ebisu Station, even with the aid of the elevated moving walkway. It's also far from Tokyo's business center. But the largely Japanese clientele favors it for its European ambience, the Westin name, and the facilities of Yebisu Garden Place, including restaurants and shopping.

The large rooms blend 19th-century Biedermeier styles with contemporary furnishings and boast high ceilings, either king-size (in the double rooms) or two double beds (in twins), a safe, cable TV with pay movies, multiline phones with voice mail, over-size desks and dataports (fax machines available upon request), separate lighted vanities, and large bathrooms with black marble counters and separate shower and tub areas. Guest Office rooms provide such additional features as a laser printer, fax machine, and office supplies; the Executive Club level includes complimentary breakfast, evening cocktails, free local calls, and free use of the fitness club. Rooms with the best view are those facing Tokyo Bay, though in winter those facing west are treated to views of Mt. Fuji.

Dining/Diversions: Nine restaurants, bars, and lounges offer a wide range of cuisine, from sushi and teppanyaki to Chinese. Victor's on the 22nd floor is the signature restaurant.

Shinjuku Accommodations, Dining & Nightlife

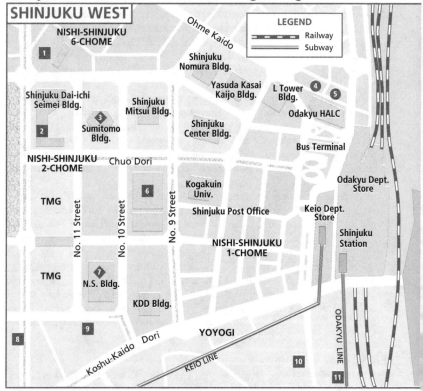

SHINJUKU WEST

SHINJUKU WEST

NISHI-SHINJUKU
6-CHOME

1

Ohme Kaido

Shinjuku
Nomura Bldg.

LEGEND
▪▪▪▪ Railway
▬▬▬ Subway

Yasuda Kasai
Kaijo Bldg.

L Tower
Bldg.

4 5

Shinjuku Dai-ichi
Seimei Bldg.

Shinjuku
Mitsui Bldg.

Odakyu HALC

3
Sumitomo
Bldg.

Shinjuku
Center Bldg.

2

NISHI-SHINJUKU
2-CHOME

Chuo Dori

Bus Terminal

Odakyu Dept.
Store

TMG

6

Kogakuin
Univ.

Keio Dept.
Store

Shinjuku Post Office

Shinjuku
Station

No. 11 Street

No. 10 Street

No. 9 Street

NISHI-SHINJUKU
1-CHOME

TMG

7
N.S. Bldg.

KDD Bldg.

ODAKYU LINE

8

9

Koshu-Kaido Dori

YOYOGI

10

KEIO LINE

11

Amenities: 24-hour room service, same-day laundry service, free newspaper. Business Center, use of nearby health club with heated indoor pool and gym (fee: ¥3,000/$25).

ROPPONGI & AKASAKA

Capitol Tokyu Hotel. 2–10–3 Nagata-cho, Chiyoda-ku, Tokyo 100-0014. ☎ **800/ 428-6598** in the U.S. and Canada, or 03/3581-4511. Fax 03/3581-5822. www.tokyuhotel. com. 459 units. A/C MINIBAR TV TEL. ¥23,000–¥26,000 ($192–$217) single; ¥35,500– ¥55,000 ($296–$458) double or twin; from ¥90,000 ($783) suite. Children under 18 stay free in parents' room. AE, DC, JCB, MC, V. Station: Kokkai Gijido-mae (1 min.) or Tameikesanno (3 min.).

Built just before the 1964 Olympics, this member of the Tokyu hotel chain is in Akasaka next to Hie Shrine, one of the city's most important Edo-Period shrines. A small hotel by Tokyo's standards, it has the unique ability to make foreign guests feel as if they're both in Asia and at home all at the same time. The level of service, provided by 400 full-time employees, is extraordinary; there are, for example, no cigarette machines in the hotel—instead, guests are requested to ask any employee to fetch them a pack of cigarettes. Fantastically large floral bouquets are the trademark of the dark and subdued lobby, which overlooks a small Japanese garden with a carp pond.

While double and twin rooms are comfortably large, the 50 single rooms are fairly small. All come with on-demand movies and traditional shoji screens; the best ones overlook the greenery of Hie Shrine. The brown and green color schemes are

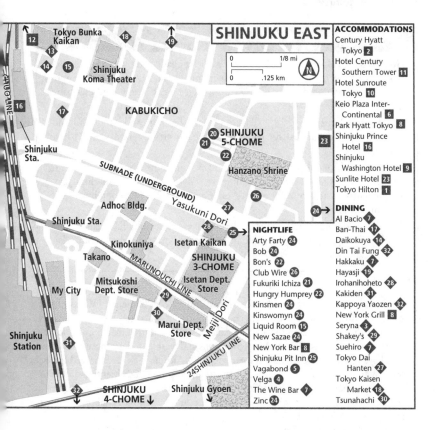

SHINJUKU EAST

Tokyo Bunka Kaikan
Shinjuku Koma Theater
KABUKICHO
SHINJUKU 5-CHOME
Hanzano Shrine
SUBNADE (UNDERGROUND)
Yasukuni Dori
Adhoc Bldg.
Shinjuku Sta.
Kinokuniya
Isetan Kaikan
Takano
MARUNOUCHI LINE
SHINJUKU 3-CHOME
Mitsukoshi Dept. Store
Isetan Dept. Store
My City
Marui Dept. Store
Meiji Dori
Shinjuku Station
24 SHINJUKU LINE
SHINJUKU 4-CHOME
Shinjuku Gyoen
CHUO LINE
Shinjuku Sta.

0   1/8 mi
0   .125 km

ACCOMMODATIONS
Century Hyatt Tokyo **2**
Hotel Century Southern Tower **11**
Hotel Sunroute Tokyo **10**
Keio Plaza Inter-Continental **6**
Park Hyatt Tokyo **8**
Shinjuku Prince Hotel **16**
Shinjuku Washington Hotel **9**
Sunlite Hotel **23**
Tokyo Hilton **1**

DINING
Al Bacio **7**
Ban-Thai **17**
Daikokuya **14**
Din Tai Fung **32**
Hakkaku **7**
Hayasji **19**
Irohanihoheto **28**
Kakiden **31**
Kappoya Yaozen **32**
New York Grill **8**
Seryna **3**
Shakey's **29**
Suehiro **7**
Tokyo Dai Hanten **27**
Tokyo Kaisen Market **18**
Tsunahachi **30**

NIGHTLIFE
Arty Farty **24**
Bob **24**
Bon's **22**
Club Wire **26**
Fukuriki Ichiza **21**
Hungry Humprey **22**
Kinsmen **24**
Kinswomyn **24**
Liquid Room **15**
New Sazae **24**
New York Bar **8**
Shinjuku Pit Inn **25**
Vagabond **5**
Velga **4**
The Wine Bar **7**
Zinc **24**

outdated, but plans for renovation over the next several years should bring the hotel up to date, with renovated rooms featuring white walls and washlet toilets. Be sure to request a room away from an adjacent construction site.

Dining/Diversions: The Keyaki Grill, famous for its steaks and continental cuisine, has some of the most attentive waiters in the world. If it's a view of the garden you want, head for the casual Origami Restaurant or the Garden View (the latter serves lunch buffets).

Amenities: 24-hour room service, free newspaper, same-day laundry service, inhouse doctor and dentist, baby-sitting, outdoor swimming pool (open June to September, no fee), barbershop, beauty salon, shopping arcade, business center, travel agency, bakery.

✪ **Hotel Okura.** 2–10–4 Toranomon, Minato-ku, Tokyo 105-0001. ☎ **800/526-2281** in the U.S., or 03/3582-0111. Fax 03/3582-3707. www.travelweb.com/thisco/okua/5084/5084.b.html. 857 units. A/C MINIBAR TV TEL. ¥28,500–¥41,500 ($237–$346) single; ¥37,000–¥57,000 ($308–$475) double; ¥40,000–¥57,000 ($333–$475) twin; from ¥75,000 ($625) suite. AE, DC, JCB, MC, V. Station: Toranomon or Kamiyacho (5 min.).

Tokyo's most venerable hotel, located across the street from the U.S. Embassy, is the favorite home-away-from-home of visiting United States dignitaries and top-level executives as well as celebrities ranging from the Rolling Stones to Yo-Yo Ma. Service is dignified, gracious, impeccable. Rich decor elegantly combines ikebana and shoji screens with an old-fashioned Western spaciousness. The atmosphere is low-key, with none of the flashiness inherent in some of the city's newer hotels.

ⓘ Family-Friendly Hotels

Holiday Inn Tokyo *(see p. 78)* This American chain hotel will seem familiar to kids, who will appreciate the rooftop swimming pool. And parents will appreciate that children under 19 can stay free in their parents' room, and that baby-sitting is available.

Hotel New Otani *(see p. 72)* This huge hotel has both indoor and outdoor swimming pools, but best for parents is the baby-sitting room, with 24-hour service.

National Children's Castle Hotel *(see p. 91)* This is the absolute best place to stay with kids, since the building contains Tokyo's best indoor/outdoor playground and activity rooms for all ages, offering everything from building blocks to computer games.

Sakura Ryokan *(see p. 89)* This modern Japanese-style inn offers a large family room that sleeps up to eight people in traditional Japanese style, on futon laid out on tatami mats.

Rooms are comfortable and offer on-demand videos, bilingual TVs, safes, fax machines with individual numbers, and dataports. My favorites are the renovated rooms in the main building facing the garden, which feature bird's-eye-maple furniture and bathrooms with marble countertops and washlet toilets; those on the 5th floor have balconies overlooking the garden. *A tip:* Although fees are charged for use of the swimming pools and health club, hotel guests can use facilities free simply by becoming a member of Okura Club International—there's no charge to become a member and membership starts immediately upon filling out an application at the hotel guest relations desk.

Dining/Diversions: Eight restaurants and four bars, including the French La Belle Epoque with 12th-floor city views; the casual Terrace Restaurant, which looks out on the garden (good for power breakfasts); and Sushi Kyubei, the signature restaurant popular with diplomats.

Amenities: 24-hour room service, daily laundry service, express pressing and laundry, three free newspapers, free shuttle service weekday mornings. Shopping arcade, tea-ceremony room, comprehensive business center open daily, private museum showcasing Japanese art, outdoor swimming pool (fee: ¥2,000/$17), health club and exercise gym with personal trainers, sauna, indoor swimming pool (fee: ¥3,500/$29 for all; ¥2,000/$17 for pool only), barbershop, beauty salon, pharmacy, massage service, steam bath, in-house doctor, post office, and a packing and shipping service.

ELSEWHERE IN THE CITY

✪ **Four Seasons Hotel Chinzan-So.** 2–10–8 Sekiguchi, Bunkyo-ku, Tokyo 112-8667. ☎ **800/332-3442** in the U.S., 800/268-6282 in Canada, or 03/3943-2222. Fax 03/3943-2300. www.fshr.com. 286 units. A/C MINIBAR TV TEL. ¥32,000–¥36,000 ($267–$300) single; ¥37,000–¥67,000 ($308–$558) double or twin; from ¥60,000 ($500) suite. Club Floor Room, ¥42,000–¥44,000 ($350–$687) single; ¥49,000–¥61,000 ($408–$508) twin or double. AE, DC, JCB, MC, V. Station: Edogawabashi (exit 1a, a 10-min. walk or a 2-min. ride).

A bit off the beaten track (about a 15-min. taxi ride from Ikebukuro on the northern end of the Yamanote Line loop), the Four Seasons is set on the 17-acre, 100-year-old Chinzan-So Garden, making it extremely inviting after a bustling day in Tokyo. The stunning interiors, created by American designer Frank Nicholson, make this one of the most beautiful European-style hotels in Japan, and prices here are lower than at other Tokyo hotels at this level. Peaceful garden views are available from both private and public spaces.

Even the smallest rooms, which occupy the lower floors, boast king-size beds and are twice the size of most Japanese hotel rooms. All rooms offer satellite TV with on-demand videos, a minimum of three phones, two lines with modem capacity, safe, bedside control panels operating curtains and lights, and oversize marble bathroom with lots of extras, including mini TV. Since the hotel embraces the park, all rooms have garden views. Club floors provide an extra measure of privacy and service, with their own lounge and concierge.

Dining/Diversions: You have your choice of seven restaurants and bars, including Yang Yuan Zhai (the first overseas outlet of the famous Beijing restaurant Diaoyutai, with chefs flown in from the mother restaurant) and Bice, featuring Italian chefs, hand-picked ingredients, and pasta made daily. A Japanese restaurant serves everything from sushi and shabu-shabu to teppanyaki, while Le Jardin is a great place for tea.

Amenities: 24-hour room service, 24-hour laundry service (including 1-hour pressing and overnight dry cleaning), complimentary shoe-shine, your choice of free newspaper (including *USA Today*), complimentary limo service (I love this) to anywhere in Tokyo (weekdays from 8am to 5pm), and complimentary in-room fax-machine use. Elegant boutiques, business center overlooking the garden, salon, and spa featuring a gorgeous indoor pool with a glass ceiling that opens in summer, sunning terrace, indoor and outdoor Jacuzzis, sauna, steam room, fitness gym with English-language instruction, and Japanese hot-springs bath (the water is shipped in from Izu Peninsula)—all free for hotel guests!

3 Expensive

GINZA

Dai-Ichi Hotel Tokyo. 1–2–6 Shimbashi, Minato-ku, Tokyo 105-8621. ☎ **800/223-6800** in the U.S. and Canada, or 03/3501-4411. Fax 03/3595-2634. 275 units. A/C MINIBAR TV TEL. ¥27,000–¥34,000 ($225–$283) single; ¥34,000–¥48,000 ($283–$432) twin; ¥38,000 ($317) double. AE, DC, JCB, MC, V. Station: Shimbashi (1 min., via underground passageway).

This hotel, located in Shimbashi on the edge of the Ginza, is a convenient choice for those conducting business in the surrounding area. It attracts mostly business travelers, of whom 30% are foreigners. There's a direct connection to the Shimbashi subway station, a plus during inclement weather. Unfortunately, the hotel's decor falls short of the European atmosphere the hotel strives for; the two-story lobby mural, an imitation of a Romantic pastoral scene, seems jarringly out of place in the Ginza, and the faux French furnishings lack character. guestrooms, decorated in French drawing-room style with imitation Louis XIV furniture, are comfortable, with windows that open, dataports, and free fax machines. The best views—appropriately enough—are of Japan's tribute to the Eiffel Tower, Tokyo Tower.

Dining/Diversions: Twelve restaurants and bars include a teppanyaki restaurant and bar on the top floor, an Italian-style cafe, and Japanese restaurants serving sushi, yakitori, shabu-shabu, sukiyaki, kaiseki, and local fare.

Amenities: 24-hour room service, same-day laundry service, free newspaper, free shoe-shine. Business center, travel agency, drugstore, beauty salon, barbershop, boutiques. indoor pool, sauna, and gym (fee: ¥3,000/$25).

Renaissance Tokyo Hotel Ginza Tobu. 6–14–10 Ginza, Chuo-ku, Tokyo 104-0061. ☎ **800/ 228-9898** in the U.S. and Canada, or 03/3546-0111. Fax 03/3546-8990. www. marriottrewards.com. E-mail: Ginza-room@group.tobu.co.jp. 206 units. A/C MINIBAR TV TEL. ¥17,000–¥23,000 ($142–$192) single; ¥28,000 ($233) double or twin. Renaissance floor, ¥24,000 ($200) single; ¥35,000 ($292) double or twin. AE, DC, JCB, MC, V. Station: Ginza (4 min.) or Higashi-Ginza (1 min.).

This small, classy, and personable hotel, located on Showa Dori behind the Ginza Matsuzakaya department store, employs an efficient and helpful full-time staff of 200, many of whom are foreigners. Each room comes equipped with three telephones, bilingual cable TV with on-demand pay videos, and massage showerhead; there are also hookups for fax machines and computers (fax machines available on request). The cheapest singles are not usually offered—they're considered too small for foreigners—but if you insist they'll let you have one; though indeed small, I personally find them more nicely appointed than those offered by most business hotels. The 10th-floor Renaissance floor, accessible only by key, offers the added luxury of complimentary breakfast.

Dining/Diversions: The five restaurants and bars include an upscale French restaurant, a Japanese restaurant, and a cafe open until 2am.

Amenities: Room service (6:30am to 2am), same-day laundry service, free newspaper. Travel and business center, hairdressing salon.

NIHOMBASHI & AROUND TOKYO STATION

Palace Hotel. 1–1–1 Marunouchi, Chiyoda-ku, Tokyo 100-0005. ☎ **800/457-4000** U.S. and Canada, or 03/3211-5211. Fax 03/3211-6987. www.palacehotel.co.jp. 389 units. A/C MINIBAR TV TEL. ¥24,000–¥29,000 ($200–$242) single; ¥33,000–¥45,000 ($275–$375) double; ¥32,000–¥60,000 ($267–$500) twin; from ¥100,000 ($833) suite. AE, DC, JCB, MC, V. Station: Otemachi (2 min.), Tokyo Station (7 min.).

Because of its proximity to Tokyo's business district, this hotel is a favorite among foreign business travelers; in fact, foreigners account for fully half of its guests. The hotel is across the street from the Imperial Palace and its lovely gardens. Its deluxe twin rooms—which are large, face the gardens, and boast VCRs, washlet toilets, and a balcony—are highly recommended. All rooms feature two-line phones, fax and computer hookups (fax machines available), soundproof windows that open, bathroom scales, magnifying mirror, safes, vanity desk, and satellite TVs with CNN and on-demand pay movies. For added security and prompt service, attendants are on call at service stations on each floor. Repeat guests are rewarded with monogrammed slippers.

Dining/Diversions: Of the hotel's seven restaurants, serving Chinese, Japanese, and French food, the French-cuisine Crown Restaurant on the 10th floor is the best, with superb views of the Imperial Palace grounds.

Amenities: 24-hour room service, same-day laundry service, free newspaper, instant coffee. Shopping arcade, business center, barbershop, beauty salon, fitness club nearby (fee: ¥3,150/$26).

Royal Park Hotel. 2–1–1 Nihombashi-Kakigara-cho, Chuo-ku, Tokyo 103-8520. ☎ **800/ 457-4000** in the U.S., or 03/3667-1111. Fax 03/3667-1115. www.royalparkhotels.co.jp/ nihonbashi. E-mail: rphfront@pluto.dti.ne.jp. 450 units. A/C MINIBAR TV TEL. ¥22,000– ¥26,000 ($183–$217) single; ¥30,000–¥41,000 ($250–$342) double or twin. Executive floor, from ¥36,000 ($300) single or double. AE, DC, JCB, MC, V. Station: Suitengu-mae (underneath the hotel).

Opened in 1989, the Royal Park is located east of Tokyo Station (about a 10-min. ride by taxi), not far from the Tokyo Stock Exchange and Japan's financial center. One of its greatest assets, however, is that it's connected via an enclosed walkway to the Tokyo City Air Terminal, the main terminus of the Airport Limousine Bus (which shuttles passengers to and from Narita Airport), making this the most convenient place for visitors with only a night or two to spend in Tokyo. But what makes it particularly attractive to business travelers are its up-to-date guestrooms, which have dataports and a sophisticated computerized TV system that allows guests to access the Internet, send e-mail, check stock-market quotes and airline schedules, watch videos on demand, play computer games, and more (fee: ¥1,300/$11 for the first hour or per video; wireless keyboards are available at the front desk). The best views are from twins facing the Sumida River. There are three executive floors, each offering complimentary breakfast and cocktails and free use of the fitness club.

Dining/Diversions: The hotel's 10 restaurants and bars include a French restaurant, a teppanyaki restaurant, and the Orpheus Sky Lounge, which offers great views from the 20th floor.

Amenities: 24-hour room service, same-day laundry service, free newspaper, baby-sitting. Fitness club with indoor pool, gym, massage, and sauna (fee: ¥3,000/$25); business center, beauty salon, and barbershop; small shopping arcade.

SHINJUKU

Tokyo Hilton. 6–6–2 Nishi-Shinjuku, Shinjuku-ku, Tokyo 160-0023. ☎ **800/HILTONS** in the U.S. or Canada, or 03/3344-5111. Fax 03/3342-6094. www.hilton.com. 807 units. A/C MINIBAR TV TEL. ¥28,000–¥37,000 ($233–$308) single; ¥32,000–¥41,000 ($267–$342) twin or double. Executive floor, ¥37,000–¥44,000 ($308–$367) single; ¥43,000–¥50,000 ($358–$417) twin or double; from ¥70,000 ($583) suite. Seasonal packages available. Children stay free in parents' room. AE, DC, JCB, MC, V. Station: Nishi-Shinjuku (2 min.) or Shinjuku (10-min. walk or free shuttle bus).

Located on Shinjuku's west side, the 38-story Tokyo Hilton opened in 1984 as the largest Hilton in the Asia/Pacific area. Today it keeps a lower profile than most of the other Shinjuku hotels, with a quiet, subdued lobby. It remains popular with business and leisure travelers alike. As with all Hiltons, the room decor here reflects traditional native style, with shoji screens instead of curtains and simple yet elegant furnishings. Rooms are up-to-date with voice mail, satellite TV with pay movies, connections for fax and computer modems, and a hands-free speakerphone. The top five floors are executive floors, where guests have their own lounge for complimentary continental breakfast and cocktail hour and rooms come with fax machines.

Dining/Diversions: Seven restaurants and bars specialize in Italian, Chinese, teppanyaki, and other cuisine.

Amenities: 24-hour room service, same-day laundry service, complimentary shuttle service to Shinjuku Station, free newspaper. Kinko's (open 24 hr.), outdoor tennis courts, fitness center with indoor pool and sauna (fee: ¥1,500/$12 for either pool or gym alone, ¥2,000/$17 for sauna; or ¥2,000/$17 for pool and gym, ¥4,000/$33 for everything), convenience store, beauty parlor, barbershop, shopping arcade.

AKASAKA & ROPPONGI

✪ **Akasaka Prince Hotel.** 1–2 Kioi-cho, Chiyoda-ku, Tokyo 102-8585. ☎ **800/542-8686** in the U.S. and Canada, or 03/3234-1111. Fax 03/3262-5163. www.princehotels.co.jp/english/. 761 units. A/C MINIBAR TV TEL. ¥27,000–¥36,000 ($225–$300) single; ¥34,000–¥40,000 ($283–$333) twin; ¥37,000–¥42,000 ($308–$350) double; from ¥100,000 ($833) suite. AE, DC, JCB, MC, V. Station: Akasaka-mitsuke or Nagatacho (2 min.).

This 40-story ultramodern white skyscraper—an Akasaka landmark with a facade that reminds me of an unfolding fan—caused quite a stir when it opened in 1983. The lobby is intentionally spacious and empty, lined with almost 12,000 slabs of white marble, so as not to compete with brilliant Japanese kimono (weddings are big business in Japanese hotels).

The guestrooms are set on a 45° angle from the center axis of the building's core, giving each one a corner view with expansive windows overlooking the city. Rooms are bright—gray, white, or soothing powder-blue—with a lot of sunshine; request one overlooking the Akasaka side, and you'll have a view of neon lights down below and Tokyo Tower in the distance. The single rooms are among the nicest in Tokyo, with three windows forming a pleasant alcove around a sofa. Sinks and vanity desks are located away from toilet and bath areas.

Dining/Diversions: There are 14 international restaurants and bars. Le Trianon, occupying a stately 65-year-old European-style building that once belonged to the imperial family, is the hotel's premier restaurant. Top of Akasaka, on the 40th floor, is Akasaka's best cocktail lounge with a view (no children allowed). The Potomac, open 24 hours, offers a bargain steak lunch (see chapter 5).

Amenities: 24-hour room service, same-day laundry and dry-cleaning service, baby-sitting, free newspaper. A fully equipped, excellent business center, with a spectacular 20th-floor view. Travel desk, souvenir shop, florist, beauty salon, convenience store, outdoor heated swimming pool open May through September (fee: ¥1,000/$8.35).

ANA Hotel Tokyo. 1–12–33 Akasaka, Minato-ku, Tokyo 107-0052. ☎ **800/262-4683** in the U.S. and Canada, or 03/3505-1111. Fax 03/3505-1155. www.ananet.or.jp/anahotels/tokyo/. 903 units. A/C MINIBAR TV TEL. ¥24,000–¥33,000 ($200–$275) single; ¥31,000–¥38,000 ($258–$317) double or twin; from ¥60,000 ($500) suite. AE, CB, DC, JCB, MC, V. Station: Tameike Sanno (1 min.); Roppongi, Akasaka, Kamiyacho, Toranomon, or Kokkai Gijido-mae (5–10 min.).

A gleaming white, triangular building rising 37 stories above the crossroads of Akasaka, Roppongi, Toranomon, and Kasumigaseki, the ANA Hotel Tokyo (an affiliate of All Nippon Airways and referred to by the Japanese as the Zenniku hotel) has given the Hotel Okura stiff competition since its grand opening in 1986. Rooms, complete with dataports and cable TV, are large, with those on the upper floors offering views of the American Embassy and Tokyo Bay (I consider this the best view), Mt. Fuji (visible usually only in winter), or the Imperial Palace. The 33rd and 34th floors feature special executive quarters, where guests have their own concierge, free continental breakfast, and an evening cocktail hour.

Dining/Diversions: A dozen restaurants and bars, serving French, Italian, Chinese, and Japanese favorites, are available. The Astral Bar on the 37th floor provides live music and fantastic views of the city. The lounge in the spacious, cream-colored marble lobby is a favorite among Tokyoites for people-watching.

Amenities: Room service (6am to 2am), free newspaper, same-day laundry service, baby-sitting. Business center with secretarial services, travel desk, shopping arcade, barbershop and beauty salon, sauna (for men only), fitness club (fee: ¥1,500/$12), outdoor swimming pool (fee: ¥1,000/$8.35).

Hotel New Otani. 4–1 Kioi-cho, Chiyoda-ku, Tokyo 102-8578. ☎ **800/421-8795** in the U.S. and Canada, or 03/3265-1111. Fax 03/3221-2619. 1,612 units. A/C MINIBAR TV TEL. ¥28,500–¥36,000 ($237–$300) single; ¥33,500–¥57,000 ($279–$475) double; ¥41,000–¥57,000 ($342–$475) twin; from ¥70,000 ($583) suite. AE, DC, JCB, MC, V. Station: Akasaka-mitsuke or Nagatacho (3 min.).

If you like quiet, small hotels, this place is not for you. Like a city unto itself, the New Otani is so big that two information desks assist lost souls searching for a particular restaurant or one of the shops in the meandering arcade; there are even two check-in desks. Its most splendid feature is its garden, the best of any Tokyo

Akasaka Accommodations, Dining & Nightlife

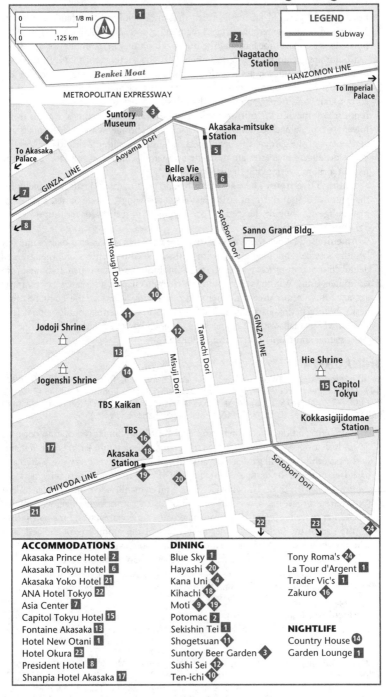

ACCOMMODATIONS
Akasaka Prince Hotel 2
Akasaka Tokyu Hotel 6
Akasaka Yoko Hotel 21
ANA Hotel Tokyo 22
Asia Center 7
Capitol Tokyu Hotel 15
Fontaine Akasaka 13
Hotel New Otani 1
Hotel Okura 23
President Hotel 8
Shanpia Hotel Akasaka 17

DINING
Blue Sky 1
Hayashi 20
Kana Uni 4
Kihachi 18
Moti 9 19
Potomac 2
Sekishin Tei 1
Shogetsuan 11
Suntory Beer Garden 3
Sushi Sei 12
Ten-ichi 10

Tony Roma's 24
La Tour d'Argent 1
Trader Vic's 1
Zakuro 16

NIGHTLIFE
Country House 14
Garden Lounge 1

73

hotel—a 400-year-old Japanese garden that once belonged to a feudal lord, with 10 acres of ponds, waterfalls, bridges, bamboo groves, and manicured bushes. The hotel also gets kudos for banning the use of cell phones in its public spaces.

Rooms are comfortable, offering English-language cable (with CNN); shoji-like screens on the windows; desks with dataports and an extra phone line for fax and Internet use (fax machines are available free of charge); and bedside controls for the curtains, air conditioner, and do not disturb sign. More expensive rooms have bathroom scales, magnifying mirrors, walk-in closets, and fax machines. Rooms in the tower are especially chic, done in jade, black, and chrome, with washlet toilets and great views of the garden, the skyscrapers of Shinjuku, and, on clear days, Mt. Fuji in the distance. Since rates are the same no matter which way you face, be sure to request a room overlooking the garden.

Dining/Diversions: There are more than 30 restaurants and bars here, including the famous La Tour d'Argent, a Trader Vic's, a revolving Chinese buffet, and a popular lounge overlooking the garden. (See chapter 5 for reviews for La Tour d'Argent, Sekishin Tei, and Blue Sky.)

Amenities: 24-hour room service, two free newspapers delivered daily, same-day laundry service. Shopping arcade with 120 stores, convenience store, medical and dental clinics, post office, tea-ceremony room, business center (open 24 hours, with computers using Windows available at no charge), chapel with daily services, travel agency, art museum (free for hotel guests; pick up tickets at the guest relations desk), beauty parlor, barbershop, a 24-hour child-care center, outdoor pool (fee: ¥2,000/$17), small workout center (free for hotel guests), health club with indoor pool, sauna, and tennis courts (fee: ¥5,000/$42).

SHINAGAWA

Le Meridien Pacific Tokyo. 3-13-3 Takanawa, Minato-ku, Tokyo 108-8567. ☎ **800/ 543-4300** in the U.S., or 03/3445-6711. Fax 03/3445-5733. 954 units. A/C MINIBAR TV TEL. ¥21,000–¥25,000 ($175–$208) single; ¥25,000–¥33,000 ($208–$275) twin or double; from ¥50,000 ($412) suite. AE, DC, JCB, MC, V. Station: Shinagawa (1 min.).

This graceful and dignified hotel across the street from Shinagawa Station occupies grounds that once belonged to Japan's imperial family, a reminder of which remains in the peaceful, tranquil garden with a pond and a waterfall that serves as a dramatic backdrop of the lobby lounge. Approximately 40% of hotel guests are foreigners. All rooms come with cable TV with CNN and on-demand video and washlet toilets; some have fax machines as well. Most bathrooms are surprisingly small, with almost no counter space to speak of. Rates are based on a variety of factors: for single rooms it's the size of the bed; for doubles it's the size of the room, size of the bed, and whether the room faces the garden or the bay (more expensive); for twins it's the height. The best views are those from the highest floors overlooking Tokyo Bay.

Dining/Diversions: Nine restaurants and bars offer Japanese, Chinese, and excellent French cuisine. The Blue Pacific lounge on the 30th floor has great views of Tokyo Bay.

Amenities: Room service (to 1am), free newspaper, same-day laundry service. Outdoor pool (fee: ¥1,500/$12), shopping arcade, travel agency, barbershop, business center, beauty salon.

Radisson Miyako Hotel Tokyo. 1-1-50 Shiroganedai, Minato-ku, Tokyo 108-8640. ☎ **800/333-3333** in the U.S and Canada, or 03/3447-3111. Fax 03/3447-3133. www.miyako-hotel-tokyo.co.jp/. 498 units. A/C MINIBAR TV TEL. ¥18,000–¥24,000 ($150–$200) single; ¥30,000–¥38,000 ($250–$317) double; ¥25,000–¥38,000 ($208–$317) twin; from ¥80,000 ($667) suite. AE, DC, JCB, MC, V. Station: Takanawadai (8 min.) or free shuttle from Meguro or Shinagawa Station.

This hotel is one of our favorites in Tokyo, for its calm peacefulness as well as its small-luxury-hotel service (when one of us didn't have time to go to the post office, the concierge offered to go herself during her lunch hour). This affiliate of the famous Miyako Hotel in Kyoto was designed by Minoru Yamasaki, the architect of New York's World Trade Center and Los Angeles' Century Plaza. Because it's a bit off the beaten path, it has a quieter, more relaxed atmosphere than more centrally located hotels, as well as more competitive rates (the expected opening of a nearby subway station in 2000 may change that). Japanese account for 70% of guests.

The rooms, with dataports, are large, with huge floor-to-ceiling windows overlooking the hotel's own lush garden, a famed garden next door, or Tokyo Tower. The singles are a good deal and are often fully booked. Rooms on the eighth floor have fax machines.

Dining/Diversions: The hotel has nine restaurants, bars, and cocktail lounges. La Clé d'Or, serving continental fare, has a view of the hotel's garden, as does the Yamatoya Sangen, which offers a variety of Japanese cuisine. Silver Hill offers great, bargain-priced lunch and dinner buffets.

Amenities: Frequent free shuttle service to and from Meguro Station (5 min. away) and to Shinagawa Station (mornings only). Room service (7am to midnight), free newspaper, complimentary shuttle bus, same-day laundry service, free parking. Health club with a 25-meter heated indoor pool, gym, Jacuzzi, and sauna (fee: ¥2,000/$17 for either pool or gym; ¥4,000/$33 for everything); shopping arcade; convenience store, dental and medical clinics; barbershop; travel agency; excellent bilingual concierge desk.

ON OR NEAR ODAIBA

Hotel Inter-Continental Tokyo Bay. 1–16–2 Kaigan, Minato-ku, Tokyo 105-8576. ☎ **800/ 327-0200** in the U.S. and Canada, or 03/5404-2222. Fax 03/5404-2111. 336 units. A/C MINIBAR TV TEL. ¥27,000–¥43,000 ($225–$358) single; ¥33,000–¥49,000 ($275–$408) double or twin; from ¥100,000 ($833) suite. Club Inter-Continental Floor, from ¥34,000 ($283) single; from ¥40,000 ($333) double or twin. AE, DC, JCB, MC, V. Station: Hamamatsucho (6 min.), Daimon Station (12 min.), or Takeshiba (1 min.).

Located on Tokyo Bay and offering the city's best views of Rainbow Bridge and Odaiba, this fairly small hotel has a cozy, comfortable lobby, which some guests find as a welcome relief from the expansive, marble lobbies favored in Tokyo proper. It caters to business travelers during the week, with leisure guests filling rooms on weekends. Its location is convenient to Haneda Airport and the international convention center (Tokyo Big Sight), though the station closest to the hotel, Takeshiba, is served only by the monorail Yurikamome Line, which connects Shimbashi with Odaiba and which can be quite crowded on weekends. Takeshiba also serves as a passenger terminal for boats to outlying islands.

The handsomely decorated rooms feature cable TV and pay movies, dataports, a safe, and well-appointed bathrooms with washlet toilets and bathroom scales. All rooms face the water, but it's worth paying extra for the bay view of Rainbow Bridge and Odaiba, which is spectacular at night. The highest-priced rooms afford harbor views even from the bathrooms. The Club rooms, which occupy the top five floors, include complimentary continental breakfast and evening cocktails served in the exclusive lounge.

Dining/Diversions: Restaurants span six continents of divergent cuisine, with presentations from Provence, California, Japan, and other Asian countries. Retire to the Sunset Lounge for great views of Tokyo Bay.

Amenities: 24-hour room service, same-day laundry service, free newspaper on request, business center.

Hotel Nikko Tokyo. 1–9–1 Daiba, Minato-ku, Tokyo 135-8625. ☎ **800/645-5687** in the U.S. and Canada, or 03/5500-5500. Fax 03/5500-2525. E-mail: info@hnt.co.jp. 453 units. A/C MINIBAR TV TEL. ¥27,000–¥35,000 ($225–$292) single; ¥32,000–¥40,000 ($267–$333) double or twin; from ¥75,000 ($625) suite. AE, DC, JCB, MC, V. Station: Daiba (1 min.).

Opened in 1996 as the first hotel on Odaiba, this grand, elegant hotel is now somewhat dwarfed by the Meridien Grand Pacific across the street. Although its claim on offering the best views of the Tokyo skyline have been usurped by its competitor, it exudes a more relaxed, resort-evoking atmosphere and offers a more inspiring view from its airy lobby. It bills itself as an "urban resort," offering incentives for both the business and leisure traveler and is especially popular with young well-to-do Japanese in search of an exotic weekend getaway. It's by far the most un-Tokyolike hotel in the city. Closer to the waterfront than the Meridien, it is surrounded by parks and gardens, with a wooden walkway linking it to the Tokyo Decks shopping mall and a sandy beach. A curved facade assures waterfront views from most rooms, which have the usual amenities like dataports, satellite TV, safe, and washlet toilet, as well as private balconies with two chairs. The most expensive rooms offer commanding views of Tokyo Bay, Rainbow Bridge, and the city skyline, while the least expensive rooms, smaller in size, face the Meridien or the Maritime Museum and Haneda airport across the bay.

Dining/Diversions: Ten restaurants and bars are on hand, most capitalizing on the great views; among these are the French Terrace on the Bay with outdoor terrace seating, the Bayside Cafe, and the Sakura serving sushi and teppanyaki. Disappointingly, however, there are no top-floor venues.

Amenities: Room service (8pm to 11am), same-day laundry service, free newspaper, business center, spa with indoor pool connected to outdoor heated tub, Jacuzzi and sun terrace overlooking Rainbow Bridge (fee: ¥3,000/$25 the first day; thereafter ¥1,000/$8.35).

Le Meridien Grand Pacific Tokyo. 2–6–1 Daiba, Minato-ku, Tokyo 135-8701. ☎ **800/543-4300** in the U.S., or 03/5500-6711. Fax 03/5500-4507. www.htl.pacific.co.jp. 884 units. A/C MINIBAR TV TEL. ¥23,000 ($192) single; ¥31,000–¥40,000 ($258–$333) double or twin; from ¥70,000 ($583) suite. Club President Floor from ¥39,000 ($325) double; ¥42,000 ($350) twin. AE, DC, JCB, MC, V. Station: Daiba (1 min.).

Opened in 1998, this soaring, 30-story hotel offers great views of the Tokyo skyline and Rainbow Bridge from its location on Odaiba, an island of reclaimed land with the Tokyo Big Sight convention center, shopping malls, beaches, and sightseeing attractions. Although the lobby's imitation Louis XIV furniture, marbled columns, and large chandeliers seem rather stuffy and out of place in this leisure destination, it nonetheless attracts many visiting Japanese, especially on weekends, and boasts an efficient, accommodating staff. Rooms repeat the French decorating theme and come with dataports, bilingual TVs with CNN, movies on demand, safes, washlet toilets, and magnifying mirrors. They offer views of either Tokyo port in the distance or, even better, Rainbow Bridge and the Tokyo skyline (but only from rooms above the 17th floor). Guests in the Club President rooms receive complimentary breakfast and evening cocktails and free entry to the fitness club. This is a great choice if you want to get away from the bustle of Tokyo, but the location can be a disadvantage; it's served only by the monorail Yurikamome Line, which can be quite crowded on weekends, as can bus and taxi travel over Rainbow Bridge.

Dining/Diversions: Eight restaurants serve Italian, French, and Chinese cuisine, as well as kaiseki, teppanyaki, sushi, and tempura.

Amenities: Room service (6am to noon and 5pm to 1am), same-day laundry service, art gallery, gift shop, outdoor swimming pool (fee: ¥2,000/$17), fitness club with indoor swimming pool (fee: ¥1,800/$15).

4 Moderate

GINZA

Ginza Nikko Hotel. 8–4–21 Ginza, Chuo-ku, Tokyo 104-0061. ☎ **03/3571-4911.** Fax 03/3571-8379. E-mail: yoyaku@g-nikkohtl.co.jp. 112 units. A/C MINIBAR TV TEL. ¥10,000–¥16,000 ($83–$133) single; ¥20,000–¥25,000 ($167–$208) double; ¥24,000–¥28,000 ($200–$233) twin. AE, DC, JCB, MC, V. Station: Shimbashi, Ginza, or Hibiya (5 min.). On Sotobori Dori.

There's nothing fancy or out of the ordinary about this small business hotel, an affiliate of Japan Airlines, but it's personable and clean and has an unbeatable location in southern Ginza. Built more than 40 years ago, it's one of the oldest hotels in the area. Rates are based on room size, with the cheapest rooms very tiny indeed; even the largest tend to be dark because of surrounding taller buildings. Facilities are limited to a cafe/restaurant and bar.

Hotel Alcyone. 4–14–3 Ginza, Chuo-ku, Tokyo 104-0061. ☎ **03/3541-3621.** Fax 03/3541-3263. E-mail: hotelalcyone@msn.com. 74 units. A/C TV TEL. ¥10,000–¥12,000 ($83–$108) single; ¥17,000–¥23,000 ($142–$192) twin or double. AE, DC, JCB, MC, V. Station: Higashi-Ginza (exit 5, 1 min.) or Ginza (exit A6, 5 min.). A few minutes' walk from the Kabukiza and a 5-min. walk from Ginza Crossing.

There's nothing exceptional about the appearance of this older hotel, but it does offer something most other Ginza hotels don't—quite a few Japanese-style rooms at reasonable prices, as well as so-called combination rooms that combine Western-style beds with tatami areas. I prefer the Japanese rooms here, since they're less cluttered, offer more space, and feature such touches as built-in Japanese-style vanities and shoji screens. All rooms have empty fridges you can stock yourself. Hotel facilities include a Swiss restaurant specializing in cheese fondue, a beauty salon, and a small public bath that can be locked for privacy. Room service is available from 3 to 9:30pm.

✪ Hotel Ginza Daiei. 3–12–1 Ginza, Chuo-ku, Tokyo 104-0061. ☎ **03/3545-1111.** Fax 03/3545-1177. 106 units. A/C MINIBAR TV TEL. ¥11,400–¥13,600 ($95–$113) single; ¥15,600 ($130) double; ¥17,500–¥20,800 ($146–$173) twin. AE, DC, JCB, MC, V. Station: Higashi-Ginza (3 min.), or Yurakucho (10 min).

A redbrick building located behind the Kabukiza Theater, this business hotel offers minuscule but well-equipped rooms, with lots of extras not usually found in this price range: three telephones in each room; bedside controls for the air-conditioning, room lights, curtains, and do not disturb sign; washlet toilets; hair dryer; trouser press; bilingual, satellite TV with English-language programs (though no CNN); and radios wired for 440 stations. The most expensive twins are so-called "Healthy Twins," corner rooms with larger bathrooms featuring jet baths and mini TV. There's one Chinese restaurant.

Mitsui Urban Hotel Ginza. 8–6–15 Ginza, Chuo-ku, Tokyo 104-0061. ☎ **03/3572-4131.** Fax 03/3572-4254. www.mitsuikanko.co.jp. 265 units. A/C TV TEL. ¥14,000–¥17,000 ($117–$142) single; ¥21,000–¥24,500 ($175–$204) double; ¥21,000–¥30,000 ($175–$250) twin. AE, DC, JCB, MC, V. Station: Shimbashi (2 min.).

Because of its great location, convenient to the Ginza and to the Hibiya and Kasumigaseki business centers, this attractive hotel caters to both business travelers and tourists. The lobby, on the second floor, has a friendly staff. The bright and modern guestrooms are tiny, but feature amenities found usually only at more expensive hotels, including safes, trouser presses, and complimentary newspapers. In addition, bathrooms are larger than in other business hotels, with a decent-size tub, a no-fog mirror, hair dryer, and, in the most expensive twins, washlet toilet. I suggest asking for a room away from the highway overpass beside the hotel. Of the hotel's four restaurants and bars, my favorite is Munakata, a pleasant Japanese restaurant offering reasonably priced mini-kaiseki lunches (see chapter 5).

NIHOMBASHI & AROUND TOKYO STATION

Holiday Inn Tokyo. 1–13–7 Hatchobori, Chuo-ku, Tokyo 104-0032. ☎ **03/3553-6161.** Fax 03/3553-6040. 119 units. A/C MINIBAR TV TEL. ¥16,500–¥17,700 ($137.50–$147.50) single; ¥18,500–¥22,400 ($154–$187) double; ¥23,400–¥23,900 ($195.60–$199) twin. Children under 19 stay free in parents' room. AE, DC, JCB, MC, V. Station: Hatchobori (1 min.). On Shinohashi Dori.

This brick hotel is popular with American solo travelers, who choose it primarily for its familiarity and large beds. Similar in atmosphere and decor to an American motel, it's smaller than its U.S. counterparts, from its tiny lobby to its small rooms (which are still fairly large for Tokyo). Pluses are the no-smoking rooms; double-size (or larger) beds throughout, even in the twin rooms; the complimentary instant coffee in addition to the usual tea; and English-language cable TV with pay movies. Other amenities include a rooftop outdoor pool, free for hotel guests (open July and Aug only); baby-sitters available on request; and a free *Japan Times* delivered to your room in the morning. There is also one Western restaurant, plus a bar. The hotel is about a 25-minute walk to Ginza.

Hotel Yaesu Ryumeikan. 1–3–22 Yaesu, Chuo-ku, Tokyo 103-0028. ☎ **03/3271-0971.** Fax 03/3271-0977. www.jnto.go.jp. E-mail: yaesu-ryumeikan@ma4.justnet.ne.jp. 30 units (25 with bathroom). A/C TV TEL. ¥8,000–¥9,500 ($67–$79) single without bathroom, ¥10,000–¥13,000 ($83–$108) single with bathroom; ¥14,000 ($117) double without bathroom; ¥17,000–¥18,000 ($142–$150) double with bathroom. Rates include Japanese breakfast. AE, DC, MC, V. Station: Tokyo Station (3 min. from the north Yaesu exit), or Nihombashi (1 min., exit A3). On the corner of Eitai Dori and Sotobori Dori.

This 30-year-old hotel is your best bet for reasonably priced lodging just minutes away from Tokyo Station. From the north Yaesu exit, turn left onto Sotobori Dori; the hotel will be on your right, just before Eitai Dori. In addition to a coffee shop and Japanese restaurant, it offers both Japanese-style tatami rooms and Western-style rooms with beds. I personally prefer the Japanese-style rooms, especially the most expensive tatami rooms, which have a nice, traditional feel and come with sitting alcove and Japanese-style deep tub. Only Japanese breakfasts are available; if you can't stomach rice and fish in the morning, opt for a room without breakfast and subtract ¥1,000 ($8.35) per person from the rates above.

Tokyo Station Hotel. 1–9–1 Marunouchi, Chiyoda-ku, Tokyo 100-0005. ☎ **03/ 3231-2511.** Fax 03/3231-3513. 58 units. A/C TV TEL. ¥10,000–¥15,000 ($83–$125) single; ¥17,000–¥24,000 ($142–$200) double; ¥17,000–¥34,000 ($142–$283) twin. AE, DC, JCB, MC, V. Station: Tokyo (1 min.). In Tokyo Station.

If you're arriving and departing Tokyo by Shinkansen bullet train, the Tokyo Station Hotel is the most convenient choice. Opened in 1915, this historic hotel occupies the Marunouchi (west) side of the original, handsome, redbrick Tokyo Station, one of Tokyo's few prewar landmarks. Its unpretentious interior has changed little over the decades, from the old-fashioned, crowded lobby to the wood staircases leading to what are probably the widest corridors in Tokyo. There is no elevator. Its rooms are large for Tokyo and offer views that could only excite a train buff. The most expensive twins are spacious, with high ceilings, floor-to-ceiling windows, and modern décor—but the red velvet furniture is a bit much. The cheaper rooms feature outdated floral wallpaper. In short, the hotel's interior amuses—it's so different from high-tech Tokyo that it's almost refreshing, if not endearing. Astonishingly, there are 10 restaurants and bars serving French, Italian, Chinese, and Japanese food; their business depends largely on travelers passing through.

Yaesu Fujiya Hotel. 2–9–1 Yaesu, Chuo-ku, Tokyo 104-0028. ☎ **03/3273-2111.** Fax 03/ 3273-2180. 377 units. A/C MINIBAR TV TEL. ¥12,500–¥13,500 ($104–$112.50) single; ¥17,000–¥18,000 ($142–$150) double; ¥24,000–¥35,000 ($200–$292) twin. AE, DC, JCB, MC, V. Stations: Kyobashi or Ginza 1–chome (3 min.), Tokyo or Yurakucho (5 min.). On Sotobori Dori, between Tokyo and Yurakucho stations and just a 5-min. walk from the Ginza.

This reliable, moderately priced hotel has a very convenient location. As many as 17 stations are within a 15-minute walk, assuring it a high occupancy rate with a mostly Japanese clientele. Otherwise, the hotel looks older than its 1986 construction date, despite new carpeting and wallpaper. Rooms are quite small, with hardly space to unpack, but feature bilingual cable TV with CNN, free instant coffee in addition to tea, and free newspaper. No-smoking rooms are available. Facilities include a convenience store, a souvenir corner, and restaurants serving French, American, and Japanese food.

ASAKUSA

Asakusa View Hotel. 3–17–1 Nishi-Asakusa, Taito-ku, Tokyo 111-8765. ☎ **03/ 3847-1111.** Fax 03/3842-2117. 342 units. A/C MINIBAR TV TEL. ¥13,000–¥18,000 ($108–$150) single; ¥21,000–¥31,000 ($175–$258) double; ¥26,000–¥31,000 ($217–$258) twin; ¥34,000 ($283) triple. Japanese-style rooms, from ¥40,000 ($333) for 2. AE, DC, JCB, MC, V. Station: Tawaramachi (8 min.).

This is the only upper-bracket and modern hotel in the Asakusa area, and it looks almost out of place rising among this famous district's older buildings. It's a good place to stay if you want to be in Tokyo's old downtown but don't want to sacrifice any creature comforts. The guestrooms are very pleasant, with sleek contemporary Japanese furnishings and bay windows that let in plenty of sunshine; rooms facing the front have views over the famous Sensoji Temple. Eight Japanese-style rooms are available, sleeping up to five people. Of the hotel's six restaurants and bars, Makie is the best known, featuring Western cuisine served in the delicate style of Japanese kaiseki. Other facilities include an indoor pool with a ceiling that opens in summer (fee: ¥3,000/$25), shopping arcade, and a Japanese-style public bath with cypress tubs (fee: ¥1,050/$8.75). Room service is available 7am to 2am.

✪ Ryokan Shigetsu. 1–31–11 Asakusa, Taito-ku 111-0032. ☎ **03/3843-2345.** Fax 03/ 3843-2348. www.roy.hi-ho.ne.jp/shigetsu. E-mail: shigetsu@roy.hi-ho.ne.jp. 24 units. A/C MINIBAR TV TEL. ¥7,300–¥9,000 ($61–$75) single; ¥14,000–¥15,000 ($117–$125) twin. Japanese or Western breakfast ¥1,200 ($10) extra, Japanese dinner ¥3,000 ($25) extra. AE, MC, V. Station: Asakusa (4 min.).

Whenever a foreigner living in Tokyo, soon to play host to first-time visitors to Japan, asks me to recommend a moderately priced ryokan in Tokyo, this is the one I most often suggest. It has a great location in Asakusa just off Nakamise Dori, a colorful, shop-lined pedestrian street leading to the famous Sensoji Temple—an area that gives you a feel for the older Japan. A member of the Japanese Inn Group, the ryokan was completely rebuilt in 1995 and represents the best of modern yet traditional Japanese design—simple yet elegant, with shoji, unadorned wood, and artwork throughout. Traditional Japanese music or the recorded chirping of birds plays softly in the background of the corridors and public spaces. Two public

Japanese baths have views of the nearby five-storied pagoda. A Japanese restaurant serves excellent Japanese breakfasts, as well as mini-kaiseki dinners (discounts given to hotel guests; reserve 5 days in advance) and lunches. There are 14 Western-style rooms, 7 singles and 7 twins, but I prefer the slightly more expensive 10 Japanese-style tatami rooms, which include Japanese-style mirrors and comfortable chairs for those who don't like relaxing on the floor. In short, this establishment costs no more than a regular business hotel but has much more class.

Sukeroku-no-yado-Sadachiyo. 2–20–1 Asakusa, Taito-ku, Tokyo 111-0032. ☎ **03/3842-6431.** Fax 03/3842-6433. www2.marinet.or.jp/~hotekyo/sada.html. E-mail: sadatiyo@marinet.or.jp. 20 units. A/C TV TEL. ¥11,500 ($96) single; ¥19,000 ($158) twin. AE, MC, V. Station: Tawaramachi (8 min.); Asakusa (15 min.).

Located in the heart of Asakusa's traditional neighborhood, this 50-year-old ryokan entices with its whitewashed walls, stone lanterns, paper lanterns, bamboo screens, and rickshaw beside the front door. Inside, antiques line hallways that lead to tatami guestrooms. Even the public lounge and lobby is Japanese style, making this inn a great choice for those wishing to experience a bit of old Edo in the modern metropolis.

UENO

✪ **Hotel Sofitel.** 2–1–48 Ikenohata, Taito-ku, Tokyo 110-0008. ☎ **800/221-4542** in the U.S. and Canada or 03/5685-7111. Fax 03/5685-6171. www.sofiteltokyo.com/. E-mail: info@sofiteltokyo.com. 71 units. A/C MINIBAR TV TEL. ¥17,000–¥27,000 ($142–$225) single; ¥22,000–¥32,000 ($183–$267) double or twin. AE, DC, JCB, MC, V. Station: Yushima (7 min.), Ueno (10 min.).

Located across from Shinobazu Pond in the heart of Ueno, this French-owned hotel is easily recognizable by its unique architecture: five pyramid-shaped trapeziums, stacked on top of each other. Inside, it's an oasis of refined beauty, excellent service, and great views. And with only four rooms on each floor, it has the atmosphere of a small luxury hotel, without the corresponding prices. Rooms, with rates based on size, boast original artwork, a safe, and satellite TV with CNN and pay movies. But there's nothing that beats the view over Shinobazu Pond, with its bird refuge and the adjoining zoo (some rooms facing the opposite side do, however, have occasional views of Mt. Fuji). I'm partial to the superior rooms on the 25th floor. Restaurants include a teppanyaki grill, a traditional Japanese restaurant specializing in kaiseki served in individual tatami rooms, and a casual Western restaurant. Services include 24-hour room service, same-day laundry, free shoeshine, free pressing service, baby-sitting, and secretarial services. All in all, a great place for the price.

① **Suigetsu Hotel Ohgaisou.** 3–3–21 Ikenohata, Taito-ku, Tokyo 110-0008. ☎ **03/3822-4611.** Fax 03/3823-4340. 124 units. A/C MINIBAR TV TEL. Western-style rooms ¥8,000–¥9,800 ($67–$82) single; ¥12,000 ($100) double; ¥14,400 ($120) twin. Japanese-style rooms ¥16,000 ($133) for 2 persons, including Japanese breakfast. AE, DC, JCB, MC, V. Station: Nezu (exit 2, 5 min.), Ueno (12 min.), Keisei (10 min.).

Located near Ueno Park with its many museums and the Keisei Skyliner Station (with service to Narita Airport), this hotel offers both Western and Japanese accommodations, but since the Western-style rooms are rather unimaginative, I heartily suggest you opt for one of the 40 Japanese-style tatami rooms in its high-tech addition, some of which have balconies. Catering mainly to Japanese, the hotel is most famous for its preservation of the former traditional wooden home of novelist Mori Ogai, set amidst a garden visible from the hotel's public spaces. Facilities include a sushi bar, a Western restaurant, tea-ceremony room, and a Japanese public cypress bath that uses a subterranean hot spring.

Asakusa Accommodations, Dining & Nightlife

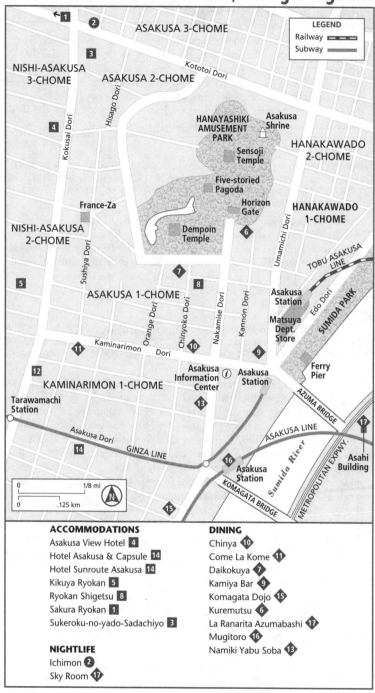

LEGEND
Railway
Subway

ASAKUSA 3-CHOME

NISHI-ASAKUSA 3-CHOME

Kototoi Dori

ASAKUSA 2-CHOME

Hisago Dori

Kokusai Dori

HANAYASHIKI AMUSEMENT PARK

Asakusa Shrine

HANAKAWADO 2-CHOME

Sensoji Temple

Five-storied Pagoda

Horizon Gate

HANAKAWADO 1-CHOME

France-Za

NISHI-ASAKUSA 2-CHOME

Sushiya Dori

Dempoin Temple

Umamichi Dori

TOBU ASAKUSA LINE

ASAKUSA 1-CHOME

Orange Dori

Chinyoko Dori

Nakamise Dori

Kannon Dori

Asakusa Station

Edo Dori

SUMIDA PARK

Matsuya Dept. Store

Kaminarimon Dori

Ferry Pier

KAMINARIMON 1-CHOME

Asakusa Information Center

Asakusa Station

AZUMA BRIDGE

Tarawamachi Station

Asakusa Dori

GINZA LINE

ASAKUSA LINE

Sumida River

METROPOLITAN EXPWY.

Asakusa Station

Asahi Building

0   1/8 mi
0   .125 km

N

KOMAGATA BRIDGE

ACCOMMODATIONS
Asakusa View Hotel 4
Hotel Asakusa & Capsule 14
Hotel Sunroute Asakusa 14
Kikuya Ryokan 5
Ryokan Shigetsu 8
Sakura Ryokan 1
Sukeroku-no-yado-Sadachiyo 3

NIGHTLIFE
Ichimon 2
Sky Room 17

DINING
Chinya 10
Come La Kome 11
Daikokuya 7
Kamiya Bar 9
Komagata Dojo 15
Kuremutsu 6
La Ranarita Azumabashi 17
Mugitoro 16
Namiki Yabu Soba 13

A Note on Japanese Symbols

Many hotels, restaurants, and other establishments in Japan do not have signs giving their names in Roman (English-language) letters. As an aid to the reader, the second appendix to this book lists the Japanese symbols for all such places described in this guide. Each set of characters representing an establishment name has a number, which corresponds to the number that appears inside the box before the establishment's name in the text. Thus, to find the Japanese symbols for, say, the **Suigetsu Hotel Ohgaisou,** refer to no. 1 in appendix B.

Yamanaka Ryokan. 4–23–1 Ikenohata, Taito-ku, Tokyo 110-0008. ☎ **03/3821-4751.** Fax 03/3821-4770. 13 units. A/C MINIBAR TV TEL. ¥7,000 ($58) single; ¥14,000 ($117) double; ¥21,000 ($175) triple. Japanese breakfast ¥1,000 ($8.35) extra. DC, JCB, MC, V. Station: Nezu (exit 2, 3 min.) or JR Ueno Station (15 min.).

A traditional wood gate and a flagstone pathway lined with bamboo mark the entry to this modern, refined Japanese inn, located in a residential neighborhood not far from Ueno Park. Rooms are nicely done, with modern bathrooms and deep Japanese-style tubs. There's a restaurant specializing in creative Chinese cuisine on the premises; if you order in advance, you can have dinners served in your room, with prices ranging from ¥3,000 ($25) to ¥7,000 ($58) per person.

SHINJUKU

✪ **Hotel Century Southern Tower.** 2–2–1 Yoyogi, Shibuya-ku, Tokyo 151-8583. ☎ **03/5354-0111.** Fax 03/5354-0100. 375 units. A/C TV TEL. ¥16,000–¥18,000 ($133–$150) single; ¥22,000–¥24,000 ($183–$200) twin; ¥22,000–¥28,000 ($183–$233) double. AE, DC, JCB, MC, V. Station: Shinjuku (2 min.).

Opened in 1998 and a welcome addition to the Shinjuku hotel scene, this hotel is located just south of the station and just a footbridge away from the huge Takashimaya Times Square shopping complex. Because it occupies the top floors of a sleek white building, it seems far removed from the hustle and bustle of Shinjuku below. Its 20th-floor lobby is simple and uncluttered and boasts almost surreal views of Tokyo stretching in the distance. Ask for a room on a high floor. Rooms facing east are considered best (and are therefore more expensive), especially at night when neon is in full regalia. Rooms facing west have views of Shinjuku's sky-scrapers and, on clear days (mostly in winter), of Mt. Fuji. Maps in each room outline the important buildings visible from your room. Otherwise, rooms have two phone lines for Internet and fax access, pay movies, safe, voice mail, washlet toilets, and empty fridge (stock up at the hotel's convenience store). Two floors are reserved for non-smokers. There's a lobby lounge, Chinese and Japanese restaurants, and Tribeks, a contemporary restaurant offering Asian- and European-influenced American food and great views of Shinjuku.

Hotel Sunroute Tokyo. 2–3–1 Yoyogi, Shibuya-ku, Tokyo 151-0053. ☎ **03/3375-3211.** Fax 03/3379-3040. www.sunroute.aska.or.jp. 538 units. A/C MINIBAR TV TEL. ¥13,500–¥14,500 ($112–$121) single; ¥17,000–¥17,500 ($142–$146) double; ¥18,000–¥27,000 ($150–$225) twin. Rates include service charge. AE, DC, JCB, MC, V. Station: Shinjuku (3 min.).

Conveniently located just a short walk southeast of Shinjuku Station, this hotel attracts a large foreign clientele and calls itself a "city hotel." While it does boast a lobby lounge, convenience store, beauty parlor, barbershop, two restaurants serving Japanese and Chinese cuisine, and two bars, its guestrooms resemble those in a business hotel rather than tourist accommodations, with just the basics.

Ueno Accommodations & Dining

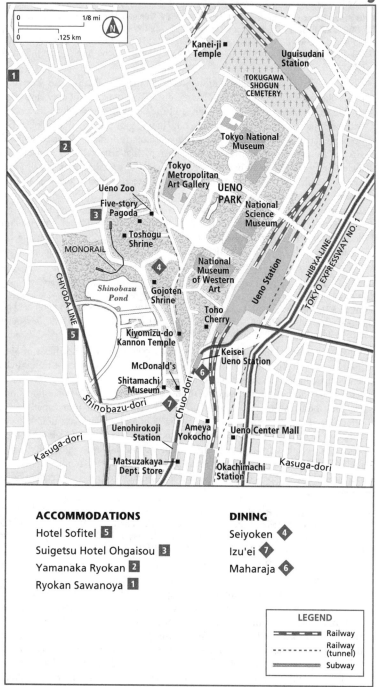

ACCOMMODATIONS

Hotel Sofitel **5**

Suigetsu Hotel Ohgaisou **3**

Yamanaka Ryokan **2**

Ryokan Sawanoya **1**

DINING

Seiyoken **4**

Izu'ei **7**

Maharaja **6**

Keio Plaza Inter-Continental Tokyo. 2–2–1 Nishi-Shinjuku, Shinjuku-ku, Tokyo 160-8330. ☎ **800/222-KEIO** in the U.S., or 03/3344-0111. Fax 03/3344-0247. www.keioplaza.co.jp. 1,485 units. A/C MINIBAR TV TEL. ¥20,000–¥36,000 ($167–$300) single; ¥24,000–¥39,000 ($200–$325) twin or double. AE, DC, JCB, MC, V. Station: Tocho-mae (2 min.), Shinjuku (5 min.).

The closest hotel to Shinjuku Station's west side, the Keio Plaza is also West Shinjuku's oldest hotel, built in 1971. It has the distinction of being not only Japan's first skyscraper, but also, at 47 stories high, still the tallest hotel in Tokyo. It's popular with both Japanese and foreign travelers, including group tours, and its lobby bustles with activity—sometimes too much so, making it difficult to get personalized service. But the hotel does boast a number of first-class facilities and services, including free access to an outdoor pool and children's pool. Guests can also use a nearby health club with an indoor pool and exercise room (fee: ¥2,520/$21). Rooms are comfortably furnished and offer cable TV with CNN and pay movies, dataports, and bathrooms with generous counter space, magnifying mirrors, and washlet toilets. Views are of the surrounding Shinjuku area. There's a no-smoking floor. With 19 restaurants and 10 bars, choices seem almost limitless; the best restaurants include Japanese and French establishments on the top floors. Room service is available 24 hours.

Shinjuku Prince Hotel. 1–30–1 Kabuki-cho, Shinjuku-ku, Tokyo 160-8487. ☎ **800/542-8686** in the U.S., or 03/3205-1111. Fax 03/3205-1952. www.princehotels.co.jp/english/. 571 units. A/C TV TEL. ¥15,000–¥16,000 ($125–$133) single; ¥17,000–¥32,000 ($142–$267) double; ¥26,000–¥32,000 ($217–$267) twin. AE, DC, JCB, MC, V. Station: Seibu Shinjuku (beneath the hotel) or Shinjuku (5 min.).

This business hotel has a great location, just a 5-minute walk northeast of Shinjuku Station, making it convenient to Shinjuku's nightlife district of Kabuki-cho. This smart-looking, streamlined brick building has shopping arcades and 10 restaurants and bars on its bottom 10 floors, while the next 20-some floors hold the guestrooms, all topped by a restaurant. The cheapest rooms are small, but all offer a great view of Shinjuku; those facing Shinjuku Station have double-paned windows to shut out noise. Each room comes with an empty refrigerator you can stock yourself, a safe, and hair dryer. There's one no-smoking floor. Services include room service from 11am until midnight, same-day laundry service, and free English newspapers on request. This is a good choice for a moderately priced hotel.

Shinjuku Washington Hotel. 3–2–9 Nishi-Shinjuku, Shinjuku-ku, Tokyo 160-8336. ☎ **03/3343-3111.** Fax 03/3342-2575. 1,301 units. A/C MINIBAR TV TEL. ¥11,300–¥14,500 ($94–$121) single; ¥17,000–¥24,000 ($142–$200) double; ¥17,500–¥43,000 ($146–$358) twin; from ¥30,000 ($250) triple. AE, DC, JCB, MC, V. Station: Shinjuku (10 min.).

This huge white building reminds me of an ocean liner—even the hotel's tiny windows look like portholes. Inside, everything is bright and white, with lots of open space. The third-floor lobby created quite a stir back in the '80s, when a row of machines were installed for automated check-in and checkout, but they proved so unpopular that now there are humans to help with the process (the annex has its own check-in desk). At check-in, you'll receive a card key to activate the electricity, after which you're pretty much left on your own—there are no bellhops here, no room service. The tiny guestrooms remind me of ship cabins, but have everything you need. There are seven bars and restaurants, including a 25th-floor steak house and bar; an adjoining shopping arcade offers more dining possibilities.

AOYAMA

President Hotel. 2–2–3 Minami Aoyama, Minato-ku, Tokyo 107-8545. ☎ **03/3497-0111.**
Fax 03/3401-4816. www.president-hotel.co.jp. 210 units. A/C MINIBAR TV TEL. ¥12,000–
¥13,000 ($100–$108) single; ¥17,000 ($142) double; ¥17,000–¥21,000 ($142–$175) twin.
AE, DC, JCB, MC, V. Station: Aoyama-Itchome (1 min.).

This small hotel is a good choice for the budget-conscious business traveler, not
only because it's a respected address in Tokyo but also thanks to its reasonable prices
and great location, between Akasaka, Shinjuku, Aoyama, and Roppongi. It offers
some of the same conveniences as the larger and more expensive hotels, like room
service (7 to 9am and 5 to 9pm), weekday same-day laundry service, and free English newspaper delivered upon request. The unpretentious lobby has a European
atmosphere. Rooms themselves, equipped with cable TV, are tiny but cheerful; ask
for a room facing the front on a high floor. There are two very good restaurants, one
Japanese and one French.

IKEBUKURO

Crowne Plaza Metropolitan Tokyo. 1–6–1 Nishi-Ikebukuro, Toshima-ku, Tokyo 171-8505.
☎ **800/227-6963** in the U.S. and Canada, or 03/3980-1111. Fax 03/3980-5600.
www.crowneplaza.com. 818 units. A/C MINIBAR TV TEL. ¥16,500–¥19,500 ($137–$154)
single; ¥22,000–¥26,500 ($183–$221) double; ¥22,000–¥30,000 ($183–$250) twin. Children under 20 stay free in parents' room (maximum of 3 persons in a room). AE, DC, JCB,
MC, V. Station: Ikebukuro (west exit, 3 min.).

This brick building, just a couple minutes' walk southwest of Ikebukuro Station,
offers the kind of service and amenities that Americans (who make up 10% of the
hotel's guests) will find familiar, though rooms are much smaller than their U.S.
counterparts. Rates are based on size and floor height; those facing west have views
of Mt. Fuji in winter. All rooms have cable TV with pay movies on demand and
hair dryers; rooms with dataports are available upon request, as are no-smoking
rooms. Facilities include a business center and an outdoor pool (fee: ¥1,500/$12);
same-day laundry service, baby-sitting, and room service (6am to 1am) are also
available. Restaurants specialize in Japanese, Chinese, and continental cuisine;
there's a cocktail lounge on the top floor.

AKASAKA & ROPPONGI

Akasaka Tokyu Hotel. 2–14–3 Nagata-cho, Chiyoda-ku, Tokyo 100. ☎ **800/428-6598** in
the U.S., or 03/3580-2311. Fax 03/3580-6066. www.akasaka-tkh.co.jp/. 535 units.
A/C MINIBAR TV TEL. ¥16,000–¥23,000 ($133–$192) single; ¥28,000 ($233) double;
¥23,000–¥37,000 ($192–$308) twin. AE, DC, JCB, MC, V. Station: Akasaka-mitsuke (1 min.).

This hotel boasts a high occupancy rate thanks to its ideal location in the middle of
Akasaka and its reasonable rates. Built in 1969, it's easily recognizable by its candy-
striped exterior (it's called the "Pajama Building" by the locals). Rooms, in a corresponding pink-and-white color scheme, include shoji screens and window panels
that slide shut for complete darkness (even in the middle of the day), windows that
can be opened (a rarity in Tokyo), and English-language cable TV with pay videos.
There are 200 single rooms, but the lower-priced ones are pretty small. Front-facing
rooms look upon the whirl and neon of Akasaka; those in the back are quieter and
face a steep slope of greenery. No-smoking rooms are available. Facilities include
five restaurants and bars, a business center, and shopping arcade. Room service is
available until midnight, and laundry service is available weekdays.

Akasaka Yoko Hotel. 6–14–12 Akasaka, Minato-ku, Tokyo 107-0052. ☎ **03/3586-4050.**
Fax 03/3586-5944. 245 units. A/C TV TEL. ¥8,900–¥9,800 ($74–$82) single; ¥14,000–
¥15,500 ($117–$129) twin. AE, JCB, MC, V. Station: Akasaka (4 min., on Akasaka Dori).

In a handy location close to the nightlife of both Roppongi (a 15-min. walk) and Akasaka (a 4-min. walk), this pleasant small business hotel caters primarily to Japanese. There are only singles and twins; for a couple of dollars more in each category, you can get a slightly larger room, which may be worth it if you're claustrophobic. If you're on a budget, two people can stay in the highest-priced single with its slightly larger bed for ¥13,000 ($113). In any case, the bathrooms are barely large enough for even one person. The hotel has a coffee shop, and there are beer- and soda-vending machines.

Hotel Ibis. 7–14–4 Roppongi, Minato-ku, Tokyo 106-0032. ☎ **03/3403-4411.** Fax 03/3479-0609. www.ibis.co.jp. E-mail: info@ibis.co.jp. 182 units. A/C MINIBAR TV TEL. ¥11,500–¥16,000 ($96–$133) single; ¥14,100–¥23,000 ($117–$192) double; ¥19,000–¥23,000 ($158–$192) twin; ¥24,000 ($200) triple. AE, DC, JCB, MC, V. Station: Roppongi (1 min.).

The Ibis is about as close as you can get to the night action of Roppongi, oddly lacking in hotels. It caters to both businessmen and couples who come to Roppongi's discos and don't make (or want to make) the last subway home. The hotel brochure promises "refreshing waking and pleasant hotel life." The lobby is on the fifth floor, with the guestrooms above. Small but comfortable, they feature modern furniture, windows that can be opened, hair dryer, and TV with English-language cable and CNN. On the 13th floor is a branch of the well-known Italian restaurant Sabatini with views of the city; on the 2nd floor is a pizza/pasta restaurant run by Sabatini. Room service is available 5pm to 10pm Monday through Saturday, to 8pm Sunday. There's a no-smoking floor.

Roppongi Prince Hotel. 3–2–7 Roppongi, Minato-ku, Tokyo 106-0032. ☎ **800/542-8686** in the U.S. and Canada, or 03/3587-1111. Fax 03/3587-0770. www.princehotels.co.jp/english/. 216 units. A/C TV TEL. ¥19,500 ($162) single; ¥23,000–¥26,500 ($192–$221) twin; ¥24,500–¥26,500 ($204–$221) double. AE, DC, JCB, MC, V. Station: Roppongi (8 min.).

This is a good choice if you want to be close to Roppongi's night action. Opened in 1984 (a welcome event in Roppongi, still woefully lacking in hotels), the hotel attracts Japanese businessmen on weekdays and vacationers aged 20 to 25 on weekends and caters to them with a young and cheerful staff, modern designs with bold colors, and a resort-like atmosphere. It's built around an inner courtyard, which features a pool with a Jacuzzi and heated deck—a solar mirror on the roof directs sun rays toward the sunbathers below, making it Tokyo's only outdoor heated pool open year-round (free for hotel guests). Unfortunately for the shy, sides of the raised pool are acrylic, giving diners at the adjacent outdoor patio unique ringside views. Rooms are small but bright and modern, with either black or white decor. Empty refrigerators let you stock up your room yourself, and there are dataports but only one line. TVs offer cable, pay movies, and video games. Facilities include Italian, tempura, sushi, and steak restaurants, as well as a coffee shop, bar, and lobby lounge. Room service is available from 7am to 2am.

Shanpia Hotel Akasaka. 7–6–13 Akasaka, Minato-ku, Tokyo 107-0052. ☎ **03/3586-0811** or 03/3583-1001 for reservations. Fax 03/3589-0575. 232 units. A/C TV TEL. ¥8,700–¥10,300 ($72.50–$86) single; ¥16,400 ($137) twin; ¥19,400 ($162) double. AE, DC, JCB, MC, V. Station: Akasaka (5 min.).

The most distinguishing feature of this hotel is that 202 of its rooms are singles, a sure sign that it caters primarily to Japanese businessmen. Although within easy walking distance to Akasaka nightlife, it has a quiet hilltop location across from the TBS high-rise. Rooms are minuscule in size, and since the single beds are tiny, you'll probably want to spring for a double bed if you're tall; however, there are only

18 twin-bedded rooms (two twin-size beds in each room) and 12 double-bedded rooms, which come with the extras of refrigerators and hair dryers. There are two restaurants, both serving Japanese and Western food, and also a bar.

Tokyo Prince Hotel. 3-3-1 Shibakoen, Minato-ku, Tokyo 105-8560. ☎ **800/542-8686** or 03/3432-1111. Fax 03/3434-5551. www.princehotels.co.jp/english/. 484 units. A/C TV TEL. ¥23,000–¥25,000 ($192–$208) single; ¥24,000–¥35,000 ($200–$292) double or twin. AE, DC, JCB, MC, V. Station: Daimon (7 min.), Kamiyacho (10 min.), Onarimon (1 min.), or Hamamatsucho (10 min.).

Set in Shiba Park near Zozoji Temple and Tokyo Tower, this is the Prince Hotel chain's oldest Tokyo property, built in 1964 for the Olympic Games and now passed over as visitors flock to the city's newer, glitzier hotels. Still, the friendly service is that of a small, luxury hotel, with facilities rivaling those of much more expensive choices. Its central location makes it possible to walk to Roppongi for nightlife (the walk home is sobering) or to Hibiya or the Tokyo Trade Center on business. Guests include many foreign business executives.

Parts of the hotel show its age (particularly in corridors and some of the lowest-priced rooms), but rooms have all the basics: cable TV with pay movies, empty refrigerators you can stock yourself, hair dryers, and marble bath areas with anti-fog mirrors. The most expensive rooms are larger and face the front of the hotel and a parking lot; opt for a cheaper, smaller room on a top floor with a view of the park and Tokyo Tower. No-smoking rooms are available, as well as a no-smoking lounge on the 11th floor with an up-close view of the Tower. Some rooms are fax/modem ready, so ask for one if you plan to use your PC. Among the 13 restaurants and lounges are the fine French restaurant Beaux Séjours, an all-weather beer garden, and Porto, which offers Western-style all-you-can-eat buffets. Facilities include a business center, outdoor pool (fee: ¥1,000/$8.35), convenience store, boutiques, vending machines, and book/magazine shop. Same-day laundry service, 24-hour room service, and complimentary newspaper round out the services of this reasonably priced hotel.

SHINAGAWA

Shinagawa Prince Hotel. 4-10-30 Takanawa, Minato-ku, Tokyo 108-8611. ☎ **800/542-8686** in the U.S. or Canada, or 03/3440-1111. Fax 03/3441-7092. 3,008 units. A/C TV TEL. ¥8,000–¥18,000 ($67–$150) single; ¥14,100–¥26,500 ($117–$221) twin; ¥14,600–¥25,500 ($122–$212) double. AE, DC, JCB, MC, V. Station: Shinagawa (2 min.).

With three gleaming white buildings added at various stages, the Shinagawa Prince is the largest hotel in Japan. This place is almost a city within a city, with nine food and beverage outlets, a travel desk, convenience shop, shopping arcade, florist, parking, conference rooms, a sports center with nine indoor tennis courts, 104-lane bowling center, indoor golf practice center, billiards, video games, indoor and outdoor pools, and a fitness center (a fee is charged for most facilities; the indoor pool in the New Tower costs ¥1,000/$8.35). It caters to Japanese businessmen on weekdays and students and family vacationers on weekends and holidays. Rooms vary widely depending upon which building you select: The Main Tower has only singles, at the cheapest rates; the Annex has singles, twins, and doubles in a medium price range; the New Tower has the best rooms, the highest prices, and the best views, including great views of Rainbow Bridge and Tokyo Bay from its upper floors. Be sure to have a drink or meal at the 39th-floor Top of Shinagawa; its views of Tokyo Bay and the rest of Tokyo are among the best in the city. With its many diversions, this hotel is like a resort getaway, but it's too big for my taste.

OTHER NEIGHBORHOODS

Akihabara Washington Hotel. 1-8-3 Kanda, Sakumacho, Chiyoda-ku, Tokyo 101-0025. ☎ **03/3255-3311.** Fax 03/3255-7343. 312 units. A/C MINIBAR TV TEL. ¥9,700–¥11,900 ($81–$99) single; ¥17,800–¥23,000 ($148–$192) twin; ¥17,000–¥23,000 ($142–$192) double. AE, DC, JCB, MC, V. Station: JR Akihabara station (1 min. from the Akihabara Electric Town exit).

This business hotel is located on the edge of Akihabara, Japan's largest retail electronics district. Rooms are modern and bright, though tiny and offering no view whatsoever. Ten single rooms on the seventh floor are so-called women's rooms, but are no different in decor or amenities from the other rooms; still, this is one of the few business hotels that acknowledges the existence of women and provides an extra amount of security for lone travelers. There's also a no-smoking floor. Facilities include a bar, coffee lounge, and a Japanese restaurant serving kaiseki and set meals.

Fairmont Hotel. 2-1-17 Kudan Minami, Chiyoda-ku, Tokyo 102-0074. ☎ **03/3262-1151.** Fax 03/3264-2476. www2.kddcom.co.p/fairmont/index-e.html. E-mail: sales@fairmont.co.jp. 207 units. A/C MINIBAR TV TEL. ¥11,000–¥13,000 ($92–$108) single; ¥20,000–¥25,000 ($167–$208) double or twin. AE, DC, JCB, MC, V. Station: Kudanshita (exit 2, 8 min.). On Chidorigafuchi.

This small hotel is beautifully situated on a quiet street on the northwest side of the Imperial Palace moat, which is lined with cherry trees—a real treat when the blossoms burst forth in spring. Guests like the Fairmont because it's an older hotel (built in 1952) and because it's centrally located, yet away from the hustle and bustle of downtown Tokyo. However, the hotel shows its age and is in need of an update (some rooms have been renovated), and it's a hike from the nearest station. In addition, the extremely low ceilings in the corridors could pose a health threat for tall travelers; the cheapest singles are barely wider than the bed; and desks are the smallest I've ever seen. Despite its drawbacks, this quiet and unassuming hotel has many faithful repeat customers. I suggest you spring for one of the larger, more expensive rooms facing the trees and palace moat. All rooms have TV with English-language cable and CNN. There's also a coffee shop, called the Brasserie de la Verdure, which has a view of the moat, and a French restaurant, Cerisiers, which looks out onto a pleasant small garden with a waterfall.

The Hilltop Hotel. 1-1 Surugadai, Kanda, Chiyoda-ku, Tokyo 101-0062. ☎ **03/3293-2311.** Fax 03/3233-4567. 75 units. A/C MINIBAR TV TEL. ¥17,000–¥20,000 ($142–$167) single; ¥24,000–¥25,000 ($200–$208) double; ¥26,000–¥32,000 ($217–$267) twin. AE, DC, JCB, MC, V. Station: Ochanomizu or Shin-Ochanomizu (8 min.) or Jimbocho (5 min.).

This is a delightfully old-fashioned, unpretentious hotel with character. Opened in 1937 and boasting an art-deco facade, it was once the favorite haunt of writers, including novelist Mishima Yukio. The hotel's brochure maintains that "oxygen and negative ions are circulated into the rooms and its refreshing atmosphere is accepted by many, including prominent individuals, as most adequate for work and for rest." I'm not sure what that means, but one guest reported that she slept like a baby here. Avoid the cheaper, more boring rooms in the annex; rooms in the main building have such endearing, homey touches as fringed lampshades, doilies, cherry-wood furniture (including mahogany desks), velvet curtains, vanity tables, and old-fashioned heaters with intricate grillwork. Some twins even combine a tatami area and shoji with beds; the most expensive twin overlooks its own terraced Japanese garden. Modern additions include washlet toilets and hair dryers; services include same-day laundry service and room service until 2am. A dozen restaurants and bars serve tempura, steaks, Chinese, and French food. Don't be surprised if the reception desk remembers you by name.

Tokyo YMCA Hotel. 7 Mitoshiro-cho, Kanda, Chiyoda-ku, Tokyo 101-0053. ☎ **03/ 3293-1911.** Fax 03/3293-1926. 40 units. A/C TV TEL. ¥10,000 ($83) single; ¥15,000– ¥22,000 ($125–$183) twin. YMCA members receive a 10% discount. Weekend discounts available. JCB, MC, V. Station: Shin-Ochanomizu or Ogawamachi (B6 exit, 1 min.), or Awajicho (5 min.). On Hongo-dori, south of Yasukuni Dori.

Where else but in Tokyo would there be a YMCA as expensive as a moderately priced hotel? However, this place is modern, and spotless, with an atmosphere better than most business hotels that fall into this price category. Fully carpeted, with reception on the second floor, it accepts both men and women, with a maximum stay of 7 nights. The rooms (mostly singles) come with hot water and tea, cotton kimono, bilingual TV, hair dryer, and tiled bathrooms. Some of the singles are larger and have a sofa at no extra charge; two people can stay in these for the cheapest twin price listed above. Vending machines dispense beer and soft drinks, and there's one Western restaurant, an indoor pool (fee: ¥1,500/$12.50), and a drug/convenience store. Laundry service is available as well.

5 Inexpensive

ASAKUSA

Hotel Sunroute Asakusa. 1-8-5 Kaminarimon, Taito-ku, Tokyo 111-0034. ☎ **03/ 3847-1511.** Fax 03/3847-1509. www.sunroute-asakusa.co.jp/english/index.htm. E-mail: webmaster@sunroute-asakusa.co.jp. 120 units. A/C MINIBAR TV TEL. ¥8,000–¥9,500 ($67–$79) single; ¥12,000 ($100) double; ¥14,000–¥16,000 ($117–$133) twin. Rates include tax. AE, DC, MC, V. Station: Tawaramachi (1 min.); Asakusa (8 min.).

Located on Kokusai Dori, this modern, pleasant hotel opened in 1998 as a business hotel but is a good choice for leisure travelers as well. Not only does it boast a good location near the sightseeing attractions of Asakusa, but it is also classier than most business hotels, with Miro reprints in the lobby and modern artwork in each guestroom. Though small, rooms come with all the comforts, including washlet toilets. Single rooms have slightly larger beds and bathrooms than found at most business hotels. The hotel's one coffee shop, serving Japanese and Western food, is on the second floor, with windows overlooking Kokusai Dori.

Kikuya Ryokan. 2-18-9 Nishi-Asakusa, Taito-ku, Tokyo 111-0035. ☎ **03/3841-4051.** Fax 03/3841-6404. 10 units (7 with bathroom). A/C TV. ¥4,900 ($41) single without bathroom, ¥6,000–¥6,500 ($50–$54) single with bathroom; ¥8,200 ($68) double without bathroom, ¥8,500–¥8,800 ($71–$73) double with bathroom; ¥12,000 ($100) triple without bathroom, ¥12,500 ($104) triple with bathroom. American breakfast ¥800 ($6.65) extra. AE, MC, V. Station: Tawaramachi (8 min.).

This friendly establishment, a member of the Japanese Inn and Welcome Inn groups, is located in Asakusa in a modern redbrick building about a 10-minute walk from Sensoji Temple, just off Kappabashi Dori (a street lined with shops specializing in wholesale restaurant cookware and tableware). The simple tatami rooms, while clean, lack the character of a more traditional ryokan. There's a communal refrigerator where you can store food and drinks; rooms with a bathroom have their own fridges. Guests are requested to leave during the daily cleaning (10:30am to 3pm).

Sakura Ryokan. 2-6-2 Iriya, Taito-ku, Tokyo 110-0013. ☎ **03/3876-8118.** Fax 03/ 3873-9456. 20 units (9 with bathroom). A/C TV TEL. ¥5,300–¥5,500 ($44–$46) single without bathroom, ¥6,300 ($52) single with bathroom; ¥9,600 ($80) double without bathroom; ¥10,600 ($88) double with bathroom; ¥12,600–¥13,500 ($105–$112) triple without bathroom; ¥13,800–¥15,600 ($115–$130) triple with bathroom. Japanese or Western break-fast ¥800 ($6.65) extra; Japanese dinner ¥1,600 ($13) extra. AE, MC, V. Station: Iriya (5 min.; exit 1 or 2).

A member of Japanese Inn and Welcome Inn groups, this modern concrete establishment is located in Asakusa just northwest of the Kappabashi Dori and Kototoi Dori intersection, about a 10-minute walk from Sensoji Temple. The reception area is on the second floor, and the friendly owner speaks some English. A combination business-tourist hotel, Sakura has both Japanese and foreign guests. Rooms are spotless, and all come with a sink and an alarm clock. Half are Western style; both Western- and Japanese-style rooms are available with or without private bathroom. The single rooms are quite spacious compared to those in business hotels. There's one Japanese-style room, complete with a terrace, large enough for a family of six or seven. Guests have use of vending machines selling drinks, a coin laundry, and an elevator.

UENO

✪ **Ryokan Sawanoya.** 2–3–11 Yanaka, Taito-ku, Tokyo 110-0001. ☎ **03/3822-2251.** Fax 03/3822-2252. www.tctv.ne.jp/members/sawanoya/. E-mail: sawanoya@tctv.ne.jp. 12 units (2 with bathroom). A/C TV TEL. ¥4,800–¥5,100 ($40–$42) single without bathroom; ¥9,000 ($75) double without bathroom, ¥9,600 ($80) double with bathroom; ¥12,300 ($102) triple without bathroom, ¥13,800 ($115) triple with bathroom. Breakfast of toast and fried eggs ¥300 ($2.50) extra; Japanese breakfast ¥900 ($7.80) extra. AE, MC, V. Closed Dec 29–Jan 3. Station: Nezu (exit 1, 7 min.).

Although this ryokan is relatively modern looking and unexciting, it's delightfully located in a wonderful residential area of old Tokyo, northwest of Ueno Park and within walking distance of the park's many attractions. The owner, English-speaking Sawa-san, gives out a map outlining places of interest in the vicinity, as well as pamphlets on inexpensive accommodations throughout Japan; if you pay for the call, he'll even make your next reservation with another Japanese Inn Group inn. Sawa-san gives a short tour of the establishment at check-in, and throughout are written explanations to help the ryokan novice. Tea and instant coffee are available all day, and facilities include a beer- and soda-vending machine, a coin-operated washing machine and dryer (with free laundry detergent), a refrigerator, and public bathrooms. Once a week, Sawa-san's son provides guests with a special treat—a traditional Japanese lion dance, free of charge. His daughter-in-law sometimes gives demonstrations of the tea ceremony. In short, this is a great place to stay thanks to Sawa-san's enthusiastic devotion to his neighborhood, which he readily imparts to his guests. Highly recommended.

SHINJUKU

Sunlite Hotel. 5–15–8 Shinjuku, Shinjuku-ku, Tokyo 160-0022. ☎ **03/3356-0391.** Fax 03/3356-1223. 197 units. A/C TV TEL. ¥8,300–¥8,900 ($69–$74) single; ¥11,500–¥15,000 ($96–$125) twin; ¥14,000 ($117) double. AE, JCB, MC, V. Station: Shinjuku (12 min.) or Shinjuku Sanchome (5 min.). The hotel is on the east side of Shinjuku Station, on Meiji Dori.

In 1985 this business hotel moved across the street from its old location into a new building, turning the older building into the Hotel Sunlite Annex (the cheaper rates above are in the older annex). Rooms are cheerful and clean, although annex rooms are small (its singles are minuscule). Feelings of claustrophobia are somewhat mitigated by windows that can be opened. The main (new) building's corner twins with windows on two sides are the best. There's a coffee shop in the main building and a restaurant serving Western food in the annex. *Note:* If you like to stay out late, beware: Doors close at 2am and don't reopen until 5:30am.

⭘ **Tokyo International Youth Hostel.** 1–1 Kagura-kashi, Shinjuku-ku, Tokyo 162-0823. ☎ **03/3235-1107.** 138 beds. ¥3,100 ($26) per person. Breakfast ¥400 ($3.35); dinner ¥800 ($6.65). No youth-hostel card required; no age limit. No credit cards. Closed Dec 29–Jan 3. Station: Iidabashi (west exit, 2 min.). Reception is on the 18th floor of the Central Plaza Building.

This hostel is definitely the best place to stay in its price range. Spotlessly clean and modern, it offers fantastic Tokyo views; in winter you can even see Mt. Fuji from rooms on the west side. Even the public baths boast good views. All beds are dormitory style, with two, four, or five bunk beds to a room. The rooms are very pleasant, with big windows, and each bed has its own curtain for privacy. There are also rooms accessible for travelers with disabilities, and two Japanese-style tatami rooms for families that sleep up to six persons. If there are vacancies, you can stay longer than the normal 3-day maximum. In summer, it's a good idea to reserve about 3 months in advance. Closed from 10am to 3pm and locked at 10:30pm (lights out). You have free use of a washer and dryer.

HARAJUKU & AOYAMA

Hotel Harajuku Trim. 6–28–6 Jingumae, Shibuya-ku, Tokyo 150-0001. ☎ **03/ 3498-2101.** Fax 03/3498-1777. 41 units. A/C TV TEL. ¥8,700–¥10,000 ($72–$83) single; ¥13,600–¥16,700 ($113–139) twin. No credit cards. Station: Meiji-Jingumae (3 min.).

It would be easy to pass this brick building on Meiji Dori and not even know there was a business hotel here. With a front desk up on the second floor and offering only 27 single rooms and 14 twins, it's the only choice in this hotel-barren shopping paradise. Rooms are clean and functional, with just the basics. The cheapest available twins are actually singles with an added bed. The most expensive singles are a bargain for single travelers. Vending machines dispense beer and soft drinks.

National Children's Castle Hotel (Kodomo-no-Shiro Hotel). 5–53–1 Jingumae, Shibuya-ku, Tokyo 150-0001. ☎ **03/3797-5677.** Fax 03/3406-7805. 27 units. A/C TV TEL. ¥6,400 ($53) single; ¥13,600–¥14,600 ($113–$122) twin; from ¥19,200 ($160) Japanese-style room. AE, DC, JCB, MC, V. Station: Omotesando (8 min.) or Shibuya (10 min.). The front desk is on the 7th floor.

The National Children's Castle Hotel, or Kodomo-no-Shiro, located on Aoyama Dori about halfway between Aoyama and Shibuya, is a great place to stay if you're traveling with children. Although the hotel itself, located on the seventh and eighth floors, isn't child-theme oriented, the complex boasts Tokyo's best and most sophisticated indoor/outdoor playground for children, complete with a clinic and restaurants. Guests range from businesspeople on weekdays to families and young college students on weekends. The rooms—mainly twins—are simple and of adequate size, with large windows. The most expensive twins, which face Shinjuku, have the best views. The hotel's three singles do not have windows, but you can pay extra to stay in a twin. The three Japanese-style rooms, available for three or more people, are a good way for families to experience the traditional Japanese lifestyle. Make reservations at least 6 months in advance, especially if you plan on being in Tokyo in the summer. Note that there's an 11pm curfew and check-in isn't until 3pm.

IKEBUKURO

⭘ **Kimi Ryokan.** 2–36–8 Ikebukuro, Toshima-ku, Tokyo 171-0014. ☎ **03/3971-3766.** 41 units (none with bathroom). A/C TEL. ¥4,500 ($37) single; ¥6,500–¥7,500 ($54–$62) double. Rates include tax. No credit cards. Station: Ikebukuro (west exit, 5 min.). The police station near the west exit of the station has maps that will guide you to Kimi.

This is a great place to stay. Spotlessly clean and with such Japanese touches as sliding screens, flower arrangements in public spaces, and traditional Japanese music playing softly in the hallways, it caters almost exclusively to foreigners and is so popular there's sometimes a waiting list to get in. Rooms are all Japanese style, with singles the size of 4½ tatami mats and the larger twins the size of 6 tatami mats (a single tatami measures about 3 ft. by 6 ft.). Facilities include a lounge with TV nook, free tea available throughout the day, and a vending machine dispensing beer and soda. There's also an international phone that accepts credit cards and a bulletin board that lists job opportunities (primarily teaching English).

AKASAKA

✪ **Asia Center of Japan.** 8–10–32 Akasaka, Minato-ku, Tokyo 107-0052. ☎ **03/3402-6111.** Fax 03/3402-0738. http://jcha.yadojozu.ne.jp/1310304. 166 units (149 with bathroom). A/C TV TEL. ¥5,100 ($42) single without bathroom, ¥6,500–¥7,500 ($54–$62) single with bathroom; ¥6,800–¥7,600 ($57–$63) twin without bathroom, ¥10,500 ($87) twin with bathroom; ¥8,500–¥9,500 ($71–$79) double with bathroom; ¥14,100 ($117) triple with bathroom. Rates include tax. JCB, MC, V. Station: Aoyama-Itchome (5 min.), Nogizaka (5 min.).

Great rates make this the top choice if you're looking for inexpensive Western-style accommodations in the center of town. However, it's so popular that it's often fully booked; be sure to reserve 6 months in advance. Everyone—from businessmen to students to travelers to foreigners teaching English—stays here; I know one teacher who lived here for years. Resembling a college dormitory, the Asia Center has rooms with or without private bathroom, as well as an inexpensive cafeteria and snack bar that's popular with area office workers. Accommodations are basic, no frills, and in the singles you can almost reach out and touch all four walls. Rooms come with the usual bed, desk, heater, coin-operated TV, and other amenities. Female travelers should avoid rooms on the ground floor—the windows can open and in Japan there are no screens. Tucked on a side street off Gaien-Higashi Dori not far from Aoyama Dori, the center is about a 15-minute walk to the nightlife of Roppongi or Akasaka.

SHINAGAWA

Keihin Hotel. 4–10–20 Takanawa, Minato-ku, Tokyo 108-0074. ☎ **03/3449-5711.** Fax 03/3441-7230. 52 units. A/C MINIBAR TV TEL. ¥8,000–¥8,500 ($67–$71) single; ¥12,500–¥14,000 ($104–$117) double; ¥13,000 ($108) twin. Japanese-style room, ¥12,000 ($100) single; ¥16,500 ($137.50) double. AE, DC, JCB, MC, V. Station: Shinagawa (1 min.). Across the street from the station.

Established in 1871, the Keihin is the oldest hotel in Shinagawa, and with the opening of much fancier luxury hotels, is about a century away from being the best hotel in the neighborhood. While the present brick building, dating from the 1930s and updated in the 1960s, doesn't have any of the graceful charm one might hope from a hotel of this age, it does possess a certain charm, and the staff is friendly and accommodating, happy to see the occasional foreign guest. Rooms tend to be dark and a bit gloomy—especially the single rooms, which are quite tiny and may face another building. The three Japanese-style rooms, in contrast, are simple but quite nice. Surprising for a hotel this size, it has four restaurants, including a Japanese restaurant serving *tonkatsu* (pork cutlets) and a cafe/bar. And its location across from Shinagawa Station, served by the Yamanote Line and commuter trains to Kamakura, makes it convenient for sightseeing.

Ryokan Sansuiso. 2–9–5 Higashi Gotanda, Shinagawa-ku, Tokyo 141-0022. ☎ **03/ 3441-7475.** Fax 03/3449-1944. 9 units (2 with bathroom). A/C TV. ¥4,900–¥5,500 ($41–$46) single without bathroom; ¥8,600 ($72) double without bathroom, ¥9,000 ($75) double with bathroom; ¥12,000 ($100) triple without bathroom. Rates include tax. AE, V. Station: Gotanda (east exit, 5 min.).

The friendly and accommodating couple who runs this Japanese-style inn doesn't speak much English but they have a poster listing all pertinent questions, such as how many nights you will be staying, etc. This ryokan, a member of the Japanese Inn Group, occupies a two-story older house on a quiet side street and offers very clean rooms with shoji screens and wood ceilings, and bilingual TVs are a plus. Some rooms have a Japanese toilet and bathroom. There's a midnight curfew.

OTHER NEIGHBORHOODS

✪ **Homeikan.** 5–10–5 Hongo, Bunkyo-ku, Tokyo 113-0033. ☎ **03/3811-1181** or 3811-1187. Fax 03/3811-1764. www.jnto.go.jp/03welcome/infomercial/homeikan/ homeikan.html. E-mail: homeikan@mcgroup.or.jp. 91 units (none with bathroom). A/C MINIBAR TV TEL. ¥6,400 ($53) single; ¥11,200 ($93) double; ¥14,400 ($120) triple. Western or Japanese breakfast ¥800 ($6.65); Japanese dinner ¥2,000 ($17). AE, DC, MC, V. Station: Hongo Sanchome (8 min.) or Kasuga (5 min.).

Located in north Tokyo, about a 30-minute hike from Ueno Park, this is a lovely place to stay if you wish to experience a traditional ryokan in a traditional neighborhood. It consists of three separate buildings, acquired over the last century by the present owner's grandfather. The main building (or *Honkan*), was purchased almost 100 years ago; today it is used mainly by school groups and senior citizens. Across the street is Daimachi Bekkan, built after World War II to serve as the family home. A beautiful, 31-room property, it boasts a private Japanese garden with a pond, nice public baths (including one open 24 hr.), and wood-inlaid and pebbled hallways leading to very nice tatami rooms adorned with such features as gnarled wood trimming and sitting alcoves. This is where most foreigners stay; if you opt for meals here, they will be served in your room in true ryokan fashion. The third and largest building, Morikawa Bekkan, 6–23–5 Hongo, about a 5-minute walk away, was built about 45 years ago and has 35 rooms.

Ryokan Toki. 5–21–1 Minami-Koiwa, Edogawa-ku, Tokyo 113-0056. ☎ **03/3657-1747.** Fax 03/3671-0655. http://village.infoweb.or.jp/~fwhf2102/tokieng.htm. E-mail: higeta1@mb. infoweb.or.jp. 17 units (3 with toilet only, 14 with bathroom). A/C TV TEL. ¥4,800 ($40) single with toilet only, ¥5,300 ($44) single with bathroom; ¥8,000 ($67) double with toilet only, ¥8,500 ($71) double with bathroom; ¥11,000 ($92) triple with toilet only, ¥12,000 ($100) triple with bathroom. Breakfast ¥700–¥800 ($5.85–$6.65) extra; Japanese dinner ¥1,500 ($12.50) extra. AE, DC, JCB, MC, V. Station: Koiwa on JR Sobu Line (south exit, 12 min.). From the south exit, walk along the covered shopping street called Flower Rd.; take the last right before the big intersection, just past the 7 Eleven.

A member of the Japanese Inn Group and Welcome Inn, this pleasant ryokan, located on a quiet residential lane beside a canal, is actually housed in several Japanese-style homes clustered together and connected by flagstone pathways. Rooms are mostly tatami, though four Western-style rooms with beds and private bathrooms are also available. All TVs offer CNN, and other amenities include free instant coffee and tea, a coin-op laundry, an international public phone, vending machines dispensing drinks, a Japanese-style public bath with whirlpool, and a tiny garden with wisteria, canal, and goldfish. The main disadvantage to staying here is the location east of the Yamanote Loop Line and the walk from the station, but the place is close to Tokyo Disneyland.

A Note on Japanese Symbols

Many hotels, restaurants, and other establishments in Japan do not have signs giving their names in Roman (English-language) letters. As an aid to the reader, the second appendix to this book lists the Japanese symbols for all such places described in this guide. Each set of characters representing an establishment name has a number, which corresponds to the number that appears inside the box before the establishment's name in the text. Thus, to find the Japanese symbols for, say, the **Hotel Asakusa & Capsule,** refer to no. 2 in appendix B.

CAPSULE HOTELS

Fontaine Akasaka. 4–3–5 Akasaka, Minato-ku, Tokyo 107-0052. ☎ **03/3583-6554.** 294 beds. A/C TV TEL. ¥4,800 ($40) per person. AE, DC, JCB, MC, V. Station: Akasaka (2 min.) or Akasaka-mitsuke (5 min.). On Hitotsuji Dori, near the TBS Building.

Located right in the heart of Akasaka's nightlife, this capsule hotel offers a sauna, public bath, no-smoking rooms, fax machine, and vending machines selling everything from beer and instant noodles to toothbrushes. The original English-language brochure read, "Persons whose bodies are tattooed are requested to keep out" (tattoos are associated with Japanese gangsters). Also, "Dead drunks are requested to keep out." Ah, the joys of Japanized English. Check-in is after 5pm, and checkout is at 10am. Though it's open only to men on weekdays, women, too, are accepted on weekends.

② **Hotel Asakusa & Capsule.** 4–14–9 Kotobuki, Taito-ku, Tokyo 111-0042. ☎ **03/3847-4477.** Fax 03/3841-1525. 72 units, 100 beds. A/C TV TEL. ¥5,200–¥7,300 ($43–$61) single; ¥2,600 ($22) per person capsule bed. No credit cards. Station: Tawaramachi (3 min.). About a 6-min. walk south of Asakusa's Sensoji Temple.

This is one of the few capsule inns that accept women. The capsules are double-decker here, with ladders leading to the top bunk. For those who desire more privacy, very basic business-hotel-style rooms are also available. They come with the smallest bathrooms I've ever seen and either single or semi-double-size beds. If you're really trying to save money, two of you can opt to share the semi-double-size bed for the same price, but the managers were very adamant that only two women or a heterosexual couple could do so. Women have a floor of their own here, accessible by a special key for added security. Unfortunately, the women's public bath is on a separate floor. The front-desk staff doesn't speak English and are a bit gruff, but at these low prices they can't be getting paid much.

Dining 5

From stand-up noodle shops and pizzerias to exclusive kaiseki restaurants and sushi bars, restaurants in Tokyo number at least 80,000—which gives you some idea of how fond the Japanese are of eating out. In a city where apartments are so small and cramped that entertaining at home is almost unheard of, restaurants serve as places for socializing, meeting friends, and wooing business associates—as well as great excuses for drinking a lot of beer, sake, and whiskey.

HOW TO DINE IN TOKYO WITHOUT SPENDING A FORTUNE I know people in Tokyo who claim they haven't cooked in years—and they're not millionaires. They simply take advantage of one of the best deals in Tokyo—the fixed-price lunch, available usually from 11am to 2pm. Called a *teishoku* in a Japanese restaurant, a fixed-price meal is likely to include a soup, a main dish such as tempura or whatever the restaurant specializes in, pickled vegetables, rice, and tea. In restaurants serving Western food, the fixed-price lunch is variously referred to as a set lunch, *seto coursu,* or simply *coursu,* and usually includes an appetizer, a main course with one or two side dishes, coffee or tea, and sometimes dessert. Even restaurants listed under **very expensive**—where you'd otherwise spend at least ¥12,000 ($100) or more for dinner (including tax and service charge but excluding drinks)—and **expensive**—where you can expect to pay ¥8,000 to ¥12,000 ($67 to $100) for dinner—usually offer set-lunch menus, allowing you to dine in style at very reasonable prices. To keep your costs down, therefore, try having your biggest meal at lunch, avoiding, if possible, the noon to 1pm weekday crush when Tokyo's army of office workers floods area restaurants. Since the Japanese tend to order fixed-price meals rather than à la carte, set dinners are also usually available (though they're not as cheap as set lunches). All-you-can-eat buffets, offered by many hotel restaurants, are also bargain meals for hearty appetites.

So many of Tokyo's good restaurants fall into the **moderate** category that it's tempting simply to eat your way through the city—and the range of cuisine is so great you could eat something different at each meal. A dinner in this category will average ¥4,000 to ¥8,000 ($33 to $67). Lunch is likely to cost half as much.

Many of Tokyo's most colorful, noisy, and popular restaurants fall into the **inexpensive** category, where meals usually go for less than ¥4,000 ($33); many offer meals for less than ¥2,000 ($17) and lunches for ¥1,000 ($8.35). The city's huge working population heads to these places to catch a quick lunch or socialize with friends after hours. In the past few years, a number of excellent yet inexpensive French bistros and Italian trattorie have burst onto the culinary scene. Ethnic restaurants, particularly those serving Indian, Chinese, and other Asian cuisine, are also plentiful and usually inexpensive. Remember to check the nightlife section in chapter 9 for suggestions on inexpensive drinking places that serve food.

OTHER DINING NOTES   The restaurants listed below are organized first by neighborhood, then by price category.

Note that a 5% consumption tax will be added to bills totaling less than ¥7,500 ($62) per person. For meals costing ¥7,500 and more per person, both the 5% consumption tax and a 3% local tax will be added to your bill. In addition, many first-class restaurants, as well as hotel restaurants, will add a 10 to 15% service charge. Unless otherwise stated, the prices I've given do not include the extra tax and charges.

Note that restaurants that have no signs in English letters are preceded by a numbered icon, which is keyed to a list of **Japanese symbols** in appendix B.

Finally, keep in mind that the **last order** is taken at least 30 minutes before the actual closing time, sometimes even an hour before at the more exclusive restaurants.

1 Restaurants by Cuisine

AMERICAN
Anderson (Harajuku, *I*)
Bamboo Sandwich House
   (Harajuku, *I*)
Farm Grill (Ginza, *I*)
Hamburger Inn (Roppongi, *I*)
Hard Rock Cafe (Roppongi, *I*)
Harvester (Harajuku, *I*)
Homework's (Aoyama, *I*)
Johnny Rockets (Roppongi, *I*)
Lunchan (Aoyama, *M*)
New York Grill (Shinjuku, *VE*)
Potomac (Akasaka, *I*)
Spago (Roppongi, *M*)
Tony Roma's (Akasaka, *I*)

CASTILIAN
El Castellano (Shibuya, *I*)

CHINESE
Blue Sky (Akasaka, *M*)
Chinese Restaurant AOI (Aoyama, *I*)
Daini's Table (Aoyama, *M*)
Din Tai Fung (Shinjuku, *I*)
Tokyo Dai Hanten (Shinjuku, *M*)
Tokyo Kaisen Market (Shinjuku, *M*)

COFFEE/TEA/DESSERTS
Aux Bacchanales (Harajuku, *M*)
Tatsutano (Ginza, *I*)

DOJO
Domburi/Kamameshi (Rice
   Casseroles)
Hayashi (Akasaka, *I*)
Komagata Dojo (Asakusa, *M*)
Tatsutano (Ginza, *I*)
Torigin (Roppongi, *I*)

EEL
Izu'ei (Ueno, *M*)
Kandagawa (Kanda, *M*)

FRENCH
Aux Bacchanales (Harajuku, *M*)
Cafe Creperie Le Bretagne
   (Aoyama, *I*)
Cafe Francais (Ebisu, *M*)
Chez Figaro (Nishi Azabu, *M*)
Crown Restaurant
   (Near Tokyo Station, *VE*)
Fugu (Blowfish)
Kana Uni (Akasaka, *E*)
Le Gaulois (Aoyama, *M*)

Key to Abbreviations: *VE* = Very Expensive   *E* = Expensive   *M* = Moderate   *I* = Inexpensive

Nagase (Harajuku, *I*)
La Terre (Roppongi, *M*)
La Tour d'Argent (Akasaka, *VE*)
Ozawa (Meguro, *E*)
Pas à Pas (Yotsuya-sanchome, *I*)
Ueno Seiyoken Grill (Ueno, *E*)
Tentake (Tsukiji, *M*)

INDIAN

Maharaja (Ueno, *I*)
Moti (Roppongi, *I*)
Tandoor (Meguro, *I*)

INDONESIAN

Bengawan Solo (Roppongi, *I*)

INTERNATIONAL

Kitchen Five (Roppongi, *I*)
Las Chicas (Aoyama, *I*)
Rainbow Room (Hibiya, *M*)
Sunset Beach Brewing Co.
  (Odaiba, *I*)
Tableaux (Daikanyama, *E*)
Taimeikan (Nihombashi, *I*)
Tea Lounge (Akasaka, *I*)
Trader Vic's (Akasaka, *E*)

ITALIAN

Al Bacio (Shinjuku, *I*)
Carmine (Ichigaya, *M*)
Come La Kome (Asakusa, *I*)
La Boheme (Shibuya, *I*)
La Ranarita Azumabashi
  (Asakusa, *M*)
Manin (Harajuku, *E*)
Ristorante Il Bianco (Roppongi, *I*)
Sabatini (Aoyama, *E*)
Selan (Aoyama, *M*)
Trattoria-Pizzeria Sabatini (Aoyama, *I*)

VARIED JAPANESE

Doka Doka (Nishi Azabu, *M*)
Donto (Hibiya, *M*)
Hakkaku (Shinjuku, *I*)
Hanezawa Beer Garden (Ebisu, *M*)
Honoji (Roppongi, *I*)
Ichioku (Roppongi, *I*)
Irohanihoheto (Shibuya, *I*)
Irohanihoheto (Shinjuku, *I*)
Kamiya Bar (Asakusa, *I*)
Suntory Beer Garden (Akasaka, *I*)

KAISEKI

Ginza Daimasu (Ginza, *M*)
Kakiden (Shinjuku, *E*)
Kappoya Yaozen (Shinjuku, *M*)
Kisso (Roppongi, *E*)
Kuremutsu (Asakusa, *E*)
Munakata (Ginza, *M*)
Rangetsu (Ginza, *M*)
Shirogane (Meguro, *E*)
Takamura (Roppongi, *VE*)
Tamura (Tsukiji, *E*)

KUSHIYAKI

Kushi Colza (Ginza, *M*)

MEXICAN

Zapata (Harajuku, *I*)

NOODLES

Kanda Yabusoba (Kanda, *I*)
Namiki Yabu Soba (Asakusa, *I*)
Shinasobaya (Nishi Azabu, *I*)
Shogetsuan (Akasaka, *I*)

ODEN (STEW)

Otako (Ginza, *I*)

PACIFIC RIM/CROSSOVER

Cardenas (Ebisu, *I*)
Doka Doka (Nishi Azabu, *M*)
Kihachi (Akasaka, *M*)
Mominoki House (Harajuku, *I*)
Nobu (Aoyama, *E*)

PIZZA

DJ's Pizzeria (Roppongi, *I*)
Hayashi (Akasaka, *E*)
Hayashi (Shinjuku, *M*)
Inakaya (Roppongi, *E*)
Kuremutsu (Asakusa, *E*)
Ohmatsuya (Ginza, *E*)
Robatayaki (Japanese Grill)
Shakey's (Shinjuku, *I*)
Trattoria-Pizzeria Sabatini
  (Aoyama, *I*)

SHABU-SHABU

Chinya (Asakusa, *I*)
Daikokuya (Shinjuku, *I*)
Hanezawa Beer Garden (Ebisu, *M*)
Hassan (Roppongi, *M*)

Rangetsu (Ginza, *M*)
Seryna (Roppongi, *VE*)
Seryna (Shinjuku, *VE*)
Shabusen (Ginza, *M*)
Shabu Zen (Roppongi, *M*)
Shirogane (Meguro, *E*)
Suehiro (Shinjuku, *M*)
Zakuro (Akasaka, *E*)
Zakuro (Nihombashi, *E*)

SUKIYAKI

Botan (Kanda, *M*)
Chinya (Asakusa, *I*)
Daikokuya (Shinjuku, *I*)
Hanezawa Beer Garden (Ebisu, *M*)
Rangetsu (Ginza, *M*)
Seryna (Roppongi, *VE*)
Seryna (Shinjuku, *VE*)
Shabu Zen (Roppongi, *M*)
Suehiro (Shinjuku, *M*)
Zakuro (Akasaka, *E*)
Zakuro (Nihombashi, *E*)

SUSHI

Bikkuri Sushi (Roppongi, *I*)
Edogin (Tsukiji, *M*)
Fukusuke (Ginza, *I*)
Fukuzushi (Roppongi, *E*)
Heiroku (Harajuku, *I*)
Hina Sushi (Roppongi, *M*)
Sushi Dai (Tsukiji, *I*)
Sushi Sei (Akasaka, *M*)
Sushi Sei (Ginza, *I*)
Sushiko (Ginza, *VE*)

TEMPURA

Daikokuya (Asakusa, *I*)
Ten-ichi (Akasaka, *E*)

Ten-ichi (Ginza, *E*)
Tsunahachi (Shinjuku, *M*)

TEPPANYAKI

Kamon (Hibiya, *VE*)
Sekishin Tei (Akasaka, *VE*)
Seryna (Roppongi, *VE*)
Seryna (Shinjuku, *VE*)

THAI

Ban-Thai (Shinjuku, *M*)
Cay (Aoyama, *M*)
Chiang Mai (Hibiya, *I*)
Siam (Shibuya, *I*)

TONKATSU (PORK CUTLET)

Tonki (Meguro, *I*)

VEGETARIAN/HEALTH FOOD

Hiroba (Aoyama, *I*)
Mominoki House (Harajuku, *I*)

WESTERN (JAPANESE VERSION)

Kamiya Bar (Asakusa, *I*)
Taimeikan (Nihombashi, *I*)

YAKITORI

Atariya (Ginza, *I*)
Ganchan (Roppongi, *I*)
Irohanihoheto (Shibuya, *I*)
Irohanihoheto (Shinjuku, *I*)
Kamakura (Roppongi, *I*)
Kushi Colza (Ginza, *M*)
Torigin (Roppongi, *I*)
Yakitori Under the Tracks (Hibiya, *I*)

YAM

Mugitoro (Asakusa, *M*)
Negishi (Shinjuku, *I*)

2 Ginza & Hibiya

Note: To locate these restaurants, see map on p. 62.

VERY EXPENSIVE

✪ **Kamon.** On the 17th floor of the Imperial Hotel, 1-1-1 Uchisaiwai-cho. ☎ **03/ 3504-1111.** Reservations recommended for dinner. Set dinners ¥12,000–¥18,000 ($100–$150); set lunches ¥3,000–¥6,000 ($25–$50). AE, DC, JCB, MC, V. Daily 11:30am–2:30pm and 5:30–9:30pm. Station: Hibiya (1 min.). TEPPANYAKI.

Kamon, which means "Gate of Celebration," has an interior that could be a statement on Tokyo itself—traditionally Japanese, yet ever so high-tech. Seating is at a single, large counter, with grills in the middle where expert chefs prepare excellent teppanyaki before your eyes. Japanese sirloin steaks or filet, seafood ranging from

A Note on Japanese Symbols

Many restaurants, hotels, and other establishments in Japan do not have signs giving their names in Roman (English-language) letters. As an aid to the reader, the second appendix to this book lists the Japanese symbols for all such places described in this guide. Each set of characters representing an establishment name has a number, which corresponds to the number that appears inside the box before the establishment's name in the text. Thus, to find the Japanese symbols for, say, **Sushiko,** refer to no. 3 in appendix B.

fresh prawn and lobster to scallops, crabmeat, and fish, and seasonal vegetables are available. The service is, of course, imperial.

(3) Sushiko. 6–3–8 Ginza. ☎ **03/3571-1968.** Reservations required. Meals ¥12,000– ¥15,000 ($100–$125). AE, JCB, MC, V. Daily 11:30am–10:30pm. Station: Ginza or Hibiya (4 min.). A block east of the elevated tracks of the JR Yamanote Line, on the Ginza side on Sukiyabashi Dori. SUSHI.

If you're in pursuit of top-quality sushi, your search will eventually take you to this place, considered by some to be one of the best sushi bars in town. There's no written menu, and the counter seats 11 customers only. Owned by a fourth-generation restaurateur, this establishment doesn't display its fish as in most sushi bars, but rather keeps it freshly refrigerated until the moment it meets the swift blade of the expert chefs.

EXPENSIVE

✪ (4) Ohmatsuya. On the 2nd floor of the modern Ail D'Or Building, behind the Sony Building on Sony St. 6–5–8 Ginza. ☎ **03/3571-7053.** Reservations required. Set dinner ¥6,500–¥9,000 ($54–$75). AE, JCB, DC, MC, V. Mon–Fri 5–10pm (last order 9:30pm); Sat 4:30–9:30pm (last order 8:30pm). Closed holidays. Station: Ginza (3 min.). JAPANESE GRILL.

Enter this second-floor restaurant and you're instantly greeted by waitresses clad in traditional countryside clothing and by an old farmhouse atmosphere. (Part of the decor is from a 17th-century samurai house in northern Japan.) Even the style of cooking is traditional, as customers grill their own food over a hibachi. Sake, served in a length of bamboo, is drunk from bamboo cups. Dinner menus include such delicacies as grilled fish, skewered meat, and vegetables. A true find—and easy to find at that, located on Sony Street, the small side street behind the Sony Building.

Ten-ichi. 6–6–5 Ginza, on Namiki Dori. ☎ **03/3571-1949.** Reservations recommended for lunch, required for dinner. Set dinners ¥8,500–¥15,000 ($71–$125); set lunches ¥7,000– ¥10,000 ($58–$83). AE, DC, JCB, MC, V. Daily 11:30am–9:30pm. Station: Ginza (3 min.). TEMPURA.

In this restaurant, located on Namiki Dori in the heart of the Ginza's nightlife, you can sit at a counter to watch the chef prepare your meal. This is the main shop of a 50-year-old restaurant chain that helped the tempura style of cooking gain worldwide recognition by serving important foreign customers. Today Ten-ichi still has one of the best reputations in town for serving the most delicately fried foods.

There are more than 10 Ten-ichi restaurants in Tokyo. Other locations include the Ginza Sony Building at the intersection of Harumi Dori and Sotobori Dori (☎ **03/3571-3837**), the Imperial Hotel's Tower basement (☎ **03/3503-1001**), 3–19–3 Akasaka on Misujidori street (☎ **03/3583-0107**), and in several department stores, including Tokyu Honten in Shibuya (☎ **03/3477-3891**), Seibu in Ikebukuro (☎ **03/3984-1930**), and Isetan in Shinjuku (☎ **03/5379-3039**).

MODERATE

✪ ⑤ **Donto.** Yurakucho Denki Building. basement, 1–7–1 Yurakucho, on Harumi Dori. ☎ **03/3201-3021.** Set dinners ¥3,500–¥7,500 ($29–$62); set lunches ¥820–¥1,500 ($6.80–$12). AE, DC, JCB, MC, V. Mon–Sat 11am–2pm and 5–10:30pm. Closed holidays. Station: Hibiya (1 min.). VARIED JAPANESE.

Located in Hibiya on Harumi Dori, this is a great place for lunch. Popular with the local working crowd (and therefore best avoided between noon and 1pm), it's pleasantly decorated with shoji screens, wooden floors, and an open kitchen. Take off your shoes at the entryway and put them into one of the wooden lockers. Choose what you want from the plastic display case, which shows various teishoku and set meals. Everything from noodles, sashimi, tempura, and obento to kaiseki is available. Unfortunately, the best deals are daily specials written in Japanese only; ask about them.

There's another Donto on the 49th floor of the Sumitomo Building in Shinjuku (☎ **03/3344-6269**).

⑥ **Ginza Daimasu.** 6–9–6 Ginza. ☎ **03/3571-3584.** Reservations required for kaiseki. Kaiseki ¥5,000–¥12,000 ($42–$100); obento ¥2,300–¥3,800 ($19–$32); set lunches ¥1,800–¥2,300 ($15–$19). DC, JCB, MC, V. Daily 11:30am–9:30pm (last order 8:30pm). Station: Ginza (2 min.). Across from Matsuzakaya department store on Chuo Dori. KAISEKI/OBENTO.

This 60-year-old restaurant has a simple, modern decor with Japanese touches. Experienced, kimono-clad waitresses serve artfully arranged set meals from the English menu. The *Fukiyose-zen obento*—many delicate dishes served in three courses—includes beautiful tempura delicacies served in an edible basket and a menu (in Japanese) explaining what you're eating. A plastic-food display in the front window will help you recognize the restaurant. Set lunches are served until 3pm.

⑦ **Kushi Colza.** 6–4–18 Ginza. ☎ **03/3571-8228.** Reservations recommended. Set dinners ¥3,300–¥4,500 ($27–$37). AE, DC, JCB, MC, V. Daily 5–10pm. Station: Hibiya (5 min.) or Ginza (10 min.). Located on a small side street between and paralleling Sotobori Dori and the elevated JR Yamanote Line tracks; look for its sign, which says "Kushi & Wine." YAKITORI/KUSHIYAKI.

Kikkoman, a well-known producer of soy sauce, maintains a few restaurants as well, including this one. It serves yakitori and *kushiyaki* (also grilled meats and vegetables on skewers), delicately seasoned with—what else?—Kikkoman soy sauce. Small, pleasant, and with an open counter where you can watch friendly chefs prepare your food, Kushi Colza has an English menu that lists three set dinners consisting of various skewered filets of beef, fish, eel, or pork, along with an appetizer, salad, soup, and dessert. There's also a special weekend and holiday set dinner for ¥3,000 ($25). À la carte selections for skewered specialties average ¥400 to ¥800 ($3.35 to $6.65) per skewer. Try the vegetable salad with soy sauce dressing.

Munakata. Mitsui Urban Hotel basement, 8–6–15 Ginza. ☎ **03/3574-9356.** Main dishes ¥1,200–¥4,000 ($10–$33); kaiseki set meals ¥8,000–¥15,000 ($67–$125); mini-kaiseki lunches ¥2,500 ($21). AE, DC, JCB, MC, V. Mon–Fri 11:30am–3pm and 5–10pm; Sat, Sun, and holidays 11:30am–10pm. Station: Shimbashi (2 min.) or Hibiya (10 min.). KAISEKI/OBENTO.

Kaiseki is one of the most expensive meals you can have in Japan, but there are some lunch specials here (served until 2pm) that make it quite reasonable. This basement restaurant is cozy, with slats of wood and low lighting that give customers a sense of privacy. In addition to mini-kaiseki meals, there are also tempura and various obento box lunches, like the Shokado bento for ¥1,300 ($11). If you come before 6:30pm on weekdays and 7pm on weekends, you can take advantage of a special kaiseki meal for ¥5,000 ($42). A great place for lunch, with an English menu, or for a dinner splurge.

A Note on Japanese Symbols

Many restaurants, hotels, attractions, and other establishments in Japan do not have signs giving their names in Roman (English-language) letters. The second appendix to this book lists the Japanese symbols for all such places described in this guide. Each set of characters representing an establishment name has a number in the appendix, which corresponds to the number that appears inside the oval before the establishment's name in the text. Thus, to find the Japanese symbol for, say, **Rangetsu** (below), refer to no. 8 in appendix B.

✪ **Rainbow Room.** Imperial Hotel, 17th floor, 1–1–1 Uchisaiwai-cho. ☎ **03/3504-1111.** Reservations recommended. Buffet dinner ¥7,500 ($62.50); buffet lunch ¥5,000 ($42). AE, DC, JCB, MC, V. Daily 11:30am–2:30pm and 5–9:30pm. Station: Hibiya (1 min.). INTERNATIONAL.

Lots of Tokyo hotels now offer all-you-can-eat buffets, but this 17th-floor restaurant has been serving buffets for more than 40 years. Its spread features more than 40 mostly European and some international dishes, which vary according to seasonal food promotions spotlighting a country's cuisine, from Indonesian to Swiss. Views are of Ginza and Hibiya Park, and there's live jazz music in the evenings. This restaurant has enjoyed great popularity for decades, making reservations a must.

⑧ **Rangetsu.** 3–5–8 Ginza. ☎ **03/3567-1021.** Reservations recommended. Beef sukiyaki or shabu-shabu ¥4,500 ($37); obento meals ¥2,200–¥4,000 ($18–$33); set lunches ¥1,200–¥1,700 ($10–$14). DC, JCB, MC, V. Mon–Sat 11:30am–10pm; Sun and holidays 11:30am–9pm. Station: Ginza (3 min.). On Chuo Dori, across from the Matsuya department store. SUKIYAKI/SHABU-SHABU/KAISEKI/OBENTO.

This well-known Ginza restaurant has been dishing out sukiyaki, shabu-shabu, obento (traditional box meals), and steaks for more than 4 decades. It uses only Matsuzaka beef (bought whole and carved up by the chefs) which ranges from costlier fine-marbled beef to cheaper cuts with thick marbling. There are also various crab dishes (including a crab sukiyaki), kaiseki, sirloin steaks, and eel dishes. Especially good deals are the obento box meals, available day and night and offering a variety of small dishes, and the various set lunches served until 2:30pm. In the basement is a sake bar, with more than 80 different kinds of sake from all over Japan, which you can also order with your meal. Outside the door is a plastic display case with descriptions in English.

⑨ **Shabusen.** Core Building. 2F, 5–8–20 Ginza. ☎ **03/3571-1717.** Set dinners ¥1,980–¥5,600 ($16.75–$47); set lunches ¥850–¥3,000 ($7.10–$25). AE, DC, JCB, MC, V. Daily 11am–10pm. Station: Ginza (1 min.). On Chuo Dori, next to the Nissan Building. SHABU-SHABU.

Located on the second floor of a fashion department store just a stone's throw from Ginza 4–chome Crossing (the Harumi Dori–Chuo-Dori intersection), this is a fun restaurant where you can cook your own sukiyaki or shabu-shabu in a boiling pot as you sit at a round counter. Orders are shouted back and forth among the staff, service is rapid, and the place is lively. There's an English menu complete with cooking instructions, so it's user-friendly. It's also one of the few restaurants that cater to individual diners (shabu-shabu is usually shared by a group). The special shabu-shabu dinner for ¥3,950 ($32), with appetizer, tomato ("super dressing") salad, beef, vegetables, noodles or rice porridge, and dessert, is enough for most voracious appetites.

You'll find a branch of Shabusen in the basement of the TBS Building at 5–3–3 Akasaka (☎ **03/3582-8161**).

INEXPENSIVE

In addition to the listings below, consider **La Boheme**, 6–4–1 Ginza (☎ **03/ 3572-5005**), a popular chain of inexpensive Italian restaurants, all open daily 11:30am to a very late 5am. See "Shibuya," below, for a complete review.

❍ ⑩ **Atariya**. 3–5–17 Ginza. ☎ **03/3564-0045**. Yakitori set courses ¥1,500–¥2,500 ($12–$21); individual skewers ¥200–¥250 ($1.65–$2.10). No credit cards. Mon–Sat 4:30–10:15pm (last order). Station: Ginza (3 min.). Near Ginza 4–chome Crossing: Take the small side street that runs behind Wako department store; Atariya is in the 2nd block on the right. YAKITORI.

Because it's open only at night and serves yakitori, this is technically a drinking establishment, but it also makes a good choice for inexpensive dining in Ginza. You have your choice of table or counter seating on the first floor, while up on the second floor you take off your shoes and sit on split-reed mats. Since set courses will include most parts of the chicken, including the liver, gizzard, and skin, you might wish to order à la carte for your favorites. Mine include asparagus wrapped in grilled pork, *tskune* (ground chicken meatballs on a skewer), and *shoniku* (chicken breast yakitori). The shop's name means "to be right on target, to score a bull's-eye," and according to its English pamphlet, eating here is certain to bring you good luck.

Chiang Mai. 1–6–10 Yurakucho. ☎ **03/3580-0456**. Main dishes ¥1,000–¥2,500 ($8.35–$21); set lunches ¥600–¥800 ($5–$6.65); set dinners from ¥4,000 ($36). No credit cards. Sun–Fri 11:30am–11pm (last order 10pm). Station: Hibiya (1 min.). In an alley 2 blocks north of the Imperial Hotel and 1 block south of Harumi Dori, down from McDonald's. THAI.

This tiny basement restaurant serves the cuisine of northern Thailand. At midday, office workers pour in for the reasonably priced set lunches; there's usually a waiting line that goes all the way up the stairs to the alley. The dinner menu is more extensive and includes all the Thai favorites, from yummy pad Thai noodles to lemongrass soup.

Farm Grill. Ginza Nine Building 3–8–5 Ginza. ☎ **03/5568-6156**. Dinner buffet ¥2,300 ($19) for men, ¥1,900 ($16) for women; lunch buffet ¥1,500 ($12). AE, JCB, MC, V. Daily 11:30am–11pm. Station: Shimbashi (exit 1, 4 min.). Near the Ginza Dai-Ichi Hotel, on the 2nd floor of a building underneath the Shuto Expressway. AMERICAN.

After all of Tokyo's cramped, tiny restaurants, what strikes you first about this place is the space—enough for 260 widely placed tables. And with its simple wood decor and (for Tokyo) incredibly cheap prices, the second thing that will come to mind is that it's just like millions of casual restaurants in the States, which is what makes this restaurant so unusual—good American food in Japan is hard to come by, and at these prices it's otherwise nonexistent. Overflowing buffets offer a variety of vegetables, casseroles, meats, and desserts. There's no time limit for lunch, available until 5pm, but there's a two-hour limit at dinner and men—presumably because of heartier appetites—pay slightly more. Add ¥1,500 to your meal, and you can drink all you want of a variety of beverages, including wine, cocktails, and beer.

⑪ **Fukusuke**. Toshiba Building B2, 5–2–1 Ginza. ☎ **03/3573-0471**. Sushi à la carte ¥120–¥300 ($1–$2.50); set dinners ¥1,300–¥3,300 ($11–$27; set lunches ¥650–¥1,300 ($5.40–$11). AE, DC, JCB, MC, V. Mon–Sat 11am–10pm; Sun and holidays 11:30–9pm. Station: Ginza or Hibiya (4 min.). In the 2nd basement below the Sukiyabashi Hankyu department store, on Sotobori Dori at Sukiyabashi Crossing. SUSHI.

In this basement full of cheap restaurants, walk all the way to the back (away from Harumi Dori) to this very inexpensive sushi bar, popular with area office workers.

It has an exceptionally long counter, which makes it a good choice if you're looking for an empty seat during the noon-to-1pm rush. It has a display counter outside with various choices of set meals, as well as an illustrated card showing various à la carte sushi. Easiest, however, is to order one of the set meals. The ¥850 ($7.10) set lunch includes soup, various sushi, Japanese pickles, and tea.

12   **Otako.** 8–6–19 Ginza. ☎ **03/3571-0751.** À la carte ¥150–¥450 ($1.25–$3.75); set meals ¥600–¥1,000 ($5–$8.35). AE, DC, JCB, MC, V. Mon–Fri 5pm–12:30am, Sat 5–10:30pm. Station: Ginza (5 min.). Near the Mitsui Urban Hotel on Namiki Dori, beside S. Watanabe art gallery. ODEN.

Located on a small street in the heart of Ginza's nightlife district, this clean and friendly establishment with blue noren curtains and a red lantern has been dishing out its own oden for more than 60 years. Oden features fish cakes, tofu, potatoes and other foods that are simmered whole for hours in a sweetened stock, and though the Japanese are especially fond of it on cold winter days, it's available here year-round. An English-language menu describes the various kinds of oden, from those with tofu to those with meatballs wrapped in cabbage. Set meals with three to five pieces of oden are available.

13   **Sushi Sei.** 8–2–13 Ginza. ☎ **03/3571-2772** or 03/3572-4770. Sushi à la carte ¥150–¥350 ($1.25–$2.90); set lunches ¥850–¥2,300 ($7.10–$19); set dinners ¥2,500–¥3,300 ($21–$27.50). AE, DC, JCB, MC, V. Mon–Sat noon–2pm and 5–10:45pm. Closed holidays. Station: Shimbashi (1 min.) or Hibiya (5 min.). Across from the elevated tracks of the JR Yamanote Line. SUSHI.

One of a dependably good chain of reasonably priced sushi bars, this place is a natural for both novices and more experienced fans of raw fish. Order à la carte for your favorites, or stick to one of the set meals if you don't know much about sushi. The chef will prepare your food and place it on a raised platform on the counter in front of you, which serves as your plate.

✪ 14   **Tatsutano.** 7–8–7 Ginza. ☎ **03/3571-1850.** Desserts ¥750–¥900 ($6.25–$7.50); kamameshi ¥1,250 ($10.40). No credit cards. Daily 11am–8pm. Station: Ginza (3 min.). On Chuo Dori, across from Yamaha. TRADITIONAL DESSERTS/KAMAMESHI.

If you'd like to try a traditional Japanese dessert, head to this 100-year-old shop, famous for its sweets. Most popular is *anmitsu*, a dessert made from beans, molasses, sweet-bean paste, and gelatin. Other traditional desserts are *oshiruko*, a hot sweet-bean porridge, and sweet-bean ice cream. If you're craving something more substantial, you might also wish to order one of the reasonably priced *kamameshi* (rice casserole) or *zosui* (rice porridge).

Yakitori Under the Tracks. Under the Yamanote Line tracks separating Ginza from Hibiya. No phone. Skewers ¥180–¥400 ($1.50–$3.35). No credit cards. Mon–Sat 5pm–midnight. Station: Hibiya or Yurakucho (3 min.). YAKITORI.

This is not a restaurant but rather a place—underneath an arch of the elevated Yamanote railway tracks. Although there are several fancier establishments that occupy an entire arch, look for the one arch located about halfway between Harumi Dori and the Imperial Hotel Tower, with about a half-dozen tiny yakitori stands, each with a table or two and a few chairs. They cater to a rather boisterous working class, mainly men. The atmosphere, unsophisticated and dingy, harks back to prewar Japan, somewhat of an anomaly in the otherwise chic Ginza. Dining here can be quite an experience, and on my last visit several stall owners enthusiastically beckoned me to join them.

3 Nihombashi & Around Tokyo Station

VERY EXPENSIVE

✪ **Crown Restaurant.** Palace Hotel, 1–1–1 Marunouchi. ☎ **03/3211-5211.** Reservations recommended. Coat required weekends and holidays, coat and tie required weekdays. Main dishes ¥4,900–¥8,900 ($41–$74); set dinners ¥10,000–¥18,000 ($83–$150); set lunches ¥5,000–¥10,000 ($42–$83). AE, DC, JCB, MC, V. Daily 11:30am–2pm and 5:30–10:30pm. Station: Otemachi (2 min.) or Tokyo Station (7 min.). FRENCH.

Elegant dining with a view is what you get at this high-class, 10th-floor French restaurant, a great choice for a romantic dinner. It features beautiful flower arrangements and three walls of windows, as well as a great view of the Imperial Palace, its gardens, a memorial fountain commemorating the crown prince's 1993 marriage, and Tokyo Tower—be sure to ask for a window seat when making your reservation. To preserve its hushed, peaceful setting, both cellular phones and children under 10 are prohibited. The menu changes with the seasons, with past dishes ranging from Maine lobster and sweetbread wrapped in light pastry to chicken breast and foie gras wrapped in buckwheat pancake. A low-calorie menu is also available, which might leave room for a sumptuous dessert like the Grand Marnier soufflé. There's live music from 6pm, and you can retire for a drink at the lounge next door.

EXPENSIVE

⑮ **Zakuro.** 3–8–2 Nihombashi. ☎ **03/3271-3791.** Set dinners ¥5,000–¥16,000 ($42–$133); set lunches ¥1,500–¥2,500 ($12.50–$21). AE, DC, JCB, MC, V. Daily 11am–10pm (last order 9pm). Station: Nihombashi (2 min.). Across from Takashimaya department store's south side, in the basement of an office building. SHABU-SHABU/SUKIYAKI.

This is the Nihombashi branch of a dependably good and well-known chain specializing in Kobe steaks. It's decorated with ceramics and woodblock prints by famous Japanese artists. The place is popular with both businesspeople and shoppers because of its location near the department store and many area offices. It serves lunch courses that include tempura, teriyaki steak, sashimi, or sukiyaki as the main entree, as well as an obento box lunch. For dinners there are set meals for shabu-shabu, teppanyaki, sukiyaki, tempura, and more. Although the main menu is in Japanese, an English brochure lists some of the set meals available.

You'll find other Zakuro restaurants in Akasaka in front of the American Embassy (☎ **03/3582-2661**) and in the TBS Kaikan Building (☎ **03/ 3582-6841**), in Kyobashi south of the Bridgestone Building (☎ **03/3563-5031**), and in the Ginza south of Matsuya department store (☎ **03/3535-4421**).

INEXPENSIVE

⑯ **Taimeikan.** 1–12–10 Nihombashi. ☎ **03/3271-2463.** Main dishes ¥800–¥2,500 ($6.65–$21); set lunch ¥800 ($6.65). No credit cards. Mon–Sat 11am–9pm (last order 8pm). Closed holidays. Station: Nihombashi (3 min.). Off Eitai Dori, 1 block east of Chuo Dori. INTERNATIONAL.

This old-fashioned, Western-style restaurant is located in the same building that houses the Kite Museum and is operated under the same management. Taimeikan has been in business since 1931. It's simple, inexpensive, and often crowded with mainly middle-aged and older Japanese. Its English-language menu lists such dishes as hamburger steak, Chinese noodles, chicken cutlet, beef fillet steak, omelet, spaghetti, and curry rice. To Western eyes, the food looks Japanese; to Japanese, it's Western fare. In other words, this restaurant serves the classic Japanese version of Western food (and even has a name for it—*yoshoku*), and in that respect has probably changed little since it opened. Diners are usually given both chopsticks and silverware, as though even the management isn't sure what it serves. It's a good place for a quick, cheap meal. Or, for slightly fancier dining, there's another restaurant up on the second floor serving pasta, roast chicken, steaks, and other Western fare, with main courses ranging from ¥2,000 to ¥9,000 ($17 to $75).

4 Tsukiji

Since Tsukiji is home to the nation's largest wholesale fish market, it's not surprising that this area abounds in sushi and seafood restaurants. In addition to the recommendations here, don't neglect the many stalls in and around the market, where you can eat everything from noodles to fresh sashimi.

EXPENSIVE

(17) **Tamura.** 2-12-11 Tsukiji. ☎ **03/3541-2591.** Reservations required for dinner, recommended for lunch. Set meals ¥6,000–¥20,000 ($50–$167); lunch obento ¥3,500–¥6,000 ($29–$50). AE, DC, JCB, MC, V. Daily noon–3pm (last order 1pm) and 5:30–10pm. Station: Tsukiji (1 min.). Off Shinohashi Dori, catercorner from Honganji Temple, down the street running between Doutour Coffee Shop and a school yard. KAISEKI.

This modern kaiseki restaurant has a friendly staff of smiling and bowing kimono-clad waitresses and hostesses who make you feel as though they've been waiting all this time just for you. Although the menu is in Japanese only, they'll help you decide what to order; but since there are only set meals, your budget will probably decide for you. Lunch is by far the most economical time to come; many Japanese housewives come for the obento lunch boxes, served in a pleasant dining room with tables and chairs. If you order one of the expensive kaiseki meals, you'll be ushered to a tatami room upstairs.

MODERATE

(18) **Edogin.** 4-5-1 Tsukiji. ☎ **03/3543-4401.** Set dinners ¥5,000–¥10,000 ($42–$83); lunch teishoku ¥1,000–¥1,500 ($8.35–$12). AE, DC, MC, V. Mon–Sat 11am–9:30pm, Sun and holidays 11:30am–9pm. Station: Tsukiji (3 min.). Located near the Harumi and Shinohashi Dori intersection behind McDonald's; anyone in the neighborhood will be able to point you in the right direction. SUSHI.

There are four Edogin sushi restaurants in Tsukiji, all located within walking distance of one another. Since they're close to the famous fish market, you can be assured the fish will be fresh. There's nothing aesthetic about the main Edogin—the lights are bright and it's noisy and busy. It's particularly crowded during lunch- and dinnertime, because the food is so dependably good and plentiful. The menu is in Japanese only, but there's a glass case outside with some of the dishes displayed, with prices for most ¥3,000 ($25) or less. As an alternative, look at what the people around you are eating or, if it's lunchtime, order the *teishoku* (served until 2pm).

(19) **Tentake.** 6-16-6 Tsukiji. ☎ **03/3541-3881.** Fugu dishes ¥1,000–¥3,900 ($8.35–$32); fugu set courses ¥3,900–¥13,500 ($32–$112); set lunches ¥800–¥1,000 ($6.65–$8.35). JCB, MC, V. Daily 11:30am–10pm. Closed Sun Apr–Sept; Wed Mar and Oct; 1st and 3rd Wed Feb and Nov. Station: Tsukiji (7 min.). From the Harumi Dori/Shinohashi intersection, walk on Harumi Dori in the opposite direction of Ginza; the restaurant is on the left just before the bridge, in a modern building. FUGU.

People who really know their *fugu*, or blowfish, will tell you that the only time to eat it is from October through March, when it's fresh. You can eat fugu year-round, however, and a good place to try this Japanese delicacy is Tentake, a place popular with the Tsukiji working crowd. There's an English menu listing fugu dishes such as tempura fugu; a complete fugu dinner with all the trimmings costs ¥9,000 ($75). Otherwise, if you want suggestions, try the fugu-chiri for ¥3,800 ($32), a do-it-yourself meal in which you cook raw blowfish, cabbage, dandelion leaves, and tofu in a pot of boiling water in front of you—this was more than I could eat, but you can make a complete meal of it by ordering the fugu-chiri course for ¥5,900 ($49), which adds tempera, yakitori, and other dishes. If someone in your party doesn't like fugu, I'd recommend the crab set menu for ¥3,900 ($32). And yes, that's fugu swimming in the fish tank.

Before you eat here, be sure you read about fugu in "Tips on Dining, Japanese Style," in appendix A.

INEXPENSIVE

✪ ⟨20⟩ **Sushi Dai.** Tsukiji Fish Market. ☎ 03/3542-1111. Sushi à la carte ¥200–¥1,000 ($1.65–$8.35); sushi seto ¥2,000 ($16). No credit cards. Mon–Sat 5am–2pm. Closed holidays. Station: Tsukiji (10 min.). Located in a row of barracks housing other restaurants and shops beside the covered market; cross the bridge that leads to the market grounds, take a right and then your first left; to your right will be the barracks. Sushi Dai is in Building 6 on the 3rd alley (just past the tiny post office), the 3rd shop on the right. SUSHI.

Located right in the Tsukiji Fish Market, this restaurant boasts some of the freshest fish in town. The easiest thing to do is order the seto, a set sushi course that usually comes with tuna, eel, shrimp, and other morsels, plus six rolls of tuna and rice in seaweed (*onigiri*). If you can't stomach sushi for breakfast, order *tamago* (a slice of layer-fried omelet).

5 Asakusa

Note: To locate these restaurants, see map on p. 81.

EXPENSIVE

✪ ⟨21⟩ **Kuremutsu.** 2-2-13 Asakusa. ☎ 03/3842-0906. Reservations required. Main dishes ¥2,500–¥5,000 ($21–$42); kaiseki courses ¥8,000–¥10,000 ($67–$83). AE, DC, JCB, MC, V. Fri–Wed 4–9:30pm (last order). Station: Asakusa (5 min.). Walk on Nakamise Dori toward Sensoji Temple, turning right after the last shop; go past the 2 stone Buddhas and then right again at the tiny Benten-do Temple with the large bell; the restaurant is on the right side of the street, across from the playground. KAISEKI/JAPANESE GRILL.

Just southeast of Sensoji Temple, Kuremutsu is actually a tiny, traditional house tucked behind a bamboo fence and inviting courtyard with willow and maple trees, a millstone covered with moss, and an entrance invitingly lit with lanterns. Inside, it's like a farmhouse in the countryside, filled with farm implements, old chests, masks, cast-iron tea kettles, hibachi, and other odds and ends. Traditionally dressed to match the mood, waitresses will automatically bring an appetizer (or table snack, for which there's a ¥1,200/$10 charge). You can then choose the menu as you eat, opting, perhaps, for fresh-grilled fish, the restaurant's specialty, a platter of assorted sashimi and fugu, or boiled vegetables. If you can afford it, order a kaiseki meal. The menu is in Japanese only, so look around at what others are eating. Most meals à la carte average ¥8,000 ($67) per person.

MODERATE

✪ ⟨22⟩ **Komagata Dojo.** 1-7-12 Komagata, Taito-ku. ☎ 03/3842-4001. Reservations recommended for dinner. Dojo dishes ¥1,000–¥1,600 ($8.35–$13); set meals ¥2,000–¥6,000 ($17–$50). DC, JCB, MC, V. Daily 11am–9pm. Station: Asakusa (3 min.). To reach the restaurant, walk south on Edo Dori (away from Kaminarimon Gate and Sensoji Temple); the restaurant—a large, old-fashioned wood house on a corner, with blue curtains at its door—is on the right side of the street, about a 5-min. walk from Kaminarimon Gate, past the Sanwa Bank. DOJO.

Following a tradition spanning almost 200 years, this old-style dining hall specializes in *dojo*, a tiny sardinelike river fish that translates as a "loach." It's served in a variety of styles, from grilled to stewed. Easiest is to order one of the set meals, which includes a popular *dojo nabe*, cooked on a charcoal burner at your table. Otherwise, look around and order what someone else is eating. The dining area is simply one large room of tatami mats, with ground-level boards serving as tables and waitresses in traditional dress moving quietly about. A restaurant very much out of the Edo Period.

(23) **Mugitoro.** 2-2-4 Kaminarimon. ☎ **03/3842-1066.** Reservations recommended. Set dinners ¥6,000–¥13,000 ($50–$108); set lunches ¥3,500–¥5,000 ($29–$42). AE, DC, JCB, MC, V. Daily 11:30am–9pm (last order). Station: Asakusa (2 min.). From Sensoji Temple, walk south (with your back to Kaminarimon Gate) until you reach the first big intersection with the stoplight; Komagata-bashi Bridge will be to your left; Mugitoro is right beside the bridge on Edo Dori, next to a tiny temple and playground. Look for the big white lantern hanging outside. YAM KAISEKI.

Founded about 60 years ago but now housed in a new building, this restaurant specializes in *tororo-imo* (yam) kaiseki and has a wide following among middle-aged Japanese women. Popular as a health food, the yams used here are imported from the mountains of Akita Prefecture and featured in almost all the dishes. The menu changes monthly, and there's an English menu.

La Ranarita Azumabashi. Asahi Beer Tower (on the opposite side of the Sumida River from Sensoji Temple), 22nd floor, 1-23-1 Azumabashi. ☎ **03/5608-5277.** Reservations recommended on weekends. Pizza ¥1,300–¥2,200 ($11–$18); pasta ¥600–¥1,800 ($5–$15); main dishes ¥1,900–¥3,400 ($16–$28); set dinners ¥6,000 and ¥12,000 ($50 and $100). AE, DC, JCB, MC, V. Mon–Sat 11:30am–2pm (last order) and 5–9pm (last order), Sun and holidays 11:20am–2pm and 4–8pm (last order). Station: Asakusa (4 min.). ITALIAN.

The Asahi Beer Tower may not mean anything to you, but if I mention the building with the golden hops poised on top, you'll certainly know it when you see it (the building was designed by Philippe Starck). The Asahi Beer Tower is the high-rise beside the golden hops, looking like . . . a beer mug with foam on top? On the top floor (in the foam), is this Italian-managed restaurant with soaring walls and great views of Asakusa. It's a perfect perch from which to watch barges on the river or the sunset over Asakusa as you dine on everything from pizza or pasta (available in half sizes) to grilled scampi or veal saltimbocca sauteed with sage and ham. The set lunches, which begin at ¥1,500 ($12) on weekdays and ¥2,500 ($21) on weekends and holidays, include an antipasta, salad, main dish, and coffee. If you want a ringside seat, make a reservation at least 3 days in advance or avoid the weekends.

There's another La Ranarita located in Harajuku at 1–13–14 Jingumae (☎ **03/3478-3310**).

INEXPENSIVE

(24) **Chinya.** 1-3-4 Asakusa. ☎ **03/3841-0010.** Set meals ¥2,300–¥6,000 ($19–$50). DC, JCB, MC, V. Thurs–Tues 11:30am–9:15pm. Station: Asakusa (1 min.). Located to the left of the Kaminarimon Gate if you stand facing Asakusa Kannon Temple (look for the sukiyaki sign). SHABU-SHABU/SUKIYAKI.

Established in 1880, Chinya is an old sukiyaki restaurant with a new home in a seven-story building to the left of Kaminarimon Gate. The entrance to this place is open-fronted; all you'll see is a man waiting to take your shoes and a hostess in

---

🏠 Family-Friendly Restaurants

Hard Rock Cafe *(see p. 131)*   This internationally known establishment should pacify grumbling teenagers. They can munch on hamburgers, gaze at famous guitars and other rock 'n' roll memorabilia, and most important, buy that Hard Rock Cafe T-shirt.

Johnny Rockets *(see p. 132)*   When your kids start asking for "real food," take them here for the best burgers in town.

Shakey's *(see p.114)*   When nothing but pizza will satisfy, head for one of these chain pizza parlors for an all-you-can-eat bargain lunch.

---

kimono ready to lead you to one of the dining areas above. It offers very good shabu-shabu or sukiyaki set lunches for less than ¥2,000 ($17), available until 4pm and including soup and side dishes. Otherwise, dinner set meals of shabu-shabu or sukiyaki, including rice and soup, begin at ¥2,300 ($19). There's a display case out front showing a few options.

Come La Kome. 1–15–10 Kaminarimon. ☎ **03/5828-3488.** Pasta and pizza ¥1,000–¥1,400 ($8.35–$12); main courses ¥1,100–¥2,200 ($9.15–$18); set lunches ¥1,000–¥1,800 ($8.35–$15). AE, JCB, MC, V. Daily 11:30am–2:30pm and 5:30pm–5am. Station: Asakusa (6 min.). Walk west on Kaminarimon Dori (away from the Sumida River); it will be on your left, across from Sushiya shopping street. ITALIAN.

This bustling, casual Italian chain offers three small floors of dining. The menu, in Japanese only, offers salads, pizza, pasta, seafood; and meat dishes. You're probably best off ordering one of the set lunches or looking around at what others are eating.

㉕ Daikokuya. 1–38–10 Asakusa. ☎ **03/3844-1111.** Set courses ¥3,000–¥4,300 ($25–$36). No credit cards. Daily 11am–8:30pm. Station: Asakusa (5 min.). Off Nakamise Dori, to the west; take the small street that passes by the south side of Dempoin Temple (also spelled Demboin); the restaurant is at the 1st intersection on the left, a white corner building with a Japanese-style tiled roof and sliding front door. TEMPURA.

This simple tempura restaurant has been popular with the locals since 1887, and though it does not offer the most refined tempura, it has atmosphere. It specializes in Edo-style tempura and *tendon* (tempura on a bowl of rice, usually ebi, or prawn), prepared using sesame oil. Although there's no English menu, there are photographs of many of the dishes. There's an annex around the corner to handle the overflow crowd.

Kamiya Bar. 1–1–1 Asakusa. ☎ **03/3841-5400.** Main dishes ¥610–¥1,300 ($5.10–$11). No credit cards. Wed–Mon 11:30am–9:30pm (last order). Station: Asakusa (1 min.). Located on Kaminarimon Dori in a plain brown-tiled building between Kaminarimon Gate and the Sumida River. JAPANESE/WESTERN.

This inexpensive eatery, established in 1880 as the first Western bar in Japan, serves both Japanese and Western fare on its three floors. The first floor is the bar, popular with tobacco-smoking older Japanese men. The second floor offers Western food of a sort (that is, the Japanese version of Western food), including fried chicken, smoked salmon, spaghetti, fried shrimp, and hamburger steak, while the third floor serves Japanese food ranging from udon noodles and yakitori to tempura and sashimi. I personally prefer the third floor, for both its food and its atmosphere. Although the menus are in Japanese only, there are extensive plastic-food display cases, showing set meals costing ¥1,500 to ¥3,500 ($12 to $29). This is a very casual restaurant, very much a place for older locals, and can be quite noisy and crowded.

⭐ 26 **Namiki Yabu Soba.** 2-11-9 Kaminarimon. ☎ **03/3841-1340.** Dishes ¥650–¥1,600 ($5.40–$13). No credit cards. Fri–Wed 11:30am–7pm. Station: Asakusa (2 min.). From Kaminarimon Gate, walk south (away from Sensoji Temple); Namiki is on the right side of the street in the 2nd block, a brown building with some bamboo trees, a small maple, and a stone lantern by the front door. NOODLES.

Asakusa's best-known noodle shop offers plain noodles in cold or hot broth as well as more substantial tempura with noodles, all listed in an English menu. Seating is at tables or on tatami mats, but since it's small you won't be able to linger if people are waiting.

6 Ueno

Note: To locate these restaurants, see map on p. 83.

EXPENSIVE

Ueno Seiyoken Grill. In Ueno Park, between Kiyomizu Temple and Toshogu Shrine. ☎ **03/3821-2181.** Main dishes ¥3,000–¥7,000 ($25–$58); set dinners ¥7,000–¥15,000 ($58–$132); set lunches ¥4,000–¥5,000 ($33–$42). AE, DC, JCB, MC, V. Daily 11am–8pm (last order). Station: JR Ueno (6 min.). CLASSIC FRENCH.

Seiyoken opened in 1876 as one of Japan's first restaurants serving Western food. Now a nondescript building dating from the 1950s, it nonetheless remains the best place to eat in Ueno Park, serving pricey but quite good classic French cuisine, with a relaxing view of greenery outside its large windows and classical music playing softly in the background. The English menu, which changes often (the set menus change either daily or weekly), includes seafood such as sole stuffed with shrimp in white wine sauce or lobster Thermidor on grilled scallops in carrot sauce, as well as meat dishes ranging from filet mignon in red wine sauce to roasted duck in green pepper sauce. There's a varied selection of French wines, as well as wines from Germany, California, and Australia. The Grill is located to the right as you enter the building and is not to be confused with the much cheaper utilitarian restaurant to the left.

MODERATE

27 **Izu'ei.** 2-12-22 Ueno. ☎ **03/3831-0954.** Reservations recommended. Main dishes ¥1,500–¥3,000 ($12–$25); set meals ¥2,000–¥8,000 ($17–$67). AE, DC, JCB, MC, V. Daily 11am–9:30pm. Station: JR Ueno (3 min.). On Shinobazu Dori, across the street from Shinobazu Pond and the Shitamachi Museum, next to KFC Home Kitchen. EEL.

Put aside all your prejudices about eels and head for this modern yet traditionally decorated restaurant with a 260-year history dating back to the Edo Period. Since eels are grilled over charcoal, the Japanese place a lot of stock in the quality of the charcoal used, and this place boasts its own furnace in the mountains of Wakayama Prefecture, which produces the best charcoal in Japan. *Unagi donburi* (rice with strips of eel on top), tempura, and sushi are available, as well as set meals. There's no English menu, but there's a display case outside and the menu has some pictures.

INEXPENSIVE

Maharaja. Nagafuji Bldg. Annex, 3rd floor, 4-9-6 Ueno. ☎ **03/3835-0818.** Main dishes ¥1,100–¥1,950 ($9.15–$16); set meals ¥1,200–¥2,900 ($10–$24); lunch buffet ¥980 ($8.15) on weekdays, ¥1,300 ($11) weekends and holidays. AE, DC, JCB, MC, V. Daily 11am–9:30pm (last order). Station: JR Ueno (2 min.). In the annex of a modern building situated between Chuo Dori and the north end of Ameyokocho shopping street. INDIAN.

Decorated in peach and pink, with etched mirrors and lots of brass, this spotless modern restaurant offers curries and tandoori at inexpensive prices, including a good all-you-can-eat lunch buffet served from 11am to 3pm.

7 Shinjuku

In addition to the suggestions below, be sure to check out the restaurant floors of several buildings in Shinjuku, where you can find restaurants in all price categories serving a variety of Japanese and international cuisine. These include the 29th and 30th floors of the **N. S. Building,** where in addition to Al Bacio and Hakkaku (described below) are restaurants serving tempura, tonkatsu, teppanyaki, and sushi, and Italian, German, and French food; the top four floors of the **Sumitomo Building,** where in addition to Seryna (described below) and Donto (see review in "Ginza & Hibiya," above) you'll find more than 20 outlets offering everything from tempura to Chinese cuisine; and the 12th, 13th, and 14th floors of **Takashimaya Times Square,** where in addition to Kappoya Yaozen (described below) are restaurants serving sushi, tonkatsu, noodles, and more.

Note: To locate these restaurants, see map on p. 66.

VERY EXPENSIVE

✪ **New York Grill.** Park Hyatt Hotel, 3–7–1–2 Nishi-Shinjuku. ☎ **03/5322-1234.** Reservations required. Main dishes ¥3,000–¥7,500 ($25–$62); set lunch ¥4,400 ($37); set dinners ¥10,000–¥15,000 ($83–$125); Sat, Sun and holiday brunch ¥5,800 ($48). AE, DC, JCB, MC, V. Mon–Sat 11:30am–2:30pm and 5:30–10:30pm; Sun and holidays 11:30am–2:30pm and 5:30–10pm. Station: Shinjuku (west exit, a 13-min. walk, or 5-min. free shuttle ride); Hatsudai on the Keio Line (7 min.); Tochomae on the Toei No. 12 Line (8 min.). AMERICAN.

On the 52nd floor of Tokyo's most exclusive hotel, the New York Grill has remained *the* place to dine ever since it opened a few years back; some swear it's the most sophisticated restaurant in all of Japan. Surrounded on four sides by glass, it features stunning views (especially at night), artwork by Valerio Adami, live jazz in the evenings, and a 1,700-bottle wine cellar (with an emphasis on California wines). The restaurant backs up its dramatic setting with generous portions of U.S. and Japanese steaks, seafood, and other fare ranging from delectable roast duck to rack of "certified organically raised" lamb, all prepared in an open kitchen. Both the set lunch, which includes main dish, appetizer, and dessert buffet, and the weekend and holiday brunch are among the city's best and most sumptuous (reservations required)—and are great options for those who don't want to pawn their belongings to eat dinner here. I wouldn't miss it.

Seryna. Shinjuku Sumitomo Building., 52nd floor, 2–6–1 Nishi-Shinjuku. ☎ **03/3344-6761.** Reservations recommended for dinner. Set dinners ¥8,000–¥18,000 ($67–$150); set lunches ¥3,800–¥6,000 ($32–$50). AE, DC, JCB, MC, V. Daily 11:30am–9:30pm (last order). Station: Nishi-Shinjuku (2 min.) or Shinjuku (west exit, 7 min.). SHABU-SHABU/SUKIYAKI/TEPPANYAKI.

Perched high above West Shinjuku in one of the city's best-known skyscrapers, Seryna has great city views and, in winter, views of Mt. Fuji from its teppanyaki corner. It's divided into two sections: one specializing in Kobe beef, shabu-shabu, and sukiyaki, the other serving teppanyaki. There's an English menu, and set lunches are reasonable (especially on weekdays when there are teppanyaki set lunches starting at ¥1,800 ($15), making it a good stopping-off place if you're exploring the west side of Shinjuku. Other set lunches feature shabu-shabu, filet steak, and mini-kaiseki.

EXPENSIVE

(28) **Kakiden.** 3-37-11 Shinjuku. ☎ **03/3352-5121.** Reservations recommended for lunch, required for dinner; required also for tatami rooms. Set dinners ¥5,000–¥15,000 ($42–$125); set lunches ¥4,000 ($33). AE, DC, JCB, MC, V. Daily 11am–9pm (last order). Station: Shinjuku (east exit, 1 min.). On the east side of Shinjuku Station, next to My City shopping complex. KAISEKI.

Although located on the eighth floor of a rather uninspiring building, Kakiden has a relaxing teahouse atmosphere, with low chairs, shoji screens, bamboo trees, and soothing traditional Japanese music playing softly in the background. Sibling restaurant to one in Kyoto, founded more than 260 years ago as a catering service for the elite, this kaiseki restaurant serves set meals that change with the seasons, according to what's fresh and available. There's an English menu listing the various set meals available, but probably the best thing to do is to simply pick a meal to fit your budget. The set lunch is available until 3pm. Set dinners include box kaiseki starting at ¥5,000 ($42), mini-kaiseki for ¥8,000 ($67), and kaiseki courses ranging from ¥8,000 to ¥15,000 ($67 to $125). Some of the more common dishes here will include fish, seasonal vegetables, eggs, sashimi, shrimp, and mushrooms, but don't worry if you can't identify everything—I've found that even the Japanese don't always know what they're eating. There are five private tatami rooms, which you must reserve in advance.

MODERATE

✪ **Ban-Thai.** 1-23-14 Kabuki-cho. ☎ **03/3207-0068.** Main dishes ¥1,200–¥1,800 ($10–$15); set dinners ¥2,500–¥6,000 ($21–$50); set lunches ¥600–¥900 ($5–$7.50) weekdays, ¥1,600–¥2,200 ($13–$18) weekends and holidays. AE, JCB, MC, V. Mon–Fri 11:30am–3pm and 5–11pm (last order); Sat–Sun and holidays 11:30am–11pm. Station: Shinjuku (east exit, 7 min.). In East Shinjuku in the seediest part of Kabuki-cho (don't worry, the interior is nicer than the exterior), on a neon-lit pedestrian street connecting the Koma Building with Yasukuni Dori (look for the red neon archway), about halfway down. THAI.

One of Tokyo's longest-running Thai restaurants and credited with introducing authentic Thai food to the Japanese, Ban-Thai still prepares excellent Thai dishes, with 90 mouthwatering items listed on the menu. My favorites are the cold and spicy meat salad, the chicken soup with coconut and lemongrass, and pad Thai noodles. Note that if you make a reservation, there's a ¥300 ($2.50) per-person table charge; also, portions are not large, so if you order several portions and add beer, your tab can really climb.

(29) **Hayashi.** Hide Building, 2-22-5 Kabuki-cho. ☎ **03/3209-5672.** Reservations recommended. Set dinners ¥4,000–¥7,000 ($33–$58). AE, JCB, MC, V. Mon–Sat 5–11:30pm. Closed holidays. Station: Shinjuku (east exit, 10 min.). On the northern edge of Kabuki-cho; you'll know you're getting close when you see Godzilla hanging from a building; the restaurant is just a bit farther to the north, on a corner. JAPANESE GRILL.

This restaurant specializes in Japanese set meals cooked over your own hibachi grill. It's small and cozy, with women in kimono overseeing the cooking operations, taking over if customers seem the least bit hesitant. The rustic interior was imported intact from the mountain region of Takayama. Four set meals are offered. Mine came with sashimi, yakitori, tofu steak, scallops cooked in their shells, shrimp, and vegetables, all grilled one after the other. Watch your alcohol intake—drinks can really add to your bill.

(30) **Kappoya Yaozen.** Takashimaya Times Square, 14th floor, 5-24-2 Sendagaya. ☎ **03/5361-1872.** Set dinners ¥3,800–¥6,000 ($32–$50); set lunches ¥1,400–¥5,000 ($12–$42). AE, JCB, MC, V. Daily 11am–11pm (last order 9:30pm). Station: Shinjuku (south exit, 1 min.). KAISEKI.

Established 280 years ago, this Shinjuku branch in a department store has a rather plain interior, but the hostesses in kimono are friendly and the view of surrounding Shinjuku is pleasant. It's also a very good choice for inexpensive kaiseki. A display case gives an approximation of some of the set meals available (they change with the seasons), but otherwise there's a pamphlet with pictures—or simply order according to your budget. This place is popular with older shoppers at the humongous Takashimaya Times Square, who, probably exhausted, come here for a civilized break.

31 **Suehiro.** N. S. Building, 29th floor, 2-4-1 Nishi-Shinjuku. ☎ **03/3343-3982.** Set dinners ¥3,500–¥8,500 ($29–$71); set lunches ¥650–¥1,750 ($5.40–$15). AE, DC, JCB, MC, V. Daily 11am–2:30pm and 5–10pm. Station: Nishi-Shinjuku (3 min.) or Shinjuku Station (west exit, 8 min.). STEAKS/SHABU-SHABU/SUKIYAKI.

This restaurant, one of many on the 29th floor of the famous Shinjuku skyscraper, offers dining with a view. There's no English-language menu, but a display case shows the various steaks, shabu-shabu, and sukiyaki dishes available. Another Suehiro on the same floor (☎ **03/3349-8788**) with the same open hours offers *ishiyaki*, which is steak cooked on a hot stone at your table.

32 **Tokyo Dai Hanten.** Oriental Wave Building 3F, 5-17-13 Shinjuku. ☎ **03/3202-0121.** Reservations recommended. Small dishes ¥1,800–¥2,800 ($15–$23); dim sum ¥600 ($5). AE, DC, JCB, MC, V. Daily 11:30am–10pm (last order). Station: Shinjuku Sanchome (2 min.). In East Shinjuku, on Yasukuni Dori near Meiji Dori and beside the orange torii leading to Hanazono Shrine). CHINESE.

This large branch of an established Chinese restaurant features an English menu offering everything from braised whole fish and rolled fried prawns to braised beef with vegetables, served up in sizes good for sharing. Set lunches costing ¥1,000 ($8.35) are available until 2:30pm. Dim sum (called *yam cha* in Japanese and served until 8pm) is available from wheeled carts that are pushed through the restaurant on weekends and holidays; the rest of the week it's available only from a Japanese menu with pictures.

Tokyo Kaisen Market. 2-36-1 Kabuki-cho, Shinjuku. ☎ **03/5273-8301.** Reservations recommended. Main dishes ¥900–¥3,000 ($7.50–$25); set dinners ¥3,500–¥6,500 ($29–$54). AE, DC, JCB, MC, V. Mon–Fri 5pm–midnight; Sat–Sun and holidays noon–midnight (last order 10:45pm). Station: Shinjuku (5 min.). In East Shinjuku on the northern edge of Kabuki-cho, a couple blocks east of the white, high-rise Hygeia Building; look for the mural of fish painted on the restaurant's facade. SEAFOOD/CHINESE.

The ground floor of this multilevel, open-beam, warehouse-style restaurant is a real fish market, with tanks of live fish and other sea creatures (I've even seen shark here). If you wish, you can choose what you want from one of the tanks, and then head upstairs to dine on your catch prepared the way you like it. Although market prices vary, a whole lobster, for example, will average ¥6,000 ($50), which you can order steamed, as sashimi, or prepared Chinese style. Not surprisingly, there's lots of sashimi on the English menu with lots of photographs, including *moriawase* (a sample platter), and seafood and other dishes with Chinese influences, including crab, scallops, chicken, pork, fried rice, noodles, dim sum, vegetables, and tofu dishes. Note that there's a ¥400 ($3.35) table charge per person.

33 **Tsunahachi.** 3-31-8 Shinjuku. ☎ **03/3352-1012.** Reservations recommended. Tempura à la carte ¥450–¥1,200 ($3.75–$10); teishoku ¥1,100–¥1,800 ($9.15–$15). AE, JCB, V. Daily 11:15am–10pm. Station: Shinjuku Sanchome (2 min.) or Shinjuku (east exit, 5 min.). Off Shinjuku Dori, on the side street that runs along the east side of Mitsukoshi department store. TEMPURA.

A small, old-fashioned brown building in the heart of fashionable East Shinjuku, this is the main shop of a restaurant that has been serving tempura since 1923. Now there are more than 40 branch restaurants in Japan, including three in Shinjuku Station alone, and others in Ginza and Akasaka. Hours may vary, but most shops are open daily from 11:30am to 10pm. This is the largest outlet, with an English menu, but the easiest option is to order the teishoku, the least expensive of which includes six pieces of tempura, including deep-fried shrimp, cuttlefish, whitefish, green pepper, conger eel, and Japanese pickles. The most expensive teishoku has 10 pieces of tempura.

INEXPENSIVE

Al Bacio. N. S. Building, 29th floor, 2–4–1 Nishi-Shinjuku. ☎ **03/3348-1393.** Pastas ¥900–¥1,400 ($7.50–$12); main dishes ¥1,600–¥2,100 ($13–$17.50); set dinners ¥3,500 and ¥4,800 ($29 and $40). AE, DC, JCB, MC, V. Daily 11:30am–3pm and 5–9:30pm. Station: Nishi-Shinjuku (3 min.) or Shinjuku Station (west exit, 8 min.). ITALIAN.

This is a good place for inexpensive European-style fish in a West Shinjuku high-rise, and the N. S. Building is one of my favorites. A friendly greeting, Italian contemporary music, and a view of the nearby TMG offices are what you get at this casual 29th-floor restaurant. Pasta portions are large enough to serve two. A large blackboard at the door lists daily specials of fresh fish, available baked, grilled, or in papillote; fish for two persons generally averages ¥2,800 ($23).

Daikokuya. Naka-Dai Building, 4th floor, 1–27–5 Kabuki-cho. ☎ **03/3202-7272.** All-you-can-eat main dishes ¥1,650–¥1,950 ($14–$16). No credit cards. Sun–Thurs 5pm–11:30pm, Fri–Sat 3pm–midnight. Station: Shinjuku (east exit, 10 min.). In Kabuki-cho, 1 block west of Koma and across from Hotel Kent. SHABU-SHABU/SUKIYAKI/YAKINIKU.

If you're a big eater traveling on a budget, you won't want to miss dining here. This place offers only three main dishes—shabu-shabu, sukiyaki, and yakiniku—and serves up as much of it as you can consume in a 2-hour period. If you want to drink beer, whiskey, or shochu with your meal, add ¥900 ($7.50) to the above prices and you'll be able to drink to your heart's content as well. Popular with students and young office workers, Daikokuya is a rather strange place (its interior is kind of cavernous—maybe harking back to cave-age gluttony?), and needless to say, can be quite rowdy.

Din Tai Fung. Takashimaya Times Square, 10th floor, 5–24–2 Sendagaya. ☎ **03/5361-1381.** Dim sum ¥400–¥1,000 ($3.35–$8.35); set meals ¥1,000–¥1,300 ($8.35–$11). JCB, MC, V. Daily 10am–7:30pm. Station: Shinjuku (south exit, 1 min.). CHINESE.

One of several dining options on the 10th floor of Takashimaya department store in the Takashimaya Times Square shopping complex, this is the Tokyo branch of one of Taipei's best-selling dim-sum spots; it's so popular that you may have to wait for a table. A display case outside the door shows the various dim sum and noodle and rice dishes available, all priced under ¥1,000 ($9), as well as three set meals from which to choose.

✪ ㉞ **Hakkaku.** N. S. Building, 29th floor, 2–4–1 Nishi-Shinjuku. ☎ **03/3345-1848.** Main dishes ¥480–¥800 ($4–$6.65); set lunches ¥700–¥900 ($5.85–$7.50). AE, DC, JCB, MC, V. Daily 11am–10pm. Station: Nishi-Shinjuku (3 min.) or Shinjuku Station (west exit, 8 min). VARIED JAPANESE.

This lively, crowded establishment has a lot going for it: a corner location in a skyscraper with expansive views over Yoyogi Park, inexpensive dishes and meals, and Kirin beer on tap. Although its decor and food resemble that of a bar, it opens much earlier than most bars and offers more variety, including sashimi, grilled fish, *nikujaga*

A Note on Japanese Symbols

Many restaurants, hotels, and other establishments in Japan do not have signs giving their names in Roman (English-language) letters. As an aid to the reader, the second appendix to this book lists the Japanese symbols for all such places described in this guide. Each set of characters representing an establishment name has a number, which corresponds to the number that appears inside the box before the establishment's name in the text. Thus, to find the Japanese symbols for, say, **Hakkaku,** refer to no. 34 in appendix B.

(a very tasty beef and potato stew), and salads. Yakitori, beginning at ¥300 ($2.50) per skewer, includes asparagus wrapped in bacon and tsukune, two of my favorites. Since the menu is only in Japanese, perhaps you'll want to sit at the Robatayaki counter, where you can point at various dishes, watch them being prepared on the open grill, and then receive them from a wooden paddle passed in your direction.

(35) **Irohanihoheto.** 3-15-15 Shinjuku, 6th floor. ☎ **03/3359-1682.** Yakitori skewers ¥350-¥450 ($2.90-$3.75); main dishes ¥350-¥650 ($2.90-$5.40). No credit cards. Sun-Thurs 5pm-midnight, Fri-Sat 5pm-4am. Station: Shinjuku Sanchome (5 min.) or Shinjuku (east exit, 10 min.). On Shinjuku's east side, on Yasukuni Dori, next to Isetan Kaikan. YAKITORI/VARIED JAPANESE.

Irohanihoheto is a chain of drinking establishments with a menu so varied, extensive, and cheap that most people eat here as well. Extremely popular with university students, it bills itself as an "Antique Pub," the meaning of which becomes even more elusive once you're inside. The main hall looks like an imitation barn to me, with rafters, hurricane lamps, and glass lanterns everywhere (a bit bright for my taste). A second room is more traditional Japanese, with tatami seating and folk crafts hanging about. People don't come here for the decor, though—it's the prices that draw them in. The menu of Japanese and Western food is in Japanese only, but there are pictures; it includes yakitori, fried noodles, french fries, sashimi, grilled meatballs, niku-jaga (potato-and-meat stew, one of my favorites), and dozens of other dishes.

(36) **Negishi.** 2-45-2 Kabuki-cho. ☎ **03/3232-8020.** Main dishes ¥600-¥1,100 ($5-$9.15); lunch teishoku ¥820-¥1,280 ($6.85-$11); set dinner ¥1,000-¥1,100 ($8.35-$9.15). No credit cards. Mon-Sat 11am-3pm and 5-11pm; Sun and holidays 11am-10pm. Station: Shinjuku (7 min.) or Seibu Shinjuku (3 min.). In East Shinjuku between America Boulevard and Hygeia (a white high-rise), on a tiny side street beside Green Plaza. JAPANESE STEWS/OX-TAIL SOUP/YAM.

You could easily overlook Negishi, a tiny hole-in-the-wall with just a counter and a few tables. It would be a shame, however, to miss its healthy, low-calorie foods and friendly atmosphere. It specializes in Japanese stews, ox-tail soup, and *mugi-toro* (boiled wheat with grated yam). You might also want to try *tan-yaki*, grilled ox tongue, which is low in calories and fat but rich in protein. There's no English menu, but there are pictures of each dish. Befitting a health-conscious store, no smoking is allowed during lunch.

Shakey's. 3-30-11 Shinjuku. ☎ **03/3341-0322.** All-you-can-eat pizza lunch ¥750 ($6.25) Mon-Sat, ¥950 ($7.90) Sun and holidays. No credit cards. Daily 11am-3pm. Station: Shinjuku Sanchome (1 min.). In East Shinjuku on Shinjuku Dori, in the basement of a building across from the Isetan department store. PIZZA.

If you want to gorge yourself on pizza, the best deal is at one of many Shakey's around town, offering all-you-can-eat pizza, spaghetti, and fried potatoes for lunch every day.

8 Harajuku & Aoyama

EXPENSIVE

✪ **Manin.** 2–22–12 Jingumae. ☎ **03/3478-3778.** Reservations recommended. Main dishes ¥3,000–¥6,000 ($25–$50); set dinners ¥8,000–¥15,000 ($67–$125); AE, DC, JCB, MC, V. Mon–Sat 6–10pm. Closed holidays. Station: Harajuku, Meiji-Jingumae, or Gaienmae (10 min.). ITALIAN.

You need both money and an appreciation for starkness and space to enjoy dining in this very modern Italian restaurant. Its dining area, one of the most unusual interiors I've ever seen, features a 30-foot-high ceiling, massive black beams, red velvet and mahogany walls, and a black floor—all designed by Philippe Starck. The menu, in Italian and Japanese, offers seafood, veal, lamb, chicken, and beef dishes in a variety of styles that change with the seasons, as well as set meals that change daily. As this place is difficult to find, you may want to come by taxi from one of the nearest stations.

✪ **Nobu.** 6–10–17 Minami Aoyama. ☎ **03/5467-0022.** Reservations recommended. Sushi and sashimi (per piece) ¥400–¥1,400 ($3.35–$12); tempura à la carte (per piece) ¥300–¥1,400 ($2.50–$12); set dinners ¥5,000–¥15,000 ($42–$125); set lunches ¥3,000–¥7,000 ($25–$58). AE, DC, JCB, MC, V. Mon–Fri 11:30am–2pm; daily 6–10pm (last order). Station: Shibuya or Omotesando (15 min.). On Roppongi Dori, near Komazawa Dori and Kotto Dori. NOUVELLE JAPANESE/PACIFIC RIM.

Everyone is talking about Nobu, a good indication that you'll need reservations to dine here. Sister restaurant to New York's Nobu, it's a classy, modern establishment, the place to see and be seen—and you can count on being seen, since the staff yells "Irashaimase!" ("Welcome!") the minute anyone is ushered into the dining room, noisily announcing each arrival. Jazz plays softly in the background, flowers sit atop each table, and the efficient staff keeps everything running smoothly. The food, beautifully presented and served one dish at a time, is a unique blend of Pacific Rim ingredients (not quite Japanese) with decidedly American/Latin influences. Sushi and sashimi are served, but so are sushi rolls, including California rolls (with avocado) and soft-shell crab rolls. Other dishes include yellowtail sashimi with jalapeno, scallop sashimi with Peruvian red chili paste, spicy sour shrimp, and black cod with miso. If ordering is too much of a chore, you can leave your meal to the discretion of Chef Matsuhisa by ordering the Omakase, a complete chef's-choice dinner starting at ¥10,000 ($83). Prices are less expensive at lunch; in fine weather, you can dine on an outdoor patio with a retractable roof.

Sabatini. Suncrest Building., 2–13–5 Kita-Aoyama. ☎ **03/3402-3812.** Reservations recommended for dinner. Pasta ¥1,800–¥3,400 ($15–$28); main dishes ¥2,100–¥6,500 ($17.50–$54); set dinner ¥15,000 ($125); set lunch ¥5,000 ($42). AE, DC, JCB, MC, V. Daily 11:30am–2:30pm and 5:30–11pm. Station: Gaienmae (2 min.). On Aoyama Dori near Gaien-Nishi Dori. ITALIAN.

This restaurant, with its Italian furniture and tableware and strolling musicians, seems as if it has been moved intact from the Old World. In fact, the only thing to remind you that you're in Tokyo is your Japanese waiter. The three Italian brothers who own Sabatini have had a restaurant in Rome for more than 30 years. They take turns overseeing the Tokyo restaurants, so one of them is always here. The menu includes soups, spaghetti, seafood, veal, steak, lamb, and a variety of vegetables. You can do it cheaper at lunch with the set menu, which gives you a choice of soup or pasta, fish or meat, salad, dessert, and coffee. There's also brunch on Saturday and Sunday for ¥5,000 ($42).

MODERATE

In addition to the choices below, also consider **La Ranarita,** 1–13–14 Jingumae (☎ 03/3478-3310); see "Asakusa," above for a review.

✪ **Aux Bacchanales.** Palais France Building, 1–6–1 Jingumae (on Meiji Dori). ☎ **03/ 5474-0076.** Main dishes ¥2,400–¥2,700 ($20–$22). AE, MC, V. Cafe, daily 10am–11pm (last order); restaurant daily 5:30–10:30pm (last order). Station: Meiji-Jingumae (2 min.) or Harajuku (7 min.). On Meiji Dori, near Takeshita Dori. FRENCH.

A real French sidewalk cafe, right in Tokyo's favorite people-watching neighborhood of Harajuku. Actually, it consists of two sections, both of which are packed on weekends: a brasserie with sandwiches and omelets priced at less than ¥650 ($5.40), strong espresso, and good cheap wine (counter prices are slightly cheaper than at one of the sit-down tables, just like in France); and a restaurant with both outdoor and indoor seating offering such dishes as grilled lobster, steak tartare, lapin á la moutarde, and lamb with thyme.

Cay. Spiral Building basement, 5–6–23 Minami-Aoyama. ☎ **03/3498-5790.** Reservations recommended. Main dishes ¥1,400–¥3,500 ($12–$29); set meal ¥3,500 ($29). AE, DC, JCB, MC, V. Mon–Sat 5:30–11pm (last order). Closed holidays. Station: Omotesando (B1 exit, 1 min.). On Aoyama Dori. THAI.

The Spiral Building, one of Aoyama Dori's most fashionable buildings, is home to this upscale Thai restaurant with an English menu. Its food, toned down for Japanese palates, includes roast-beef salad, hot-and-sour shrimp soup, deep-fried fish with coconut or chili sauce, deep-fried chicken Thai-style, fried duck with lime sauce, and Thai curries and noodles. Live music—ranging from Hawaiian or Okinawan to jazz and rock— is offered about once a week, for which there's an extra admission charge of ¥800 to ¥2,000 ($6.65 to $17).

Daini's Table. 6–3–14 Minami Aoyama. ☎ **03/3407-0363.** Reservations recommended. Main dishes ¥1,800–¥3,500 ($15–$29); set dinners ¥5,000–¥12,000 ($42–$100). AE, DC, MC, V. Daily 5:30–11pm (last order). Station: Omotesando (6 min.). NOUVELLE CHINESE.

This elegant Chinese restaurant, located next to the Blue Note jazz club off Kotto Dori, serves intriguing dishes that are nicely presented one dish at a time rather than all at once as in most Chinese restaurants. It offers both traditional dishes (roast Peking duck, steamed chicken with sesame sauce, boiled prawns with red chili sauce, and hot-and-sour Peking-style soup) and more unusual combinations (stirfried tiger prawns with spinach and garlic and stir-fried shredded beef with soybean paste in a pancake roll). Everything I've had here has been delicious. Expect to spend about ¥7,000 ($58) per person.

✪ **El Castellano.** 2–9–11 Shibuya. ☎ **03/3407-7197.** Reservations recommended. Main dishes ¥2,300–¥2,500 ($19–$21). No credit cards. Mon–Sat 6–11pm. Station: Omotesando or Shibuya (10 min.). On Aoyama Dori, about halfway between Aoyama and Shibuya, across and down the street from the National Children's Castle (not a big sign, so look). CASTILIAN.

Señor Vicente Garcia is El Castellano and a true host; leave Tokyo, return four years later—and he still remembers who you are. And we, his faithful clients, how can we forget his smiling face? The walls of this very tiny place are covered in signatures of happy customers, some of whom (having drunk a little too much red wine) may be dancing on the tables to flamenco music. In short, this place makes us feel at home. The custom is to let Señor Garcia order for you (although not de rigueur); he'll choose the best appetizer (tortilla or gambas, perhaps) and, of course, paella, the best this side of Sevilla. Though you can eat for less, expect to spend ¥5,000 ($42) per person for dinner with wine.

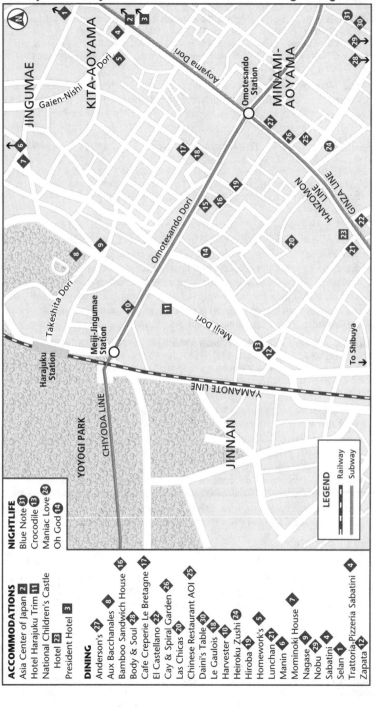

Harajuku & Aoyama Accommodations, Dining & Nightlife

ACCOMMODATIONS
Asia Center of Japan **2**
Hotel Harajuku Trim **11**
National Children's Castle
Hotel **23**
President Hotel **3**

NIGHTLIFE
Blue Note **31**
Crocodile **13**
Maniac Love **24**
Oh God **14**

DINING
Anderson's **27**
Aux Bacchanales **8**
Bamboo Sandwich House **16**
Body & Soul **28**
Cafe Creperie Le Bretagne **17**
El Castellano **22**
Cay & Spiral Garden **26**
Las Chicas **20**
Chinese Restaurant AOI **25**
Daini's Table **30**
Le Gaulois **18**
Harvester **10**
Heiroku Zushi **19**
Hiroba **19**
Homework's **5**
Lunchan **21**
Manin **6**
Mominoki House **7**
Nagase **9**
Nobu **29**
Sabatini **1**
Selan **4**
Trattoria-Pizzeria Sabatini **4**
Zapata **12**

117

Le Gaulois. 4–3–21 Jingumae. ☎ **03/3404-0820.** Reservations recommended. Main dishes ¥2,000–¥2,400 ($17–$20); set dinners ¥3,800–¥6,000 ($32–$50); set lunch ¥2,400 ($20). AE, DC, MC, V. Mon–Sat noon–2pm and 6–9pm (last order). Closed 2nd Mon of each month. Station: Omotesando (4 min.). Off Omotesando Dori; take the side street opposite the Hanae Mori Building and turn left. FRENCH.

This pleasant, unpretentious bistro is so tiny there's only one table and a counter, where diners can watch the owner-chef prepare fresh fish of the day, beef in red wine, grilled lamb with basil and other dishes from the open kitchen. You almost feel like an invited guest in a private home.

Lunchan. 1–2–5 Shibuya. ☎ **03/5466-1398.** Reservations required for Sun brunch. Pizza ¥1,400–¥1,600 ($12–$13); main dishes ¥1,600–¥2,800 ($13–$23); set lunches ¥1,200–¥2,800 ($10–$23); Sun brunch ¥2,500 ($21). AE, DC, JCB, MC, V. Mon–Sat 11:30am–10pm; Sun 11am–9pm. Station: Omotesando or Shibuya (10 min.). Easy to find, halfway between Shibuya and Aoyama and just off Aoyama Dori on the side street south of the National Children's Castle. AMERICAN.

Good American food is the forte of this contemporary, open, and airy bistro, with a dinner menu that includes pasta, pizza, sandwiches, and meat entrees. Choose from among such dishes as pizza al forno with Italian smoked ham, fresh mushrooms, oregano and hot peppers; meat loaf; grilled snapper with lentil saffron sauce; steak; or a smoked-chicken pita sandwich. A wide selection of lunch specials is offered, including sandwiches with all the trimmings. Sunday brunch, which includes a glass of champagne and is served until 3pm, features breakfast treats like eggs Benedict, turkey chili omelet, and Belgian waffles.

Selan. 2–1–19 Kita-Aoyama. ☎ **03/3478-2200.** Pasta and pizza ¥1,200–¥2,200 ($10–$18); main dishes ¥2,200–¥2,800 ($18–$23); set lunches ¥1,800–¥5,000 ($15–$42). AE, DC, JCB, MC, V. Mon–Fri 11:30am–2:30pm and 6–9:30pm; Sat–Sun 10am–2:30pm and 6–9:30pm. Station: Gaienmae or Aoyama-Itchome (5 min.). At the entrance to Meiji-Jingu-gaien Park. ITALIAN.

This restaurant has one of the most envied spots in all of Tokyo—on a gingko-lined street that serves as the entrance of Meiji-Jingu-gaien Park. The food, Italian with Japanese and French influences, is rather ordinary, with such main dishes as veal cutlet Milanese style, grilled Japanese steak, and roasted chicken in a garlic sauce, plus an assortment of pizzas and pastas—but on a warm summer's day, there's nothing more sublime than sitting on the outdoor terrace and reveling in all that greenery. The hours above are for the first-floor restaurant, with large picture windows; the ground floor cafe, which offers the same menu, boasts an outdoor terrace open throughout the day—make that throughout the year, thanks to outdoor heaters.

INEXPENSIVE

In addition to the choices below, also consider the Aoyama branch of **Honoji,** 5–50–2 Jingumae (☎ **03/5467-6770;** open Monday to Saturday 11:30am to 2pm and 5:30 to 11pm), serving up good homestyle Japanese cooking. It's off Aoyama Dori on the second side street past Kinokuniya grocery, on the right as you walk from Omotesando Station (the closest station) in the direction of Shibuya. See "Roppongi & Nishi Azabu," below, for a complete review. Also, **La Boheme,** 6–7–18 Jingumae (☎ **03/3400-3406**) serves pasta and pizza daily from 11:30am to 5am. See "Shibuya," below, for a review.

Anderson. 5–1–26 Minami-Aoyama. ☎ **03/3407-4833.** Sandwiches ¥550–¥800 ($4.60–$6.65). No credit cards. Mon–Fri 8am–10pm, Sat–Sun 9am–10pm. Closed 3rd Mon of each month. Station: Omotesando (1 min.). On Aoyama Dori. SANDWICHES.

This popular bakery has a self-serve deli and sandwich bar in its basement, where you can choose from a variety of salads and cold and warm sandwiches, including ham and cheese, chicken salad, and lobster and avocado. On the second and third floors is a restaurant, with waitress service, featuring more elaborate, open-faced sandwiches and stews and seating near big windows, good for people-watching.

Bamboo Sandwich House. 5–8–8 Jingumae. ☎ **03/3407-8427.** Sandwiches ¥340–¥700 ($2.85–$5.85). No credit cards. Daily 11am–10pm. Station: Omotesando or Meiji-Jingumae (5 min.), Harajuku (8 min.). Off Omotesando Dori, on a side street that runs beside the Paul Stuart shop. SANDWICHES.

Although its sandwiches aren't as good as Anderson's (see above), its setting is much more hip; it even boasts an outdoor terrace. You can select from 20 sandwich fillings on your choice of bread. In addition, this may be the only place in town to offer a bottomless cup of coffee (every day except Sundays and holidays), for a mere ¥220 ($1.85), a price that hasn't changed in a dozen years. The sandwich fillings can be a bit odd (if you've been searching for chicken with tuna sauce or a potato-and-meat-sauce gratin filling, you've found your place), but there are also more mundane choices like tuna or roast pork, and with the great outdoor seating, even a weird sandwich seems okay here.

✪ **Las Chicas.** 5–47–6 Jingumae. ☎ **03/3407-6865.** Main dishes ¥1,350–¥2,700 ($11–$22.50). AE, DC, JCB, V. Mon–Sat 11am–11pm, Sun 10am–11pm. Station: Omotesando (5 min.). Take the Kinokuniya exit and head down Aoyama Dori toward Shibuya, taking a right at Citibank; Las Chicas is down this small street, near the end on the left. INTERNATIONAL.

Opened by fashion house Vision Network, Las Chicas is the trendy cafe/bar in a complex housing several alternative bars and shops, including a hairdresser specializing in outrageous colors and styles, a tattoo artist, and stores selling original clothing, world music, and coffee-table books. Popular as a hangout for young foreigners and those in the fashion/design business, Las Chicas has an English-language menu and foreign waiters and cooks. Its food is fun and eclectic, borrowing ingredients and recipes from around the world, with appetizers ranging from lemon myrtle pancake with smoked salmon and wasabi mayonnaise to skewered prawns and lotus root with a Thai dippping sauce. In addition to lighter fare like focaccia, pizzetta, and pasta, it also offers a limited selection of main dishes that might include a New Zealand rack of lamb with pumpkin, sweet potato and coconut mash or rotisserie chicken with potato and thyme cake. Top off your meal with one of the best homemade desserts in town, such as a brownie or carrot cake. It's also a good spot for espresso, fruit smoothies, wine, or beer. There's outdoor seating as well. Be sure to explore the rest of the complex.

Chinese Restaurant AOI. 5–9–1 Minami-Aoyama. ☎ **03/3407-9727.** Main dishes ¥1,200–¥3,000 ($10–$25); dim sum ¥600–¥1,200 ($5–$10). DC, JCB, MC, V. Mon–Sat 11:30am–11pm, Sun 11:30am–10pm. Station: Omotesando (B1 exit, 1 min.). On a small side street off Aoyama Dori. CHINESE.

This popular, casual, noisy restaurant offers more than 100 items on its regular English-language menu, which has pictures. Two different sizes of plates are available for the selections of chicken, pork, beef, shark's fin, tofu, seafood, vegetables, and casserole dishes. I especially like this place for a dim-sum lunch, with about 30 different varieties from which to choose.

Cafe Creperie Le Bretagne. 4–9–8 Jingumae. ☎ **03/3478-7855.** Crepes ¥600–¥1,400 ($5–$12). No credit cards. Tues–Thurs 11:30am–11pm; Fri–Sat 11:30–midnight; Sun 11:30am–10pm (last order). Station: Omotesando. Off Omotesando Dori; take the side street opposite the Hanae Mori Building and turn left. CREPES.

With an inviting open-fronted shop, posters of Brittany, natural wood and brick, and a French staff, this is *the* place for crepes, filled with yummy fruit or chocolate or such irresistible combinations as banana, chocolate, and rum, or orange sorbet, vanilla ice cream, and Grand Marnier. Kids love this place, too.

Harvester. 1–13–13 Jingumae. ☎ **03/5411-7621.** Main dishes ¥320–¥800 ($2.65–$6.65). No credit cards. Daily 8am–10:30pm. Station: Harajuku or Meiji-Jingumae (1 min.). On Omotesando Dori, between Harajuku and Meiji-Jingumae stations. ROAST CHICKEN.

Here's an inexpensive, quick stop for light fare and people-watching. Airy, with open seating on Omotesando Dori, this is the KFC chain's upscale version of fast-food chicken, specializing in roasted chicken at reasonable prices. In addition to ordering a quarter, half, three-quarters, or a whole chicken, you can also order chicken curry, pita sandwiches, and side dishes. From 11am to 2pm Monday through Friday, you can get a roasted chicken plate which includes a side dish, bagel, and dessert for ¥700 ($5.85).

(37) **Heirokuzushi.** 5–8–5 Jingumae. ☎ **03/3498-3968.** Sushi ¥120 and ¥240 ($1 and $2) each. No credit cards. Daily 11am–9pm. Station: Meiji-Jingumae (2 min.) or Omotesando (5 min.). On Omotesando Dori, close to the Oriental Bazaar. SUSHI.

Bright (a bit too bright), clean, and modern, this is another one of those fast-food sushi bars where plates of food are conducted along the counter on a conveyor belt. Customers help themselves to whatever strikes their fancy. To figure your bill, the cashier simply counts the number of plates you took from the conveyor belt. There's a plastic display case of take-out sushi, which you might want to eat in nearby Yoyogi Park.

Hiroba. Crayon House, 3–8–15 Kita Aoyama. ☎ **03/3406-6409.** Dishes ¥300–¥500 ($2.50–$4.15). No credit cards. Daily 11am–2pm and 5–10pm. Station: Omotesando (2 min.). Off Omotesando Dori, on the side street to the right of the Hanae Mori Building. JAPANESE HEALTH FOOD.

Located in the basement of the Crayon House, which specializes in Japanese children's books, this self-service natural food restaurant offers organic veggies, fish, brown rice, and other health foods. Simply go through the line and pick up the dishes you want (three or four will probably be enough). When you're done eating, clear your own tray and pay at the cash register near the coffee shop across the hall. The dining hall is very simple (its atmosphere reminds me of a potluck supper in a church basement), and because of the upstairs bookstore, there are likely to be families here.

Homework's. 3–1–28 Jingumae. ☎ **03/3497-1515.** Hamburgers and sandwiches ¥850–¥1,500 ($7.10–$12.50). No credit cards. Mon-Sat 11am–9pm, Sun and holidays 11am–6pm. Station: Gaienmae (3 min.). From the station, walk on Aoyama Dori in the direction of Shibuya; turn right at Bell Commons onto Gaien-Nishi Dori; it will be on your left. HAMBURGERS.

How far will you go for a decent burger? After opening its first shop a few years back in a largely ex-pat residential area (where it quickly gained a faithful clientele), Homework's has since expanded into tourist areas, including this one not too far off the beaten path. Simple, with an open-fronted facade and an interior of natural wood, it offers more than a dozen different hamburgers in three sizes with various toppings as well as sandwiches, soups, and salads.

✪ **Mominoki House.** 2–18–5 Jingumae. ☎ **03/3405-9144.** Main dishes ¥1,000–¥2,000 ($8.35–$17); set lunches ¥1,000–¥1,500 ($8.35–$12.50). No credit cards. Mon–Sat 11am–10pm (last order); holidays 3–10pm. Station: Meiji-Jingumae (10 min.) or Harajuku (15 min.). From the Meiji Dori/Omotesando intersection, walk north on Meiji Dori, turning right at the pedestrian overpass; it will be on the left, at the 2nd street on the corner. NOUVELLE JAPANESE/MACROBIOTIC.

Mominoki House dishes could be described as French, except they're the creations of a very busy chef who uses lots of soy sauce, ginger, Japanese vegetables, and macrobiotic foods. This alternative restaurant, in a category by itself, features hanging plants and split-level dining, allowing for more privacy than one would think possible in such a tiny place. Its recorded jazz collection is extensive, and on occasional Saturday nights there's live music beginning at 8pm (music charge: ¥1,000/$8.35). Dinner features approximately 50 dishes à la carte, and may include the likes of tofu steak, duck, sole, escargots, eggplant gratin (delicious), salads, and homemade sorbet. Note that there's a dinner table charge of ¥500 ($4.15) per person. Especially good deals are the five daily lunch specials, featuring brown rice, miso soup, seasonal vegetables, fish or another main dish, and a glass of wine. There's an English menu, but daily specials are written on the blackboard, in Japanese only. The owner speaks English, so if in doubt ask him what he recommends.

Nagase. 3–21–12 Jingumae. ☎ **03/3423-1925.** Reservations required weekends. Set dinners ¥2,300 and ¥3,500 ($19–$29); set lunches ¥1,000–¥2,300 ($8.35–$19). No credit cards. Tues–Sat 11:30am–2pm and 5:30–9:30pm; Sun and holidays 11:30am–2pm and 5:30–8:30pm (last order). Station: Meiji-Jingumae (3 min.) or Harajuku (8 min.). On the opposite side of Meiji Dori from Takeshita Dori, on a side street nicknamed Harajuku Dori; it's on the left side of the street, up on the 2nd floor. FRENCH.

This is another one of those casual neighborhood bistros offering great food at very reasonable prices that made its debut following the economic recession. Like most of the others, a cut in prices means a crowding of tables to accommodate as many diners as possible, but except for the most special of occasions, I'll gladly settle for cheaper prices over spaciousness. A French menu lists set menus that give a choice of a half-dozen main dishes, which might include fish of the day, beef Burgundy, *confit de canard,* or *noisettes de lamb au thym,* along with a salad or side dish, bread, and coffee. My ¥1,000 ($9) lunch was one of the best Western meals I've ever had in Japan at that price—a salad with boiled egg, chicken, mushrooms, and tomato, followed by whitefish on mashed potatoes with an eggplant-tomato sauce subtly flavored with curry.

Trattoria-Pizzeria Sabatini. Suncrest Building., 2–13–5 Kita-Aoyama. ☎ **03/3402-2027.** Pasta and pizza ¥1,400–¥1,800 ($12–$15); main dishes ¥2,200–¥3,000 ($18–$25); set lunches ¥2,100–¥3,500 ($17.50–$29). AE, DC, JCB, MC, V. Daily 11:30am–2:30pm and 5:30–11pm. Station: Gaienmae (1 min.). At the intersection of Aoyama Dori and Gaien-Nishi Dori. ITALIAN.

This basement restaurant, opened in 1984 and owned by three brothers from Rome who also operate an expensive Italian restaurant in the same building (called Sabatini; see review above), offers the closest thing to real pizza in town. Many ingredients are flown in from Italy, including olive oil, huge slabs of Parmesan and other cheeses, as well as the restaurant's large wine selection; they've even shipped in a pasta machine. In addition to pizzas, there's also spaghetti, lasagne, fettuccine, and meat and seafood dishes. All you need order, however, is pizza.

Zapata. 6–18–10 Jingumae. ☎ **03/3499-5888.** Main dishes ¥1,400–¥2,600 ($12–$22); set lunches ¥900–¥1,500 ($7.50–$12.50) weekdays, ¥1,000–¥3,500 ($8.35–$29) weekends and holidays. MC V. Daily 11:45am–1am. Station: Meiji-Jingumae or Shibuya (7 min.) On Meiji Dori, about halfway between Shibuya and Harajuku. MEXICAN.

I've never found a Mexican restaurant in Japan I can heartily recommend without reservations. This one advertises its food as Tex-Mex but doesn't quite live up to its claims. As elsewhere, its dishes are a Japanese interpretation of Mexican food, which in this case doesn't mean it's necessarily bad. With an upbeat, modern interior—a kind of Aztec meets Southwestern chic—and a friendly staff, it offers mainly seafood, including jumbo prawns with corn meal and crab meat and fish mousse with chili curry sauce, as well as such standbys as mole poblano, enchiladas, and tacos. The best deal by far is the all-you-can-eat dinner available Sunday and Monday for ¥1,980 ($16.50): Simply choose among the many dishes on offer, which are cooked to order, and feast to your heart's content.

9 Shibuya

Shibuya serves as a major commuter nucleus and boasts the largest concentration of fashion department stores in Tokyo. It caters primarily to students and young office workers, with a lively nightlife scene offering inexpensive dining and drinking. In addition to the suggestions below, consider **Honoji,** 1–11–3 Shibuya (☎ **03/3407-4430**), open Monday to Saturday 11:30am to 2pm and 5:30 to 11pm (see "Roppongi & Nishi Azabu," below).

INEXPENSIVE

㉟ **Irohanihoheto.** 1–19–3 Jinnan, Shibuya-ku. ☎ **03/3476-1683.** Main dishes ¥380–¥980 ($3.15–$8.15). AE, DC, MC, V. Sun–Thurs 5pm–3am; Fri–Sat 5pm–4am. Station: Shibuya (Hachiko exit, 7 min.). In the basement of a modern building on the street that runs downhill from Parco I and II department stores to the JR Yamanote overhead tracks. YAKITORI/VARIED.

This boisterous drinking establishment offers inexpensive dining and is very popular with university students; if you get here after 7pm, you may have to wait for a place to sit. The extensive menu of both Japanese and Western food is in Japanese, but with pictures, and features *nikujaga* (potato-and-meat stew), fried tofu, *oden* (a tofu, fishcake, and vegetable stew), yakitori, fried noodles, potato salad, sashimi, and much more.

La Boheme. 1–6–8 Jinnan. ☎ **03/3477-0481.** Pizza and pasta ¥800–¥1,450 ($6.65–$12). AE, DC, JCB, MC, V. Daily 11:30am–5am. Station: Shibuya (10 min.). At the top of Koen Dori, across from NHK. ITALIAN.

The food is passable, but what sets La Boheme apart is that it's open every day until 5am (ditto for Zest Cantina in the same building, under the same management and serving Mexican food). The pasta ranges from lasagne to bolognese, along with some Japanese-style versions that include steamed breast of chicken with Japanese baby leek, spinach, and sesame oil, and fresh shrimp and basil with garlic, olive oil, and shimeji mushrooms.

You'll find other La Boheme restaurants in Harajuku at 6–7–18 Jinguma (☎ **03/3400-3406**) and in the Ginza at 6–4–1 Ginza (☎ **03/3572-5005**), both open daily from 11:30am to 5am.

Siam. 1–15–8 Jinnan. ☎ **03/3770-0550.** Main dishes ¥900–¥1,500 ($7.50–$12.50); lunch buffet ¥1,000 ($8.35). AE, DC, JCB, MC, V (accepted at dinner only). Daily 11:30am–3pm and 5:30–10:30pm. Station: Shibuya (8 min.). On Koen Dori, the road leading uphill past Seed, Loft, Parco, and the Tobacco and Salt Museum, on the right side. THAI.

This Thai-staffed restaurant packs them in with one of the city's best lunchtime deals—an all-you-can-eat lunch buffet of salad, a few noodle and curry dishes, rice, and soup. Dishes may not be as spicy as one might like, as they're toned down to suit the Japanese palate, but it's a good place to fill up on Thai cuisine. Dinner is à la carte from an English menu.

There's another branch in the Ginza at 5–8–17 Ginza (☎ **03/3572-4001**).

10 Ebisu & Meguro

EXPENSIVE

✪ **Ozawa.** 4–9–23 Shiroganedai. ☎ **03/3442-1171.** Reservations required. Set dinners ¥7,500–¥10,000 ($62.50–$83); set lunches ¥3,500–¥5,000 ($29–$42). AE, DC, JCB, MC, V. Tues–Sun noon–3pm and 6–11pm. Station: Meguro (east exit, 7 min.). On Gaien-Nishi Dori, near Meguro Dori. FRENCH.

There's no mistaking this unusual building, a striking green modern structure designed by Philippe Starck. In the basement is this smart-looking restaurant, with a small open kitchen and limited seating. Only set meals are served, but diners select courses from various hot and cold hors d'oeuvres and seafood and meat dishes that might include lobster flan, lamb cutlet with herbs, or grilled pigeon.

Shirogane. 6–16–28 Shirogane. ☎ **03/3449-0033.** Set dinners ¥6,000–¥14,000 ($50–$117); set lunches ¥2,000–¥10,000 ($17–$83). AE, MC, V. Mon–Sat 11:30am–2pm and 5:30–10pm (last order), Sun and holidays 11:30am–2pm and 5:30–9pm (last order). Station: Meguro or Ebisu (15 min.). On Gaien-Nishi Dori. SHABU-SHABU/KAISEKI.

Located on the third floor of a modern building that also contains a Mercedes-Benz showroom, this upscale Japanese restaurant is decorated with such traditional touches as an entry flagstone pathway with lit lanterns, wooden floors, and bamboo screens between the tables. It's popular with both Japanese business types and foreigners living in the pricey surrounding neighborhood; those who really want to impress their guests reserve one of the private rooms, which cost an extra ¥5,000 to ¥8,000 ($42 to $67). An English-language menu lists various kaiseki and shabu-shabu courses available for dinner. Lunch offers several obento box lunches and more substantial kaiseki courses.

MODERATE

Cafe Francais. Yebisu Garden Place, 1–13–1 Mita. ☎ **03/5424-1338.** Reservations recommended. Main dishes ¥2,500–¥3,800 ($21–$32); set dinners ¥4,000–¥7,500 ($33–$62.50); set lunches ¥3,200–¥4,000 ($27–$33). AE, DC, JCB, MC, V. Daily 11:30am–2:30pm and 5:30–9pm (last order). Station: Ebisu (6 min.). FRENCH.

Housed in a reproduction 18th-century French château planted in the midst of swanky Yebisu Garden Place, this ground-floor brasserie offers nouveau French cuisine at a fraction of what the same food costs at the more expensive and more formal La Salle à Manger upstairs. The only difference is that you'll get a course or two less for lunch and dinner. Otherwise, Cafe Francais is fancy enough for most tastes, with its Louis XV paneled dining room complete with portraits. On warm sunny days, you can dine outdoors on the terrace. The wine list is extensive, with more than 300 vintages from throughout France, and at reasonable prices to boot. On weekdays, a special set lunch is available for ¥2,800 ($23) in addition to the choices above, and from 2 to 5pm a teatime cake set is offered for ¥1,200 ($10).

✪ **Hanezawa Beer Garden.** 3–12–15 Hiroo, Shibuya-ku. ☎ **03/3400-6500.** Reservations required. Shabu-shabu, sukiyaki, or barbecues ¥3,000–¥5,500 ($25–$46); à la carte dishes ¥500–¥800 ($4.15–$6.65). AE, DC, JCB, MC, V. Mon–Fri 5–9pm (last order), Sat–Sun 3–9pm. Station: Ebisu, Omotesando, or Shibuya; then take a taxi. SHABU-SHABU/SUKIYAKI/VARIED JAPANESE.

This is a lovely place to go for a meal and drinks. Tucked away in a sleepy residential neighborhood, it's an outdoor garden, spread under trees and paper lanterns, that looks very traditionally Japanese. In winter you can sit in a heated tent, though the atmosphere isn't nearly as romantic. The place specializes in sukiyaki, shabu-shabu, and Mongolian barbecue, all cooked at your table (you must order sukiyaki or shabu-shabu at least a day in advance). There are also beer-drinking snacks such as french fries, yakitori, smoked cheeses, and a mixed pizza which you can order à la carte; my favorite is the *edamame*, soy beans boiled in salt (why don't we eat this in the States?).

INEXPENSIVE

Cardenas. 5–22–3 Hiroo. ☎ **03/5447-1287.** Reservations recommended. Main dishes ¥1,600–¥2,500 ($13–$21). AE, DC, JCB, MC, V. Daily 11:30am–2am. Station: Ebisu or Hiroo (8 min.). On Meiji Dori, about halfway between Ebisu and Hiroo. PACIFIC RIM.

My Tokyo friends can rarely be persuaded to go anywhere else for Pacific Rim cuisine, one of the most recent food fads to sweep the capital. For one, the food is dependably creative and delicious. Secondly, prices are astonishingly low, only a fraction of what one pays at trendier venues across town. Thirdly, the staff treats its customers right, which has earned it a fierce and loyal clientele. The changing menu tempts with such appetizers as braised *anago* (broiled eel) on top of a couscous omelette with a port wine sauce, shrimp and crab cakes in a sweet chili sauce, or a green tea soba noodle salad with baby shrimp and a spicy Oriental dressing. There's also a great Ceasar salad. Entrees may include seared Aki tuna with three peppercorns in a chili brown butter sauce and grilled free-range chicken with mashed potatoes in a Pomery mustard sauce.

Tandoor. 2–1–4 Kami-Osaki. ☎ **03/3449-0901.** Main dishes ¥880–¥1,700 ($7.35–$14); set dinners ¥1,980–¥5,000 ($16.50–$42); set lunches ¥950–¥2,980 ($7.90–$25). AE, DC, JCB, MC, V. Daily 11am–10pm. Station: Meguro (1 min.). Easily reached by taking the east exit of the JR station and then turning left. INDIAN.

This simply decorated restaurant charges rock-bottom prices for Indian curries. On weekdays, daily specials of vegetable, chicken, prawn, or mutton curries are offered for lunch, while on weekends and holidays, the all-you-can-eat buffet for ¥1,000 ($8.35) including tax has to be the cheapest deal in town. The curries tend to be a bit runny and not as spicy as in India, but the service is friendly, and at these prices, who's complaining?

(38) **Tonki.** 1–1–2 Shimo Meguro. ☎ **03/3491-9928.** Teishoku ¥1,650 ($14). JCB, V. Wed–Mon 4–10:45pm. Closed 3rd Mon of each month. Station: Meguro (west exit, 1 min.). On the west side of the station, behind the Sakura bank; look for white curtains over sliding glass doors. TONKATSU.

This is perhaps the best-known *tonkatsu* (pork cutlet) restaurant in town. You'll probably have to wait for a seat at the counter, but it's worth it. A man will ask whether you want the *hirekatsu* (a filet cut of lean pork) or the *rosukatsu* (loin cut). If you're uncertain, he'll hold up the two slabs of meat and you just point to one. No matter which you pick, ask for the *teishoku*, the set meal, featuring soup, rice, cabbage, pickled vegetable, and tea. The man will scribble your order down on a piece of paper and put it with all the other scraps of paper, miraculously keeping track of not only which order belongs to whom but also which customers have been waiting for a seat the longest. The open kitchen behind the counter takes up most of the space in the restaurant, and as you eat you can watch the dozen or so cooks scrambling to turn out orders. Never a dull moment here. You can also get free refills of tea and cabbage.

A Tonki annex (☎ **03/3443-1577**) is on the east side of Meguro station, across the street, on the second floor.

11 Roppongi & Nishi Azabu

Because Roppongi is such a popular nighttime hangout for young Tokyoites and foreigners, it boasts a large number of both Japanese and Western restaurants. To find the location of any of the Roppongi addresses below, stop by the tiny police station on **Roppongi Crossing** (Roppongi's main intersection of Roppongi Dori and Gaien-Higashi Dori), where you'll find a map of the area. If you still don't know where to go, ask one of the policemen.

About a 10-minute walk west of Roppongi (via Roppongi Dori in the direction of Shibuya) is **Nishi Azabu.** Once primarily a residential neighborhood, Nishi Azabu has slowly changed over the years as it began absorbing the overflow of Roppongi. It has restaurants and a few bars, yet remains mellower and much less crowded than Roppongi.

Note: To locate these restaurants, see map on p. 127.

VERY EXPENSIVE

○ ⟨39⟩ **Inakaya.** 7–8–4 Roppongi. ☎ **03/3405-9866.** Meals average ¥12,000 ($100). AE, DC, JCB, MC, V. Daily 5pm–5am. Station: Roppongi (4 min.). On Gaien-Higashi Dori, in the direction toward Akasaka, just past the Ibis Hotel on the left. ROBATAYAKI.

Whenever I'm playing hostess to foreign visitors in Tokyo, I always take them to this festive restaurant, and they've never been disappointed. Although tourist-oriented and pricey, it's still great fun; the drama of the place alone is worth it. Customers sit at a long, U-shaped counter, on the other side of which are mountains of fresh vegetables, beef, and seafood. And in the middle of all that food, seated in front of a grill, are male chefs—ready to cook whatever you point to, in the style of robatayaki. Orders are yelled out by your waiter and are repeated in unison by all the other waiters, with the result that there's always this excited yelling going on. Sounds strange, I know, but actually it's a lot of fun. Food offerings may include yellowtail, red snapper, sole, king crab legs, giant shrimp, steak, meatballs, gingko nuts, potatoes, eggplant, and asparagus, all piled high in wicker baskets and ready for the grill. There's another nearby branch at 5–3–4 Roppongi (☎ **03/3408-5040**), open the same hours.

Seryna. 3–12–2 Roppongi. ☎ **03/3402-1051.** Reservations required. Set dinners ¥10,000–¥16,000 ($83–$133); set lunches ¥3,500–¥7,000 ($29–$58). AE, DC, JCB, MC, V. Mon–Sat noon–10:30pm (last order), Sun and holidays noon–9:30pm (last order). Station: Roppongi (2 min.). From Roppongi Crossing, head toward Tokyo Tower on Gaien-Higashi Dori and take the 1st left. SHABU-SHABU/SUKIYAKI/TEPPANYAKI.

Popular with Japanese entertaining business clientele, this large, modern establishment features Kobe beef and is divided into three sections. Seryna Honten, the main restaurant, specializes in shabu-shabu and sukiyaki and offers a view of a small indoor rock garden. Mon Cher Ton Ton, in the basement, serves Kobe beef, shrimp, fish, shellfish, and vegetables grilled teppanyaki-style right before your eyes. Kani Seryna offers crab and seafood dishes as well as *ishiyaki* steak, which is beef cooked at your table on a heated stone. Note, however, that only Seryna Honten is open for lunch. English-language menus are available.

○ ⟨40⟩ **Takamura.** 3–4–27 Roppongi. ☎ **03/3585-6600.** Reservations required (1 day in advance for lunch, a week in advance for dinner, at which time you must order your meal). Set dinners ¥17,000, ¥20,000, and ¥25,000 ($142, $165, and $208); set lunches ¥13,000, ¥15,000, and ¥17,000 ($108, $125, and $142). AE, DC, JCB, MC, V. Tues–Sat noon–3pm and Mon–Sat 5–10:30pm. Closed for lunch the day following a holiday. Station: Roppongi

(4 min.). The restaurant has 2 entrances, each marked by wooden gate with a little roof. The sign on the restaurant is in Japanese only, but look for the credit-card signs. From Roppongi Crossing, take Roppongi Dori in the direction of Kasumigaseki; turn right after the Fuji photo shop. KAISEKI.

Takamura is a must for anyone who can afford it. Located on the edge of Roppongi, this wonderful 50-year-old house, perched on a hill and hidden by greenery, is like a peaceful oasis that time forgot. Each of its eight rooms is different, with bamboo and charcoal hearths built into the floor and windows looking out onto miniature gardens. Takamura has a very Japanese feeling, which intensifies proportionately with the arrival of your meal—seasonal kaiseki food arranged so artfully you almost hate to destroy it. Your pleasure increases, however, as you savor the various textures and flavors of the food. Specialties may include quail, sparrow, or duck, grilled on the hearth in your own private tatami room. Seating is on the floor, as it is in most traditional Japanese restaurants, but with leg wells. The price of dinner here usually averages about ¥27,000 to ¥33,000 ($225 to $275) by the time you add drinks, tax, service charge, and table charge (¥2,000/$17 per person) Dinner is for parties of two or more, while lunch is available only for parties of four or larger.

EXPENSIVE

(41) **Fukuzushi.** 5-7-8 Roppongi. ☎ **03/3402-4116.** Reservations recommended, especially for dinner. Set dinners ¥6,000–¥8,000 ($50–$67); set lunches ¥2,500–¥4,500 ($21–$37.50). AE, DC, JCB, MC, V. Mon–Sat 11:30am–2pm and 5:30–11pm; holidays 5:30–10pm. Station: Roppongi (4 min.). From Roppongi Crossing, walk toward Tokyo Tower on Gaien-Higashi Dori, turning right after McDonald's and left in front of Hard Rock Cafe. SUSHI.

This is one of the classiest sushi bars, attracting a cosmopolitan crowd. Although it has a traditional entrance through a small courtyard with lighted lanterns and the sound of trickling water, the interior is slick and modern with bold colors of black and red. Some people swear it has the best sushi in Tokyo, although with 7,000 sushi bars in the city, I'd be hard-pressed to say which one is tops. Certainly, you can't go wrong here. Five different set lunches are available that feature sushi, *chirashi-zushi* (assorted sashimi with rice), or eel as the main course. Dinners are more extensive, with the ¥8,000 ($72) set course consisting of salad, sashimi, steamed egg custard, grilled fish, sushi, miso soup, dessert, and coffee.

✪ **Kisso.** Axis Building, 5-17-1 Roppongi. ☎ **03/3582-4191.** Reservations recommended for dinner. Set dinners ¥8,000–¥13,000 ($65–$108); set lunches ¥1,200–¥5,000 ($10–$42). AE, DC, JCB, MC, V. Mon–Sat 11:30am–2pm and 5:30–9pm (last order). Closed holidays. Station: Roppongi (5 min.). From Roppongi Crossing, walk toward Tokyo Tower on Gaien-Higashi Dori; the Axis Building will be on your right. KAISEKI.

I love eating here because Kisso represents all that is best about modern Japan—understated elegance and a successful marriage between the contemporary and the traditional. There should be more places like this in Tokyo. This thoroughly modern establishment sells Japanese gourmet cookware, including expensive ceramics, utensils, and lacquerware of contemporary design, in its shop on the third floor. The restaurant, in the basement of this interesting building filled with shops dedicated to the best in interior design, is simple but elegant, with heavy tables, sprigs of flowers, and soft lighting. The food is kaiseki and comes only in set meals, served (as you might guess) on beautifully lacquered bowls and trays and ceramic plates.

Roppongi

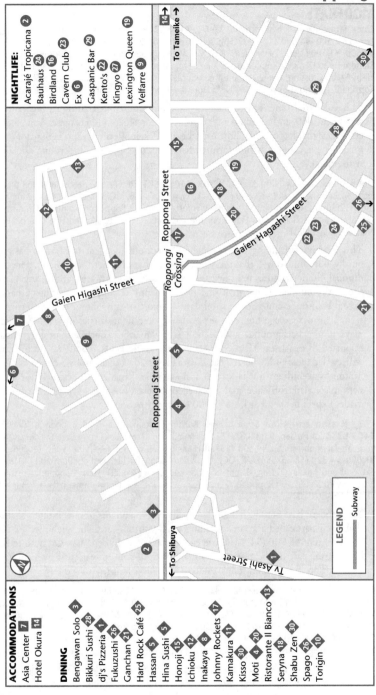

ACCOMMODATIONS
Asia Center 7
Hotel Okura 14

DINING
Bengawan Solo 3
Bikkuri Sushi 28
dj's Pizzeria 1
Fukuzushi 26
Ganchan 21
Hard Rock Café 25
Hassan 5
Hina Sushi 5
Honoji 15
Ichioku 12
Inakaya 8
Johnny Rockets 17
Kamakura 11
Kisso 30
Moti 4 20
Ristorante Il Bianco 13
Seryna 18
Shabu Zen 30
Spago 26
Torijin 10

NIGHTLIFE:
Acarajé Tropicana 2
Bauhaus 24
Birdland 16
Cavern Club 23
Ex 6
Gaspanic Bar 29
Kento's 22
Kingyo 27
Lexington Queen 19
Velfarre 9

Gaien Higashi Street
Roppongi Street
Roppongi Crossing
Gaien Hagashi Street
Roppongi Street
Tv Asahi Street
To Shibuya
To Tameike
To Tameike

LEGEND
Subway

MODERATE

Chez Figaro. 4–4–1 Nishi Azabu. ☎ **03/3400-8718.** Reservations recommended. Main dishes ¥2,500–¥4,500 ($21–$37.50); set dinners ¥6,000–¥10,000 ($50–$83); set lunches ¥2,500–¥3,500 ($21–$29). AE, DC, JCB, MC, V. Daily noon–2pm and 6–9:30pm (last order). Station: Hiroo (7 min.); Roppongi (15 min.). From Hiroo, take exit 3 and walk straight toward Nishi-Azabu Crossing; the restaurant is on your left. From Roppongi, walk toward Shibuya on Roppongi, turning left onto Gaien-Nishi Dori; it will be on your right. TRADITIONAL FRENCH.

This Tokyo old-timer has been serving the same authentic, traditional French cuisine since 1969, and it's still popular with both foreigners and Japanese. A small and cozy place that has changed little over the decades, it offers such specialties as homemade pâté, escargots, saffron-flavored fish soup, pepper steak, and young duckling with orange sauce.

Doka Doka. 4–2–14 Nishi Azabu. ☎ **03/3406-1681.** Reservations recommended weekends. Main dishes ¥1,000–¥3,800 ($8.35–$32). AE, DC, JCB, MC, V. Mon–Sat 6pm–2am (last order 12:30pm). Closed holidays. Station: Hiroo (7 min.) or Roppongi (15 min.). On a small side street across Gaien-Nishi Dori from the gas station, next to Kitchen Five (see below). NOUVELLE JAPANESE.

This restaurant/drinking establishment is a curious blend of the traditional and quirky, but done so well that the atmosphere intrigues rather than annoys. The traditional interior features mud-textured walls, heavy wood beams, and an open coal fire in the middle of the small first floor. Balcony seating upstairs rings a hand-carved balustrade and antique shoji dating from the early Showa Period (retrieved from a former Geisha house in the Yoshiwara red-light district of yore). Soft jazz plays in the background, and seating is on an odd assortment of tiny chairs imported from Africa, Tibet, Bali, and other exotic lands. The food, on a hand-written Japanese-only menu (ask the manager for explanations), changes every 3 months according to what's fresh and available. Past dishes have included duck with miso salad, fish nabe, and an excellent chicken cassoulet. The bread is homemade. Expect to spend at least ¥5,000 ($42) per person.

㊷ **Hassan and Hina Sushi.** Denki Building basement, 6–1–20 Roppongi. ☎ **03/3403-8333** for Hassan, 03/3403-9112 for Hina Sushi. Reservations suggested for dinner. All-you-can-eat shabu-shabu ¥4,500 ($37.50); all-you-can-eat sushi ¥4,300 ($36); set lunches ¥1,000–¥4,300 ($8.35–$36). AE, DC, JCB, MC, V. Mon–Fri 11:30am–2:30pm and 5–10pm; Sat, Sun and holidays 11:am–10pm. Station: Roppongi (1 min.). From Roppongi Crossing, head toward Shibuya on Roppongi Dori; the 2 restaurants are almost immediately to your left. SHABU-SHABU/SUSHI.

This modern basement restaurant is actually two restaurants in one. It offers shabu-shabu in a part called Hassan, including an all-you-can-eat shabu-shabu for ¥4,500 ($37.50). For ¥5,900 ($49) you can eat your fill of sushi here, too. Or, head to the Hina Sushi part of the restaurant for its own all-you-can-eat sushi, which costs ¥4,300 ($36) for 90 minutes or ¥4,800 ($40) for 2 hours.

La Terre. 1–9–20 Azabu-Dai, Minatoku. ☎ **03/3583-9682.** Reservations recommended. Main dishes ¥2,500–¥3,600 ($21–$30); set dinners ¥6,000–¥10,000 ($50–$83); set lunches ¥2,000–¥4,000 ($17–$33). AE, DC, JCB, MC, V. Lunch Mon–Sat 11:30am–2pm and 6–8:30pm (last order). Closed holidays. Station: Kamiyacho (exit 2, 4 min.). Near the Sakura Dori and Gaien-Higashi Dori intersection. Turn right out of the station, right at the 1st big intersection (Iikura Crossing), and then the 1st right. FRENCH.

The service is adequate but a bit reserved (if you're not a regular) at this hidden-away French bistro with red-and-white-checked tablecloths. Dinner features food bordering on nouvelle French, but to avoid the 10% service charge added to your bill at night, consider going for lunch, when the food is more standard fare. The basic lunch for ¥2,500 ($22.50) includes an appetizer or potage du jour (such as pumpkin soup), a choice of a main dish like canard au poivre vert, baskets of fresh French bread and butter, dessert, and tea or coffee. Particularly delightful are the five small tables alfresco underneath a cherry tree; during cherry-blossom season, reserve well in advance. Otherwise, the small indoor dining room overlooks greenery and the Reiyukai Shakaden Temple, which looks like a misplaced spaceship.

43) **Shabu Zen.** 5-17-16 Roppongi. ☎ **03/3585-5388** or 3585-5600. Reservations recommended. Sukiyaki ¥4,800–¥6,500 ($40–$54); all-you-can-eat shabu-shabu ¥4,500–¥7,800 ($37.50–$65). AE, DC, JCB, MC, V. Mon–Sat 5–11:30pm; Sun and holidays 5–11pm. Station: Roppongi (5 min.). From Roppongi Crossing, walk toward Tokyo Tower on Gaien-Higashi Dori, turning right at the Axis Building. SHABU-SHABU/SUKIYAKI.

Come here for all the shabu-shabu you can eat, which begins at ¥4,500 ($37.50) per person on weekdays and includes an unlimited amount of meat and vegetables, plus noodles and rice. If you want Kobe beef, considered the best, you'll pay ¥6,500 ($54). On weekends and holidays, the price for shabu-shabu begins at ¥5,000 ($42). The sukiyaki features Kobe beef.

Spago. 5-7-8 Roppongi. ☎ **03/3423-4025.** Reservations required. Pizza and pasta ¥1,900–¥2,000 ($16–$17); main dishes ¥2,900–¥4,900 ($24–$41); set lunches ¥1,900–¥4,100 ($16–$34); Sun brunch ¥1,900–¥2,600 ($16–$22). AE, DC, JCB, MC, V. Mon–Fri 11:30am–2pm and 6–10pm; Sat 11:30am–2pm and 6–9:30pm; Sun 11am–2:30pm and 6–9:30pm. Station: Roppongi (4 min.). From Roppongi Crossing, walk toward Tokyo Tower on Gaien-Higashi Dori, turning right after McDonald's and left in front of Hard Rock Cafe. CALIFORNIAN.

Like its sister restaurant in Los Angeles, Spago serves innovative California cuisine made famous by its owner, world-famous Austrian-born chef Wolfgang Puck. The atmosphere here is bright, airy, and cheerful—very California—with huge bouquets of flowers, potted palms, ferns, white walls, and a colorful mural. The menu changes every 3 months to reflect what's in season; expect the likes of angel-hair pasta with fresh thyme in goat cheese sauce and broccoli, grilled swordfish with jalapeno cilantro cumin vinaigrette, and roasted baby lamb with marsala wine sauce and mashed potatoes. If you order pizza, it will come not with tomato sauce but with olive oil, making it much lighter, so the emphasis is on the toppings. Needless to say, the main dishes are always imaginative, and the service is great. Dining here is a pleasure; I especially like the no-smoking terrace. As you might expect, Spago has one of the largest selections of California wines in town. For dessert, try the homemade ice cream.

INEXPENSIVE

Bengawan Solo. 7-18-13 Roppongi. ☎ **03/3408-5698.** Main dishes ¥1,000–¥1,800 ($8.35–$15); set lunches ¥800–¥1,300 ($6.65–$11); set dinners ¥3,500–¥5,500 ($29–$46). AE, JCB, MC, V. Daily 11:30am–3pm and 5–11pm (last order 10pm). Station: Roppongi (C2 exit, 2 min.). On Roppongi Dori, on the right side of the street if you're walking from Roppongi Crossing toward Shibuya, across from the Wave Building. INDONESIAN.

This was one of the first ethnic restaurants to open in Tokyo (in 1957), and you're likely to find some old Tokyo hands dining here. Friendly Indonesian waiters and decor add to the spicy goodness of Bengawan's traditional Indonesian food, with perennial favorites including beef in hot sauce and shrimp in coconut cream. There are lots of healthy vegetarian choices, too, such as tempe (Indonesian tofu) and gado-gado salad (with peanut sauce).

(44) **Bikkuri Sushi.** 3–14–9 Roppongi. ☎ **03/3403-1489.** Dishes ¥130–¥650 ($1.10–$5.40). No credit cards. Daily 11am–5am. Station: Roppongi (3 min.). On the left-hand side of Gaien-Higashi Dori (the road leading to Tokyo Tower), across the street from the Roi Building. SUSHI.

This is one of the cheapest places to eat in this popular nightlife district. Plates of sushi move along a conveyor belt past customers seated at the counter, who simply help themselves to whichever plates strike their fancy; this makes dining a cinch, since it's not necessary to know the name of anything. The white plates of sushi are all priced at ¥130 ($1.10), while the colored dishes cost ¥250 ($2.10) and ¥650 ($5.40). Your bill is tallied according to the number of plates you've taken.

DJ's Pizzeria. 6–4–5 Roppongi. ☎ **03/3479-5711.** Pizza and pasta ¥1,100–¥1,850 ($9.15–$15); main dishes ¥1,600–¥2,300 ($13–$19); set lunch ¥980 ($8.15). AE, DC, JCB, MC, V. Mon–Fri 11:30am–11pm, Sat–Sun and holidays noon–11pm. Station: Roppongi (7 min.). On Terebi Asahi Dori; from Roppongi Crossing, walk toward Shibuya on Roppongi Dori and turn left at the 1st big intersection. PIZZA/PASTA.

This casual but fashionable pizzeria, with its breezy, modern decor, offers 20 different kinds of pizza and 30 varieties of pasta that are very good for the price. It's popular with both foreigners living in nearby neighborhoods and others who come to Roppongi to play. Hardly anyone comes to Roppongi during the day, but if you find yourself here, take advantage of the daily lunch special that includes a pizza or pasta of the day. A window facade, opened on nice days, gives the illusion of a sidewalk cafe.

(45) **Ganchan.** 6–8–23 Roppongi. ☎ **03/3478-0092.** Yakitori skewers ¥200–¥400 ($1.65–$3.35); yakitori set course ¥2,500 ($21). AE, JCB, V. Mon–Sat 6pm–2am; Sun and holidays 6pm–midnight. Station: Roppongi (7 min.). From Roppongi Crossing, take the small street going downhill to the left of the Almond Coffee Shop; Ganchan is at the bottom of the hill on the right. YAKITORI.

This is one of my favorite yakitori-ya, and I've spent many a night here. Small and intimate, it's owned by a friendly and entertaining man who can't speak English worth a darn but keeps trying with the help of a worn-out Japanese-English dictionary he keeps behind the counter. His staff is young and fun loving. There's an eclectic cassette collection—I never know whether to expect Japanese pop tunes or Simon and Garfunkel. Seating is along just one counter, with room for only a dozen or so people. Though there's an English menu, it's easiest to order the yakitori seto, a set course that comes with salad and soup and eight skewers of such items as chicken, beef, meatballs, green peppers, and asparagus with rolled bacon. Be aware that there's a table charge of ¥700 ($5.85) per person, which includes an appetizer.

Hamburger Inn. 3–15–22 Roppongi. ☎ **03/3405-8980.** Main dishes ¥350–¥1,080 ($2.90–$9). No credit cards. Mon–Fri 11:30am–5am; Sat–Sun 11:30am–6am. Station: Roppongi (3 min.). From Roppongi Crossing, walk on Gaien-Higashi Dori toward Tokyo Tower; it will be on your left, on a corner across from the Roi Building. SNACKS/ HAMBURGERS.

In a city that constantly re-invents itself, this totally uncool, decades-old hamburger joint is something of a surprise in trendy Roppongi. With its U-shaped counter and booth seating, it's the closest Roppongi has to an old-fashioned diner. The food— hamburgers, hot dogs, sandwiches, tacos, curry rice, spaghetti—is only for the desperate (I've tried the hamburger and couldn't identify the meat), but late hours and a great corner location make it a safe and convenient haven from which to observe Roppongi's parade of drunken revelry.

A Note on Japanese Symbols

Many restaurants, hotels, and other establishments in Japan do not have signs giving their names in Roman (English-language) letters. As an aid to the reader, the second appendix to this book lists the Japanese symbols for all such places described in this guide. Each set of characters representing an establishment name has a number, which corresponds to the number that appears inside the box before the establishment's name in the text. Thus, to find the Japanese symbols for, say, **Ichioku,** refer to no. 47 in appendix B.

Hard Rock Cafe. 5–4–20 Roppongi. ☎ **03/3408-7018.** Main dishes ¥1,380–¥3,000 ($12–$25). AE, DC, JCB, MC, V. Mon–Thurs 11:30am–2am; Fri–Sat 11:30am–4am; Sun and holidays 11:30am–11:30pm. Station: Roppongi (3 min.). From Roppongi Crossing, walk on Gaien-Higashi Dori toward Tokyo Tower and take a right at McDonald's. AMERICAN.

Founded by two American ex-patriates in London in 1971, Hard Rock Cafe now has five locations in Japan; this was the first. If you have disgruntled teenagers in tow, bring them to this world-famous hamburger joint dedicated to rock 'n' roll to ogle the memorabilia on the walls, chow down on a burger, and look over the T-shirts for sale. In addition to hamburgers, the menu includes salads, sandwiches, steak, barbecued ribs, barbecued chicken, a fish of the day, and fajitas. The music, by the way, is loud.

46 **Honoji.** 3–4–33 Roppongi. ☎ **03/3588-1065.** Main dishes ¥350–¥600 ($2.90–$5). Set dinner ¥3,800 ($32). No credit cards. Mon–Fri 11:30am–1:30pm (last order); Mon–Sat 5:30–11pm (last order 10:15pm). Station: Roppongi (3 min.). On the right side of Roppongi Dori as you walk from Roppongi Crossing in the direction of Akasaka. JAPANESE.

A plain wooden facade and a no-nonsense interior of concrete walls with wire-mesh screens set the mood for what this restaurant offers: good, homestyle Japanese cooking, along with some Japanese interpretations of Western food. Although it looks small at first glance, there are backroom nooks and crannies, giving diners a sense of privacy as they enjoy grilled fish, sashimi, yakitori, *nikujaga* (a beef and potato stew), spareribs, and a few Western dishes like a cream spinach and scallop gratin. It serves the kinds of food offered by neighborhood *nomiya* (drinking establishments) all over Japan, which isn't exactly the kind of fare you'd expect to find in trendy Roppongi. Still, the crowds that wait at the door, especially on weekend nights, attest to its success. Probably the best deal is the set dinner, which includes sashimi, a main dish such as grilled fish, seasonal vegetables, and several other side dishes. Otherwise, expect to spend ¥3,000 to ¥3,500 ($27 to $31.50) per person. The lunch teishoku, available for ¥900 ($7.50) and the only item offered for lunch, draws Japanese from all walks of life.

You'll find other branches in Harajuku at 5–50–2 Jingumae (☎ **03/5467-6770;** open Monday to Saturday 11:30am to 2pm and 5:30 to 11pm); and in Shibuya at 1–11–3 Shibuya (☎ **03/3407-4430;** open Monday to Saturday 11:30am to 2pm and 5:30 to 11pm).

✪ 47 **Ichioku.** 4–4–5 Roppongi. ☎ **03/3405-9891.** Main dishes ¥800–¥2,200 ($6.65–$18). AE, DC, MC, V. Mon–Sat 5pm–1am; holidays 5–11pm. Station: Roppongi (4 min.). On a side street in the neighborhood behind the police station; look for the Rastafarian colors and a yin/yang sign. JAPANESE ORIGINALS.

This is one of my favorite restaurants in Tokyo for casual dining. It's a tiny, cozy place with only eight tables, and you fill out your order yourself from the menu in

English, complete with pictures, glued onto your table underneath clear glass. The food, featuring organically grown vegetables, can best be called Japanese nouvelle cooking, with original creations offered at very reasonable prices. There's tuna and ginger sauté, mushroom sauté, shrimp spring rolls, asparagus salad, fried potatoes, and a dish of crumbled radish and tiny fish. I recommend the tofu steak (fried tofu and flakes of dried fish), as well as the cheese gyoza (a fried pork dumpling with cheese melted on it). The average check here is ¥2,500 to ¥3,000 ($21 to $25).

☉ **Johnny Rockets.** 3–11–10 Roppongi, Roppongi Crossing. ☎ **03/3423-1955.** Hamburgers ¥600–¥1,200 ($5–$10); set lunches ¥700–¥1,000 ($5.85–$8.35). No credit cards. Sun–Thurs 11am–11pm; Fri and Sat 11am–6am. Station: Roppongi. HAMBURGERS.

Quite simply the best burgers in town. Since the regular burgers are huge (I've seen sumo wrestlers stocking up here), I was glad when smaller versions were added to the menu. Perched on the second floor of a building on Roppongi Crossing, Johnny Rockets is decorated like an American '50s diner. Seating is on a first-come, first-served basis at the counters, and smoking is not allowed. Other goodies on the menu include sandwiches, fries (which you can get topped with chili), malts, shakes, floats, and pie á la mode. It definitely hits the spot, especially after a night of carousing. From 11am to 4pm daily, a fixed-price lunch offers a hamburger or sandwich, fries, and a drink (unlimited refills).

Kamakura. 4–10–11 Roppongi. ☎ **03/3405-4377.** Yakitori skewers ¥180–¥350 ($1.50–$2.90); set dinners ¥2,300–¥4,300 ($19–$36). AE, DC, JCB, MC, V. Mon–Sat 5–midnight. Station: Roppongi (2 min.). Off Gaien-Higashi Dori, on a side street opposite Ibis Hotel; from Roppongi Crossing, walk on Gaien-Higashi Dori in the direction of Akasaka and take the 2nd right. YAKITORI.

Much more refined than most yakitori-ya, this basement establishment is decorated with paper lanterns and sprigs of fake but cheerful spring blossoms, with traditional koto music playing softly in the background. The English menu lists yakitori set courses, and à la carte sticks include those with shrimp, meatballs, gingko, squid, eggplant, and mushrooms.

☮ **Kitchen Five.** 4–2–15 Nishi-Azabu. ☎ **03/3409-8835.** Dishes ¥1,300–¥1,850 ($11–$15). No credit cards. Tues–Sat 6–9:45pm (last order). Closed holidays, Golden Week, and late July–early Sept. Station: Hiroo (7 min.) or Roppongi (15 min.). Opposite Gaien-Nishi Dori from the gas station, down a side street. MEDITERRANEAN/ETHNIC.

If it's true that cooking with love is the best spice, then perhaps that's why Yuko Kobayashi's 13-year-old, 16-seat restaurant is so popular. She goes to market every morning to fetch ingredients for a dozen main dishes, which can include stuffed eggplant, moussaka, and various other casseroles and curries. Every summer Kobayashi goes off to search for recipes in Sicily, South America, northern Africa, and other countries that feature garlic, tomatoes, and olive oil in their cuisine. The love for what she does shines in her eyes as she cooks, serves, and walks you through the menu of daily dishes displayed. A word of warning: The food is so delicious, it's tempting to over-order. Highly recommended.

☮ **Moti.** 3–12–6 Roppongi. ☎ **03/5410-6871.** Main dishes ¥1,300–¥1,750 ($11–$15); set dinners ¥2,600–¥3,000 ($22–$25); set lunches ¥950–¥1,350 ($7.90–$11) Mon–Sat, ¥1,250–¥1,650 ($10–$14) Sun and holidays. AE, DC, JCB, MC, V. Mon–Sat 11:30am–11pm (last order); Sun and holidays noon–10pm. Station: Roppongi (1 min.). From Roppongi Crossing, walk toward Tokyo Tower on Gaien-Higashi Dori and take the 1st left. INDIAN.

This is my favorite Indian restaurant in town. Dishes include vegetable curries, chicken and mutton curries (I usually opt for the sag mutton—lamb with spinach), and tandoori chicken. Set lunches, served until 2:30pm, offer a choice of vegetable, chicken, or mutton curry, along with Indian bread (nan) and tea or coffee.

A second Roppongi location is at 6–2–35 Roppongi (☎ **03/3479-1939**), on Roppongi Dori in the direction of Shibuya.

Ristorante Il Bianco. 4–5–2 Roppongi. ☎ **03/3470-5678.** Reservations a must for dinner. Pasta ¥1,000–¥1,700 ($8.35–$14); main dishes ¥1,500–¥2,500 ($12.50–$21); set dinners ¥4,000–¥8,000 ($33–$67); set lunches ¥1,200–¥3,800 ($10–$32). AE, DC, JCB, MC, V. Mon–Sat 11:30am–2pm and 5–10pm (last order). Station: Roppongi (3 min.). From Roppongi Crossing, take Gaien-Higashi Dori in the direction of Aoyama; turn right at the 2nd street (opposite Ibis Hotel) and walk several blocks to the end of the nightlife district (and a slightly busier street), then left. ITALIAN.

My friends and I don't know how they do it (or why, considering that they probably lose money on us), but this tiny Italian restaurant offers an incredible deal for wine drinkers—for a mere ¥600 ($5) extra at dinner, you can drink all the house red or white wine you wish (mostly from Chile). Even more amazing, you can bring in your own favorite bottle without paying a corkage fee. Pasta comes in three sizes, with the smallest size perfect as a starter for one person. Main courses include veal and spinach gratin, roast chicken, wrapped whitefish with potato, wild roast duck, and grilled filet mignon. The only problem is finding the place—stop at the police station at Roppongi Crossing to look at the map or ask for directions. And once you get here, be sure to take the stairs to the second-floor restaurant unless you want a cheap thrill—the elevator deposits you directly into the kitchen.

48 Shinasobaya. 4–3–7 Nishi Azabu. ☎ **03/3406-5298.** Main dishes ¥400–¥1,000 ($3.35–$8.35). No credit cards. Daily 11:30am–4am. Station: Hiroo (6 min.) or Roppongi (12 min.). From Nishi Azabu Crossing, head south on Gaien-Nishi Dori and turn right and then left; it's on the street that parallels Gaien-Nishi Dori to the west. RAMEN.

Looking for inexpensive food in the middle of the night? Head for this simple but clean ramen shop, with a red lantern outside its door and only four tables inside. Its name translates as "Chinese Noodle House," and that's what it serves, along with fried rice, wonton soup, and very tasty *gyoza* (fried dumplings).

49 Torigin. 4–12–6 Roppongi. ☎ **03/3403-5829.** Yakitori skewers ¥140–¥250 ($1.15–$2.10); kamameshi ¥800–¥1,200 ($6.65–$10). No credit cards. Mon–Sat 11:30am–2pm and 5–11pm. Station: Roppongi (2 min.). From Roppongi Crossing, take Gaien-Higashi Dori in the direction of Akasaka, taking the 3rd right. YAKITORI/RICE CASSEROLES.

Part of a chain of yakitori establishments, this no-frills place is typical of the smaller Japanese restaurants all over the country patronized by the country's salarymen, who stop off for a drink and bite to eat before boarding the commuter trains for home. An English menu includes skewers of grilled chicken, gingko nuts, green peppers, quail eggs, and asparagus with rolled bacon, as well as various *kamameshi* (rice casseroles cooked and served in their own little pots and topped with chicken, bamboo shoots, mushrooms, crab, salmon, or shrimp).

12 Akasaka

Note: To locate these restaurants, see map on p. 73.

VERY EXPENSIVE

✪ **La Tour d'Argent.** Hotel New Otani, 4–1 Kioi-cho. ☎ **03/3239-3111.** Reservations required. Main dishes ¥6,200–¥12,000 ($52–$100). AE, CB, DC, JCB, MC, V. Tues–Sun 5:30–10:30pm (last reservation accepted for 8:30pm). Station: Akasaka-mitsuke or Nagatacho (3 min.). CLASSIC FRENCH.

Here's the place to dine if you're celebrating a very special occasion, are on a hefty expense account, or fancy yourself a jet-setter. Opened in 1984, La Tour d'Argent is the authentic sister to the one in Paris, which opened back in 1582 and was visited twice by Japan's former emperor Hirohito. Entrance to the Tokyo restaurant is through an impressive hallway with a plush interior and displays of tableware used in the Paris establishment throughout the centuries. The dining hall looks like an elegant Parisian drawing room. The service is superb, and the food is excellent. The specialty here is roast duckling—it meets its untimely end at the age of 3 weeks and is flown to Japan from Brittany. Other dishes on the menu, which changes seasonally, may include sea bass, médaillons of veal in light curry sauce, young pigeon, beef tenderloin, or fricassee of lobster and morels.

Sekishin Tei. Hotel New Otani, 4–1 Kioi-cho, Chiyoda-ku. ☎ 03/3238-0024. Reservations recommended for dinner. Set dinners ¥10,000–¥20,000 ($83–$167); set lunches ¥3,500–¥6,000 ($29–$50). AE, DC, JCB, MC, V. Daily 11:30–2pm and 6–9pm. Station: Nagatacho or Akasaka-mitsuke (3 min.). TEPPANYAKI.

Nestled in the New Otani's 400-year-old garden, this teppanyaki restaurant is composed of three glass-enclosed pavilions, all with the same menu of Kobe beef, fish, lobster, and vegetables cooked on a grill right in front of you. If you order a salad, try the soy-sauce dressing; it's delicious. You'll eat surrounded by peaceful views, making this place a good lunchtime choice.

EXPENSIVE

✪ ⟨29⟩ **Hayashi.** Sanno Kaikan Building., 3rd and 4th floors, 2–14–1 Akasaka. ☎ 03/3582-4078. Reservations recommended for dinner. Set dinners ¥6,000, ¥8,000, and ¥10,000 ($50, $67, and $83); lunches ¥900 ($7.50). AE, DC, JCB, MC, V. Mon–Fri 11:30am–2pm and 5:30–11pm; Sat 5:30–11pm. Closed holidays. Station: Akasaka (exit 2, 1 min.). Just south of Misuji Dori, on the 3rd and 4th floors of a nondescript, improbable-looking building. JAPANESE GRILL/RICE CASSEROLES.

One of the most delightful old-time restaurants I've been to, this cozy, rustic-looking place serves home-style country cooking and specializes in grilled food that you prepare yourself over your own square hibachi. Altogether, there are 10 grills in this small restaurant, some of them surrounded by tatami mats and some by wooden stools or chairs. As the evening wears on, the one-room main dining area can get quite smoky, but somehow that just adds to the ambience. Other nice touches are the big gourds and memorabilia hanging about and the waiters in traditional baggy pants. Hayashi serves three set menus, which change with the seasons. The ¥6,000 ($50) meal—which will probably end up being closer to ¥8,000 ($67) by the time you add drinks, tax, and service charge—may include such items as sashimi and vegetables, chicken, scallops, and gingko nuts, which you grill yourself. At lunch, only *oyakodomburi* is served: literally, "parent and child," a simple rice dish topped with egg and chicken.

Kana Uni. 1–1–16 Moto-Akasaka. ☎ 03/3404-4776. Reservations recommended. Main dishes ¥2,000–¥4,900 ($17–$41). AE, DC, JCB, MC, V. Mon–Fri 6pm–2:30am; Sat 6–11pm. Closed holidays. Station: Akasaka-mitsuke (3 min.). In the block behind the Suntory Building (look for the key-shaped logo). FRENCH.

This cozy and intimate restaurant/bar is owned and managed by a man who speaks excellent English and loves to have foreign guests. In fact, because the place is a little hard to find, they'll even come and fetch you if you call from Akasaka-mitsuke Station. Open since 1966, Kana Uni features such main dishes as sliced raw tenderloin, steaks, beef stew, grilled fish, sautéed scallops, and poached filet of sole with sea-urchin sauce. But the real treat is the soft live jazz nightly from

7 to 11pm (music charge: ¥1,000/$8.35 per person), so after dinner, relax with cocktails and enjoy the ambience. The red rose on each table, by the way, symbolizes the owner's favorite song, which is also the nightly closing number. Guesses, anyone?

Ten-ichi. 3–19–3 Akasaka. ☎ **03/3583-0107.** Reservations recommended at dinner. Set dinners ¥7,000–¥15,000 ($58–$125); set lunches ¥3,800–¥10,000 ($32–$83). AE, DC, JCB, MC, V. Mon–Sat 11:30am–9:30pm. Station: Akasaka or Akasaka-mitsuke (5 min.). On Misuji Dori. TEMPURA.

This is the Akasaka branch of one of Tokyo's best-known and oldest tempura establishments. The set dinner for ¥10,000 ($90) (it's on the English menu) includes deep-fried prawns and other seafood, vegetables, salad, rice, miso soup, fruit, and pickled vegetables (refer to the Ten-ichi restaurant in Ginza for more information).

✪ **Trader Vic's.** New Otani Hotel, 4–1 Kioi-cho. ☎ **03/3265-4707.** Reservations recommended. Main dishes ¥3,000–¥6,500 ($25–$54); set dinners ¥9,000–¥14,000 ($75–$117); set lunches ¥3,700–¥4,500 ($31–$37.50); Sun and holidays brunch (including tax and service charge) ¥6,000 ($50). AE, DC, JCB, MC, V. Daily 11:30am–2:30pm and 5–10pm. Station: Akasaka-mitsuke (3 min.) or Yotsuya (5 min.). SEAFOOD/STEAKS/INTERNATIONAL.

Part of an American chain operating out of California, the decor is Hollywood-set Polynesian, and the extensive menu offers salads, seafood, Chinese dishes, curries, steak, and chicken. At lunch, lighter fare such as sandwiches is also available. A few tables boast views of the hotel's famous gardens (reserve in advance). For a major feast, come for the all-you-can-eat-and-drink sparkling wine brunch on Sundays and holidays. Otherwise, a limited, less expensive menu is served at the bar, including a very popular U.S. rib-eye steak set dinner for ¥3,500 ($29).

⑮ **Zakuro.** TBS Kaikan Building. basement, 5–3–3 Akasaka. ☎ **03/3582-6841.** Reservations recommended. Set dinners ¥5,500–¥15,800 ($46–$132); set lunches ¥1,500–¥3,800 ($12.50–$32). AE, DC, JCB, MC, V. Daily 11am–10pm (last order). Station: Akasaka (TBS exit, 1 min.). SHABU-SHABU/SUKIYAKI.

Zakuro, a local chain, is one of several restaurants claiming to have introduced shabu-shabu in Japan. It's decorated with folk art, including works by famous Japanese artists Shiko Munakata and Shoji Hamada. Friendly, kimono-clad hostesses serve shabu-shabu, sukiyaki, tempura, and teriyaki beef, all available as set dinners with various side dishes. Kobe beef is available. At lunch there are set meals of tempura, sashimi, sukiyaki, and teriyaki beef. Since Zakuro (which means "pomegranate") has an English menu, ordering is no problem. This is a popular place to bring visiting foreign clients.

You'll find other Zakuro restaurants in Akasaka in front of the American Embassy (☎ **03/3582-2661**), in Nihombashi south of the Takashimaya department store (☎ **03/3271-3791**), in Kyobashi south of the Bridgestone Building (☎ **03/3563-5031**), and in the Ginza south of the Matsuya department store (☎ **03/3535-4421**).

MODERATE

There's a branch of ⑬ **Sushi Sei** at 3–11–14 Akasaka (☎ **03/3586-9503**). See the listing in the "Ginza & Hibiya" section for a description.

Blue Sky. Hotel New Otani, 4–1 Kioi-cho, Chiyoda-ku. ☎ **03/3238-0028.** Dinner buffet ¥6,300 ($52.50); lunch buffet ¥3,500 ($29). AE, DC, JCB, MC, V. Daily 11:30am–2pm and 5–9pm. Station: Akasaka-mitsuke or Nagatacho (3 min.). CHINESE.

Located on the 17th floor of the New Otani's main building with great views of the city, this revolving restaurant provides panoramic views and all-you-can eat buffets, primarily Chinese. The food, tasty and varied, consists of approximately 40 different items for lunch and 50 for dinner and includes spicy Szechuanese cuisine, dim sum, Japanese food, and freshly baked pizza. My only complaint is that the restaurant revolves at a breakneck speed that matches fast-paced Tokyo, making a complete turn every 45 minutes. If the thought makes you dizzy, there's another buffet-style restaurant called **Top of the Tower** on the 40th floor of the New Otani's tower, also with spectacular views of the city and offering continental buffet lunches for ¥4,800 ($40) and dinners for ¥7,500 ($62.50).

Kihachi. 5–3–9 Akasaka. ☎ **03/3224-2521.** Reservations recommended. Main dishes ¥2,200–¥2,800 ($18–$23); set dinner ¥3,500 ($29); set lunches ¥980–¥1,500 ($8.15–$12.50). AE, DC, JCB, MC, V. Mon–Sat 11:45am–1:30pm and 5–10:30pm. Closed holidays. Station: Akasaka (exit 1, 1 min.). Located on the 2nd floor above Starbucks. NOUVELLE JAPANESE.

With a cool, breezy interior accented with palm trees, bamboo shades, and wicker furniture, this restaurant offers an interesting English menu that changes monthly and combines flavors of the West with Japanese and Chinese ingredients. Past dishes have included a swordfish and vegetable salad flavored with wasabi; an appetizer of tuna, bean curd and avocado; and main dishes ranging from Japanese steak with a green pepper sauce to steamed sea bream and bamboo shoots with a black bean sauce.

INEXPENSIVE

Don't forget to consider **Hayashi,** on the third and fourth floors of the Sanno Kaikan Building, 2–14–1 Akasaka, described above as an expensive restaurant. I mention it again here simply because I don't want those of you on a budget to miss it. This is one of the coziest and most delightful restaurants in town. Although dinner is costly, you can enjoy the same atmosphere for much, much less at lunch, when only one dish, *oyakodomburi* (rice with chunks of chicken and omelet on top), is served, with pickled vegetables, clear soup, and tea for ¥900 ($7.50). Open for lunch Monday through Friday from 11:30am to 2pm.

Akasaka is also home to two branches of **Moti,** my favorite Indian restaurant: on the second floor of the Akasaka Floral Plaza, 3–8–8 Akasaka (☎ 03/3582-3620); and on the third floor of the Kinpa Building, 2–14–31 Akasaka (☎ 03/3584-6640). See "Roppongi & Nishi Azabu," above, above for a complete review. Finally, a branch of **Shabusen,** specializing in inexpensive shabu-shabu, is located in the basement of the TBS basement at 5–3–3 Akasaka (☎ 03/3582-8161). See " Ginza & Hibiya," above, for a complete review.

Potomac. Akasaka Prince Hotel, 1–2 Kioi-cho Chiyoda-ku. ☎ **03/3234-1111.** Main dishes ¥1,500–¥2,800 ($12.50–$23); set lunches ¥1,200–¥1,800 ($10–$15). AE, DC, JCB, MC, V. Open 24 hr. daily. Station: Akasaka-mitsuke or Nagatacho (2 min.). AMERICAN.

A traditional American coffee shop open an astonishing 24 hours, Potomac offers a teriyaki-style sirloin steak, fish, broiled chicken, spaghetti, and sandwiches, along with set meals for lunch and dinner, including a Japanese-style set menu for ¥2,000 ($17). But its real value is what is arguably the best lunchtime deal in town: steak, vegetables, and french fries for $10, based on the daily exchange rate. That, plus the fast service, draws everyone from American businesspeople to Japanese housewives.

⑤⓪ **Shogetsuan.** 3–19–8 Akasaka. ☎ **03/3583-1181.** Main dishes ¥650–¥1,400 ($5.40–$12). No credit cards. Mon–Fri 11am–9pm; Sat 11am–3pm. Closed holidays. Station: Akasaka (2 min.). On Hitosugi Dori, across from a pachinko parlor (look for the shop's purple noren and plastic-food display case outside its door). NOODLES.

If all you're looking for is a quick, inexpensive bite in the heart of Akasaka, head to this simple soba shop. Choices include tempura soba, *tenzaru* (cold soba with tempura), *tendon* (tempura on rice), *wakame* (noodles with seaweed), and *katsudon* (pork cutlet on rice).

Suntory Beer Garden. Suntory Building rooftop, 1–2–3 Moto-Akasaka. ☎ **03/3401-4367.** Reservations recommended. Main dishes ¥1,300–¥2,400 ($11–$20). No credit cards. May–Aug Mon–Sat 5–10pm. Closed holidays and Sept–Apr. Station: Akasaka-mitsuke (1 min.). VARIED JAPANESE/BARBECUE.

This rooftop beer garden is better and more sophisticated than most, with real palms and bushes circling the dining area instead of the usual plastic. It even has a great view of surrounding Akasaka. Even more astounding, there's no Astroturf! In addition to its draft Suntory beer, it also offers a barbecue of sirloin, beef, or lamb you grill at your own table, as well as the usual beer snacks (spring rolls, yakitori) listed on an English-language menu. Purchase what you want from the ticket booth upon entering, sit down, and then hand the waiter your ticket.

Tony Roma's. 2–3–4 Akasaka. ☎ **03/3585-4478.** Main dishes ¥1,280–¥3,580 ($11–$30). AE, DC, MC, V. Mon–Fri 11:45am–2:30pm and 5:30–11pm, Sat noon–11pm, Sun and holidays noon–10:30pm. Station: Tameike-Sanno (1 min.), Akasaka (7 min.) or Kokkai Gijido-mae (4 min.). On Sotobori Dori, near Roppongi Dori. BARBECUED RIBS.

This well-known U.S. chain dishes out large portions of the same barbecued baby-back ribs served back home, in a similar setting. It's popular with staff from the nearby American embassy, as well as area office workers. You can order ribs alone or in combination with barbecued chicken, grilled lamb, steamed lobster, or other entrees, all of which include coleslaw and a choice of side dish such as baked potato or french fries. Steaks, seafood, and hamburgers are also available.

Other Tokyo locations include 3–1–30 Minami-Aoyama (☎ **03/3479-5214**) and 5–4–20 Roppongi (☎ **03/3408-2748**), below the Hard Rock Cafe.

13 Other Neighborhoods

EXPENSIVE

✪ **Tableaux.** Sunroser Daikanyama Building, 11–6 Sarugaku-cho. ☎ **03/5489-2201.** Reservations required. Main dishes ¥2,100–¥4,800 ($17.50–$40). AE, DC, JCB, MC, V. Daily 5:30–11pm (last order). Station: Daikanyama (5 min.). INTERNATIONAL.

This place is just too cool. Designer Margaret O'Brien must have had fun here—it's a medieval Russian tearoom gone slightly mad, with bead-fringed curtains, mosaics of cracked mirrors, chandeliers, stars and moons, animal-skins, and red velvet upholstery. There's even a subterranean courtyard for alfresco dining. The effect is fantastical and a bit surreal; eating here is like playing a two-bit part in your own murky dreams. Luckily, the professional staff and excellent, beautifully presented food live up to the fantasy-provoking setting. For the health-conscious, there's a large selection of vegetarian dishes, fish, and charcoal-grilled free-range chicken. For the rest, order zuwai crab cakes topped with caviar and Dijon balsamic sauce or a mixed dim sum plate, followed by lobster risotto or filet mignon grilled with mustard and tomatoes in a gorgonzola port wine sauce. An adjoining cigar lounge offers live jazz (avoid the cover charge by sitting at the bar).

MODERATE

(51) **Botan.** 1–15 Kanda Sudacho. ☎ **03/3251-0577.** Tori sukiyaki ¥6,700 ($56). No credit cards. Mon–Sat 11:30am–8pm (last order). Closed holidays. Station: Ogawamachi or Awajicho (exit A3, 3 min.) or Akihabara (10 min.). Down the street from Kanda Yabusoba (see below). CHICKEN SUKIYAKI.

Whereas most sukiyaki consists of beef, this famous restaurant, housed in a traditional Japanese-style house with a maple tree gracing its entrance, has been serving only one dish—chicken sukiyaki—for more than a century. Take your shoes off at the entrance, where the friendly staff will then guide you past a huge rock and stone lantern to a tatami room. If there are two of you, you'll share a room with others; if your party is larger, you'll probably have your own private room (make reservations for parties of more than four persons). You'll cook your chicken sukiyaki yourself over the table-side charcoal grill, making for a fun, convivial evening.

✪ **Carmine.** 1–19 Saiku-cho, Shinjuku-ku. ☎ **03/3260-5066.** Reservations required. Pasta ¥1,000 ($8.35); set dinners ¥3,800–¥5,000 ($32–$42); set lunches ¥1,800–¥2,500 ($15–$21). No credit cards. Mon–Sat noon–2pm and 6–9pm. Station: Ichigaya (12 min.) or Kagurazaka (8 min.); then take a taxi. TUSCAN.

During the bubble economy of the '80s, when most Italian restaurants charged exorbitantly and got away with it, this tiny Italian restaurant was revolutionary in offering great food at almost shockingly low prices, drawing crowds despite its out-of-the-way location. Carmine Cozzolino, the chef and gregarious host, received his training in the Tuscan style of cooking in Florence. Specialties include the antipasto misto del giorno, the penne al salmone or al gorgonzola, the scaloppine al marsala, and the filetto di manzo al scalogno. The four-course set dinner for ¥3,800 ($32) is a steal. The one-room dining hall is minuscule, simply decorated with artwork supplied by one of Carmine's friends. Since there are only 48 seats, you won't get more than your foot in the door without a reservation.

✪ ㊝ **Kandagawa.** 2–5–11 Soto-Kanda. ☎ **03/3251-5031.** Reservations required. Main dishes ¥2,200–¥3,600 ($19.80–$32.40). MC, V. Mon–Sat 11:30am–2pm and 5–8pm. Closed holidays. Station: Akihabara (5 min.). On Sotobori Dori. EEL.

Dining in this beautiful, old-fashioned, traditional Japanese restaurant, famous for its eel dishes since the Edo Period, is unforgettable. A Japanese-style wooden house, hidden behind a wooden gate, it offers seven private tatami rooms, as well as a larger tatami dining room. The menu, in Japanese only, offers side dishes of soup, rice, and Japanese pickles, and such main dishes as kabayaki (broiled and basted eel), unaju (broiled eel on rice with a sweet sauce), shiroyaki ("white" eel, broiled without soy sauce or oil), and umaki (eel wrapped in an omelet). There's also grilled eel's liver, plus sashimi. Expect to spend a minimum of ¥7,500 ($62.50) per person, including drinks, appetizers, tax, and service. Since no one here speaks English, it's best to have a Japanese make your reservation, at which time you must order the dishes you'd like to be served.

INEXPENSIVE

✪ **Kanda Yabusoba.** 2–10 Awajicho, Kanda. ☎**03/3251-0287.** ¥600–¥1,700 ($5–$14). No credit cards. Daily 11:30am–7pm. Station: Awajicho or Ogawamachi (exit A3, 3 min.) or Akihabara (10 min.). Northeast of the Sotobori Dori and Yasukuni Dori intersection; from Sotobori Dori, take the side street that runs between the Tokyo Green Hotel and the New Kanda Hotel. NOODLES.

Soba (noodle) shops are among the least expensive restaurants in Japan, and this is one of Tokyo's most famous, established in 1880 and rebuilt after the 1923 Great Kanto Earthquake. The house, which is surrounded by a wooden gate with an entryway through a small grove of bamboo, features shoji screens, a wooden ceiling, and a dining area with tatami mats and tables. Since it's often filled with middle-aged businessmen and housewives, you'll probably have to wait for a seat if you come during lunchtime. There's a menu in English. The specialties are hot and cold wheat noodles, which you can order with shredded yam, grilled eel, or a crispy shrimp tempura. Listen to the woman sitting at a small counter by the kitchen—she sings out orders to the chef, as well as hellos and good-byes to customers.

Pas á Pas. 5 Funamachi, Shinjuku-ku. ☎ **03/3357-7888.** Reservations required. Lunch menu ¥1,500 ($12.50); dinner menu ¥2,500 ($21). AE, DC, MC, V. Mon–Sat noon–1:30pm and 6–9pm (last order). Closed holidays. Station: Yotsuya-sanchome (exit 4; 4 min.). Walk north on Shinjuku Dori, take the 2nd right (just before Fuji Bank), and look for a white building and a little sign on the 2nd floor. FRENCH.

Steep stairs lead to this second-floor, (too) crowded bistro, wildly popular for its very cheap prices yet very good food. To compensate for the low prices, its tables, with their red-and-white checkered tablecloths, are too close together, but all is forgiven the moment your confit de canard or joue de boeuf au vin rouge arrives. Only three-course set meals are served, but a choice of about four entrees for lunch and 10 for dinner leaves room for personal preference. Add a bottle of wine for about ¥4,000 ($33).

Sunset Beach Brewing Company. Tokyo Decks Beach, 1–6–1 Daiba. ☎ **03/5500-5066.** Lunch buffet ¥1,500 ($12.50); dinner buffet ¥2,480 ($21). AE, DC, JCB, MC, V. Daily 11am–3:30pm and 5–10pm (last order). Station: Odaiba Kaihin Koen (2 min.). INTERNTIONAL.

Located in Tokyo Decks Beach, a shopping/dining complex on the man-made island of Odaiba, this microbrewery is one of my favorites for outdoor dining, with great views of the beach, the bay, and Rainbow Bridge. Although the food—which runs the gamut from lasagne and pizza to salads and vegetables—is mediocre at best, the price is right, the beer is good, and the location is a great summertime escape from the concrete jungle.

6

What to See & Do in Tokyo

Many Westerners grow up with a highly romanticized view of Japan, picturing it as a woodblock print—exquisite, mysterious, and ancient.

What a shock, then, to come to Tokyo. In a country known around the world for its appreciation of the aesthetic, Tokyo is disappointingly unimpressive. Some foreigners, unable to reconcile unrealistic expectations with the cold facts of reality, summarily dismiss Tokyo as a monstrosity of the 21st century and go off in search of the "real" Japan. What they don't realize is that beneath Tokyo's concrete shell is a cultural life left very much intact. In fact, Tokyo is the best place in the world for experiencing Japanese performing arts, such as Kabuki, as well as such diverse activities as the tea ceremony and flower arranging. It's also the nation's foremost repository for Japanese art and crafts and boasts a wide range of both first-class and unique museums.

SEEING THE CITY BY GUIDED TOUR   With the help of this book and a good map, you should be able to visit Tokyo's major attractions easily on your own. However, should you be pressed for time, consider taking one of the several group tours offered by the **Japan Travel Bureau (JTB)** (☎ **03/5620-9500**) or **Japan Gray Line** (☎ **03/3433-5745** and 03/3436-6881). Day tours may include Tokyo Tower, the Imperial Palace district, Asakusa Sensoji Temple, Meiji Jingu Shrine, and Ginza. There are also a number of organized evening tours that take in such activities as Kabuki. Be warned, however, that tours are very tourist-oriented and are more expensive than touring Tokyo on your own. Prices range from about ¥3,600 ($30) for a morning tour to about ¥10,800 ($90) for a night tour with dinner and Kabuki. You can easily book tours through most tourist hotels and travel agencies.

One tour you might consider is a **boat trip on the Sumida River** between Hama Rikyu Garden and Asakusa. Commentary on the 40-minute trip is in both Japanese and English (be sure to pick up the English leaflet, too). You'll get descriptions of the 12 bridges you pass along the way and views of Tokyo you'd otherwise miss. Boats depart Hama Rikyu Garden hourly or more frequently between 10:15am and 4:05pm, with the fare to Asakusa costing ¥620 ($5.15) one way. Other cruises are also available, with boats departing from Hinode Pier (closest station: Hamamatsucho, about a 7-min. walk) for Asakusa (fare: ¥660/$5.50), Tokyo Sea Life Park

---

● **Did You Know?**

- Tokyo has been the capital of Japan only since 1868; before that, Kyoto served as capital for more than 1,000 years.
- Ten percent of Japan's total population lives in Tokyo—more than 12 million residents. Almost a quarter of Japan's total population lives within commuting distance.
- Tokyo's workers commute to work an average of 90 minutes one-way. Shinjuku Station handles the most train and subway passengers in all of Japan, more than one million people a day; more than 60 exits lead out of the station.
- Tokyo has suffered widespread destruction twice in the past century—in the 1923 Great Kanto Earthquake and in World War II firebombings. In both instances, more than 100,000 people lost their lives.
- During the Edo Period (1603–1867), Edo (former Tokyo) witnessed almost 100 major fires, not to mention countless smaller fires.
- Tokyo sprawls over 800 square miles, and yet most streets are not named.
- The average life span in Japan is 83½ years for women and 77 years for men, the longest in the world. By 2015, an estimated one-fourth of Japanese will be older than 65.
- Rickshaws originated in Tokyo in 1869; 4 years later, there were 34,000 of the people-propelled vehicles in the capital city.
- Park space in Tokyo is woefully inadequate—just 4.52 square meters (5.40 sq. yd.) per capita, compared to 45.7 square meters (54.7 sq. yd.) per person in Washington, D.C.
- Tokyo Disneyland, which opened in 1983, is 1½ times larger than Disneyland in California and is visited by more than 10 million people annually.

(fare: ¥800/$6.65), and Odaiba (fare: ¥520/$4.35). Fifty-minute **harbor cruises,** also departing Hinode Pier, cost ¥800 ($6.65). For more information, contact the **Tourist Information Center** (☎ 03-3201-3331) or the **Tokyo Cruise Ship Co.** (☎ 03/3457-7830).

Suggested Itineraries

There are two things to remember in planning your sightseeing itinerary: The city is huge, and it takes time to get from one end to the other. Plan your days so you cover Tokyo neighborhood by neighborhood, coordinating sightseeing with dinner and evening plans. To help you get the most out of your stay, the suggested itineraries below will guide you to the most important attractions. Note, however, that some attractions are closed 1 day of the week, so plan your days accordingly.

If You Have 1 Day   Start by getting up in the wee hours of the morning (if you've just flown in from North America, you'll be suffering from jet lag anyway and will find yourself wide awake by 5am) and head for the **Tsukiji Fish Market,** Japan's largest wholesale fish market (closed Sun and holidays). Be brave and try a breakfast of the freshest sushi you'll ever have. By 9am you should be on the Hibiya Line on your way to Ueno, where you should head to the **Tokyo National Museum,** the country's largest and most important museum (closed Mon). From there, move on

Tokyo Attractions

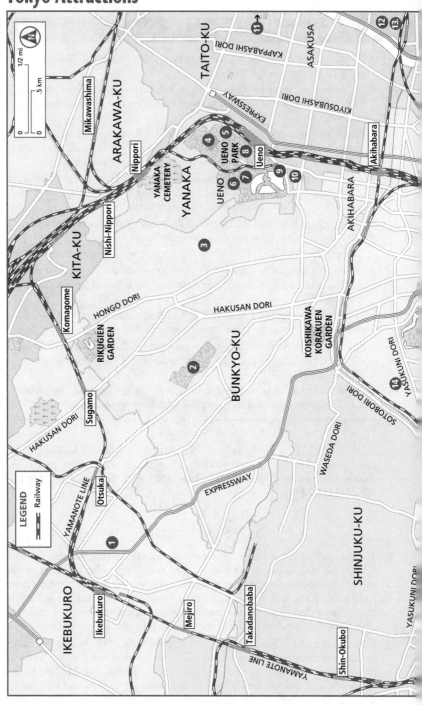

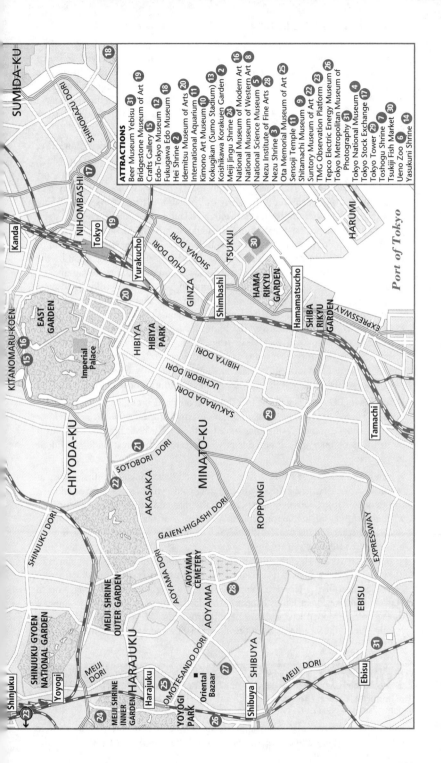

ATTRACTIONS

Beer Museum Yebisu **19**
Bridgestone Museum of Art **15**
Crafts Gallery **12**
Edo-Tokyo Museum **18**
Fukugawa Edo Museum **18**
Hei Shrine **2**
Idemitsu Museum of Arts **20**
International Aquarium **11**
Kimono Art Museum **10**
Kokugikan (Sumo Stadium) **13**
Koishikawa Korakuen Garden **2**
Meiji Jingu Shrine **24**
National Museum of Modern Art **16**
National Museum of Western Art **8**
National Science Museum **5**
Nezu Institute of Fine Arts **28**
Nezu Shrine **3**
Ota Memorial Museum of Art **25**
Sensoji Temple **11**
Shitamachi Museum **9**
Suntory Museum of Art **22**
TMC Observation Platform **23**
Tepco Electric Energy Museum **26**
Tokyo Metropolitan Museum of Photography **31**
Tokyo National Museum **4**
Tokyo Stock Exchange **17**
Tokyo Tower **7**
Toshogu Shrine **29**
Tsukiji Fish Market **30**
Ueno Zoo **6**
Yasukuni Shrine **14**

SUMIDA-KU

SHINOBAZU DORI

NIHOMBASHI

Kanda

Tokyo **19**

Yurakucho

KITANOMARU-KOEN

EAST GARDEN **15 16**

Imperial Palace

CHIYODA-KU

SHINJUKU DORI

SHINJUKU GYOEN NATIONAL GARDEN

Shinjuku

Yoyogi

MEIJI SHRINE INNER GARDEN

HARAJUKU

MEIJI DORI

MEIJI SHRINE OUTER GARDEN

Harajuku **25**

YOYOGI PARK **26**

Oriental Bazaar

OMOTESANDO DORI

Shibuya

SHIBUYA

AOYAMA DORI

AOYAMA CEMETERY

AOYAMA **28**

27

SOTOBORI DORI **21**

AKASAKA **22**

GAIEN-HIGASHI DORI

MINATO-KU

ROPPONGI

MEIJI DORI

Ebisu

EBISU **31**

EXPRESSWAY

CHUO DORI

SHOWA DORI

GINZA

HIBIYA

HIBIYA PARK **20**

HIBIYA DORI

UCHIBORI DORI

SAKURADA DORI

29

Tamachi

TSUKIJI

Shimbashi

Hamamatsucho

HAMA RIKYU GARDEN **30**

SHIBA RIKYU GARDEN

EXPRESSWAY

HARUMI

Port of Tokyo

143

to **Asakusa** for lunch in one of the area's traditional Japanese restaurants, followed by a walk on Nakamise Dori (good for souvenirs) to **Sensoji Temple.** In the late afternoon you might want to head for **Ginza** for some shopping, followed by dinner in a restaurant of your choice. Drop by a yakitori-ya, a typical Japanese watering hole, for a beer and a snack. You might be exhausted by the end of the day, but you'll have seen some of the city's highlights.

If You Have 2 Days   On the first day, get up early and go to **Tsukiji Fish Market** to eat sushi for breakfast. Next, head for the nearby **Hama Rikyu Garden,** which opens at 9am (closed Monday). It's about a 20-minute walk from Tsukiji, or a short taxi ride away. After touring the garden, one of the city's best, board the ferry that departs from inside the grounds for a trip up the Sumida River to **Asakusa,** where you can visit **Sensoji Temple** and shop along Nakamise Dori, and then have lunch in a traditional Japanese restaurant. You might even wish to follow my recommended walking tour of Asakusa, covered in Chapter 7. In the afternoon, head to the **Ginza** with its many department stores. If there's a performance, drop by the Kabukiza Theater for part of a Kabuki play. Have dinner at a Ginza restaurant.

On your second day, go early in the morning to the **Edo-Tokyo Museum** (located next to the sumo stadium), a great museum that illuminates the city's tumultuous history. Next, head to Ueno, where you should walk through **Ueno Park** to the **Tokyo National Museum.** From there, board the JR Yamanote Line to **Harajuku,** where you can visit **Meiji Jingu Shrine,** Tokyo's most famous Shinto shrine; the **Ota Memorial Museum of Art,** with its collection of woodblock prints; and the **Oriental Bazaar,** a great place to shop for souvenirs. Spend the evening in one of Tokyo's famous nightlife districts, such as **Shinjuku** or **Roppongi.**

If You Have 3 Days   Spend the first 2 days as outlined above, and on the 3rd day head for **Kamakura,** one of Japan's most important historical sites. Located an hour south of Tokyo by train, Kamakura served as the capital back in the 1100s and is packed with temples and shrines, one of which features the Great Buddha outdoor bronze statue.

If You Have 4 Days or More   Consider yourself lucky. Spend the first 3 days as outlined above; devote the 4th day to pursuing your own interests, such as taking a trip to one of Tokyo's numerous art or specialty museums, making an appointment with an acupuncturist, shopping, or following one of the recommended walking tours in chapter 7. This may be the evening to spend in wild partying, staying out until the first subways start running at 5am.

If you have a 5th day, you might visit **Nikko,** approximately 2 hours north of Tokyo, to see the sumptuous **mausoleum of Tokugawa Ieyasu,** the shogun who succeeded in unifying Japan in the 1600s. Or you might consider a 2-day trip to **Hakone,** famous for its fantastic open-air sculpture museum and home to some of the best old-fashioned Japanese inns near Tokyo. It also offers unparalleled views of Mount Fuji, if the weather is clear. See chapter 10 for more ideas on side trips from Tokyo.

1 The Top Attractions

The Imperial Palace (Kokyo). Located on Hibiya Dori Ave. in the heart of the city. Station: Nijubashi-mae (1 min.) or Hibiya (5 min.).

The Imperial Palace is the heart and soul of Tokyo. Built on the very spot where Edo Castle used to stand during the days of the Tokugawa shogunate, it became the imperial home at its completion in 1888 and is now the residence of Emperor Aki-hito, 125th emperor of Japan. Destroyed during air raids in 1945, the palace was rebuilt in 1968 using the principles of traditional Japanese architecture. But don't expect to get a good look at it; the palace grounds are off-limits to the public, with the exception of 2 days a year when the royal family makes an appearance before the throngs: New Year's Day and on the Emperor's Birthday (December 23). Still, all Japanese tourists make brief stops here to pay their respects. You'll have to con-sole yourself with a camera shot of the palace from the southeast side of **Nijubashi Bridge,** with the moat and the palace turrets showing above the trees. The wide moat, lined with cherry trees, is especially beautiful in the spring. You might even want to spend an hour strolling the 3 miles around the palace and moat.

But the most important thing to do while in the vicinity of the palace is to visit its **Higashi Gyoen** (East Garden), where you'll find what's left of the central keep of old Edo Castle, the stone foundation; see "Parks & Gardens," below.

✪ **Sensoji Temple.** 2–3–1 Asakusa, Taito-ku. ☎ **03/3842-0181.** Free admission. Open 24 hr. Station: Asakusa (2 min.).

This is Tokyo's oldest and most popular temple, with a history dating back to 628. That was when, according to popular lore, two brothers fishing in the nearby Sumida River netted the catch of their lives—a tiny golden statue of Kannon, the Buddhist goddess of mercy and happiness, who is empowered with the ability to release humans from all suffering. Sensoji Temple (also popularly known as Asakusa Kannon) was erected in her honor, and although the statue is housed here, it's never shown to the public. Still, through the centuries worshippers have flocked here, seeking favors of Kannon, and when Sensoji Temple burned down during a 1945 bombing raid, the present structure was rebuilt with donations by the Japanese people.

Colorful **Nakamise Dori,** a pedestrian lane leading to the shrine, is lined with traditional shops and souvenir stands, while nearby **Demboin Garden** remains an insider's favorite as a peaceful oasis away from the bustling crowds. See the walking tour in chapter 7 for more on this fascinating part of old Tokyo.

✪ **Meiji Jingu Shrine.** Meiji Shrine Inner Garden, 1–1 Kamizono-cho, Yoyogi, Shibuya-ku. ☎ **03/3379-5511.** Free admission. Daily sunrise–sunset (until 4:30pm in winter). Station: Harajuku (2 min.).

This is Tokyo's most venerable Shinto shrine, opened in 1920 in honor of Emperor and Empress Meiji, who were instrumental in opening Japan to the outside world a hundred years ago. Two torii (the traditional entry gate of a shrine), Japan's largest, built of cypress more than 1,700 years old, give dramatic entrance to the grounds, once the estate of a daimyo lord. The shaded pathway is lined with trees, shrubs, and a dense wood. In June, the **Iris Garden** is in spectacular bloom (separate admis-sion fee charged). The shrine itself, about a 10-minute walk from the first torii, is a fine example of dignified and refined Shinto architecture. It's made of plain Japanese cypress and topped with green-copper roofs. Meiji Jingu Shrine is the place to be on New Year's Eve, when more than two million people crowd onto the grounds to usher in the New Year.

If you'd like to see more pertaining to Emperor Meiji, about a 10-minute walk from the shrine at the north end of the garden is the **Meiji Jingu Treasure Museum,** which displays personal items that belonged to the emperor. It's open daily except the third Friday of the month from 9am to 4:30pm (4pm in winter), and charges ¥500 ($4.15) admission for adults and ¥250 ($2.10) for children.

✪ **Tokyo National Museum (Tokyo Kokuritsu Hakubutsukan).** Ueno Park, Taito-ku. ☎ **03/3822-1111.** Admission ¥420 ($3.50) adults, ¥130 ($1.10) students, ¥70 (60¢) children, free for senior citizens (except during special exhibitions). Free for everyone 2nd Sat of every month (except during special exhibitions). Oct–Mar, Tues–Sun 9:30am–5pm (enter by 4:30pm); Apr–Sept, Tues–Thurs and Sat–Sun 9:30am–5pm and Fri 9:30am–8pm. Closed Dec 26–Jan 3. Station: Ueno (10 min.). Walk through Ueno Park to its north end.

The National Museum is not only the largest and oldest museum in Japan, but it also boasts the largest collection of Japanese art in the world. This is where you go to see antiques from Japan's past—old kimono, samurai armor, priceless swords, lacquerware, pottery, scrolls, screens, ukiyo-e (woodblock prints), calligraphy, ceramics, archaeological finds, and more. Items are shown on a rotating basis, with about 4,000 on display at any one time—so no matter how many times you visit the museum, you'll always see something new.

The museum is composed of four buildings. The **Main Gallery** (Honkan), straight ahead as you enter the main gate, is the most important one, devoted to Japanese art. Here you'll view a comprehensive history of Japanese ceramics, from the Jomon Period 3,000 B.C. to Imari ware produced during the Meiji Era. You'll also see Buddhist sculptures dating from about A.D. 538 to 1192; samurai armor, helmets, and decorative sword mountings; swords, which throughout Japanese history were considered to embody spirits all their own; textiles and kimono; lacquerware; and paintings, calligraphy, ukiyo-e, and scrolls. Be sure to check out the museum shop in the basement; it sells reproductions from the museum's collections, as well as traditional crafts by contemporary artists.

The **Gallery of Eastern Antiquities** (Toyokan) houses art and archaeological artifacts from everywhere in Asia outside Japan. There are Buddhas from China and Gandhara; stone reliefs from Cambodia; embroidered wall hangings and cloth from India; Iranian and Turkish carpets; Thai and Vietnamese ceramics; and more. Chinese art—including jade, paintings and calligraphy, and ceramics—makes up the largest part of the collection, illustrating China's tremendous influence on Japanese art, architecture, and religion. You'll also find Egyptian relics in this gallery, including a mummy dating from around 751 to 656 B.C. and wooden objects from the 20th century B.C.

The **Heiseikan Gallery** holds special exhibitions on its second floor, while the first floor is where you'll find archaeological relics of Japan, including pottery and objects from old burial mounds, as well as items used in daily life by the Ainu, the indigenous ethnic group of Hokkaido. The **Gallery of Horyuji Treasures** (Horyuji Homotsukan) displays priceless Buddhist treasures from the Horyuji Temple in Nara, founded by Prince Shotoku in 607. Displays, representing some of Japan's oldest Buddhist artifacts, include bronze scultpure, ceremonial Gigaku masks used in ritual dances, lacquerware, and paintings.

✪ **Edo-Tokyo Museum (Edo-Tokyo Hakubutsukan).** 1–4–1 Yokoami, Sumida-ku. ☎ **03/3626-9974.** Admission ¥600 ($5) adults, ¥300 ($2.50) children. Tues–Wed and Sat–Sun 10am–6pm; Thurs–Fri 10am–8pm. Station: Ryogoku on the JR Sobu Line (3 min.).

The building housing this impressive museum is said to resemble a rice granary when viewed from afar, but to me it looks like a modern torii, the entrance gate to a shrine. This is the metropolitan government's ambitious attempt to present the history, art, disasters, science, culture, and architecture of Tokyo from its humble beginnings in 1590—when the first shogun, Tokugawa Ieyasu, made Edo (old Tokyo) the seat of his domain—to 1964, when Tokyo hosted the Olympics. All in all, the museum's great visual displays create a vivid portrayal of Tokyo through the centuries. I wouldn't miss it.

After purchasing your tickets and taking the escalator to the sixth floor, you'll enter the museum by walking over a replica of Nihombashi Bridge, the starting point for all roads leading out of old Edo. Exhibits covering the Edo Period portray the lives of the shoguns, merchants, craftsmen, and townspeople. The explanations are mostly only in Japanese, but there's plenty to look at, including a replica of an old Kabuki theater, a model of a daimyo mansion, portable floats used during festivals, maps of old Edo, and—perhaps most interesting—a rowhouse tenement, where Edo commoners lived in cramped quarters measuring only 10 square meters. Other displays cover the Meiji Restoration, the Great Kanto Earthquake of 1923, and the bombing raids of World War II (Japan's own role as aggressor is disappointingly glossed over).

✪ **Tsukiji Fish Market.** 5-2-1 Tsukiji, Chuo-ku. ☎ **03/3542-1111.** Free admission. Mon–Sat 5–10am (best time 5–8am). Closed some Wed, holidays, New Year's, and Aug 15–16. Station: Tsukiji (Honganji Temple exit, 10 min.).

This huge wholesale fish market—the largest in Japan, and one of the largest in the world—is a must for anyone who has never seen such a market in action. And the action here starts early: At about 3am, boats begin arriving from the seas around Japan, from Africa, and even from America, with enough fish to satisfy the demands of a nation where seafood reigns supreme. To give you some idea of its enormity, this market handles almost all the seafood consumed in Tokyo. The king is tuna, huge and frozen, unloaded from the docks, laid out on the ground, and numbered. Wholesalers then walk up and down the rows, jotting down the numbers of the best-looking tuna, and by 5:15am the tuna auctions are well under way. The wholesalers then transfer what they've bought to their own stalls in the market, subsequently selling the fish to their regular customers, usually retail stores and restaurants.

The market is held in a cavernous, hangarlike building, which means that you can visit it even on a dismal rainy morning. There's a lot going on—men in black rubber boots rushing wheelbarrows and carts through the aisles, hawkers shouting, knives chopping and slicing. Wander the aisles and you'll see things you never dreamed were edible. This is a good place to bring your camera if you have a flash: The people working here burst with pride if you single them out for a photograph. The floors are wet, so leave your fancy shoes at the hotel.

Tsukiji is also a good place to come if you want sushi for breakfast. Beside the covered market are rows of barracklike buildings divided into sushi restaurants and shops related to the fish trade. **Sushi Dai,** for example, offers a *seto* for ¥2,000 ($17); it's open every day the fish market is open, from 5am to 2pm (see chapter 5 for more information).

As you walk the distance between the Tsukiji subway station and the fish market, you'll find yourself in a delightful district of tiny retail shops and stalls where you can buy the freshest seafood in town, plus dried fish and fish products, seaweed, vegetables, and cooking utensils. Also in this area, and beside the market, are stalls selling cheap sushi, noodles, and fish, catering mainly to buyers and sellers at the market who come for a quick breakfast. There are also a lot of pottery shops and stores that sell plastic and lacquered trays, bowls, and cups. Although they usually sell in great quantities to restaurant owners, shopkeepers will usually sell to the casual tourist as well.

2 Five Unforgettable Ways to Immerse Yourself in Japanese Culture

Just walking down the street could be considered a cultural experience in Japan. But there are a few more concrete ways to learn more about this country's cultural life: The best is by participating in some of its time-honored rituals and traditions.

IKEBANA   Instruction in ikebana, or flower arranging, is available at a number of schools in Tokyo, several of which offer classes in English on a regular basis. (Note that you should call beforehand to enroll.) **Sogetsuryu Ikebana School,** 7–2–21 Akasaka (☎ **03/3408-1151;** station: Aoyama-Itchome, a 5-minute walk from exit 4), offers instruction in English on Monday from 10am to noon (closed in August). The cost of one lesson for first-time participants is ¥4,850 ($41), including the cost of the flowers and materials. The **Ohararyu Ikebana School,** 5–7–17 Minami Aoyama (☎ **03/3499-1200;** station: Omotesando, 3 min.), offers 2-hour instruction in English at 10am on Wednesday and Thursday and at 1:30pm on Tuesday, charging ¥4,000 ($33) for instruction and materials. You can also come just to observe for ¥800 ($6.65). Finally, the **Ikenobo Ochanomizu Gakuin,** 2–3 Kanda Surugadai (☎ **03/3292-3071;** station: Ochanomizu, a 3-min. walk), offers 1½-hour classes on Wednesday at 11am, 2pm, and 4pm, charging ¥3,700 ($31), including cost of the flowers.

If you wish to see ikebana, ask at the Tourist Information Office whether there are any special exhibitions on while you're in town. Department stores sometimes have special ikebana exhibitions in their galleries. Another place to look is Yasukuni Shrine, located on Yasukuni Dori, northwest of the Imperial Palace (closest station: Ichigaya or Kudanshita). Dedicated to Japanese war dead, the shrine also has ongoing exhibitions of ikebana on its grounds.

TEA CEREMONY   Several first-class hotels hold tea ceremonies in special tea-ceremony rooms with instruction in English. Reservations are usually required, and since they're often booked by groups, you'll want to call in advance to see whether you can participate. **Seisei-an,** on the seventh floor of the Hotel New Otani, 4–1 Kioi-cho, Chiyoda-ku (☎ **03/3265-1111,** ext. 2443; station: Nagatacho or Akasaka-mitsuke, a 3-min. walk from both), holds 20-minute lessons on Thursday through Saturday from 11am to noon and 1 to 4pm. The cost is ¥1,050 ($8.75), including tea and sweets. **Chosho-an,** on the seventh floor of the Hotel Okura, 2–10–4 Toranomon, Minato-ku (☎ **03/3582-0111;** station: Toranomon or Kamiyacho, a 10-min. walk from both), gives 30-minute classes anytime between 11am and noon and between 1 and 4pm Monday through Saturday. Appointments are required; the cost is ¥1,050 ($8.75) for tea and sweets. At **Toko-an,** on the fourth floor of the Imperial Hotel, 1–1–1 Uchisaiwaicho, Chiyoda-ku (☎ **03/3504-1111;** station: Hibiya, 1 min.), instruction is given from 10am to noon and 1 to 4pm, daily except Sunday and holidays. Reservations are required. The fee is ¥1,500 ($12.50) for tea and sweets.

ACUPUNCTURE & SHIATSU   Although most Westerners have heard of acupuncture, they may not be familiar with *shiatsu* (Japanese pressure-point massage). Most first-class hotels in Japan offer shiatsu. There are acupuncture clinics everywhere in Tokyo, and the staff of your hotel may be able to tell you of one nearby. As it's not likely the clinic's staff will speak English, it might be a good idea to have the guest relations officer at your hotel not only make the reservation but specify the treatment you want.

Go halfway around the world.
Sound like you're halfway around the block.

Global connection with the AT&T Network

AT&T
direct
service

Calling home from far away? With the world's most powerful network, **AT&T Direct** Service connects you clear and fast, plus gives you the option of an English-speaking operator. All you need is your AT&T Calling Card or credit card.* Sounds good, especially from the middle of nowhere. FOR A LIST OF **AT&T ACCESS NUMBERS**, TAKE THE ATTACHED WALLET GUIDE.

Pachinko Parlors

Brightly lit and garish, pachinko parlors are packed with upright pinball-like machines, with row upon row of Japanese businessmen, housewives, and students sitting intently immobile in front of them. Originating in Nagoya and popular since the 1950s, pachinko is a game in which ball bearings are flung into a kind of vertical pinball machine, one after the other. Humans control the strength with which the ball is released, but otherwise there's very little to do. Some players even wedge a matchstick under the control and just watch the machine with folded arms. Points are amassed according to which holes the ball bearings fall into. If you're good at it, you win ball bearings back, which you can subsequently trade in for food, cigarettes, watches, calculators, and the like.

It's illegal to win money in Japan, but outside many pachinko parlors and along back alleyways, there are slots where you can trade in the watches, calculators, and other prizes for cash. The slots are so small that the person handing over the goods never sees the person who hands back money. Police, meanwhile, just look the other way.

Pachinko parlors compete in an ever-escalating war of themes, lights, and noise. Step inside, and you'll wonder how anyone could possibly think; the noise level of thousands of ball bearings clanking is awesome. Perhaps that's the answer to its popularity: You can't think, making it a getaway pastime. Some people seem to be addicted to the mesmerizing game, newspaper articles talk of errant husbands who never come home anymore, and psychologists analyze its popularity. At any rate, every hamlet seems to have a pachinko parlor, and major cities like Tokyo are inundated with them. You'll find them in nightlife districts and clustered around train stations, but with their unmistakable clanging and clanking, you'll hear them long before you notice their brightly lit, gaudy facades.

For acupuncture, try **Ido-no-Nihonsha,** on the second floor of the Kokushin Building, 1–10–2 Sinjuku (☎ 03/3341-3470); station: Shinjuku-Gyoenmae, 5 min.). Hours here are 10am to 6pm Monday through Friday; call for an appointment and a schedule fee, but note that no English is spoken. For shiatsu, try **Namikoshi Shiatsu Center,** with several branches in Tokyo. Those where some English is spoken include the **Shibuya branch,** on the second floor of No. 2 Okuno Building, 2–18–8 Shibuya (☎ 03/3409-1731; station: Shibuya, 5 min.), open Monday through Saturday 10am to 7pm. It charges ¥8,200 ($68) an hour for the first visit, ¥7,200 ($60) per hour on subsequent visits. Some English is also spoken at the **Asakusabashi branch,** on the second floor of the Isoe Building, 1–29–7 Yanagibashi (☎ 03/3861-3963; station: Asakusabashi, 5 min.), open Monday through Saturday 9am to 7pm. The rates here are ¥7,000 ($58) per hour on the first visit and ¥6,000 ($50) per hour on subsequent visits. Although no English is spoken, there's a more convenient branch in Yurakucho, on the third floor of the Kotsu Kaikan Building, 2–10–1 Yurakucho (☎ 03/3211-8008; station: Yurakucho, 1 min.). It's open Monday through Saturday 10am to 6:30pm and charges ¥7,800 ($65) per hour.

PUBLIC BATHS I suggest that you go at least once to a neighborhood *sento* (public bath). Altogether, Tokyo has an estimated 1,450 sento—which may sound like a lot but is nothing compared to the 2,687 the city used to have just 30 years ago. Easily recognizable by a tall chimney and shoe lockers just inside the door, a sento sells about anything you might need at the bathhouse—soap, shampoo, towels, even underwear.

Since there are so many public baths spread throughout the city, it's best simply to go to the one most convenient to you. If you prefer a suggestion, however, the **Azabu Juban Onsen**, 1–5 Azabu Juban, Minato-ku (☎ **03/3404-2610**; station: Roppongi), is one of the more luxurious and is the one I used to go to when I lived for a while in an apartment without a tub or shower. Its brownish water actually comes from a hot spring 500 meters underground. It's closed on Tuesday but open the rest of the week from 11am to 9pm; admission is ¥1,260 ($10.50).

The **Asakusa Kannon Onsen**, 2–7–26 Asakusa, Taito-ku (☎ **03/3844-4141**; station: Asakusa), is located just west of Sensoji Temple in an ivy-colored building. This one also boasts water from a hot spring and has the atmosphere of a real neighborhood bath. It's particularly popular with the older generation. Open Friday through Wednesday from 6:30am to 6pm (closed Friday if Thursday is a holiday). The fee is only ¥700 ($5.85).

For bathing in hot springs, visit the mountain resort area of **Hakone,** described in detail in chapter 10.

ZAZEN   A few temples in the Tokyo vicinity occasionally offer sitting meditation with instruction in English. Approximately 30 minutes east of Akihabara on the Sobu Line is **Ida Ryogoku-do Zazen Dojo** of the Sotoshu Sect, 5–11–20 Minami Yawata, Ichikawa City (☎ **0473/79-1596**; station: Moto-Yawata, 5 min.). Zazen is held daily at 5:30 and 10am and 3 and 8:30pm, generally for 45 minutes. A Dogen-Sangha meeting is held the fourth Saturday of the month from 1 to 2:30pm, consisting of 30 minutes for zazen followed by a 1-hour lecture. Participation is free, and if you call from Moto-Yawata Station, someone will come for you. You can also stay at the dojo for longer periods to practice zen; call Mr. Nishijima at ☎ 03/3435-0701 for more information.

In addition, the **Young Men's Buddhist Association of Tokyo University,** of the Sotoshu Sect, second floor of the Nippon Shimpan Building, 3–33–5 Hongo (☎ **03/3235-0701** for Mr. Nishijima or 03/3929-4680 for Mr. Leutchford; station: Hongo-Shanchome, 3 min.) holds a Dogen-Sangha meeting the first, third, and fifth Saturday of each month from 1 to 2:30pm, including 30 minutes of zazen and a 1-hour lecture in English. There's a ¥300 ($2.50) fee.

3 Parks & Gardens

Although Japan's most famous gardens are not in Tokyo, most of the places listed below use principles of Japanese landscaping and give visitors at least an idea of the scope and style of these gardens. The fifth listing, **Ueno Park,** is Tokyo's largest city park and contains a number of museums and attractions, making it one of the city's most visited places.

✪ **Hama Rikyu Garden.** 1–1 Hamarikyuteien, Chuo-ku. ☎ **03/3541-0200.** Admission ¥300 ($2.50). Tues–Sun 9am–5pm. Station: Shimbashi (10 min.).

Considered by some to be the best garden in Tokyo, this peaceful oasis has origins stretching back 300 years, when it served as a retreat for a former feudal lord and as duck-hunting grounds for the Tokugawa shoguns. In 1871, possession of the garden passed to the imperial family, who used it to entertain such visiting dignitaries as General Ulysses S. Grant. Come here to see how the upper classes enjoyed themselves during the Edo Period. Located on Tokyo Bay and surrounded by water on three sides, the garden contains an inner tidal pool, spanned by three bridges draped with wisteria. There are also other ponds; a refuge for ducks, herons, and migratory birds; a promenade along the bay lined with pine trees and offering views of Rainbow Bridge; a 300-year-old pine; moon-viewing pavilions; and tea-houses. From a boarding pier inside the garden's grounds, ferries depart for Asakusa every hour (or more often) between 10:15am and 4:05pm; the fare is ¥620 ($5.15) one-way.

East Garden (Higashi Gyoen). 1–1 Chiyoda, Chiyoda-ku. ☎ **03/3213-1111.** Free admission. Mar–Oct Tues–Thurs and Sat–Sun 9am–4:30pm (enter by 4pm); Nov–Feb Tues–Thurs and Sat–Sun 9am–4pm (enter by 3:30pm). Closed Dec 25–Jan 3. Station: Otemachi (3 min.).

The 53 acres of the formal Higashi Gyoen—once the main grounds of Edo Castle—are a wonderful respite in the middle of the city. Yet surprisingly, it's hardly ever crowded. **Ninomaru,** my favorite part, is laid out in Japanese style with a pond, stepping stones, and winding paths; it's particularly beautiful when the wisteria, azaleas, irises, and other flowers are in bloom. Near Ninomaru is the **Sannomaru Shozokan,** which displays changing exhibitions of art treasures belonging to the imperial family free of charge.

On the highest spot of Higashi Gyoen is the **Honmaru** (inner citadel), where Tokugawa's main castle once stood. Built in the first half of the 1600s, the castle was massive, surrounded by a series of whirling moats and guarded by 23 watchtowers and 99 gates around its 10-mile perimeter. At its center was Japan's tallest building at the time, the five-story castle keep, soaring 168 feet above its foundations and offering an expansive view over Edo. This is where Tokugawa Ieyasu would have taken refuge, had his empire ever been seriously threatened. Although most of the castle was a glimmering white, the keep was black with a gold roof, which must have made quite a sight in old Edo as it towered above the rest of the city. Today all that remains of Tokugawa's castle are a few towers, gates, stone walls, moats, and the stone foundation of the keep.

Koishikawa Korakuen Garden (identified as Korakuen Garden on the TIC map). 1–6–6 Koraku, Bunkyo-ku. ☎ **03/3811-3015.** Admission ¥300 ($2.50). Daily 9am–5pm (enter by 4:30pm). Station: Iidabashi or Korakuen (8 min.). Entrance is at the southwestern edge of the garden.

Constructed in the 17th century by a member of the Tokugawa clan with the assistance of a Chinese scholar refugee, this lovely, circular-pathed garden once spread over 63 acres but has been whittled away by urbanization to only 16 acres. Still, it remains Tokyo's oldest and one of its most celebrated stroll gardens, known for its miniature replicas of famous scenic spots in Japan and China. With its bridges, maple and pine groves, wisteria, ponds, flowering shrubs and trees, and other feasts for the eyes, little wonder it's been designated an Outstanding Scenic Place of Historical Importance. Indeed, the name *Korakuen* translates as "a pleasure afterward," reference to a Chinese poem with the verse "Be the first to take the world's trouble to heart, be the last to enjoy the world's pleasure."

Shinjuku Gyoen. 11 Naitocho, Shinjuku-ku. ☎ **03/3350-0151.** Admission ¥200 ($1.65). Tues–Sun 9am–4:30pm (enter by 4pm). Station: Shinjuku Gyoen-mae (2 min.).

Formerly the private estate of a feudal lord and then of the imperial family, this is considered one of the most important parks of the Meiji Era. It's wonderful for strolling because of the variety of its planted gardens; styles range from French and English to Japanese traditional. This place amazes me every time I come here. The park's 144 acres make it one of the city's largest, and each bend in the pathway brings something completely different: Ponds and sculpted bushes give way to a promenade lined with sycamores, which opens up into a rose garden. Cherry blossoms, azaleas, chrysanthemums, and other flowers provide splashes of color from spring through autumn. There are also wide grassy expanses, popular for picnics and playing, and a greenhouse filled with tropical plants.

Ueno Park. 3 Ikenohata, Taito-ku. ☎ **03/3827-7752.** Free admission to the park; separate admissions to each of its attractions. Ueno Park daily 24 hr. Station: Ueno (1 min.).

Ueno Park—on the northeast edge of the Yamanote Line—is one of the largest parks in Tokyo, and one of the most popular places in the city for Japanese families on a day's outing. It's a cultural mecca with a number of attractions, including the prestigious Tokyo National Museum and the delightful Shitamachi Museum, Ueno Zoo, and Shinobazu Pond (a bird sanctuary). The busiest time of the year at Ueno Park is in April, during the cherry-blossom season.

Other well-known landmarks in Ueno Park are **Toshogu Shrine**, erected in 1651 and dedicated to Tokugawa Ieyasu, founder of the Tokugawa shogunate; and **Kiyomizu-do Kannon Temple**, completed in 1631 as a copy of the famous Kiyomizu-do Kannon Temple in Kyoto (see "Shrines & Temples," below).

For more information on Ueno Park, see the walking tour of Ueno in chapter 7.

4 Shrines & Temples

In addition to the temples and shrines listed here, don't forget **Sensoji Temple** and **Meiji Jingu Shrine** (see "The Top Attractions," above).

Kiyomizu-do Kannon Temple. Ueno Park, Taito-ku. ☎ **03/3821-4749.** Free admission. Daily 7am–5pm. Station: Ueno (3 min.).

Established in 1631 and moved to its present site overlooking Shinobazu Pond in 1698, this small but important structure is a copy of the famous Kiyomizu Temple in Kyoto (but on a much less grand scale). It was once part of the Kan'eiji Temple precincts that covered Ueno Hill during the Edo Period. Remarkably, the temple survived both the 1868 battle between imperial and shogunate forces and bombings during World War II. Today, it's one of Tokyo's oldest temples. It enshrines Kosodate Kannon, protectoress of childbearing and child-raising; women hoping to become pregnant come here to ask for the goddess's mercy, and those whose wishes have been fulfilled return to pray for their child's good health and protection. Many leave behind dolls as a symbol of their children—if you take your shoes off and walk to the door to the right of the main altar, you'll see some of them. Once a year, on September 25, a requiem service is held for all the dolls at the temple, after which they are cremated.

Nezu Shrine. 1–28–9 Nezu, Bunkyo-ku. ☎ **03/3821-4817** or 03/3822-0753. Free admission. Precincts daily 24 hr.; shrine daily 5:30am–6pm. Station: Nezu (3 min.).

Nezu Shrine is just enough off the beaten path to remain one of Tokyo's best-kept secrets. Built in 1706, it features an ornate front courtyard gate of red lacquer with joists in gilt, green, blue, orange, and black. Inside are beautiful vermilion-colored buildings, venerable cedars, and thousands of manicured azalea bushes. When the azalea is in bloom, this place is heaven.

Toshogu Shrine. Ueno Park, Taito-ku. ☎ **03/3822-3455.** Admission ¥200 ($1.65) adults, ¥100 (85¢) children. Summer daily 9am–6pm; winter daily 9am–4:30pm. Station: Ueno (4 min.).

Cherry-Blossom Viewing in Ueno Park

If you happen to come to Ueno Park during that brief single week in April when the cherry blossoms burst forth in glorious pink, consider yourself lucky. Cherry blossoms have always been dear to the Japanese heart as a symbol of beauty, fragility, and the transitory nature of life. Ueno Park, with its 1,000 cherry trees, has been popular as a viewing spot since the Edo Period. Today, Tokyoites throng here en masse to celebrate the birth of the new season. It's not, however, the spiritual communion with nature you might think. In the daytime on a weekday, Ueno Park may be peaceful and sane enough, but on the weekends and in the evenings during cherry-blossom season, havoc prevails as office workers break out of their winter shells.

Sending underlings to stake out territory early in the day, whole companies of workers later converge on Ueno Park to sit under the cherry trees on plastic or cardboard, their shoes neatly lined up along the perimeter. They eat obento box lunches and drink sake and beer; many get drunk and can be quite rowdy. The worst offenders are those singing karaoke. Still, visiting Ueno Park during cherry-blossom season is a cultural experience no one should miss. It's more than likely that you'll be invited to join one of the large groups—and by all means do so. You'll all sit there drinking and making merry, seemingly oblivious to the fragile pink blossoms shimmering above.

Come here to pay respects to the man who made Edo (present-day Tokyo) the seat of his government and thus elevated the small village to the most important city in the country. The only shrine in Tokyo that's been designated a National Treasure, Toshogu Shrine was erected in 1651 and is dedicated to Tokugawa Ieyasu, founder of the Tokugawa shogunate. Like Toshogu Shrine in Nikko, it was built by Ieyasu's grandson, Iemitsu, and boasts some of the same richly carved, ornate design favored by the Tokugawas. Remarkably, it survived the civil war of 1868, the Great Kanto Earthquake of 1923, and even World War II. The pathway to the shrine is lined with massive stone lanterns, as well as 50 copper lanterns donated by *daimyo* (feudal lords) from all over Japan. Inside the shrine, you'll see some exquisite art, including murals by a famous Edo artist, Kano Tan-yu, and samurai armor worn by Ieyasu. On a more somber note, there's also a display on the grounds appealing for world peace, with photographs of Hiroshima following its destruction by the atom bomb and of victims dead and alive.

Yasukuni Shrine. 3–1–1 Kudan-kita, Chiyoda-ku. ☎ **03/3261-8326.** Free admission to shrine; Yushukan ¥300 ($2.50) adults, ¥200 ($1.65) junior and senior high-school students, ¥100 (85¢) children. Shrine, daily 24 hr.; Yushukan, daily 9am–5pm (to 4:30pm Nov–Feb). Station: Kudanshita (5 min.) or Ichigaya (10 min.).

Built in 1869 to commemorate Japanese war dead, Yasukuni Shrine is constructed in classic Shinto style, with a huge steel torii gate at its entrance. During times of war, soldiers were told that if they died fighting for their country, their spirits would find glory here; even today, it's believed that the spirits of some 2.5 million Japanese war dead are at home here, where they are worshipped as deities. During any day of the week, you're likely to encounter older Japanese, paying their respects to friends and families who perished in World War II. But every August the shrine is thrust into the national spotlight when World War II memorials are held. In 1985, then prime minister Yasuhiro Nakasone caused a national uproar when he put in an appearance (some thought it improper for a prime minister to visit—and thereby condone—a shrine so closely tied to Japan's nationalistic and militaristic past).

On the shrine's grounds is a small war memorial museum, the **Yushukan,** containing weapons, uniforms, and other memorabilia left by war dead from the Sino-Japanese War, Russo-Japanese War, and World Wars I and II. Included are samurai armor, swords, bows and arrows, tanks, guns, and artillery, as well as such thought-provoking displays as a human torpedo (a tiny submarine guided by one occupant and loaded with explosives) and a suicide attack plane. But the most chilling displays are the seemingly endless photographs of war dead, some of them very young teenagers. In stark contrast to the somberness of the museum, temporary exhibits of beautiful ikebana (Japanese flower arrangements) and bonsai are often held on the shrine grounds in rows of glass cases. Yasukuni Shrine is also famous for its cherry blossoms.

5 More Museums

For details on the **Tokyo National Museum** and the **Edo-Tokyo Museum,** see "The Top Attractions," above.

ART MUSEUMS

Bridgestone Museum of Art (Bridgestone Bijutsukan). Bridgestone Building, 1–10–1 Kyobashi, Chuo-ku. ☎ **03/3563-0241.** Admission ¥500 ($4.15) adults, ¥400 ($3.35) students, ¥200 ($1.65) children. Tues–Sun 10am–6pm. Closed during exhibit changes. Station: Tokyo (Yaesu Central exit, 5 min.), Kyobashi (Meiji-ya exit, 5 min.) or Nihombashi (Takashimaya exit, 5 min.). On Chuo Dori (with an entrance around the corner on Yaesu Dori), a short walk directly east of Tokyo Station.

This privately owned museum contains a small but impressive collection of French impressionist art, as well as Japanese paintings in the Western style dating from the Meiji Period onward. This is one of the best of Tokyo's private art museums, and since there are only five rooms of displays, it makes a quick and worthwhile detour if you're in the vicinity. The permanent collection includes works by Monet, Manet, Degas, Sisley, Cézanne, Pissarro, Renoir, Corot, Gauguin, van Gogh, Matisse, Picasso, Modigliani, and Rousseau, as well as Japanese painters Asai Chu, Kuroda Seiki, Aoki Shigeru, Kuniyoshi Wasuo, and Saeki Yuzo. Special exhibitions are mounted three or four times a year.

✪ **Hara Museum of Contemporary Art (Hara Bijutsukan).** 4–7–25 Kita-Shinagawa, Shinagawa-ku. ☎ **03/3445-0651.** Admission ¥1,000 ($8.35) adults, ¥700 ($5.85) students 16 and older, ¥500 ($4.15) children, free for seniors. Tues, Thurs–Sun and holidays 11am–5pm, Wed 11am–8pm. Closed during exhibition changes. Station: Shinagawa (15 min.).

Japan's oldest museum devoted to contemporary international and Japanese art is housed in a tiled, Bauhaus-style art deco home that once belonged to the current director's grandfather; the building alone is worth the trip. It stages three or four exhibitions annually, some on the cutting edge of international art and at least one featuring works from its own collection, which focuses on paintings and sculptures mainly from the 1950s and 1960s by Japanese and foreign artists and includes works by Andy Warhol, Roy Lichtenstein, Claes Oldenburg, Jackson Pollock, Karel Appel, Robert Rauschenberg, and Frank Stella. *A tip:* There's a "Secret Room" with explicit S&M photographs by Araki Nobuyoshi. Be sure, too, to check out the downstairs toilet by Morimura Yasumasu. Afterward, relax at the lovely greenhouse-like cafe with outdoor seating.

Museum Tips

Note that most museums in Tokyo are closed on Monday and for New Year's, generally the last few days in December and the first 3 days of January. If Monday happens to be a national holiday, most museums will remain open but will close Tuesday instead. Some of the privately owned museums may also be closed the day following every national holiday, as well as for exhibition changes. Call beforehand to avoid disappointment. Remember, too, that you must enter museums at least 30 minutes before closing time. For a listing of current special exhibitions, including those being held at major department stores, consult the *Tokyo Journal*, published monthly.

Idemitsu Museum of Arts (Idemitsu Bijutsukan). Teigeki Building, 9th floor, 3-1-1 Marunouchi, Chiyoda-ku. ☎ **03/3272-8600.** Admission ¥500 ($4.15) adults, ¥300 ($2.50) students. Tues–Sun 10am–5pm. Closed during exhibition changes. Station: Yurakucho or Hibiya (3 min.). On Hibiya Dori, across from the Imperial Palace moat.

This privately owned museum is dedicated to the preservation and display of Japanese and Chinese art, primarily paintings, calligraphy, and ceramics. It mounts approximately seven exhibitions a year. Past exhibits have included works by Kosugi Hoan, a Japanese- and Western-style painter during the Meiji and Taisho periods; treasures excavated from China during the Cultural Revolution; and paintings and calligraphy by Sengai, a Zen master during the Edo Period. A plus is the view of the imperial palace, moat, and gardens.

Museum of Contemporary Art, Tokyo (MOT; Tokyo-to Gendai Bijutsukan). 4-1-1 Miyoshi, Koto-ku. ☎ **03/5245-4111.** Admission to permanent collection ¥500 ($4.15) adults, ¥250 ($2.10) students and children; special exhibits ¥700–¥1,000 ($5.85–$8.35). Tues–Thurs and Sat–Sun 10am–6pm; Fri 10am–9pm. Station: Kiba, on the Tozai Line (15 min.) or Kikukawa, on the Shinjuku Line (15 min.). Between Kiba and Kikukawa stations on Mitsume Dori; you're best off taking a taxi from the station.

The MOT is inconveniently located between Kiba and Kikukawa stations on Mitsume Dori but is well worth the trek if you're a fan of the avant-garde. This modern structure of glass and steel, with a long corridor entrance that reminds me of railroad trestles, houses both permanent and temporary exhibits of Japanese and international postwar art in large rooms that lend themselves to large installations. While temporary exhibits, which occupy most of the museum space, have ranged from Southeast Asian art to a retrospective of Jasper Johns, the smaller permanent collection presents a chronological study of 50 years of contemporary art, beginning with Japanese postwar avant-garde and continuing with anti-artistic trends and pop art in the 1960s, Minimalism, and art after the 1980s. Included are works by Andy Warhol, Gerhard Richter, Roy Lichtenstein, David Hockney, Frank Stella, Sandro Chia, and Julian Schnabel, with individual works changed frequently during the year.

National Museum of Modern Art (Tokyo Kokuritsu Kindai Bijutsukan). 3 Kitanomaru Koen Park, Chiyoda-ku. ☎ **03/3214-2561.** Admission to permanent collection ¥420 ($3.80) adults, ¥130 ($1.15) students, ¥70 (65¢) children; more for special exhibits. Tues–Sun 10am–5pm (Fri in summer to 8pm). Station: Takebashi (5 min.).

Here you'll find the largest collection of modern Japanese art housed under one roof, including both Japanese- and Western-style paintings, prints, watercolors, drawings, and sculpture, all dating from the Meiji Period to World War II. Names to look for include Munahata Shiko, Kuroda Seiki, and Yokoyama Taikan. To provide a wider context, a few Western artists are also represented, among them Klee, and Richter. *Note:* The museum is closed for renovation until sometime in 2001; contact the TIC for exact opening date.

National Museum of Western Art (Kokuritsu Seiyo Bijutsukan). Ueno Park, Taito-ku. ☎ **03/3828-5131.** Admission ¥420 ($3.50) adults, ¥130 ($1.10) students, ¥70 (60¢) children; special exhibits require separate admission fee. Free admission to permanent collection 2nd and 4th Sat of the month. Tues–Thurs and Sat–Sun 9:30am–5pm, Fri 9:30am–7pm. Station: Ueno (4 min.).

Japan's only national museum dedicated to Western art owes its small but impressive collection to Kojiro Matsukata, a shipbuilding magnate and National Diet member who began his collection just before World War I in an effort to introduce European art to young Japanese painters. The museum is housed in a main building designed by Le Corbusier and two recent additions. It presents a chronological study of sculpture and art from the end of the Middle Ages through the 20th century, beginning with works by Old Masters, including Lucas Cranach the Elder, Rubens, El Greco, Murillo, and Tiepolo. French modern painters and Impressionists are well represented, including Monet (with a whole room of his work), Manet, Renoir, Pissarro, Sisley, Courbet, Cezanne, and Gauguin. The museum's 20th-century collection includes works by Picasso, Max Ernst, Miro, Dubuffet, and Pollock. The museum is also famous for its 50-odd sculptures by Rodin, one of the largest collections in the world, encompassing most of his major works, including *The Kiss, The Thinker, Balzac,* and *The Gates of Hell.*

Nezu Institute of Fine Arts (Nezu Bijutsukan). 6–5–1 Minami Aoyama, Minato-ku. ☎ **03/3400-2536.** Admission ¥1,000 ($8.35) adults, ¥700 ($5.85) students and children. Tues–Sun 9:30am–4:30pm. Closed days following holidays and during exhibit changes. Station: Omotesando (8 min.).

This is one of Tokyo's best private museums. It houses a fine collection of Oriental art, including Chinese bronzes, Japanese calligraphy, Korean ceramics, and other artwork ranging from paintings and sculpture to lacquerware, Buddhist and Shinto art, and items used in tea ceremonies. Among its works are two famous paintings, the 13th-century *Nachi Waterfall* from the Kamakura Period, shown only every five years to protect its fragility (the next display will be in spring 2001); and irises stenciled on gold by Ogata Korin from the Edo Period, displayed for two weeks at the end of April. In addition to the permanent displays, special exhibits highlight specific art such as antique Imari ware or decorative Chinese clocks. Admission includes entrance to a delightful small garden with a pond.

Ota Memorial Museum of Art (Ota Kinen Bijutsukan). 1–10–10 Jingumae, Shibuya-ku. ☎ **03/3403-0880.** Admission ¥500–¥900 ($4.15–$7.50) adults, ¥400–¥700 ($3.35–$5.85) high school and college students, ¥300–¥500 ($2.50–$4.15) junior high students, ¥100–¥300 (85¢–$2.50) children; price depends on the exhibit. Tues–Sun 10:30am–5:30pm (enter by 5pm). Closed from the 27th to the end of each month. Station: Harajuku (2 min.) or Meiji-Jingumae (1 min.). Near the intersection of Omotesando Dori and Meiji Dori, behind La Foret.

This great museum features the private *ukiyo-e* (woodblock print) collection of the late Ota Seizo, who early in life recognized the importance of ukiyo-e as an art form and dedicated his life to its preservation. Exhibitions of the museum's 12,000 prints are changed monthly, with descriptions of the displays in English. The museum itself is small but delightful, with such traditional touches as bamboo screens, stone pathways, and even a small tearoom that sells Japanese sweets.

SPECIALTY MUSEUMS & EXHIBITION HALLS
✪ **Asakura Choso Museum.** 7–18–10 Yanaka, Taito-ku. ☎ **03/3821-4549.** Admission ¥300 ($2.50) adults, ¥150 ($1.25) children. Tues–Thurs and Sat–Sun 9:30am–4:30pm. Station: Nippori (4 min.).

This unique museum is one of my favorites and is well worth a visit if you haven't been to a Japanese home. It served as the residence and studio of sculptor Asakura Fumio (1883–1964), famous for his statues of statesmen, women, and cats, many of which are on display here. The house, which combines modern and traditional architecture, wraps around an inner courtyard pond, fed by a natural spring, and contains some furniture and antiques in its many tatami rooms, including a beautiful library, a tearoom, and a room for enjoying the morning sun. There's even a rooftop garden. See the recommended stroll of Yanaka in chapter 7 for more information.

Beer Museum Yebisu. Yebisu Garden Place, 4–20–1 Ebisu, Shibuya-ku. ☎ **03/5423-7255.** Free admission. Tues–Sun 10am–6pm (enter by 5pm). Station: Ebisu (8 min.).

If you are in Yebisu Garden Place (perhaps to see the Museum of Photography), you may wish to take a spin through this showcase of Sapporo breweries. Named after Yebisu Beer, which made its debut in 1890 and to which both Ebisu Station and the surrounding neighborhood owe their names, it presents a high-tech explanation (in Japanese only) of an age-old process, including a "virtual brewery" which lets viewers observe the brewing process through 3–D glasses, with such startling close-ups that it's almost like swimming in the brew. I especially like the gallery of old beer advertisements. Alas, there are no free samples; visitors must purchase tickets from vending machines at the tasting lounge.

Crafts Gallery (Bijutsukan Kogeikan). Kitanomaru Koen Park, Chiyoda-ku. ☎ **03/3211-7781.** Admission ¥420–¥830 ($3.50–$6.90) adults, ¥130–¥450 ($1.10–$3.75) students, ¥70–¥330 (60¢–$2.75) children; price depends on the exhibit. Tues–Sun 10am–5pm. Station: Takebashi (7 min.).

Housed in a handsome Gothic-style brick building constructed in 1910 as headquarters of the Imperial Guard, this gallery exhibits contemporary crafts, including pottery, ceramics, kimono, metalworks, glassware, lacquerware, bamboo works, and more; objects are changed approximately four times a year to reflect the changes of the seasons. Most exhibitions concentrate on a specific theme, such as bamboo ware or the works of a single artist, usually one noted for skill in traditional arts. Unfortunately, exhibition space is very limited; you can tour the place in less than an hour.

Daimyo Clock Museum (Daimyo Tokei Hakubutsukan). 2–1–27 Yanaka, Taito-ku. ☎ **03/3821-6913.** Admission ¥300 ($2.50) adults, ¥200 ($1.65) students, ¥100 (85¢) children 6–11. Tues–Sun 10am–4pm. Closed Dec 25–Jan 15 and July–Sept. Station: Nezu (10 min.).

This one-room display of clocks and watches of the Edo Period (1603–1867) features about 50 examples from the museum's extensive collection at any given time (displays change annually). Rather than measuring 24 hours a day, Edo clocks were based on the length of time between sunrise and sunset, so that time varied greatly with the seasons. On display are huge freestanding clocks, sundials, alarm clocks, pocket watches, and small watches that were attached to obi (the sash worn with a kimono). The museum's name stems from the fact that clocks were so expensive that only *daimyo* (feudal lords) could afford them. See the recommended walking tour of Yanaka in chapter 7 for more information.

Drum Museum (Taikokan). Miyamoto Japanese Percussion and Festival Store, 2–1–1 Nishi-Asakusa, Taito-ku. ☎ **03/3842-5622.** Admission ¥300 ($2.70) adults, ¥150 ($1.35) children. Wed–Sun 10am–5pm. Closed holidays. Station: Tawaramachi (2 min.) or Asakusa (5 min.). On Kokusai Dori, north of Kaminarimon Dori.

This fourth-floor museum is a collection of more than 600 instruments, displayed on a rotating basis and including traditional Japanese drums as well as a variety of drums from all over the world. With the exception of some of the rare, older pieces, many of the drums can be touched and played, making this a good bet with children. There are also videos of drumming from Japan and around the world. On the ground floor is a shop specializing in Japanese percussion instruments and items used in Japanese festivals, including decorative Japanese drums, lion heads for the lion dance, Japanese flutes, and masks.

Edo-Tokyo Open Air Architectural Museum (Edo-Tokyo Tatemono-en). 3–7–1 Sakura-cho, Koganei-shi **042/388-3300.** Admission ¥300 ($2.50) adults, ¥150 ($1.25) children. Apr–Sept Tues–Sun 9:30am–5:30pm; Oct–Mar Tues–Sun 9:30am–4:30pm. Directions: From Shinjuku Station, take the rapid Chuo Line about 30 min. to Musashi-Koganei Station. Take the north exit and board bus no. or no. 21 for a 5-min. ride to Koganei Koen Nishi Guchi stop, from which it's a 5-min. walk, or bus no. 14 to Edo-Tokyo Tatemono-en-mae stop, from which it's a 3-min. walk.

Although located on the far western outskirts of Tokyo, this branch of the Edo-Tokyo Museum is a must for architecture buffs. Spread on 17 acres in the middle of an expansive park, it showcases some two dozen buildings from the late Edo Period to the 1950s, arranged along streets in a village setting. Included are 200-year-old thatch-roofed farmhouses, traditional Japanese and Western-style residences, a teahouse, soy sauce shop, a bathhouse, police box, flower shop, and more, filled with related objects and furniture.

✪ Fukugawa Edo Museum (Fukagawa Edo Shiryokan). 1–3–28 Shirakawa, Koto-ku. ☎ **03/3630-8625.** Admission ¥300 ($2.50) adults, ¥50 (40¢) children 6–14. Daily 9:30am–5pm. Closed 2nd and 4th Mon of each month. Station: Monzen-Nakacho or Morishita; then a 15-min. walk or bus no. 33 toward Kiyosumi Garden to the Kiyosumi Teien-mae bus stop.

This is the Tokyo of your dreams, the way it appears in all those samurai flicks on Japanese TV: a reproduction of a 19th-century neighborhood in Fukagawa, a prosperous community on the east bank of the Sumida River during the Edo Period. This delightful museum is located off Kiyosumi Dori, on a pleasant tree-lined, shop-filled street called Fukagawa Shiryokan Dori. The museum's hangarlike interior contains 11 full-scale replicas of traditional houses, vegetable and rice shops, a fish store, two inns, a fire watchtower, and tenement homes, all arranged to resemble an actual neighborhood. There are lots of small touches and flourishes to make the community seem real and believable—a cat sleeping on a roof, a snail crawling up a fence, a dog relieving itself on a pole, sounds of birds, a vendor shouting his wares, horses' hooves clattering, and a dog barking. Of Tokyo's museums, this one is probably the best for children, though the hike from the station is a bit long. Don't confuse this museum with the much larger Edo-Tokyo Museum, which traces the history of Tokyo.

Japanese Sword Museum (Nippon Bijutsu Token Hozon Kyokai). 4–25–10 Yoyogi, Sumida-ku. ☎ **03/3379-1386** or 3379-1388. Admission ¥525 ($4.35) adults, ¥315 ($2.60) for students, free for children under 12. Tues–Sun 9am–4pm. Station: Sangubashi, on the Odakyu Line (10 min.).

This small, one-room museum has more than 120 swords and sword fittings in its collection, of which only 30 or so are on display at any one time. Considered by the Japanese to embody spirits all their own, Japanese swords rank as an art form of the highest degree, and in feudal Japan sword makers were respected masters. Be sure to pick up the English-language pamphlets that describe how to care for swords and how to identify various types of blades, temper patterns, and file markings, as these will greatly increase your appreciation and understanding of this ancient craft.

A Note on Japanese Symbols

Many hotels, restaurants, and other establishments in Japan do not have signs giving their names in Roman (English-language) letters. As an aid to the reader, the second appendix to this book lists the Japanese symbols for all such places described in this guide. Each set of characters representing an establishment name has a number, which corresponds to the number that appears inside the box before the establishment's name in the text. Thus, to find the Japanese symbols for, say, the **Kimono Art Museum,** refer to no. 53 in appendix B.

Japan Folk Crafts Museum (Nippon Mingeikan). 4–3–33 Komaba, Meguro-ku. ☎ **03/ 3467-4527.** Admission ¥1,000 ($8.35 adults, ¥500 ($4.15) students, ¥200 ($1.65) children 6–11. Tues–Sun 10am–5pm. Station: Komaba-Todaimae, on the local (not express) Keio-Inokashira Line (west gate exit, 5 min.).

Occupying an interesting traditional building dating from 1936, this museum displays temporary exhibits of folk art gathered from around Japan, including furniture, pottery, and textiles, much of it dating from the Edo and Meiji eras. Crafts from other Asian (as well as from European) countries are also on display in this special museum, with displays changing every 3 months. Past exhibits have included works by Bernard Leach and his contemporaries, Korean crafts, and Japanese pottery used in daily life. Buy a copy of *Tokyo Journal* to find out what's currently on display.

(53) **Kimono Art Museum (Kimono Hakubutsukan).** 7th floor, 1–20–11 Ueno, Taito-ku. ☎ **03/3839-8620.** Admission ¥300 ($2.50) adults, ¥200 ($1.65) students, ¥150 ($1.25) children. Wed–Mon 11am–5pm. Closed during exhibit changes. Station: Ueno-Hirokoji (1 min.). On Chuo Dori, across the street from Matsuzakaya department store.

This one-room showroom is dedicated to the kimono, which has changed little since its creation in the 8th century. Displays change monthly, with themes ranging from modern designs to those used in Kabuki theater or everyday life. This museum is worth a look if you're visiting the nearby Ameya Yokocho shopping street.

Kite Museum (Tako-no-Hakubutsukan). Taimeiken Building, 5th floor, 1–12–10 Nihombashi, Chuo-ku. ☎ **03/3275-2704.** Admission ¥200 ($1.65) adults, ¥100 (85¢) children. Mon–Sat 11am–5pm. Closed holidays. Station: Nihombashi (3 min.). Off Eitai Dori.

This private collection consists of more than 3,000 kites, mainly Japanese, all jam-packed in a few small rooms. They range from miniature kites the size of postage stamps to kites dating from the Taisho Period, some ornately decorated with Kabuki stars, samurai, and animals. There are even hand-painted kites by ukiyo-e master Hiroshige.

Museum of Maritime Science (Fune-no-Kagakukan). 3–1 Higashi-Yashio, Shinagawa-ku. ☎ **03/5500-1111.** Combination ticket to everything, ¥1,000 ($8.35) adults, ¥600 ($5) children; main museum and the Soya, ¥700 ($5.85) adults, ¥400 ($3.35) children. Daily 10am–5pm. Station: Fune-no-Kagakukan, on the Yurikamome Line from Shimbashi (1 min.). On Odaiba.

The building housing the Museum of Maritime Science is a perfect match—it's in the shape of a passenger liner, complete with an observation tower atop its bridge. Appropriately enough, it's located on Odaiba, reclaimed land in Tokyo Bay, and offers a good view of Tokyo's container port nearby. The museum contains an excellent collection of model boats, including warships like the 1898 battleship *Shikishima,* submarines, ferries, supertankers, container ships, and wooden ships used during the Edo Period. Technical explanations, unfortunately, are mostly in Japanese. Children love the radio-controlled boats they can direct in a pond. Moored nearby is the *Soya,* constructed in 1938 as a cargo icebreaker; it served as Japan's first Antarctic observation ship.

Those with a lot of time on their hands can also visit the *Yotei Maru,* which once ferried the waters between Aomori and Hokkaido before the opening of an underwater tunnel made its job obsolete. Today, oddly enough, it serves as a floating amusement center of sorts; my favorite is its re-creation of Aomori Station of the late 1950s, with lifelike models of passengers, ticket collectors, and street vendors. Beside the museum is a public swimming pool open in summer, making this area of Odaiba a good destination for families.

National Science Museum (Kokuritsu Kagaku Hakubutsukan). Ueno Park, Taito-ku. ☎ **03/3822-0111.** Admission ¥420 ($3.50) adults, ¥70 (60¢) children; more for special exhibits. Tues–Sun 9am–4:30pm. Station: Ueno (5 min.).

This is a sprawling complex, comprising three buildings and covering everything from the evolution of life to electronics in Japan. Unfortunately, most displays are in Japanese (be sure to pick up the museum's English pamphlet), but the museum is still worth visiting. There are plenty of exhibits geared toward children. Dinosaurs greet visitors on the ground floor of the main hall, while up on the third floor plants and animals of Japan are featured, including marine life such as huge king crabs, the Japanese brown bear, the Japanese crested ibis, and the Japanese monkey. Other highlights include a display on the origin, development, and history of the Japanese people; a hands-on discovery room for children; and a map of Japan showing the location of all its active volcanoes.

Open-Air Folk House Museum (Nihon Minka-en). 7–1–1 Masugata, Tama-ku, Kawasaki. ☎ **044/922-2181.** Admission: ¥300 ($2.50) adults, ¥100 (85¢ students and children. Tues–Sun 9:30am–4pm. Station: Mukogaoka Yuen (15 min.)

Whereas the Edo-Tokyo Tatemono-en (above) is an open-air museum of traditional and modern Tokyo homes and buildings, mostly dating from the late Edo Period to the 1950s, this architectural museum concentrates on rural Japan from centuries past. Located in the neighboring city of Kawasaki, 30 minutes by express train on the Odakyu Line from Shinjuku, it features 23 traditional houses and other historical buildings, in a lovely setting spread along wooded hillsides. Most are heavy-beamed thatched houses, but there are also warehouses, a samurai's residential gate, a water wheel, and a Kabuki stage from a small fishing village, all originally from other parts of Honshu and reconstructed here. The oldest houses date from about 300 years ago. An English pamphlet tells about each of the buildings, and there are many explanations throughout in English.

Shitamachi Museum (Shitamachi Fuzoku Shiryokan). Ueno Park, Taito-ku. ☎ **03/3823-7451.** Admission ¥200 ($1.65) adults, ¥100 (85¢) children. Tues–Sun 9:30am–4:30pm. Station: Ueno (3 min.).

Shitamachi means "downtown" and refers to the area of Tokyo in which commoners used to live, mainly around Ueno and Asakusa. There's very little left of old downtown Tokyo; and with that in mind, the Shitamachi Museum seeks to preserve for future generations a way of life that was virtually wiped out by the great earthquake of 1923 and by World War II. There are shops set up as they may have looked back then, including a merchant's shop and a candy shop, as well as one of the Shitamachi tenements common at the turn of the century. These tenements—long, narrow buildings with one roof over a series of dwelling units separated by thin wooden walls—were the homes of the poorer people. Everyone knew everyone else's business; few secrets could be kept in such crowded conditions. The narrow back alleyways where they were located served as communal living rooms. The museum also displays relics relating to the life of these people, including utensils, toys, costumes, and tools, most of which are simply lying around so that you can pick them up and examine them more closely. Individuals, many living in Shitamachi, donated all the museum's holdings.

Sony Building. 5-3-1 Ginza, Chuo-ku. ☎ **03/3573-2371.** Free admission. Daily 11am-7pm. Station: Ginza (B9 exit, 1 min.). At the intersection of Harumi Dori and Sotobori Dori.

A popular place to kill an hour or two of free time in the Ginza, the Sony Building offers six floors of showrooms and amusements, as well as restaurants and shops. The latest in Sony video and digital cameras, high-definition TVs, CD players, laptops, and computers are all on display for public inspection. A Play Station on the sixth floor has Sony games you can interact with for free; HiVision Theater presents free programs throughout the day, though only in Japanese.

Sugino Costume Museum (Sugino Gakuen Isho Hakubutsukan). 4-6-13 Kami-Osaki, Shinagawa-ku. ☎ **03/3491-8151.** Admission ¥200 ($1.65) adults, ¥100 (85¢) children. Mon–Sat 10am–4pm. Closed holidays and Aug to mid-Sept. Station: Meguro (west exit, 6 min.). On the left side of the street behind Sakura Bank.

This private museum belongs to Sugino College, a school of clothing design. Its three floors contain mostly European antique clothing from the 19th and 20th centuries, including everyday dress, gowns, flapper dresses, and men's clothing, as well as folk costumes from such diverse countries as Holland, Cambodia, Korea, and Guatemala. On the fourth floor are antique Japanese costumes, including samurai armor, kimono, and dress worn by the Ainu, a native people of Hokkaido.

Sumo Museum (Sumo Hakubutsukan). 1-3-28 Yokoami, Sumida-ku. ☎ **03/3622-0366.** Free admission, but during tournaments you must have sumo tickets to enter the stadium and museum. Mon–Fri 10am–4:30pm. Closed holidays. Station: Ryogoku (1 min.).

This museum, located in the Kokugikan sumo stadium, shows the history of sumo since the 18th century, with portraits and mementos of past and present grand champions (called *yokozuna*), the highest rank of sumo wrestler. Ask for the museum's English-language pamphlet.

Tepco Electric Energy Museum. 1-12-10 Jinnan, Shibuya-ku. ☎ **03/3477-1191.** Free admission. Thurs–Tues 10am–6pm. Station: Shibuya (5 min.).

If you have children with you, or are interested in electricity, drop by Tokyo Electric Power Company's (TEPCO) public-service facility. TEPCO operates thermal electric, nuclear, and hydroelectric power plants that supply Tokyo and its vicinity with electricity; this showroom was established to teach urban dwellers how electricity is generated, supplied to homes, and consumed (since a 1999 nuclear accident 70 miles outside Tokyo, it has also worked toward alleviating public fears of nuclear disaster). Five floors of displays include a model of a nuclear reactor, a "house of the future" geared toward Japan's aging population, and a children's play area with computers and games. Although displays are in Japanese only, there are English-language pamphlets on each floor that answer all the technological questions that may arise.

Tokyo Metropolitan Museum of Photography (Tokyo-to Shashin Bijutsukan). Yebisu Garden Place, 1-13-3 Mita, Meguro-ku. ☎ **03/3280-0031.** Admission to permanent collection ¥500 ($4.15) adults, ¥250 ($2.10) students and children, free for seniors. Sun, Tues, Wed, Sat 10am–6pm; Thurs–Fri 10am–8pm. Station: Ebisu (8 min.).

This museum has an impressive 16,000 works in its collection of photographs, ranging from the historical to the contemporary, with about 70% by Japanese photographers. Exhibitions from Japan and abroad, many on the cutting edge of contemporary photography, are shown in the changing Exhibition Gallery, while the Permanent Collection features a rotating exhibit of the museum's holdings. In the basement is the Images & Technology Gallery, which displays materials and equipment from the earliest days of filming to the latest technological advances.

Tokyo Stock Exchange. 2–1 Nihombashi-Kabutocho, Chuo-ku. ☎ **03/3665-1881.** Free admission. Exhibition Plaza Mon–Fri 9am–4pm. Closed holidays. Station: Kayabacho (exit 11, 5 min.) or Nihombashi (exit A2, 5 min.).

Established in 1878, the Tokyo Stock Exchange is one of the busiest exchanges in the world. It's located in the Nihombashi/Kyobashi district, known as the Wall Street of Japan; the district was a commercial area even during the Edo Period. Although computers have rendered the frenetic trading floor obsolete, an Exhibition Plaza provides an overview of the Japanese securities market with an array of audiovisual displays, with explanations in English. There are computers that deliver the latest stock-market information, and another computer that takes you through the steps of investing in securities. Investment idiots like me appreciate the Kabuto Theater, which uses simple explanations even a child can understand to describe the securities market and what bonds, securities, and dividends all mean.

Toyota Auto Salon Amlux. 3–3–5 Higashi Ikebukuro, Toshima-ku. ☎ **03/5391-5900.** Free admission. Tues–Sun 11am–8pm. Station: Higashi Ikebukuro (2 min.) or Ikebukuro (5 min.).

I'm not a big car fan, but even I have fun at Amlux. Japan's largest automobile showroom, this sophisticated facility boasts five floors of exhibition space with more than 70 vehicles (be sure to stop by the information desk on the first floor for an English-language pamphlet). Everything from sports and racing cars to family and luxury cars are on view, all open so that potential customers can climb inside and play with the dials. There are also educational and entertainment programs, including a display using holograms to show what goes into making a car. A specially designed, high-definition 3-D theater, free on a first-come, first-served basis, features a 6-axle motion ride that simulates a car, complete with bodysonic seats and a Surround Sound system.

6 Spectacular City Views

✪ **Tokyo Metropolitan Government Office (TMG).** 2–8–1 Nishi-Shinjuku. ☎ **03/5321-1111.** Free admission. Tues–Fri 9:30am–5:30pm (you must enter by 5pm); Sat–Sun and holidays 9:30am–7:30pm (you must enter by 7pm). Closed Tues when Mon is a holiday, and Dec 29–Jan 3. Station: Shinjuku (10 min.) or Nishi-Shinjuku (4 min.).

Tokyo's new city hall—designed by one of Japan's most well-known architects, Kenzo Tange—is an impressive addition to the skyscrapers of West Shinjuku. Three buildings comprise the complex—TMG No. 1, TMG No. 2, and the Metropolitan Assembly Building—and together they contain everything from Tokyo's Disaster Prevention Center to the governor's office. Most important for visitors, however, is TMG No. 1, the tall building to the north, which offers one of the best views of Tokyo. This 48-story, 800-foot structure, the tallest building in Shinjuku, boasts two observatories, located on the 45th floors of both the North and South Towers, with access from the first floor. Both observatories offer the same great views—on clear winter days you can even see Mt. Fuji—as well as a small souvenir shop and coffee shop.

Tokyo Tower. 4–2 Shiba Koen, Minato-ku. ☎ **03/3433-5111.** Admission to main observatory, ¥820 ($6.85) adults and ¥460 ($3.85) children; top observatory, ¥1,420 ($11.85) adults and ¥860 ($7.15) children. Mid-Mar to mid-Nov, daily 9am–8pm; mid-Nov to mid-Mar, daily 9am–7pm. Station: Onarimon or Kamiyacho (5 min.).

Japan's most famous observation tower was built in 1958 and modeled after the Eiffel Tower in Paris. Lit up at night, this 1,099-foot tower is a familiar and beloved landmark in the city's landscape; but with the construction of skyscrapers over the past few decades (including the TMG, above, with its free observatory), it has lost some of its appeal as an observation platform.

The tower has two observatories: the main one at 495 feet, and the top observatory at 825 feet. The best time of year for viewing is said to be during Golden Week, at the beginning of May. With many Tokyoites gone from the city and most factories and businesses closed down, the air at this time is thought to be the cleanest and clearest. There are, by the way, several off beat tourist attractions in the tower's base building, including a wax museum (where you can see the Beatles, a wax rendition of Leonardo's *Last Supper,* and a medieval torture chamber), a small aquarium, a museum of holography, and a trick art gallery, all with separate admission fees.

7 Especially for Kids

In addition to its observatories, **Tokyo Tower** (see above) also contains a few other attractions that might be worth a visit if you have children in tow, including a small aquarium and a wax museum. Other attractions listed above that are good for children include the **Edo-Tokyo Museum, Fukugawa Edo Museum, Museum of Maritime Science, National Science Museum,** and **Tepco Electric Energy Museum.**

Hanayashiki. 2–28–1 Asakusa (northwest of Sensoji Temple), Taito-ku. ☎ **043/3842-8780.** Admission ¥900 ($7.50) adults, ¥400 ($3.35) children 5–12 and senior citizens, free for children 4 and younger. Wed–Mon 10am–6pm (5pm in winter). Station: Asakusa (7 min.).

Opened in 1853, this small and rather corny amusement park is Japan's oldest. It offers a small roller coaster, a kiddie Ferris wheel, carousel, haunted house, 3-D theater, and other diversions that appeal to children. Note, however, that after paying admission, you must still buy tickets for each ride; tickets are ¥100 (85¢) each and most rides require two or three.

✪ International Aquarium. World Import Mart Building., 10th floor, Sunshine City, 3–1–3 Higashi Ikebukuro. ☎ **043/3989-3466.** Admission ¥1,600 ($13.35) adults, ¥800 ($6.65) children 4–12 (under 4 free). Mon–Sat 10am–6pm; Sun and holidays 10am–6:30pm. Station: Higashi Ikebukuro (3 min.) or Ikebukuro (7 min.).

Claiming to be the world's highest aquarium, this Sunshine City complex is the unlikely home to more than 20,000 fish and animals, including dolphins, octopuses, eels, piranhas, sea horses, sea otters, seals, giant crabs, and rare—and rather weird—species of fish. There are several shows, including performances by sea lions and what's probably the world's only "fish circus," featuring an electric eel and an archer fish.

National Children's Castle (Kodomo-no-Shiro). 5–53–1 Jingumae, Shibuya-ku. ☎ **03/3797-5666.** Admission ¥500 ($4.15) adults, ¥400 ($3.35) children 3–17 (free for children under 3); ¥200 ($1.65) extra for pool use. Tues–Fri 12:30–5:30pm; Sat, Sun, and holidays (including school holidays) 10am–5:30pm. Station: Omotesando (exit B2, 8 min., on Aoyama Dori in the direction of Shibuya) or Shibuya (10 min.).

Here's a great place to bring the kids. Conceived by the Ministry of Health and Welfare to commemorate the International Year of the Child in 1979, the Children's Castle holds various activity rooms designed to appeal to children of all ages. The third floor, designed for spontaneous and unstructured play, features a large climbing gym, computer play room, building blocks, play house, dolls, and books, and a teen corner with table tennis and other age-appropriate games; there's also an art room staffed with instructors to help children with projects suitable to their ages. On the fourth floor is a music room, which holds mini-concerts and special events and also has instruments the kids are invited to play (during my last visit, a band composed of junior-high-aged kids was playing for an enthusiastic audience of dancing toddlers), as well as a video room with private cubicles where visitors can make selections from a stocked library of English and Japanese videos. On the roof is an outdoor playground complete with tricycles and a small wading pool. Various programs are presented throughout the week, including puppet shows, fairy tales, and origami presentations.

○ **Shinjuku Joypolis Sega.** Takashimaya Times Square, 11th floor. ☎ **03/5361-3040.** Admission ¥300 ($2.50) adults, ¥100 (85¢) children 7 to 14 (free for children under 7); individual attractions an additional ¥500–¥700 ($4.15–$5.85) each. Daily 10am–midnight. Station: Shinjuku (south exit, 2 min.).

Bored teenagers in tow, grumbling at yet another temple or shrine? Bring them to life at Tokyo's most sophisticated virtual amusement arcade, outfitted with the latest in video games and high-tech virtual reality attractions, courtesy of Sega. Video games include skiing races, in which participants maneuver curves utilizing virtual reality equipment, as well as numerous aeronautical battle games. There's also a 3-D sightseeing tour of an underwater city, with seats that move with the action on the screen; a 3-D haunted house called Murder Lodge; and, most popular of all, the Mission Q-Zar, in which participants are divided into two teams, armed with laser guns, and pitted against each other in darkened rooms where they hide and shoot. Most harmless are the Print Club machines, which have taken Japan by storm and will print your face on stickers with the background (Mt. Fuji, perhaps?) of your choice. If you think your kids will want to try everything, you can buy them a passport for ¥2,800 ($23).

There's another Joypolis at **Tokyo Decks** in Odaiba (☎ **03/5500-2820**), open daily from 5 to 11:30pm. Its admission is ¥500 ($4.15) for adults and ¥300 ($2.50) for children; a children's passport costs ¥3,200 ($27).

Tokyo Disneyland. 1–1 Maihama, Urayasu-shi, Chiba Prefecture. ☎ **047/354-0001.** Disneyland Passport, including entrance to and use of all attractions: ¥5,200 ($43) adults, ¥4,490 ($37) senior citizens, ¥4,590 ($38) junior high and high school students, ¥3,570 ($30) children 4–11 (under 4 free). Starlight admission after 5pm, ¥4,180 ($35) adults, ¥3,670 ($31) juniors, ¥2,850 ($24) children. *Note:* Only JCB accepted. Daily 8 or 9am to 9 or 10pm, with slightly shorter hours in winter. Schedule is subject to change, so call in advance. Tickets can be purchased in advance at the Tokyo Disneyland Ticket Center, in the Hibiya Mitsui Building, 1–1–2 Yurakucho (station: Hibiya), and at major travel agencies. Station: Maihama Station, on the JR Keiyo Line from Tokyo Station (1 min.).

If you (or your kids) have your heart set on visiting all the world's Disney parks, then head to Tokyo Disneyland. Virtually a carbon copy of the back-home version, this one also boasts the Jungle Cruise, Pirates of the Caribbean, Haunted Mansion, and Space Mountain. The hottest attractions include the Fantillusion, a spectacular night parade of thousands of lights using state-of-the-art fiber optics, light-emitting costumes, and electroluminescence techniques; Toontown, a wacky theme park where Mickey, Minnie, Donald, and other Disney characters work and play;

MicroAdventure, in which visitors, wearing 3-D glasses, participate in a mock awards ceremony gone amok with various special effects; and Star Tours, a thrill adventure created by Disney and George Lucas.

Tokyo IMAX Theatre. Takashimaya Times Square, 12th floor, 5–24–2 Sendagaya, Shibuya-ku. ☎ **03/5361-3030.** Admission ¥1,300 ($11) adults, ¥1,000 ($8.35) seniors and students, ¥800 ($6.65) children 4 to 12. 9 shows daily 10:50am–9:20pm (last showing). Station: Shinjuku (south exit, 2 min.).

IMAX theaters are now so common they almost seem old hat. Leave it to the Tokyo IMAX Theatre, however, to offer something different—a six-story-high 3-D format made amazingly realistic through viewer headsets complete with individual speakers (English headsets available for most films). Luckily, IMAX films deal mainly with nature and adventure—a horror film would be more than I could bear.

Tokyo Sea Life Park. 6–2–3 Rinkai-cho, Edogawa-ku. ☎ **03/3869-5152.** Admission ¥700 ($5.85) adults, ¥250 ($2.10) children 12 to 14, free for children 11 and younger and seniors. Tues–Sun 9:30am–5pm (you must enter by 4pm). Directions: On weekdays, take the JR Keiyo Line rapid service from Tokyo Station to Shin-Kiba, change to the local Keiyo Line, and get off at the next station, Kasairinkai Koen, from which it's a 5-min. walk. On weekends and holidays, take the rapid service directly to Kasairinkai Koen. There are also boats departing 7 times daily from Hinode Pier near Hamamatsucho Station, costing ¥800 ($6.65) and taking 1 hour.

Located on the shore of Tokyo Bay in Kasai Rinkai Park, this public facility is Tokyo's largest—yet cheapest—aquarium, with tanks displaying marine life of Tokyo Bay and beyond, including the Pacific, Indian, and Atlantic oceans. Hammerhead sharks, bluefin tuna, the giant sunfish, penguins, a touch tide pool, and a 3-D movie are some of the highlights. The park also contains a beach, small Japanese garden, and a bird sanctuary, making it a good family outing. I suggest coming by train and returning via boat to Hamatsucho.

Toshimaen. 3–25–1 Koyama, Nerima, Tokyo. ☎ **03/3990-8800.** Entrance to amusements, all rides, and pools ¥3,990 ($33) adults, ¥3,360 ($28) children. Summer, daily 9am–9pm (pool closes at 5pm); winter, daily 10am–5pm. Station: Toshima-en (3 min.). Take the local (not express) Seibu Ikebukuro Line to Nerima (5th stop); transfer to track 5 for Toshima-en Station.

This is an old-timer in the world of amusement parks. Its 40 attractions include a carousel carved by German craftsmen at the turn of the century, four roller coasters, a Japanese-style haunted house with its own assortment of ghosts, and a safari ride. In summer, there are also seven swimming pools, including water slides, wave pools, children's pool, and an Olympic-size pool, making it a cool place to hang out on a hot day (avoid weekends).

Ueno Zoo. Ueno Park, Taito-ku. ☎ **03/3828-5171.** Admission ¥500 ($4.15) adults, ¥200 ($1.65) children 12–14, free for children under 12 and senior citizens. Tues–Sun 9:30am–5pm (you must enter by 4pm). Closed some holidays. Station: Ueno (4 min.).

Founded back in 1882, Japan's oldest zoo is small by today's standards but remains one of the most well-known in Japan, due in part to its giant pandas, donated by the Chinese government to mark the re-establishment of diplomatic relations between the two countries following World War II. A vivarium, opened in 1999, houses amphibians, fish, and reptiles, including Komodo dragons, green tree pythons, and dwarf crocodiles. Personally, I can't help but feel sorry for some of the animals in their small spaces, but children will enjoy the Japanese macaques, polar bears, California sea lions, penguins, gorillas, giraffes, zebras, elephants, deer, and tigers.

8 Spectator Sports

For information on current sporting events taking place in Tokyo, ranging from kickboxing and pro wrestling to soccer, table tennis, and golf, check the monthly magazine *Tokyo Journal* or contact the **Tourist Information Center.** Tickets for many events, including baseball and sumo, can be purchased at one of many **Playguide** ticket outlets in Tokyo, including Matsuya department store in the Ginza, Isetan and Keio department stores in Shinjuku, and Seibu department store in Shibuya and Ikebukuro.

BASEBALL   Introduced into Japan from the United States in 1873, baseball is as popular among Japanese as it is among Americans. Even the annual high-school play-offs keep everyone glued to their television sets.

As with other imports, the Japanese have added their own modifications. Some of the playing fields are smaller (new ones tend to have American dimensions), and, borrowing from American football, each team has its own cheerleaders. There are several American players who have proved very popular with local fans; but according to the rules, no more than four foreigners may play on any one team.

While playing one's hardest is at a premium in the United States, in Japan any attempt at excelling individually is frowned upon. As in other aspects of life, it is the group, the team, that counts. To what extent that's so may be illustrated by the case of an American player: When he missed opening day at training camp due to a life-or-death operation on his son at a hospital, his contract was immediately canceled. And rather than let a foreign player break the hitting record set by a Japanese, American Randy Bass was thrown only balls and walked.

There are two professional leagues, the Central and the Pacific, which play from April to October and meet in the final play-offs. In Tokyo, the home teams are the **Yomiuri Giants** and the **Nippon Ham Fighters,** both of which play at the Tokyo Dome (☎ 03/3811-2111; station: Suidobashi); and the **Yakult Swallows,** which play at Jingu Stadium (station: Gaienmae). Other teams playing in the vicinity of Tokyo are the **Chiba Lotte Marines,** who play at Kawasaki Stadium, Kanagawa (☎ 044/244-1171; station: Kawasaki Station on the JR Tokaido Line, then by bus no. 16, 19, 21, 22, or 23); the **Seibu Lions,** Seibu Lions Stadium, Tokorozawa City (☎ 0429/24-1151; station: JR to Seibu Kyujo-mae, on the Seibu Sayama Line); and the **Yokohama Bay Stars,** Yokohama Stadium, Yokohama (☎ 045/661-1251; station: Kannai, on the JR Keihin Tohoku Line). Advance tickets go on sale on Friday, 2 weeks prior to the game, and can be purchased at the stadium or, for Tokyo teams, at any **Playguide** ticket outlet (☎ 03/3257-9999, with counters throughout the city). Prices for the Tokyo Giants begin at about ¥2,000 ($17) for an unreserved seat.

✪ **SUMO**   The Japanese form of wrestling known as sumo began perhaps as long as 1,500 years ago and is still the nation's most popular sport, with wrestlers—often taller than 6 feet and weighing well over 300 pounds—revered as national heroes. A sumo match takes place on a sandy-floored ring less than 15 feet in diameter; the object is for a wrestler either to eject his opponent from the ring or to cause him to touch the ground with any part of his body other than his feet. This is accomplished by shoving, slapping, tripping, throwing, and even carrying the opponent. Altogether, there are 48 holds and throws, and sumo fans know them all.

Sumo matches are held in Tokyo at the **Kokugikan,** 1–3–28 Yokoami, Sumida-ku (☎ 03/3623-5111; station: Ryogoku, then a 1-min. walk). Matches are held in January, May, and September for 15 consecutive days, beginning at around 10am and lasting until 6pm; the top wrestlers compete after 3:30pm. The best seats are ringside box seats, but they're bought out by companies and by friends and families of sumo wrestlers. Usually available are balcony seats, which can be purchased at any **Playguide** ticket outlet (☎ **03/3257-9999,** with counters throughout Tokyo), or at ticket counters in several department stores, including Matsuya in Ginza, Isetan in Shinjuku, and Seibu or Tobu in Ikebukuro. You can also purchase tickets directly at the Kokugikan ticket office beginning at 9am every morning of the tournament. Prices range from about ¥2,100 ($17.50) for an unreserved seat to ¥8,200 ($68) for a good reserved seat.

If you can't make it to a match, watching on TV is almost as good. Tournaments in Tokyo, as well as those that take place annually in Osaka, Nagoya, and Fukuoka, are broadcast on the NHK channel from 4 to 6pm daily during matches.

7

Tokyo Strolls

Because Tokyo is a jigsaw puzzle of distinct neighborhoods, it makes sense to explore the city section by section. Below are walking tours of four of Tokyo's most fascinating and easily explored neighborhoods. For information on sightseeing and attractions outside these neighborhoods or for additional information on attractions described below, see chapter 6.

Walking Tour 1
Asakusa

Start: Hama Rikyu Garden (near Shimbashi Station); or Asakusa Station (exit 1 or 3).
Finish: Kappabashi Dori (station: Tawaramachi).
Time: Allow approximately 5 hours, including the boat ride.
Best Times: Tuesday through Friday, when the crowds aren't as big.
Worst Times: Monday, when Hama Rikyu Garden is closed, and Sunday, when Demboin Garden and the shops on Kappabashi Dori are closed.

If anything remains of old Tokyo, Asakusa is it. This is where you'll find narrow streets lined with small residential homes, women in kimono, Tokyo's oldest and most popular temple, and quaint shops selling boxwood combs, fans, sweet pastries, and other products of yore. With its temple market, old-fashioned amusement park, traditional shops, restaurants, and theaters, Asakusa preserves the charm of old downtown Edo better than anyplace else in Tokyo. For many older Japanese, a visit to Asakusa is like stepping back to the days of their childhood; for tourists, it provides a glimpse of the way things were.

Pleasure-seekers have been flocking to Asakusa for centuries. Originating as a temple town back in the 7th century, it grew in popularity during the Tokugawa regime, as merchants grew wealthy and whole new forms of popular entertainment arose to cater to them. Theaters for Kabuki and Bunraku flourished in Asakusa, as did restaurants and shops. By 1840, Asakusa had become Edo's main entertainment district. In stark contrast to the

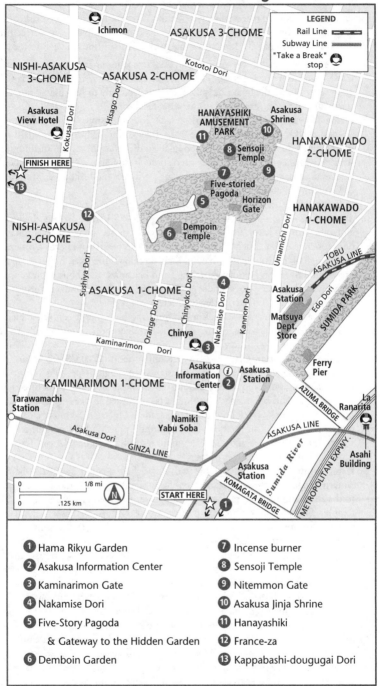

LEGEND
Rail Line ▭▭▭
Subway Line ▬▬▬
"Take a Break" stop 🌀

Ichimon

ASAKUSA 3-CHOME

Kototoi Dori

NISHI-ASAKUSA 3-CHOME

ASAKUSA 2-CHOME

Hisago Dori

Kokusai Dori

Asakusa View Hotel

FINISH HERE

13

12

NISHI-ASAKUSA 2-CHOME

Sushiya Dori

HANAYASHIKI AMUSEMENT PARK

11

8 Sensoji Temple

7

5 Five-storied Pagoda

Horizon Gate

6 Dempoin Temple

Asakusa Shrine

10

9

HANAKAWADO 2-CHOME

HANAKAWADO 1-CHOME

Umamichi Dori

TOBU ASAKUSA LINE

ASAKUSA 1-CHOME

Orange Dori

Chinyoko Dori

Nakamise Dori

Kannon Dori

4

Chinya 3

Kaminarimon Dori

KAMINARIMON 1-CHOME

Asakusa Information Center 2 Asakusa Station

Tarawamachi Station

Asakusa Dori

GINZA LINE

Namiki Yabu Soba

Asakusa Station

Edo Dori

SUMIDA PARK

Matsuya Dept. Store

Ferry Pier

AZUMA BRIDGE

ASAKUSA LINE

Sumida River

La Ranarita

Asahi Building

METROPOLITAN EXPWY.

Asakusa Station

KOMAGATA BRIDGE

START HERE

1

0   1/8 mi
0   .125 km

N

1 Hama Rikyu Garden
2 Asakusa Information Center
3 Kaminarimon Gate
4 Nakamise Dori
5 Five-Story Pagoda
 & Gateway to the Hidden Garden
6 Demboin Garden

7 Incense burner
8 Sensoji Temple
9 Nitemmon Gate
10 Asakusa Jinja Shrine
11 Hanayashiki
12 France-za
13 Kappabashi-dougugai Dori

solemnity surrounding places of worship in the West, Asakusa's temple market had a carnival atmosphere reminiscent of medieval Europe, complete with street performers and exotic animals. It retains some of that festive atmosphere even today.

The most dramatic way to arrive in Asakusa is by boat from Hama Rikyu Garden (see stop no. 1, below), just as people used to arrive in the olden days. If you want to forgo the boat ride, take the subway directly to Asakusa Station and start your tour from stop no. 2. Otherwise, head to:

1. **Hama Rikyu Garden,** at the south end of Tokyo (station: Shimbashi, then a 13-min. walk). Considered by some to be Tokyo's finest garden, it was laid out during the Edo Period in a style popular at the time, in which surrounding scenery was incorporated in its composition. It contains an inner tidal pool, bridges draped with wisteria, moon-viewing pavilions, and teahouses. (See "Parks & Gardens," in chapter 6, for more details.)

Boats depart the garden hourly or more frequently between 10:15am and 4:05pm, with the fare to Asakusa costing ¥620 ($5.15), and make their way along the Sumida River. Although much of what you see along the river today is only concrete embankments, I recommend the trip because it affords a different perspective of Tokyo—barges making their way down the river, high-rise apartment buildings with laundry fluttering from balconies, warehouses, and superhighways. The boat passes under approximately a dozen bridges during the 40-minute trip, each one completely different.

Upon arrival in Asakusa, walk away from the boat pier a couple of blocks inland, where you'll soon see the colorful Kaminarimon Gate on your right. Across the street on your left is the:

2. **Asakusa Information Center,** 2–18–9 Kaminarimon (☎ 03/3842-5566). It's open daily from 9:30am to 8pm, and staffed by English-speaking volunteers from 10am to 5pm. Stop here to pick up a map of the area and to ask directions to restaurants and other sights you might be interested in visiting. In addition, note that huge Seiko clock on the center's facade—a mechanical music clock that performs every hour on the hour from 10am to 7pm. Mechanical dolls reenact scenes from several of Asakusa's most famous festivals, including dances. Then it's time to head across the street to the:

3. **Kaminarimon Gate,** unmistakable with its bright red colors and a 220-pound lantern hanging in the middle. The statues inside the gate are the gods of wind to the right and thunder to the left, ready to protect the deity enshrined in the temple. The god of thunder is particularly fearsome—he has an insatiable appetite for human navels. Once past the gate, you'll find yourself immediately on a pedestrian lane called:

4. **Nakamise Dori,** which leads straight to the temple. Nakamise means "inside shops," and historical records show that vendors have sold wares here since the late 17th century. Today Nakamise Dori is lined on both sides with tiny stalls, many owned by the same family for generations. If you're expecting austere religious artifacts, however, you're in for a surprise: Fabrics, shoes, barking toy dogs, Japanese crackers (called *sembei*), bags, umbrellas, Japanese dolls, T-shirts, fans, masks, and traditional Japanese accessories are all available. How about a brightly colored straight hairpin—and a black hairpiece to go with it? Or a temporary tattoo in the shape of a dragon? This is a great place to shop for souvenirs, gifts, and items you have no earthly need for—a little bit of unabashed consumerism on the way to spiritual purification.

☕ **TAKE A BREAK**   If you're hungry for lunch, there are a number of possibilities in the neighborhood. **Chinya,** 1–3–4 Asakusa, just west of Kaminarimon Gate on Kaminarimon Dori, has been serving sukiyaki and shabu-shabu since 1880. To the south of Kaminarimon Gate is **Namiki Yabu Soba,** 2–11–9 Kaminarimon, Asakusa's best-known noodle shop. For Western food, head to the other side of the Sumida River, where on the 22nd floor of the Asahi Beer Tower you'll find **La Ranarita,** 1–23–1 Azumabashi, a moderately priced Italian restaurant with great views of Asakusa. (See chapter 5 for complete reviews.)

Near the end of Nakamise Dori, as you head toward the temple, you'll pass a kindergarten on your left, followed by a:

5. Five-story red-and-gold pagoda. It's a 1970 remake of one constructed during the time of the third shogun, Iemitsu, in the 17th century.

A low-lying building connected to the pagoda is the gateway to the gem of this tour: a **hidden garden,** one of Asakusa's treasures, just a stone's throw from Nakamise Dori and barely visible on the other side of the kindergarten. Most visitors to Asakusa pass it by, unaware of its existence, primarily because it isn't open to the general public. And yet, anyone can visit it for free simply by asking for permission, which you can obtain by entering the building connected to the pagoda at the left. Go inside, turn right, and walk to the third door to the left; you'll be asked to sign your name and will be given a map showing the entrance to the garden, open Monday through Saturday from 9am to 3pm. However, because the garden is on private grounds belonging to the Demboin Monastery, it's occasionally closed due to functions. There's no way of telling until you get here whether you'll be able to see it, so you'll just have to trust to luck. Once you've obtained permission, retrace your steps down Nakamise past the kindergarten, take the first right onto Demboin Dori, and then enter the second gate on your right. This is the entrance to:

6. Demboin Garden (also spelled Dempoin Garden). If the gate is locked, ring the doorbell to be let in. Soon you'll find yourself in a peaceful oasis in the midst of bustling Asakusa, in a countryside setting that centers on a pond filled with carp and turtles. It was designed in the 17th century by Enshu Kobori, a tea-ceremony master and famous landscape gardener who also designed a garden for the shogun's castle. Because most people are unaware that the garden exists or that it's accessible, you may find yourself the sole visitor. The best view is from the far side of the pond, where you can see the temple building and pagoda above the trees.

Return to Nakamise Dori and resume your walk north to the second gate, which opens onto a square filled with pigeons and a large:

7. Incense burner, where worshippers "wash" themselves to ward off or help against illness. If, for example, you have a sore throat, be sure to rub some of the smoke over your throat for good measure. But the dominating building of the square is:

8. Sensoji Temple, Tokyo's oldest temple. Founded in the 7th century and thus already well established long before Tokugawa settled in Edo, Sensoji Temple is dedicated to Kannon, the Buddhist goddess of mercy, and is therefore popularly called the Asakusa Kannon Temple. According to legend, the temple was founded after two fishermen pulled up a golden statue of Kannon from the sea. The sacred statue is still housed in the temple, carefully preserved inside three boxes; even though it's never on display, people still flock to the temple to pay their respects.

The Floating World of Yoshiwara

During the Edo Period (1603–1867), prostitution in Japan was not only allowed, it was also—along with everything else in feudal Japan—regulated and strictly controlled by the Tokugawa shogunate. Licensed quarters arose in various parts of Edo (former Tokyo), but none was as famous or as long-standing as **Yoshiwara,** the "floating world of pleasure." Opened in 1657 in the midst of rice fields, far outside the city gates upriver from Asakusa, Yoshiwara rose to such prominence that at its height, as many as 3,000 prostitutes, referred to as "courtesans," worked their trade here. The services they rendered depended on how much their customers were willing to spend. Some men, so they say, stayed for days. Stories abound of how more than a few lost their entire fortunes.

The top-ranked courtesan, known as Tayu, was distinguished by her gorgeous costume, which often weighed as much as 40 pounds and included a huge *obi* (sash) knotted in front. Many of the courtesans, however, had been sold into prostitution as young girls. To prevent their escape, a moat surrounded Yoshiwara, which could be entered or exited only through a guarded gate. The courtesans were allowed out of the compound only once a year, during an autumn festival. Such virtual imprisonment was abolished only in 1900. Yoshiwara itself was closed down in 1957, when prostitution became illegal.

Within the temple is a counter where you can buy your fortune by putting a 100-yen coin into a wooden box and shaking it until a long bamboo stick emerges from a small hole. The stick will have a number on it, which corresponds to one of the numbers on a set of drawers. Take out the fortune from the drawer that has your number. Most fortunes are in both English and Japanese, but if not, ask the man sitting at the counter to the left whether he has a translation. (If the counter is unoccupied, you can also ask at the Asakusa Information Center.) But don't expect the translation to clear things up; my fortune contained such cryptic messages as "Getting a beautiful lady at your home, you want to try all people know about this," and "Stop to start a trip." If you find your fortune raises more questions than it answers or you simply don't like what it has to say, you can conveniently negate it by tying it to one of the wires provided for this purpose just outside the main hall.

To the right (east) of the temple is the rather small:

9. **Nitemmon Gate.** Built in 1618, it is the only structure on temple grounds remaining from the Edo Period; all other buildings, including Sensoji Temple and the pagoda, were destroyed in a 1945 air raid.

On the northeast corner of the grounds is a small orange shrine, the:

10. **Asakusa Jinja Shrine,** built in 1649 by Iemitsu Tokugawa, the third Tokugawa shogun, to commemorate the two fishermen who found the statue of Kannon and their village chief. From Asakusa Jinja Shrine, walk around the back side of Sensoji northwest to:

11. **Hanayashiki,** a small and corny amusement park that first opened in 1853 and still draws in the little ones. (See "Especially for Kids," in chapter 6, for more details.)

Most of the area west of Sensoji Temple (the area to the left if you stand facing the front of the temple) is a small but interesting area of Asakusa popular among

Tokyo's older working class. This is where several of Asakusa's old-fashioned pleasure houses remain, including bars, restaurants, strip shows, traditional Japanese vaudeville, and so-called "love hotels," which rent out rooms by the hour. One of the most famous strip shows is:

12. France-za, 1–43–12 Asakusa (☎ **03/3841-6631**), located on a small side street that leads west from Sensoji Temple. Shows run throughout the day from 11:30am to 9pm—and leave nothing to the imagination. The entrance fee is ¥3,000 ($25). If you keep walking west, within 10 minutes you'll reach:

13. Kappabashi-dougugai Dori, generally referred to simply as Kappabashi Dori. Tokyo's wholesale district for restaurant items, it has shop after shop selling pottery, chairs, tableware, cookingware, lacquerware, rice cookers, noren, and everything else needed to run a restaurant. And yes, you can even buy those models of plastic food you've been drooling over in restaurant displays. Ice cream, pizza, sushi, mugs foaming with beer—they're all here, looking like the real thing. My favorite is one of spaghetti with a fork hovering above it, supported by a few strands of noodles.

🍲 **WINDING DOWN**   The **Asakusa View Hotel,** on Kokusai Dori Avenue between Sensoji Temple and Kappabashi Dori, has several restaurants and bars. In the basement is the clubby **Ice House,** the hotel's main bar, while on the ground floor is a casual coffee shop. There are also Japanese, Chinese, and French restaurants. Another good place to end a day of sightseeing in Asakusa is **Ichimon,** 3–12–6 Asakusa, near the intersection of Kokusai and Kototoi avenues. Decorated like a farmhouse, it specializes in different types of sake (see "The Bar Scene," in chapter 9 for more details).

Walking Tour 2
Harajuku & Aoyama

Start: Meiji Jingu Shrine (station: Harajuku).

Finish: Japan Traditional Craft Center (station: Gaienmae).

Time: Allow approximately 5 hours, including stops along the way.

Best Times: The 1st and 4th Sundays of every month, when there's an antiques flea market at Togo Shrine.

Worst Times: Monday, from the 27th to the end of every month (when the Ota Memorial Museum of Art and the Nezu Institute of Fine Arts are closed), and Thursday (when the Oriental Bazaar and Japan Traditional Craft Center are closed).

Harajuku is one of my favorite neighborhoods in Tokyo, though I'm too old to really fit in. In fact, anyone over 25 is apt to feel ancient here, since this is Tokyo's most popular hangout for Japanese high school and college students. The young come here to see and be seen; you're sure to spot Japanese punks, girls decked out in the fashions of the moment, and young couples looking their best. I like Harajuku for its vibrancy, its sidewalk cafes, its street hawkers, and its trendy clothing boutiques. It's also the home of Tokyo's most important Shinto shrine, as well as a woodblock-print museum and an excellent souvenir shop of traditional Japanese items.

Nearby is **Aoyama,** a yuppified version of Harajuku, where the upwardly mobile shop and dine. It has a number of designer shops, a museum for Asian art, and a lovely shop selling handcrafted traditional items. Connecting Harajuku and

Aoyama is **Omotesando Dori,** a tree-lined avenue that forms the heart of this area and is a popular promenade for people-watching.

From Harajuku Station, take the south exit (the one closer to Shibuya) and turn right over the bridge, where you will immediately see the huge cypress torii marking the entrance to:

1. **Meiji Jingu Shrine,** the most venerable shrine in Tokyo. Dedicated to Emperor and Empress Meiji, Meiji Jingu Shrine opened in 1920. (See "The Top Attractions," in chapter 6, for more details.) On the 10-minute walk along the tree-shaded path to the shrine, stop off at the Iris Garden, spectacular for its irises in late June. North of the shrine complex is the Meiji Jingu Treasure Museum, which houses personal items that belonged to the emperor.

After visiting the shrine, retrace your steps back to Harajuku Station and continue walking north beside the station to its north exit. Across the street from Harajuku Station's north exit is:

2. **Takeshita Dori,** a pedestrian-only street lined nonstop with stores that cater to teenagers. It's packed—especially on Sunday afternoons—with young people hunting for bargains on inexpensive clothing, shoes, music, sunglasses, jewelry, watches, cosmetics, and more.

After inching your way along this narrow lane with its flow of humanity, you will eventually find yourself on a busy thoroughfare, Meiji Dori. If it's the first or fourth Sunday of the month, turn left (north) onto Meiji Dori, where in a couple minutes on your left you'll see:

3. **Togo Shrine,** dedicated to Admiral Heihachiro Togo, who was in charge of the fleet that defeated the Russian navy in 1905 in the Russo-Japanese War. Nowadays, the shrine is most popular for its flea market held the 1st and 4th Sundays of every month, when everything from old chests, dolls, porcelain, and kimono are for sale, spread out on a tree-shaded sidewalk that meanders around the shrine.

Head back south on Meiji Dori, where to your right, just before the big intersection, is:

4. **La Forêt,** a building filled with trendy shoe and clothing boutiques. The less expensive boutiques tend to be on the lower floors, more exclusive boutiques higher up. (See chapter 8 for details on the shops and department stores listed in this walking tour.) Behind La Forêt is one of my favorite museums, the:

5. **Ota Memorial Museum of Art,** 1–10–10 Jingumae, featuring the private *ukiyo-e* (woodblock prints) collection of the late Ota Seizo. Exhibitions of the museum's 12,000 prints change monthly and are always worth checking out. (See "More Museums," in chapter 6, for details.)

Across Omotesando Dori is:

6. **Chicago,** which specializes in used American clothing but also stocks hundreds of used and new kimono and yukata in a corner of its basement.

☕ **TAKE A BREAK** On Meiji Dori, near Takeshita Dori, is **Aux Bacchanales,** 1–6–1 Jingumae, Harajuku's trendiest address for people-watching from its Parisian-style sidewalk cafe. On the other side of Meiji Dori, down the street, is **Café des Près,** 4–31–9 Jingumae, one of several branches of this popular chain of sidewalk cafes that has taken Tokyo by storm.

Near La Forêt is Harajuku's major intersection, Meiji Dori and Omotesando Dori. Heading east on Omotesando Dori (away from Harajuku Station), you'll soon see, to your right:

Walking Tour–Harajuku & Aoyama

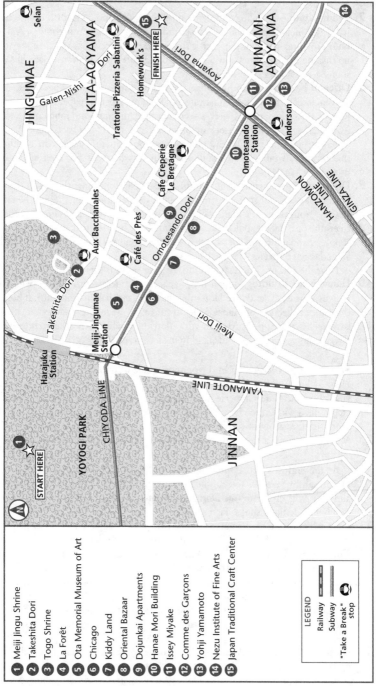

JINGUMAE

Selan

KITA-AOYAMA

Dori

Gaien-Nishi

Trattoria-Pizzeria Sabatini

Homework's

FINISH HERE

Aoyama Dori

MINAMI-AOYAMA

Omotesando Station

Anderson

Café Creperie
Le Bretagne

Aux Bacchanales

Omotesando Dori

Café des Prés

Takeshita Dori

Meiji-Jingumae Station

Harajuku Station

Meiji Dori

CHIYODA LINE

YOYOGI PARK

HANZOMON LINE

GINZA LINE

YAMANOTE LINE

JINNAN

START HERE

N

① Meiji Jingu Shrine
② Takeshita Dori
③ Togo Shrine
④ La Forêt
⑤ Ota Memorial Museum of Art
⑥ Chicago
⑦ Kiddy Land
⑧ Oriental Bazaar
⑨ Dojunkai Apartments
⑩ Hanae Mori Building
⑪ Issey Miyake
⑫ Comme des Garçons
⑬ Yohji Yamamoto
⑭ Nezu Institute of Fine Arts
⑮ Japan Traditional Craft Center

LEGEND

Railway

Subway

"Take a Break" stop

175

7. **Kiddy Land,** 6–1–9 Jingumae, which sells gag gifts and a great deal more than just toys, including much to amuse undiscerning adults. You could spend an hour browsing here, but the store is so crowded with teenagers that you may end up rushing for the door. Continuing east on Omotesando Dori, to your right will soon be Harajuku's most famous store:

8. **Oriental Bazaar,** 5–9–13 Jingumae, Tokyo's best one-stop shopping for Japanese souvenirs. Four floors hold chinaware, old kimono, Japanese paper products, fans, jewelry, woodblock prints, vases, screens, antique furniture, and much more, all at reasonable prices. I always stock up on gifts here for the folks back home.

As you continue walking east on Omotesando Dori, on your left are buildings that probably wouldn't catch your attention anywhere else but look highly unusual in Tokyo:

9. **Dojunkai Apartments,** built in the mid-1920s following the Great Kanto Earthquake. Several such apartment complexes were built for the middle class, but few from that era remain. With their ivy-covered walls and clump of shady trees, the apartments look quite cozy; some have been turned into galleries and shops. With land prices the way they are, the Dojunkai Apartments may well be an endangered species.

Near the end of Omotesando Dori, to your right, is the:

10. **Hanae Mori Building,** designed by Japanese architect Kenzo Tange (who also designed the Akasaka Prince Hotel and the TMG city hall in Shinjuku). It houses the entire collection of Hanae Mori, from casual wear to evening wear. In the basement is the Antique Market, with individual stallkeepers selling china, jewelry, clothing, watches, swords, and items from the 1930s.

TAKE A BREAK   On the oppposite side of Omotesando Dori from the Hanae Mori Building is a small side street. If you take this and then turn left, you'll find the **Cafe Creperie Le Bretagne,** 4–9–8 Jingumae, a great place for crepes filled with fruit, chocolate, or liqueur concoctions. For something slightly more substantial, walk to Aoyama Dori and turn right for **Anderson,** 5–1–26 Minami-Aoyama, a bakery that also sells sandwiches from its basement cafeteria.

At the end of Omotesando Dori, where it connects with Aoyama Dori, is **Omotesando Station.** You can board the subway here, or, for more sightseeing and shopping, cross Aoyama Dori and continue heading east, where you'll pass a number of designer shops. First comes:

11. **Issey Miyake** on the left at 3–18–11 Minami-Aoyama. The clothes here are known for their fabrics and richness in texture. To the right is:

12. **Comme des Garçons,** 5–2–1 Minami-Aoyama, showcase of Rei Kawakubo's designs for both men and women. Farther down the street, on the right, is:

13. **Yohji Yamamoto,** 5–3–6 Minami-Aoyama. As with all Yamamoto shops, this one has an interesting avant-garde interior.

Continue walking in the same direction, curving to the left, until you come to a stoplight. Cross the street and turn right, following the sign that directs you to the:

14. **Nezu Institute of Fine Arts,** 6–5–1 Minami-Aoyama. It houses a fine collection of Asian art and boasts a delightful small garden with a pond.

Retrace your steps to Aoyama Dori, turn right, and head north about 5 minutes to the corner of Aoyama Dori and Gaien-Nishi-Dori, where, to your right, is the:

15. Japan Traditional Craft Center, 3–1–1 Minami-Aoyama, a lovely shop devoted to beautifully crafted traditional items from all over Japan. Crafts for sale may include bamboo products, lacquerware, ceramics, metalwork, boxes made from cherry bark, chopsticks, fans, and much more.

☕ **WINDING DOWN**   **Trattoria-Pizzeria Sabatini,** 2–13–5 Kita-Aoyama has great pizzas, as well as pastas and heartier dishes. **Selan,** 2–1–9 Kita-Aoyama, has a wonderful outdoor terrace on a leafy tree-lined street; it's a wonderful place for a drink or light meal. If you're dying for a burger, head to **Homework's,** 3–1–28 Jingumae.

Walking Tour 3
Ueno

Start: South end of Ueno Park (station: Ueno).
Finish: Ameya Yokocho flea market, along the tracks of the Yamanote Line (station: Ueno or Okachimachi).
Time: Allow approximately 2 hours, not including stops along the way.
Best Times: Weekdays, when museums and shops aren't as crowded.
Worst Time: Monday, when the museums and zoo are closed.

Located on the northeast end of the Yamanote Line loop, Ueno is one of the most popular places in Tokyo for Japanese families on a day's outing. Unlike sophisticated Ginza, Ueno has always been favored by the working people of Tokyo and visitors from Tokyo's rural north. During the Edo Period, the area around Ueno was where merchants and craftpeople lived, worked, and played. Ueno was also the site of the enormous Kan'eiji Temple compound, which served as the private family temple and burial ground of the Tokugawa shoguns. Today, Ueno's main drawing card is Ueno Park, the largest park in Tokyo. It's famous throughout Japan for its cluster of historic monuments, zoo, and excellent museums, including the prestigious Tokyo National Museum.

You will probably arrive in Ueno by either subway or the JR Yamanote Line. Regardless, make your way to the main entrance of Keisei Ueno Station (terminus of the Skyliner train from the Narita Airport). If you wish, stop by one of the many obento counters that stretch along the road between the Keisei Ueno Station and JR Ueno Station. Sushi, sandwiches, and traditional obento can be purchased here for a picnic later in the park; there are few restaurants in the park itself. Outside Keisei Ueno Station's main entrance are two steep flights of stone stairs leading up to an area of trees. This is the south entrance to:

1. Ueno Park. Located atop a broad hill, this was once part of the precincts of Kan'eiji Temple, a huge, 300-acre complex consisting of one main temple and 36 subsidiary temples. Unfortunately, most of the complex was destroyed in 1868, when 2,000 diehard shogun loyalists gathered on Ueno Hill for a last stand against the advancing forces of the imperial army. Ueno Park opened in 1873 as one of the nation's first public parks.

Although quite small compared to New York City's Central Park, this is Japan's largest city park and Tokyo's most important museum district, making it a favorite destination for families and school groups in search of culture, relaxation, and fun. With its 1,000 cherry trees, it's also one of the most famous cherry-blossom–viewing spots in the country. By the way, it's also a popular hangout for Tokyo's down-and-out population, so don't be surprised if you see a few of them snoozing away on park benches. (Yes, even Tokyo has its homeless people, who are largely ignored by Japanese society, outcasts in a country where hard work and uniformity are revered; since the recession, Japan's homeless population has markedly grown).

A landmark near the south entrance to the park is a bronze:

2. **Statue of Takamori Saigo,** a samurai born in 1827 near Kagoshima on Kyushu island. Rising through the ranks as a soldier and statesman, he helped to restore the emperor to power after the Tokugawa shogunate's downfall. Later, he became disenchanted with the Meiji regime when rights enjoyed by the samurai class were suddenly rescinded. He led a revolt against the government that failed, and ended up taking his own life in ritual suicide. The statue was erected in the 1890s but later became controversial when Gen. Douglas MacArthur, leader of the U.S. occupation forces in Japan after World War II, demanded its removal because of its nationalistic associations. Today, the statue, saved by public outcry, still depicts the stout Saigo dressed in a simple cotton kimono with his hand on his sword. It is the best-known monument in Tokyo, if not all of Japan.

Ironically, behind the statue of Saigo and slightly to the left is a memorial dedicated to those very men Saigo originally opposed. Here lie the:

3. **Tombs of the Shogitai Soldiers,** the diehard Tokugawa loyalists who resisted imperial forces on Ueno Hill in 1868. Tended by descendants of the soldiers, the grounds contain small paintings depicting the fierce battle.

Behind and to the left of the war memorial, on the other side of the pathway, is:

4. **Kiyomizu-do Kannon Temple,** completed in 1631 as a copy of the famous Kiyomizu Temple in Kyoto and one of the few buildings left standing after the battle of 1868, making it one of the oldest temples in Tokyo. The temple houses the protectoress of childbearing and child-raising, and attracts both women hoping to become pregnant and those whose wishes have been fulfilled. To the right of the main altar is a room full of dolls, left by women to symbolize their children in a gesture they hope will further protect them.

☕ **TAKE A BREAK** Located between Kiyomizu Temple and Toshogu Shrine, **Ueno Seiyoken Grill** opened in 1876 as one of Japan's first restaurants serving Western food. It remains the best place for a meal in Ueno Park, serving pricey but quite good classic French cuisine. At the other end of the spectrum are a number of small kiosks and huts throughout Ueno Park selling drinks, snacks, and ice cream. If the weather is fine, I suggest you head for **Toho Cherry,** located just a stone's throw behind the Saigo statue—look for its hedge and string of lanterns, which encircle a beer garden, perfect for a snack or beer.

Walking north from Kiyomizu-do Kannon Temple, you'll soon pass orange torii (made, horrendously enough, out of plastic) and Seiyoken restaurant on your left. Following signs that say Ueno Zoo, turn left at the Lions Club totem pole. Soon, to your left, you'll see the stone torii that marks the entrance to:

5. **Toshogu Shrine,** Ueno Park's most famous religious structure, dedicated to Tokugawa Ieyasu, founder of the Tokugawa shogunate. The shrine was erected in 1651 by Ieyasu's grandson and, like Nikko's Toshogu Shrine (see chapter 10), is ornately decorated with brilliant red, blue, green, and gold ornamentation. The

Walking Tour–Ueno

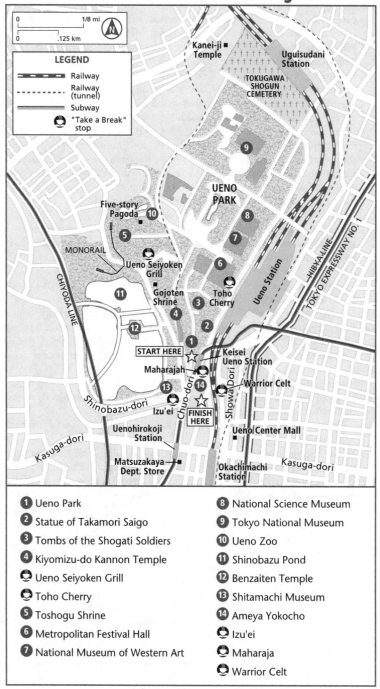

1 Ueno Park

2 Statue of Takamori Saigo

3 Tombs of the Shogati Soldiers

4 Kiyomizu-do Kannon Temple

☕ Ueno Seiyoken Grill

☕ Toho Cherry

5 Toshogu Shrine

6 Metropolitan Festival Hall

7 National Museum of Western Art

8 National Science Museum

9 Tokyo National Museum

10 Ueno Zoo

11 Shinobazu Pond

12 Benzaiten Temple

13 Shitamachi Museum

14 Ameya Yokocho

☕ Izu'ei

☕ Maharaja

☕ Warrior Celt

pathway leading to the shrine is lined with massive stone lanterns, plus 50 copper lanterns donated by feudal lords from throughout Japan. To the right of the pathway is a five-storied pagoda (located on zoo grounds), covered entirely in lacquer and constructed in 1639. Also on shrine grounds are the charred remains of a tree discovered in nearby Nishi-Nippori in 1991; it was burned during the bombing raids of 1945 and placed here as an appeal for peace. Nearby are photographs of the war's destruction in Hiroshima and Nagasaki. The shrine grounds are also famous for their peonies, which bloom both in spring and in winter.

But the most important thing to see here is the shrine itself, which contains murals by a famous Edo artist, Kano Tan-yu, and armor worn by Ieyasu. Note the lions decorating the arched, Chinese-style Karamon Gate—legend has it that when night falls, they sneak down to Shinobazu Pond for a drink. On a lighter note, you'll also see signs asking you to refrain from making a bonfire, just in case you were contemplating a cookout on these sacred grounds.

Across from Toshogu Shrine is a miniature amusement park for young children. Walk through it or around it to Ueno Park's main square, marked by an artificial pond with a spouting, dancing fountain. Keep walking straight, past the people feeding the pigeons and the *koban* police box. That building to your right is the:

6. **Metropolitan Festival Hall,** opened in 1961 as a venue for classical music, ballet, and dance. The building to the left is the very good:

7. **National Museum of Western Art (Kokuritsu Seiyo Bijutsukan),** built in 1959 with a main building designed by French architect Le Corbusier. It features works by such Western artists as Renoir, Monet, Sisley, Manet, Delacroix, Cézanne, Degas, El Greco, and Goya; but it's probably most famous for its 50-some sculptures by Rodin.

Just north of this museum is the:

8. **National Science Museum (Kokuritsu Kagaku Hakubutsukan),** a good attraction if you're traveling with children.

The most important museum in Ueno Park, however, is the one farthest to the north, the:

9. **Tokyo National Museum (Tokyo Kokuritsu Hakubutsukan),** Japan's largest museum and the world's largest repository of Japanese art. This is the place to see antiques from Japan's past, including lacquerware, pottery, scrolls, screens, *ukiyo-e* (woodblock prints), samurai armor, swords, kimono, Buddhist statues, and much more. If you go to only one museum in Tokyo, this should be it!

Assuming you don't spend the entire day in museums, walk south from the National Museum past the dancing fountain, turn right, and follow signs for:

10. **Ueno Zoo,** which opened in 1882 and remains Japan's oldest zoo. Although it seems rather small by today's standards, it's famous for its two giant pandas, which were donated by the Chinese government. These two celebrities are so popular that there are always long lines to their cages on weekends, and there are all kinds of panda souvenirs for sale. When one of the zoo's pandas died some years back, the entire nation went into mourning, until the Chinese quickly sent a replacement. There are also Japanese macaques, polar bears, California sea lions, penguins, gorillas, giraffes, zebras, elephants, deer, and tigers. Be sure, too, to see the five-story pagoda mentioned earlier in the walk. End your tour of the zoo at:

11. **Shinobazu Pond** (you can also get to Shinobazu Pond without entering the zoo by retracing your steps to those orange plastic torii and walking downhill toward the pond, passing the Gojoten Shrine along the way). This marshy pond was

constructed in the 17th century; teahouses used to line its banks. Now part of the pond has literally gone to the birds: It's a bird sanctuary. The pond is filled with lotus plants, a lovely sight when they bloom in August. There are small boats for rent, and on an island in the middle of the pond, connected to the bank with walkways, is the:

12. Benzaiten Temple, dedicated to the goddess of fortune. At the southeastern edge of Shinobazu Pond is the:

13. Shitamachi Museum (Shitamachi Fuzoku Shiryokan). Shitamachi means "downtown" and refers to the area of Tokyo where commoners used to live, mainly around Ueno and Asakusa. Displays here include a Shitamachi tenement house, as well as everyday objects used in work and play, all donated by people living in the area.

From the Shitamachi Museum, head south on Chuo Dori and turn left on Kasuga Dori, passing Matsuzakaya department store and Ueno Center Mall. Here, at Okachimachi Station, is:

14. Ameya Yokocho, a narrow shopping street under and along the west side of the elevated tracks of the Yamanote Line between Ueno and Okachimachi stations. Originally a wholesale market for candy and snacks, and after World War II a black market in U.S. Army goods, Ameya Yokocho (also referred to as Ameyacho or Ameyoko) today consists of hundreds of stalls and shops selling at a discount everything from fish and vegetables to handbags and clothes. Early evening is the most crowded time as workers rush through on their way home. Some shops close on Wednesdays, but otherwise most are open from about 10am to 7pm.

WINDING DOWN Across from the Shitamachi Museum, next to KFC, is **Izu'ei,** 2–12–22 Ueno, a modern restaurant that has served eel since the Edo Period. If Indian food is more to your taste, head to nearby **Maharaja,** 4–9–6 Ueno, located on the third floor of the Nagafuji Building Annex next to the Ameya Yokocho market. For a drink, head to **Warrior Celt,** 6–9–2 Ueno, a friendly bar with a nightly happy hour and free, live music; it's just a stone's throw from Ameya Yokocho.

Walking Tour 4
Yanaka

Start: Tennoji Temple (station: Nippori, then the north exit).
Finish: Nezu Temple (station: Nezu).
Time: Allow approximately 4 hours, including stops along the way.
Best Times: There is no "best" time, as such, for this walk.
Worst Time: Monday and Friday, when museums are closed.

Yanaka has been famous for its many temples ever since the Edo Period, when most temples and shrines were removed from the inner city and relocated to the outskirts in an attempt to curb the frequent fires that ravaged the crowded shogunate capital. Not only did the religious structures' thatched roofs ignite like tinder, but the land they formerly occupied would subsequently be cleared and left empty, to act as fire breaks in the otherwise densely populated city. Furthermore, temples on the edge of town could double as forts to protect Edo from invasion. The only invasions Yanaka suffered, however, were friendly ones, as townspeople flocked here to enjoy its peacefulness, wooded hills, paddies, clear streams, and majestic temple compounds. It wasn't long before the wealthy began building country estates here, followed by artists and writers who favored Yanaka's picturesque setting and cool breezes.

One of Tokyo's few old quarters to have survived both the 1923 Kanto earthquake and firebombs of World War II, Yanaka today still boasts Tokyo's greatest concentration of temples, most dating from the Edo Period. It's also largely residential, with narrow lanes, small houses, and a few unique museums and traditional shops tucked here and there among the gently sloping hills. Because there are no major attractions or department stores here, the atmosphere of this stroll is markedly different from the bustling liveliness of the previous walking tours—there are no crowds here and there's very little traffic. Rather, a trip to Yanaka is like visiting a small town, where the pace of life is slow and the people have time for each other. If Tokyo is starting to wear on your nerves, come here to refresh yourself.

The easiest way to get to Yanaka is on the Yamanote Line. Disembark at Nippori Station, exiting at the north end of the platform (the end closest to Nishi-Nippori Station) and turning left for the west exit. Look for the flight of steps up the hill, beside the public telephones and a map of the area. Walk through the cemetery, following the cement footpath until it turns left and joins a paved road. Across this street to the left is:

1. **Tennoji Temple,** founded more than 500 years ago. It used to be a grand and impressive complex, 10 times its present size and popular among townspeople as one of Edo's three temples authorized to hold lotteries. The lotteries, however, drew such huge crowds and got so out of hand that they were banned in the mid-19th century by the Tokugawa shogunate. Then, in 1868, most of the complex was destroyed in the battle between the Tokugawa loyalists and imperial forces on nearby Ueno Hill. Today, Tennoji is quiet and peaceful, with neatly swept grounds and the soothing sounds of chirping birds and chanting monks. The first thing you see upon entering the compound is a seated bronze Buddha, which dates from 1690 and is one of the temple's dearest treasures. Nearby is a standing bronze *jizo,* guardian of children's spirits. It was erected by a grieving father more than 60 years ago, following the death of his son in a playground accident; a relief at the base depicts boys playing in school uniform. There's also a stone statue of the Kannon, goddess of mercy.

Walk out of the temple compound's main entrance and continue walking on the paved road straight through:

2. **Yanaka Cemetery,** once the burial grounds of Kanei-ji and Tennoji temples and opened to the public in 1874. As one of Tokyo's largest cemeteries, it has more than 7,000 tombstones, including graves belonging to famous public figures, artists and writers, some of whom lived in the area. Among the most famous writers buried here are Soseki Natsume (1867-1916) and Ogai Mori (1862-1922), both novelists of the Meiji Era and longtime Yanaka residents. Natsume, whose portrait is featured on the 1,000-yen note, became famous after writing *I am a Cat,* a humorous look at the follies of human society as seen through the eyes of a cat. Ogai, who at 19 was the youngest graduate ever from the medical school at Tokyo University and who later became surgeon general, was a foremost figure of modern Japanese literature. His works tried to bridge the gap between the traditional and the modern, as Japan moved away from its feudal agrarian past and plunged headlong into its role as an industrialized nation.

Today the cemetery is quite peaceful and empty, but it wasn't always so. During the Edo Period, teahouses along its edge served more than tea, with

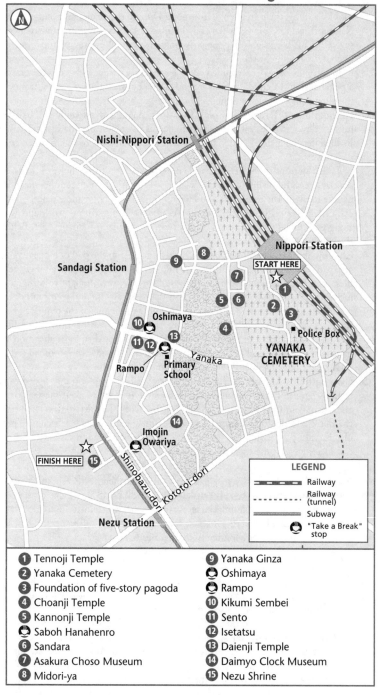

Nishi-Nippori Station

Sandagi Station

Nippori Station

START HERE

Oshimaya

Rampo

Primary School

Yanaka

Police Box

YANAKA CEMETERY

Imojin Owariya

FINISH HERE

Shinobazu-dori

Kototoi-dori

Nezu Station

LEGEND

- Railway
- Railway (tunnel)
- Subway
- "Take a Break" stop

1. Tennoji Temple
2. Yanaka Cemetery
3. Foundation of five-story pagoda
4. Choanji Temple
5. Kannonji Temple
- Saboh Hanahenro
6. Sandara
7. Asakura Choso Museum
8. Midori-ya
9. Yanaka Ginza
- Oshimaya
- Rampo
10. Kikumi Sembei
11. Sento
12. Isetatsu
13. Daienji Temple
14. Daimyo Clock Museum
15. Nezu Shrine

monks among their frequent customers. One of the teahouse beauties, Osen Kasamori, achieved fame when ukiyo-e master Harunobu immortalized her in several of his works. Most poor girls were always looking for patrons, but not necessarily one-night stands.

In a minute or two, on your left you'll see two very strange sights in a cemetery— a police box and a children's playground. Here, between the two and surrounded by a low bamboo fence and hedge, is the:

3. **Foundation of Tennoji Temple's five-story pagoda.** First built in 1644 but burned down in 1772, it was reconstructed as the tallest pagoda in Edo. It met its final demise in 1957, when it was burned down by two lovers who then committed suicide.

Take a right at the police box and continue through the cemetery into a residential street, following it one block until it ends at a T-intersection. Ahead is a plaque marking the tomb of Kano Hogai (1828-1888), a Japanese painter of the early Meiji Period who incorporated western techniques in his work and who, along with Okakura Tenshin, is credited for "modernizing" Japanese art. Behind the plaque is:

4. **Choanji Temple,** established in 1669 and dedicated to the god of longevity, one of Japan's seven lucky gods. During the Edo Period, a pilgrimage to all seven temples, each housing one of the seven gods of fortune, was thought to bring good luck. Now that such pilgrimages have lost their appeal, Choanji seems rather forgotten. In addition to Kano's tomb, located near the center of the temple's graveyard, the temple is notable for its three stone *stupas* dating from the 1200s, erected for the repose of departed souls. They are located straight ahead on the main path, near the end to the left, by the statues and under the groomed cedars.

Turn left out of Choanji. Presently, to your left, will be:

5. **Kannonji Temple.** A small pagoda to the right of its front entrance is dedicated to the 47 ronin (*akoroshi*), masterless samurai who avenged their master's death and then committed ritual suicide in 1702 (see "The Masterless Samurai," chapter 2). Their story captured the public's imagination and has become a popular Kabuki play. Two of the ronin were brothers of a head priest here, and several meetings plotting their revenge allegedly took place on this spot.

☕ **TAKE A BREAK**   Just a stone's throw farther north, on the right, is **Saboh Hanahenro,** 7–17–11 Yanaka (☎ **03/3822-6387**), which translates as "Teahouse Flower Temple-pilgrimage." A modern, two-floor teahouse decorated with international folk crafts, it serves Japanese green tea, coffee, beer, cakes, and sweets every day except Monday from 11am to 6pm.

Just past the teahouse, also on the right, is:

6. ㊼ **Sandara,** 7–18–6 Yanaka, a small crafts shop selling pottery, baskets, and other crafts. It's open every day except Monday from 10am to 6pm. Its name comes from the sacks once used to hold rice.

Past this shop, also on the right, is one of the highlights of this stroll, the:

7. ✪ **Asakura Choso Museum,** 7–18–10 Yanaka. With its modern black facade, it looks rather out of place in this traditional neighborhood, but its interior is a delightful mix of modern and traditional architecture. This is one of Tokyo's most intriguing homes open to the public. Built in 1936, it was the home and studio of Asakura Fumio, a western-style sculptor known for his realistic statues of statesmen, women, and cats (a lover of felines, Asakura once had as many as a

A Note on Japanese Symbols

Many hotels, restaurants, attractions, and shops in Japan do not have signs giving their names in Roman (English-language) letters. The second appendix to this book lists the Japanese symbols for all such places described in this guide. Each set of characters representing an establishment name has a number in the appendix, which corresponds to the number that appears inside the oval before the establishment's name in the text. Thus, to find the Japanese symbol for, say, **Sandara,** refer to no. 54 in appendix B.

---

dozen cats running around his studio, which he used as models). After passing through his studio with its soaring ceilings, you'll find yourself in a traditional Japanese house, which wraps itself around an inner courtyard pond, famous for its large stones arranged to reflect the Five Confucian Virtues. There's even a rooftop garden with views over the surrounding neighborhood. On display are several of Asakura's kimono, which he much preferred over Western-style dress. See chapter 6 for more information.

Take a right out of the museum, turning left at the next street (if you take a right here, you will end up back at Nippori Station). Keep to the right and walk down the steps. Then take the first right, located just past Lawson convenience store and the arched entryway marking the neighborhood's pedestrian-only shopping lane. Here, to your right, is:

8. (55) **Midori-ya,** 3–13–5 Nishi-Nippori (☎ **03/3828-1746**), an exquisite basket shop with several samples on display outside its front door. It's the store and workshop of Suigetsu Buseki and his son Sui Koh, a charming father-and-son team who coax flexible strands of bamboo into beautifully crafted baskets, some of them signed. The shop is known for its use of smoked bamboo, which is taken from the underside of thatched farmhouses and exhibits a beautiful gloss and subtle color gradation attained from years of indoor fire pits. Since such antique pieces of bamboo are increasingly hard to come by, some of the baskets here are rightfully expensive, but are still less expensive than at the major department stores. Freshly cut bamboo is also used for some of the less expensive pieces. You can linger here; the Busekis are happy to discuss their trade and their love with Japanese-speakers. The imperial family and visiting dignitaries, including a former U.S. ambassador to Japan, have been among their customers.

The shop is open daily 10am to 6pm.

Retrace your steps to the corner and turn right onto:

9. Yanaka Ginza, an ambitious name for an otherwise old-fashioned shopping lane. It's pleasant because it's free from cars and, unlike many shopping streets nowadays, isn't a covered arcade. Lining the lane are shops selling both modern and traditional toys, obento lunch boxes, sweets, household goods, Japanese tea, and vegetables. Look for the tofu shop, a must in any Japanese neighborhood.

At the end of the shopping street, turn left and walk about 5 minutes, passing the Sendagi business hotel on the way, until you come to a stoplight and a slightly larger road.

TAKE A BREAK Immediately to the left of the stoplight, on the corner, is a noodle shop called (56) **Oshimaya,** 3–2–5 Yanaka (☎ **03/3821-5052**). It's located on the second floor of a modern building but has traditional touches of bamboo screens at the window and an indoor pond with fish. It offers two different kinds of noodles—soba and udon—served in a variety of ways, including tempura soba, sansai udon (with mountain vegetables), and tanuki soba (cold noodles served with vegetables, seaweed, crab and egg). Open every day except Thursday from 11am to 8pm (closed from 4 to 5pm on weekdays). If all you want is a drink, farther down the street on the right-hand side is 57 **Rampo,** 2-9-14 Yanaka (☎ **03/3828-9494**), a coffee shop packed with knicknacks, kitsch, and folk art. It offers soft drinks, coffee, tea, and beer, with jazz playing softly in the background. Open every day except Monday from 10am to 8pm. Look for the wooden "Coffee Snack" sign above its door.

If you take a right at the stoplight mentioned above, to your right you will soon see:

10. 58 **Kikumi Sembei,** 3–37–16 Sendagi (☎ **03/3821-1215**). You can't miss it—look for the beautiful, 110-year-old wooden building, with its traditional open-fronted shop selling Japanese crackers. It's definitely worth a photograph. You might even want to buy some of its square-shaped sembei. It's open every day except Monday from 10am to 7pm.

Just beyond the cracker shop is Sendagi Station. Unless you're ready to call it quits, however, turn around and head back in the opposite direction, passing the stoplight and the noodle shop listed above. Almost immediately on your right will be a:

11. **sento,** or public bathhouse, easily recognizable by its lockers for shoes just in the entranceway and the chimney rising in the back. Although on the decline, public bathhouses still serve as important gathering places, especially for those who live without private bathrooms.

Farther along, on your right on a corner, is:

12. 59 **Isetatsu,** 2–18–9 Yanaka (☎ **03/3823-1453**), a crafts store that sells items made from Japanese paper, including paper fans, papier mâché objects, and boxes. Founded in the mid-1800s and run by the Hirose family for four generations, it specializes in *chiyogami,* handmade decorative paper printed with wood blocks. Some of the designs are the family's own creations; others are taken from family crests used by samurai and members of the court and worn on kimono and armor. The most expensive papers are rare and cannot be reproduced. The store is open daily from 10am to 6pm.

Continuing in the same direction (east), in the next block on the left side is:

13. **Daienji,** 3–1–2 Yanaka, located opposite the grade school. Famous for its chrysanthemum fair, this temple honors ukiyo-e master Harunobu, one of Edo's most famous artists, and Osen Kasamori, who worked at one of the many teahouses near Tennoji in the 1760s and achieved fame when Harunobu singled her out as a model for many of his portraits. The larger stone marker is a monument to Harunobu; the smaller one to the left is Osen's.

Cross back to the other side of the street at the crosswalk, turn left to continue walking in the same direction you've been going, and then take the first immediate right (after the elementary school). Turn left at the end of the street, and presently, to your right, will be the:

14. **Daimyo Clock Museum (Daimyo Tokei Hakubutsukan),** 2–1–27 Yanaka, with its one-room display of clocks and watches of the Edo Period (1603-1867). About 50 examples from the museum's extensive collection are on display at any one time, with exhibitions changing annually. Objects on display range from huge freestanding clocks to sundials, alarm clocks, pocket watches, and small watches that were attached to *obi* (the sash worn with a kimono). The first clock was brought to Japan by a missionary in the 16th century, and in typical Japanese fashion, was quickly modified to suit local needs. Rather than measuring 24 hours a day, Edo clocks were based on the length of time between sunrise and sunset, so that time varied greatly with the seasons. Clocks had to be set once or twice a day, and were so expensive that only daimyo, or feudal lords, could afford them. Most daimyo had both a clock maker and clock setter under their employ, since castles were large and generally contained several huge clocks on their grounds. Apparently, time was of the essence in Japan even back then. Unfortunately, explanations in the museum are in Japanese only. See chapter 6 for more information.

Take a right out of the museum to return to the street you were on, turn left and then left again (note the weirdly shaped pine tree on the corner), and walk down one of the many slopes for which Yanaka is famous and which still has some traditional wooden homes (including a beautiful one on your right). On the left-hand side of the slope, at the end of the street just before the stoplight, is Imojin Owariya, a Japanese sweet shop (see "Winding Down," below). Cross the busy street, Shinobazu-Dori Avenue, at the stoplight and continue straight (you'll pass another sento to your left). The road will begin to slope upward, and then, to your right, will be:

15. **Nezu Shrine,** one of Tokyo's best-kept secrets. With its brightly colored oranges, venerable cedars, and manicured azalea bushes, it's a welcome contrast to the austerity of the Buddhist temples that dominate Yanaka. It was built in 1706 by the fifth Tokugawa shogun and features a front courtyard gate of red lacquer with joists in gilt, green, blue, orange, and black. Take a rest here on the shrine's serene grounds.

To reach Nezu Station, return to Shinobazu-Dori and turn right.

WINDING DOWN   On the slope upward from Shinobazu-Dori in the direction of the clock museum is ⑥⓪ **Imojin Owariya,** 2–30–4 Nezu (☎ 03/ 3821-5530), a tiny shop selling Japanese sweets and ice cream. Look for the small display case outside its front door. Inside it's very plain, with just a few tables, kind of like a Japanese version of a small-town ice cream parlor. You can get homemade ice cream here, as well as shaved ice with flavorings of sweet-bean paste, lemon, strawberry, or melon. The shop is open daily from 11am to 7pm.

8 Shopping

I have never seen people shop as much as the Japanese do. Judging from the crowds that surge through Tokyo's department stores every day, I'm convinced it's the country's number one pastime. Women, men, couples, and even whole families go on shopping expeditions in their free time, making Sunday the most crowded shopping day of the week.

1 The Shopping Scene

BEST BUYS   Tokyo is the country's showcase for everything from the latest in camera or stereo equipment to original woodblock prints. Traditional Japanese crafts and souvenirs that make good buys include toys (both traditional and the latest in technical wizardry), kites, Japanese dolls, carp banners, swords, lacquerware, bamboo baskets, ikebana accessories, ceramics, chopsticks, fans, masks, knives, scissors, sake, and silk and cotton kimono. And you don't have to spend a fortune: You can pick up handmade Japanese paper (washi) products, such as umbrellas, lanterns, boxes, and stationery, or other souvenirs for a fraction of what they would cost in import shops in the United States. In Harajuku it's possible to buy a fully lined dress of the latest fashionable craze for $60, and I can't even count the number of pairs of shoes I've bought in Tokyo for a mere $30. Used cameras can be picked up for a song, reproductions of famous woodblock prints make great inexpensive gifts, and many items—from pearls to electronic video and audio equipment—can be bought tax free (see "Taxes," below).

Japan is famous for its electronics, but if you're buying new you can probably find these products just as cheaply, or even more cheaply, in the United States. If you think you want to shop for electronic products while you're in Tokyo, it pays to do some comparison shopping before you leave home so you can spot a deal when you see one. On the other hand, one of the joys of shopping for electronics in Japan is discovering new, advanced models; you might decide you want that new Sony portable CD player simply because it's the coolest thing you've ever seen, no matter what the price.

GREAT SHOPPING AREAS   Another enjoyable aspect of shopping in Tokyo is that specific areas are often devoted to certain goods, sold wholesale but also available to the individual shopper.

Kappabashi Dori (station: Tawaramachi), for example, is where you'll find shops specializing in kitchenware, while **Kanda** (station: Jimbocho), is known for its bookstores. ✪ **Akihabara** (station: Akihabara), is packed with stores selling the latest in electronics. **Ginza** (station: Ginza), is the chic address for clothing boutiques as well as art galleries. **Shibuya** (station: Shibuya), has several stores devoted to designer clothing, while **Harajuku** (stations: Harajuku, Meiji-Jingu-mae, Omontesando), is the place to go for youthful, fun, and inexpensive fashions.

SALES   Department stores have sales throughout the year, during which you can pick up bargains on everything from electronic goods and men's suits to golf clubs, toys, kitchenware, food, and lingerie; there are even sales for used wedding kimono. The most popular sales are for **designer clothing,** usually held twice a year, in July and December or January. Here you can pick up fantastic clothing at cut-rate prices—but be prepared for the crowds. To find out about current sales, check the *Tokyo Journal*, the monthly guide to what's going on in Tokyo.

Items on sale in department stores are usually found on one of the top floors in what's usually labeled the "Exhibition Hall" or "Promotion Hall" in the store's English brochure, which you can obtain by stopping by the information desk located near the main entrance. Sometimes an entire floor is devoted to a sale.

TAXES   Remember that a 5% consumption tax will be added on to the price marked, but all major department stores in Tokyo will refund the tax to foreign visitors if total purchases amount to more than ¥10,001 ($83.35) on that day. Exemptions include food, beverages, tobacco, pharmaceuticals, cosmetics, film, and batteries. When you've completed your shopping, take the purchased goods and receipts to the tax refund counter in the store. There are forms to fill out (you will need your passport). Upon completion, a record of your purchase is placed on the visa page of your passport and you are given the tax refund on the spot. When leaving Japan, make sure you have your purchases with you; you may be asked by Customs to show them (pack them in your carry on).

SHIPPING IT HOME   Many first-class hotels in Tokyo provide a packing and shipping service. In addition, most large department stores, as well as tourist shops such as the Oriental Bazaar and antique shops, will ship your purchases overseas.

If you wish to ship packages yourself, the easiest method is to go to a post office and purchase an easy-to-assemble cardboard box, available in three sizes (along with the necessary tape and string). Keep in mind that packages mailed abroad cannot weigh more than 20 kilograms (about 44 lb.), and that only the larger international post offices accept packages to be mailed overseas. Remember, too, that mailing packages from Japan is expensive. Ask your hotel concierge for the closest international post office.

2 Shopping A to Z

ANTIQUES & CURIOS

In addition to the listings here, other places to look for antiques include the **Oriental Bazaar** and Tokyo's **outdoor flea markets** (see below).

Antique Gallery Meguro. Stork Mansion Meguro Building, 2nd floor, 2–24–18 Kami-Osaki. ☎ **03/3493-1971.** Daily 11am–7pm. Station: Meguro (west exit, 2 min.).

About 50 dealers under one roof make this a good bet for one-stop shopping for a wide range of Japanese antiques and collectibles.

Antique Market. Hanae Mori Building basement, Omotesando Dori, 3–6–1 Kita-Aoyama, Minato-ku. ☎ **03/3406-1021.** Daily 11am–8pm (some shops closed on Thurs). Station: Omotesando (A1 exit, 1 min.).

More than 30 individual stalls carry both Japanese and European antiques, including china, jewelry, clothing, swords, dolls, watches, woodblock prints, vases, lamps, and lots of art-nouveau and art-deco pieces, at very high prices.

Kurofune. 7–7–4 Roppongi. ☎ **03/3479-1552.** Mon–Sat 10am–6pm. Station: Roppongi (5 min.). From Roppongi Crossing, walk away from Tokyo Tower on Gaien-Higashi Dori and take the diagonal street to the left opposite the Defense Agency, and then a right at 7 Eleven.

Located in a large house in Roppongi, Kurofune is owned by an American, John Adair, who for 20 years has specialized in Japanese antique furniture in its original state, with the largest collection in Tokyo of mid- to top-quality pieces. Browsing here is a delight, even if you can't afford to buy, though the stock does include hibachi, fabrics, prints, maps, lanterns, and folk art. Fax Adair (03/3479-0719) for a map of how to get here.

Mayuyama. 2–5–9 Kyobashi, Chuo-ku. ☎ **03/3561-5146.** Mon–Sat 10am–6pm. Closed holidays. Station: Kyobashi (2 min.). In a stone building between Kyobashi and Takaracho stations, within walking distance of Tokyo Station.

One of the best-known names in fine antiques, this shop was established in 1905 and is one of Tokyo's oldest and most exclusive antique shops. It deals in ceramics, pottery, scrolls, and screens from Japan, China, and Korea—at predictably high prices.

Tokyo Antique Hall (Komingu Kottokan). 3–9–5 Minami Ikebukuro. ☎ **03/ 3982-3433.** Fri–Wed 11am–7pm (some stalls may close early if business is slow). Station: Ikebukuro (east exit, 10 min.). Take a right out of the station's east side, walking south on Meiji Dori; the shop will be on your left.

This is one of the best places for one-stop hunting, with approximately 32 dealers offering mostly Japanese antiques and bric-a-brac. Although most articles are marked, it's okay to try bargaining. You could spend hours here, looking over everything from woodblock prints and lacquerware to hair pins, ceramics, pottery, and samurai gear.

ARCADES & TAX-FREE SHOPS

IN HOTELS   Shopping arcades are found in several of Tokyo's first-class hotels. While they don't offer the excitement and challenge of going out and rubbing elbows with the natives, they do offer convenience, English-speaking clerks, and consistently top-quality merchandise. The **Imperial Hotel Arcade** (station: Hibiya) is one of the best, with shops selling pearls, woodblock prints, porcelain, antiques, and expensive name-brand clothing like Hanae Mori. The **Okura** and **New Otani** hotels also have extensive shopping arcades.

UNDERGROUND ARCADES   Underground shopping arcades are found around several of Tokyo's train and subway stations; the biggest are at **Tokyo Station** (the Yaesu side) and **Shinjuku Station** (the east side). They often have great sales and bargains on clothing, accessories, and electronics. My only complaint is that once you're in them, it sometimes seems like you'll never find your way out again.

DUTY-FREE ARCADES   Other good places to shop if you're short of time are duty-free stores. To qualify, you must present your passport, whereupon you'll be issued a piece of paper to surrender at the Customs desk when departing Japan (the Customs desk at the Narita Airport is well marked, so you can't miss it). At that time, you may also be requested to show your purchases to Customs officials, so be sure to put them in your carry on.

The best-known tax-free arcade is the **International Arcade,** near the Imperial Hotel under the elevated JR Yamanote train tracks (☎ **03/3571-1528;** station: Hibiya). It features merchandise from pearls to electronics. Narita Airport's duty-free shops, located past the security machines and Customs, are also good places to shop for alcohol. Prices aren't cheaper and selections are limited, but I usually buy my sake here before boarding the plane just so I don't have to lug it around.

ART GALLERIES

The Ginza has the highest concentration of art galleries in Tokyo, with more than 200 shops dealing in everything from old woodblock prints to silk screens, lithographs, and contemporary paintings. The *Tokyo Journal,* the city's monthly magazine, lists current exhibitions in more than two dozen galleries in the Ginza alone, as well as those in other parts of Tokyo. In addition, Japanese department stores almost always contain art galleries, with exhibitions ranging from works by European masters to contemporary Japanese pottery.

Creation Gallery G8. Recruit Ginza 8 Building, 8-4-17 Ginza, Chuo-ku. ☎ **03/ 3575-6918.** Mon–Fri 11am–7pm. Station: Shimbashi (1 min.). Across the elevated tracks from the Daiichi Hotel Tokyo.

Cartoons, illustrations, digital images, posters, and other high-tech and pop art by mostly Japanese artists are regularly featured in this ground-floor gallery.

Nishimura Gallery. Nishi Ginza Building basement, 4-3-13 Ginza, Chuo-ku. ☎ **03/ 3567-3906.** Tues–Sat 10:30am–6:30pm. Station: Ginza (1 min.).

This gallery represents an even mix of established Japanese and foreign (mainly British) painters and sculptors, including David Hockney, Peter Blake, and Funakoshi Katsura.

S. Watanabe. 8-6-19 Ginza, Chuo-ku. ☎ **03/3571-4684.** Mon–Sat 9:30am–8pm. Station: Shimbashi (2 min.). On Namiki Dori.

This shop deals mostly in modern and some antique woodblock prints.

Satani Gallery. Dai-ni Asahi Building basement, 4-2-6 Ginza, Chuo-ku. ☎ **03/3564-6733.** Tues–Sat 10:30am–6:30pm. Station: Ginza (1 min.).

This gallery presents paintings and sculpture by young Japanese contemporary artists, and also represents such well-known international artists as Christo, Max Ernst, Paul Klee, and Joan Miró.

Tokyo Gallery. Dai-go Shuwa Building, 2nd floor, 8-6-18 Ginza, Chuo-ku. ☎ **03/3571-1808.** Mon–Fri 10am–7pm, Sat 10am–5pm. Station: Shimbashi (2 min.). On Namiki Dori.

This tiny gallery specializes in one-man shows of avant-garde art, mostly by Japanese artists.

Yoseido Gallery. 5-5-15 Ginza, Chuo-ku. ☎ **03/3571-1312.** Mon–Sat 10am–6:30pm. Station: Ginza (1 min.). On Namiki Dori near Harumi Dori.

This shop deals in modern woodblock prints, etchings, silk screens, copper plates, and lithographs.

BOOKS

Yasukuni Dori in Jimbocho, Kanda (station: Jimbocho), is lined with bookstores selling both new and used books, with several dealing in English-language books. Keep in mind, however, that English-language books are usually more expensive in Japan than back home. Still, no bibliophile should pass this street up, especially if your interest is in books related to Japan.

Jena. 5–6–1 Ginza, Chuo-ku. ☎ **03/3571-2980.** Mon–Sat 10:30am–9pm, Sun and holidays 11am–7:30pm. Station: Ginza (1 min.). On Harumi Dori.

This bookstore carries foreign titles on its third floor, including magazines, novels, and books on Japan. Although it's smaller than Maruzen in Nihombashi or Kinokuniya in Shinjuku, it's conveniently located in Ginza and is worth a quick look.

○ Kinokuniya. Takashimaya Annex, Takashimaya Times Square complex, 5–24–2 Sendagaya, Shinjuku-ku. ☎ **03/5361-3301.** Daily 10am–8pm. Closed some Wed. Station: Shinjuku (south exit, 2 min.).

This is one of Tokyo's best-known bookstores, with a good selection of books and magazines in English on its sixth floor, including books on Japan and dictionaries and textbooks for students of Japanese.

Kitazawa. 2–5 Jimbocho, Kanda, Chiyoda-ku. ☎ **03/3263-0011.** Mon–Sat 10am–6pm. Closed holidays. Station: Jimbocho (1A exit then turn right, 1 min.). On Yasukuni Dori.

The largest of several English-language bookstores in Kanda, Kitazawa boasts an overwhelming selection of books, including the most recently published novels, American and English classic literature, topical books ranging from history and philosophy to politics, books on Japan, and antiquarian books. Don't neglect the bargain-priced books in the trolleys outside the front door.

Maruzen. 2–3–10 Nihombashi, Chuo-ku. ☎ **03/3272-7211.** Mon–Sat 10am–7pm, Sun 10am–6pm. Closed some Sun. Station: Kyobashi (3 min.). On Chuo Dori across from Takashimaya department store, within walking distance of the Ginza and Tokyo stations.

This is Japan's oldest bookstore, founded in 1869. Its English-language section, on the second floor, offers everything from dictionaries and travel guides to special-interest books on Japan, while the basement contains an office-supply shop with printing and copying services. The fourth-floor Craft Center sells traditional handmade products.

Ohya Shobo. 1–1 Jimbocho, Kanda, Chiyoda-ku. ☎ **03/3291-0062.** Mon–Sat 10am–6:30pm. Closed holidays. Station: Jimbocho (A7 exit, 3 min.). Turn right (east) onto Yasukuni Dori; it will be on your right, one of the last bookstores.

Established in 1882, this delightfully cramped shop in Kanda doesn't have any English-language books, but it does claim to have the world's largest stock of 18th- and 19th-century Japanese illustrated books, woodblock prints, and maps, including maps from the Edo Period.

○ Tower Records and Books. 1–22–14 Jinnan, Shibuya-ku. ☎ **03/3496-3661.** Daily 10am–10pm. Closed some Mon. Station: Shibuya (Hachiko exit, 5 min.).

My friends in Tokyo don't shop anywhere else for their books and magazines. Why? Prices here are much lower than elsewhere, with magazines about half-price. The seventh floor is devoted to imported books and magazines, with a good selection of English-language books, as well as magazines and newspapers from around the world, from *Spin* to *Wine Spectator*, and the Sunday editions of major newspapers.

Tuttle Book Shop. 1–3 Jimbocho, Kanda, Chiyoda-ku. ☎ **03/3291-7072.** Mon–Fri 10:30am–6:30pm, Sat and national holidays 10:30am–6:30pm. Station: Jimbocho (A7 exit, 3 min.). Turn right (east) onto Yasukuni Dori; it will be on your right.

This shop, the Tokyo branch of a Vermont firm, has a wide selection of books on Japan and the Far East written in English, as well as English translations of Japanese novels, guidebooks, and instructional books on the Japanese language.

A Note on Japanese Symbols

Many hotels, restaurants, attractions, and shops in Japan do not have signs giving their names in Roman (English-language) letters. The second appendix to this book lists the Japanese symbols for all such places described in this guide. Each set of characters representing an establishment name has a number in the appendix, which corresponds to the number that appears inside the oval before the establishment's name in the text. Thus, to find the Japanese symbol for, say, **Camera No Kimura**, refer to no. 61 in appendix B.

CAMERAS & FILM

You can purchase cameras at many duty-free shops, including those in Akihabara, but if you're really serious about photographic equipment or want to stock up on film, make a trip to a shop dealing specifically in cameras. If purchasing a new camera is too formidable an expense, consider buying a used camera. New models come out so frequently in Japan that older models can be grabbed up for next to nothing.

61 **Camera no Kimura.** 1–18–8 Nishi Ikebukuro, Toshima-ku. ☎ **03/3981-8437.** Mon–Sat 8am–8pm; Sun and holidays 10am–7pm. Station: Ikebukuro (1 min.). West of the station.

This store has a small but good selection of used cameras and lenses. Since there's no telling what may be available, most camera bugs stop by frequently just to look over the stock.

Matsuzakya Camera. 1–27–34 Takanawa, Minato-ku. ☎ **03/3443-1311.** Mon–Sat 10am–7pm; Sun and holidays 10am–6pm. Station: Shinagawa or Meguro (15 min.).

A great place to head for used Japanese and foreign cameras. It also stocks new equipment.

Yodobashi Camera. 1–11–1 Nishi-Shinjuku, Shinjuku-ku. ☎ **03/3346-1010.** Daily 9:30am–9pm. Station: Shinjuku (west exit, 3 min.). 1 block west of the station.

Shinjuku is the photographic equipment center for Tokyo, and this store is the biggest in the area. In fact, it ranks as one of the largest discount camera shops in the world, with around 30,000 items in stock, and reputedly sells approximately 500 to 600 cameras daily. In addition to cameras, it also has watches, calculators, typewriters, cassette players, and more. Although prices are marked, you can bargain here. This is the place to stock up on film; you can also have film developed here.

CRAFTS & TRADITIONAL JAPANESE PRODUCTS

If you want to shop for traditional Japanese folk crafts in the right atmosphere, nothing beats **Nakamise Dori** (station: Akasaka), a pedestrian lane leading to Sensoji Temple in Asakusa. It's lined with stall after stall selling souvenirs galore, from wooden geta shoes and hairpins worn by geisha to T-shirts, fans, toy swords, and dolls. Most stalls are open from 10am to 6pm; some may close 1 day a week.

Ando. 5–6–2 Ginza. ☎ **03/3572-2261.** Mon–Fri 9am–6pm, Sat–Sun 11am–7pm. Closed holidays. Station: Ginza (1 min.). On Harumi Dori, between Chuo Dori and Sotobori Dori.

Opened in 1880, this shop has probably Tokyo's largest selection of Japanese cloisonné, including jewelry, vases, and plates.

Arai Bunsendo. On Nakamise Dori (about halfway down on the west side), Asakusa. ☎ **03/3844-9711.** Daily 10:30am–6pm. Closed Sun after the 20th of each month. Station: Asakusa (3 min.).

This 100-year-old stall sells paper dance fans, including special orders for Kabuki stars.

(62) **Bengara.** 2–35–11 Asakusa, Taito-ku. ☎ **03/3841-6613.** Fri–Wed 10am–6pm, holidays 11am–6pm. Station: Asakusa (3 min.). 1 block east of Sensoji Temple's main building, on Umamichi Dori (also spelled Umamiti), the 1st busy street that parallels Nakamise Dori to the east.

Noren are the doorway curtains hanging in front of Japanese restaurants, public bathhouses, and shops, signaling that the establishment is open. Bengara sells more than 100 different models of both traditional and modern noren of various sizes and colors, including those bearing *kanji* (Chinese characters) or scenes from famous woodblock prints. There are catalogues you can look through, or you can even have a noren custom-made with your own name.

(63) **Beniya Mingeitan.** 2–16–8 Shibuya, Shibuya-ku. ☎ **03/3400-8084.** Fri–Wed 10am–7pm. Station: Shibuya (6 min.). Off Aoyama Dori, to the left behind a gas station.

This shop, located on three narrow floors of a modern concrete building, offers artisanal goods from all over Japan, including bamboo baskets, rattan slippers, pottery, chopsticks, wooden rice bowls, glassware, jewelry, lacquerware, noren, and bolts of dyed Japanese Yuzen cloth. No credit cards are accepted.

Bingoya. 10–6 Wakamatsucho, Shinjuku-ku. ☎ **03/3202-8778.** Tues–Sun 10am–7pm. Station: Akebonobashi (15 min.) or Shinjuku (west exit, then bus no. 74 or 76 to the Kawadacho bus stop).

Folk art and crafts are sold on six floors of this small building, including traditional toys such as tops and dolls, handmade paper products, baskets, straw boots, items made from cherry bark, chopsticks, pottery, glassware, lacquerware, and fabrics from all over Japan.

Blue & White. 2–9–2 Azabu Juban, Minato-ku. ☎ **03/3451-0537.** Mon–Sat 10am–6pm. Closed holidays. Station: Roppongi (exit 3, 12 min.).

American Amy Katoh has been the driving force behind this unique, 25-year-old shop specializing in Japanese modern and traditional crafts, including textiles, *yukata*, porcelain, and more, mostly in colors of blue and white.

(64) **Hyakusuke.** 2–2–14 Asakusa, Taito-ku. ☎ **03/3841-7058.** Wed–Mon 11am–5pm. Station: Asakusa (3 min.). Just east of Nakamise Dori; walking toward Sensoji Temple, turn right after the last shop on Nakamise, pass the 2 Buddha statues, and turn right again at Benten-do Temple; the shop is on your right, across from the playground.

For traditional Japanese cosmetics (*kesho hin*), come to Hyakusuke, a 200-year-old, family-owned shop. During the Edo Period, this shop did a brisk trade in teeth blackener (white teeth were considered ugly), but today it offers some rather mundane products, as well as such traditional treatments as *kombu to funori* (a seaweed hair treatment), *tsubaki* (camelia) oil for healthy hair, and—perhaps most interesting—*uguisu no hun*, which is nightingale droppings that are said to leave your skin soft and smooth. Simply mix it with a little soap to wash your face. A purchase of ¥1,000 ($8.35) will last about 1 month of daily use. Makeup used by geisha and Kabuki actors is also sold here, attracting customers in these traditional professions.

Japan Sword. 3–8–1 Toranomon, Minato-ku. ☎ **03/3434-4321.** Mon–Fri 9:30am–6pm, Sat 9:30am–5pm. Closed holidays. Station: Toranomon (exit 2, 5 min.).

This is the best-known sword shop in Tokyo, with an outstanding collection of fine swords, daggers, sword guards and fittings, and other sword accessories, as well as some antique samurai armor. Coming here is like visiting a museum. The shop also sells copies and souvenir items of traditional swords at prices much lower than the very expensive historic swords. You can also have swords cleaned and polished here.

✪ **Japan Traditional Craft Center (Zenkoku Dentoteki Kogeihin Senta).** Plaza 246 Building, 3-1-1 Minami Aoyama, Minato-ku. ☎ **03/3403-2460.** Fri–Wed 10am–6pm. Station: Gaienmae (1 min.). On the corner of Gaien-Nishi Dori and Aoyama Dori (above a Häagen-Dazs).

This place is worth a trip even if you can't afford to buy anything. Established to publicize and distribute information on Japanese crafts, the center is a great introduction to both traditional and contemporary Japanese design. It sells various top-quality crafts from all over Japan on a rotating basis, so there are always new items on hand. Crafts for sale usually include lacquerware, ceramics, fabrics, paper products, bamboo items, writing brushes, metalwork, and more. Prices are high, but rightfully so.

Kokkusai Kanko Kaikan. 1-8-3 Marunouchi, Chiyoda-ku, and on the 9th floor of the Daimaru department store. ☎ **03/3215-1181.** Mon–Fri 9am–5pm. Closed holidays. Station: Tokyo (North Yaesu Exit, 1 min.). Look for Kokusai Kanko Kaikan on the small square with the clock; its entrance is opposite the JR Travel Service Center. In Daimaru, take the left-hand elevator just off the square with the clock (the elevator on the right side will *not* deliver you to the prefecture offices).

These two places are real finds! Located right beside each other, practically on top of Tokyo Station, they contain tourism promotional offices for almost every prefecture in Japan. Many of the offices also sell a few goods and products unique to their prefecture. Altogether, there are several dozen of these little shops, spread along the first through fourth floors of the Kokusai Kanko Kaikan Building and on the ninth floor of the Daimaru department store. You won't find such a varied collection anywhere else in Japan—and prices are very reasonable, cheaper than at department stores. What's more, no one shops here. You don't have time to go to Okayama to buy its famous Bizen pottery? You forgot to buy your clay ningyo doll while in Fukuoka? You can find those here, as well as toys, lacquerware, pottery, glassware, paper products, sake, food items, kokeshi dolls, bamboo ware, pearls, china, and everything else Japan makes.

Kotobukiya. 3-18-17 Minami-Aoyama, Minato-ku. ☎ **03/3408-4187.** Daily 10am–7pm. Closed the 1st and 3rd Tues of each month. Station: Omotesando (1 min.). On Aoyama Dori, opposite Omotesando Dori.

This crowded shop specializes in vases and accessories for flower arranging, of mostly contemporary designs.

Kurodaya. 1-2-5 Asakusa, Taito-ku. ☎ **03/3844-7511.** Tues–Sun 11am–7pm. Station: Asakusa (1 min.). Next to Kaminarimon Gate, to the east.

If you're visiting Asakusa, you might want to stop in at this shop. First opened back in 1856, it sells traditional Japanese paper and paper products, including kites, papier-mâché masks, boxes, and more.

Kyugetsu. 1-20-4 Yanagibashi, Taito-ku. ☎ **03/3861-5511.** Daily 9:15am–6pm. Station: Asakusabashi (1 min.). In front of the station.

Asakusabashi is Tokyo's wholesale district for retailers of dolls, with several stores lining Edo Dori. This is one of the area's biggest stores, founded in 1830. It sells both modern and traditional dolls; its Japanese dolls range from elegant creatures with porcelain faces, delicate coiffures, and silk kimono to wooden dolls called kokeshi.

🔾 **Oriental Bazaar.** 5–9–13 Jingumae, Shibuya-ku. ☎ **03/3400-3933.** Fri–Wed 9:30am–6:30pm. Station: Meiji-Jingumae (3 min.), Harajuku (4 min.), or Omotesando (5 min.). On Omotesando Dori in Harajuku; look for an Asian-looking facade of orange and green.

If you have time for only one souvenir shop in Tokyo, this should be it. It's the city's best-known and largest souvenir/crafts store, offering four floors of products at reasonable prices. Shop for cotton yukata, polyester and silk kimono (new and used), T-shirts, woodblock prints, paper products, stationery, fans, chopsticks, swords, lamps and vases, Imari chinaware, sake sets, Japanese dolls, lacquered jewelry boxes, pearls, books on Japan, and even antique furniture. This store will also ship things home for you.

Sakai Kokodo Gallery. 1–2–14 Yurakucho, Chiyoda-ku. ☎ **03/3591-4678.** Daily 11am–6pm. Station: Hibiya (1 min.). Across from the Imperial Hotel's Tower.

This gallery claims to be the oldest woodblock-print shop in Japan. The first shop was opened back in 1870 in the Kanda area of Tokyo by the present owner's great-grandfather, and altogether four generations of the Sakai family have tended the store. It's a great place for original prints as well as for reproductions of such great masters as Hiroshige. (If you're really a woodblock print fan, you'll want to visit the Sakai family's excellent museum, Japan Ukiyo-e Museum, in the small town of Matsumoto in the Japan Alps.)

⑥⑤ **Sukeroku.** Nakamise Dori, Asakusa. ☎ **03/3844-0577.** Fri–Wed 10am–6pm. Station: Asakusa (3 min.). The next to last shop on the right as you walk from Kaminarimon Gate toward Sensoji Temple.

This tiny, truly unique shop sells handmade figures of traditional Japanese characters, from mythological figures to priests, farmers, entertainers, and animals, including people of the many castes from the Edo Period, ranging from peasants to feudal lords. Most are in the ¥3,000 to ¥5,000 ($25 to $42) price range, though some are much higher than that.

Tsutaya. 5–10–5 Minami-Aoyama, Minato-ku. ☎ **03/3400-3815.** Open daily 9:30am–6:30pm. Closed the 2nd and 3rd Sun of each month. Station: Omotesando (2 min.).

Tsutaya has everything you might need for *ikebana* (flower arranging) or the Japanese tea ceremony, including vases of unusual shapes and sizes, scissors, and tea whisks.

Washikobo. 1–8–10 Nishi Azabu, Minato-ku. ☎ **03/3405-1841.** Mon–Sat 10am–6pm. Closed holidays. Station: Roppongi (7 min.). On the right side of the street as you walk on Roppongi Dori toward Shibuya.

This store deals almost exclusively in handmade Japanese paper and handcrafts from various parts of Japan, including paper and cardboard boxes, cardboard chests of drawers, paper wallets, pencil boxes, paper dolls, woodblock prints, kites, notebooks, paper lamps, toys, and sheets of beautifully crafted paper.

⑥⑥ **Yamamoto Soroban Ten.** 2–35–12 Asakusa, Taito-ku. ☎ **03/3841-7503.** Fri–Wed 10am–6pm. Station: Asakusa (5 min.). 1 block east of Sensoji Temple's main building, on Umamichi Dori (also spelled Umamiti); look for the giant abacus outside the front door.

You can still see older Japanese doing accounts with an abacus, although the sight is not as common as it was even a decade ago. This shop has been in business for over 60 years and is now in its third generation of owners. One wonders, however, how long the shop will survive in the world of computers and calculators (Japanese children no longer learn how to use the abacus in school). The founder's granddaughter speaks English, and English explanations of how an abacus works are available.

Yonoya. 1–37–10 Asakusa, Taito-ku. ☎ **03/3844-1755.** Thurs–Tues 10am–7pm. Station: Asakusa (3 min.). On Demboin Dori (also spelled Dempoin Dori), just off Nakamise Dori.

This unique shop specializes in handmade boxwood combs. Its history stretches back 300 years, to a time when women's hairstyles were elaborate and complicated, as many woodblock prints testify. Today such handcrafted combs are a dying art. The combs here range in price from about ¥3,000 to more than ¥25,000 ($25 to $208).

Yoshitoku. 1–9–14 Asakusabashi, Taito-ku. ☎ **03/3863-4419.** Daily 9:30am–6pm. Closed holidays. Station: Asakusabashi (1 min.).

Yoshitoku has had a shop at this location since 1711, making it Tokyo's oldest wholesale doll and traditional crafts store. It carries a variety of Japanese dolls on its first floor, most traditionally dressed as samurai, geisha, Kabuki actors, sumo wrestlers, and other Japanese personalities. There are also fine—and expensive— dolls representing the imperial court, dressed in silk kimono that follow the originals down to the minutest detail. Obviously, these dolls are meant not for children's play but for display by collectors. Upstairs are more mundane modern dolls, including stuffed animals.

DEPARTMENT STORES

Japanese department stores are institutions in themselves. Usually enormous, well-designed, and chock-full of merchandise, they have about everything you can imagine, including museums and art galleries, pet stores, rooftop playgrounds or greenhouses, travel agencies, restaurants, grocery markets, and flower shops. You could easily spend a whole day in a department store—eating, attending cultural exhibitions, planning your next vacation, and, well, shopping. Microcosms of Japanese society, these department stores reflect the affluence of modern Japan.

One of the most wonderful aspects of the Japanese department store is the courteous service. If you arrive at a store as its doors open at 10 or 10:30am, you'll witness a daily rite: Lined up at the entrance are staff who bow in welcome. Some Japanese shoppers arrive just before opening time so as not to miss this favorite ritual. Sales clerks are everywhere, ready to help you. In many cases you don't even have to go to the cash register once you've made your choice; just hand over the product, along with your money, to the sales clerk, who will return with your change, your purchase neatly wrapped, and an "*arigatoo gozaimashita*" (thank you very much). A day spent in a Japanese department store could spoil you for the rest of your life.

The basement of the store is usually devoted to foodstuffs: fresh fish, produce, and pre-prepared snacks and dinners. There are often free samples of food; if you're feeling slightly hungry, walking through the food department could do nicely for a snack. Many department stores include boutiques by such famous Japanese and international fashion designers as Issey Miyake, Rei Kawakubo (creator of Comme des Garçons), Hanae Mori, Christian Dior, Calvin Klein, and Brooks Brothers, as well as a department devoted to the kimono. Near the kimono department may also be the section devoted to traditional crafts; department stores are convenient places to shop for these. To find out what's where, stop by the store's information booth, located on the ground floor near the front entrance, and ask for the floor-by-floor pamphlet in English. Be sure, too, to check out the sales on the promotional floor—you never know what bargains you may chance upon. All major credit cards are accepted in department stores.

Department Store Hours

Japanese department stores are generally open from 10 or 10:30am to 7, 7:30, or 8pm. They used to close 1 day a week, but now they close irregularly, always on the same day of the week (say, on Tuesday), but in no apparent pattern. One month they may be closed the second and third Tuesday of the month, but the next month only the first. In any case, you can always find several that are open, even on Sundays and holidays (major shopping days in Japan).

IN GINZA & NIHOMBASHI

✪ **Matsuya.** 3–6–1 Ginza, Chuo-ku. ☎ **03/3567-1211.** Sun–Tues 10:30am–7:30pm, Wed–Sat 10:30am–8pm. Closed some Tues. Station: Ginza (2 min.). On Chuo Dori Ave., just a long block north of Ginza 4–chome Crossing.

This is one of my favorite department stores in Tokyo, with a good selection of Japanese folk-craft items, kitchenware, kimono, and beautifully designed contemporary household goods, in addition to the usual clothes and accessories. I always make a point of stopping by the seventh floor's Design Collection, which displays items from around the world selected by the Japan Design Committee as examples of fine design, from the Alessi teapot to Braun razors. If I were buying a wedding gift, Matsuya is one of the first places I'd look.

Matsuzakaya. 6–10–1 Ginza, Chuo-ku. ☎ **03/3572-1111.** Mon–Sat 10:30am–7:30pm, Sun and holidays 10:30am–7pm. Closed some Wed. Station: Ginza (2 min.). 1 block from Ginza 4–chome Crossing on Chuo Dori in the direction of Shimbashi.

Established more than 300 years ago, this was the first department store in Japan that did not require customers to take off their shoes at the entrance. It appeals mainly to Tokyo's older generation with its mostly men's and women's clothing.

✪ **Mitsukoshi.** 1–4–1 Nihombashi Muromachi, Chuo-ku. ☎ **03/3241-3311.** Daily 10am–7pm. Closed some Mon. Station: Mitsukoshimae (1 min.).

This Nihombashi department store is one of Japan's oldest, founded in 1673 by the Mitsui family as a kimono store. In 1683 it became the first store in the world to deal only in cash sales; it was also one of the first stores in Japan to begin displaying goods on shelves rather than having merchants fetch bolts of cloth for each customer, as was the custom of the time. And it was also among the first shops to employ female clerks. Today, housed in a building dating from 1914, it remains one of Tokyo's loveliest department stores, with a beautiful and stately Renaissance-style facade and an entrance guarded by two bronze lions, replicas of those in Trafalgar Square. It carries many name-brand boutiques, including Givenchy, Dunhill, Chanel, Hanae Mori, Oscar de la Renta, Christian Dior, and Tiffany. Its kimono, by the way, are still hot items.

Another branch, located right on Ginza 4–chome Crossing (☎ **03/3562-1111;** Monday through Saturday 10am to 7:30pm, Sunday 10am to 7pm; closed some Mondays), is popular with young shoppers.

Printemps. 3–2–1 Ginza, Chuo-ku. ☎ **03/3567-0077.** Mon–Sat 10am–8pm, Sun 10am–7pm. Closed some Wed. Station: Yurakucho or Ginza (2 min.).

This store, a branch of Paris's fashionable Au Printemps, is a relative newcomer on the Ginza scene. A fun store with announcements in both French and Japanese, it's very popular with Tokyo's younger generation. A main building contains mostly fashion and accessories, while an annex has household goods.

Seibu. 2–5–1 Yurakucho, Chiyoda-ku. ☎ **03/3286-0111.** Daily 11am–8pm. Closed some Tues. Station: Yurakucho (1 min.) or Hibiya and Ginza (2 min.). In Yurakucho near the elevated tracks of the JR Yamanote Line, between the Hibiya and Ginza stations.

This store consists of two buildings, one selling clothing and accessories, the other specializing in interior design and kitchenware.

Takashimaya. 2–4–1 Nihombashi (on Chuo Dori Ave.), Chuo-ku. ☎ **03/3211-4111.** Mon–Fri 10am–7pm; Sat and Sun 10am–6:30pm. Closed some Wed. Station: Nihombashi (1 min.). On Chuo Dori.

This department store provides stiff competition for Mitsukoshi, with a history just as long. It was founded as a kimono shop in Kyoto during the Edo Period and opened in Tokyo in 1933. Today it's one of the city's most attractive department stores, with boutiques by such famous designers as Chanel, Laroche, Dunhill, Céline, Lanvin, Louis Vuitton, Gucci, Christian Dior, Issey Miyake, and Kenzo.

Wako. 4–5–11 Ginza, Chuo-ku. ☎ **03/3562-2111.** Mon–Sat 10:30am–6pm. Closed holidays. Station: Ginza (1 min.). On the corner of Ginza 4–chome Crossing.

This is one of the Ginza's smallest department stores, but also one of the classiest, housed in one of the few area buildings that survived World War II. It was erected in 1932 and is famous for its distinctive clock tower, graceful curved facade, and innovative window displays. The owners are the Hattori family, founders of the Seiko watch company. The store's ground floor carries a wide selection of Seiko watches and clocks, while the upper floors carry imported and domestic fashions and luxury items, with prices to match. It caters to older, well-to-do customers; you won't find hordes of young Japanese girls shopping here.

Yurakucho Hankyu. 2–5–1 Yurakucho, Chiyoda-ku. ☎ **03/3575-2233.** Mon–Sat 10:30am–8pm, Sun and holidays 10:30am–7:30pm. Closed some Tues. Station: Yurakucho (1 min.) or Hibiya and Ginza (2 min.). In Yurakucho, just east of the elevated JR Yamanote Line tracks and between the Hibiya and Ginza subway stations, beside Seibu.

This relative newcomer to the area has the usual food, clothing, accessory, and household-goods departments. Nearby is the even newer H2 Sukiyabashi Hankyu annex, which attracts young shoppers with its GAP, Eddie Bauer, and Tommy Hilfiger outlets, as well as music stores.

IN IKEBUKURO

Seibu. 1–28–1 Minami Ikebukuro, Toshima-ku. ☎ **03/3981-0111.** Daily 10am–8pm. Closed some Tues. Station: Ikebukuro (underneath the store).

Seibu, once the nation's largest department store and still one of the biggest, has 47 entrances, thousands of sales clerks, dozens of restaurants, 12 floors, 31 elevators, and an average of 170,000 shoppers a day. Two basement floors are devoted to foodstuffs—you can buy everything from taco shells to octopus to seaweed. Dishes are set out so that you can nibble and sample the food as you move along, and hawkers yelling out their wares give the place a marketlike atmosphere. Fast-food counters sell salads, grilled eel, chicken, sushi, and other ready-to-eat dishes. The rest of the floors offer clothing, furniture, art galleries, kitchenware, and a million other things. Loft, Seibu's department for household goods and interior design, and Wave, Seibu's CD department, occupy the top four floors of the main building. Many of the best Japanese and Western designers have boutiques here; Size World and Queen's Coordination, both on the fourth floor, specialize in large and petite women's sizes, respectively.

Tobu/Metropolitan Plaza. 1–1–25 Nishi-Ikebukuro, Toshima-ku. ☎ **03/3981-2211.** Daily 10am–8pm. Closed some Wed. Station: Ikebukuro (west exit, 1 min.).

Once overshadowed by nearby Seibu, this flagship of the Tobu chain expanded and reopened in 1993 as Japan's largest department store, employing 3,000 clerks to serve the 180,000 customers who enter its doors daily. It consists of a main building, a connecting central building, and Metropolitan Plaza. You'll find here everything from luxury goods and the latest international fashions to hardware, software, toys, daily necessities, and traditional Japanese products (good for souvenirs). The basement food floor is massive—food accounts for nearly 20% of Tobu's total sales. The Tobu Museum of Art, in the Metropolitan Plaza, showcases impressive collections of international works.

IN SHINJUKU

Isetan. 3–14–1 Shinjuku, Shinjuku-ku. ☎ **03/3352-1111.** Daily 10am–7:30pm. Closed some Wed. Station: Shinjuku Sanchome (1 min.) or Shinjuku (east exit, 6 min.). On Shinjuku Dori, east of Shinjuku Station.

Isetan is a favorite among foreigners living in Tokyo. It has a good line of conservative clothing appropriate for working situations, as well as contemporary and fashionable styles, including designer clothes (Issey Miyake, Kenzo, Comme des Garçons, Paul Smith) and large dress sizes (on the second floor). In addition, it boasts a New Creator's Space on the ground floor, unique among Japanese department stores (which are generally reluctant to carry anything but the tried-and-true), that showcases clothing by up-and-coming Japanese designers. It also has a great kimono section, along with all the traditional accessories (obi, shoes, purses), a well-known art gallery on the eighth floor of its annex, and an arts and crafts section with changing exhibits.

✪ **Takashimaya Times Square.** 5–24–2 Sendagaya, Shinjuku-ku. ☎ **03/5361-1122.** Daily 10am–7:30pm. Closed some Wed. Station: Shinjuku (1 min.). Across the street from Shinjuku Station's south exit.

Since its opening in 1996, Takashimaya Times Square has been the number one draw in Shinjuku and is packed on weekends. Much larger than Takashimaya's Nihombashi flagship, this huge complex is anchored by Takashimaya department store, which boasts 14 floors of clothing and restaurants. There's also Tokyu Hands, with everything imaginable for the home hobbyist; Kinokuniya bookstore, with English-language books on the sixth floor; Shinjuku Joypolis, a sophisticated games arcade by Sega; and Tokyo IMAX Theater, a huge screen with 3-D films.

IN SHIBUYA

In recent years, Shibuya has emerged as a shopping mecca for the fashionable young, and so many stores have opened lately that there's a bona fide store war going on. Tokyu and Seibu are the two big names. In addition to the big stores here, see the "Fashions," section, below.

Seibu. 21–1 Udagawacho. ☎ **03/3462-0111.** Sat–Thurs 10am–8pm, Fri 10am–9pm. Closed some Wed. Station: Shibuya (Hachiko exit, 3 min.).

Shibuya's largest department store consists of two buildings connected by pedestrian skywalks, with lots of designer boutiques; see listing for main store in Ikebukuro, above.

Tokyu Honten (Main Store). 2–24–1 Dogenzaka. ☎ **03/3477-3111.** Daily 10am–8pm. Closed some Tues. Station: Shibuya (Hachiko exit, 7 min.).

The Tokyu chain's flagship store appeals mainly to a 30s-and-older age group with its conservative styles in clothing and housewares. Here you'll find women's fashions (including departments for larger sizes), men's fashions, children's clothing and toys, arts and crafts, and restaurants. It adjoins the ultramodern Bunkamura complex, the largest cultural center in Tokyo, with cinemas, theater and concert halls, a museum, bookstore, and cafes.

ELECTRONICS

The largest concentration of electronics and electrical-appliance shops in Japan is in an area of Tokyo called **Akihabara Electric Town (Denkigai),** centered around Chuo Dori. Although you can find good deals on video and audio equipment elsewhere, Akihabara is special simply for its sheer volume. With more than 600 multilevel stores, shops, and stalls, Akihabara accounts for one-tenth of the nation's electronics and electrical-appliance sales. An estimated 50,000 shoppers come here on a weekday, 100,000 per day on a weekend. Even if you don't buy anything, it's great fun walking around. If you do intend to buy, make sure you know what the item would cost back home—with the present exchange rate, there are few bargains in Japanese electronics products, but you may be able to pick up something that's unavailable back home. Most of the stores and stalls are open-fronted and many are painted neon green and pink. Inside, lights are flashing, fans are blowing, washing machines are shaking and shimmying, and stereos are blasting. Salesmen yell out their wares, trying to get customers to look at their rice cookers, refrigerators, computers, cellular phones, video equipment, cameras, CD players, TVs, calculators, and watches. This is the best place to go to see the latest models of everything electronic, an educational experience in itself.

If you are buying, be sure to bargain, and don't buy at the first place you go to. One woman I know who was looking for a portable cassette player bought it at the third shop she went to for ¥4,000 ($33) less than what was quoted to her at the first shop. Make sure, too, that whatever you purchase is made for export—that is, with instructions in English, an international warranty, and the proper electrical connectors. All the larger stores have duty-free floors where products are made for export. Some of the largest are **Yamagiwa,** 3–13–10 Soto-Kanda (☎ **03/3253-2111**); **Laox,** 1–2–9 Soto-Kanda (☎ **03/3253-7111**); and **Hirose Musen,** 1–10–5 Soto Kanda (☎ **03/3255-2211**). If you're serious about buying, check these stores first.

The easiest way to get to Akihabara is via the Yamanote Line or the Keihin Tohoku Line to the JR Akihabara Station. You can also take the Hibiya subway line to Akihabara Station, but it's farther to walk. In any case, take the Akihabara Electric Town exit. Most shops are open daily from about 10am to 7pm.

FASHIONS

The department stores listed above are all good places for checking out the latest trends. If you want the Japanese-designer look without the corresponding price tags, the **Harajuku** area has hundreds of small shops selling inexpensive knockoffs. **Takeshita Dori,** a street described in the walking tour of Harajuku and Aoyama (see chapter 7), is lined with shops catering to young, fashion-conscious Japanese. Otherwise, **Harajuku** and **Shibuya** are the places to go for fashion department stores, which are multistoried buildings filled with concessions of various designers and labels. The stores below are some of the largest.

La Forêt. 1–11–6 Jingumae, Shibuya-ku. ☎ **03/3475-0411.** Daily 11am–8pm. Station: Meiji-Jingumae (1 min.) or Harajuku (3 min.). Just off the intersection of Omotesando Dori and Meiji Dori.

This is not only the largest store in Harajuku, but also one of the most fashionable, appealing mostly to teenage and twenty-something shoppers. Young and upcoming Japanese designers are here, as well as names like Plantation by Issey Miyake. You'll find the most reasonably priced fashions and accessories in the basement and on the fourth floor. There's a lot to see; you could easily spend a couple of hours here.

Parco. 15–1 Udagawacho, Shibuya-ku. ☎ **03/3464-5111.** Daily 10am–8:30pm. Station: Shibuya (Hachiko exit, 4 min.).

A division of Seibu, Parco is actually three buildings clustered together (called Parco Part 1, Part 2, and Part 3). Parco Part 1 is the place to go for designer boutiques for men and women, with clothes by such avant-garde Japanese designers as Yohji Yamamoto, Issey Miyake, Tsumori Chisato, Junya Watanabe, and Takeo Kikuchi, as well as international designers like Paul Smith, Jean Paul Gaultier, Katharine Hamnett, and Helmut Lang. Part 2 has children's clothing as well as Polo Ralph Lauren and Eddie Bauer lines, while Part 3 is devoted to sports clothes. Parco has two sales a year that you shouldn't miss if you're here—one in January and one in July.

Seed. 21–1 Udagawacho, Shibuya-ku. ☎ **03/3462-0111.** Sat–Thurs 11am–8pm, Fri 11am–9pm. Station: Shibuya (Hachiko exit, 4 min.).

This is my favorite fashion department store in Shibuya, with five small floors devoted to the newest of the new in design talent. There will be a lot of names you're probably not familiar with, along with such notables as Katharine Hamnett, Jean Paul Gaultier, and Kenzo. In the basement is J. Crew, currently very popular in Japan (there's also a new Gap nearby).

DESIGNER BOUTIQUES

The block between Omotesando Crossing and the Nezu Museum in **Aoyama** (station: Omotesando, 2 min.) has become the Rodeo Drive of Japan, the showcase of top designers. Even if you can't buy here (steep prices for most pocketbooks), a stroll is *de rigueur* for clothes hounds and those interested in design. Most shops are open daily 11am to 8pm. **Comme des Garçons,** on the right side as you walk from Aoyama Dori (☎ 03/3406-3951), is Rei Kawakubo's showcase for her daring— and constantly evolving—men's and women's designs. The goddess of Japanese fashion and one of the few females in the business, Kawakubo has remained on the cutting edge of design for more than a decade. Across the street is **Issey Miyake** (☎ 03/3423-1407), with two floors of cool, spacious displays of Miyake's interestingly structured designs for men and women, including his very popular Pleats Please line. Miyake's **Permanente** (☎ 03/3499-6476) collection of classics is farther down the street, toward the Nezu Museum, on the opposite side in the From-1st building. One of Japan's newer designers, **Tsumori Chisato,** has a shop on the left side of the street (☎ 03/3423-5170). Also worth seeking out along this stretch is **Yohji Yamamoto** across the street (☎ 03/3409-6006), where Yamamoto's unique, classically wearable clothes are sparingly hung, flaunting the avant-garde interior space.

On the other side of Aoyama Dori, on Omotesando Dori, is **Hanae Mori** (☎ 03/3400-3301), the granddame of Japanese design, with everything from separates and men's golf wear to haute couture and wedding gowns on display on three floors of a building designed by Japanese architect Kenzo Tange.

SECONDHAND SHOPS

Recently, perhaps in light of Japan's recession, a number of secondhand consignment shops have opened up near **Ebisu Station,** in the direction of Hiroo. Prices here will be half—or maybe even a third or fourth—of what you'd pay in a designer boutique for this season's fashions, and you can expect the secondhand clothes to have little or no wear, though they may be several seasons away from being the newest of the new. The shops below are open daily from 11am to 8pm (Garret closes at 9pm).

Take the east exit from JR Ebisu Station (the one closest to Yebisu Garden Place) for Ebisu 1– and 4–chome and continue walking straight away (east) from the station one block to the busy street. Cross the street and turn right to the Fuji and Sakura banks. Then cross the busy street that runs between them, turn left, and continue walking east. Nearby, at the end of the block on a corner on your right, is **Garret** (☎ 03/3446-6187), which stocks new and used clothing and accessories for men and women. I've seen men's sport coats by Paul Smith and Hugo Boss, Hermès and Chanel jewelry, Prada handbags, Rolex watches, and some women's tricot from Comme des Garçons, as well as many other Japanese fashions. Take a right out of Garret and continue walking. On the right, before the stoplight, is **FL & Always** (☎ 03/3446-9652), which carries the frilly, very feminine clothing of Pink House, as well as Ingeborg and Karl Helmut.

Catty-corner across the street is **One Fifth** (☎ 03/3442-7366), which receives new inventory almost daily of mostly foreign designers. I've seen women's clothing by Alexander McQueen, Versace, Max Mara, Fendi, and Chanel, as well as accessories by Louis Vuitton, Celine, Prada, Versace, and Fendi. It's a good place to look for serious work clothes. Take a left out of One Fifth and then left again at the stoplight. After a few blocks, at the first stoplight, you'll see on the right **Ultra Queen** (☎ 03/3449-9531), which caters to young shoppers and carries an amusing mix of women's used casual clothing, designer clothes, and new imports, as well as accessories from the United States. I've seen clothing by Agnes B, Gaultier, and Betsy Johnson.

Walk straight out of Ultra Queen, crossing the road and walking past the gas station, until you come to **Keymissbeemy** (☎ 03/3446-0094) on the right. This shop carries new but discounted men's clothing, 50% of it by Paul Smith. From here, take a right and walk straight to Ebisu Station; it will take about 8 minutes.

FLEA MARKETS

Flea markets are good opportunities to shop for antiques as well as for delightful junk. You can pick up secondhand kimono at very reasonable prices, as well as kitchenware, vases, cast-iron tea pots, small chests, dolls, household items, and odds and ends. (Don't expect to find any good buys in furniture.) The markets usually begin as early as 6am and last until 4pm or so, but go early if you want to pick up bargains. Bargaining is expected.

In addition to these regularly scheduled markets, check the *Tokyo Journal* for a list of others. Note that since most are outdoors, they tend to be canceled if it rains.

Togo Shrine, on Meiji Dori in Harajuku (near Meiji-Jingumae or Harajuku stations), has an antique market on the first, fourth and, when there is one, the fifth Sunday of every month from 4am to 2pm. It's great for used kimono as well as small furniture and curios. For more information, see the walking tour of Harajuku and Aoyama in chapter 7.

Nogi Shrine, a 1-minute walk from Nogizaka Station, has an antique market the second Sunday of each month, except November, from dawn to dusk.

Hanazono Shrine, on Yasukuni Dori east of Shinjuku Station (a 5-min. walk from Shinjuku Sanchome Station), has a flea market every Sunday from dawn to dusk (except in May and November, due to festivals).

Finally, the closest thing Tokyo has to a permanent flea market is **Ameya Yokocho** (also referred to as Ameyokocho or Ameyacho), a narrow street near Ueno Park that runs along and underneath the elevated tracks of the JR Yamanote Line between Ueno and Okachimachi stations. There are about 400 stalls here selling discounted items ranging from fish, seaweed, and vegetables to handbags, tennis shoes, cosmetics, watches, and casual clothes. The scene retains something of the *shitamachi* spirit of old Tokyo. Although housewives have been coming here for years, young Japanese recently discovered the market as a good place for bargains on fashions, accessories, and cosmetics. Some shops close Wednesday, but hours are usually daily 10am to 7pm; early evening is the most crowded time. Don't even think of coming here on a holiday—it's a standstill pedestrian traffic jam.

INTERIOR DESIGN

The department stores listed above have furniture and interior-design sections: Ike-bukuro's **Seibu** has an especially well-known and popular department, but my favorite is the Design Collection on the seventh floor of Ginza's **Matsuya.**

Loft. 21–1 Udagawacho, Shibuya-ku. ☎ **03/3462-0111.** Daily 10am–8pm. Closed some Wed. Station: Shibuya (Hachiko exit, 4 min.). Behind Seibu B.

Loft is Seibu's store for the homeowner and hobbyist, with tableware, cookware, glassware, bathroom accessories, bed linen, office supplies, stationery, and more. Don't miss the sixth-floor variety goods department, filled with an amazing amount of Japanese and American kitsch, party goods, and costumes. If you've yearned for an ashtray in the shape of a toilet, this is the place for you.

Tokyu Hands. 12–18 Udagawacho, Shibuya-ku. ☎ **03/5489-5111.** Daily 10am–8pm. Closed 2nd and 3rd Mon of each month. Station: Shibuya (Hachiko exit, 6 min.). Near the trio of Parco buildings.

Billing itself the "Creative Life Store," Tokyu Hands, part of the Tokyu chain, is a huge department store for the serious homeowner and hobbyist, with everything from travel accessories, *noren* (doorway curtains), chopsticks, and kitchen knives to equipment and materials for do-it-yourselfers, including paper for shoji. If there's a practical, Japanese product you've decided you can't live without (lunch box? bathroom slippers? laundry rack?), this is a good place to look.

You'll also find Tokyu Hands in Higashi Ikebukuro near the Sunshine City Building (☎ **03/3980-6111**) and in the Takashimaya Times Square complex in Shinjuku (☎ **03/5361-3111**).

KIMONO

The **Oriental Bazaar** (see "Crafts & Traditional Japanese Products," above) has a good selection of new and used kimono, including elaborate wedding kimono. In addition, department stores sell kimono, notably **Takashimaya** and **Mitsukoshi** in Nihombashi and **Isetan** in Shinjuku. They also have yearly sales of used, rental wedding kimono. Flea markets are another good option for used kimono and yukata, particularly the antique market at **Togo Shrine** (see above).

Chicago. 6–31–21 Jingumae, Shibuya-ku. ☎ **03/3409-5017.** Daily 11am–8pm. Station: Meiji-Jingumae (1 min.) or Harajuku (2 min.). On Omotesando Dori, between Meiji Dori and Harajuku Station.

This is the place to go for used kimono. It stocks hundreds of affordable used kimono (including wedding kimono), cotton *yukata* (for sleeping), and *obi* (the sash worn around a kimono), all located in its Kimono Corner, in the very back of the shop past the 1950s American clothing.

Hayashi Kimono. 2 locations in the International Arcade (underneath the JR Yamanote Line's elevated tracks), 2–1–1 Yurakucho, Chiyoda-ku. ☎ **03/3501-4012.** Mon–Sat 10am–7pm; Sun 10am–6pm. Station: Yurakucho (2 min.).

Established in 1913, Hayashi sells all kinds of kimono, including wedding kimono, cotton yukata, and *tanzen* (the heavy winter overcoat that goes over the yukata), as well as used and antique kimono. If you're buying a gift for someone back home, this is the best place to start.

KITCHENWARE & TABLEWARE

In addition to the department stores and interior design shops listed above, there are two areas in Tokyo with a number of shops filled with items related to cooking and serving. In **Tsukiji,** along the streets stretching between Tsukiji Station and Tsukiji Fish Market, are shops selling pottery, serving trays, bowls, dishes, wonderful fish knives, and lunch boxes. The second place to look is ✪ **Kappabashi-dougugai Dori** (station: Tawaramachi), popularly known as Kappabashi and Japan's largest wholesale area for cookware. There are approximately 150 specialty stores here selling cookware, including sukiyaki pots, woks, lunch boxes, pots and pans, aprons, knives, china, lacquerware, rice cookers, and disposable wooden chopsticks in bulk. Although stores in Tsukiji and Kappabashi are wholesalers selling mainly to restaurants, you're welcome to browse and purchase as well. Stores in both areas are closed on Sunday.

MUSIC

HMV. 24–1 Udagawacho, Shibuya-ku. ☎ **03/5458-3411.** Thurs–Tues 10am–10pm, Wed 10am–11pm. Station: Shibuya (Hachiko exit, 4 min.).

HMV offers five floors of music, from Japanese pop to dance, soul, reggae, rock, and New Age to jazz, classical and opera, with listening stages so you can hear before you buy.

✪ **Tower Records and Books.** 1–22–14 Jinnan, Shibuya-ku. ☎ **03/3496-3661.** Daily 10am–10pm. Closed some Mon. Station: Shibuya (Hachiko exit, 5 min.).

From classical to new releases to Japanese pop to games and CD-ROMs, it's all here, on six floors. On the seventh floor are imported books and magazines.

Virgin Megastore. Marui 101 Building basement, 3–30–16 Shinjuku, Shinjuku-ku. ☎ **03/ 3353-0056.** Daily 11am–8pm. Closed some Wed. Station: Shinjuku Sanchome (1 min.). On Shinjuku Dori, across from Isetan department store.

Virgin stocks 150,000 CD titles and 15,000 videos, and also offers 50 listening stations, where you can hear the latest hits.

Wave. 6–2–27 Roppongi, Minato-ku. ☎ **03/3408-0111.** Sun 11:30am–8pm; Mon–Sat 11:30am–8:30pm. Closed 2nd Sun of each month. Station: Roppongi (4 min.). On the left side of Roppongi Dori as you walk from Roppongi Station toward Shibuya.

This innovative store, a branch of Seibu, has a computerized record-reference system and a comprehensive selection of music and videos. On the first floor are headphones to help you select from 200 of the top hits. In the basement is Ciné Vivant, a minitheater that shows foreign films four or five times daily.

PEARLS

Mikimoto, on Chuo Dori not far from Ginza 4–chome Crossing, past Wako department store (☎ **03/3535-4611**), is Japan's most famous pearl shop. It was founded by Mikimoto Koichi, the first to produce a really good cultured pearl, in 1905. Open daily 10:30am to 6:30pm, closed the third Wednesday of every month. Otherwise, there's a Mikimoto branch (☎ **03/3591-5001**), in the Imperial Hotel Arcade, under the Imperial Hotel (station: Hibiya), where you'll also find **Asahi Shoten** (☎ **03/3503-2528**), with a good selection in the modest-to-moderate price range; and **K. Uyeda Pearl Shop** (☎ **03/3503-2587**), with a wide selection of pearls in many different price ranges.

SHOES

Here are two shops where you may find shoes in your size.

Diana. 1–8–6 Jingumae, Minato-ku. ☎ **03/3478-4001**. Daily 10:30am–8:30pm. Station: Omotesando (2 min.). Near La Forêt, on Meiji Dori in Harajuku.

Diana has long been a refuge for foreigners, with larger sizes on the second floor. Still, don't count on finding anything larger than a women's size 8. The shop does, however, have all the latest styles. There's another store at 6–9–6 Ginza (☎ **03/ 3573-4001**), open daily from 11am to 8pm.

Ginza Washington. 5–7–7 Ginza, Chuo-ku. ☎ **03/3572-5911**. Daily 10:30am–8pm. Station: Ginza (1 min.). On Chuo Dori, near the Ginza 4–chome Crossing.

This is one of Tokyo's largest shoe stores. You'll find the larger sizes on the fifth floor, but if none of these fit and you're desperate, you can also have shoes custom made.

TOYS

Hakuhinkan Toy Park. 8–8–11 Ginza. ☎ **03/3571-8008**. Daily 11am–8pm. Station: Shimbashi or Ginza (4 min.). On Chuo Dori, near the overhead expressway.

This is one of Tokyo's largest and best toy stores, with six floors. In addition to the usual dolls, puzzles, games, and other items, there's also a large assortment of gag gifts, and a video arcade on the fourth floor.

Kiddy Land. 6–1–9 Jingumae. ☎ **03/3409-3431**. Daily 10am–8pm. Closed the 3rd Tues of each month. Station: Meiji-Jingumae (2 min.) or Harajuku and Omotesando (5 min.). On Omotesando Dori in Harajuku, near Oriental Bazaar.

Toys, games, puzzles, dolls, action figures, Pokémon cards, and much more are packed into this immensely popular shop, usually so crowded with teenagers that it's impossible to get in the front door. It also has a large selection of gag gifts, including temporary tattoos, fake breasts made of rubber, and who knows what else.

Tokyo After Dark 9

Come dusk, Tokyo blossoms into a profusion of giant neon lights and paper lanterns, the streets filling with millions of overworked Japanese out to have a good time. Tokyo at night is one of the craziest cities in the world, a city that never gives up and never seems to sleep. Entertainment districts can be as crowded at 3am as they are at 10pm, and many places stay open until the first subways start running, after 5am. Whether it's jazz, reggae, gay bars, sex shows, dance clubs, hostess bars, mania, or madness you're searching for, Tokyo has it all.

GETTING TO KNOW THE SCENE   Tokyo has no one center of nighttime activity. There are many nightspots spread throughout the city, each with its own atmosphere, price range, and clientele. Most famous are probably **Ginza**, **Kabuki-cho** in Shinjuku, and **Roppongi.** Before visiting any of the locales listed in this chapter, be sure just to walk around one of these neighborhoods and absorb the atmosphere. The streets will be crowded, the neon lights will be overwhelming, and you never know what you might discover on your own.

Although there are many bars, discos, and clubs packed with both men and mostly young women, nightlife in Japan is still pretty much a man's domain, just as it has been for centuries. At the high end of this domain are the **geisha bars,** where highly trained women entertain by playing traditional Japanese instruments, singing, and holding witty conversations—and nothing more risqué than that. Such places are located mainly in Kyoto, and generally speaking, are both outrageously expensive and closed to outsiders. As a foreigner, you'll have little opportunity to visit a geisha bar unless you're invited by a business associate.

More common than geisha bars, and generally not quite as expensive, are the so-called **hostess bars,** many of which are located in Ginza and Akasaka. A woman will sit at your table, talk to you, pour your drinks, listen to your problems, and boost your ego. You buy her drinks as well, which is one reason the tab can be so high. Hostess bars in various forms have been a part of Japanese society for centuries. Most of you will probably find the cost of visiting one not worth the price, as the hostesses usually speak only Japanese, but such places provide Japanese males with sympathetic ears and the chance to escape the worlds of both work and family. Men usually

Then I saw for the first time the true beauty of Tokyo, and of all Japanese cities. They are only beautiful at night, when they become fairylands of gorgeous neon: towers and sheets and globes and rivers of neon, in stunning profusion, a wild razzle-dazzle of colors and shapes and movements, fierce and delicate, restrained and violent against the final afterglow of sunset.

—James Kirkup, *These Horned Islands* (1962)

have their favorite hostess bar, often a small place with just enough room for regular customers. In the more exclusive hostess bars, only those with an introduction are allowed entrance.

The most popular nightlife spots are **drinking establishments,** where most office workers, students, and ex-patriates go for an evening out. These places include Western-style bars, most commonly found in Roppongi, as well as Japanese-style watering holes, called *nomi-ya*. *Yakitori-ya,* bars that serve yakitori and other snacks, are included in this group. At the low end of the spectrum are topless bars, sex shows, massage parlors, and porn shops, with the largest concentration of such places in Shinjuku's Kabuki-cho district.

In addition to the establishments listed in this chapter, be sure to check the restaurants listed in the inexpensive category in chapter 5 for a relatively cheap night out on the town. Many places serve as both eateries and watering holes, especially yakitori-ya.

EXTRA CHARGES & TAXES   One more thing you should be aware of is the "table charge" that some bars and many cocktail lounges charge their customers. Included in the table charge is usually a small appetizer—maybe nuts, chips, or a vegetable; for this reason, some locales call it an *otsumami*, or snack charge. At any rate, the charge is usually between ¥300 and ¥500 ($2.70 and $4.50) per person. Some establishments levy a table charge only after a certain time in the evening; others may add it only if you don't order food from the menu. If you're not sure and it matters to you, be sure to ask before ordering anything. Remember, too, that a 5% consumption tax will be added to your bill. Some higher-end establishments, especially nightclubs, hostess bars, and some dance clubs, will also add a 10% to 20% service charge.

FINDING OUT WHAT'S ON   To find out what's happening in the entertainment scene—contemporary and traditional music and theater, exhibitions in museums and galleries, films, and special events—buy a copy of the *Tokyo Journal.* It's published monthly and is available for ¥600 ($5) at foreign-language bookstores, restaurants, and bars. It also has articles of interest to foreigners in Japan. Keep an eye out also for the free *Tokyo Classified,* which carries a nightlife section, covering concerts and events, and is available at bars and other venues around town.

GETTING TICKETS FOR EVENTS   If you're staying in one of the higher-class hotels, the concierge or guest-relations manager can usually get tickets for you. Otherwise, you can always head to the theater or hall itself. An easier way is to go through one of many ticket services available. **Ticket PIA** (☎ 03/5237-9999) is probably your best bet, as it has an English-language service. You can also try **Ticket Saison** (☎ 03/5990-9999) or **Playguide** (☎ 03/5802-9999). Department stores also often have ticket counters for concerts, sporting events, and other happenings.

1 The Performing Arts

KABUKI   Probably Japan's best-known traditional theater art, Kabuki is also one of the country's most popular forms of entertainment. Visit a performance and it's easy to see why—in a word, Kabuki is fun! The plays are dramatic, the costumes are gorgeous, stage settings can be fantastic, and the themes are universal—love, revenge, and the conflict between duty and personal feelings. Probably one of the reasons Kabuki is so popular even today is that it originated centuries ago as a form of entertainment for the common people in feudal Japan, particularly the merchant group. One of Kabuki's interesting aspects is that all roles—even those depicting women—are portrayed by men.

Altogether, there are more than 300 Kabuki plays, all written before the 20th century. For a Westerner, one of the more arresting things about a Kabuki performance is the audience itself. Because this has always been entertainment for the masses, the spectators can get quite lively, adding yells, guffaws, and laughter. Also contributing to the festive atmosphere are the box lunches and drinks available during intermission.

One of Japan's most prestigious theaters for Kabuki is ✪ **Kabukiza,** 4–12–15 Ginza (☎ **03/3541-3131,** or 03/5565-6000 for reservations). Conveniently located within easy walking distance of the Ginza 4–chome Crossing (directly above the Higashi-Ginza subway station), this impressive theater with a Momoyama-style facade (influenced by 16th-century castle architecture) is a remake of the 1924 original building. It seats almost 2,000 and features the usual Kabuki stage fittings, including a platform that can be raised and lowered below the stage for dramatic appearances and disappearances of actors, a revolving stage, and a runway stage extending into the audience.

The Kabukiza stages about eight or nine Kabuki productions a year, with each production beginning its run between the first and third of each month and running about 25 days, with performances daily from 11 or 11:30am to about 9pm (there are no shows in August). Usually, there are two different programs being shown; matinees run from about 11 or 11:30am to 4pm, and evening performances run from about 4:30 or 5pm to about 9pm. It's considered perfectly okay to come for only part of a performance.

Of course, you won't be able to understand what's being said, but that doesn't matter; the productions themselves are great entertainment. For an outline of the plot, you can purchase an **English program,** which costs ¥1,000 ($8.35); or, you can rent **English earphones** for ¥650 ($5.40), plus a ¥1,000 ($8.35) refundable deposit—these provide a running commentary on the story, music, actors, stage properties, and other aspects of Kabuki. Buying a program or renting earphones will add immensely to your enjoyment of the play.

Tickets generally range from ¥2,400 to ¥16,000 ($20 to $133), depending on the program and seat location. Advance tickets can be purchased at the **Advance Ticket Office,** to the right side of Kabukiza's main entrance, from 10am to 6pm. You may also make advance reservations by phone (same-day bookings are not accepted). Otherwise, tickets for each day's performance are placed on sale 1 hour before the start of each performance.

If you don't have time for an entire performance or wish to view Kabuki only for a short while, it's possible to watch only one act, with tickets costing only ¥600 to ¥1,000 ($5 to $8.35), depending on the time of day and length of the show. One-acts generally last about 1 or 1½ hours; note that English-language earphones are not available here, but you can buy a program. Note, also, that seats are a bit far from the stage, on the very top two rows of the theater (on the fourth floor; there is no elevator). On the other hand, I have seen several acts this way, sometimes simply dropping by when I'm in the area. Tickets, sold at the smaller entrance to the left of the main entrance, are available on a first-come, first-served basis and go on sale 20 minutes prior to each act. If you liked the act so much that you wish to remain for the next one, it's possible to do so if the act is not sold out; tickets in these cases are usually available on the fourth floor.

If you're in Tokyo in August, you can usually see Kabuki instead at the **National Theater of Japan** (Kokuritsu Gekijo), 4–1 Hayabusacho, Chiyoda-ku (☎ **03/ 3265-7411; station:** Hanzomon, 6 min.). Kabuki is scheduled here throughout the year except during May, September, and December, when Bunraku (see below) is being staged instead. Matinees usually begin at noon and evening performances at 5pm. Tickets range from about ¥1,500 to ¥8,500 ($12.50 to $71).

NOH   Whereas Kabuki developed as a form of entertainment for the masses, Noh was a much more traditional and aristocratic form of theater. In contrast to Kabuki's extroverted liveliness, Noh is very calculated and restrained. The oldest form of theater in Japan, it has changed very little in the past 600 years. The language is so archaic that today the Japanese cannot understand it at all, which explains in part why Noh does not have the popularity that Kabuki does.

As in Kabuki, all the performers are men. Altogether there are about 240 Noh plays, often concerned with supernatural beings, beautiful women, mentally confused and tormented people, or tragic-heroic epics.

Because the action is slow, sitting through an entire performance can be quite tedious unless you are particularly interested in Noh dance and music. In addition, most Noh plays do not have English translations. You may just want to drop in for a short while. Definitely worth seeing, however, are the short comic reliefs, called *kyogen,* that make fun of life in the 1600s and are performed between Noh dramas.

Noh is performed at a number of locations in Tokyo, with tickets generally ranging from ¥2,500 to ¥6,000 ($21 to $50). Performances are usually in the early afternoon, around 1pm, or in the late afternoon, at 5 or 6:30pm; check the *Tokyo Journal* for exact times. The **National Noh Theater** (Kokuritsu Nohgakudo), 4–18–1 Sendagaya, Shibuya-ku (☎ **03/3423-1331; station:** Sendagaya, 5 min.), is Tokyo's most famous. Other Noh theaters worth checking out are: **Hosho Nohgakudo,** 1–5–9 Hongo, Bunkyo-ku (☎ **03/3811-4843; station:** Suidobashi, 5 min.); **Kanze Nohgakudo,** 1–16–4 Shoto, Shibuya-ku (☎ **03/3469-5241; station:** Shibuya, 10 min.); **Kita Nohgakudo,** 4–6–9 Kami-Osaki, Shinagawa-ku (☎ **03/3491-8813; station:** JR Meguro, 10 min.); and **Tessenkai Nohgaku-do Kenshujo,** 4–21–29 Minami Aoyama, Minato-ku (☎ **03/3401-2285; station:** Omotesando, exit A4, 5 min.).

BUNRAKU   Bunraku is traditional Japanese puppet theater, but contrary to what you might expect, the dramas are for adults, with themes centering on love, revenge, sacrifice, and suicide.

Popular in Japan since the 17th century, Bunraku is fascinating to watch because the puppeteers, dressed in black, are always right on stage with their puppets. They're wonderfully skilled in making the puppets seem like living beings. It usually takes three puppeteers to work one puppet, which is about three-quarters human size: One puppeteer is responsible for movement of the puppet's head, facial expressions, and right arm and hand; another operates the puppet's left arm and hand; the third moves its legs. A narrator recites the story and speaks all the various parts, accompanied by the *samisen,* a traditional three-stringed Japanese instrument.

Although the main Bunraku theater in Japan is in Osaka, the **National Theatre of Japan (Kokuritsu Gekijo)** in Tokyo, 4–1 Hayabusacho, Chiyoda-ku (☎ **03/ 3265-7411;** station: Hanzomon, 6 min.), stages about three Bunraku plays a year—in May, September, and December. There are usually two to three performances daily, at 11am, 2:30pm, and 6pm, with tickets costing ¥4,800 to ¥5,800 ($40 to $48). Earphones with English explanations are available for ¥650 ($5.40).

WESTERN CLASSICAL MUSIC   Among the best-known orchestras in Tokyo are the **Tokyo Philharmonic Orchestra** (Tokyo Phil Jimukyoku; ☎ 03/3256-9696), the **Japan Philharmonic Symphony** (Nihon Phil; ☎ 03/5378-5991), the **Tokyo City Philharmonic Orchestra** (Tokyo City Phil; ☎ 03/3822-0727), and the **NHK Philharmonic Orchestra** (NHK Phil; ☎ 03/3465-1780). They play in various theaters throughout Tokyo, with the majority of performances in Suntory Hall in Akasaka, Bunkamura Orchard Hall in Shibuya, or the Tokyo Geijutsu Gekijo in Ikebukuro. Since the schedule varies, it's best to call the orchestra directly or check with the *Tokyo Journal* to see whether there's a current performance. Tickets generally start at ¥3,000 or ¥4,000 ($25 or $33).

✪ **TAKARAZUKA KAGEKIDAN**   This world-famous, all-female troupe stages elaborate musical revues, with dancing, singing, and gorgeous costumes. The first Takarazuka troupe, formed in 1912 at a resort near Osaka, gained instant notoriety because all its performers were women, in contrast to the all-male Kabuki. When I went to see this troupe perform, I was surprised to find that the audience too consisted almost exclusively of women.

Performances are held generally in March, April, July, August, November, December, and sometimes in June in a temporary, tent-like auditorium called **Takarazuka 1000 Days,** set up just northeast of JR Yurakucho Station (☎ **03/ 5251-2001**). Tickets generally range from about ¥2,000 to ¥8,000 ($17 to $67). In 2001, Takarazuka will move back into its renovated, permanent theater at Tokyo Takarazuka Gekijo, 1–1–3 Yurakucho (station: Yurakucho or Hibiya). Inquire at the Tourist Information Center for more information.

2 The Club & Music Scene

THE MAJOR ENTERTAINMENT DISTRICTS

GINZA   A chic and expensive shopping area by day, Ginza transforms itself into a dazzling entertainment district of restaurants, bars, and first-grade hostess bars at night. It's the most sophisticated of Tokyo's nightlife districts and also one of the most expensive. Almost all the Japanese businessmen you see out carousing in Ginza are paying by expense account; the prices are ridiculously high.

Since I'm not wealthy, I prefer Shinjuku and Roppongi. However, because Ginza does have some fabulous restaurants and several hotels, I've included some recommendations in the area if you happen to find yourself here after dinner. The cheapest way to absorb the atmosphere in Ginza is simply to wander about, particularly around Namiki Dori, Suzuran Dori, and their side streets. The "Ginza & Hibiya Accommodations, Dining & Nightlife" map on page 62 will help you locate the Ginza clubs and bars mentioned in this chapter.

✪ **SHINJUKU**   Northeast of Shinjuku Station is an area called **Kabuki-cho,** which undoubtedly has the craziest nightlife in all of Tokyo, with block after block of strip joints, massage parlors, pornography shops, peep shows, bars, restaurants, and lots of drunk Japanese men. A world of its own, it's sleazy, chaotic, crowded, vibrant, and fairly safe. Despite its name, Shinjuku's primary night hot spot has nothing to do with Kabuki, though at one time there was a plan to bring some culture to the area by introducing a Kabuki theater. The plan never materialized, but the name stuck. Although Kabuki-cho has always been the domain of salarymen out on the town, in recent years young Japanese, including college-age men and women, have claimed parts of it as their own, with the result that there are a few inexpensive drinking establishments well worth a visit. Although most of the night action in Shinjuku is east of the station, the west side also has an area of inexpensive restaurants and bars. The "Shinjuku Accommodations, Dining & Nightlife" map on page 66 will help you locate the Shinjuku clubs and bars mentioned in this chapter.

To the east of Kabuki-cho, just west of Hanazono Shrine, is a smaller district called **Goruden Gai**, which is "Golden Guy" mispronounced. It's a warren of tiny alleyways leading past even tinier bars, each consisting of just a counter and a few chairs. Generally closed to outsiders, these bars cater to regular customers. On hot summer evenings the mama-sans of these bars sit outside on stools and fan themselves, with soft red lights melting out of the open doorways. Things aren't as they appear, however. These aren't brothels—they're simply bars, and the "mama"-sans are as likely to be men as women. Although most cater to regular customers, a few accept foreigners (see "The Bar Scene," below). Unfortunately, Goruden Gai sits on such expensive land that many of the bar owners are being forced to sell their shops to land developers; some are already boarded up. It's a shame, because this tiny neighborhood is one of the most fascinating in all of Tokyo.

Even farther east is **Shinjuku 2–chome** (called Ni–chome; pronounced "knee-chomay"), officially recognized as the gay-bar district of Shinjuku. It's here that I was once taken to a host bar featuring young men in crotchless pants. Strangely enough, the clientele included both gay men and groups of young, giggling office girls. The place has since closed down, but Shinjuku is riddled with other spots bordering on the absurd.

The best thing to do in Shinjuku is simply to walk about. In the glow of neon light, you'll pass everything from smoke-filled restaurants to hawkers trying to get you to step inside so they can part you from your money. If you're looking for strip joints, topless or bottomless coffee shops, peep shows, or porn, I leave you to your own devices, but you certainly won't have any problems finding them. In Kabuki-cho alone, there are an estimated 200 sex businesses in operation, including bathhouses where women are available for sex, usually at a cost of around ¥30,000 ($250). Although prostitution is illegal in Japan, everyone seems to ignore what goes on behind closed doors. Just be sure you know what you are getting into; your bill at the end may add up to be much more than you figured.

A word of **warning** for women traveling alone: Forgo the experience of Shinjuku. Although you're relatively safe here, with so many people milling about, you won't feel comfortable with so many inebriated men stumbling around. If there are two of you, however, you'll be okay. I took my mother to Kabuki-cho for a spin around the neon, and we escaped relatively unscathed. You're also fine walking alone to one of my recommended restaurants or to meet someone here.

ROPPONGI   To Tokyo's younger crowd, Roppongi is the city's most fashionable place to hang out. It's also a favorite with the foreign community, including models, business types, and English teachers. Roppongi has more than its fair share of live-music houses, restaurants, discos, ex-patriate bars, and pubs. Some Tokyoites complain that Roppongi is too crowded, too trendy, and too commercialized (and has too many foreigners), but for the casual visitor I think Roppongi offers an excellent opportunity to see what's new and hot in the capital city and is easy to navigate because nightlife activity is so concentrated.

The center of Roppongi is **Roppongi Crossing** (the intersection of Roppongi Dori and Gaien-Higashi Dori), at the corner of which sits the garishly pink Almond Coffee Shop. The shop itself has mediocre coffee and desserts at terribly inflated prices, but the sidewalk in front of the store is the number-one meeting spot in Roppongi.

If you need directions, there's a conveniently located *koban* (police box) catty-corner from the Almond Coffee Shop and next to the Bank of Tokyo-Mitsubishi. It has a big outdoor map of the Roppongi area, showing the address system, and someone is always there to help. The "Roppongi Accommodations, Dining & Nightlife" map on page 127 will help you locate the Ropppongi clubs and bars mentioned in this chapter.

Recently, the action of Roppongi has spilled over into neighboring **Nishi-Azabu,** which has several restaurants and bars catering to both Japanese and foreigners. The center of Nishi-Azabu is the next big crossroads, Nishi-Azabu Crossing (the intersection of Roppongi Dori and Gaien-Nishi Dori). Nishi Azabu is about a 10-minute walk from Roppongi Station; walk on Roppongi Dori in the direction of Shibuya.

OTHER HOT SPOTS   Not quite as sophisticated as Ginza, **Akasaka** nonetheless has its share of exclusive geisha and hostess bars, hidden away behind forbidding walls and exquisite courtyards. More accessible are the many drinking bars, restaurants, and inexpensive holes-in-the-wall. Popular with both executive tycoons and ordinary office workers as well as foreigners staying in one of Akasaka's many hotels, this district stretches from the Akasaka-mitsuke subway station along three narrow streets, called Hitotsugi, Misuji, and Tamachi, all the way to the Akasaka station. For orientation purposes, stop by the *koban* (police box) at the huge intersection of Aoyama Dori and Sotobori Dori at Akasaka-mitsuke station. The "Akasaka Accommodations, Dining & Nightlife" map on page 73 will help you locate the Akasaka establishments mentioned in this chapter.

One of the most popular districts for young Japanese by day, **Harajuku** doesn't have much of a nightlife district because of the city zoning laws. There are a few places scattered through the area, however, that are good alternatives if you don't like the crowds or the commercialism of Tokyo's more famous nightlife districts. There are also a fair number of sidewalk cafes open late into the night.

Shibuya's **Shibuya Center Gai,** a pedestrian lane just a minute's walk from the Hachiko exit of Shibuya Station, is popular with young Japanese for its inexpensive restaurants, bars, fast-food joints, and pachinko parlors. **Ebisu** also has a few very popular ex-patriate bars.

NIGHTCLUBS & HOSTESS BARS

Club Maiko. Aster Plaza Building, 4th floor, 7-7-6 Ginza. ☎ **03/3574-7745.** Cover ¥8,000 ($67), a special package deal for foreigners, including entrance and show charge, snacks, and free drinks. Hostess drinks ¥1,000 ($8.35). Mon–Sat 6pm–midnight. Closed holidays. Station: Ginza (3 min.). On Suzuran Dori.

Here's a hostess bar in the heart of Ginza that's receptive to foreigners and not prohibitively expensive. The hostesses here are geisha and maiko, who are young women training to be geisha. At this small bar, consisting of a few tables and a long counter, the women put on dancing shows and between performances sit and talk with customers. With its traditional music and atmosphere, this may be the closest you'll get to Japan's geisha bars.

A Guide to Tokyo Maps

Once you've chosen a nightlife spot that appeals to you, you can locate it using the following neighborhood maps:

To locate bars and clubs in **Asakusa,** see map on page 81.

To locate bars and clubs in **Shinjuku,** see map on pages 66.

To locate bars and clubs in **Harajuku,** see map on page 117.

To locate bars and clubs in **Roppongi,** see map on page 127.

To locate bars and clubs in **Akasaka,** see map on page 73.

✪ **Kingyo.** 3–14–17 Roppongi. ☎ **03/3478-3000.** Cover ¥4,000 ($33). Shows daily at 7:30 and 10pm; also at 1:30am Fri and Sat. Reservations advised. Station: Roppongi (4 min.). Near the Roppongi cemetery.

This sophisticated nightclub stages one of the most high-energy, visually charged acts I've ever seen—nonstop action of ascending and receding stages and stairs, fast-paced choreography, elaborate costumes, and loud music. There are a few female dancers, but most of the dancers are males assuming female parts, just like in Kabuki. In fact, many of the performances center on traditional Japanese themes, with traditional dress and kimono, but the shows take place in a very technically sophisticated setting. There are also satires; one recent performance included a piece on Microsoft vs. Apple; another featured aliens from outer space. Great fun.

LIVE MUSIC

Bauhaus. Reine Roppongi, 2nd floor, 5–3–4 Roppongi. ☎ **03/3403-0092.** Cover ¥3,500 ($29), including 1 drink, plus 20% service charge. Mon–Sat 7pm–12:30am; music begins at 8pm. Station: Roppongi (3 min.). From Roppongi Crossing, walk toward Tokyo Tower on Gaien-Higashi Dori, turning right at McDonald's.

This small club, featuring mostly '70s and '80s British and American hard rock, is owned and operated by the house band, which plays 30-minute sets every hour on the hour from 9pm, and then serves drinks to the regular clientele, mostly for-eigners. The band is led by singer Kay-chan, a kind of Japanese David Bowie, who puts on quite a show—a bit raunchy in places. He'll come and sit at your table between sets if you ask him.

Birdland. Square Building (in the basement), 3–10–3 Roppongi. ☎ **03/3478-3456.** Cover ¥1,500 ($12.50), plus ¥800 ($6.65) drink minimum, and 10% service charge. Mon–Thurs 6pm–midnight; Fri–Sat 6pm–1am. Station: Roppongi (2 min.). From Roppongi Crossing, walk toward Tokyo Tower on Gaien-Higashi Dori and take the 1st left.

Down to earth and featuring good jazz performed by Japanese musicians, Birdland has been a welcome refuge from Roppongi's madding crowd for more than 26 years. It's small and cozy, with candles and soft lighting, and attracts an older, knowl-edgeable, and appreciative crowd.

Blue Note. 6–3–16 Minami Aoyama. ☎ **03/5485-0088.** Cover ¥7,000–¥12,000 ($58–$100). Mon–Sat 5:30pm–1am, with shows at 7 and 9:30pm. Station: Omotesando (8 min.).

Tokyo's most expensive, elegant jazz venue is cousin to the famous Blue Note in New York and has proven so popular it outgrew its original 1988 location and moved into this larger location 10 years later. Still, with 300 seats, it follows the frustrating practice of selling tickets good for only one set (there are two sets nightly). The musicians are top-notch; Oscar Peterson, Sarah Vaughan, Tony Bennett, David Sanborn, and the Milt Jackson Quartet have all performed here.

Body & Soul. 6–13–9 Minami Aoyama. ☎ **03/5466-3348.** Cover ¥3,000–¥3,500 ($25–$29). Mon–Sat 7–midnight. Station: Omotesando (7 min.).

This low-ceilinged, cozy basement club gives everyone a good view of its mostly jazz performances by Japanese and foreign musicians.

✪ **Cavern Club.** 5–3–2 Roppongi. ☎ **03/3405-5207.** Cover ¥1,300 ($11), music charge, plus 1 drink minimum, and a 22% service charge. Mon–Sat 6pm–2:30am; Sun and holidays 6pm–midnight. Station: Roppongi (4 min.). Take the side street going downhill on the left side of Almond Coffee Shop, then the 1st left; the club will be on the right.

If you know your Beatles history, you'll know Cavern is the name of the Liverpool club where the Fab Four got their start. The Tokyo club features house bands performing Beatles music exclusively, and very convincingly at that. Extremely popular with both Japanese and foreigners, it's packed on weekends—expect long lines. Reservations are taken, but are good for only two sets—then you have to leave.

Country House. 5–1–4 Akasaka. ☎ **03/3583-9287.** Cover ¥1,000 ($8.35). Mon–Sat 6pm–midnight. Closed holidays. Station: Akasaka (TBS exit, 1 min.). On Hitotsugi Dori.

This country-music spot is a fun place to spend an evening in Akasaka. The owner, Mr. Hirao, plays steel guitar in the house band and is always happy to see foreigners walk through the doors. There's a cover charge, but a better deal is the optional ¥4,000 ($33) charge, which includes cover, a choice of two dishes from a menu that includes pizza, sausage, corned beef and potatoes, and salad, and all the beer or cocktails you can consume in a 2-hour period. There's also a snack menu listing Tex-Mex dishes, pasta, Southern fried chicken, and more.

Crocodile. 6–18–8 Jingumae, on Meiji Dori between Harajuku and Shibuya. ☎ **03/3499-5205.** Cover ¥2,000–¥2,500 ($17–$21); occasionally more for big acts. Daily 6pm–2am; music starts at 8pm. Station: Meiji-Jingumae or Shibuya (10 min.).

Popular with a young crowd, Crocodile describes itself as a casual rock 'n' roll club, with live bands ranging from rock and blues to jazz-fusion, reggae, soul, experimental, and even country. It's a good place to check out new Japanese bands. It has an interesting interior and a good, laid-back atmosphere; depending on the music, the clientele ranges from Japanese with bleached-blond hair and earrings to foreign English teachers.

Liquid Room. Humax Pavilion, 7th floor, 1–20–1 Kabuki-cho. ☎ **03/3200-6831.** Cover ¥3,000–5,500 ($25–$46) for most. Concert dates vary, but generally Wed–Sat from 6pm. Station: Shinjuku (east exit, 10 min.). Located just west of Koma Theater.

This is one of Tokyo's best-known venues for live music, ranging from alternative and hard rock to hip-hop. There are also DJ nights, all-night parties, and other events. Check *Tokyo Journal* or *Tokyo Classified* for a concert schedule; tickets bought in advance are cheaper.

✪ **New York Bar.** Park Hyatt Hotel, 52nd floor, 3–7–1–2 Nishi-Shinjuku. ☎ **03/5322-1234.** Cover ¥1,700 ($14). Daily from 5pm, with live music 8pm–midnight. Station: Shinjuku (13 min.); Hatsudai on the Keio Line (7 min.); Tochomae on the Toei No. 12 Line (8 min.).

This is one of Tokyo's most sophisticated venues, boasting Manhattan-style jazz and breathtaking views of glittering West Shinjuku. Unfortunately, it's also one of the city's smallest. Consider coming for dinner in the adjacent **New York Grill** (see chapter 5) and you'll save the cost of the cover.

Piga Piga. Nanshin Building, 1–8–16 Ebisu Minami. ☎ **03/3715-3431.** Cover ¥1,000 ($8.35) Mon–Thurs, ¥2,000 ($17) Fri–Sat and holidays. Mon–Thurs 6pm–1am, Fri–Sat 6pm–3am. Station: JR Ebisu (2 min.). From the west exit, turn left down the 2nd street away from and parallel to the tracks (there's a bank here with a heart logo); it's almost immediately on the right.

Piga Piga offers African food, African drinks, and great African music, with live bands from Tanzania, Zaire, and Kenya—the real thing. There are three to four sets beginning at 8pm, except on Monday and Wednesday when there's a DJ. Since the music is irresistible, people also come here to dance, usually in the aisles between the tables.

Roppongi Pit Inn. 3–17–7 Roppongi (in the basement). ☎ **03/3585-1063.** Cover ¥3,000–¥4,500 ($25–$37.50), including 1 drink. Daily from 6:30pm, with shows about 7:30 and 9pm. Station: Roppongi (7 min.).

Another well-known music house, this no-frills joint has been catering to a younger crowd of jazz enthusiasts for almost 25 years. It boasts some of the finest in native and imported jazz, as well as fusion and jazz rock.

Shinjuku Pit Inn. 2–12–4 Shinjuku, southeast of the Yasukuni Dori/Meiji Dori intersection. ☎ **03/3354-2024.** Cover (including 1 drink) from ¥1,300 ($11) for the 2:30pm show (¥2,500/$21 weekends and holidays), ¥3,000–¥4,000 ($25–$33) for the evening shows. Station: Shinjuku Sanchome (4 min.).

This is one of Tokyo's most famous jazz, fusion, and blues clubs, featuring both Japanese and foreign musicians. There are three programs daily—at 2:30, 7:30, and 9:30pm—making it a great place to stop for a bit of music in the middle of the day. Since only a few snacks (such as potato chips and sandwiches) are available, eat before you come.

Sweet Basil. 6–7–11 Roppongi. ☎ **03/5474-013.** Cover ¥5,000–¥10,000 ($42–$83). Daily 5:30–11:30pm. Station: Roppongi (3 min.). From Roppongi Crossing, take the road downhill from the left side of Almond Coffee Shop; it will be on the right.

Popular with well-heeled Japanese, this classy venue in a modern brick building offers a wide range of musical entertainment, from jazz and R&B to nostalgia and Japanese pop. There's one set on Sunday and Tuesday at 7:30pm; otherwise, there are two sets, at 7 and 9:30pm. Most people come here to dine as well, from a menu that includes seafood, pasta, and lighter fare.

DANCE CLUBS & DISCOS

Discos have lost much of their popularity since their heyday in the 1980s, but Roppongi still boasts more dance clubs than anywhere else in the city. Sometimes the set cover charge includes drinks and occasionally even food, which makes for an inexpensive way to spend an evening. Keep in mind, however, that prices are usually higher on weekends and are sometimes higher for men than for women. Although discos are required by law to close at midnight, many of them ignore the rule and simply stay open until dawn.

Club Wire. 5–17–6 Shinjuku. ☎ **03/3207-6953.** Cover ¥2,000 ($17) Sun–Thurs, including 1 drink; ¥2,500 ($21) Fri–Sat, including 2 drinks. Daily 9pm–4am. Station: Shinjuku Sanchome (5 min.). Off Yasukuni Dori, on the pathway leading to Hanazono Shrine.

This simple basement disco caters primarily to Japanese in their early 20s. It plays mainly hard rock and punk, with occasional live music.

Kento's. Daini Building, 5–3–1 Roppongi. ☎ **03/3401-5755.** Also at 6–7–12 Ginza. ☎ **03/ 3572-9161.** Cover ¥1,300 ($11), plus 22% service and 1 drink minimum. Mon–Sat 6pm–2:30am; Sun and holidays 6pm–midnight. Station: Roppongi (4 min.).

Kento's was one of the first places to open when the wave of 1950s nostalgia hit Japan in the '80s; it has even been credited with creating the craze. This is the place to come to if you feel like dancing the night away to tunes of the '50s and '60s, played by live bands. Although there's hardly room to dance, that doesn't stop the largely over-30 Japanese audience from twisting in the aisles. Snacks such as chicken, pizza, spaghetti, and salads are available.

Lexington Queen. Daisan Goto Building, 3–13–14 Roppongi. ☎ **03/3401-1661.** Cover (including 12 tickets for food—including sushi—and drinks) ¥3,000 ($25) for women, ¥4,000 ($33) for men. Men unaccompanied by women are not allowed. Daily 8pm–midnight (sometimes as late as 5am). Station: Roppongi (3 min.).

Opened in 1980, Lexington Queen has been the reigning queen of disco in Tokyo for two decades. In fact, it's so much smaller than the newer, glitzier discos, it seems almost quaint. Its list of past guests reads like a Who's Who of foreign movie and rock stars, from Rod Stewart to Stephen Dorff to Dustin Hoffman; one night when I was there, Duran Duran walked in. This is the best place to be on Halloween and New Year's if you can stand the crowds. Women are admitted free Monday and Thursday.

Maniac Love. 5–10–6 Minami Aoyama. ☎ **03/3406-1166.** Cover ¥2,000 ($17) Sun–Thurs; ¥2,500 ($21), including 1 drink, Fri and Sat. Mon–Fri 10pm–5am, Sat 10pm–10am. Station: Omotesando (2 min.). From Aoyama Dori, take the street opposite and leading away from Kinokuniya grocery store and turn right at the 1st alley; it's opposite the "Wood You Like Company" shop (there's no sign).

This tiny basement venue has none of the glitz favored by some Tokyo discos; it relies instead on a great sound system to attract a vibrant young crowd. In fact, the music is so loud that you can feel the beat pulsing through your body, commanding you to dance. If you're still up, come at 5am on Sunday, when the ¥1,000 ($8.35) cover includes free coffee. This is a place with soul.

Milk. 1–13–3 Ebisu Nishi. ☎ **03/5458-2826.** Cover ¥3,000 ($25) Sun–Thurs, including 2 drinks; ¥3,500 ($29) Fri and Sat, including 2 drinks. Daily 8pm–4am. Station: Ebisu (west exit, 2 min.). Take the side street after Wendy's; it will be on your right.

This split-level, psychedelic basement disco packs 'em in with loud, loud, loud hard rock and alternative music. On Thursday, Friday, and Saturday nights, it features live bands from 10:30pm. In the same building is the very popular **What the Dickens** ex-pat bar (see "The Bar Scene," below).

Velfarre. 7–14–22 Roppongi. ☎ **03/3402-8000.** Cover ¥2,000 ($17) for women and ¥3,000 ($25) for men Sun–Thurs, including 2 drinks; ¥3,000 ($25) for women and ¥4,000 ($33) for men Fri and Sat, including 3 drinks. Sun–Thurs 6pm–midnight, Fri–Sat 6pm–1am. Station: Roppongi (3 min.). From Roppongi Crossing, walk toward Aoyama (away from Tokyo Tower) on Gaien-Higashi Dori and take the 1st left after Ibis Hotel.

If you're looking for the disco scene, search no further. This huge, plush venue claims to be Japan's largest disco, and has all the latest technical gadgetry to match. Tokyo's disco of the moment, it attracts young Japanese dressed to kill. The dance floor is absolutely gigantic; stage dancers help set the pace. The music ranges from pop to techno and hard house. *Note:* The place does close promptly at closing time.

Yellow. 1–10–11 Nishi-Azabu. ☎ **03/3479-0690.** Cover (including 1 or 2 drinks) from ¥3,000 ($25), depending on the DJ and the event. Daily 9pm–midnight (often until 4am); may close on Sun, Mon, and Tues for private functions, so call ahead. Station: Roppongi (10 min.). From Roppongi Crossing, head toward Shibuya on Roppongi Dori; turn right at the next-to-last street before Gaien-Nishi Dori; it's in the 2nd block on the right.

Closed on and off by the boys in blue, this is the closest thing Tokyo has to a true underground disco, staging the city's most progressive events, from *butoh* performances (avant-garde dance) to gay nights. Guest DJs from abroad make appearances, playing a variety of music from salsa and reggae to hip-hop, soul, and techno. Only the in-the-know are supposed to come here, so there's no sign—just a blank, yellow neon square.

3 The Bar Scene

GINZA

See the map on p. 62 for the bars listed in this section.

Atariya. 3–5–17 Ginza. ☎ **03/3564-0045.** Mon–Sat 4:30–10:30pm. Station: Ginza (3 min.). Near Ginza 4–chome Crossing; take the small side street that runs behind the Wako department store; it will be on the right in the second block.

With its typical Japanese setting, this is a convivial place for an evening of yakitori and beer, made easy with an English menu.

✪ ⑥⑦ **Lupin.** 5–5–11 Ginza. ☎ **03/3571-0750.** Mon–Sat 5–11pm. Station: Ginza (2 min.). In a tiny alley behind Ketel, a German restaurant on Namiki Dori.

You couldn't find a more subdued place than this tiny basement bar. First opened back in 1928, it features a long wooden bar and booths and has changed little over the decades. Even the staff looks like they've been here since it opened. Because no music is ever played here, it's a great place for conversation. Very civilized. There's a table charge of ¥500 ($4.50) per person, which includes a small snack.

Nanbantei. 5–6–6 Ginza. ☎ **03/3571-5700.** Daily 5–10pm. Station: Ginza (2 min.). On Suzuran Dor not far from Harumi Dori.

Foreigners are cheerfully welcomed at this chain of yakitori-ya, which combines the modern with the traditional in its decor. Its English menu lists skewers of pork with asparagus, Japanese mushroom, large shrimp, quail eggs, gingko nuts, chicken meatballs, and many other yakitori, including yakitori set courses starting at ¥3,000 ($25).

Old Imperial. Imperial Hotel, 1–1–1 Uchisaiwai-cho. ☎ **03/3504-1111.** Daily 11:30am–midnight. Station: Hibiya (1 min.).

This is the Imperial Hotel's tribute to its original architect, Frank Lloyd Wright, and is the only place in the hotel that contains Wright originals—the art deco terracotta wall behind the bar, the mural, and the small desk at the entrance. Its clubby atmosphere, low lighting, and comfortable chairs and tables (copies of Wright originals) make it perfect for a quiet drink. Try the Mount Fuji, which is the bar's own creation of dry gin, lemon juice, pineapple juice, egg white, and maraschino cherry.

Pronto. 8–6–25 Ginza. ☎ **03/3571-7864.** Mon–Sat 7:30am–11pm, Sun 8am–10pm. Station: Ginza (3 min.). On Namiki Dori.

Tokyo is riddled with outlets of this popular chain of utilitarian "dining cafes," which serve as coffee shops during the day and bars at night. The menu ranges from salads and pastas to pizza and sandwiches. This place is popular with couples and area office workers, most of whom seem to smoke.

Ginza Sapporo Lion. 7–9–20 Ginza. ☎ **03/3571-2590.** Mon–Sat 11:30am–11pm, Sun and holidays 11:30am–10:30pm. Station: Ginza (3 min.). On Chuo Dori not far from the Matsuzakaya department store.

Sapporo beer is the draw at this large beer hall with its mock Gothic ceiling. A large display of plastic foods and an English-language menu help you choose from snacks ranging from yakitori to sausage and spaghetti. The place is popular with older Japanese.

ASAKUSA

See the map on p. 81 for the bars listed in this section.

Ichimon. 3–12–6 Asakusa. ☎ **03/3875-6800.** Mon–Sat 6–10:30pm. Closed holidays. Station: Tawaramachi (10 min.) or Asakusa (15 min.). Just northeast of the Kokusai Dori/Kototoi Dori intersection; from the intersection, walk 1 block north on Kokusai Dori and turn right; it's almost immediately on your right, with a big sake barrel above its door.

Ichimon takes its name from *mon*, which was the lowest piece of currency used by common people during the Edo Period. Ichimon means "one mon." This quirky place, specializing in sake, has a unique system whereby each customer is required to purchase at least ¥5,000 ($42) worth of mon, issued here in wooden tokens at the rate of ¥100 (85¢) for each mon; the tokens are then used to pay for your sake, meal, and ¥800 ($6.65) snack charge. It's usually enough to cover the cost of a couple of flasks of sake, a tray of appetizers, and a main dish that might include sashimi, steak, fried fish, *nabe* (a one-pot stew of meat and vegetables), udon noodles, a tofu dish, or chicken. Mon you don't use can be exchanged for the real thing when you leave. This is a cozy place, decorated like an old farmhouse with wooden beams, shoji screens, and antiques.

Sky Room. Asahi Beer Tower, 22nd floor, 1–23–1 Azumabashi. ☎ **03/5608-5277.** Daily 10am–9pm. Station: Asakusa (4 min.). On the opposite side of the Sumida River from Sensoji Temple.

This is a great place for an inexpensive drink after an active day in historic Asakusa. The Asahi Beer Tower, which sits next to the distinctive building with the golden hops perched on top, belongs to the Asahi Beer company; it's thought to represent a mug of foaming beer. The cafeteria-style bar, perched at the top of the building in the foam next to **La Ranarita** (see chapter 5), offers great views as well as different kinds of Asahi beer, wine, coffee, tea, and cider, all priced at only ¥500 ($4.15). With seating for only 26 at a window-side counter, it can be crowded on weekends.

UENO

Warrior Celt. 6–9–2 Ueno. ☎ **03/3836-8588.** Daily 5pm–5am. Station: Okachimachi (north exit, 5 min.) or Ueno (5 min.). One block east of the Yamanote elevated train tracks, between Okamachi and Ueno stations and just a stone's throw from the Ameya Yokocho market.

This third-floor pub is somewhat of a novelty in Ueno, especially for its nightly happy hour until 7pm (when all drinks are priced at just ¥500/$4.15) and free, live music most nights of the week, including a Celtic jam on Wednesdays. With its international, friendly mix, it's a good place to while away some hours if you find yourself in Ueno after the museums close.

SHINJUKU

See the map on p. 66 for the bars listed in this section.

⑥⑧ **Anyo.** 1–1–8 Kabuki-cho. ☎ **03/3209-7253.** Mon–Sat 7pm–2am. Closed holidays and in mid-Aug. Station: Shinjuku Sanchome (8 min.). Just west of Hanazono Shrine in Goruden Gai; look for its lighted sign of a girl in red with a red-dotted cap.

This gem of a place affords a different view of Japanese life. The tiny bar, with room for only a dozen or so people, is typical of a multitude of miniature establishments that line the narrow alleyways of Goruden Gai, a fascinating, unique nightlife neighborhood east of Kabuki-cho (see "The Major Entertainment Districts," above). However, unlike most of the establishments here, this place welcomes foreigners. It's run by a friendly husband-and-wife team who speak some English. There's a ¥500 ($4.15) table charge per person.

Bob. 2–16–11 Shinjuku. ☎ **03/3341-9355.** Cover (including food) ¥2,000 ($17). Mon–Sat 7:30pm–2am or later. Station: Shinjuku Sanchome (4 min.). Southeast of the Yasukuni Dori and Gyoen Dori intersection, behind Bygs, in Shinjuku Ni–chome.

Karaoke pros will love this tiny, Japanese-style bar, with room for only a dozen people or so, a gracious host, and an extensive library of English-language hits, including songs by the Beatles, Carole King, Billy Joel, Bon Jovi, the Doors, Duran Duran, Elvis Presley, and more. Bob, who lived in the United States and Taiwan for 27 years, speaks English and loves having foreign guests; if prompted, he'll belt out some songs himself. I've seen even anti-karaoke diehards melt after a few hours here and end up singing their hearts out. A fun place to spend an evening.

Bon's. 1–1–10 Kabuki-cho. ☎ **03/3209-6334.** Daily 7pm–5am. Station: Shinjuku Sanchome (7 min.). In Goruden Gai, near Hanazono Shrine.

This is another accessible place in Shinjuku's Goruden Gai, a warren of tiny alleyways and even tinier bars. Larger than most of the bars here, the establishment caters to a 30-ish Japanese clientele and boasts a Mickey Mouse collection behind a glass case. There's a table charge of ¥600 ($5).

⟨69⟩ Fukuriki Ichiza. 1–1–10 Kabuki-cho. ☎ **03/5291-5139.** Daily 6pm–3am. Station: Shinjuku Sanchome (7 min.). In Goruden Gai.

This tiny, funky bar, under the laid-back patronage of owner Dragon Shibata, attracts a young clientele with its Latin American music, Corona beer, pictures of Che Guevera, and kitsch. The first drink here costs ¥1,000 ($8.35); thereafter, they're ¥500 ($4.15).

Hungry Humphrey. 1–1–10 Kabuki-cho. ☎ **03/3200-6156.** Mon–Sat 6:30pm–1:30am. Closed holidays. Station: Shinjuku-Sanchome (7 min.). Upstairs from Bon's (see above), on the edge of Goruden Gai across from Hanazono Shrine.

This place, which specializes in various kinds of vodka, also tolerates foreigners and has a rustic, European feel to it. If you wish, you can keep a bottle here with your name on it (a common custom in Japan for regulars who frequent a favorite bar), properly frozen until your next visit. There's a ¥300 ($2.50) table charge.

⟨35⟩ Irohanihoheto. 3–15–15 Shinjuku. ☎ **03/3359-1682.** Sun–Thurs 5pm–midnight, Fri–Sat 5pm–4am. Station: Shinjuku Sanchome (5 min.). In E. Shinjuku on Yasukuni Dori, next to Isetan Kaikan, on the 6th floor.

If you're young and don't have much money, head for this place. One in a chain of inexpensive yakitori-ya that attracts a young college crowd, it offers a multitude of snacks as well as beer.

New Sazae. Ishikawa Building, 2nd floor, 2–18–5 Shinjuku. ☎ **03/3354-1745.** Sun–Thurs 10pm–5am, Fri–Sat 10pm–6am. Station: Shinjuku Sanchome (4 min.). Southeast of the Yasukuni Dori and Gyoen Dori intersection, behing Bygs, in Shinjuku Ni–chome.

After other bars close, those who refuse to call it quits migrate around the corner to this dive. The crowd is a bit rowdy, but if you get this far you're probably right where you belong. A ¥1,000 cover ($8.35) includes the first drink.

✪ Vagabond. 1–4–20 Nishi Shinjuku. ☎ **03/3348-9109.** Daily 5:30–11:30pm. Station: Shinjuku (west exit, 2 min.). In W. Shinjuku, in the 2nd alley behind (north of) Odakyu Halc.

Although most of the night action in Shinjuku is east of the station, the west side also has an area of inexpensive restaurants and bars. This second-floor nightspot has been in operation for more than 20 years and is owned by the effervescent Mr. Matsuoka, who can be found either here or over at nearby Volga (see below). Vagabond features a jazz pianist nightly, beginning at 7:30pm. Although there's no music charge per se, after 7:30pm there is an obligatory snack charge of ¥500 ($4.15) for the bowl of chips automatically brought to your table. Small and cozy, this place is popular with foreigners who live near Shinjuku Station and with Japanese who want to rub elbows with them; its Guinness brings in customers from the United Kingdom. Simple snacks range from yakitori to spring rolls and fried tofu.

✪ ⑦⓪ **Volga.** 1–4–18 Nishi Shinjuku. ☎ **03/3342-4996.** Mon–Sat 5:30–10:30pm. Closed holidays. Station: Shinjuku (west exit, 2 min.). In W. Shinjuku, on the corner down the street from Vagabond (see above).

Volga, a yakitori-ya housed in an ivy-covered two-story brick building, features an open grill facing the street and a smoky and packed drinking hall typical of older establishments that once dotted the country. Its unrefined atmosphere has changed little since it opened here in the 1950s. Rooms are tiny and simply decorated with wooden tables and benches, and the clientele is middle-aged. Very Japanese. Since it's often packed, get here soon after it opens to be assured a seat. Recommended yakitori includes the *tsukune* (meatballs) or *agedofu* (deep-fried tofu).

The Wine Bar. N. S. Building, 30th floor, 2–4–1 Nishi-Shinjuku. ☎ **03/3348-8993.** Daily 4pm–2:30am. Station: Shinjuku (west exit, 8 min.).

This bar is part of a successful chain of inexpensive wine bars catering to Japanese interested in tasting different wines. Choices range from domestic vintages to imports from Germany, Italy, France, and the United States. A glass of house wine starts at ¥380 ($3.15) and a bottle of wine at ¥2,200 ($18), but note that there's a table charge of ¥500 ($4.15) per person. Western food is also served, including pastas, steaks, and light fare. The bar is located on the 30th floor, but the view is blocked by surrounding skyscrapers.

HARAJUKU

See the map on p. 117 for the bar listed in this section.

Oh God. 6–7–18 Jingumae. ☎ **03/3406-3206.** Daily 6pm–6am. Station: Meiji-Jingumae (3 min.) or Harajuku (5 min.). From the Meiji/Omotesando Dori intersection, walk on Omotesando Dori toward Aoyama and turn right at Cafe de Rope; it's in the building at the end of the alley.

This mellow, dimly lit bar is a godsend for travelers on a budget looking for a casual place to hang out in Harajuku. It features a mural of a city at sunset and shows free foreign films every night at 9pm, midnight, and 3am (also at 6pm on Fri and Sat).

A Note on Japanese Symbols

Many hotels, restaurants, attractions, and other establishments in Japan do not have signs giving their names in Roman (English-language) letters. The second appendix to this book lists the Japanese symbols for all such places described in this guide. Each set of characters representing an establishment name has a number in the appendix, which corresponds to the number that appears inside the oval before the establishment's name in the text. Thus, to find the Japanese symbol for, say, **Volga**, refer to no. 70 in appendix B.

I've seen everything from James Bond to Fassbinder to grade-B movies here. There are also two pool tables.

EBISU

Beer Station. Yebisu Garden Place, 4-20 Ebisu. ☎ **03/3442-5111.** Mon–Sat 11:30am–11pm, Sun and holidays 11:30am–10pm. Station: Ebisu (7 min.). At the entrance to Yebisu Garden Place if arriving via the moving walkway from Ebisu Station.

This attractive beer hall is a good imitation of a century-old Bavarian brewery—oompah music even greets you at the entrance. Among the several floors of dining and drinking—each with its own display of plastic food—the most attractive is the huge basement beer hall, the Festbrau, with its vaulted ceiling and huge pillars. The outdoor terrace seating is good for people-watching.

Bodeguita. 1-7-3 Ebisu Minami, Shibuya-ku. ☎ **03/3715-7721.** Mon–Sat 6pm–midnight. Station: Ebisu (west exit, 1 min.). Turn left on the 2nd street away from and parallel to the tracks (there's a bank on the corner with a heart logo).

This very small, crowded Cuban club features Latin music videos (that usually induce customers to dance) and good food, including *arroz con frijoles* (the classic rice and beans) and *arroz saltado* (rice, fried potatoes, and meat). Quiet during the week, it fills up with Latinos on weekends. A single woman will feel welcome at this family-run place.

Enjoy House. 2-9-9 Ebisu Nishi. ☎ **03/5489-1591.** Sun, Tues–Thurs 1pm–1am, Fri–Sat 1pm–3am. Closed 3rd Sun of every month. Station: Ebisu (west exit, 3 min.). From Komazawa Dori, turn right on the street just before Wendy's; when you reach a juncture where several streets converge, it will be on a diagonal street to the left.

With its '60s-reminiscent decor, efficient yet relaxed and funky staff, friendly atmosphere, and tiny dance floor, the inimitable Enjoy House is a great place to—well, enjoy yourself. Everyone here seems high and happy; the place is aptly named.

What the Dickens! 1-13-3 Ebisu Nishi, 4th floor. ☎ **03/3780-2099.** Tues–Wed 5pm–1am, Thurs–Sat 5pm–2am, Sun 3pm–midnight. Station: Ebisu (west exit, 2 min.). From Komazawa Dori, turn right after Wendy's; it's at the end of the 2nd block on the left, on the corner.

Possibly Tokyo's most popular ex-pat bar of the moment, What the Dickens! is undisputed proof that Ebisu is no longer the sleepy backwater it once was. This bar packs 'em in with live bands nightly (everything from rock and pop to reggae, jazz, blues, Dixieland, and folk), no cover, British beer on tap, and hearty servings of pub grub, including lamb pie, steak and kidney, beef Guinness, and a Sunday roast.

ROPPONGI

See the map on p. 127 for the bars listed in this section.

✪ **Acarajé Tropicana.** 1-1-1 Nishi Azabu. ☎ **03/3479-4690.** Tues–Thurs 6pm–3am, Fri–Sat 6pm–5am, Sun 7pm–3am. Station: Roppongi (7 min.). From Roppongi Crossing, head toward Shibuya on Roppongi Dori, turning right at the 1st major street (Terebi Asahi Dori); it's immediately on your left.

This basement Brazilian bar is a friendly place, filled with regulars, Latin music and dancing, a TV screen showing Brazil's two great passions (Carnival and soccer), and Brazilian cocktails and beer. Highly recommended, but it gets crowded.

Dusk to Dawn. 3-13-8 Roppongi. ☎ **03/5771-2258.** Mon–Sat 6pm–5am. Station: Roppongi (3 min.). On the left side of Gaien-Higashi Dori as you walk from Roppongi Crossing toward Tokyo Tower, catty-corner from Starbuck's.

If you're looking for a convivial bar with elbow room, a professional, thirty-something international crowd, and a welcoming atmosphere, try this second-floor bar. Happy hour is until 9pm; on Wednesdays, women receive happy hour prices on drinks all night long.

Ex. 7–7–6 Roppongi. ☎ **03/3408-5487.** Mon–Sat 5pm–2am. Station: Roppongi (5 min.). From Roppongi Crossing, take Gaien-Higashi Dori toward Aoyama (away from Tokyo Tower), turning onto the diagonal street that veers off the left (opposite the former Defense Agency); it will be on the right, past 7-Eleven.

Ex, whose name, appropriately enough, means "bottoms up," is a bit of old Germany right in the heart of Tokyo. Hearty helpings of German food are on hand, with plenty of beer to wash it all down. There's no menu, so you just have to ask what's cooking; common dishes are schnitzel, wurst, meat loaf, sauerkraut, and fried potatoes. Ex is a tiny place, but it's usually packed with German businessmen and ex-pats who don't mind standing to drink their favorite German brew.

Gaspanic Bar. 3–15–24 Roppongi. ☎ **03/3405-0633.** Daily 6pm–5am. Station: Roppongi (4 min.). From Roppongi Crossing, walk towards Tokyo Tower on Gaien-Higashi Dori, turning left at Hamburger Inn.

This is the bar of the moment for foreign and Japanese twenty-somethings. The music is loud, and after midnight the place gets so crowded that female patrons have been known to start dancing on the countertops. Thursdays are especially packed, since all drinks go for only ¥300 ($2.50). Gaspanic Miller, downstairs, sells pizza by the slice, while in the basement is Club Panic 99, open only on Thursday, Friday, and Saturday for dancing. Large bouncers at the door serve as clues that this place can get rough.

Hard Rock Cafe. 5–4–20 Roppongi. ☎ **03/3408-7018.** Mon–Thurs 11:30am–2am, Fri–Sat 11:30am–4am, Sun and holidays 11:30am–11:30pm. Station: Roppongi (3 min.). From Roppongi Crossing, walk toward Tokyo Tower on Gaien-Higashi Dori and turn right at McDonald's.

If you like your music loud, the Hard Rock Cafe is the place for you. The outside is easily recognizable by King Kong scaling an outside wall; the inside looks like a modern yuppie version of the local hamburger joint, except, of course, there's the added attraction of all that rock-'n'-roll paraphernalia. The food includes barbecued chicken, burgers, and fajitas. During happy hour (Mon through Thurs from 4 to 6:30pm), drinks are half price. Otherwise, a beer will set you back ¥800 ($6.65).

Hideout Bar. 3–14–9 Roppongi. ☎ **03/3497-5219.** Daily 6pm–6am. Station: Roppongi (3 min.). From Roppongi Crossing, head toward Tokyo Tower on Gaien-Higashi Dori; it's on the left, catty-corner from McDonald's and opposite the Roi Building.

This small basement bar packs 'em in like the Yamanote Line during rush hour with its loud music. It gets so crowded in here after midnight—mostly with thirty-somethings—that everyone just dances where they are. A fun, party kind of place.

Paddy Foley's. Roi Building basement. 5–5–1 Roppongi. ☎ **03/3423-2250.** Daily 5pm–2am. Station: Roppongi (3 min.). On Gaien-Higashi Dori, on the right as you walk from Roppongi Crossing toward Tokyo Tower.

Easy to find, this lively Irish pub is popular with both Japanese and foreigners. The Celt, next door and under the same management, offers dancing and live music, with never a cover charge.

AKASAKA

See the map on p. 73 for the bars listed in this section.

Garden Lounge. Hotel New Otani, 4–1 Kioi-cho. ☎ **03/3265-1111.** Daily 7am–10pm. Station: Nagata-cho or Akasaka-mitsuke (3 min.).

If you prefer the view of a Japanese landscape garden to that of neon lights, get to this place before sunset, where you can look out over a 400-year-old garden complete with waterfall, pond, bridges, and manicured bushes. Cocktails begin at a pricey ¥1,300 ($11). There's live music from 5pm with a ¥300 ($2.50) cover charge.

Top of Akasaka. Akasaka Prince Hotel, 40th floor, 1–2 Kioi-cho. ☎ **03/3234-1111.** Daily noon–2am. Station: Nagata-cho or Akasaka-mitsuke (2 min.).

I like to start out evenings in Akasaka with a quiet drink at this fancy and romantic cocktail lounge. With the city of Tokyo as a dramatic backdrop, I can watch the day fade into darkness as millions of lights and neon signs twinkle in the distance. Cocktails average ¥1,500 ($12.50), and after 5pm there's a cover charge of ¥800 ($6.65) for the piano music. Note that no children are allowed.

SHINAGAWA

Top of Shinagawa. Shinagawa Prince Hotel, 4–10–30 Takanawa. ☎ **03/3440-1111.** Daily 11:30am–2am. Station: Shinagawa (2 min.).

Occupying the whole top floor of this 39-story hotel, the Top of Shinagawa boasts one of the best views of any hotel bar in Tokyo. It offers unparalleled panoramas of Tokyo Bay, Odaiba, the Rainbow Bridge, Mt. Fuji, and the Tokyo cityscape. The bar itself is divided into various sections; only the East Lounge (facing the bay) is open during the day, offering a dessert, fruit, and sandwich buffet for ¥1,650 ($14) from 11:30am to 5pm. There's an open restaurant called Prince Court at the center; it offers a fixed-price dinner for ¥5,000 ($42).

4 Gay & Lesbian Bars

Shinjuku Ni–chome (pronounced "knee-chomay"), southeast of the Yasukuni Dori and Gyoen Dori intersection, is Tokyo's gay and lesbian quarter, with numerous establishments catering to a variety of age groups and preferences. The following are good starting points; you'll find a lot more in the immediate area just exploring on your own.

Arty Farty. 2–17–4 Shinjuku. ☎ **03/3356-5388.** Mon–Fri 5pm–5am, Sat–Sun 3pm–5am. Station: Shinjuku Sanchome (4 min.). Behind Bygs, on a corner.

This gay bar allows only men, except on Sundays when women with gay companions are also welcome.

Kinsmen. 2–18–5 Shinjuku. ☎ **03/3354-4949.** Wed–Mon 9pm–5am. Station: Shinjuku Sanchome (4 min.). Down the street from Arty Farty, behind Bygs.

This second-floor gay bar welcomes customers of all persuasions. It's a pleasant oasis, small and civilized, with a huge flower arrangement dominating the center of the room. Occasionally there's live music.

Kinswomyn. 2–15–10 Shinjuku. ☎ **03/3354-8720.** Wed–Mon 8pm–4am. Station: Shinjuku Sanchome (4 min.). On a street behind Kinsmen.

This casual, welcoming, women-only bar attracts a regular clientele of mainly Japanese lesbians.

Zinc. 2–14–6 Shinjuku. ☎ **03/3352-6297.** Tues–Sun 8pm–4:30am. Station: Shinjuku Sanchome (4 min.). In the 2nd block behind Bygs.

This basement disco, with a high-charged energetic atmosphere, attracts young gays and lesbians, both Japanese and foreign, but heterosexuals are welcome (occasional special events are restricted to either men or women). Weekdays it has a relaxed atmosphere, but dancing and DJs on Fridays and Saturdays bring in the crowds. There's usually a ¥800 to ¥3,000 ($6.65 to $25) cover charge, including one or two drinks, on weekends. Otherwise, drinks cost ¥500 ($4.15), with reduced prices on Thursdays.

5 Beer Gardens

If you're in Tokyo during the summer months, take advantage of the very popular beer gardens. These sprout up all over Japan when the weather turns warm, often atop office buildings. In addition to the places below, another good spot for an outdoor beer is **Hibiya Park,** across from the Imperial Hotel, where there are various beer gardens and bars open from about April through October, daily from 11am to 8pm.

✪ **Hanezawa Beer Garden.** 3–12–15 Hiroo, Shibuya-ku. ☎ **03/3400-6500.** Mon–Fri 5–9pm, Sat–Sun 4–9pm. Reservations required. Station: Ebisu, Omotesando, or Shibuya; then take a taxi.

This traditional Japanese outdoor garden, spread under trees and paper lanterns, is a lovely place for a meal and drinks. It serves sukiyaki, shabu-shabu, Mongolian barbecue (cooked at your table), and a variety of snacks and other dishes. Note that if you want shabu-shabu or sukiyaki, you should notify the restaurant the day before. You can also come just for the beer, which starts at ¥450 ($3.75), and light fare like yakitori, french fries, and *edamame* (boiled soy beans). The place is open throughout the year, though in winter you'll sit in a tarp enclosure, not nearly as romantic as under the stars.

Suntory Beer Garden. Suntory Building, 1–2–3 Moto-Akasaka. ☎ **03/3401-4367.** May–Aug Mon–Sat 5–10pm. Closed holidays. Station: Akasaka-mitsuke (1 min.).

This rooftop beer garden, which has a great view of surrounding Akasaka, is better and more sophisticated than most, with real palms and bushes circling the dining area instead of the usual plastic that seems to plague most such places. In addition to its draft Suntory beer, it also offers a barbecue meal you can grill at your table, as well as beer snacks (spring rolls, yakitori) listed on an English-language menu. Purchase what you want from the ticket booth, sit down, and then hand the waiter your ticket.

6 Films

Going to the movies is an expensive pastime in Tokyo, with admission averaging about ¥1,800 ($15) for adults, ¥1,500 ($12.50) for senior-high and college students, ¥1,300 ($11) for junior-high students, and ¥1,000 ($8.35) for children and seniors over 60. If you want to see one of Hollywood's latest releases (which usually take a few months to reach Japan), you may also have to contend with long lines and huge crowds. To see what's on and where, pick up a free copy of *Tokyo Classifieds* or purchase the monthly *Tokyo Journal,* which is sold in bookstores for ¥600 ($5) and lists addresses for more than 100 cinemas. Note that theaters in Tokyo close early, with the last showing usually around 7pm. Movies are shown in the original language, with Japanese subtitles.

One of my favorite theaters is **Ciné Vivant** (☎ **03/3403-6061**), in the Wave Building, 6–2–27 Roppongi (station: Roppongi; 1 min.), which specializes in European films, mostly new works. There are about four or five showings daily, starting around 11am or noon.

Another good place to see films—albeit mostly of the B-grade variety, with the occasional classic or newer release—is at the bar **Oh God** (see above). It charges no admission, although beer starts at a high ¥700 ($5.85). Movies, which generally start at 9pm on weekdays and 6pm on weekends, are shown throughout the evening, with the last one beginning at 3am. I've seen everything from sci-fi horror flicks to James Bond here. Call to see what's playing.

If you're interested in seeing Japanese classics, your best bet is the **National Film Center** (☎ **03/3561-0823**), a division of the National Museum of Modern Art in Kitanomaru Koen Park (station: Takebashi). Movies, shown on Saturday and Sunday, include both Japanese and foreign films (some with English subtitles), with programs featuring specific directors or historical retrospectives. Since programs change often, call to see what's playing and to check show times. A ticket here is ¥410 ($3.40).

Side Trips from Tokyo 10

If your stay in Tokyo is 3 days or more, you should consider excursions in the vicinity. **Kamakura** and **Nikko** rank as two of the most important historical sites in Japan, each representing a completely different but equally exciting period of Japanese history. **Yokohama,** with its thriving port, waterfront development, and several museums and attractions, makes an interesting day trip, while the **Fuji-Hakone-Izu National Park** serves as a huge recreational playground for the residents of Tokyo. For overnight stays, I recommend **Hakone,** both for its atmosphere and its Japanese-style inns (*ryokan*), where you'll be able to experience a bit of old Japan. (For more information on ryokan, see chapter 4.) Active travelers may want to hike to the top of **Mt. Fuji,** while shoppers may want to head for the pottery village of **Mashiko.**

Before departing Tokyo, stop by the **Tourist Information Center (TIC)** for a color brochure called "Side Trips from Tokyo," which carries information on Kamakura, Nikko, Hakone, and the Mt. Fuji area. The TIC also has a map of Tokyo's vicinity, as well as pamphlets on individual destinations, some of which give train schedules and other useful information (see "Visitor Information," in chapter 3 for the TIC location).

1 Kamakura

32 miles (57.5km) S of Tokyo

If you take only one day trip outside Tokyo, it should be to Kamakura, especially if you're unable to include the ancient capitals of Kyoto and Nara in your travels. Kamakura is a delightful hamlet with no fewer than 65 Buddhist temples and 19 Shinto shrines spread throughout the village and the surrounding wooded hills. Most of these were built centuries ago, when a warrior named Yoritomo Minamoto seized political power and established his shogunate government in Kamakura back in 1192. Wanting to set up his seat of government as far away as possible from what he considered to be the corrupt imperial court in Kyoto, Yoritomo selected Kamakura because it was easy to defend. The village is enclosed on three sides by wooded hills and on the fourth by the sea—a setting that lends a dramatic background to its many temples and shrines.

Although Kamakura remained the military and political center of the nation for a century and a half, the Minamoto clan was in power for only a short time. After Yoritomo's death, both of his sons were assassinated, one after the other, after taking up military rule. Power then passed to the family of Yoritomo's widow, the Hojo family, who ruled until 1333, when the emperor in Kyoto sent troops to crush the shogunate government. Unable to stop the invaders, 800 soldiers retired to the Hojo family temple at Toshoji, where they all disemboweled themselves in ritualistic suicide known as *seppuku.*

Today a thriving seaside resort with a population of 175,000, Kamakura—with its old wooden homes, temples, shrines, and wooded hills—makes a pleasant 1-day trip from Tokyo. (There's also a beach in Kamakura called Yuigahama Beach, but I find it unappealing; it's often litter-strewn and unbelievably crowded in summer. Skip it.)

ESSENTIALS

GETTING THERE   Take the **JR Yokosuka Line** bound for Zushi, Kurihama, or Yokosuka; it departs every 10 to 15 minutes from the Yokohama, Shinagawa, Shimbashi, and Tokyo JR stations. The trip takes almost 1 hour from Tokyo Station and costs ¥890 ($7.40) one-way to Kamakura Station.

VISITOR INFORMATION   In Kamakura, there's a **tourist information window** (☎ **0467/22-3350;** open daily 9am to 6pm, 5pm in winter) immediately to the right outside Kamakura Station's east exit, in the direction of Tsurugaoka Hachimangu Shrine. It sells a color brochure with a map of Kamakura for ¥200 ($1.65); there's also a free map (in both English and Japanese), but it's not always in stock. Ask here for directions on how to get to the village's most important sights by bus.

ORIENTATION & GETTING AROUND   Kamakura's major sights are clustered in two areas: **Kamakura Station,** the town's downtown, with the tourist office, souvenir shops, restaurants, and Tsurugaoka Hachimangu Shrine; and **Hase,** with the Great Buddha and Hase Kannon Temple. You can travel between Kamakura Station and Hase Station via the **Enoden Line,** a wonderful small train, or you can walk the distance in about 15 minutes. Destinations in Kamakura are also easily reached by buses that depart from Kamakura Station.

SEEING THE SIGHTS

The most worthwhile places of interest in Kamakura are generally considered to be **Tsurugaoka Hachimangu Shrine, the Great Buddha,** and **Hase Kannon Temple;** visitors with more time on their hands should take in a few other sights as well. Keep in mind that most temples and shrines open about 8 or 9am and close between 4 and 5pm.

AROUND KAMAKURA STATION   About a 10-minute walk from Kamakura Station, ✪ **Tsurugaoka Hachimangu Shrine** (☎ **0467/22-0315**) is the spiritual heart of Kamakura and one of its most popular attractions. It was built by Yoritomo and dedicated to Hachiman, the Shinto god of war who served as the clan deity of the Minamoto family. The pathway to the shrine is along Wakamiya Oji, a cherry tree-lined pedestrian lane that was also constructed by Yoritomo back in the 1190s, so that his oldest son's first visit to the family shrine could be accomplished in style with an elaborate procession. The lane stretches from the shrine all the way to Yuigahama Beach, with three massive torii gates set at intervals along the route to signal the approach to the shrine. On both sides of the pathway are souvenir and antique shops selling lacquerware, pottery, and folk art.

As you ascend the 62 steps to the vermilion-painted shrine, note the gingko tree to the left, thought to be about 1,000 years old. This is supposedly the site where Yoritomo's second son was ambushed and murdered back in 1219; his head was

Side Trips from Tokyo

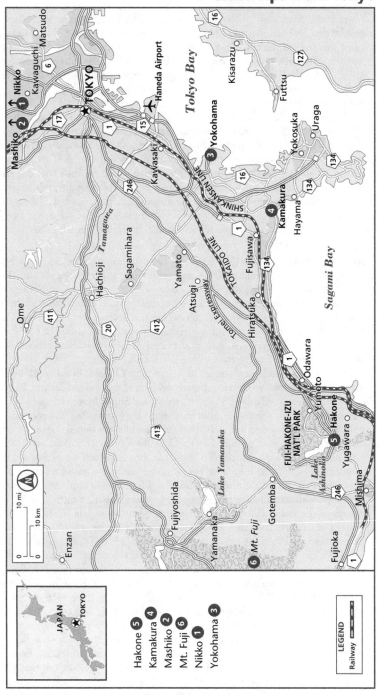

Railway

LEGEND
Railway

Hakone **5**
Kamakura **4**
Mashiko **2**
Mt. Fuji **6**
Nikko **1**
Yokohama **3**

JAPAN
TOKYO

never found. Such stories of murder and betrayal were common in feudal Japan. Fearful that his charismatic brother had designs on the shogunate, Yoritomo banished him and ordered him killed. Rather than face capture, the brother committed *seppuku.* When the brother's mistress gave birth to a boy, the baby was promptly killed. Today the lotus ponds, arched bridge, pigeons, and bright vermilion sheen of the shrine give little clue to such violent history. The shrine grounds are free to the public and are always open.

Although it's a bit out of the way, it might pay to visit **Zeniarai-Benten Shrine** (☎ **0467/25-1081**), about a 20-minute walk west of Kamakura Station. This shrine is dedicated to the goddess of good fortune. On Asian zodiac days of the snake, worshippers believe that if you take your money and wash it in spring water in a small cave on the shrine grounds, it will double or triple itself later on. This being modern Japan, don't be surprised if you see a bit of ingenuity; my Japanese landlady told me that when she visited the shrine she didn't have much cash on her, so she washed something she thought would be equally as good—her credit card. As a shrine dedicated to the goddess of fortune, it's fitting that admission is free. Open daily 8am to 5pm.

AROUND HASE STATION   To get to these attractions, you can go by bus, which departs from in front of Kamakura Station (take any bus from platform 2 or 7 to the Daibutsuen-mae stop). Or, for a more romantic adventure, you can go by the **Enoden train line,** a tiny train that putt-putts its way seemingly through backyards on its way from Kamakura Station to Hase and beyond. Since there's only one track, trains have to take turns going in either direction. I would suggest taking the bus from Kamakura Station directly to the Great Buddha, walking to Hase Shrine, and then taking the Enoden train back to Kamakura Station.

Probably Kamakura's most famous attraction is the ✪ **Great Buddha** (☎ **0467/ 22-0703**), called the Daibutsu in Japanese and located at Kotokuin Temple. Thirty-seven feet high and weighing 93 tons, it's the second-largest bronze image in Japan. The largest Buddha is in Nara, but in my opinion the Kamakura Daibutsu is much more impressive: For one thing, the Kamakura Buddha sits outside, against a dramatic backdrop of wooded hills. Cast in 1252, the Kamakura Buddha was indeed once housed in a temple like the Nara Buddha, but a huge tidal wave destroyed the wooden structure—and the statue has sat under sun, snow, and stars ever since. I also prefer the face of the Kamakura Buddha; I find it more inspiring and divine, as though with its half-closed eyes and calm, serene face it's somehow above the worries of the world. It seems to represent the plane above human suffering, the point at which birth and death, joy and sadness merge and become one. Open daily from 7am to 6pm (to 5:30pm in winter). Admission is ¥200 ($1.65) for adults and ¥150 ($1.25) for children, and your entry ticket is a bookmark, a nice souvenir. If you want, you can pay an extra ¥20 (15¢) to go inside the statue—it's hollow.

About a 10-minute walk from the Daibutsu is ✪ **Hase Kannon Temple** or Hasedera (☎ **0467/22-6300**), located on a hill with a sweeping view of the sea. This is the home of an 11-headed gilt statue of Kannon, the goddess of mercy, housed in the Kannon-do (Kannon Hall). More than 30 feet high and the tallest wooden image in Japan, it was made from a single piece of camphorwood back in the 8th century. The legend surrounding this Kannon is quite remarkable. Supposedly two wooden images were made from the wood of a huge camphor tree. One of the images was kept in Hase, not far from Nara, while the second was given a short ceremony and then duly tossed into the sea to find a home of its own. The image drifted 300 miles eastward and washed up on shore, but was thrown back in

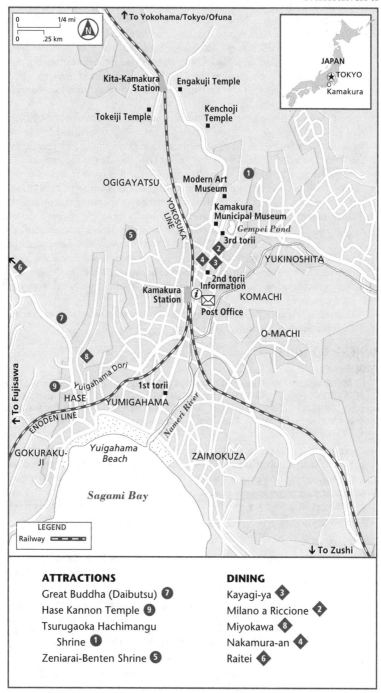

Kamakura

To Yokohama/Tokyo/Ofuna

0   1/4 mi
0   .25 km

N

JAPAN

TOKYO

Kamakura

Kita-Kamakura Station

Engakuji Temple

Tokeiji Temple

Kenchoji Temple

OGIGAYATSU

Modern Art Museum

Kamakura Municipal Museum

Gempei Pond

3rd torii

YOKOSUKA LINE

2nd torii

Information

YUKINOSHITA

Kamakura Station

Post Office

KOMACHI

O-MACHI

To Fujisawa

Yuigahama Dori

1st torii

HASE

YUMIGAHAMA

ENODEN LINE

Nameri River

GOKURAKU-JI

Yuigahama Beach

ZAIMOKUZA

Sagami Bay

LEGEND
Railway

To Zushi

ATTRACTIONS

Great Buddha (Daibutsu) 7
Hase Kannon Temple 9
Tsurugaoka Hachimangu
  Shrine 1
Zeniarai-Benten Shrine 5

DINING

Kayagi-ya 3
Milano a Riccione 2
Miyokawa 8
Nakamura-an 4
Raitei 6

again because all who touched it became ill or incurred bad luck. Finally, the image reached Kamakura, where it gave the people no trouble. This was interpreted as a sign that the image was content with its surroundings, and Hase Kannon Temple was erected at its present site. Note how each face has a different expression, representing the Kannon's compassion for various kinds of human suffering. In the Kannon-do you'll also find the **Treasure House,** with relics from the Kamakura, Heian, Muromachi, and Edo periods.

Another statue housed here is of **Amida,** a Buddha who promised rebirth in the Pure Land to the West to all who chanted his name. It was created by orders of Yoritomo Minamoto upon his 42nd birthday, considered an unlucky year for men. You'll find it housed in the Amida-do (Amida Hall), beside the Kannon-do.

As you climb up the steps to the Kannon-do, you'll encounter statues of a different sort. All around you will be likenesses of **Jizo,** the guardian deity of children. Although parents originally came to Hase Temple to set up statues to represent their children in hopes the deity would protect and watch over them, through the years the purpose of the Jizo statues has changed. Now they represent miscarried, stillborn, or, most frequently, aborted children. More than 50,000 Jizo statues have been offered here since the war, but the thousand or so you see now will remain only a year before being burned or buried to make way for others. Some of the statues, which can be purchased on the temple grounds, are fitted with hand-knitted caps and sweaters. The effect is quite chilling.

Hase Temple is open daily 8am to 5pm (to 4:30pm in winter); admission is ¥300 ($2.50) for adults, ¥100 (85¢) for children.

WHERE TO DINE
MODERATE

71　**Miyokawa.** 1–16–17 Hase. ☎ **0467/25-5556.** Reservations recommended. Mini-kaiseki ¥5,500–¥10,000 ($46–$83); obento ¥2,300–¥5,000 ($19–$42); Japanese steak set meal ¥3,500 ($29). MC, V. Daily 11am–9pm. Station: Hase (5 min.). On the main road leading from Hase Station to the Great Buddha (about a 5-min. walk from each). MINI-KAISEKI/OBENTO.

This modern, casual restaurant specializes in kaiseki, including beautifully prepared mini-kaiseki set meals that change with the seasons. It also offers a great obento lunch box, the least expensive of which is served in a container shaped like a gourd, as well as a set meal featuring steak prepared Japanese style. You can also order takeout obento, priced at ¥700–¥1,500 ($5.85–$12.50), which you could eat at the pavilion at Hase Temple.

INEXPENSIVE

In addition to the suggestions below, there's a pavilion at **Hase Temple,** described above, that serves noodles, beer, and soft drinks, with both indoor and outdoor seating. It offers a great view, making it a good place for a snack on a fine day.

72　**Kayagi-ya.** 2–11–16 Komachi. ☎ **0467/22-1460.** Dishes ¥1,200–¥3,000 ($10–$25); teishoku ¥2,000–3,000 ($17–$25). No credit cards. Sat–Thurs noon–6pm. Station: Kamakura (5 min.). On Wakamiya Oji, on the left side if you're walking from Kamakura Station to Tsurugaoka Hachimangu Shrine, next to a lumberyard. EEL.

This modest, older-looking restaurant serves several different kinds of inexpensive eel dishes, my favorite of which is the *unagi donburi* (eel served on top of rice).

Milano a Riccione. 2–12–30 Komachi. ☎ **0467/24-5491.** Pizza and pasta ¥950–¥1,800 ($7.90–$15); main dishes ¥1,800–¥2,300 ($15–$19); set dinner ¥4,500 ($37.50); set lunches ¥1,300–¥2,500 ($11–$21). AE, DC, JCB, MC, V. Thurs–Tues 11:30am–4:30pm and

A Note on Japanese Symbols

Many hotels, restaurants, attractions, and other establishments in Japan do not have signs giving their names in Roman (English-language) letters. The second appendix to this book lists the Japanese symbols for all such places described in this guide. Each set of characters representing an establishment name has a number in the appendix, which corresponds to the number that appears inside the oval before the establishment's name in the text. Thus, to find the Japanese symbol for, say, **Miyokawa,** refer to no. 71 in appendix B.

5:30–10:30pm. Station: Kamakura (6 min.). On the left side of Wakamiya Oji hen walking from Kamakura Station to Tsurugaoka Hachimangu Shrine. ITALIAN.

This is the Japanese branch of a restaurant from Milan, known for its handmade pasta, seafood, and good selection of wines. Although located in a basement, it opens onto a subterranean courtyard, making it brighter and more cheerful than one would expect. There's an English, seasonal menu, but the best bargain is the daily set lunch for ¥1,300 ($11.70), which gives you a choice of pasta, an appetizer, and coffee, espresso, or tea. It's also the quickest meal you can order; otherwise, if you're in a hurry, you should dine elsewhere, as care and time are devoted to the preparation of such meals as grilled scallops and leeks and roast chicken with zucchini and ham.

(73) **Nakamura-an.** 1–7–6 Komachi. ☎ **0467/25-3500.** Noodles ¥700–¥1,600 ($5.85–$13). No credit cards. Fri–Wed noon–6pm. Station: Kamakura (2 min.). From Kamakura Station, walk under the mock orange torii visible across the square and take the 2nd right; the shop is on the right, on a side street between the pedestrian-only shopping street and Wakamiya Oji. NOODLES.

This is Kamakura's most famous noodle shop; it often has a queue of hungry customers lined up outside. It's easy to spot thanks to the front window, where you can watch noodles being made. There's a display of plastic food to help you in making your selection. I can never resist ordering the tempura soba.

✪ (74) **Raitei.** Takasago. ☎ **0467/32-5656.** Reservations required for kaiseki. Noodles ¥850–¥1,500 ($7.10–$12.50); obento lunch boxes ¥3,500–¥4,500 ($29–$37.50); soba set meals ¥2,500 ($21); kaiseki feasts from ¥6,000 ($50). At the front gate, you must pay an entry fee of ¥500 ($4.15), which counts toward the price of your meal. AE, DC, JCB (on meals costing more than ¥10,000 only). Daily 11am–sundown (about 7pm in summer). Bus: 4 or 6 from platform 2 to Takasago stop. NOODLES/OBENTO.

Though it's a bit inconveniently located, this is the absolute winner for a meal in Kamakura. Visiting Raitei is as much fun as visiting the city's temples and shrines. The restaurant is situated in the hills on the edge of Kamakura, surrounded by verdant countryside, and the wonder is that it serves inexpensive *soba* (Japanese noodles) as well as priestly kaiseki feasts, which you must reserve in advance. If you're here for soba or one of the obento lunch boxes, go down the stone steps on the right to the back entry, where you'll be given an English menu with such offerings as noodles with chicken, mountain vegetables, tempura, and more. The pottery used here comes from the restaurant's own specially made kiln, and you'll dine sitting on roughly hewn wood stools or tatami. When you've finished your meal, be sure to walk the path circling through the garden past a bamboo grove, stone images, and a miniature shrine. The stroll takes about 20 minutes, unless you stop for a beer at the refreshment house, which has outdoor seating and a view of the countryside. Incidentally, buses going to Takasago stop also at the Great Buddha.

2 Nikko

90 miles (144km) N of Tokyo

Since the publication of James Clavell's novel *Shogun*, many people have become familiar with Tokugawa Ieyasu, the powerful real-life shogun of the 1600s on whom Clavell's fictional shogun was based. Quashing all rebellions and unifying Japan under his leadership, Tokugawa established such a military stronghold that his heirs continued to rule Japan for the next 250 years without serious challenge.

If you'd like to join the millions of Japanese who through the centuries have paid homage to this great man, travel 90 miles north of Tokyo to Nikko, where **Toshogu Shrine** was constructed in his honor in the 17th century and where Tokugawa's remains were laid to rest in a mausoleum. Nikko means "sunlight"—an apt description of the way the sun's rays play upon this sumptuous shrine of wood and gold leaf. Nearby are another mausoleum containing Tokugawa's grandson, a temple, a shrine, and a garden. Surrounding the sacred grounds are thousands of majestic cedar trees in the 200,000-acre ✪ **Nikko National Park.**

I've included a few recommendations for an overnight stay. Otherwise, you can see Nikko in a full day.

ESSENTIALS

GETTING THERE   The easiest, fastest, and most luxurious way to get to Nikko is on the Tobu Line's Limited Express, called the **Spacia,** which departs every hour or more frequently from Asakusa Station and costs ¥2,750 ($23) one-way for the 1-hour and 50-minute trip. All seats are reserved, which means you are guaranteed a seat; if you're traveling on a holiday or a summer weekend, you may wish to reserve your ticket in advance. Another plus is that there's usually an English-speaking hostess on board who passes out pamphlets on the area and can answer sightseeing questions about Nikko.

Otherwise, you can also reach Nikko on Tobu's slower **rapid train** from Asakusa, which costs ¥1,330 ($11) one-way and takes 2 hours and 10 minutes, with trains departing every hour or more frequently. There are no reserved seats, which means you might have to stand if trains are crowded.

If you're visiting **Mashiko** (see below) and don't have a Japan Rail Pass, you can save yourself the hassle of buying train tickets from different rail companies by taking the Tobu Railway from Asakusa to Tobu Utsunomiya Station for the bus to Mashiko, and then continuing onward from Tobu Utusnomiya Station to Nikko. If you have a Japan Rail Pass, take the Shinkansen bullet train from Ueno to Utsunomiya (there are departures every 15 to 30 min. and the trip takes about 47 min.) and change there for Nikko (45 min.).

VISITOR INFORMATION   Before leaving Tokyo, pick up the leaflet "Nikko" from the **Tourist Information Center (TIC).** It gives the train schedule for both the Tobu Line, which departs from Asakusa Station, and JR trains that depart from Ueno Station. The TIC also has some color brochures with maps of the Nikko area.

Nikko's Tobu and JR stations are located almost side by side in the village's downtown area. The **Nikko Tobu Station tourist information counter** (☎ **0288/ 53-4511**), located inside Tobu Station to the right after passing through the wicket gate, is staffed by a friendly woman who speaks enough English to give you a map, answer basic questions, and point you in the right direction. You can also make hotel and ryokan reservations here for free. Open daily 9am to noon and 1 to 5pm.

Nikko

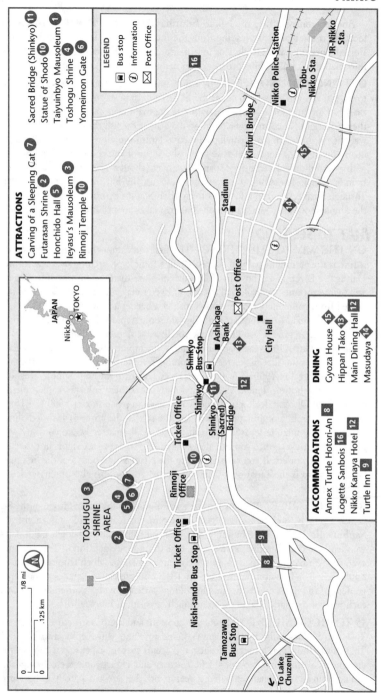

ATTRACTIONS

Carving of a Sleeping Cat **7**
Futarasan Shrine **2**
Honchido Hall **5**
Ieyasu's Mausoleum **3**
Rinnoji Temple **10**

Sacred Bridge (Shinkyo) **11**
Statue of Shodo **10**
Taiyuinbyo Mausoleum **1**
Toshogu Shrine **4**
Yomeimon Gate **6**

LEGEND

🚏 Bus stop
ⓘ Information
⊠ Post Office

JAPAN
Nikko ● ★ TOKYO

ACCOMMODATIONS

Annex Turtle Hotori-An **8**
Logette Sanbois **16**
Nikko Kanaya Hotel **12**
Turtle Inn **9**

DINING

Gyoza House **15**
Hippari Tako **13**
Main Dining Hall **12**
Masudaya **14**

TOSHUGU SHRINE AREA

Rinnoji Office

Ticket Office

Nishi-sando Bus Stop

Tamozawa Bus Stop

To Lake Chuzenji

Shinkyo (Sacred) Bridge

Shinkyo

Shinkyo Bus Stop

Ashikaga Bank

Post Office

City Hall

Stadium

Kirifuri Bridge

Nikko Police Station

Tobu-Nikko Sta.

JR-Nikko Sta.

1/8 mi
.125 km

235

Another tourist office, the **Nikko Information Center** (☎ 0288/54-2496), is located on the main road leading from the train station to Toshogu Shrine. It has English-speaking staff and lots of information in English about Nikko, including information on public hot springs. Open daily from 8:30am to 5pm.

GETTING AROUND   Toshogu Shrine and its mausoleum are on the edge of town, but you can walk from either the JR or Tobu train stations to the shrine in less than half an hour. Simply head straight out the main exit, pass the bus stands, and then turn right. There are signs pointing the way in English throughout town. Keep walking on this main road (you'll pass the Nikko Information Center about halfway down, on the left side, as well as souvenir shops) until you come to a T intersection with a vermilion-colored bridge spanning a river (about a 15-minute walk from the train stations). The stone steps opposite lead up the hill into the woods and to Toshogu Shrine. You can also travel from Tobu Station by bus, getting off at either the Shinkyo or Nishi Sando bus stop. The trip takes about 5 minutes.

WHAT TO SEE & DO

ON THE WAY TO THE SHRINE   The first indication that you're nearing the shrine is the vermilion-painted **Sacred Bridge** (Shinkyo), arching over the rushing Daiyagawa River. It was built in 1636, and for more than 3 centuries only shoguns and their emissaries were allowed to cross it. Even today, mortal souls like us are prevented from completely crossing it because of a barrier at one end.

Across the road from the Sacred Bridge are some steps leading uphill into a forest of cedar, where after a 5-minute walk you'll see a statue of **Shodo,** a priest who founded Nikko 1,200 years ago, at a time when mountains were revered as gods. Behind him is the first major temple, Rinnoji Temple, where you can buy a combination ticket for ¥900 ($7.50) that allows entry to Rinnoji Temple, Toshogu Shrine, neighboring Futarasan Shrine, and the other Tokugawa mausoleum, Taiyuinbyo. Once at Toshogu Shrine, you'll have to pay an extra ¥500 ($4.15) to see Ieyasu's tomb. Combination tickets are also sold at the entry to Toshogu Shrine which already include Ieyasu's tomb. It doesn't really matter where you buy your combination ticket, since you can always pay the extra fee to see sights not covered. A note for bus riders: If you take the bus to the Nishi Sando bus stop, the first place you'll come to is the Taiyuinbyo Mausoleum, where you can also purchase a combination ticket.

RINNOJI TEMPLE   Rinnoji Temple was founded by the priest Shodo in the 8th century, long before the Toshogu clan came onto the scene. Here you can visit the **Sanbutsudo Hall,** a large building that enshrines three 28-foot-high, gold-plated wooden images of Buddha. Perhaps the best thing to see at Rinnoji Temple, however, is its **Shoyo-en Garden** (opposite Sanbutsudo Hall), which requires a separate ¥300 ($2.50) admission. Completed in 1815 and typical of Japanese landscaped gardens of the Edo Period, this small strolling garden provides a different vista with each turn of the path, making it seem much larger than it actually is.

✪ TOSHOGU SHRINE   The most important and famous structure in Nikko is Toshogu Shrine, built by Tokugawa's grandson (and third Tokugawa shogun), Tokugawa Iemitsu, as an act of devotion. It seems that no expense was too great in creating the monument: Some 15,000 artists and craftspeople were brought to Nikko from all over Japan, and after 2 years' work they erected a group of buildings more elaborate and gorgeous than any other Japanese temple or shrine. Rich in colors and carvings, Toshogu Shrine is gilded with 2.4 million sheets of gold leaf

Impressions

(they could cover an area of almost 6 acres). The mausoleum was completed in 1636, almost 20 years after Ieyasu's death, and was most certainly meant to impress anyone who saw it as a demonstration of the Tokugawa shogunate's wealth and power.

Toshogu Shrine is set in a grove of magnificent ancient **Japanese cedars** planted over a 20-year period during the 1600s by a feudal lord named Matsudaira Masatsuna. Some 13,000 of the original trees are still standing, adding a sense of dignity to the mausoleum and the shrine.

You enter Toshogu Shrine via a flight of stairs that pass under a huge stone torii gateway, one of the largest in Japan. On your left is a five-story, 115-foot-high **pagoda.** Although normally pagodas are found only at temples, this pagoda is just one example of how both Buddhism and Shintoism are combined at Toshogu Shrine. After climbing a second flight of stairs, turn left, where you'll see the **Sacred Stable,** which houses a sacred white horse. Horses have long been dedicated to Shinto gods and are kept at shrines. Shrines also kept monkeys as well, since they were thought to protect horses from disease; look for the three monkeys carved above the stable door, fixed in the pose of "see no evil, hear no evil, speak no evil"— they're considered guardians of the sacred horse. Across from the stable is **Kami-Jinko,** famous for its carving by Kano Tanyu, who painted the images of the two elephants after reading about them but without ever seeing what they actually looked like.

At the next flight of stairs is **Yomeimon Gate,** considered to be the central showpiece of Nikko and popularly known as the Twilight Gate, implying that it could take you all day (until twilight) to see everything carved onto it. Painted in red, blue, and green, and decorated with gilding and lacquerwork, this gate has about 400 carvings of flowers, dragons, birds, and other animals. It's almost too much to take in at once and is very un-Japanese in its opulence, having more in common with Chinese architecture than the usual austerity of most Japanese shrines.

To the left of the Yomeimon Gate is the hall where the portable shrines are kept, as well as **Honchido Hall,** famous for its dragon painting on the ceiling. If you clap your hands under the painting, the echo supposedly resembles a dragon's roar. You also can visit the shrine's main sanctuary, the **Hai-den,** comprised of three halls: One was reserved for the imperial family, one for the shogun, and one (the central hall) for conducting ceremonies.

To the right of the main hall is the entrance to **Tokugawa Ieyasu's mausoleum.** If it's not already included in your combination ticket, admission is ¥500 ($4.15). After the ticket counter, look for the carving of a sleeping cat above the door, dating from the Edo Period and famous today as a symbol of Nikko (you'll find many reproductions in area souvenir shops). Beyond that are 200 stone steps leading past cedars to Tokugawa's tomb. After the riotous colors of the shrine, the tomb seems surprisingly simple.

Toshogu Shrine is open daily from 8am to 5pm (to 4pm in winter); you must enter by 4:30pm (by 3:30pm in winter).

FUTARASAN SHRINE   Directly to the west of Toshogu Shrine is Futarasan Shrine, the oldest building in the district (from 1617), which has a pleasant garden and is dedicated to the gods of mountains surrounding Nikko. On the shrine's grounds is the so-called **ghost lantern,** enclosed in a small wooden structure. According to legend, it used to come alive at night and sweep around Nikko in the form of a ghost. It apparently scared one of the guards so much that he struck it with his sword, the marks of which are still visible on the lamp's rim.

Past Futarasan Shrine is **Taiyuinbyo Mausoleum,** the final resting place of Iemitsu, the third Tokugawa shogun. Completed in 1653, it's not nearly so ornate as Toshogu Shrine—nor as crowded, making it a pleasant last stop on your tour of Nikko.

WHERE TO STAY

If it's peak season or a weekend, it's best to reserve a room in advance. Otherwise, in the off-season you can also make a reservation upon arrival at Nikko Tobu Station, either at the **tourist information counter,** where the service is free, or the **accommodation-reservation window** (☎ 0288/54-0864), which charges a ¥200 to ¥500 ($1.65 to $4.15) fee but is familiar with the accommodations in the area and will make all arrangements for you.

MODERATE

✪ **Nikko Kanaya Hotel.** 1300 Kami-Hatsuishi, Nikko City, Tochigi Prefecture 321-1401. ☎ **0288/54-0001.** Fax 0288/53-2487. www.kanayahotel.co.jp/. 76 units (65 with shower/tub and toilet, 11 with toilet only). MINIBAR TV TEL. ¥8,000 ($67) single with toilet only, ¥10,000 ($83) single with shower and toilet, ¥11,000–¥35,000 ($92–$292) single with bathroom; ¥10,000 ($83) twin with toilet only, ¥12,000 ($100) twin with shower and toilet, ¥13,000–¥40,000 ($108–$333) twin with bathroom. ¥3,000 ($25) extra on Sat and eve before national holidays; ¥5,000–¥10,000 ($42–$83) extra in peak season. AE, DC, JCB, MC, V. Bus: From Nikko Tobu Station to the Shinkyo stop, a 5-min. ride. On foot: 15 min. from Tobu Station.

This distinguished-looking, old-fashioned place on a hill above the Sacred Bridge is the most famous hotel in Nikko, combining the rustic heartiness of a European country lodge with elements of old Japan. It was founded in 1873 by the Kanaya family, who wished to offer accommodations to foreigners, mainly missionaries and businessmen looking to escape the heat and humidity of Tokyo. The present complex, built in spurts over the past 100 years, has a rambling, delightfully old-fashioned atmosphere that fuses Western architecture with Japanese craftsmanship. Through the decades it has played host to a number of VIPs, from Charles Lindbergh to Indira Gandhi to Shirley MacLaine; Frank Lloyd Wright left a sketch for the bar fireplace, which was later built and is still there.

All rooms are Western-style twins, with the differences in price based on room size, view, and facilities. They're rather simple, but are cozy and have character; some have antiques. None have air-conditioning, since the high altitude of Nikko rarely warrants it. If you want to stay in the best room in the house, a corner room in the 62-year-old wing where the emperor once stayed, you'll pay the highest price above.

Dining: A small shabu-shabu restaurant, a wonderful dining hall serving Western food (see "Where to Dine," below), an inexpensive coffee shop with a nice view, and a bar.

Amenities: Souvenir shops, small outdoor heated pool free for hotel guests (open in summer only), outdoor skating rink (in winter), Japanese garden.

INEXPENSIVE

✪ **Annex Turtle Hotori-An.** 8–28 Takumi-cho, Nikko City, Tochigi Prefecture 321-1433. ☎ **0288/53-3663** for reservations or 0288/53-5828. Fax 0288/53-3883. www. sunfield.ne.jp/~turtle. E-mail: turtle@sunfield.ne.jp. 11 units (all with bathroom). TV TEL. ¥5,800 ($48) per person. AE, MC, V. Bus: From Nikko stations to the Sogo Kaikan-mae stop, a 7-min. ride; then a 9-min. walk.

Owned by the friendly family that runs Turtle Inn (see below), this is one of my favorite places to stay in Nikko. One dip in the hot-springs bath overlooking the river will tell you why; at night, you're lulled to sleep by the sound of the rushing waters. A modern structure, it's located in a nice rural setting on a quiet street with a few other houses. A plentiful Western-style breakfast costs ¥1,000 ($8.35) in the pleasant living area/dining room. For dinner, you can go to the nearby Turtle Inn, or buy a pizza from the freezer and microwave it yourself. There's also a communal refrigerator where you can store your own food and drink, as well as a coin-operated laundry. All rooms except one are Japanese style.

Logette Sanbois. 1560 Tokorono, Nikko City, Tochigi Prefecture 321-1421. ☎ **0288/ 53-0082.** Fax 0288/53-5212. www.sunfield.ne.jp/~sanboa/. E-mail: l-sanboa@sunfield.ne.jp. 9 units (4 with bathroom). A/C TEL. ¥5,000 ($42) single without bathoom, ¥5,500 ($46) single with bathroom; ¥9,000 ($75) twin without bathroom, ¥10,000 ($83) twin with bathroom. Japanese breakfast ¥800 ($6.65) extra; Japanese dinner ¥2,700 ($22.50) extra. AE, DC, JCB, MC, V. A 15-min. walk from Tobu Station, on the opposite side of the Daiyagawa River.

This two-story wooden establishment, with a rustic, cabin-like interior, has an idyllic spot on a mountainside, surrounded by forest. It's owned by the friendly Ogihara family. Two of the rooms are Japanese style, with a private bathroom and even a balcony. The rest are Western style with and without bathrooms. Even if you have a private bath, you might want to use the public one—it boasts a large window overlooking the woods.

Turtle Inn. 2–16 Takumi-cho, Nikko City, Tochigi Prefecture 321-1433. ☎ **0288/53-3168.** Fax 0288/53-3883. www.sunfield.ne.jp/~turtle. E-mail: turtle@sunfield.ne.jp. 10 units (3 with bathroom). TV. ¥8,400 ($70) double without bathroom, ¥10,000 ($83) double with bathroom. AE, MC, V. Bus: From Nikko stations to the Sogo Kaikan-mae stop, a 7-min. ride; then a 5-min. walk.

This excellent pension, a Japanese Inn Group member, is located within walking distance of Toshogu Shrine, in a new two-story house on a quiet side street beside the Daiyagawa River. It's run by the friendly Fukuda family. Mr. Fukuda speaks English and is very helpful in planning a sightseeing itinerary for the area. Rooms are bright and cheerful, in both Japanese and Western styles; the five tatami rooms are without bath. Excellent Western dinners (with Japanese touches) and Japanese dinners are available for ¥2,000 ($17), as are Western breakfasts for ¥1,000 ($8.35). Mashiko pottery is used for tableware. Be sure to order dinner by 10am; dinner is not available on Sunday.

WHERE TO DINE
MODERATE

✪ **Main Dining Hall.** Nikko Kanaya Hotel, 1300 Kami-Hatsuishi. ☎ **0288/54-0001.** Reservations recommended during peak season. Main dishes ¥2,500–¥6,000 ($21–$50); set lunches ¥3,500–¥10,000 ($29–$83). AE, DC, JCB, MC, V. Daily noon–3pm and 6–8pm. A 15-min. walk from Nikko Tobu Station. CONTINENTAL.

Even if you don't spend the night here, you might want to come for a meal in the hotel's quaint dining hall with its wood-carved pillars, one of the best places in town for lunch. Since it's beside the Sacred Bridge, only a 10-minute walk from Toshogu Shrine, you can easily combine it with your sightseeing tour of Nikko. I suggest Nikko's specialty, locally caught rainbow trout, available in three different styles of cooking. I had mine cooked Kanaya style, covered with soy sauce, sugar, and sake, grilled and served whole. The best bargain is the set lunch, available until 3pm, which comes with soup, salad, a main dish such as trout, bread or rice, and dessert. Lobster, salmon, chicken, and other Western fare are also listed on the English menu.

Masudaya. 439 Ichiyamachi. ☎ **0288/54-2151.** Reservations recommended for private rooms. Set meals ¥3,950 ($33) and ¥5,340 ($44.50). No credit cards. Fri–Wed 11am–4pm (open Thurs if a holiday). A 5-min. walk from Nikko Tobu Station. On the left side of the main street leading from Tobu Station to Toshogu Shrine, just before the fire station. YUBA.

Only two fixed-price meals are served at this Japanese-style, 80-year-old restaurant, both featuring *yuba*. A high-protein food made from soybeans, yuba is a local specialty produced only in Kyoto and Nikko. Until 100 years ago it could be eaten only by priests and members of the imperial family. Now you can enjoy it, too, along with such sides as rice, sashimi, soup, fried fish, and vegetables. Dining is either in a common dining hall or, for the more expensive meals, in private tatami rooms upstairs, for which you should make a reservation.

INEXPENSIVE

Gyoza House. 257 Matsubara-cho. ☎ **0288/53-0494.** Main dishes ¥450–¥1,050 ($3.75–$8.75). No credit cards. Summer, daily 11am–8pm. Winter, daily 11am–7:30pm. A 2-min. walk from Nikko Tobu Station. On the left side of the main street leading from Tobu Station to Toshogu Shrine. GYOZA.

This simple restaurant serving up *gyoza* (Chinese dumplings) and *ramen* (noodle-and-vegetable soup) is easy to spot, with its red awning and bright green facade. An English menu and pictures on the wall make ordering a cinch, whether it's the typical *yaki-gyoza* (sauteed gyoza) or one of the more unique dishes like curry gyoza, shoyu gyoza (in a soup broth), or spicy ramen.

⑦⑤ **Hippari Tako.** 1011 Kami-Hatsuishi. ☎ **0288/53-2933.** Main dishes ¥500–¥800 ($4.15–$6.65). No credit cards. Daily 11am–8pm. A 15-min. walk from Nikko Tobu Station. On the left side of the main street leading from Toshogu Shrine, 1 min. before the Nikko Kanaya Hotel and the Sacred Bridge. NOODLES.

This tiny, three-table establishment is under the caring supervision of motherly Miki-san, who serves a limited selection of noodle dishes, including ramen and stir-fried noodles with vegetables as well as *onigiri* (rice balls) and yakitori. The walls, covered with business cards and messages left by appreciative guests from around the world, are testimony to both the tasty meals and Miki-san's warm hospitality. There's an English menu.

3 Mashiko

62 miles (99km) N of Tokyo

Mashiko is a small village known throughout Japan for its *Mashiko-yaki*, distinctive, heavy, country-style pottery. A visit to Mashiko can be combined with an overnight trip to Nikko (see above), since both are not far from the town of Utsunomiya, north of Tokyo. Since the major attraction in Mashiko is its pottery shops and kilns and there's little in the way of restaurants and accommodations, I suggest coming here just for the day, returning to Tokyo or traveling on to Nikko before nightfall. Plan on spending about three hours in Mashiko itself, plus several hours for transportation.

Mashiko's history as a pottery town began in 1853, when a potter discovered ideal conditions, with the nearby mountain clay and red pine wood for firing. It wasn't until 1930, however, that Mashiko gained national fame, when the late Hamada Shoji, designated a "living national treasure," built a kiln here and introduced Mashiko ware throughout Japan. Other potters have since taken up his technique, producing ceramics for everyday use, including plates, cups, vases, and tableware. Altogether, there are about 50 pottery shops in Mashiko, along with about 300 kilns, where you can simply wander in, watch the craftspeople at work, and even try your own hand at throwing or glazing a pot. Pottery fairs, held twice a year in May and November, attract visitors from throughout Japan.

ESSENTIALS
GETTING THERE
By Train   You must first take a train from Tokyo to Utsunomiya, and then transfer there for a bus that will take you to Mashiko. If you have a Japan Rail Pass, the easiest and fastest way to reach Utsunomiya is aboard the **Tohoku Shinkansen,** which departs from Tokyo Station every 15 to 30 minutes and arrives in Utsunomiya approximately 50 minutes later (you can also catch the Shinkansen at Ueno Station). If you don't have a Rail Pass, the cost of the Shinkansen from Tokyo Station to Utsunomiya is ¥4,290 ($36). Otherwise, take the **JR Tohoku Honsen** rapid train from Ueno Station, which departs approximately every hour, takes 90 minutes to reach Utsunomiya JR Station, and costs ¥1,890 ($16) one-way. If you're stopping off in Mashiko on your way to or from Nikko, you may wish to save yourself the hassle of buying extra tickets by taking the **Tobu train** from Asakusa to Tobu Utsunomiya Station and Nikko Tobu Station (see "Nikko," above).

By Bus   Upon reaching Utsunomiya JR Station, take the west exit, go down the stairs and walk straight out of the station one block to the bridge and turn left. The bus stop, called **Miyanohashi,** is on the left (about a 3-minute walk from the station). Buses operated by the Toya Bus company depart from here (and from Tobu Utsunomiya Station) approximately every hour, taking about one hour to reach Mashiko and costing ¥1,100 ($9.15) one-way.

VISITOR INFORMATION   Although inconveniently located when arriving from Tokyo by bus, there's a **tourist information office** located at the tiny Mashiko train station, open daily 8:30am to 5pm (☎ **0285/70-1120**).

WHAT TO SEE & DO
Upon reaching Mashiko, get off the bus at the **Sankokanmae bus stop.** Here, to the left if continuing in the same direction as you've been going, is the **Mashiko Reference Collection Museum,** or ⑦⑥ **Mashiko Sankokan** (☎ **0285/72-5300**), a small compound of several thatch-roofed farmhouses and exhibition halls that served as Hamada Shoji's workshop and home from 1925 until his death in 1978 at the age of 83. Galleries here showcase about 30 of his works, as well as his private collection of Eastern and Western glass, ceramics, fabrics, furniture, and paintings, including pieces by Bernard Leach and Kanjiro Kawai. You can also see his "climbing kiln," built along the slope of a hill. Admission is ¥800 ($6.65) for adults, half price for children. Open Tuesday through Sunday 9:30am to 4:30pm; closed New Year's and the month of February.

A seven-minute walk from Mashiko Sankokan (reached by backtracking in the direction of Tokyo and turning left at the first stoplight) is the **Ceramic Art Messe Mashiko,** or Togei Messe Mashiko (☎ **0285/72-7555**), a visitor's complex devoted to pottery. The Togei-kan Museum displays works by Hamada, as well as pottery from Mashiko and other areas of Japan. A former thatched home belonging to Hamada is also here, as well as a pottery school and kiln. Admission is ¥600 ($5) for adults, half price for children. It's open Thursday to Tuesday 9:30am to 5pm (to 4pm in winter).

SHOPPING

The main reason people come to Mashiko is to shop. Beside the Togei Messe complex is one of the largest shops, the (77) **Mashikoyaki Kyohan Center** (☎ 0285/72-4444), open daily from 8:30am to 6pm. On the other side of the Kyohan Center is the main street of Mashiko, where you'll find dozens of shops offering a wide variety of pottery produced by the town's potters. Simply wander in and out—you're sure to find something that pleases you. Hiroshi Higeta's shop and indigo-dying thatched cottage, filled with 72 indigo vats using techniques passed down from generation to generation for more than 200 years, also make an interesting stop (☎ 0285/72-3162).

4 Yokohama

20 miles (32km) S of Tokyo

There are few attractions in Yokohama to warrant a visit if you're just in Japan for a short time. However, if you find yourself in Tokyo for an extended period, Yokohama is a pleasant destination for an easy day trip.

A rather new city in Japan's history books, Yokohama was nothing more than a tiny fishing village when Commodore Perry arrived in the mid-1800s and demanded that Japan open its doors to the world. The village was selected by the shogun as one of several ports to be opened for international trade, transforming it from a backwater to Japan's most important gateway. Yokohama subsequently grew by leaps and bounds, and was a pioneer when it came to Western goods and services, boasting Japan's first bakery (1860), photo studio (1862), telephone (1869), beer brewery (1869), cinema (1870), daily newspaper (1870), public rest room (1871), and ice cream (1879).

Now Japan's second-largest city, with a population of 3.3 million, Yokohama is still an important international port and supports a large international community, with many foreigners residing in the section called the Bluff. Yokohama has an especially large Chinese population and Japan's largest Chinatown, whose restaurants serve as a mecca for hungry Tokyoites. Befitting a city known for its firsts, Yokohama has been developing Japan's largest urban development project to date, the **Minato-Mirai 21,** with a conference center, museums, hotels, and restaurants. Yokohama also boasts a beautiful garden, a handful of specialty museums, and several amusement parks. Hard to imagine that a mere 140-some years ago, Yokohama was a village of 100 houses.

ESSENTIALS

GETTING THERE Because many Yokohama residents work in Tokyo, it's as easy to get to Yokohama as it is to get around Tokyo. Fares average ¥300 to ¥450 ($2.50 to $4.15), depending on which line you take and which station you start from. Most convenient is probably the **JR Keihin-Tohoku Line,** which travels through Ueno, Tokyo, Yurakucho, Shimbashi, and Shinagawa stations before continuing on to Yokohama and Kannai stations, with the journey from Tokyo Station to Yokohama Station taking approximately 40 minutes. The **JR Yokosuka Line** and **JR Tokaido Line** are the quickest, traveling between Tokyo Station and

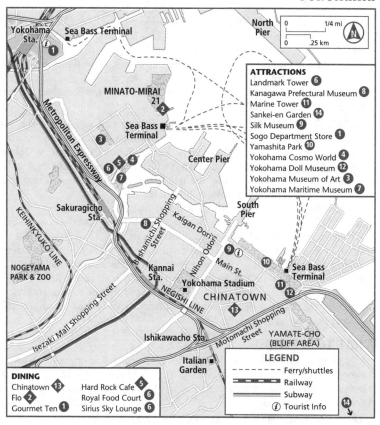

ATTRACTIONS
Landmark Tower 6
Kanagawa Prefectural Museum 8
Marine Tower 11
Sankei-en Garden 14
Silk Museum 9
Sogo Department Store 1
Yamashita Park 10
Yokohama Cosmo World 4
Yokohama Doll Museum 12
Yokohama Museum of Art 3
Yokohama Maritime Museum 7

LEGEND
- - - - - Ferry/shuttles
▬▬▬ Railway
═══ Subway
ⓘ Tourist Info

DINING
Chinatown 13   Hard Rock Cafe 5
Flo 2   Royal Food Court 6
Gourmet Ten 1   Sirius Sky Lounge 6

Yokohama Station in about 30 minutes, with stops in Shimbashi and Shinagawa along the way. The **Keihinkyuko Line** (also shortened to Keikyu) stops at Asakusa, Shimbashi, and Shinagawa stations before continuing to Yokohama Station, with the trip from Shinagawa taking about 50 minutes. From Shibuya, take the express (not the local, which makes too many stops) **Tokyu-Toyoko Line** to Yokohama in about 30 minutes.

VISITOR INFORMATION   There are several tourist information centers in Yokohama. At Yokohama Station, take the east exit to the front of Sogo department store, where you'll find the **Yokohama Tourist Information office** (☎ 045/441-7300; open daily 10am to 6pm). Probably the most convenient and easiest-to-find branch of the **Yokohama Municipal Tourist Association** (☎ 045/211-0111; open Sunday through Thursday 9am to 6pm; Friday, Saturday and holidays except New Year's 9am to 8pm) is in a kiosk outside the Sakuragi-cho subway station, in the direction of Minato-Mirai 21 and its Landmark Tower. A larger office is located in the Sangyo Boeki Center, 2 Yamashita-cho, Naka-ku (☎ 045/641-4759; open Monday to Saturday 10am to 6pm), an easy walk from Kannai Station and close to the Silk Center and Yamashita Park. All offices are among the best and most efficient I've come across in Japan, and the English-language map and city brochure are excellent. The staff speaks English, gives directions, and can give you all kinds of brochures on the city. It can also arrange for you to visit with a Japanese family under Yokohama's **Home-Visit System** (see "Minding Your P's & Q's," in appendix A), but be sure to call to set up the appointment at least 2 hours in advance of your intended visit (a day in advance is even better).

Next door to the city tourist office, in the Silk Center, is the **Kanagawa Prefectural Tourist Office** (☎ 045/681-0007; open Monday through Friday 9am to 5:30pm), where you can also get information on Hakone and Kamakura, both in Kanagawa Prefecture.

GETTING AROUND　Yokohama Station is connected to Sakuragi-cho and Kannai stations, which are close to most of Yokohama's attractions, by commuter train, subway, bus, and boat. Both the **JR Keihin-Tohoku Line** and the **Tokyu-Toyoko Line** from Tokyo pass through Yokohama Station and continue on to Sakuragi-cho and Kannai stations. Sakuragi-cho Station is the second stop from Yokohama Station by train or subway, Kannai the third.

The most fun way to get from Yokohama Station to the attractions around Sakuragi-cho and Kannai is via the **Sea Bass shuttle boat.** Take the east exit from Yokohama Station and follow the signs; boats depart every 15 to 30 minutes from a pier outside the second floor of Sogo department store. They deposit passengers at Minato-Mirai 21 (near Sakuragi-cho Station) in 10 minutes or at Yamashita Park (near Kannai Station) in 20, with fares costing ¥350 ($2.90) and ¥600 ($5) respectively (children pay half-fare). The trip affords a good view of Yokohama's skyline, especially the ongoing development of Minato-Mirai 21, and is considerably cheaper than the harbor cruises offered.

WHAT TO SEE & DO

A good plan for sightseeing would be to visit Sogo department store with its *ukiyo-e* (woodblock print) museum, take the Sea Bass to Minato-Mirai 21 for the sights there, take the subway or walk to Kannai and Yamashita Park, and then board bus no. 8 for Sankei-en Garden.

AROUND YOKOHAMA STATION　The biggest attraction here is **Sogo,** 2–18–1 Takashima (☎ 045/465-2111; take the east exit from the station), Japan's second-largest department store (Tokyo's Tobu in Ikebukuro is the largest, while Ikebukuro's Seibu is third). It employs 5,000 sales clerks, who serve as many as 150,000 customers a day—a number that can swell to double that on weekends. On the sixth floor is the **Sogo Museum of Art,** which features changing exhibitions as well as a traditional crafts department where you can shop for pottery, traditional blue-dyed clothing, kimono, chopsticks, and souvenirs. On the 10th floor are branches of famous restaurants.

But probably the best thing to do in Sogo is to visit the sixth-floor **Hiraki Ukiyo-e Museum** or Hiraki Ukiyoe Bijitsukan (☎ 045/465-2233), a delightful museum devoted exclusively to woodblock prints. It has an impressive 8,000 prints in its collection; exhibits in the one room change monthly. Tickets, purchased at vending machines outside the museum entrance, cost ¥500 ($4.15) for adults, ¥400 ($3.35) for students, and ¥300 ($2.50) for children.

Sogo is open daily from 10am to 7pm (closed some Tuesdays). From here, you can take the Sea Bass shuttle boat, described above, to Minato-Mirai 21 or Yamashita Park, or take the subway or commuter train.

AROUND SAKURAGICHO STATION　There's no mistaking the **Minato-Mirai 21** when you see it. If you approach from the harbor via the Sea Bass, it will look like a vision of the future, a city not of this planet, with its awe-inspiring monolithic buildings. Already boasting a huge state-of-the-art convention facility, three first-class hotels, Japan's tallest building, office buildings, two great museums, and an amusement park, the area is still under construction; upon completion, it will encompass 460 acres housing 10,000 residents and employing 190,000. It's all a bit too sterile for my taste, but its two museums make a visit here worthwhile.

If you arrive by train or subway, take the moving walkway that connects Sakuragi-cho Station to the Landmark Tower in Minato-Mirai 21 in 5 minutes.

For a bird's-eye view of not only Minato-Mirai 21 but all of Yokohama, head for Japan's tallest skyscraper, the **Landmark Tower.** The fastest elevator in the world will whisk you up 900 feet in about 40 seconds to the 69th floor, where there's an observation room called **Sky Garden** (☎ 045/222-5030). From here you can see the harbor with its container port and Yokohama Bay Bridge, as well as almost the entire city and even, on clear days in winter, Mt. Fuji. It costs ¥1,000 ($8.35) for adults, ¥800 ($6.65) for seniors, ¥500 ($4.15) for elementary and junior-high students, and ¥200 ($1.65) for children. Open daily from 10am to 10pm (to 9pm October through June). For dining options in Landmark Tower, see "Where to Dine," below.

It would be hard to miss **Yokohama Cosmo World** (☎ 045/221-0232), an amusement park spread along both sides of a canal: It boasts one of the largest Ferris wheels in the world. Other diversions include a roller coaster that looks like it dives right into a pond (but vanishes instead into a tunnel), a haunted house, a simulation theater with seats that move with the action, kiddie rides, a games arcade, and much more. Admission is free, but rides cost extra, usually ¥500 ($4.15) each. It's open daily 11:30am to 8pm (11am to 10pm July 20 through August).

The most important thing to see at Minato-Mirai 21 is the **Yokohama Museum of Art,** 3–4–1 Minato-Mirai (☎ 045/221-0300), which emphasizes works by Western and Japanese artists since the 1850s. The museum's ambitious goal is to collect and display works reflecting the mutual influence between the modern art of Europe and that of Japan since the opening of Yokohama's port in 1859. The light and airy building, designed by Kenzo Tange and Urtec Inc., features exhibits from its permanent collection—which includes works by Cézanne, Picasso, Matisse, Leger, Max Ernst, and Dali—that change three times a year, as well as special exhibits on loan from other museums. Open Friday through Wednesday from 10am to 6pm. Admission for the permanent collection is ¥500 ($4.15) for adults, ¥300 ($2.50) for high-school and college students, and ¥100 (85¢) for children, with special exhibitions costing more.

Maritime buffs should check out the **Yokohama Maritime Museum,** 2–1–1 Minato-Mirai (☎ 045/221-0280), which concentrates on Yokohama's history as a port, beginning with the arrival of Perry's "Black Ships." Other displays chart the evolution of ships from Japan and around the world from the 19th century to the present, with lots of models of everything from passenger ships to oil tankers. Kids like the three telescopes connected to cameras placed around Yokohama and the captain's bridge with a steering wheel; sailing fans enjoy touring the 320-foot, 4-masted Nippon-maru moored nearby, built in 1930 as a sail training ship for students of the merchant marines. Admission is ¥600 ($5) for adults and ¥300 ($2.50) for children. Open Tuesday through Sunday from 10am to 5pm (to 6:30pm in July and August, to 4:30pm November through February).

History buffs should wander over to the **Kanagawa Prefectural Museum,** 5–60 Minaminaka-dori (☎ 045/201-0926), about a 7-minute walk from either Sakuragi-cho or Kannai Station. It's housed in a Renaissance-style building constructed in 1904 as the nation's first modern foreign-exchange bank, but the interior has been completely renovated. Start by taking the escalator up to the third floor, where you'll begin a chronological odyssey through Kanagawa Prefecture's history, from the Paleolithic Period 30,000 years ago to the opening of Yokohama Port and the modernization of Japan. I found the model villages throughout the various periods especially fascinating. Check out the four large-scale drawings of foreigners dating from the 19th century—they have distinct Japanese features despite blue eyes. (The one on the left is Commodore Perry.) There are also models of both Perry's ships and of Japan's first train, which ran between Tokyo and Yokohama. Open Tuesday through Sunday from 9:30am to 5pm; admission is ¥300 ($2.50) for adults, ¥200 ($1.65) for students, free for seniors and children.

AROUND KANNAI STATION & YAMASHITA PARK   Kannai Station is three stops by subway from Yokohama Station. A more picturesque method of transportation is the Sea Bass shuttle boat, which connects Yamashita Park with Yokohama Station and Minato-Mirai 21. (See "Getting Around," above.)

Laid out after the huge 1923 earthquake that destroyed much of Tokyo and Yokohama, Yamashita Park is Japan's first seaside park, a pleasant place for a stroll along the waterfront, where you have a view of the city's mighty harbor.

Across the gingko-lined street from Yamashita Park are two worthwhile special-interest museums. At the west end (closest to Minato-Mirai 21) is the Silk Center, where you'll find both the prefectural tourist office and the excellent ✪ **Silk Museum,** 1 Yamashita-cho, Naka-ku (☎ **045/641-0841**). For many years after Japan opened its doors, silk was its major export, and most of it was shipped to the rest of the world from Yokohama, the nation's largest raw-silk market. In tribute to the role silk has played in Yokohama's history, this museum has displays showing the metamorphosis of the silkworm and process by which silk is obtained from cocoons, all well-documented in English; from April to October you can even observe live cocoons and silk worms at work (compared to the beauty they produce, silk worms are amazingly ugly). The museum also displays various kinds of silk fabrics as well as gorgeous kimono and antique Japanese costumes, many dating from the Nara and Heian periods. Don't miss this museum; surprisingly, it's never crowded. Open Tuesday through Sunday from 9am to 4:30pm; admission is ¥300 ($2.50) for adults, ¥200 ($1.65) for students, ¥100 (85¢) for children 6 to 11.

At the opposite end of Yamashita Park is the **Yokohama Doll Museum,** 18 Yamashita-cho (☎ **045/671-9361**), which houses approximately 2,000 dolls from 130 countries around the world. Its main floor displays antique dolls, including those produced by such famous doll makers as Lenci and Jumeau, as well as dolls from around the world dressed in native costume. The upstairs floor is devoted to Japanese dolls, including folk dolls traditionally sold at shrines and temples, classical Edo-Period dolls, *hina* (elaborate dolls representing the empress and emperor, used for the March Hina festival) and *kokeshi* (simple wooden dolls). Open Tuesday through Sunday 10am to 5pm (to 7pm mid-July through August). Admission is ¥300 ($2.50) for adults, ¥150 ($1.25) for children.

Not far from Yamashita Park is **Chukagai,** Japan's largest Chinatown; see "Where to Dine," below.

✪ **SANKEI-EN GARDEN**   In my opinion, **Sankei-en Garden** (☎ **045/ 621-0634**) is the best reason to visit Yokohama. Although not old itself, this lovely park contains a number of historical buildings that were brought here from other parts of Japan, including Kyoto and Nara. All the buildings are situated around streams and ponds and surrounded by Japanese-style landscape gardens. The park, which is divided into an Inner Garden and Outer Garden, was laid out back in 1906 by Tomitaro Hara, a local millionaire who made his fortune exporting silk. As you wander along the gently winding pathways, you'll see a villa built in 1649 by the Tokugawa Shogunate clan, tea arbors, a 500-year-old three-story pagoda, and a farmhouse built in 1650 without the use of nails. The gardens are well-known for their blossoms of plums, cherries, and water lilies, but no matter what the season, the views here are beautiful.

Sankei-en is open daily from 9am to 5pm (you must enter the Inner Garden by 4pm, the Outer Garden by 4:30pm); admission is ¥300 ($2.50) for the Outer Garden, another ¥300 ($2.50) for the Inner Garden. The easiest way to reach Sankei-en Garden is by bus no. 8, which departs from platform No. 2 at Yokohama Station's east exit and winds its way past Sakuragi-cho Station, Chinatown, and through Kannai before reaching the Honmoku-Sankeien-mae bus stop 20 minutes later.

GREAT FOR KIDS   If you have children, you may wish to get on their good side by taking them to **Hakkeijima Sea Paradise,** Hakkeijima (☎ **045/788-8888**), a combination seaside amusement park and aquarium. Among the dozen thrill rides are a roller coaster that juts out over the sea, a fiber-glass boat that shoots the currents, a tower ride that lets you "fall" 350 feet at a scream-invoking speed, and a carousel. The aquarium features such popular animals as sea otters, Atlantic puffins, polar bears, penguins, and belugas; an underwater tunnel moves visitors past stingrays, moray eels, and exotic tropical fish. There are also marine mammal shows featuring dolphins, belugas, and seals. Admission is free, with separate charges for activities. The aquarium and its shows cost ¥2,450 ($20) for adults, ¥1,400 ($12) for children 6 to 15, and ¥700 ($5.85) for children 4 and 5. Individual thrill rides range from ¥300 to ¥1,000 ($2.50 to $8.35). Otherwise, a combination "free" pass good for everything (available only April through November) costs ¥4,900 ($41), ¥3,500 ($29) and ¥2,000 ($17) respectively.

The aquarium is open March through November, Monday through Friday from 10am to 8pm and weekends 9am to 9pm; December through February, Monday through Friday from 10am to 6pm and weekends from 10am to 8pm. It takes approximately 1 hour to reach Hakkeijima Sea Paradise from Yokohama Station. Take the Keihin Tohoku Line from Tokyo, Yokohama, Sakuragi-cho or Kannai stations to Shin-sugita, and then transfer to the Seaside Line to Hakkeijima Station; you can also take a shuttle boat that departs Minato-Mirai 21 every hour on the hour (less frequently in winter) for the 50-minute ride to Hakkeijima (¥2,000/$17 for adults, ¥1,000/$8.35 for children).

WHERE TO DINE

AROUND YOKOHAMA STATION   The most convenient place for a meal close to the station is **Gourmet Ten,** on the 10th floor of Sogo department store (☎ **045/465-2111;** open 11am to 10pm, closed some Tuesdays), which you can reach by taking the east exit from Yokohama Station. It features branches of many famous restaurants, including Tenichi, serving tempura; Shisen, a Chinese restaurant; Chikuyotei, a famous eel restaurant; and Sabatini, an Italian restaurant from Rome, with another branch in Tokyo. Other restaurants serve a range of Japanese specialties, from udon to Kobe beef. Since all restaurants have plastic-food displays outside their doors, ordering is easy. Set meals average ¥1,200 to ¥4,500 ($10 to 37.50). Most restaurants accept credit cards (those that do display them on the door).

MINATO-MIRAI 21'S LANDMARK TOWER   For casual, inexpensive, and fast dining, head to the Landmark Plaza shopping mall at the base of Landmark

Tower, where on the fifth floor you'll find the large, American-style **Royal Food Court,** with a half-dozen self-serve counters offering different kinds of foods. You can dine here for less than ¥1,200 ($10). Among the options are pizza, a salad bar, and Chinese. Some seats have a view of the harbor and Yokohama Bay Bridge. Open daily from 11am to 9:30pm.

I was a bit skeptical about a restaurant located in a convention center, but **Flo,** in the Pacifico Yokohama Exhibition Hall with an entrance on the seaward side (☎ 045/221-2615), is a classy yet reasonable choice for French cuisine, with white tablecloths, tall ceiling, and large windows overlooking Rinko Seaside Park and the bay. Lunch, served daily noon to 4pm, offers set meals ranging from ¥1,700 to ¥3,800 ($14 to $32) along with á-la-carte choices, while the dinner menu, available from 4 to 10pm daily, includes set courses starting at ¥3,800 ($32) and main dishes starting at ¥2,200 ($18) that include seafood and steaks.

For even more sophisticated surroundings, or just a romantic evening cocktail, take the elevator up to the 70th floor of Landmark Tower, where you'll find the Yokohama Royal Park Hotel Nikko's **Sirius Sky Lounge** (☎ 045/221-1111), with stunning seaside views. It serves a buffet lunch daily, from 11:30am to 2:30pm, with choices of Asian and continental dishes, costing ¥4,000 ($33) Monday through Friday and ¥5,000 ($42) weekends and holidays. At tea time, from 11:30am to 5pm daily, tea and cake sets start at ¥1,300 ($11), plus a ¥500 ($4.15) cover charge per person. From 5pm to 1am daily, Sirius is a cocktail lounge, with a very limited snack menu and cocktails starting at ¥1,100 ($9.15). There's live music, and a cover charge of ¥1,000 to ¥2,000 ($8.35 to $17) per person.

Finally, another good place for a drink or a hamburger is the local branch of the **Hard Rock Cafe,** located on the first floor of Queen's Square Yokohama Tower A (☎ 045/682-5626). Open Monday to Friday 11am to 1am, Friday and Saturday 11am to 3am, and Sunday and holidays 11am to 11pm.

CHUKAGAI (CHINATOWN)   Located in Yamashita-cho, a couple blocks inland from Yamashita Park, Chinatown has more than 100 restaurants and shops, lining one main street and dozens of offshoots. Tokyoites have long been coming to Yokohama just to dine here; many of the restaurants have been owned by the same family for generations. Most serve Cantonese food, with plastic-food displays, English menus, or pictures of their dishes, so your best bet is to simply wander around and let your budget be your guide. Most dishes run ¥800 to ¥3,000 ($6.65 to $25), and set lunches go for ¥800 to ¥1,200 ($6.65 to $10). Larger restaurants accept credit cards; those that do display them on the front door. Most Chinatown restaurants are open from 11am or 11:30am to 9:30pm or later; some close Tuesday or Wednesday, but there are always restaurants open. Among the larger, better-known ones are **Manchinro** (☎ 045/681-4004) and **Heichinro** (☎ 045/681-3001), both of which serve Cantonese food, including dim sum; and **Kaseiro** (☎ 045/681-2918), which serves Pekinese food.

Chinatown is about a 15-minute walk from Kannai Station or a 10-minute walk from Ishikawacho Station. For more information, call the **Chinatown Information Office** (☎ 045/662-1252).

5 Hakone

60 miles (96km) SW of Tokyo

Part of the Fuji-Hakone-Izu National Park, ✪ **Hakone** is one of the closest and most popular destinations for residents of Tokyo. Beautiful Hakone has about

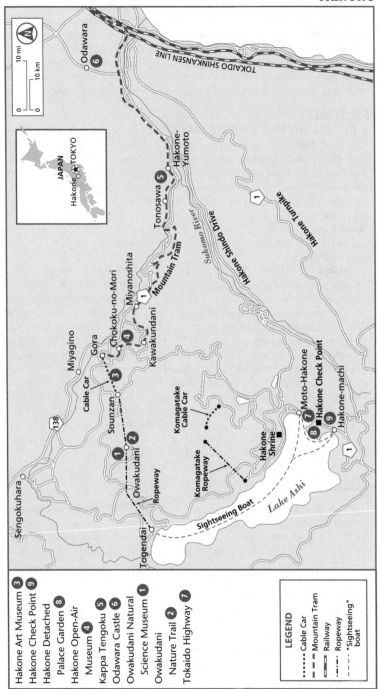

Hakone

LEGEND

- ▪▪▪▪ Cable Car
- ▬ ▬ ▬ Mountain Tram
- ▬▬ Railway
- ·—·—· Ropeway
- - - - "Sightseeing" boat

Hakone Art Museum ③
Hakone Check Point ⑨
Hakone Detached
Palace Garden ⑧
Hakone Open-Air
Museum ④
Kappa Tengoku ⑤
Odawara Castle ⑥
Owakudani Natural
Science Museum ①
Owakudani
Nature Trail ②
Tokaido Highway ⑦

everything a vacationer could wish for—hot-spring resorts, mountains, lakes, breathtaking views of Mt. Fuji, and interesting historical sites. You can tour Hakone as a day trip if you leave early in the morning and limit your sightseeing to a few key attractions, but adding an overnight stay near Lake Ashi or in the mountains is much more pleasant. If you plan to return to Tokyo, I suggest leaving your luggage in storage at your Tokyo hotel and traveling to Hakone with only an overnight bag.

ESSENTIALS

GETTING THERE & GETTING AROUND　　Getting to and around Hakone is half the fun! There's an easy, circular tour you can follow through Hakone that includes various forms of unique transportation: Starting out by train from Tokyo, you then switch to a small two-car tram that zigzags up the mountain, change to a cable car and then to a smaller ropeway, and end your trip with a boat ride across Lake Ashi, stopping off to see major attractions along the way. From Lake Ashi (from the villages of Togendai, Hakone-machi, or Moto-Hakone), you can then board a bus bound for Odawara Station (an hour's ride), where you can take the train back to Tokyo. From Togendai, there are also buses that go directly to Shinjuku Station.

Odakyu (☎ 03/3481-0103) operates the most convenient network of trains, buses, trams, cable cars, and boats to and around Hakone. The most economical way to see Hakone is with Odakyu's **Hakone Free Pass,** which, despite its name, isn't free but does give you a round-trip ticket on the express train from Shinjuku Station to Odawara or Hakone Yumoto and includes all modes of transportation in Hakone listed above and covered below. The pass avoids the hassle of having to buy individual tickets and also provides nominal discounts on most of Hakone's attractions. Several variations of the pass are available; the most common, valid for 3 days, costs ¥5,500 ($46) for adults (half-fare for children). The trip from Shinjuku to Odawara takes 1½ hours, with trains running approximately every 30 minutes. In Odawara you then transfer to the electric mountain tram. Some express trains go all the way to Hakone Yumoto, where you can then board the mountain tram, with the trip from Shinjuku taking 2 hours.

If you can, travel on a weekday. The **Hakone Weekday Pass,** which is good only Monday through Thursday, is valid for 2 days and costs ¥4,700 ($39) for adults, half-price for children. Not only are weekdays less crowded, but some hotels offer cheaper weekday rates, which means you'll save all around.

If time is of the essence, you can take the faster **Odakyu Romance Car,** which travels from Shinjuku all the way to Hakone Yumoto in 1½ hours and costs an extra ¥870 ($7.25), on top of the cost of the pass above. Passes can be purchased at any station of the Odakyu Railway, including Shinjuku Station and Odawara.

If you wish to start your trip in the opposite direction from the route I recommend below (say, if you're staying in one of the accommodations near Lake Ashi), take one of the **Odakyu buses** that departs every hour from Shinjuku Station's west exit bound for Togendai on Lake Ashi. The trip takes 2 hours and 10 minutes, with stops at Moto-Hakone on the way. Reservations are recommended.

VISITOR INFORMATION　　Before leaving Tokyo, stop off at the Tourist Information Center and pick up the "Hakone and Kamakura" leaflet, which lists the schedules for the extensive transportation network throughout the Hakone area. There's also a color brochure called "Hakone National Park," which includes sightseeing information and contains a map of the Hakone area. See "Visitor Information," in chapter 3 for TIC locations.

In Shinjuku Station, stop by the **Odakyu Sightseeing Service Center,** located on the ground floor near the west exit of Odakyu Shinjuku Station (☎ **03/5321-7887**); open daily 8am to 6pm, where you can obtain sightseeing information, purchase Hakone Free Pass tickets, and, if you wish, buy one- or two-day do-it-yourself package tours that include round-trip transportation to Hakone, meals, sightseeing, and hotel stays.

In Hakone Yumoto, there's the **Yumoto Tourist Office** (☎ **0460/5-5700**), open daily from 9am to 5:30pm (staffed by English-speaking volunteers only on weekdays). You can pick up more pamphlets on Hakone here and ask directions. It's a 2-minute walk from the Hakone Yumoto Station. Take a right out of the station onto the town's main street; the office is on the left.

WHAT TO SEE & DO

If you plan on spending only a day in Hakone, you should leave Tokyo very early in the morning and plan on visiting only a few key attractions—I recommend the **Hakone Open-Air Museum,** the **Owakudani Nature Trail,** and, if time permits, the **Hakone Check Point** and adjacent **Hakone Detached Palace Garden.**

If you're spending the night—and I strongly urge that you do—you can arrange your itinerary in a more leisurely fashion and devote more time to Hakone's attractions. You may wish to travel only as far as your hotel the first day, stopping at sights along the way and in the vicinity. The next day you could continue with the rest of the circuit through Hakone. If you want to do most of your sightseeing the first day, or are staying 2 nights in Hakone, you can travel all the way to Hakone-machi or Moto-Hakone on Lake Ashi and from there take a bus to all accommodations recommended below.

SCENIC RAILWAY TO GORA

Regardless of whether you travel via Shinkansen, the Odakyu Romance Car, or the ordinary Odakyu express, you'll end up at either Odawara Station, considered the gateway to Hakone, or Hakone Yumoto Station, located in Hakone itself. At either station, you can transfer to the **Hakone Tozan Railway,** a delightful, mountain-climbing two-car electric tram that winds its way through forests and over streams and ravines as it travels upward to Gora, making several switchbacks along the way. The entire trip from Hakone Yumoto Station to Gora takes only 45 minutes, but it's a beautiful ride, on a narrow track through the mountains. This is my favorite part of the whole journey. The trains, which run every 10 to 15 minutes, make about a half-dozen stops before reaching Gora, including **Tonosawa** and **Miyanoshita,** two hot-spring spa resorts with a number of old ryokan and hotels. Some of these ryokan date back several centuries, from the days when they were on the main thoroughfare to Tokyo, the old Tokaido Highway. Miyanoshita is also the best place for lunch. See "Where to Dine," and "Where to Stay," below.

As for things to do along the way, if you're changing from the Odakyu train to the electric tram in Odawara, consider making a short excursion to **Odawara Castle,** Odawara Joshi-koen (☎ **0465/23-1373**), especially if you won't have the opportunity to see any of Japan's more famous castles. A 10-minute walk from Odawara Station (take the east exit out of the station and turn right), this three-tiered, four-storied castle dates from 1416 but was rebuilt in 1960. Its keep contains a small historical museum relating to the castle, while the tower affords a panoramic view of the surrounding park. Admission is ¥400 ($3.35) for adults and ¥150 ($1.25) for children. It's open daily from 9am to 5pm.

In Hakone Yumoto, you can relax at ⑦⑧ **Kappa Tengoku** (☎ **0460/5-6121**), an open-air, hot-spring public bath located on a hill just a 2-minute walk behind Hakone Yumoto Station. It's probably the closest outdoor bath in the vicinity of Tokyo. Admission is ¥700 ($5.85) for those over 6, ¥400 ($3.35) for 2- to 6-year-olds. Open daily from 10am to 10pm. To get there from Hakone Yumoto Station, take a right, walk along the tracks, take the first right and go under the train tracks, and then take an immediate right again. Walk uphill and follow the sign (in kanji only) up the long flight of steps to what looks like a house. The baths, separated for men and women, are behind the house, set against a cliff under some trees. After your bath, you can recuperate at the small snack bar.

The most important stop on the Hakone Tozan Railway is the next-to-the-last stop, Chokoku-no-Mori, where you'll find the famous ✪ **Hakone Open-Air Museum** (*Chokoku-no-Mori Bijutsukan;* ☎ **0460/2-1161**) a minute's walk from the station. With the possible exception of views of Mt. Fuji, this museum is, in my opinion, Hakone's number-one attraction. Using nature itself as a dramatic back-drop, it showcases sculpture primarily of the 20th century in a spectacular setting of glens, formal gardens, ponds, and meadows. There are 700 sculptures on display, both outdoors and in several buildings, with works by Carl Milles, Emilio Greco, Manzu Giacomo, Jean Dubuffet, Willem de Kooning, Barbara Hepworth, and more than 20 pieces by Henry Moore. The Picasso Pavilion contains more than 200 works by Picasso, from pastels to ceramics, while the Picture Gallery displays paint-ings by Miro, Renoir, Kandinsky, Vlaminck, Utrillo, and Takeshi Hayashi. There are several installations geared toward children, where they can climb and play. I could spend all day here; count on staying at least two hours. Open daily from 9am to 5pm (until 4:30pm December through February). Admission is ¥1,600 ($13) for adults, ¥1,100 ($9.15) for students, and ¥800 ($6.65) for children. Your Hakone Free Pass gives you a ¥100 (85¢) discount.

BY CABLE CAR TO SOUNZAN

Cable cars leave Gora every 15 minutes and arrive 9 minutes later at the end sta-tion of Sounzan, making several stops along the way as they travel steeply uphill. One of the stops is Koen-Kami, which is only a minute away from the **Hakone Art Museum** (☎ **0460/2-2623**). This museum displays Japanese pottery and ceramics from the Jomon Period (around 4000 to 2000 B.C.) to the Edo Period. What makes this place particularly rewarding is the small but lovely moss garden, with a teahouse where you can sample some Japanese tea for ¥630 ($5.25). Open Friday through Wednesday from 9am to 4:30pm (to 4pm in winter). Admission is ¥900 ($7.50) for adults, ¥500 ($4.15) for students, and ¥300 ($2.50) for children.

BY ROPEWAY TO TOGENDAI

From Sounzan you board a ropeway with gondolas for a long haul over a mountain to Togendai on the other side, which lies beside Lake Ashi, known as Lake Ashinoko in Japanese. Note that the ropeway stops running at 5pm in summer and 4pm in winter.

Before reaching Togendai, get off at the first stop, Owakudani, the ropeway's highest point, to hike the 30-minute **Owakudani Nature Trail.** Owakudani means "Great Boiling Valley," and you'll soon understand how it got its name when you see (and smell) the sulfurous steam escaping from fissures in the rock, testimony to volcanic activity still present here. Most Japanese commemorate their trip here by buying boiled eggs cooked in the boiling waters, available at the small hut midway along the trail. Also located here is the **Owakudani Natural Science Museum**

(☎ 0460/4-9149), with displays on the fauna, flora, geology, and volcanic origins of Hakone. You can watch a 7-minute video covering the seasonal changes on Owakudani, learn about poisonous and edible local plants, and see the 23 different kinds of fish in Lake Ashi that make it such a popular destination for fishing fanatics. Most dramatic is the simulated eruption of Mt. Kami-yama in Hakone, which blew its top about 20,000 years ago, vividly portrayed with actual ground shaking, explosive sounds, and a light show. Open daily from 9am to 4:30 (to 4pm in winter); admission is ¥400 ($3.35) for adults, and ¥250 ($2.10) for children under 12.

ACROSS LAKE ASHI BY BOAT

From Togendai you can take a pleasure boat across Lake Ashi, also referred to as "Lake Hakone" in some English brochures. Believe it or not, two of the boats plying the waters are replicas of man-of-war pirate ships; a third is a replica Mississippi paddleboat. It takes about half an hour to cross the lake to Hakone-machi (also called simply Hakone; *machi* means city) and Moto-Hakone, two resort towns right next to each other on the southern edge of the lake. This end of the lake affords the best view of Mt. Fuji, one often depicted in tourist publications. Boats are in operation all year (though they run less frequently in winter and not at all in stormy weather), with the last boat departing around 5pm from the end of March to the end of November. There are also buses that connect Togendai with Moto-Hakone, Odawara, and Shinjuku.

If you're heading back to Tokyo, buses depart for Odawara near the boat piers in both Hakone-machi and Moto-Hakone. Otherwise, for more sightseeing, get off the boat in Hakone-machi, take a left, and then walk about 5 minutes on the town's main road, following the signs to the **Hakone Check Point** (☎ 0460/3-6635), or *Hakone Sekisho*, on a road lined with some souvenir shops. This is a reconstructed guardhouse, originally built in 1619 to serve as a checkpoint along the famous Tokaido Highway, which connected Edo (present-day Tokyo) with Kyoto. In feudal days, local lords, called *daimyo*, were required to spend alternate years in Edo, and their wives were kept on in Edo as hostages so that the lords wouldn't plan rebellions while in their homelands. This was one of the points along the highway where female travelers and guns were checked, primarily to keep women from fleeing Edo. Passes were necessary for travel, and although it was possible to sneak around it, male violators who were caught were promptly executed, while women suffered the indignation of having their heads shaven and were then given away to anyone who wanted them. You'll see displays relating to the Edo Period, including items used for travel, samurai armor, and life-size models re-enacting scenes inside a checkpoint. Open daily from 9am to 4pm (until 4pm in winter); admission is ¥200 ($1.65) for adults and ¥100 (85¢) for children.

Just beyond the Hakone Check Point, at the big parking lot with the traditional gate, is the **Hakone Detached Palace Garden** (*Onshi-Hakone-Koen*), which lies on a small promontory on Lake Ashi and has spectacular views of the lake and, sometimes, Mt. Fuji. Originally part of an imperial summer villa built in 1886, the garden is open free to the public 24 hours daily. It's a great place for wandering. On its grounds is the **Lakeside Observation Building** (open daily 9am to 4:30pm), with displays relating to the Hakone Palace, which was destroyed by earthquakes. For more information on either the Hakone Checkpoint or the Detached Palace Garden, call the **Hakone Tourist Office** (☎ 0460/5-5700).

If you take the northernmost exit from the garden, crossing a bridge, you'll see the neighboring resort town, **Moto-Hakone.** Across the highway and lined with ancient and mighty cedars is part of the old **Tokaido Highway** itself. During the

Edo Period, more than 400 cedars were planted along this important road, which today stretches 1¼ miles along the curve of Lake Ashi and makes for a pleasant stroll (unfortunately, though, a modern road has been built right beside the original one). Moto-Hakone is a 5-minute walk from the Detached Palace Garden.

WHEN YOU'RE DONE SIGHTSEEING FOR THE DAY

Buses depart for Odawara from both Hakone-machi and Moto-Hakone two to four times an hour. Be sure to check the time of the last departure; generally, it's around 8pm, but this can change with the season and day of the week. The bus to Odawara passes by several of the accommodations recommended below: the Fujiya Hotel, Ichinoyu, Naraya, and Moto-Hakone Guest House. Otherwise, the trip from Moto-Hakone takes approximately 30 minutes to Hakone Yumoto, where you can catch the Romance Car bound for Shinjuku, or 50 minutes to Odawara, where you can then catch the Odakyu express train back to Shinjuku.

WHERE TO STAY

Japan's ryokan sprang into existence to accommodate the stately processions of daimyo and shogun as they traversed the roads between Edo and the rest of Japan. Many of these ryokan were built along the Tokaido Highway, and some of the oldest are found in Hakone.

EXPENSIVE

✪ **The Fujiya Hotel.** 359 Miyanoshita, Hakone-machi, Ashigarashimo-gun 250-0404. ☎ **0460/2-2211.** Fax 0460/2-2210. www.fujiyahotel.co.jp. 146 units. A/C MINIBAR TV TEL. $122 single or double special foreigners' rate in 2000, $123 in 2001; $50 extra Sat. ¥20,000–¥35,000 ($167–$292) single or double; ¥5,000 ($42) extra weekends; ¥10,000 ($83) extra mid-Aug and New Year's. AE, DC, JCB, MC, V. Station: Miyanoshita, Hakone Tozan Railway (5 min.). Bus: From Odawara or Moto-Hakone to Miyanoshita Onsen stop (1 min.).

The Fujiya, which was established in 1878, is quite simply the grandest, most majestic old hotel in Hakone and one of the oldest and loveliest Western-style hotels in Japan. I love this hotel for its comfortably old-fashioned atmosphere, including such Asian touches as a Japanese-style roof, lots of windows, and wooden corridors. Staying here transports me to a gentler, and more genteel, past. There are five separate buildings, all different and added on at various times in the hotel's long history, but management has been meticulous in retaining its historic traditions; you get the feeling that almost nothing has changed through the decades. A land-scaped garden out back, with a waterfall, pond, greenhouse, and stunning views over the valley, is great for strolls and meditation. An outdoor pool, fed by thermal springs, occupies a corner of the garden, and there's also an indoor thermal pool and hot-spring public baths.

The rooms are old-fashioned and spacious, with high ceilings and antique furnishings; some even have claw-foot tubs. The most expensive rooms are the largest, but my favorite are those in the Flower Palace, which has an architectural style that reminds me of a Japanese temple. Note that the special rate for foreigners, which is based on the age of the hotel, is higher on weekends and is not available during Golden Week, the month of August, or New Year's. The accommodating front-desk personnel, all of whom have spent at least 1 year abroad, speak very good English. Even if you don't stay here, do come for a meal or tea. Highly recommended.

Dining/Diversions: The main dining hall is perhaps the best place for a meal in Hakone (see "Where to Dine," below). Afternoon high tea with scones and cinnamon toast is served in the charming tea lounge, which overlooks the garden, for ¥1,200 ($10). There's also a casual Western restaurant, a bar, and a Japanese restaurant.

A Note on Japanese Symbols

Many hotels, restaurants, attractions, and other establishments in Japan do not have signs giving their names in Roman (English-language) letters. The second appendix to this book lists the Japanese symbols for all such places described in this guide. Each set of characters representing an establishment name has a number in the appendix, which corresponds to the number that appears inside the oval before the establishment's name in the text. Thus, to find the Japanese symbol for, say, **Ichinoyu,** refer to no. 79 in appendix B.

Amenities: Indoor and outdoor pools (free for hotel guests), sauna, Jacuzzi, hot-spring public baths, landscaped garden, souvenir shops, mahjong room, game room, golf course.

(79) **Ichinoyu.** 90 Tonosawa, Hakone-machi, Ashigarashimo-gun 250-0315. ☎ **0460/ 5-5331.** Fax 0460/5-5335. 24 units. (12 with bathroom). A/C FRIDGE TV TEL. ¥9,800–¥14,800 ($82–$123) per person, including 2 meals. ¥1,500–¥6,000 ($12.50–$50) extra per person in Aug, Sat and holidays. AE, DC, JCB, MC, V. Station: Tonosawa, Hakone Tozan Railway (6 min.). Bus: From Odawara or Moto-Hakone to Tonosawa bus stop (2 min.).

Located near Tonosawa Station (on the Hakone Tozan Line) next to a roaring river, this delightful, rambling wooden building stands on a tree-shaded winding road that follows the track of the old Tokaido Highway. First opened more than 365 years ago, Ichinoyu is now in its 15th generation of owners. It claims to be the oldest ryokan in the area and was once honored by the visit of a shogun during the Edo Period.

The ryokan has only tatami rooms. The oldest rooms here date from the Meiji Period, more than 100 years ago. The two rooms I like the most are called Seseragi and Matsu. They're old-fashioned, consisting mainly of seasoned and weathered wood, and face the river. All rooms have refrigerators and safes. Old artwork, wall hangings, and paintings decorate the place, and some of the rooms have old wooden bathtubs. Both the communal tubs and the tubs in the rooms have hot water supplied from a natural spring. The price you pay depends on your room, the meals you select, and the time of year.

✪ **Naraya.** 162 Miyanoshita, Hakone-machi, Ashigarashimo-gun 250-0404. ☎ **0460/ 2-2411.** Fax 0460/7-6231. 20 units (19 with bathroom). TV TEL. ¥28,000–¥60,000 ($233–$500) per person, including 2 meals. AE, DC, JCB, MC, V. Station: Miyanoshita, Hakone Tozan Railway (5 min.). Bus: From Odawara or Moto-Hakone to Miyanoshita Onsen (1 min.).

Across the street from the Fujiya Hotel is Naraya, an elegant traditional Japanese inn with tiled roof, wooden walls, shoji screens, and hot-spring baths. Although the inn's history stretches back several hundred years, the present building is about a century old. The tatami rooms, all of which have refrigerators and tubs fed with hot-spring water, have inspiring views of the inn's large and beautiful landscape garden, open only to staying guests. This is a great place to relax and revel in nature's beauty, and the meals served are well worth the price of staying here.

INEXPENSIVE

Fuji-Hakone Guest House. 912 Sengokuhara, Hakone, Kanagawa 250-0631. ☎ **0460/ 4-6577.** Fax 0460/4-6578. hakone@pop21.odn.ne.jp. 12 units (none with bathroom). ¥5,000–¥6,000 ($42–$50) single; ¥10,000–¥12,000 ($83–$100) double; ¥15,000–¥16,000 ($125–$133) triple. Plus ¥150 ($1.25) local tax per person. Peak season and weekends ¥1,000–¥2,000 ($8.35–$17) extra. Western breakfast ¥800 ($6.65) extra. Minimum 2-night stay preferred. AE, MC, V. **Bus:** Hakone Tozan Bus (included in the Hakone Free Pass) from Togendai (10 min.) or from Odawara Station (50 min.) to the Senkyoro-mae stop (announced in English), then a 1-min. walk.

It's a bit isolated, but this Japanese Inn Group member offers inexpensive, spotlessly clean lodging in tatami rooms. This modern house, situated in tranquil surroundings set back from a tree-shaded road, is run by a man who speaks very good English and is happy to provide sightseeing information. Some of the rooms face the Hakone mountain range. Facilities include a public hot-spring bath, coin-operated laundry and dryer, a large lounge area with bilingual TV, and a communal refrigerator.

WHERE TO DINE

✪ **Main Dining Room.** In the Fujiya Hotel, 359 Miyanoshita. ☎ **0460/2-2211.** Reservations required for dinner. Set dinners ¥10,000–¥15,000 ($83–$125); lunch main dishes ¥1,500–¥3,000 ($12.50–$25). AE, DC, JCB, MC, V. Daily noon–2pm; 2 seatings (6 and 8pm) for dinner. **Station:** Miyanoshita, on the Hakone Tozan Railway (5 min.). CONTINENTAL.

Hakone's grandest, oldest hotel, conveniently located near a stop on the two-car Hakone Tozan Railway, is a memorable place for a good Western meal. The main dining hall, dating from 1930, is very bright and cheerful, with a high, intricately detailed ceiling, large windows with Japanese screens, a wooden floor, and white tablecloths. The views of the Hakone hills are impressive, and the service by bow-tied wait staff is attentive. For lunch you can have such dishes as pilaf, spaghetti, sandwiches, fried chicken, rainbow trout, and sirloin steak. The excellent dinners feature elaborate set courses or à la carte dishes ranging from scallops and grilled lamb to steaks. Afterward, be sure to tour the landscaped garden.

Restaurant Peacock Boat House. 3 Lake View Dr., Moto-Hakone. ☎ **0460/3-6668.** Set meals ¥2,000–¥2,400 ($17–$20). AE, DC, V. Fri–Wed 11am–7pm. Go right if exiting from the boat dock; if you're walking from Hakone-machi, it's to the left just after you've emerged from the old Tokaido Hwy. WESTERN.

This casual restaurant, which is decorated (as its name implies) as a boathouse, sits on the shore of Lake Ashi. It offers inexpensive set meals that include rainbow trout and chicken teriyaki, as well as some à la carte items such as beef curry rice and sandwiches. In summer, you can relax on the deck and watch the boats come and go.

6 Mount Fuji

62 miles (99km) SW of Tokyo

Mt. Fuji, affectionately called "Fuji-san" by the Japanese, has been revered since ancient times. Throughout the centuries Japanese poets have written about it, painters have painted it, pilgrims have flocked to it, and more than a few people have died on it. Without a doubt, this mountain has been photographed more than anything else in Japan.

Mt. Fuji is stunningly impressive. At 12,388 feet, it towers far above anything else around it, a cone of almost perfectly symmetrical proportions. Mt. Fuji is majestic, grand, and awe-inspiring. To the Japanese it symbolizes the very spirit of their country. Though it's visible on clear days from as far as 100 miles away, Fuji-san is, unfortunately, almost always cloaked in clouds. If you catch a glimpse of this mighty mountain (which you can sometimes do from the bullet train between Tokyo and Nagoya), consider yourself extremely lucky. One of the best spots for views of Mt. Fuji is **Hakone** (see above).

ESSENTIALS

GETTING THERE BY TRAIN & BUS   There are five ascending trails to the summit of Mt. Fuji (and five descending trails), each divided into 10 stages of unequal length, with most climbs starting at the Go-go-me, or the Fifth Stage. From Tokyo, Kawaguchiko Trail is the most popular and most easily accessible. The easiest way to reach Kawaguchiko Trail's Fifth Stage is by **bus** from Shinjuku Station, with most trips requiring a change of buses at Kawaguchiko Station. There are some 18 buses a day in operation between Shinjuku and Kawaguchiko Station from mid-July to the end of August, with less frequent service April through mid-July and September through October. The bus ride from Shinjuku Station, with departures a 2-minute walk from the west side of the station at the No. 50 bus stop of the Shinjuku Highway Bus Terminal (in front of the Yasuda Seimi No. 2 Building), takes about 1 hour and 45 minutes and costs ¥1,700 ($14) one way to Kawaguchiko Station. Note that you must make a reservation for this bus, through **Keio Teito Dentetsu** (☎ 03/5376-2222) or a travel agency.

From Kawaguchiko Station there are buses onward to the Fifth Stage, with the trip taking approximately 50 minutes and costing ¥1,700 ($14). During the official climbing season (mid-July through August), there are also three buses daily that travel directly from Shinjuku Station to Kawaguchiko Trail's Fifth Stage, costing ¥2,600 ($22) one way and taking almost 2½ hours. Note that bus service is suspended in winter, when Mt. Fuji is blanketed in snow and is considered too dangerous for the novice climber. Otherwise, buses generally run from April through October, unless there is inclement weather, though far less frequently than during the official season.

VISITOR INFORMATION   More information and train and bus schedules can be obtained from the **Tokyo Tourist Information Center** in leaflets called "Mt. Fuji and Fuji Five Lakes" and "Climbing Mt. Fuji"; see "Visitor Information" in chapter 3.

CLIMBING MOUNT FUJI

Mt. Fuji is part of **Fuji-Hakone-Izu National Park.** The most popular trails are the **Kawaguchiko Trail** for the ascent and the **Subashiri Trail** for the descent. All trails are divided into 10 different stages, with the Fifth Stage located about 8,250 feet up. From the Fifth Stage, it takes about 5 hours to reach the summit and 3 hours for the descent.

PREPARING FOR YOUR CLIMB   You don't need climbing experience to ascend Mt. Fuji, but you do need stamina and a good pair of walking shoes. It's possible to do it in tennis shoes, but if the rocks are wet they can get awfully slippery. You should also bring a light plastic raincoat (which you can buy at souvenir shops at the Fifth Stage) since it often rains on the mountain, a sun hat, a bottle of water, and a sweater for the evening. It gets very chilly on Mt. Fuji at night. Even in August, the average temperature on the summit is 43.6°F.

Because of snow and inclement weather from fall through late spring, the best time to make an ascent is during the "official" climbing season, from mid-July to August 31. It's also when buses run most frequently. However, it's also the most crowded time of the year. Consider the fact that there are more than 120 million Japanese, most of whom wouldn't dream of climbing the mountain outside the "official" 1½ months it's open, and you begin to get the picture. About 400,000 people climb Fuji-san every year, mostly in July and August and mostly on weekends—so if you plan on climbing Mt. Fuji on a Saturday or a Sunday in summer, go to the end of the line, please.

Climbing Through the Years

The first documented case of someone scaling Mt. Fuji is from the early 8th century. During the Edo Period, pilgrimages to the top were considered a purifying ritual, with strict rules governing dress and route. Women, thought to defile sacred places, were prohibited from climbing mountains until 1871.

Don't be disappointed when your bus deposits you at **Kawaguchiko Fifth Stage,** where you'll be bombarded with souvenir shops, restaurants, and busloads of tourists; most of these tourists aren't climbing to the top. As soon as you get past them and the blaring loudspeakers, you'll find yourself on a steep rocky path, surrounded only by scrub brush and with hikers on the path below and above you. After a couple of hours, you'll probably find yourself above the roily clouds, which stretch in all directions. It will be as if you were on an island, barren and rocky, in the middle of an ocean.

STRATEGIES FOR CLIMBING TO THE TOP   The usual procedure for climbing Mt. Fuji is to take a morning bus, start climbing in early afternoon, spend the night near the summit, get up early in the morning to watch the sun rise, and then climb the rest of the way to the top, where there's a 1-hour hiking trail that circles the crater. Hikers then begin the descent, reaching the Fifth Stage about noon.

There are about 20 **mountain huts** along the Kawaguchiko Trail above the Fifth Stage, but they're very primitive, providing only a futon and toilet facilities. The cost is ¥5,000 ($42) per person without meals, ¥7,000 ($58) with meals. When I stayed in one of these huts, dinner consisted of dried fish, rice, bean-paste soup, and pickled vegetables; breakfast was exactly the same. Still, unless you want to carry your own food, I'd opt for the meals. Note that huts are open only July and August. I recommend the **Toyokan Hut** at the Seventh Stage (☎ 0555/22-1040) or the **Taishikan Hut** at the Eighth Stage (☎ 0555/22-1947). Call the **Fujiyoshida Tourist Information Service** at ☎ 0555/22-7000 for more information.

In recent years, a new trend has started in which climbers arrive at the Fifth Stage late in the evening and then climb to the top through the night with the aid of flashlights. After watching the sun rise, they then make their descent. That way, they don't have to spend the night in one of the huts.

Climbing Mt. Fuji is definitely a unique experience, but there's a saying in Japan: "Everyone should climb Mt. Fuji once; only a fool would climb it twice."

Appendix A: Tokyo in Depth

1 Tokyo Today

With a population of about 12 million, Tokyo is one of the largest cities in the world—and one of the most intriguing. As the nation's capital and financial nerve center, Tokyo is where it's happening in Asia. In a nation of overachievers, Tokyo has more than its fair share of intelligentsia, academics, politicians, businesspeople, artists, and writers, and it's the country's showcase for technology, fashion, art, music, and advertising. People rush around here with such purpose and determination, it's hard not to feel that you're in the midst of something important, that you're witnessing history in the making.

As for innovation, Tokyo has long been recognized as a leader. Indeed, Japan, once dismissed as merely an imitator with no imagination of its own, has long been at the forefront of all things technological, from computers and cars to audiovisual equipment and kitchen and office gadgetry. Walking through the stores of Akihabara, Tokyo's electronics center, provokes an uneasiness few visitors can shake, for it's here that the latest goods are sold long before they reach Western markets.

Yet despite outward appearances, all is not rosy in the land of the rising sun. Its unparalleled economic growth, considered invincible in the 1980s and generating both admiration and envy worldwide, came to an abrupt halt in 1992 with the burst of the economic bubble and the onset of the country's worst recession since World War II. Political scandal, rising unemployment, an increased crime rate, Kobe's catastrophic 1995 earthquake, the release of nerve gas on a Tokyo subway, a nuclear power accident only 70 miles from the capital, and a declining birth rate coupled with an aging population have all conspired to add a sense of anxiety to the Japanese people.

For the short-term visitor to Tokyo, however, problems that loom in the public psyche are not readily apparent—unless you go to Ueno or Yoyogi parks, where the growing number of homeless is nothing short of astounding. Moreover, while Tokyo remains one of the most expensive cities in the world, it now offers something that would have been unthinkable during the spending-happy 1980s: bargains. Tony French restaurants serve value-conscious fixed-price lunches, secondhand clothing stores sell last year's designer wear, and many hotels haven't raised their rates in more than 5 years. For many Japanese, the recession has an unexpected benefit—because

The Japanese are in general intelligent and provident, free and unconstrained, obedient and courteous, curious and inquisitive, industrious and ingenious, frugal and sober, cleanly, good-natured and friendly, upright and just, trusty and honest, mistrustful, superstitious, proud, and haughty, unforgiving, brave, and invincible.

—Charles Peter Thunberg, *Travels in Europe, Africa, and Asia* (1795)

companies are no longer willing to pay their workers overtime, families are spending more time together than they did a decade ago.

And what is life like for a typical Tokyoite? For one thing, living quarters are much tinier than in the Western world, with many families confined to two- or three-room flats. Because apartments in the center of Tokyo are prohibitively expensive, the day usually begins with a long commute from the suburbs. It's not uncommon for commuters to spend 2 to 3 hours a day traveling to and from work on the city's trains and subways, which are often packed beyond belief. For the average white-collar company employee, known as a "salaryman," the day can be long, since in addition to commuting and work hours he may also join fellow workers for an evening out, which he considers necessary for promoting understanding and closeness. Through the years, he will receive a pay raise according to his age and promotion according to the number of years he has worked for the company.

For Japanese women, being a housewife and full-time mother is considered the most honored position. Many will go to college and then work for a few years, but the ultimate goal is to find a husband and have children, ideally before reaching the old age of 25, though more and more couples are postponing marriage these days. Those who fail to find mates can always resort to arranged marriages, which still make up about 15% of the matches in Japan.

As ruler of the home front, the Japanese mother's job is to make sure her children study hard enough to pass the tough entrance exam to one of the country's best universities, from which graduates are recruited into the country's top companies. Thus, she will strive to get her children into the best kindergarten and thereafter into the best schools, and it's not unusual for students to attend evening or weekend cram schools in an attempt to get an edge over their peers. Ironically, once in college, students are under little pressure to study and the college years are basically viewed as four short years of freedom before a lifetime of servitude to the company or the home.

Of course, as elsewhere, there are people who do not fit the traditional mold, including female professionals, fathers who are more involved with their children's upbringing, and teenagers who bleach their hair blonde and sport body piercings. But while Tokyo boasts more free-thinking individualists than any other Japanese metropolis, for the most part everyone follows the rules set before them. Such regimentation certainly has its flaws, but it also assures orderliness, dependability, and safety from crime.

While in recent years many Japanese will tell you that crime is regrettably on the increase, it still remains negligible compared to American cities. This is perhaps best illustrated by what I witnessed on a visit to Tokyo's crowded Asakusa district: A street vendor who was hawking jewelry dashed across the street for a quick lunch, confident that his wares were safe, even though they were within easy grasp of multitudes of pedestrians strolling by. Tokyo is so safe that an American friend of mine was told by her daughter's first-grade teacher that all children should walk to and from the local public school on their own, unaccompanied by parents.

Despite the recession, life in Tokyo remains much as it's always been— humming with energy, crowded beyond belief, and filled with acts of human kindness. Japanese department stores are still full of shoppers and a dazzling array of goods. Some financial experts believe that Japan is already on the road to economic recovery.

2 A Look at the Past

EARLY HISTORY Archaeological finds show that the region was inhabited as early as 30,000 B.C., but it wasn't until the 6th century that Japan began spreading its cultural wings. Taking its cues from China, its great neighbor to the west, Japan adopted Buddhism, the character system of writing, and Chinese art forms and architecture, and molded them into a style of its own.

In A.D. 794 the Japanese imperial family established a new capital in Heiankyo (present-day Kyoto), where it remained for more than 1,000 years. The arts flourished, and extravagant temples and pavilions were erected. Noh drama, the tea ceremony, flower arranging, and landscape gardening developed. But even though Kyoto served as the cultural heart of the nation, it was often the nation's capital in name only. Preoccupied by their own luxurious lifestyle, the nobles and royal court of Kyoto were little match for rebellious military clans in the provinces.

THE FEUDAL PERIOD The first successful clan uprising took place at the end of the 12th century, when a young warrior named Minamoto Yoritomo won a bloody civil war that brought him supremacy over the land. Wishing to set up his rule far away from the imperial family in Kyoto, he made his capital in a remote and easily defendable fishing village called Kamakura, not far from today's Tokyo. He created a military government, a shogunate, ushering in a new era in Japan's history in which the power of the country passed from the aristocratic court into the hands of the warrior class. In becoming the nation's first shogun, or military dictator, Yoritomo laid the groundwork for military governments in Japan which lasted for another 700 years.

Dateline

- **794** Kyoto becomes Japan's capital.
- **1192** Minamoto Yoritomo becomes shogun and establishes his shogunate government in Kamakura.
- **1333** The Kamakura shogunate falls and the imperial system is restored.
- **1457** Edo Castle constructed in Tokyo (destroyed during World War II).
- **1603** Tokugawa Ieyasu becomes shogun and establishes his shogunate in Edo (present-day Tokyo), marking the beginning of a 264-year rule by the Tokugawa clan.
- **1612** Silver mint opens in the Ginza.
- **1633** Japan closes its doors to foreign trade and subsequently forbids all foreigners from landing in Japan and all Japanese from leaving.
- **1787** The population of Tokyo reaches 1.3 million.
- **1853** Commodore Matthew C. Perry of the U.S. Navy succeeds in persuading the Japanese to sign a trade agreement with the United States.
- **1867** Tokugawa regime is overthrown, bringing Japan's feudal era to a close.
- **1868** Emperor Meiji assumes power, moves his imperial capital from Kyoto to Tokyo, and begins the industrialization of Japan.

continues

- **1873** Ueno Park opens to the public as Tokyo's first city park.
- **1878** Establishment of the Tokyo Stock Exchange.
- **1922** The Imperial Hotel, designed by Frank Lloyd Wright, opens in Hibiya, opposite the Imperial Palace.
- **1923** Tokyo and Yokohama are devastated by a major earthquake in which more than 100,000 people lose their lives.
- **1937** Japan goes to war with China and conquers Nanking.
- **1940** Japan forms a military alliance with Germany and Italy.
- **1941** The Pacific War begins as Japan bombs Pearl Harbor.
- **1945** Hiroshima and Nagasaki suffer atomic bomb attacks; Japan agrees to surrender.
- **1946** The emperor renounces his claim to divinity; Japan adopts a new, democratic constitution; women gain the right to vote.
- **1952** The Allied occupation of Japan ends; Japan regains its independence.
- **1956** Japan is admitted to the United Nations.
- **1964** The XVIII Summer Olympic Games are held in Tokyo.
- **1989** Emperor Hirohito dies after a 63-year reign.
- **1990** Hirohito's son, Akihito, formally ascends the throne and proclaims the new "Era of Peace" (Heisei).
- **1991** Tokyo's new city hall, the Tokyo Metropolitan Government Office, designed by Kenzo Tange, opens in Shinjuku.

continues

The Kamakura Period, from 1192 to 1333, is perhaps best known for the unrivaled ascendancy of the warrior caste, called samurai. Ruled by a rigid code of honor, the samurai were bound in loyalty to their feudal lord and would defend him to the death. If they failed in their duties, they could redeem their honor by committing ritualistic suicide, or *seppuku*. Spurning the soft life led by the noble court in Kyoto, the samurai embraced a harsher and simpler set of ideals and a Spartan lifestyle, embodied in the tenets of Zen Buddhism's mental and physical disciplines.

The Kamakura Period was followed by 200 years of vicious civil wars and confusion as *daimyo* (feudal lords) staked out their fiefdoms throughout the land and strove for supremacy. Not unlike a baron in medieval Europe, a daimyo had absolute rule over the people who lived in his fiefdom and was aided in battles by his samurai retainers.

THE RISE OF TOKUGAWA   In the second half of the 16th century, several brilliant military strategists rose to power, but none proved as shrewd as Tokugawa Ieyasu, a statesman so skillful in eliminating his enemies that his heirs would continue to rule Japan for the next 250 years. It was with him that Tokyo's history began.

For centuries, present-day Tokyo was nothing more than a rather obscure village called Edo, which means simply "mouth of the estuary." Then, in 1590, Tokugawa acquired eight provinces surrounding Edo, much of it marsh and wilderness, with little freshwater available. Undaunted, Tokugawa chose Edo as his base and immediately set to work correcting the area's shortcomings by reclaiming land, building a conduit for fresh water, and constructing a castle surrounded by moats.

In 1603, Tokugawa succeeded in defeating all his rivals in a series of brilliant battles, becoming shogun over all of Japan. He declared the sleepy village of Edo the seat of his shogunate government, leaving the emperor intact but virtually powerless in Kyoto. He then set about expanding Edo Castle to make it the most impressive castle in the land, surrounding it with an ingenious system of moats that radiated out from the castle in a great swirl, giving him access to the sea and thwarting enemy attack.

THE EDO PERIOD   Edo grew quickly as the shogunate capital. For greater protection, and to ensure that no daimyo in the distant provinces could grow strong enough to usurp the shogun's power, the Tokugawa government ordered every daimyo to reside in Edo for a prescribed number of months every other year, thus keeping the feudal lords under the watchful eye of the shogunate. Furthermore, all daimyo were required to leave their families in Edo as permanent residents, to serve as virtual hostages. There were as many as 270 daimyo in Japan in the 17th century, with each maintaining several mansions in Edo for family members and retainers, complete with elaborate compounds and expansive landscaped gardens. Together with their samurai, who made up almost half of Edo's population in the 17th century, the daimyo and their entourage must have created quite a colorful sight on the dusty streets of old Edo. By expending so much time and money traveling back and forth and maintaining residences in both the provinces and Edo, a daimyo would have been hard put to wage war against the shogun.

To cater to the needs of the shogun, daimyo and samurai, merchants, and craftsmen from throughout Japan swarmed to Edo. To accommodate them, hills were leveled and marshes filled in, creating what is now the Ginza, Shimbashi, and Nihombashi. By 1787 the population had reached 1.3 million, making Edo one of the largest cities in the world.

- **1992** The worst recession since World War II hits Japan. The Diet approves use of military forces for United Nations peace-keeping efforts.
- **1993** Liberal Democratic party loses election for the first time since 1955. Akebono, a Hawaiian, becomes first non-Japanese to reach sumo's highest rank of yokozuna.
- **1995** Japan's sense of security is shaken by the Great Hanshin Earthquake (and the subsequent mishandling of rescue aid), which flattens the city of Kobe, and by the sarin-gas attack upon Tokyo's crowded commuter trains.
- **1997** New Shinkansen bullet train connects Tokyo with Nagano in the Japan Alps, site of the 1998 Winter Olympics.
- **1999** A nuclear plant 70 miles northeast of Tokyo suffers Japan's worst nuclear accident, exposing dozens to radiation.

However, it was a city few outsiders were ever permitted to see. Fearing the spread of Western influence and Christianity in Japan, the Tokugawa shogunate adopted a policy of complete isolation in 1633, slamming Japan's doors to the outside world for more than 200 years. The shogunate forbade foreigners to enter Japan and forbade the Japanese to leave. Those who defied the strict decrees paid with their lives. The only exception to this policy of isolation was a colony of tightly controlled Chinese merchants in Nagasaki and a handful of Dutch, confined to a small trading post on a tiny island in Nagasaki.

The Edo Period (1603–1867) was a time of political stability with all policy dictated by the shogunate government. Japanese society was divided into four distinct classes: the court nobles, the samurai, the farmers, and the merchants. Although the nobles occupied the most exalted social position, it was the samurai who wielded the real power, for they were the only ones allowed to carry weapons.

At the bottom of the social ladder were the merchants and townspeople. They occupied squalid tenements, which were typically long row houses constructed of wood and facing narrow meter-wide alleys, with open sewers running down the middle. Family homes were unimaginably small, consisting of a tiny entryway which also doubled as the kitchen and a single room about 100 square feet in size. Since most of Edo was built of wood, it goes without saying that fires were a constant threat. In fact, rare indeed was the person who didn't lose his house at least several times during his lifetime. Between 1603 and 1868, almost 100 major fires swept through Edo, along with countless smaller fires. One of the most tragic fires occurred in 1657, after a severe drought had plagued the city for almost 3 months. Buffeted by strong winds, the flames ignited wooden homes and thatched roofs like tinder, raging for 3 days and reducing three-fourths of the city to smoldering ruins. More than 100,000 people lost their lives.

Despite such setbacks, the merchants of Tokyo grew in number and became so wealthy that new forms of luxury and entertainment arose to occupy their time. Kabuki drama and woodblock prints became the rage, while stone and porcelain ware, silk brocade for elaborate and gorgeous kimono, and lacquerware were elevated to wondrous works of art. Japan's most famous pleasure district was an area in northeast Edo called Yoshiwara, the "floating world of pleasure," where rich merchants spent fortunes to cavort with beautiful courtesans.

THE OPENING OF JAPAN   By the mid-19th century it was clear that the feudal system was outdated. With economic power in the hands of the merchants, money rather than rice became the primary means of exchange. Many samurai families found themselves on the brink of poverty, and discontent with the shogunate grew widespread.

In 1854, Commodore Matthew C. Perry of the U.S. Navy succeeded in forcing the shogun to sign an agreement granting America trading rights, thus ending 2 centuries of isolation. Then, in 1868, the Tokugawas were overthrown and Emperor Meiji was restored as ruler. The feudal era drew to an end.

THE MEIJI RESTORATION   Rather than remain in Kyoto, Emperor Meiji decided to take Edo for his own and moved his imperial capital to its new home in 1868. Renaming Edo Tokyo, or "Eastern Capital," (to distinguish it from the "western" capital of Kyoto), the emperor was quick to welcome ideas and technology from the West. The ensuing years, known as the Meiji Period (1868–1911), were nothing short of amazing, as Japan progressed rapidly from a feudal agricultural society of samurai and peasants to an industrial nation. The samurai were stripped of their power and were no longer permitted to carry swords; a prime minister and cabinet were appointed; a constitution was drafted; and a parliament, called the Diet, was elected. The railway, postal system, and even specialists and advisers were imported from the West. Between 1881 and 1898, 6,177 British, 2,764 Americans, 913 Germans, and 619 French were retained by the Japanese government to help transform Japan into a modern society.

As the nation's capital, Tokyo was hardest hit by this craze for modernization. Ideas for fashion, architecture, food, and department stores were imported from the West—West was best, and things Japanese were forgotten or pushed aside. It didn't help that Tokyo was almost totally destroyed twice in the first half of this century. In 1923 a huge earthquake, measuring 7.9 on the Richter scale and known as the Great Kanto Earthquake, struck the city, followed by tsunami (tidal waves). More than 100,000 people died and a third of Tokyo was in ruins. Disaster struck again during World War II, when incendiary bombs laid more than half the city to waste and killed another 100,000 people.

WORLD WAR II & its AFTERMATH   Japan's expansionist policies in Asia during the 1930s and early 1940s spread the flag of the rising sun over

Hong Kong, China, Singapore, Burma, Malaysia, the Philippines, the Dutch East Indies, and Guam. However, World War II halted Japan's advance. Shortly after the United States dropped the world's first atomic bombs—over Hiroshima on August 6, 1945, and over Nagasaki 3 days later—surrender came, on August 14, 1945.

The end of the war brought American occupation forces to Japan, where they remained until 1952. It was the first time in Japan's history that the island nation had suffered defeat and occupation by a foreign power. The experience had a profound effect on the Japanese people. Emerging from their defeat, they began the long effort to rebuild their cities and economy. In 1946, under the guidance of the Allied military authority, headed by U.S. general Douglas MacArthur, they adopted a new, democratic constitution that renounced war and divested the emperor of his claim to divinity. A parliamentary system of government was set up, and in 1947 the first general elections were held. The following year, the militarists and generals who had carried out the Pacific War were tried and many of them were convicted. To the younger generation of Japanese, the occupation was less a painful burden that had to be suffered than an opportunity to remake their country, with American encouragement, into a modern, peace-loving, and democratic state.

A special relationship developed between the Japanese and their American occupiers. In the early 1950s, as the cold war between the United States and the Communist world erupted in hostilities in Korea, that relationship grew into a firm alliance, strengthened by a security treaty between Tokyo and Washington. In 1956, Japan joined the United Nations as an independent country.

POSTWAR JAPAN　Perhaps unsurprising in a city trained in natural calamities, Tokyo was so adept at rebuilding that a decade later not a trace of wartime destruction remained. Avoiding involvement in foreign conflicts, the Japanese concentrated on economic recovery. Through a series of policies that favored domestic industries and shielded Japan against foreign competition, the country achieved rapid economic growth. By the mid-1960s—only a century after Japan had opened its doors to the rest of the world and embraced modernization—the Japanese had transformed their nation into a major industrial power, with Tokyo riding the crest of the economic wave. In 1964, in recognition of Japan's increasing importance, the Summer Olympic Games were held in Tokyo, thrusting the city into the international limelight.

As their economy continued to expand, the Japanese sought new markets abroad; by the early 1970s, they had attained a trade surplus, as Japanese products—cars and electronic goods—attracted more and more foreign buyers. By the 1980s, Japan Inc. seemed on the economic brink of ruling the world, as Japanese companies bought prime real estate around the world, books flooded the Western market expounding Japanese business principles, and Japan enjoyed unprecedented financial growth.

In 1992, recession hit Japan, bursting the economic bubble and plunging the country into its worst recession since World War II. Since then, bankruptcies have reached an all-time high, Tokyo real-estate prices have plummeted 70% from what they were in 1990, the Nikkei 225 index sank 65% from what it was in 1989, and the country has rocked with one political scandal after another. Public confidence was further eroded in 1995, first by a major earthquake in Kobe that killed 5,000 people and proved that Japan's cities are not as safe as the government had maintained, and then by an attack by an obscure religious sect that released the deadly nerve gas sarin on Tokyo's subway system during rush hour, killing 12 people and sickening thousands. A feeling of helplessness and vulnerability grew after North Korea lobbed a missile over Japan in 1998, followed by a 1999 accident at a nuclear power plant only 70 miles from Tokyo that exposed dozens to radiation. Meanwhile, Japanese workers must now fear for their jobs—lifetime employment is no longer a guarantee.

Despite the recession, Tokyo continues to set the pace for the rest of the nation. Construction and development continue, with ever new areas of recreation and commerce opening on reclaimed land in Tokyo Bay. In April 1999, Tokyo elected Ishihara Shintaro as its outspoken governor, a nationalist writer who, together with former Sony chairman Morita Akio, penned the 1989 best-selling *The Japan That Can Say No*. His election is regarded as a clear rejection of the status quo and a belief that change in Japan must come from within, with Tokyo clearly at the forefront of change.

3 Social Skills 101

Because of its physical isolation and the fact that it was never successfully invaded before World War II, Japan is one of the most homogeneous nations in the world. Almost 99% of Japan's population is Japanese, with hardly any influx of other genes into the country since the 8th century. The Japanese feel they belong to one huge tribe different from any other people on earth. A Japanese will often preface a statement or opinion with the words "We Japanese," implying that all Japanese think alike and that all people in the world can be divided into two groups, Japanese and non-Japanese.

While in the West the recipe for a full and rewarding life seems to be in that elusive attainment of "happiness," in Japan it's in the satisfactory performance of duty and obligation. Individuality in Japan is equated with selfishness and a complete disregard for the feelings and consideration of others. The Japanese are instilled with a sense of duty toward the group—whether it be family, friends, co-workers, or Japanese society as a whole. In a nation as crowded as Japan, such consideration of others is essential, especially in Tokyo, where space is particularly scarce.

MEETING THE JAPANESE

If you've been invited to Japan by some organization or business, you will receive the royal treatment, and most likely be wined and dined so wonderfully and thoroughly that you'll never want to return home. If you've come to Tokyo on your own as an ordinary tourist, however, your experiences will depend largely on you. Although the Japanese will sometimes approach you to ask whether they might practice some English with you, for the most part you are left pretty much on your own unless you make the first move.

The best way to meet the Japanese is to participate in a super program launched by the Japan National Tourist Organization called the **Home Visit System,** which offers overseas visitors the opportunity to visit an English-speaking Japanese family in their home. Upon request, you might even be paired with a family with the same occupation as yours. It doesn't cost anything, and the visit usually takes place for two hours in the evening beginning at 7pm (dinner is not served). It's a good idea to bring a small gift, such as flowers, fruit, or something from your hometown. To apply, drop by the

Tourist Information Center in the Tokyo International Forum, 3–5–1 Marunouchi (☎ 03/3201-3331; station: Yurakucho), at least a day (preferably 2 days) in advance. You must bring your passport with you. Applications are accepted Monday to Friday from 9am to noon and 1 to 4pm; it takes about one hour for staff to complete arrangements, after which you'll be given detailed directions to your host family's home.

In addition to Tokyo, Yokohama also has a Home Visit network (see chapter 10, "Side Trips from Tokyo," for details on its tourist offices).

Another way to meet Japanese is to go where they play, namely Tokyo's countless bars and eateries. There, you'll often find people who know some English and will want to practice it on you, as well as more inebriated people who want to talk to you whether they know English or not. If you're open to it, such chance encounters may prove to be a highlight of your trip.

MINDING YOUR P'S & Q'S

When European merchants and missionaries began arriving in Japan almost 400 years ago, the Japanese took one look at them and immediately labeled them barbarians. After all, these hairy and boisterous outsiders rarely bathed and didn't know the first thing about proper etiquette and behavior.

The Japanese, on the other hand, had a strict social hierarchy which dictated exactly how a person should speak, sit, bow, eat, walk, dress, and live. Failure to comply with the rules could bring swift punishment and sometimes even death. More than one Japanese literally lost his head for committing a social blunder.

Of course, things have changed since then, and the Japanese have even adopted some of the Western barbarians' customs. However, what hasn't changed is that the Japanese still attach much importance to rules of proper behavior and etiquette, which developed to allow relationships to be as frictionless as possible—important in a country as crowded as Japan. The Japanese don't like confrontations, and although I'm told they do occur, I've never seen a fight in Japan.

One aspect of Japanese behavior that sometimes causes difficulty for foreigners is that the Japanese find it very hard to say no. They're much more apt to say that your request is very difficult to fulfill or they'll simply beat around the bush without giving a definite answer. At this point you're expected to let the subject drop. Showing impatience, anger, or aggressiveness rarely gets you anywhere in Japan. Apologizing sometimes does. And if someone does give in to your request, you can't say thank you often enough.

BOWING The main form of greeting in Japan is the bow rather than the handshake. Although at first glance it may seem simple enough, the bow—together with its implications—is actually quite complicated. The depth of the bow and the number of seconds devoted to performing it, as well as the total number of bows, depend on who you are and to whom you're bowing. In addition to bowing in greeting, the Japanese also bow upon departing and to express gratitude. The proper form for a bow is to bend from the waist with a straight back and to keep your arms at your sides, but as a foreigner you'll probably feel foolish and look pretty stupid if you try to imitate what the Japanese have spent years learning. A simple nod of the head is enough. Knowing that foreigners shake hands, a Japanese may extend a hand, but probably won't be able to stop from giving a little bow as well. The Japanese will bow even when speaking to an invisible someone on the telephone.

VISITING CARDS   You're a nonentity in Japan if you don't have a business or visiting card, called a *meishi*. Everyone from housewives to plumbers to secretaries to bank presidents carries meishi with them to give out upon introduction. If you're trying to conduct business in Japan, you'll be regarded suspiciously if you don't have business cards. As a tourist you don't have to have business cards, but it certainly doesn't hurt, and the Japanese will be greatly impressed by your preparedness. The card should have your address and occupation on it. As a nice souvenir, you might consider having your meishi made in Japan with the Japanese syllabic script (katakana) written on the reverse side.

The proper way to present a meishi depends on the status of the two people involved. If you are both of equal status, you exchange meishi simultaneously; otherwise, the lower person on the totem pole presents the meishi first. Turn it so that the other person can read it (that is, upside down to you) and present it with both hands and a slight bow. Afterwards, don't simply put the meishi away. Rather, it's customary for both of you to study the meishi for a moment, and, if possible, to comment on it (such as, "You're from Kyoto? My brother lived in Kyoto!" or "Sony! What a famous company!").

SHOES   Nothing is so distasteful to the Japanese as the bottoms of shoes, and therefore shoes are taken off before entering a home, a Japanese-style inn, a temple, and even some museums and restaurants. Usually, there will be some plastic slippers at the entranceway for you to slip on, but whenever you encounter tatami floors you should remove even these slippers—only bare feet or socks (you'll be much happier if yours are clean and hole-less) are allowed to tread upon tatami.

Bathrooms present a whole other set of slippers. If you're in a home or Japanese inn, you'll notice another pair of slippers—again plastic or rubber—sitting right inside the bathroom at the door. Step out of the hallway plastic shoes and into the bathroom slippers and wear these the whole time you're in the bathroom. When you're finished, change back into the hallway slippers. If you forget this last changeover, you'll regret it—nothing is as embarrassing as walking in wearing bathroom slippers and not realizing what you've done until you see the mixed looks of horror and mirth on the faces of the Japanese.

GUEST ETIQUETTE   If you are invited to a Japanese home, you should know it is both a rarity and an honor. Most Japanese consider their homes too small and humble for entertaining guests, which is why there are so many restaurants, coffee shops, and bars. If you are lucky enough to get an invitation, don't show up empty-handed. Bring a small gift, such as candy, fruit, flowers, or a souvenir of your hometown. Alcohol is also appreciated.

Instead of being invited to a private home, you may be invited out to dinner and drinks, especially if you're in Japan on business, in which case your hosts will most likely have an expense account. In any event, it's nice to reciprocate by taking them out later to your own territory, say, a French or other Western-style restaurant, where you'll feel comfortable playing host.

If you're among friends, the general practice is to divide the check equally among everyone, no matter how much or little each consumed.

In any case, no matter what favor a Japanese has done for you—whether it was giving you a small gift, buying you a drink, or even just making a telephone call for you—be sure to give your thanks profusely the next time you meet. The Japanese think it odd and rude not to be remembered and thanked upon the next meeting, even if a year has elapsed.

OTHER CUSTOMS   When the Japanese give back change, they hand it to you in a lump sum rather than counting it out. Trust them. It's considered insulting for you to sit there and count it in front of them because it insinuates that you think they might be trying to cheat you. The Japanese are honest. It's one of the great pleasures of being in their country.

Don't blow your nose in public if you can help it, and never at the dinner table. It's considered disgusting. On the other hand, even though the Japanese are very hygienic, they are not all averse to spitting on the sidewalk. And even more peculiar, men often urinate when and where they want, usually against a tree or a wall and most often after a night of carousing in the bars.

This being a man's society, men will walk in and out of doors and elevators before women, and in subways will often sit down while their wives stand. Some Japanese men, however, who have had contact with the Western world, will make a gallant show of allowing a Western woman to step out of the elevator or door first.

THE JAPANESE BATH

On my very first trip to Japan, I was certain that I would never get into a Japanese bath. I was under the misconception that men and women bathed together, and I couldn't imagine getting into a tub with a group of smiling and bowing Japanese men. I needn't have worried. In almost all circumstances, bathing is gender-segregated. There are some exceptions, primarily at outdoor hot-spring spas in the countryside, but the women who go to these are usually grandmothers who couldn't care less. Young Japanese women wouldn't dream of jumping into a tub with a group of male strangers.

Japanese baths are delightful—and I, for one, am addicted to them. You'll find them at Japanese-style inns, at hot-spring spas, and at neighborhood baths (not everyone has his or her own bath in Japan). Sometimes they're elaborate affairs with many tubs, plants, and statues, and sometimes they're nothing more than a tiny tub. Public baths have long been regarded as social centers for the Japanese—friends and co-workers will visit hot-spring resorts together; neighbors exchange gossip at the neighborhood bath. Sadly, however, the neighborhood bath has been in great decline over the past decades, as more and more Japanese own private baths. In 1968, Tokyo alone had 2,687 neighborhood baths; today that number has dropped to less than 1,400.

In any case, whether large or small, the procedure at all Japanese baths is the same. After completely disrobing in the changing room and putting your clothes in either a locker or a basket, hold your washcloth in front of you so that it covers the vital parts and walk into the bath area. There you'll find plastic basins and stools (they used to be made of wood), and faucets along the wall. Sit on the stool in front of the faucet and repeatedly fill your basin with water, splashing it all over you. If there's no hot water from the faucet, it's acceptable to dip your plastic basin into the hot bath. Soap yourself down completely—and I mean completely—and then rinse away all traces of soap. I have never seen a group of people wash themselves so thoroughly as the Japanese, from their eyes to their toes. Only after you're squeaky-clean are you ready to get into the bath. When you've finished bathing, do not pull the plug. The same bathwater is used by everyone, which is why it's so important to soap down and rinse before entering the tub.

Your first attempt at a Japanese bath may be painful—simply too scalding for comfort. It helps if you ease in gently and then sit perfectly still. You'll notice all tension and muscle stiffness ebbing away, a decidedly relaxing way to end the day. The Japanese are so fond of baths that many take them nightly, especially in winter, when a hot bath keeps one toasty warm for hours afterward. With time, you'll probably become addicted, too.

4 Dealing with the Language Barrier

Without a doubt, the hardest part of being in Tokyo is the language barrier. Suddenly you find yourself transported to a crowded city of 12 million people, where you can neither speak nor read the language. To make matters worse, many Japanese cannot speak English, and signs, menus, and shop names are often in Japanese only.

Realizing the difficulties foreigners have with the language in Japan, the **Japan National Tourist Organization** (**JNTO**) puts out a nifty booklet called **"The Tourist's Language Handbook,"** with sentences in English and their Japanese equivalents for almost every activity, from asking directions and shopping to ordering in a restaurant and staying in a Japanese inn. In addition, a glossary of common phrases and words appears in appendix B of this book.

If you need to ask directions in Tokyo, your best bet is to **ask younger people.** They have all studied English in school and are most likely to be able to help you. Japanese businessmen also often know some English. And as strange as it sounds, if you're having problems communicating with someone, try writing your question instead of speaking it. The emphasis in schools is on written rather than oral English (even many English teachers can't speak English very well), so Japanese who can't understand a word you say may know all the subtleties of syntax and English grammar. If you still have problems communicating, you can always call the **Travel-Phone,** a toll-free nationwide help line set up by JNTO to help foreigners in distress or in need of information (for information on Travel-Phone, see "Visitor Information," in chapter 3). And if you're heading out for a particular restaurant or shop, have your destination written out in Japanese by someone at your hotel to show to taxi drivers or passersby. If you get lost along the way, look for one of the police boxes, called *koban,* found in virtually every neighborhood. They have maps of their district and can pinpoint exactly where you want to go if you have the address with you.

THE WRITTEN LANGUAGE   No one knows the exact origins of the Japanese language, but we do know that it existed only in spoken form until the 6th century. It was then that the Japanese borrowed the Chinese characters, called **kanji,** and used them to develop their own form of written language. Later, two phonetic alphabet systems, **hiragana** and **katakana,** were added to kanji to form the existing Japanese writing system. Thus, Chinese and Japanese use some of the same pictographs, but otherwise there's no similarity between the languages; while they may be able to recognize some of each other's written language, the Chinese and Japanese cannot communicate verbally.

The Japanese written language—a combination of kanji, hiragana, and katakana—is probably one of the most difficult systems of written communication in the modern world. As for the spoken language, there are many levels of speech and forms of expression relating to a person's social status, age, and sex. Even nonverbal communication is vital to understanding Japanese, since what isn't said is often more important than what is. It's little wonder that Saint Francis Xavier, a Jesuit missionary who came to Japan in the 16th century, wrote that Japanese was an invention of the devil designed to thwart the spread of Christianity. And yet, astoundingly, adult literacy in Japan is estimated to be 99%.

A note on establishment names: Many hotels, restaurants, and sight-seeing attractions in Tokyo now have signs in **romanji** (Roman, or English-language, characters); many others do not. For places mentioned in this book that have only Japanese signs, I've included an appendix of the Japanese character names so you'll be able to recognize them. When you see a number in an oval before the name of any restaurant, Japanese-style inn, or other establishment, turn to appendix B, section 2, "A Japanese-Character Index of Establishment Names," and look for the corresponding number to find the Japanese character name of that establishment.

PRONUNCIATION   If you're having difficulty communicating with a Japanese, it may help to pronounce an English word in a Japanese way. Foreign words, especially English, have penetrated the Japanese language to such an extent that they're now estimated to make up 20% of everyday vocabulary. The problem is that these words change in Japanese pronunciation, because words always end in either a vowel or an n, and because two consonants in a single syllable are usually separated by a vowel. Would you recognize *terebi* as "television," *koohi* as "coffee," or *rajio* as "radio"?

OTHER HELPFUL TIPS   It's worth noting that Japanese nouns do not have plural forms; thus, for example, *ryokan*, a Japanese-style inn, can be both singular and plural. Plural sense is indicated by context. In addition, the Japanese custom is to list the family name first, followed by the given name. That is the format I have followed in this book, but note that many things published in English—business cards, city brochures, etc.—may follow the Western custom of listing family name last.

And finally, you may find yourself confused because of suffixes attached to Japanese place names. For example, *dori* can mean street, avenue, or road, and sometimes it's attached to the proper noun with a hyphen while at other times it stands alone. Thus, you may see Chuo-dori, Chuo Dori, or even Chuo-dori Avenue on English maps and street signs, but they are all one and the same street. Likewise, *dera* means "temple" and is often included at the end of the name, as in Kiyomizudera; *ji* means shrine.

WRITTEN ENGLISH IN JAPAN   You'll see English on shop signs, bill-boards, posters, shopping bags, and T-shirts. However, words are often wonderfully misspelled or used in such unusual contexts that one can only guess at the original intent. My days have been brightened innumerable times by the discovery of some zany or unfathomable English. What, for example, could possibly be the meaning behind "Today birds, tomorrow men," which appeared under a picture of birds on a shopping bag? I have treasured ashtrays that read "The young boy grasped her heart firmly" and "Let's Trip in Hokkaido." In Matsue a "Beauty Saloon" conjures up images of beauties chugging mugs of beer, while in Gifu one can only surmise at the pleasures to be had at the Hotel Joybox. And imagine my consternation upon stepping on a bathroom scale that called itself the "Beauty-Checker."

But the best one I saw was at Narita airport. At all check-in counters was a sign telling passengers they would be required to pay a departure tax at "the time of check in for your fright." I explained the cause of my amusement to the person behind the counter, and when I came back 2 weeks later, I was almost disappointed to find that all signs had been corrected. That's Japanese efficiency.

5 Tips on Dining, Japanese Style

Whenever I leave Japan, it's the food I miss the most. Sure, there are sushi bars and other Japanese specialty restaurants in many major cities elsewhere, but they don't offer nearly the variety available in Japan (and often aren't nearly as good). For just as America has more to offer than hamburgers and steaks, Japan has more than just sushi and tempura. For both the gourmet and the uninitiated, Tokyo is a treasure trove of culinary surprises.

JAPANESE CUISINE

Altogether, there are more than a dozen different and distinct types of Japanese cuisine, plus countless regional specialties. A good deal of what you eat may be completely new to you, as well as completely unidentifiable. No need to worry—often the Japanese themselves don't even know what they're eating, so varied and so wide is the range of available edibles. The rule is simply to enjoy, and enjoyment begins even before you raise your chopsticks to your mouth.

To the Japanese, presentation of food is as important as the food itself, and dishes are designed to appeal to the eye as well as to the palate. In contrast to the American way of piling as much food as possible onto a single plate, the Japanese often use many small plates, each arranged artfully with bite-size morsels of food. After you've seen what can be done with maple leaves, flowers, bits of bamboo, and even pebbles to enhance the appearance of food, your relationship with what you eat may be changed forever.

Below are explanations of some of the most common types of Japanese cuisine. Generally, only one type of cuisine is served in a given restaurant—for example, only raw seafood is served in a sushi bar, while tempura is served at a tempura counter. There are some exceptions to this, especially in those restaurants where raw fish may be served as an appetizer. In addition, some of Japan's drinking establishments offer a wide range of foods, from soups to sushi to skewered pieces of chicken known as yakitori.

For a quick rundown of individual dishes, refer to the menu terms in appendix B.

FUGU Known as blowfish, puffer fish, or globefish in English, fugu is one of the most exotic and adventurous foods in Japan—if it's not prepared properly, it means almost certain death for the consumer! In the past decade, some 50 people in Japan have died from fugu poisoning, usually because they tried preparing it at home. The ovaries and intestines of the fugu are deadly and must be entirely removed without being punctured. So why eat fugu if it can kill you? Well, for one thing, it's delicious, and for another, fugu chefs are strictly licensed by the government and greatly skilled in preparing fugu dishes. You can order fugu raw (*fugu-sashi*), when it's sliced paper-thin and dipped into soy sauce with bitter orange and chives; in a stew (*fugu-chiri*) cooked with vegetables at your table; and as a rice porridge (*fugu-zosui*). The season for fresh fugu is from October or November through March, but some restaurants serve it throughout the year.

KAISEKI The king of Japanese cuisine, kaiseki is the epitome of delicately and exquisitely arranged food, the ultimate in aesthetic appeal. It's

There is a saying that the Chinese eat with their stomachs and the Japanese with their eyes.

—Bernard Leach, *A Potter In Japan* (1960)

also among the most expensive meals you'll ever find. A kaiseki dinner can cost ¥25,000 ($208) or more per person; some restaurants, however, do offer more affordable mini-kaiseki courses, beginning at ¥3,500 or ¥5,000 ($29 or $42). The cost is so high because much time and skill are involved in preparing each of the many dishes, with the ingredients cooked to preserve natural flavors. Even the plates are chosen with great care to enhance the color, texture, and shape of each piece of food.

Kaiseki cuisine, both in selection and presentation, is based on the four seasons. The kaiseki gourmet can tell what time of year it is just by looking at a meal.

A kaiseki meal is usually a lengthy affair, with various dishes appearing in set order. First come the appetizer, clear broth, and one uncooked dish. These are followed by boiled, broiled, fried, steamed, heated, and vinegared dishes, and finally by another soup, rice, pickled vegetables, and fruit. Although meals vary greatly depending on what's fresh, common dishes include some type of sashimi, tempura, cooked seasonal fish, and an array of bite-size pieces of various vegetables. Since kaiseki is always a set meal, there's no problem in ordering; simply let your budget be your guide.

KUSHIAGE Kushiage foods are breaded and deep-fried on skewers and include chicken, beef, seafood, and lots of seasonal vegetables (snow peas, green pepper, gingko nuts, lotus root, and the like). They're served with a slice of lemon and usually a specialty sauce. The result is delicious, and I highly recommend trying it. I don't understand why this style of cooking isn't better known abroad—maybe someday it will be. Ordering the set meal is easiest, and what you get is often determined by both the chef and the season. A restaurant serving kushiage, called a kushiage-ya, is often open only for dinner.

OKONOMIYAKI Okonomiyaki, which originated in Osaka after World War II and literally means "as you like it," is often referred to as Japanese pizza. Basically, it's a kind of pancake to which meat or fish, shredded cabbage, and vegetables are added, topped with Worcestershire sauce. Since it's a popular offering of street vendors, restaurants specializing in this type of cuisine are very reasonably priced. At some places the cook makes it for you, but at other places it's do-it-yourself, which can be quite fun if you're with a group. Yakisoba (fried Chinese noodles and cabbage) are also usually on offer at okonomiyaki restaurants.

RICE As in other Asian countries, rice has been a Japanese staple for about 2,000 years. There are no problems here—everyone is familiar with rice. The difference, however, is that in Japan it's quite sticky, making it easier to pick up with chopsticks. It's also just plain white rice (called *gohan*)—no salt, no butter, no soy sauce (it's considered rather uncouth to dump a lot of sauces in your rice). In the old days, not everyone could afford the expensive white kind, which was grown primarily to pay taxes or rent to the feudal lord; the peasants had to be satisfied with a mixture of brown rice, millet, and greens. Today, some Japanese still eat rice three times a day, although they're now just as apt to have bread and coffee for breakfast.

ROBATAYAKI   Robatayaki refers to restaurants in which seafood and vegetables are cooked over an open charcoal grill. In the olden days, an open fireplace (*robata*) in the middle of an old Japanese house was the center of activity for cooking, eating, socializing, and simply keeping warm. Therefore, today's robatayaki restaurants are like nostalgia trips back into Japan's past and are often decorated in rustic farmhouse style, with staff dressed in traditional clothing. Robatayaki restaurants, often open only in the evening, are popular among office workers for both eating and drinking.

There's no special menu in a robatayaki restaurant—rather, it includes just about everything eaten in Japan. The difference is that most of the food will be grilled. Favorites of mine include gingko nuts (*ginnan*), asparagus wrapped in bacon (known simply as asparagus bacon), green peppers (*piman*), mushrooms (various kinds), potatoes (*jagabataa*), and just about any kind of fish. You can also usually get skewers of beef or chicken as well as a stew of meat and potatoes (*nikujaga*)—delicious in cold winter months. Since ordering is usually à la carte, you'll just have to look and point.

SASHIMI & SUSHI   It's estimated that the average Japanese eats 38 kilograms (83½ lb.) of seafood a year—that's six times the average American consumption. Although this seafood may be served in any number of ways, from grilled to boiled, a great deal of it is eaten raw. The idea of eating raw fish might seem a little strange at first, but if you try it, you'll probably like it.

Sashimi is simply raw seafood, usually served as an appetizer and eaten alone (that is, without rice). If you've never tried it, a good choice to start out with is *maguro*, or lean tuna, which doesn't taste fishy at all and is so delicate in texture that it almost melts in your mouth. The way to eat sashimi is first to put *wasabi* (pungent green horseradish) into a small dish of soy sauce and then dip the raw fish in the sauce using your chopsticks.

Sushi, which is raw fish with vinegared rice, comes in many varieties. The best known is *nigiri-zushi*: raw fish, seafood, or vegetables placed on top of vinegared rice with just a touch of wasabi. It's also dipped in soy sauce. Use chopsticks or your fingers to eat sushi; remember, you're supposed to eat each piece in one bite—quite a mouthful, but about the only way to keep it from falling apart. Another trick is to turn it upside down when you dip it in the sauce, to keep the rice from crumbling.

Also popular is *maki-zushi*, which consists of seafood, vegetables, or pickles rolled with rice inside a sheet of nori seaweed. *Inari-zushi* is vinegared rice and chopped vegetables inside a pouch of fried tofu bean curd.

Typical sushi includes tuna (*maguro*), flounder (*hirame*), sea bream (*tai*), squid (*ika*), octopus (*tako*), shrimp (*ebi*), sea eel (*anago*), and omelet (*tamago*). Ordering is easy because you usually sit at a counter, where you can see all the food in a refrigerated glass case in front of you. You also get to see the sushi chefs at work. The typical meal begins with sashimi and is followed by sushi, but if you don't want to order separately, there are always various set courses (*seto*).

By the way, the least expensive sushi is **chiraishi,** which is a selection of fish, seafood, and usually tamago on a large flat bowl of rice. Because you get more rice, those of you with bigger appetites may want to order chiraishi. Another way to enjoy sushi without spending a fortune is at a **kaiten sushi** shop, in which plates of sushi circulate on a conveyor belt on the counter—customers simply reach for the dishes they want and pay for the number of dishes they take.

SHABU-SHABU & SUKIYAKI   Until about a hundred years ago, the Japanese could think of nothing so disgusting as eating the flesh of animals (fish was okay). Considered unclean by the Buddhists, meat consumption was banned by the emperor in the 7th century. It wasn't until a century ago, when Emperor Meiji himself announced his intentions to eat meat, that the Japanese accepted the idea. Today, the Japanese have become skilled in preparing a number of beef dishes, and according to a survey conducted a few years ago by the Japan Fisheries Association, grilled meat, curry rice, and hamburger were the three favorite dishes among senior-high-school boys living in Tokyo. (Girls, by the way, still preferred sushi.)

Sukiyaki is among Japan's best-known beef dishes and is one many Westerners seem to prefer. Sukiyaki is thinly sliced beef cooked, at the table, in a broth of soy sauce, stock, and sake, along with scallions, spinach, mushrooms, tofu, bamboo shoots, and other vegetables. All diners serve themselves from the simmering pot and then dip their morsels into their own bowl of raw egg. You can skip the raw egg if you want, but it adds to the taste and also cools the food down enough so that it doesn't burn your tongue.

Shabu-shabu is also prepared at your table and consists of thinly sliced beef cooked in a broth with vegetables, in a kind of Japanese fondue. (It's named for the swishing sound the beef supposedly makes when cooking.) The main difference between the two dishes is the broth: Whereas in sukiyaki it consists of stock flavored with soy sauce and sake and is slightly sweet, in shabu-shabu it's relatively clear and has little taste of its own. The pots used are also different.

Using their chopsticks, shabu-shabu diners hold pieces of meat in the watery broth until they're cooked. This usually takes only a few seconds. Vegetables are left in longer, to swim around until fished out. For dipping, there's either sesame sauce with diced green onions or a more bitter fish stock sauce. Restaurants serving sukiyaki usually serve shabu-shabu as well.

SOBA & UDON NOODLES   The Japanese love eating noodles, and I suspect at least part of the joy comes from the way they eat them—they slurp, sucking in the noodles with gravity-defying speed. What's more, slurping noodles is considered proper etiquette. Fearing that it would stick with me forever, however, I've neglected to learn the technique. Establishments serving noodles range from stand-up eateries—often found at train and subway stations and the ultimate in fast food—to more refined noodle restaurants with tatami seating. Regardless of where you eat them, noodles are among the least expensive dishes in Japan.

There are many different kinds of noodles—some are eaten plain, some in combination with other foods such as shrimp tempura, some served hot, others served cold. **Soba,** made from buckwheat flour, is eaten hot (*kake-soba*) or cold (*zaru-soba*). **Udon** is a thick, white, wheat noodle originally from Osaka; it's usually served hot. **Somen** is a fine, white noodle eaten cold in the summer and dunked in a cold sauce.

TEMPURA   Today a well-known Japanese food, tempura was actually introduced by the Portuguese in the 16th century. Tempura is fish and vegetables delicately coated in a batter of egg, water, and wheat flour, and then deep-fried; it's served piping hot. To eat tempura, you usually dip it in a sauce of soy, fish stock, radish (*daikon*), and grated ginger; in some restaurants, only some salt, powdered green tea, and perhaps a lemon wedge are provided as accompaniments. Various tempura specialties include eggplant (*nasu*), mushroom (*shiitake*), sweet potato (*satsumaimo*), small green pepper (*shishito*), sliced lotus root (*renkon*), shrimp (*ebi*), squid (*ika*), lemon-mint leaf (*shiso*), and many kinds of fish. Again, the easiest thing to do is to order the set meal, the *teishoku*. If you're still hungry, you can always order something extra à la carte.

TEPPANYAKI A teppanyaki restaurant is a Japanese steak house. As in the well-known Benihana restaurants in many U.S. cities, the chef slices, dices, and cooks your meal of tenderloin or sirloin steak and vegetables on a smooth hot grill right in front of you—though with much less fanfare than in the U.S. Because beef is relatively new in Japanese cooking, some people categorize teppanyaki restaurants as "Western." However, I consider this style of cooking and presentation unique, and throughout this book I refer to such restaurants as Japanese. Teppanyaki restaurants tend to be expensive, simply because of the price of beef in Japan, with Kobe beef the most prized.

TONKATSU Tonkatsu is the Japanese word for "pork cutlet," made by dredging pork in wheat flour, moistening it with egg and water, dipping it in bread crumbs, and deep-frying it in vegetable oil. Since restaurants serving tonkatsu are generally inexpensive, they're popular with office workers and families. The easiest order is the teishoku, which usually features either the pork fillet (*hirekatsu*) or the pork loin (*rosukatsu*). In any case, your tonkatsu is served on a bed of shredded cabbage, and one or two different sauces will be at your table—a Worcestershire sauce and perhaps a specialty sauce. If you order the teishoku, it will come with rice, miso soup, and pickled vegetables.

UNAGI I'll bet that if you ate unagi without knowing what it was, you'd find it very tasty—and probably be very surprised to learn you'd just eaten eel. Popular as a health food because of its high vitamin A content, eel is supposed to help fight fatigue during hot summer months but is eaten year-round. Broiled eel (*kabayaki*) is prepared by grilling fillet strips over a charcoal fire; the eel is repeatedly dipped in a sweetened barbecue soy sauce while cooking. A favorite way to eat broiled eel is on top of rice, in which case it's called unaju. Do yourself a favor and try it.

YAKITORI Yakitori is chunks of chicken or chicken parts basted in a sweet soy sauce and grilled over a charcoal fire on thin skewers. Places that specialize in yakitori (*yakitori-ya*, often identifiable by a red paper lantern outside the front door) are technically not restaurants but, rather, drinking establishments; they usually don't open until 5 or 6pm. Most yakitori-ya are popular with workers as inexpensive places to drink, eat, and be merry.

The cheapest way to dine on yakitori is to order a set course, which will often include various parts of the chicken, including the skin, heart, and liver. Since this may not be entirely to your taste, you may wish to order à la carte, which is more expensive but gets you exactly what you want. In addition to chicken, other skewered, charcoaled delicacies are usually offered (called *kushi-yaki*). If you're ordering by the stick, you might want to try chicken breast (*sasami*), chicken meatballs (*tsukune*), green peppers (*piman*), chicken and leeks (*negima*), mushrooms (*shiitake*), or gingko nuts (*ginnan*).

OTHER CUISINES   During your travels you might also run into these types of Japanese cuisine: **Kamameshi** is a rice casserole, served in individual-size cast-iron pots, with different kinds of toppings that might include seafood, meat, or vegetables. **Domburi** is also a rice dish, topped with tempura, eggs, and either chicken or pork. **Nabe,** a stew cooked in an earthenware pot at your table, consists of chicken, sliced beef, pork, or seafood; noodles; and vegetables. **Oden** is a broth with fish cakes, tofu, eggs, and vegetables, served with hot mustard. If a restaurant advertises that it specializes in **Kyodo-Ryori,** it serves local specialties for which the region is famous and is often very rustic in decor. In recent years, the big Tokyo craze has been restaurants serving **crossover cuisine**—creative dishes inspired by ingredients from both sides of the Pacific rim.

Although technically Chinese fast-food restaurants, **ramen shops** are a big part of inexpensive dining in Japan. Serving what I consider to be generic Chinese noodles, soups, and other dishes, ramen shops can be found everywhere; they're easily recognizable by red signs, flashing lights, and quite often pictures of various dishes displayed right by the front door. Many are stand-up affairs—just a high counter to rest your bowl on. In addition to ramen (noodle and vegetable soup), you can also get such things as **yakisoba** (fried noodles) or—my favorite—**gyoza** (fried pork dumplings). What these places lack in atmosphere is made up for in cost: Most dishes average about ¥550 ($4.60), making them one of the cheapest places in Japan for a meal.

JAPANESE DRINK

All Japanese restaurants serve complimentary Japanese **green tea** with meals. If that's a little too weak for your taste, you may want to try **sake** (pronounced sah-kay), also called *Nihon-shu,* an alcoholic beverage made from rice and served either hot or cold. It goes well with most forms of Japanese cuisine. Produced since about the 3rd century, sake varies by region, production method, alcoholic content, color, aroma, and taste. Altogether, there are about 2,000 brands of sake produced in Japan. Miyabi is a prized classic sake; other popular brands are Gekkeikan, Koshinokanbai, Hakutsuru (meaning "white crane"), and Ozeki.

Japanese **beer** is also very popular. The biggest sellers are Kirin, Sapporo, Asahi, and Suntory, and each brand offers a bewildering variety of brews. In an attempt to capture the newest drinking market—women—beer companies continually come out with new products, most on sale at sidewalk vending machines. Ironically enough, Budweiser is also a big hit among young Japanese. Businessmen are fond of **whiskey,** which they usually drink with ice and water. **Wine,** usually available only at restaurants serving Western food, has gained in popularity in recent years, with both domestic and imported brands available. Although cocktails are available in discos, hotel lounges, and fancier bars at a rather inflated price, most Japanese stick with beer, sake, or whiskey.

Popular in recent years is **shochu,** an alcoholic beverage usually made from rice but sometimes from wheat, sweet potatoes, or sugar cane. It used to be considered a drink of the lower classes, but sales have increased so much that it's threatening the sake and whiskey businesses. A clear liquid, comparable, perhaps, to vodka, it can be consumed straight but is often combined with soda water in a drink called *chu-hai,* but watch out—the stuff can be deadly.

RESTAURANT ESSENTIALS

ORDERING   The biggest problem facing the hungry foreigner in Tokyo is ordering a meal in restaurants without English-language menus. This book alleviates the problem to a large extent by giving some sample dishes and prices for recommended restaurants. I've also noted which restaurants have English menus.

One aid to simplified ordering is the common use of **plastic food models** in glass display cases either outside or just inside the front door of many restaurants. Sushi, tempura, daily specials, spaghetti—they're all there in mouth-watering plastic replicas, along with the corresponding prices. Simply decide what you want and point it out to your waiter.

Unfortunately, not all restaurants in Japan have plastic display cases, especially the more exclusive or traditional ones. In fact, you'd be missing a lot of Tokyo's best cuisine if you restricted yourself to eating only at those with displays. If there's no display from which to choose, the best thing to do is to look at what people around you are eating and order what looks best. An alternative is simply to order the *teishoku*, or daily special meal (also called "set course" or simply "course," especially in restaurants serving Western food); these are fixed-price meals that consist of a main dish and several side dishes, often including soup, rice, and Japanese pickles. Although most restaurants have special set courses for dinner as well, lunch is the usual time for the teishoku; you can help keep your costs down by eating your big meal in the middle of the day. Even a restaurant that may be prohibitively expensive at dinnertime can be perfect for a lunchtime treat, when specials may cost as little as a fourth of what a dinner would be. The usual time for the teishoku is from about 11 or 11:30am to about 2pm.

HOURS   Restaurants are usually open from about 11am to 10 or 11pm. Of course, some establishments close earlier, while others stay open past midnight; many close for a few hours in the afternoon as well. Try to avoid the lunchtime rush, which is from noon to 1pm.

Keep in mind that the closing time posted for most restaurants is exactly that—everyone is expected to pay his or her bill and leave. A general rule of thumb is that the last order is taken at least a half hour before closing time, sometimes an hour or more for kaiseki restaurants. To be on the safe side, therefore, try to arrive at least an hour before closing time so that you have time to relax and enjoy your meal.

SMOKING   Sorry, nonsmokers—you won't find many nonsmoking areas in restaurants. Some 60% of Japanese men smoke (15% of women), and although this figure is down from 85% in 1965, those who do smoke have little consciousness of nonsmokers' rights. However, now that lung cancer has surpassed stomach cancer as the leading cause of cancer-related death in Japan, perhaps nonsmokers will gain more rights.

DINING PROCEDURE & ETIQUETTE

UPON ARRIVAL   As soon as you're seated in a Japanese restaurant (that is, a restaurant serving Japanese food), you'll be given a wet towel, which will be steaming hot in winter or pleasantly cool in summer. Called an **oshibori,** it's for wiping your hands. In all but the fanciest restaurants, men can get away with wiping their faces as well, but women are not supposed to (I ignore this if it's hot and humid outside). The oshibori is a great custom, one you'll wish would be adopted back home. Sadly, some cheaper Japanese restaurants now resort to a paper towel wrapped in plastic, which isn't nearly the same. Oshibori are generally not provided in Western restaurants.

CHOPSTICKS The next thing you'll probably be confronted with are chopsticks. The proper way to use them is to place the first chopstick between the base of the thumb and the top of the ring finger (this chopstick remains stationary) and the second one between the top of the thumb and the middle and index fingers (this second chopstick is the one you move to pick up food). The best way to learn to use chopsticks is to have a Japanese show you how. It's not difficult, but if you're having trouble, some restaurants might have a fork as well. How proficiently foreigners handle chopsticks is a matter of great curiosity for the Japanese, and they're surprised if you know how to use them; even if you were to live in Japan for 20 years, you would never stop receiving compliments on how talented you are with chopsticks.

As for etiquette involving chopsticks, if you're taking something from a communal bowl or tray, you're supposed to turn your chopsticks upside down and use the part that hasn't been in your mouth. After transferring the food to your plate, you turn the chopsticks back to their proper position. The exception is shabu-shabu and sukiyaki. Never stick your chopsticks down vertically into your bowl of rice and leave them there—that is done only when a person has died. Also, don't pass anything from your chopsticks to another person's chopsticks, as that's done only to pass the bones of the cremated.

EATING SOUP If you're eating soup, you won't use a spoon. Rather, you'll pick up the bowl and drink from it. Use your chopsticks to fish out larger morsels of food. It's considered in good taste to slurp with gusto, especially if you're eating noodles. Noodle shops in Japan are always well orchestrated with slurps and smacks.

DRINKING If you're drinking in Japan, the main thing to remember is that you never pour your own glass. Bottles of beer are so large that people often share one. The rule is that, in turn, one person pours for everyone else in the group, so be sure to hold up your glass when someone is pouring for you. Only as the night progresses do the Japanese get sloppy about this rule. It took me a while to figure this out, but if no one notices your empty glass, the best thing to do is to pour everyone else a drink so that someone will pour yours. If someone wants to pour you a drink and your glass is full, the proper thing to do is to take a few gulps so that he or she can fill your glass. Because each person is continually filling everyone else's glass, you never know exactly how much you've had to drink, which (depending on how you look at it) is either very good or very bad.

PAYING THE BILL If you go out with a group of friends (not as a visiting guest of honor and not with business associates), it's customary to split the dinner bill equally, even if you all ordered different things. This makes it difficult if you're trying to spend wisely, especially if others had a lot more to eat and drink. But even foreigners living in Japan adopt the practice of splitting the bill; it certainly makes figuring everyone's share easier, especially since there's no tipping in Japan.

OTHER TIPS It's considered bad manners to walk down the street in Japan eating or drinking (except at a festival). You'll notice if a Japanese buys a drink from a vending machine, he'll stand there, gulp it down, and throw away the container before moving on. To the chagrin of the elders, young Japanese sometimes ignore this rule.

HOW TO EAT WITHOUT SPENDING A FORTUNE

Even with today's economy in Japan, Tokyo is still an extremely expensive city. During your first few days here, money will seem to flow out of your pockets like water. Many people become convinced they must have lost some of it somehow. At this point, almost everyone panics (I've seen it happen again and again), but then they slowly realize that since prices are markedly different here (steeper), a bit of readjustment in thinking and habits is necessary. Coffee, for example, is something of a luxury, and some Japanese are astonished at the thought of drinking four or five cups a day. By following the advice here, you'll be able to cut down on needless expenses, saving your money for special things.

BREAKFAST & COFFEE BREAKS   If you're on a tight budget, avoid eating breakfast at your hotel (after a week of buffet breakfasts consisting of scrambled eggs, processed ham, and lettuce, you'll probably tire of them anyway). Coffee shops offer what's called "morning service" until 10 or 11am; it generally consists of a cup of coffee, a small salad, a boiled egg, and toast, for about ¥550 ($4.60). That's a real bargain when you consider that just one cup of coffee can cost ¥300 to ¥600 ($2.50 to $5), depending upon where you order it (with the exception of some hotel breakfast buffets, there's no such thing as the bottomless cup in Japan).

For a coffee break later in the day, look for an inexpensive chain such as Doutour or Pronto, where a cup of coffee runs about ¥200 ($1.65). Starbucks has also conquered Japan, with more than 40 locations in Tokyo alone (and probably a good deal more by the time you read this); it charges from ¥250 ($2.10) for a short to ¥370 ($3.10) for a grande caffe latte (per company policy, smoking is banned).

SET LUNCHES   Eat your biggest meal at lunch. Many restaurants serving Japanese food offer a daily set lunch (*teishoku*) at a fraction of their set dinner's cost. Usually ranging in price from ¥700 to ¥1,500 ($5.85 to $12.50), they're generally available from 11 or 11:30am to 2 or 2:30pm. A Japanese teishoku will often include the main course (such as tempura, grilled fish, or the specialty of the house), soup, pickled vegetables, rice, and tea, while the set menu in a Western-style restaurant (often called set lunch) usually consists of a main dish, salad, bread, and coffee.

CHEAP EATS   Places in which to look for inexpensive restaurants include department stores (often one whole floor will be devoted to various kinds of restaurants, most with plastic food displays), underground shopping arcades, nightlife districts, and around train and subway stations. Some of the cheapest establishments for a night out on the town are the countless **yakitori-ya** across Japan—drinking establishments that also sell skewered meats and vegetables. **Noodle shops** are also generally inexpensive, ranging from stand-up stalls seen around train stations to more traditional restaurants, where guests sit at low tables on tatami. **Ramen shops** specializing in Chinese noodles and soups are even cheaper. For **sushi,** the cheapest places are those that deliver food via a conveyor belt; you simply reach out and take the plate that interests you. **Coffee shops** often offer inexpensive Western food, including sandwiches. Japan also has American fast-food chains, such as McDonald's (where Big Macs cost about ¥280/$2.35), Wendy's, and Kentucky Fried Chicken, as well as Japanese chains—Morninaga, Lotteria, and First Kitchen among them—that sell hamburgers and french fries.

PRE-PREPARED FOODS   You can save even more money by avoiding restaurants altogether. There are all kinds of pre-prepared foods you can buy; some are even complete meals, perfect for picnics in the park or right in your hotel room.

Perhaps the best known is the **obento,** or box lunch, commonly sold in major train stations and on train-station platforms, in food sections of department stores, and at counter windows of tiny shops throughout Tokyo. Costing usually between ¥800 and ¥1,500 ($6.65 and $12.50), the basic obento contains a piece of meat (generally fish or chicken), various side dishes, rice, and pickled vegetables. Sushi boxed lunches are also available.

My favorite place to shop for pre-prepared foods is to go to a **department store** and head for the food and produce section, usually in the basement. These places hearken back to Japanese markets of yore, with vendors yelling out their wares and crowds of housewives deciding on the evening's dinner. Different counters specialize in different items—tempura, yakitori, eel, Japanese pickles, cooked fish, sushi (sometimes made by robots!), salads, vegetables, and desserts. Almost the entire spectrum of Japanese cuisine is available, and there are numerous samples available (some travelers have been known to "dine" in department-store basements for free). What I love about buying my dinner in a department store is that I can compose my own meal exactly as I wish—perhaps some sushi, some mountain vegetables, boiled soy beans, maybe even some Chinese food—in combinations never available in most restaurants. There are also counters selling obento box meals. In any case, you can eat for less than ¥1,200 ($10), and there's nothing like milling with Japanese housewives to make you feel like one of the locals. Though not as colorful, 24-hour convenience stores also sell packaged foods, including sandwiches and obento.

Street-side stalls, called **yatai,** are also good sources for inexpensive meals. These restaurants-on-wheels sell a variety of foods, including *oden* (fish cakes), *yakitori* (skewered barbecued chicken), and *yakisoba* (fried noodles), as well as sake and beer. They appear mostly at night, lighted by a single lantern or a string of lights, and many have a counter with stools as well, protected in winter by a wall of tarp. These can also be great places for rubbing elbows with the locals.

6 Shrines & Temples: Religion in Japan

The main religions in Japan are Shintoism and Buddhism, and many Japanese consider themselves believers in both. Most Japanese, for example, will marry in a Shinto ceremony, but when they die, they'll have a Buddhist funeral.

A native religion of Japan, **Shintoism** is the worship of ancestors and national heroes, as well as of all natural things, both animate and inanimate. These natural things are thought to embody gods and can be anyone or anything—mountains, trees, the moon, stars, rivers, seas, fires, animals, rocks, even vegetables. Shintoism also embraces much of Confucianism, which entered Japan in the 5th century and stressed the importance of family and loyalty. There are no scriptures in Shintoism, nor any ordained code of morals or ethics.

The place of worship in Shintoism is called a *jinja,* or shrine. The most obvious sign of a shrine is its *torii,* an entrance gate, usually of wood, consisting of two tall poles topped with either one or two crossbeams. Another feature common to shrines is a water trough with communal cups, where

If the most celebrated cathedrals of Europe were situated in the Black Forest, and were all simple wooden structures resembling very large but plain log cabins, Christianity would approximate to Shinto in its aesthetic appeal.
—Alexander Campbell, *The Heart of Japan,* 1962, on the Ise Jingu Shrine

the Japanese will rinse out their mouths and wash their hands. Purification and cleanliness are important in Shintoism because they show respect to the gods. At the shrine itself, worshippers will throw a few coins into a money box, clap their hands three times to get the gods' attention, and then bow their heads and pray for whatever they wish—good health, protection, the safe delivery of a child, or a prosperous year. The most famous shrine in Tokyo is **Meiji Shrine.**

Founded in India in the 5th century, **Buddhism** came to Japan in the 6th century via China and Korea, bringing with it the concept of eternal life, and by the end of the 6th century had gained such popularity that it was declared the state religion. Of the various Buddhist sects in Japan today, Zen Buddhism is probably the most well known in the West. Considered the most Japanese form of Buddhism, Zen is the practice of meditation and a strictly disciplined lifestyle to rid oneself of desire so that one can achieve enlightenment. There are no rites in Zen Buddhism, no dogmas, no theological conceptions of divinity. One does not analyze rationally, but rather knows things intuitively. The strict and simple lifestyle of Zen appealed greatly to Japan's samurai warrior class, and many of Japan's arts, including the tea ceremony, arose from the practice of Zen.

Whereas Shintoists have shrines, Buddhists have temples, called *otera.* Instead of torii, temples will often have an entrance gate with a raised doorsill and heavy doors. Temples may also have a cemetery on their grounds (which Shinto shrines never have) as well as a pagoda. Tokyo's most famous temple is **Sensoji Temple** in Asakusa.

7 Recommended Reading

There are a vast number of books in English covering every aspect of Japan. **Kodansha International,** a Japanese publishing company, has probably published more books on Japan in English—including Japanese-language textbooks—than any other company. Available at major bookstores in Japan, you can also order them over the Internet from www.amazon.com.

HISTORY   The definitive work of Japan's history through the ages is *Japan: The Story of a Nation* (Alfred A. Knopf, 1991), by Edwin O. Reischauer, a former U.S. ambassador to Japan. For overview of Tokyo's history, refer to Edward G. Seidensticker's *Low City, High City* (Harvard University Press, 1991), which covers the period from 1867 to 1923, when the city rapidly grew from an isolated and ancient shogun's capital into a great modern city; and its sequel, *Tokyo Rising* (Harvard University Press, 1991), which describes the metropolis since the Great Earthquake of 1923 and follows its remarkable development through the postwar years until the end of the 1980s. Arthur Sadler's *The Maker of Modern Japan: The Life of Shogun Tokugawa Ieyasu* (Tuttle, 1987) is a biography of the first Tokugawa shogun, the man responsible for transforming the sleepy town of Edo (Tokyo) into the bustling capital of the shogunate government.

SOCIETY & CULTURE   Reischauer's *The Japanese Today* (Tuttle, 1993) offers a unique perspective of Japanese society, including the historical events that have shaped and influenced Japanese behavior and the role of the individual in Japanese society. Other books pertaining to Japanese society and psychology are Kurt Singer's *Mirror, Sword and Jewel: The Geometry of Japanese Life* (Kodansha, 1981) and Chie Nakane's *Japanese Society* (University of California Press, 1970). A classic description of the Japanese and their culture is found in Ruth Benedict's brilliant *The Chrysanthemum and the Sword: Patterns of Japanese Culture* (New American Library, 1967), first published in the 1940s but reprinted many times since. For a more contemporary approach, look into *The Japanese Mind: The Goliath Explained* (Linden Press/Simon & Schuster, 1983), by Robert C. Christopher; I consider this book compulsory reading for anyone traveling to Japan because it describes so accurately the Japanese and the role history has played in developing their psyche. On the other hand, debunking many commonly held theories on Japanese society (many of which are espoused by the books above) is *Japan: A Reinterpretation* (Pantheon, 1997), by former *International Herald Tribune* Tokyo bureau chief Patrick Smith, who provides a spirited new look into Japan's economic miracle and recent demise. Tokyo's growing homeless population is tackled in *Tokyo's Homeless: A City in Denial* (Nova Science Publishers, 1999) by Tony D. Guzewicz.

For advice on Japanese etiquette, refer to *Japanese Etiquette Today: A Guide to Business and Social Customs* (Tuttle, 1994), by James M. Vardaman and Michiko Sasaki Vardaman, which covers everything from bowing and bathing to eating and dining customs, office etiquette, and the complicated art of giving gifts. Business travelers may also want to read *Business Japan: A Practical Guide to Understanding Japanese Business Culture* by Peggy Kenna and Sonra Lacy (NTC Publishing, 1994), which compares American and Japanese business styles, practices, and social customs.

For information on religions in Japan, two beautifully illustrated books are *Shinto: Japan's Spiritual Roots* (Kodansha, 1980) and *Buddhism: Japan's Cultural Identity* (Kodansha, 1982), both by Stuart D. B. Picken, with introductions by Edwin O. Reischauer.

THE ARTS   For a general rundown on the development of literature, religion, and art through the ages, see George B. Sansom's *Japan: A Short Cultural History* (Charles E. Tuttle, 1997).

Kabuki and other stage arts are covered in Faubion Bowers's *Japanese Theater* (Greenwood Press, 1976), while *The Kabuki Handbook* (Charles E. Tuttle, 1998) by Aubrey and Giovanna Halford summarizes popular plays. The history and philosophy of the tea ceremony, beginning with its origins in the 12th century, are explained in *The Tea Ceremony* (Kodansha, 1998), by Sen'o Tanaka. Another worthwhile read is *The Japanese Way of Tea: From its Origins in China to Sen Rikyu*, by Sen Soshitsu (University of Hawaii Press, 1998).

CONTEMPORARY CHRONICLES   For contemporary experiences of foreigners in Japan, there's the inimitable Dave Barry, who describes his whirlwind trip to the land of the rising sun in the comical *Dave Barry Does Japan* (Random House, 1992). A delightful account of the Japanese and their customs is given by the irrepressible George Mikes in *The Land of the Rising Yen* (Penguin, 1973); I doubt you'll be able to find the book in the United States; it's in major bookstores in Japan, however, and would make enjoyable reading during your trip. Rick Kennedy, a longtime resident of

Japan, gives a lighthearted view of life in the capital in *Home, Sweet Tokyo: Life in a Weird and Wonderful City* (Kodansha, 1988).

FICTION In Tokyo bookstores, you'll find whole sections dedicated to English translations of Japan's best-known modern and contemporary authors, including Mishima Yukio, Soseki Natsume, Abe Kobo, Tanizaki Junichiro, and Nobel Prize winners Kawabata Yasunari and Oe Kenzaburo. An overview of Japanese classical literature is provided in *Anthology of Japanese Literature* (Grove Press, 1955), edited by Donald Keene. *Modern Japanese Stories: An Anthology* (Tuttle, 1962), edited by Ivan Morris, introduces short stories by some of Japan's top modern writers, including Mori Ogai, Tanizaki Junichiro, Kawabata Yasunari, and Mishima Yukio.

Soseki Natsume, one of Japan's most respected novelists of the Meiji Era, writes of Tokyo and its tumultuous time of change in *And Then* (Putnam, 1982), translated by Norma Moore Field, and *Kokoro* (Regnery Gateway Co., 1985), translated by Edwin McClellan. His first novel, *I am a Cat* (Charles E. Tuttle, 1972), describes the foibles of upper-middle-class Japanese during the Meiji Era through the eyes of a cat.

Oe Kenzaburo gained international recognition when he became the second Japanese to win the Nobel Prize for Literature in 1994. He has written such well-known novels as *A Personal Matter* (Grove Press, 1968), about a Tokyo man in search of himself after the birth of a handicapped son, as well as *A Healing Family* (Kodansha, 1996), a collection of essays written over several years dealing primarily with Oe's severely handicapped autistic son, Hikari, who has become a celebrity in his own right as a composer of classical music. Other favorite writers of Japan's baby-boom generation include Murakami Ryu, who burst onto the literary scene with *Almost Transparent Blue* (Kodansha, 1977) and later captured the undercurrent of decadent urban life in his best-selling *Coin Locker Babies* (Kodansha, 1995), and Murakami Haruki, whose writings include *Dance Dance Dance* (Kodansha, 1994), about a 30-something protagonist living in a glittering high-rise but searching for more meaning in life, and *South of the Border, West of the Sun* (Knopf, 1999), the story of a bewildered man in contemporary Tokyo.

Among works of fiction about Japan by Western writers, most Westerners are familiar with James Clavell's *Shogun* (Dell, 1975), a fictional account based on the lives of Englishman William Adams and military leader Tokugawa Ieyasu around 1600 and later made into a television miniseries.

For fictional yet personal contemporary accounts of what it's like for Westerners living in Tokyo, two entertaining novels are John D. Morley's *Pictures from the Water Trade* (Harper & Row, 1986) and Robert J. Collins's *Max Danger: The Adventures of an Expat in Tokyo* (Tuttle, 1987). Finally, *Audrey Hepburn's Neck* (Simon & Schuster, 1996), by Alan Brown, is a poignant portrait of Japan's mishmash of Western and Japanese culture, as seen through the eyes of a confused young Japanese comic illustrator living in Tokyo.

Appendix B: The Japanese Language

1 A Glossary of Useful Japanese Terms

Needless to say, it takes years to become fluent in Japanese, particularly in written Japanese, with its thousands of kanji, or Chinese characters, and many hiragana and katakana characters. Knowing just a few words of Japanese, however, is not only useful but will delight the Japanese people you meet in the course of your trip.

PRONUNCIATION

In pronouncing the following vocabulary, keep in mind that there's very little stress on individual syllables (pronunciation of Japanese is often compared to Italian). Here's an approximation of some of the sounds of Japanese:

a   *as in* father
e   *as in* pen
i   *as in* see
o   *as in* oh
oo *as in* oooh
u   *as in* boo
g   *as in* gift at the beginning of words; like ng in sing in the middle or at the end of words

Vowel sounds are almost always short unless they are pronounced double, in which case you hold the vowel a bit longer. *Okashi*, for example, means "a sweet," whereas *okashii* means "strange." As you can see, even slight mispronunciation of a word can result in confusion or hilarity. (Incidentally, jokes in Japanese are nearly always plays on words.) Similarly, double consonants are given more emphasis than only one consonant by itself.

USEFUL WORDS & PHRASES
BASIC TERMS

Good morning
   Ohayo gozaimasu
Good afternoon
   Konnichiwa
Good evening   **Konbanwa**
Good night   **Oyasuminasai**

Hello   **Haro**
   (or **Konnichiwa**)
How are you?
   Ogenki desu ka?
How do you do?
   Hajimemashite?

Good-bye **Sayonara (**
or **Bye-bye!)**
Excuse me/Pardon me/I'm sorry
Sumimasen
Please (when offering something)
Dozo
Please (when requesting some-
thing) **Kudasai**

Thank you **Domo arigatoo**
You're welcome **Doo-
itashimashite**
Please (go ahead) **Doozo**
Yes **Hai**
No **Iie**

BASIC QUESTIONS & EXPRESSIONS

I'm American **Amerikajin desu**
I'm Canadian **Canadajin desu**
I'm English **Eikokujin desu**
Sorry, I don't speak Japanese
**Sumimasen, Nihongo was
wakarimasen**
Do you understand English?
Eigo wa wakarimasu ka?
Do you understand?
Wakarimasu ka?
I understand **Wakarimasu**
I don't understand
Wakarimasen
Can I ask you a question?
Otazune shitaino desu ka?
Just a minute, please
Chotto matte kudasai

How much is it? **Ikura desu ka?**
It's expensive **Takai desu**
It's cheap **Yasui desu**
Where is it? **Doko desu ka?**
When is it? **Itsu desu ka?**
What is it?
Kore-wa, nan-desu-ka?
I like it **Suki desu**
(pronounced "ski")
Where is the toilet?
Toire wa, doko desu ka?
My name is . . .
[Your name] **to mo shimasu**
What is your name?
O-namae wa, nan desu ka?

TRAVEL EXPRESSIONS & DIRECTIONALS

Where is . . . ?
Doko desu ka . . . ?
Where is the train station?
Eki wa, doko desu ka?
Train station **Eki**
Airport **Kuukoo**
Subway **Chika-tetsu**
Bus **Bus-u**
Taxi **Takushi**
Airplane **Hikooki**
Train **Densha**
Bullet train **Shinkansen**
Limited express train (long
distance) **Tokkyu**
Ordinary express train (doesn't
stop at every station)
Kyuko
Rapid train **Kaisoku densha**
Local train (one that stops at
every station)
Kakueki teisha (or **futsu**)
I would like a reserved seat, please.
Shiteiseki o kudasai.

I would like a seat in the
no-smoking car, please.
**Kinensha no shiteiski o
kudasai.**
Unreserved seat **Jiyuseki**
Platform **Platt-homu**
Ticket **Kippu**
Destination **Ikisaki**
One-way ticket
Katamichi-kippu
(or **katamichiken**)
Round-trip ticket **Ofuku-kippu**
(or **ofukuken**)
I would like to buy a ticket.
**Kippu ichimai o kaitai no
desu kedo.**
I would like to buy two tickets.
**Kippu nimai o kaitai no desu
kedo.**
Exit **Deguchi**
Entrance **Iriguchi**
North **Kita**
South **Minami**

The Japanese Language

East **Higashi**
West **Nishi**
Left **Hidari**
Right **Migi**
Straight ahead **Massugu** (or **zutto**)
Is it far? **Toi desu ka?**
Is it near? **Chikai desu ka?**
Can I walk there? **Aruite ike-masu ka?**
Street **Dori** (or **michi**)
Tourist Information Office **Kanko annaijo** (or **kanko kyokai**)
Where is the tourist office? **Kanko annaijo, doko desu ka?**

May I have a map, please? **Chizu o kudasai?**
Police **Keisatsu**
Police box **Koban**
Post office **Yubin-kyoku**
I'd like to buy a stamp. **Kitte o kaitai no desu kedo.**
Bank **Ginko**
Hospital **Byooin**
Drug store **Yakkyoku**
Convenience store **Konbiniensu stoa**
Embassy **Taishkan**
Department store **Depaato**
Downtown area **Hanka-gai**

LODGING TERMS

Hotel **Hoteru**
Japanese-style inn **Ryokan**
Youth hostel **Yusu hosuteru**
Cotton kimono **Yukata**
Room **Heya**
Do you have a room available? **Heya ga arimasu ka?**
Does that include meals? **Shokuji wa tsuite imasu ka?**
Tax **Zei**
Service charge **Saavice**

Key **Kagi**
Balcony **Baranda**
Hot-spring spa **Onsen**
Outdoor hot-spring bath **Roten-buro**
Bath **Ofuro**
Public bath **Sento**
Where is the nearest public bath? **Ichiban chikai sento wa, doko desu ka?**

DINING TERMS & PHRASES

Restaurant **Resutoran** (serves Western-style food)
Dining hall **Shokudo** (usually serves Japanese food)
Coffee shop **Kissaten**
Japanese pub **Izakaya**
Western food **Yoshoku**
Japanese food **Washoku**
Breakfast **Chosoku**
Dinner **Yushoku**
I'd like to make a reservation **Yoyaku oneigai shimasu**
Menu **Menyu**
Japanese green tea **Ocha**
Black (Indian) tea **Kocha**
Coffee **Koohi**
Water **Mizu**
Lunch or daily special, set menu **Teishoku** (Japanese food)
Lunch or daily special, set menu **Cosu**, or **seto** (usually Western food)

This is delicious. **Oishii desu.**
Thank you for the meal. **Gochisoo-sama deshita.**
I would like a fork, please. **Foku o kudasai.**
I would like a spoon, please. **Saji o kudasai.**
I would like a knife, please. **Naifu o kudasai.**
May I have some more, please? (if you're asking for liquid, such as more coffee, or food) **Mo skoshi o kudasai?**
May I have some more, please? (if you're asking for another bottle—say, of soda or sake) **Mo ipon o kudasai?**
May I have some more, please? (if you asking for another cup—say, of coffee or tea) **Mo ippai o kudasai?**

The Japanese Language

I would like sake, please. **Osake o kudasai.**

I would like a cup of coffee. **Koohii o ippai o kudasai.**

I would like the set meal, please. **Seto o kudasai** or **Teishoku o kudasai.**

FOOD TERMS

Ayu A small river fish; a delicacy of western Japan.

Anago Conger eel.

Chu-hai Shochu Mixed with soda water and flavored with syrup and lemon (see below).

Dengaku Lightly grilled tofu (see below) coated with a bean paste.

Dojo A small, eel-like river fish.

Fugu Pufferfish (also known as blowfish or globefish).

"Genghis Khan" Mutton and vegetables grilled at your table.

Gohan Rice.

Gyoza Chinese fried pork dumplings.

Kaiseki A formal Japanese meal consisting of many courses and served originally during the tea ceremony.

Kamameshi A rice casserole topped with seafood, meat, or vegetables.

Kushiage (also **kushikatsu** or **kushiyaki**) Deep-fried skewers of chicken, beef, seafood, and vegetables.

Maguro Tuna.

Makizushi Sushi (see below), vegetables, and rice rolled inside dried seaweed.

Miso A soybean paste, used as a seasoning in soups and sauces.

Miso-shiru Miso soup.

Mochi Japanese rice cake.

Nabemono A single-pot dish of chicken, beef, pork, or seafood, stewed with vegetables.

Natto Fermented soybeans.

Nikujaga A beef, potato, and carrot stew, flavored with sake (see below) and soy sauce; popular in winter.

Oden Fish cakes, hard-boiled eggs, and vegetables, simmered in a light broth.

Okonomiyaki A thick pancake filled with meat, fish, shredded cabbage, and vegetables or noodles, often cooked by diners at their table.

Ramen Thick, yellow Chinese noodles, served in a hot soup.

Sake (also **Nihon-shu**) Rice wine.

Sansai Mountain vegetables, including bracken and flowering fern.

Sashimi Raw seafood.

Shabu-shabu Thinly sliced beef quickly dipped in boiling water and then dipped in a sauce.

Shochu Japanese whiskey, made from rice, wheat, or potatoes.

Shojin-ryoori Japanese vegetarian food, served at Buddhist temples.

Shoyu Soy sauce.

Shumai Steamed Chinese pork dumplings.

Soba Buckwheat noodles.

Somen Fine white wheat vermicelli, eaten cold in summer.

Sukiyaki A Japanese fondue of thinly sliced beef cooked in a sweetened soy sauce with vegetables.

Sushi (also **nigiri-zushi**) Raw seafood placed on top of vinegared rice.

Tempura Deep-fried food coated in a batter of egg, water, and wheat flour.

Teppanyaki Japanese-style steak, seafood, and vegetables cooked by a chef on a smooth, hot tableside grill.

Tofu Soft bean curd.

Tonkatsu Deep-fried pork cutlets.

Udon Thick white wheat noodles.

The Japanese Language

Unagi   Grilled eel.
Wasabi   Japanese horseradish, served with sushi.
Yakisoba   Chinese fried noodles, served with sautéed vegetables.

Yakitori   Charcoal-grilled chicken, vegetables, and other specialties, served on bamboo skewers.
Yudofu   Tofu simmered in a pot at your table.

MATTERS OF TIME

Now   **Ima**
Later   **Sto de**
Today   **Kyoo**
Tomorrow   **Ashita**
Day After Tomorrow   **Asatte**
Yesterday   **Kinoo**
Which day?   **Nan-nichi desu ka?**

Daytime   **Hiruma**
Morning   **Asa**
Night   **Yoru**
Afternoon   **Gogo**
Holiday   **Yasumi** (or **kyujitsu**)
Weekdays   **Heijitsu**

Days of the Week

Sunday   **Nichiyoobi**
Monday   **Getsuyoobi**
Tuesday   **Kayoobi**
Wednesday   **Suiyoobi**

Thursday   **Mokuyoobi**
Friday   **Kinyoobi**
Saturday   **Doyoobi**

Months of the Year

January   **Ichi-gatsu**
February   **Ni-gatsu**
March   **San-gatsu**
April   **Shi-gatsu**
May   **Go-gatsu**
June   **Roku-gatsu**

July   **Shichi-gatsu**
August   **Hachi-gatsu**
September   **Kyuu-gatsu**
October   **Juu-gatsu**
November   **Juuichi-gatsu**
December   **Juuni-gatsu**

NUMBERS

1	**Ichi**	20	**Nijuu**
2	**Ni**	30	**Sanjuu**
3	**San**	40	**Shijuu** (or **yonjuu**)
4	**Shi**	50	**Gojuu**
5	**Go**	60	**Rokujuu**
6	**Roku**	70	**Nanajuu**
7	**Shichi** (or **nana**)	80	**Hachijuu**
8	**Hachi**	90	**Kyuuju**
9	**Kyuu**	100	**Hyaku**
10	**Juu**	1,000	**Sen**
11	**Juuichi**	10,000	**Ichiman**
12	**Juuni**		

OTHER GENERAL NOUNS

Fusuma   Sliding paper doors.
Gaijin   Foreigner.
Geta   Wooden sandals.
Haori   A short coat worn over a kimono.
Irori   Open-hearth fireplace.
Jinja   Shinto shrine.

Kotatsu   A heating element placed under a low table (which is covered with a blanket) for keeping one's legs warm; used in place of a heater in traditional Japanese homes.

Minshuku Inexpensive lodging in a private home; the Japanese equivalent of a European pension.

Nihonjin Japanese person.

Nomi-ya A drinking establishment.

Shoji White paper sliding windows.

Tatami Rice mats.

Tera (or **dera**) Temple.

Tokonoma A small, recessed alcove in a Japanese room used to display a flower arrangement, scroll, or art object.

Torii Entrance gate of a Shinto shrine, consisting usually of two poles topped with one or two crossbeams.

Yukata A cotton kimono worn for sleeping.

Zabuton Floor cushions.

2 A Japanese-Character Index of Establishment Na

The Japanese Language

Index

See also Accommodations and Restaurants indexes, below.

General Index

General Index

Restaurant Index

FROMMER'S® COMPLETE TRAVEL GUIDES

Alaska
Amsterdam
Arizona
Atlanta
Australia
Austria
Bahamas
Barcelona, Madrid &
  Seville
Beijing
Belgium, Holland &
  Luxembourg
Bermuda
Boston
British Columbia & the
  Canadian Rockies
Budapest & the Best of
  Hungary
California
Canada
Cancún, Cozumel &
  the Yucatán
Cape Cod, Nantucket &
  Martha's Vineyard
Caribbean
Caribbean Cruises & Ports
  of Call
Caribbean Ports of Call
Carolinas & Georgia
Chicago
China
Colorado
Costa Rica
Denmark
Denver, Boulder & Colorado
  Springs
England
Europe

European Cruises & Ports
  of Call
Florida
France
Germany
Greece
Greek Islands
Hawaii
Hong Kong
Honolulu, Waikiki &
  Oahu
Ireland
Israel
Italy
Jamaica
Japan
Las Vegas
London
Los Angeles
Maryland & Delaware
Maui
Mexico
Miami & the Keys
Montana & Wyoming
Montréal & Québec City
Munich & the Bavarian
  Alps
Nashville & Memphis
Nepal
New England
New Mexico
New Orleans
New York City
New Zealand
Nova Scotia, New Brunswick
  & Prince Edward Island
Oregon
Paris

Philadelphia & the
  Amish Country
Portugal
Prague & the Best of the
  Czech Republic
Provence & the Riviera
Puerto Rico
Rome
San Antonio & Austin
San Diego
San Francisco
Santa Fe, Taos & Albuquerque
Scandinavia
Scotland
Seattle & Portland
Singapore & Malaysia
South Africa
Southeast Asia
South Pacific
Spain
Sweden
Switzerland
Thailand
Tokyo
Toronto
Tuscany & Umbria
USA
Utah
Vancouver & Victoria
Vermont, New Hampshire
  & Maine
Vienna & the Danube Valley
Virgin Islands
Virginia
Walt Disney World &
  Orlando
Washington, D.C.
Washington State

FROMMER'S® DOLLAR-A-DAY GUIDES

Australia from $50 a Day
California from $60 a Day
Caribbean from $70 a Day
England from $70 a Day
Europe from $60 a Day

Florida from $60 a Day
Hawaii from $70 a Day
Ireland from $60 a Day
Italy from $70 a Day
London from $85 a Day

New York from $80 a Day
Paris from $85 a Day
San Francisco from $60 a Day
Washington, D.C.,
  from $60 a Day

FROMMER'S® PORTABLE GUIDES

Acapulco, Ixtapa &
  Zihuatanejo
Alaska Cruises & Ports of Call
Bahamas
Baja & Los Cabos
Berlin
California Wine Country
Charleston & Savannah
Chicago

Dublin
Hawaii: The Big Island
Las Vegas
London
Maine Coast
Maui
New Orleans
New York City
Paris

Puerto Vallarta, Manzanillo
  & Guadalajara
San Diego
San Francisco
Sydney
Tampa & St. Petersburg
Venice
Washington, D.C.

FROMMER'S® NATIONAL PARK GUIDES

Family Vacations in the
   National Parks
Grand Canyon

National Parks of the
   American West
Rocky Mountain

Yellowstone & Grand Teton
Yosemite & Sequoia/
   Kings Canyon
Zion & Bryce Canyon

FROMMER'S® MEMORABLE WALKS

Chicago
London

New York
Paris

San Francisco
Washington, D.C.

FROMMER'S® GREAT OUTDOOR GUIDES

New England
Northern California

Southern California & Baja
Southern New England

Washington & Oregon

FROMMER'S® BORN TO SHOP GUIDES

Born to Shop: China
Born to Shop: France

Born to Shop: Italy
Born to Shop: London

Born to Shop: New York
Born to Shop: Paris

FROMMER'S® IRREVERENT GUIDES

Amsterdam
Boston
Chicago
Las Vegas

London
Los Angeles
Manhattan
New Orleans

Paris
San Francisco
Seattle & Portland
Vancouver

Walt Disney World
Washington, D.C.

FROMMER'S® BEST-LOVED DRIVING TOURS

America
Britain
California

Florida
France
Germany

Ireland
Italy
New England

Scotland
Spain
Western Europe

THE UNOFFICIAL GUIDES®

Bed & Breakfasts in
   California
Bed & Breakfasts in
   New England
Bed & Breakfasts in
   the Northwest
Beyond Disney
Branson, Missouri
California with Kids
Chicago

Cruises
Disneyland
Florida with Kids
Golf Vacations in the
   Eastern U.S.
The Great Smoky &
   Blue Ridge
   Mountains
Inside Disney

Hawaii
Las Vegas
London
Miami & the Keys
Mini Las Vegas
Mini-Mickey
New Orleans
New York City
Paris

Safaris
San Francisco
Skiing in the West
Walt Disney World
Walt Disney World
   for Grown-ups
Walt Disney World
   for Kids
Washington, D.C.

SPECIAL-INTEREST TITLES

Frommer's Britain's Best Bed & Breakfasts and
   Country Inns
Frommer's Britain's Best Bike Rides
The Civil War Trust's Official Guide
   to the Civil War Discovery Trail
Frommer's Caribbean Hideaways
Frommer's Food Lover's Companion to France
Frommer's Food Lover's Companion to Italy
Frommer's Gay & Lesbian Europe
Frommer's Exploring America by RV
Hanging Out in Europe
Israel Past & Present

Mad Monks' Guide to California
Mad Monks' Guide to New York City
Frommer's The Moon
Frommer's New York City with Kids
The New York Times' Unforgettable
   Weekends
Places Rated Almanac
Retirement Places Rated
Frommer's Road Atlas Britain
Frommer's Road Atlas Europe
Frommer's Washington, D.C., with Kids
Frommer's What the Airlines Never Tell You